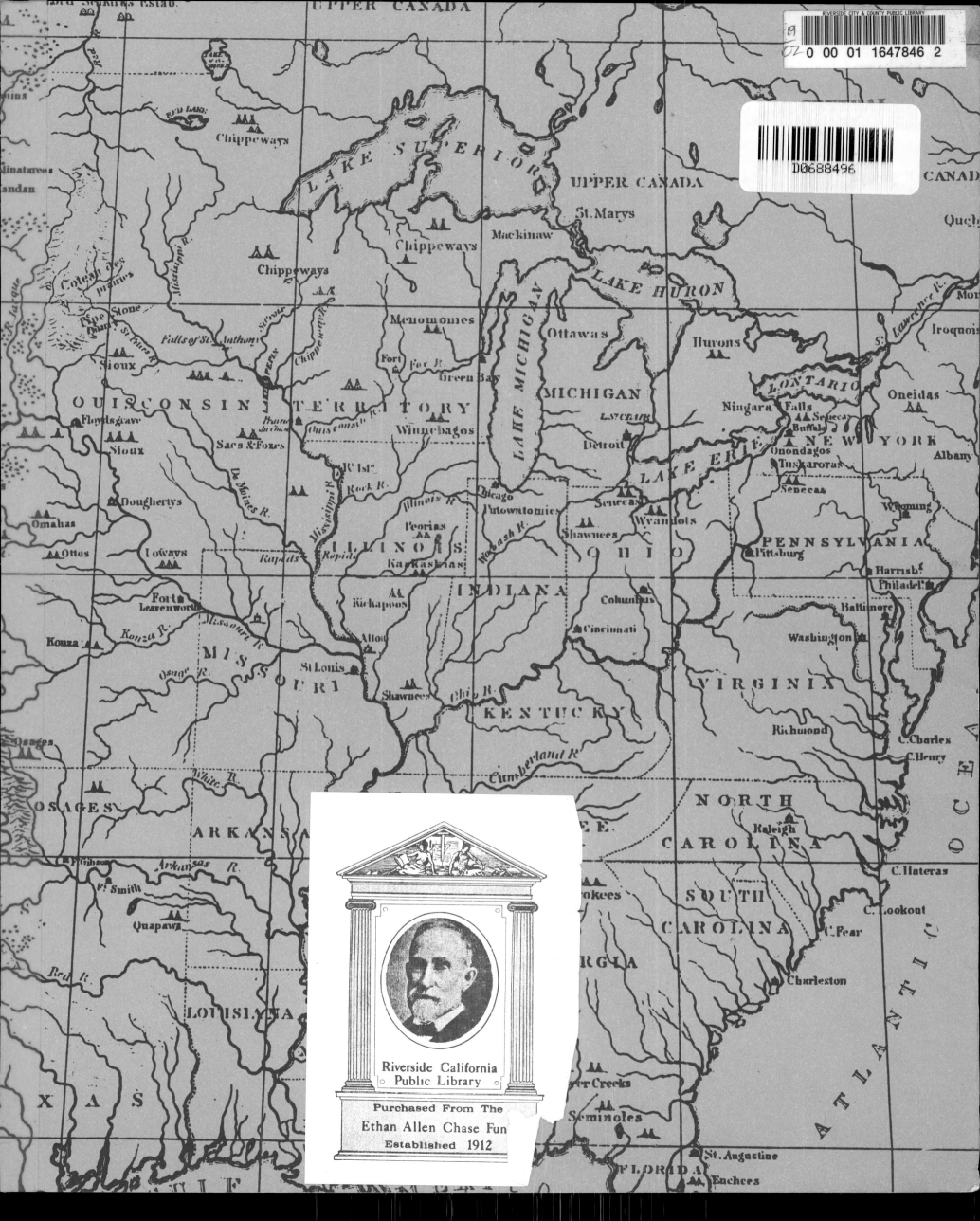

Art · of · the Golden · West

ALAN AXELROD

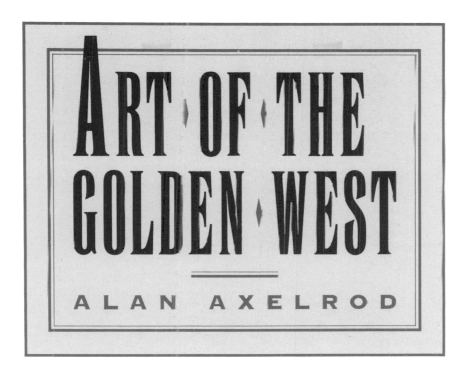

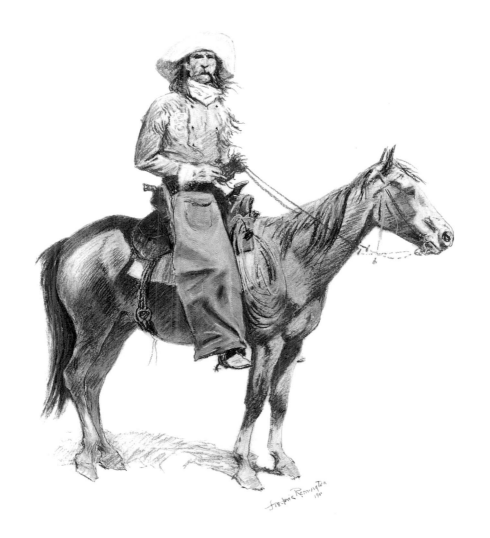

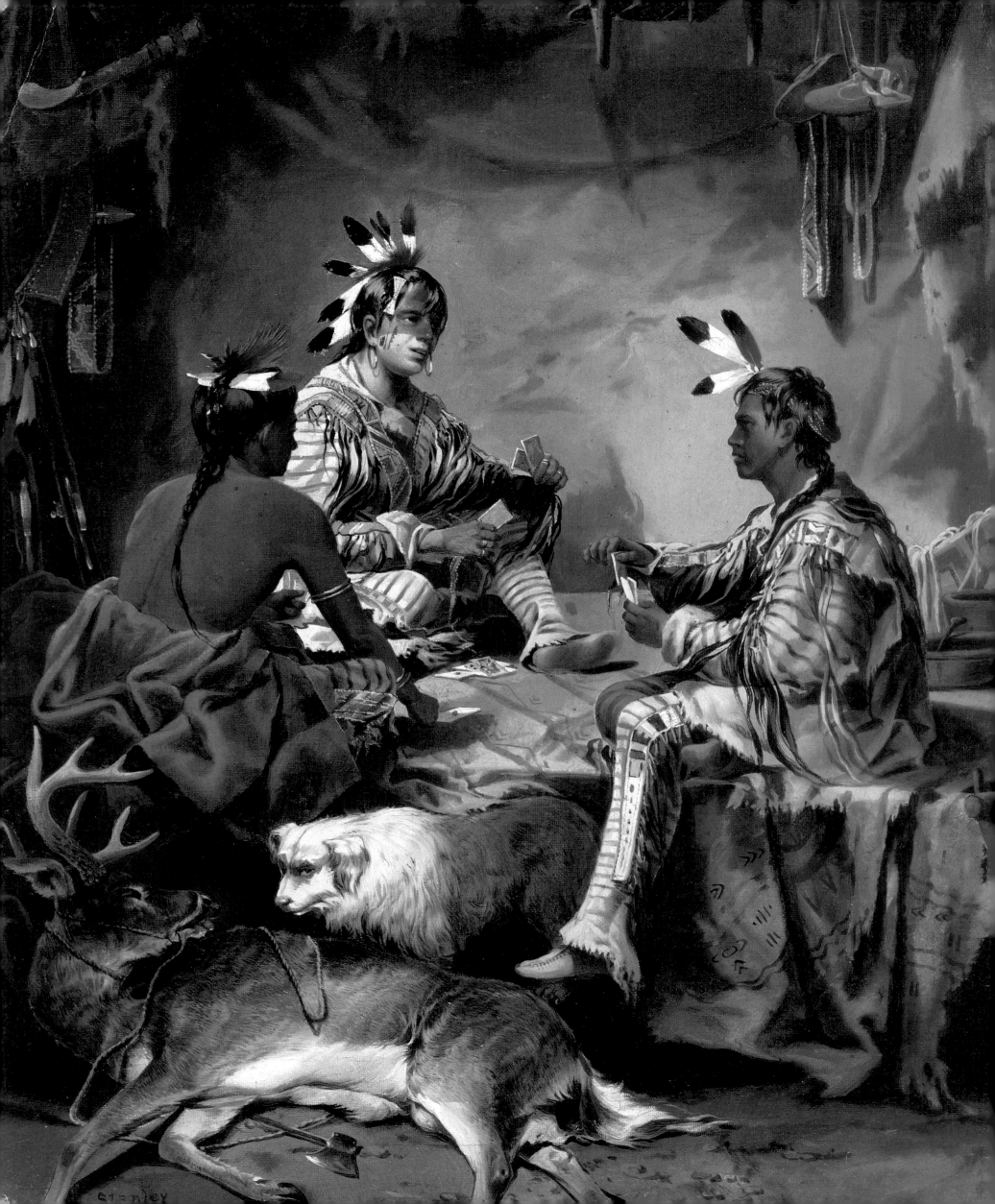

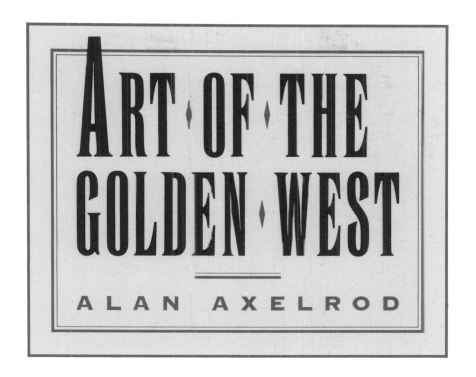

Art of the Golden West

Alan Axelrod

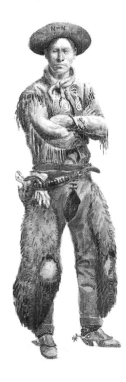

ABBEVILLE PRESS

PUBLISHERS

NEW YORK

FOR ANITA AND IAN

Project editor: Walton Rawls
Manuscript editor: Elaine Luthy
Designer: Julie Rauer
Picture editor: Massoumeh Farman-Farmaian
Copy chief: Robin James
Production supervisor: Hope Koturo

The author and publisher gratefully acknowledge the contribution of the Amon Carter Museum, Fort Worth, Texas, to the visual content of this book.

First edition

Library of Congress Cataloging-in-Publication Data

Axelrod, Alan, 1952–
    Art of the Golden West / Alan Axelrod.
        p.   cm.
    Includes bibliographical references (p.) and index.
    ISBN 1-55859-103-6
    1. West (U.S.)—History.   2. West (U.S.) in art,   3. Art, American.   I. Title.
F591.A53   1990   90-997
978—dc20   CIP

Jacket illustration: Charles M. Russell, *Jerked Down,* 1907. See page 339

Half-title page: Frederic Remington, *An Arizona Cowboy, 1901.* See page 336

Frontispiece: John Mix Stanley (1814–1872), *Gambling for the Buck,* 1867. Oil on canvas, 20 × 15⅞ in. Stark Museum of Art, Orange, Texas

Title page: Olaf Carl Seltzer, *Horse Wrangler,* 1929. See page 350

Epigraph: Albert Bierstadt, *The Oregon Trail,* 1869. See page 151

Contents: Charles M. Russell, *Bronco Busting. Driving in. Cow Puncher,* 1889–90. See page 347.

Preface: Frederic Remington (1861–1909), *American, Mexican and French Pioneer Types,* 1891. Pen and ink and graphite on paper, 10¾ × 14 in. Amon Carter Museum, Fort Worth, Texas

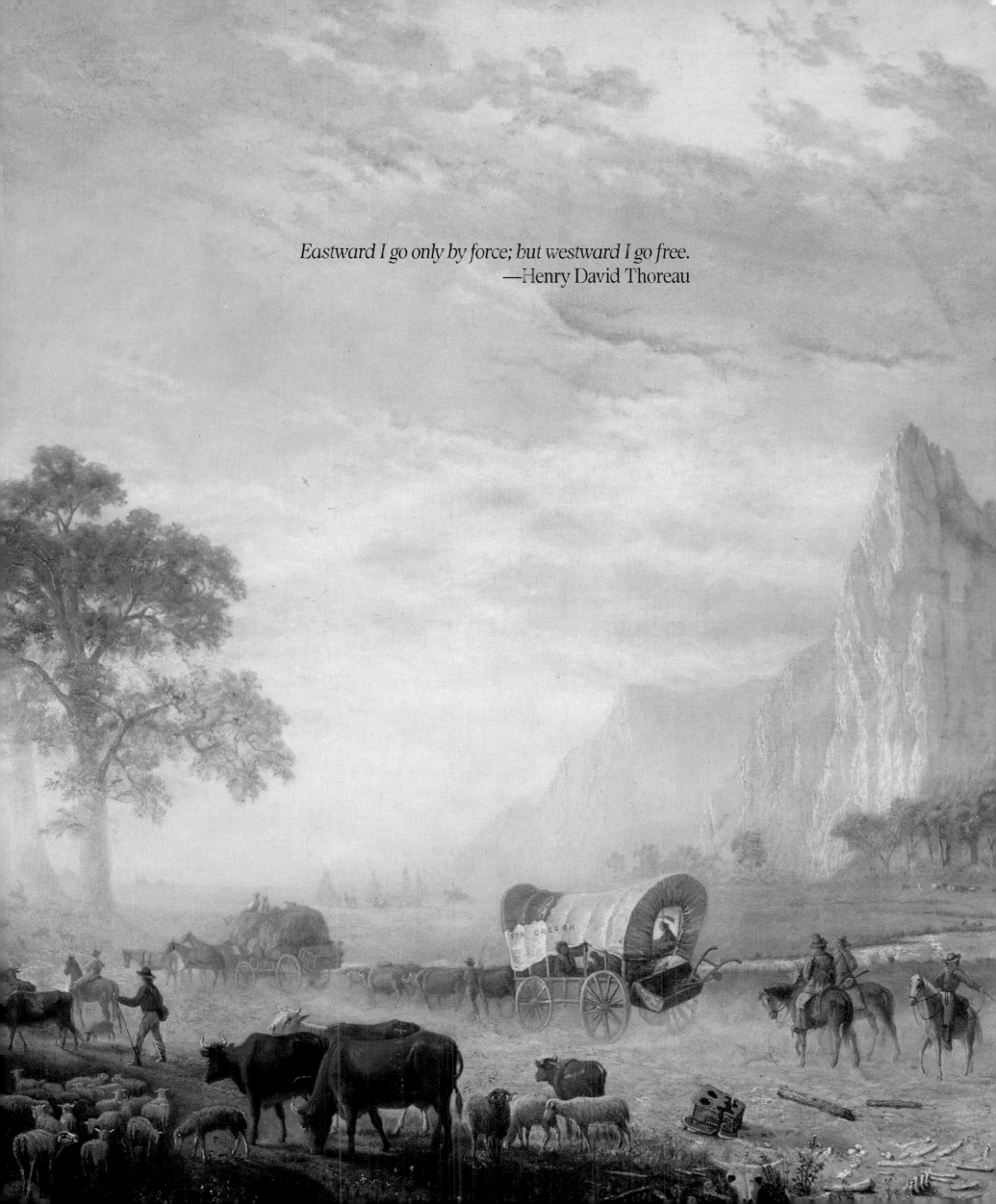

Eastward I go only by force; but westward I go free.
—Henry David Thoreau

Contents

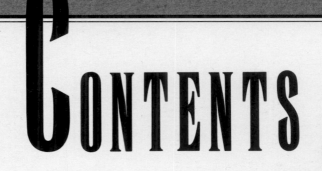

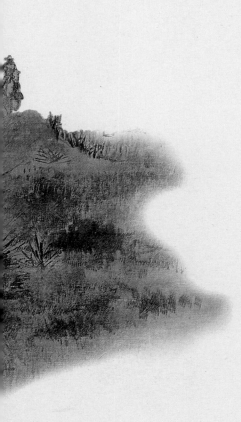

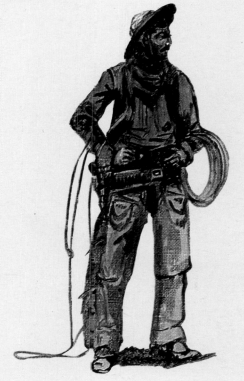

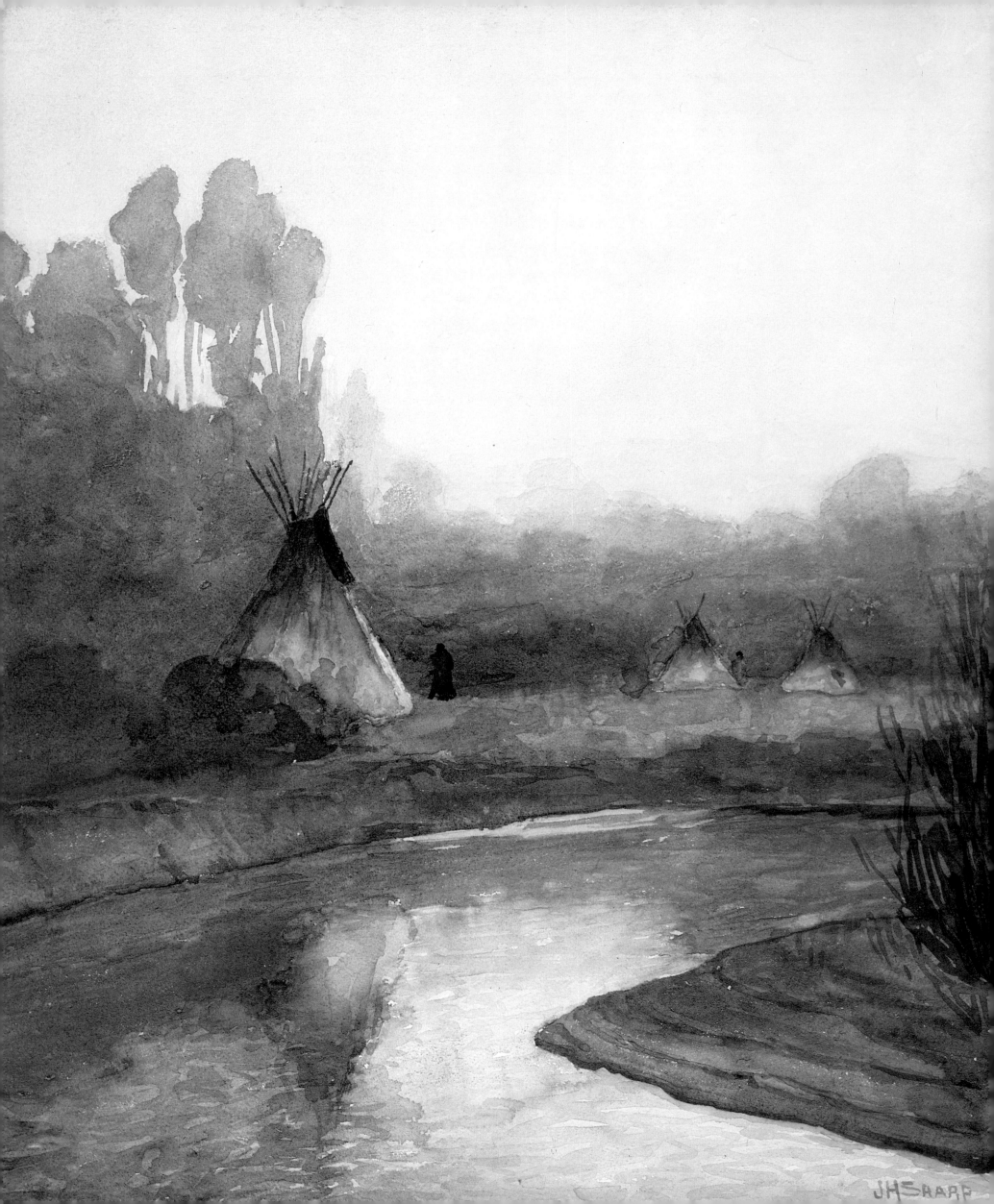

PREFACE

This is not a work of art history, but one of history with art. While it is not my intention to cast the extraordinary paintings and sculptures reproduced here in the role of "mere" illustrations to a historical text, neither can we pretend that they were created by entirely self-inspired geniuses working in isolation. It is axiomatic that the understanding and enjoyment of any artwork is heightened by knowledge of the world in which it was created, and nowhere is this more true than in the case of western American art. At the same time, no body of art more brilliantly illuminates the places and moments of its creation than that of the West. The paintings and sculptures presented here are as essential to the plot of the western story as the mountains, rivers, prairies, deserts, trappers, prospectors, range riders, Indians, cavalry troopers, gamblers, desperadoes, and pioneers they have helped transmute into legend. *Art of the Golden West* offers a narrative of western American history—together with biographical sketches of some of the West's most important artists—and more than four hundred works of art. The book was created in the belief that the words and the pictures are elements of a single story, as inseparable, one from the other, as a cowboy and his Stetson.

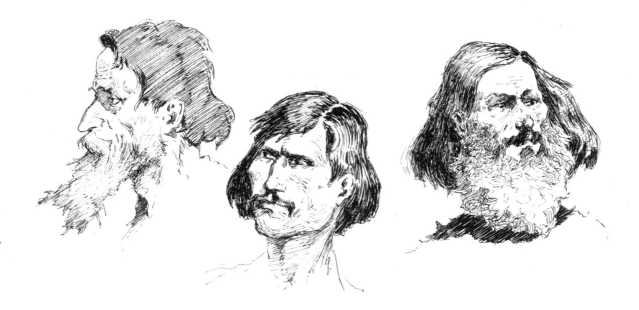

Joseph Henry Sharp, *Early Moonlight, Little Horn, Montana*, n.d. Detail; see page 317

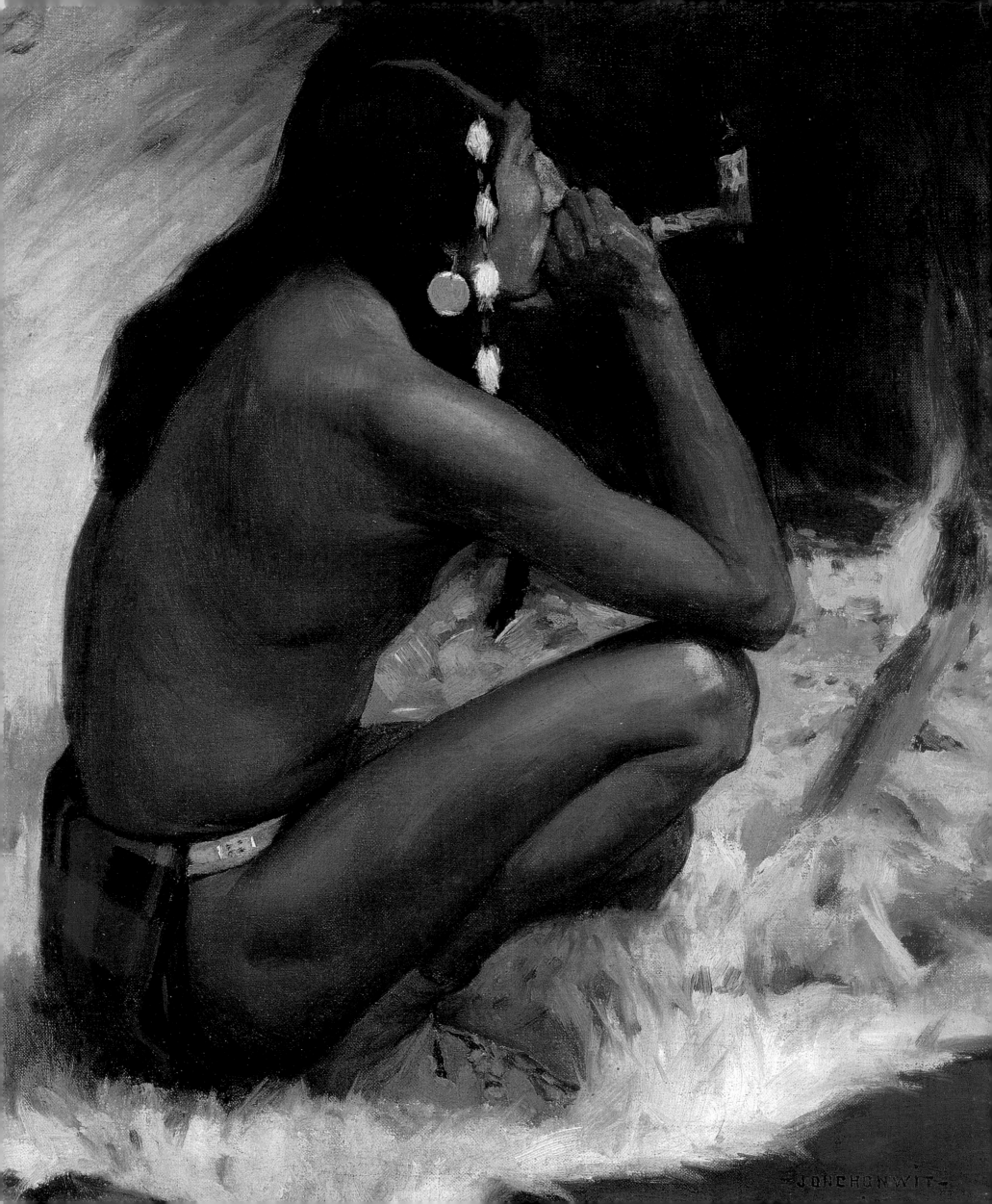

EMPIRES

E. Irving Couse
(1866–1936)
Jonchonwit, 1897
Oil on canvas,
17 ½ × 14 ½ in.
The Rockwell Museum,
Corning, New York

When does the history of the West begin? With the first fur trappers and traders? With Lewis and Clark? With the cowboys? There is no end to the beginnings we might propose—if we insist on finding a particular time and place and person or people. Better to guess that the West began with an idea or, more precisely, with that alloy of feeling and idea we call myth. The West began when men first conceived of a place other than where they were and what they knew, a place of danger and wealth, of death and renewal, the eternal destination of the sun.

But if we will be satisfied with nothing less than a name and a date, we could do worse than to seize upon Columbus and October 12, 1492, a date as exact as it is familiar. Perhaps it is the beginning of the West, perhaps not, but it *is* a point of great moment in the western story; for it is the point at which myth, which lives in imagination and longing, converged with history, which lives in deed and fulfillment. Norsemen explored the "New World" almost five hundred years before Columbus set sail; the Portuguese, inspired by their sovereign, Prince Henry the Navigator, explored the Azores—about a thousand miles from Newfoundland—between 1451 and 1470; and German mariners, on commission from King Christian of Denmark, probed Greenland in 1472. But it was with the voyages of Columbus that men realized they could actually go west, could translate myth and imagination into geography and history.

It is a peculiar fact that the translation has never been completed; where the West is concerned, historical and geographical facts have never wholly supplanted the workings of myth and imagination. Even today, "our" West remains (in the phrase stamped on New Mexico license plates) a land of enchantment, so that, whether we live in Tombstone, Tucson, Dayton, or Boston, we live with images of the American West. They are images compounded of myth and history, of fantastic geography and a factual topography whose real features—great deserts and mountains, mesas and canyons, badlands and grasslands—are scarcely less fantastic. They are images that have nourished a rich and varied body of art, which in turn has multiplied the images from which yet more art has been created. Like everything else western—at least since October 12, 1492—the art of the West is founded firmly on fact and just as firmly on myth. We prize the art for its details of horses, of saddles, of blankets, and boots, of moccasins, rifles, and ropes. Of such things was—and is—the "real West" made. But it is myth that in the first place vitalized those details, that reality, and it is myth that has propelled the West into our own otherwise computerized, sorted, and filed day.

THE FIRST WESTERNER

On July 12, 1212, during one of countless dusty battles between Spaniard and Moor, a peasant named Alhaja found an unguarded pass in the Sierra Morenas and marked it with a cow's skull. The Spanish force made a surprise attack over this pass and decisively defeated the Moors. A grateful King Sancho of Navarre ennobled Alhaja with the surname Cabeza de Vaca, Head of a Cow. Many years later, around 1490, in the Andalusian town of Jerez, one Alvar Núñez was born and, on reaching his majority, would proudly adopt his mother's surname, Cabeza de Vaca.

The boy's grandfather had conquered the Canary Islands and, amid a household staffed with Guanche slaves, regaled Alvar Núñez with tales of heroism and conquest. With Jerez just a few miles from Cádiz, to which Columbus returned—in chains—after his third New World voyage, and even closer to Sanlúcar de Barrameda, the port from which Magellan set sail in 1519, Alvar Núñez's destiny was forged. He became first a sol-dier, seeing action in the Battle of Ravenna (April 11, 1512), in which some twenty thousand died, and, following service in Gaeta near Naples, served the duke of Medina-Sidonia in Seville during the Comuneros civil war and against the French in Navarre. His services were rewarded in 1527 by a royal appointment as second in command, under Pánfilo de Narváez, of an expedition to conquer Florida.

That, we shall see, turned out to be some reward.

Between 1492 and 1580 (when Philip II temporarily united Spain and Portugal, thereby consolidating the vast New World holdings of both nations), Spain established a virtual monopoly on American conquest and thereby controlled the largest empire the world had ever seen. It was an empire founded on agriculture—the cultivation of cotton, sugar, and tobacco, and the raising of cattle—and maintained by slaves, Indian as well as black. But its motive force was the pursuit of the twin goals of propagating Christianity and mining gold—gold and God, but especially gold.

Few New World expeditions, Spanish or otherwise,

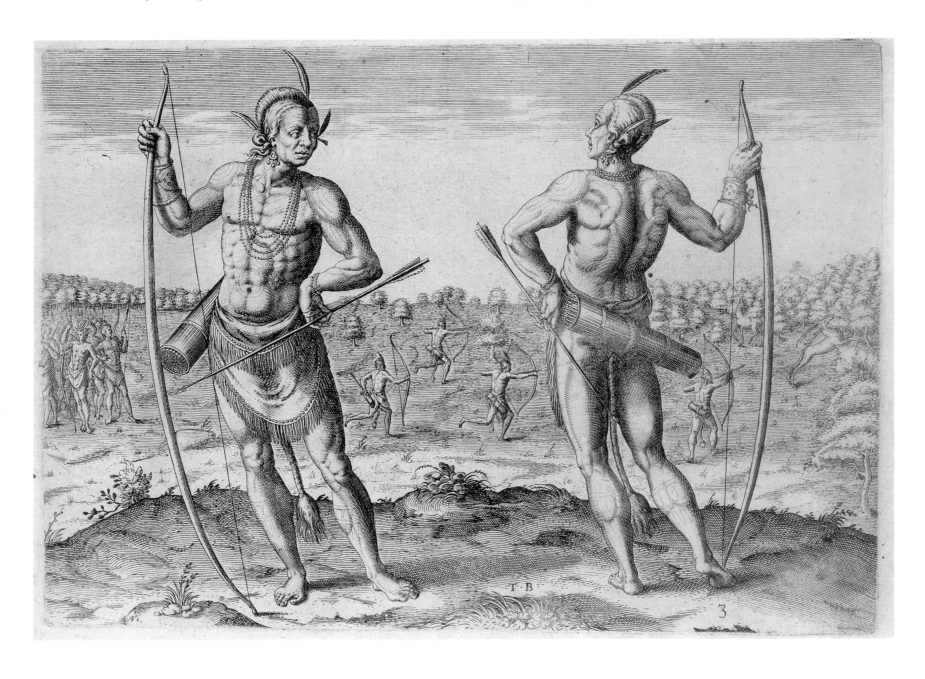

actually turned up the coveted ore, but a handful of discoveries were sufficient to inspire many expeditions. And the most celebrated discoveries were those of Hernán Cortés. When, in 1519, he landed a small force at what is today Veracruz, Mexico, he was greeted by ambassadors of the Aztec king Moctezuma II, who bore dazzling gifts, mostly of gold. Cortés was hardly sated: "Send me some [more] of it," the conquistador declared, "because I and my companions suffer from a disease of the heart which can be cured only with gold." And so Cortés marched upon Tenochtitlán—Mexico City. He began his campaign by boring holes in the hulls of his own ships (he told his men it was the work of worms) so that there could be no turning back, and by recruiting allies among the ever-warring city-states of the far-flung Aztec empire. Recruitment was not a peaceful exercise. The people of Cholula were won over after Cortés slaughtered some three thousand of them in the space of two hours. Perhaps at the news of this, Moctezuma lost any heart he may have had for a fight. Perhaps he believed Cortés to be the incarnation of the birdlike god Quetzalcoatl, who created man out of his own blood. In any case, he opened his city to him and his band.

The Spaniards could justly boast of the magnificence of their cities, cathedrals, castles, of the administrative complexity of their ever-growing empire, of the baroque subtleties of their Catholic religion. They were, however, quite unprepared for the imperial majesty of Tenochtitlán: a city the size of Córdoba or Seville, entirely within Lake Texcoco two miles from the mainland. Access was by four artificial causeways constructed of beautifully hewn beams exquisitely fitted together. Magnificent buildings abounded; drinking water flowed into the city through a system of aqueducts as sophisticated as anything that might have been found in ancient Rome. Great public squares afforded market space, wherein were offered for sale gold, silver, jewels; game of every description; vegetables; cloth; pottery of every kind, use, and degree of decoration. There was a street given over to the selling of herbs. There were barbershops and restaurants.

So far as anyone can tell, the Aztec empire as Cortés found it in 1519 was relatively new. Prior to the fourteenth century, apparently, the Aztecs were but one of several nomadic tribes wandering through and about Central America. Then, from the war god Huitzilopochtli, came revelation and commandment: conquer, and harvest the blood of the conquered. Within the space of two centuries, the demands and the fruits of continual warfare had created a vast, complex, and darkly beautiful empire extending from the Gulf of Mexico to the Pacific and from the Valley of Mexico south into Guatemala. All was ruled with solemn and unremitting tyranny from Tenochtitlán, and the supreme tyrant in the early sixteenth century was Moctezuma II.

For all its magnificence, the empire was founded in

blood and existed for the purpose of shedding blood, a purpose with which the Spaniards were wholly familiar themselves. By the time Columbus first voyaged to America, Spain had been engaged in some eight centuries of brutal warfare with the Moors—like the "Indians" of Central America, a people of different religion and different race from the Spanish. Rapacity at arms had become a way of life; the New World conquistadors were but the latest incarnation of a millennium-old standing army of conquest.

Enter the man who would command the expedition that sent Cabeza de Vaca on an eight-year odyssey through the West. Pánfilo de Narváez was as inept as he was covetous, and he was most covetous of the conquests of Hernán Cortés. Narváez conducted an expedition from Cuba to Mexico with the object of arresting the successful conquistador. Cortés set out from Tenochtitlán to meet Narváez's forces, leaving the imperial city in the hands of one Pedro de Alvarado. Overcoming Narváez's army proved no great task; Cortés suborned fully nine hundred of his opponent's men and employed them in defeating the balance of the expeditionary army. It was Narváez who was placed under arrest—having also lost an eye in the battle.

While Spaniard fought Spaniard in the Mexican countryside, Pedro de Alvarado, back in Tenochtitlán, initiated an action that was to typify white-Indian relations for the next four centuries. According to a native account, it was during the feast of the war god Huitzilopochtli that "the Spaniards were seized with an urge to kill the celebrants. They all ran forward, armed as if for battle. . . . They posted guards so that no one could escape, and then rushed into the Sacred Patio to slaughter the celebrants." Alvarado's men seized the ritual drummer, hacking off his arms and then his head. Others they eviscerated. They pursued all who tried to run; they searched buildings and the rooms inside the buildings, killing whomever they found.

Whereas the citizens had at first meekly submitted to the invaders, they now rose up in rebellion against them, laying siege to the palace in which the soldiers had taken refuge and were holding Moctezuma captive. Cortés returned in the midst of the rebellion, managed to supervise the plunder of the palace treasure room, and fought his way out, out of the palace, and out of the city.

As for Moctezuma, he was dead. Spanish accounts say that he had been assassinated by his own people; Aztec accounts attribute his death to the Spanish. But Cortés was by no means finished. Ten months after their hasty retreat, the conquistadors returned to the city and laid heavy siege, destroying Tenochtitlán's aqueducts and choking off its food supply. Then, weakened by thirst and starvation, the Aztecs began to succumb to smallpox—apparently carried to Mexico by a black slave in the service of Narváez. Still, the battle wore on for three months before Cortés at last retook the city.

Theodor de Bry (after John White) *Regulorum aut Principum in Virginia*, Plate 3 from *Ad Miranda, Narratio Fida Tamen de Commodis et Incolarum Ritibus Virginiae* by Thomas Hariot. Frankfurt: Johann Wechel, 1590
Engraving, 13 × 9 ¾ in.
The Metropolitan Museum of Art; The Elisha Whittelsey Collection, The Elisha Whittelsey Fund, 1962

John White, a "skilful painter" whom Sir Walter Raleigh commissioned as artist and surveyor for two expeditions to Virginia in 1585 and 1588, produced this idealized portrait, front and rear, of an "Indian prince." Along with the other White paintings engraved by Theodor de Bry, this was the Old World's first look at an inhabitant of the New.

Tenochtitlán—or what remained of it—was looted by Cortés, his soldiers, and their native allies. Large numbers of Indians were enslaved and branded, probably the first instance of this most "western" means of identifying chattel. The new king, Cuauhtémoc—successor to Cuitlahuac (dead of smallpox), who had briefly succeeded Moctezuma—was tortured in an effort to extract the whereabouts of the hoard of silver and gold the Spanish had left behind in their hasty withdrawal from the city the previous year. It was to no avail. As was to happen to many in the West—to many Spanish and, centuries later, to many Americans—the full and final promise of gold was to elude Cortés, although he grew very wealthy and powerful nonetheless, establishing mining operations that yielded a fortune in tin, iron, and other metals and harvesting cocoa and cotton not directly from tree and field, but as tribute paid by the vanquished Aztecs.

Seven years after his defeat at the hands of the great conquistador, Pánfilo de Narváez received a royal commission to conquer Florida, which meant all the New World north of the country Cortés had appropriated. Narváez's second in command, Cabeza de Vaca, kept a remarkable journal of the expedition—the first journal by America's first westerner.

Cabeza de Vaca chafed under the incompetent leadership of Narváez, who combined all the rapacity of the Spanish conquerors with none of their undeniable courage or tactical skill. Like others who sought to eclipse the success of Cortés, to find what medieval legend called the Seven Cities of Cibola, the Seven Cities of Gold, Narváez failed to realize that Cortés had not merely conquered territory, but had looted a *civilization,* which was, among other things, a nexus of great wealth. To the north of this civilization lay the borderlands, sparsely populated by small groups who barely survived, let alone accumulated gold.

North of the now-ruined Aztec empire lay the Wild West.

Narváez, Cabeza de Vaca, and some six hundred men set sail on June 17, 1527, from the port of Sanlúcar de Barrameda; they arrived in Santo Domingo on September 17, and the troubles began. During the month and a half the expedition spent on the island gathering provisions and supplying themselves with horses, 140 men deserted to live with the natives. After a stop in Santiago de Cuba, where Narváez recruited replacements, Cabeza de Vaca was sent with two of the expedition's ships to Trinidad, Cuba, for further provisioning. A hurricane wrecked both vessels, killing sixty men and

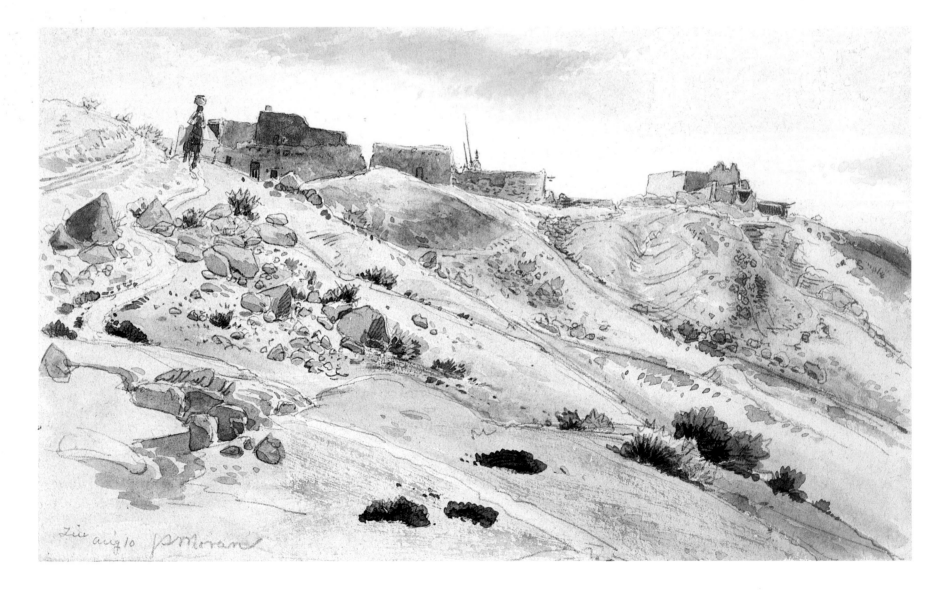

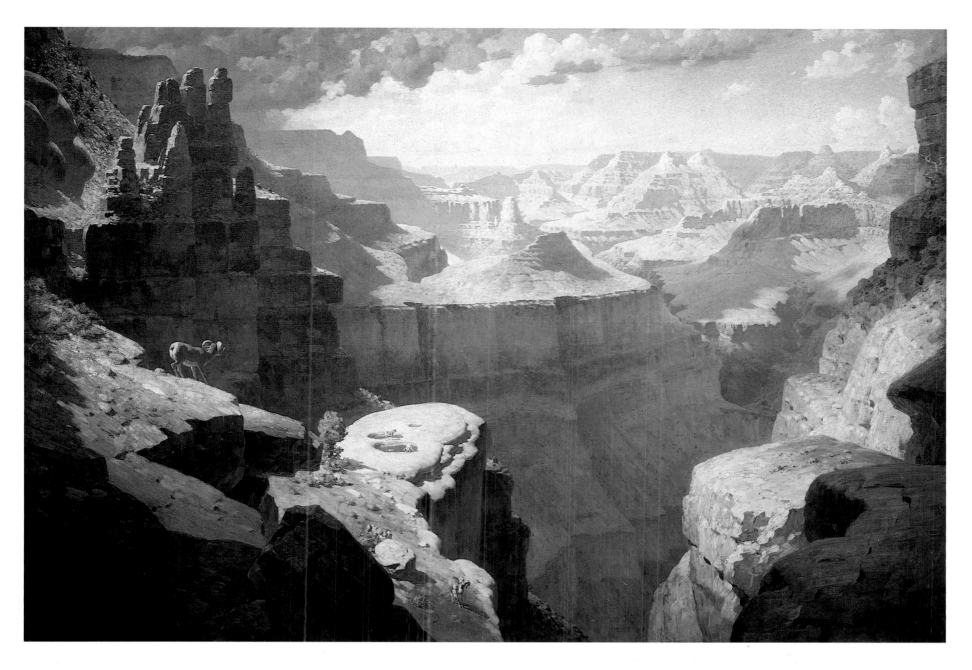

William Robinson Leigh
(1866–1955)
Grand Canyon, 1911
Oil on canvas, 66 × 99 in.
Collection of The Newark Museum;
Gift of Henry Wallington Wack

Many artists turned their talents to
this 217-mile-long icon of the
western landscape.

twenty horses. After a delay of some four months, the expedition set out for the mainland with four hundred men and eighty horses. The ships promptly ran aground on shoals off the western point of Cuba, stranding the entire party for fifteen days, until yet another storm floated them off.

It was the middle of April 1528 when the expedition at last touched Florida. Of the eighty horses, only forty-two had survived the storms and other rigors of the sea passage, and most of those "were too thin and run down to be of much use." But the men found "a gold rattle" amid some Indian fishnets. In a solemn but efficient ceremony, Narváez claimed the country for Charles v, king of Spain.

Near present-day Tampa, they "found pieces of linen and woolen cloth and bunches of feathers like those of New Spain"—country of the fabulously wealthy Cortés. "And we saw some nuggets of gold. . . . We inquired of the Indians by signs where these things came from. They gave us to understand that very far from here was a province called Apalachen, where was much gold and plenty of everything we wanted."

Narváez was all haste. He decided to march inland

while the ships continued to coast on to a port. But what port? Cabeza de Vaca argued that "under no circumstances should we forsake the ships before they rested in a secure harbor." After all, the pilots "did not so much as know where we then were." The expedition would want for horses and, lacking an interpreter, could not even count on communication with the Indians; nor were supplies sufficient for a "march we knew not where." Better to reembark, find a port, secure it, and *then* set out in search of gold. But when Narváez proposed that Cabeza de Vaca take the ships to port while the main party marched inland, the conquistador refused, explaining that he felt certain the inland party was doomed, therefore "I would rather hazard the danger that lay ahead in the interior than give any occasion for questioning my honor by remaining safely aboard behind."

Lust for gold—the phrase by now is such a cliché that we find it hard to hear as an expression of the madness that would drive three hundred men (one hundred manned the ships) to abandon their lifeline of supplies and march they "knew not where." After about a month on foot, they reached the Apalachicola River. A certain Juan Velasquez, native of Cuellar, attempted to ford the

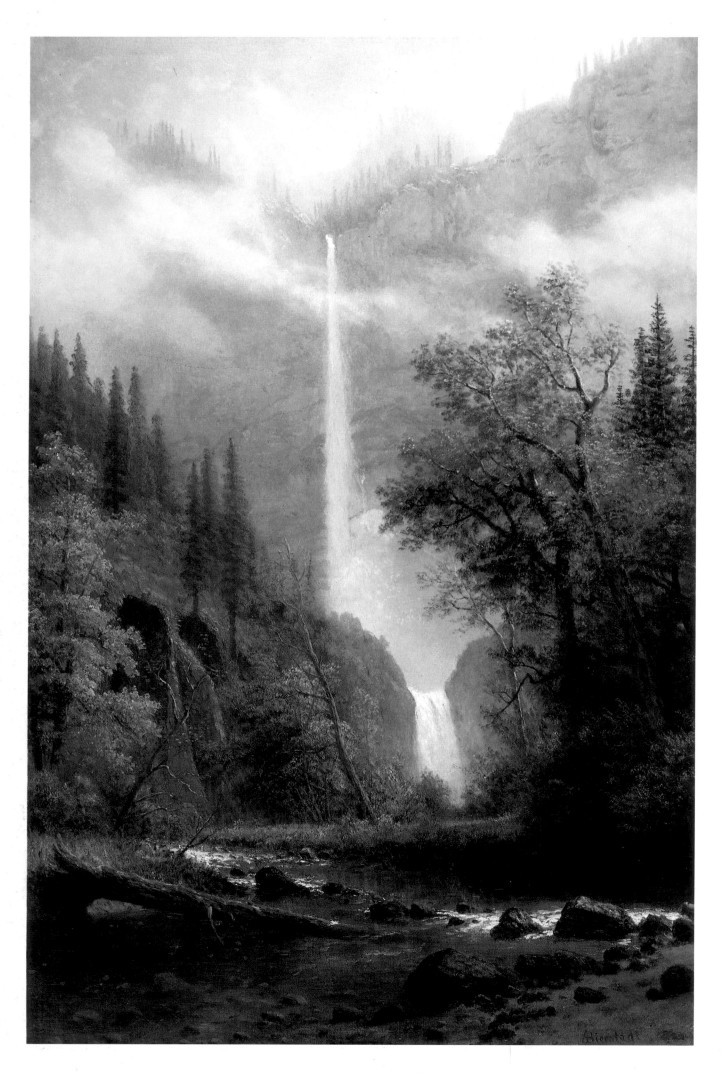

Albert Bierstadt (1830–1902)
Multnomah Falls, n.d.
Oil on canvas, 44 ½ × 30 in.
Gilcrease Museum, Tulsa, Oklahoma

Multnomah is the most spectacular
of the eleven waterfalls of the
Columbia River Gorge.

ALBERT BIERSTADT

**BORN 1830, SOLINGEN NEAR DÜSSELDORF,
GERMANY
DIED 1902, NEW YORK CITY**

Among the first artists to portray the western landscape as a subject of spectacular, overpowering scenic beauty, Albert Bierstadt enjoyed two decades of tremendous popular success only to suffer a final twenty years of decline and eclipse.

His parents brought him to New Bedford, Massachusetts, in 1831. By age twenty, he was teaching drawing and painting and was exhibiting his own crayon landscapes. Unable to find satisfactory training in the United States, Bierstadt returned to Düsseldorf in 1853 to study at the academy, where he was imbued with the prevailing aesthetic of grandiose landscape depiction. He indulged his taste for the sublime on sketching trips along the Rhine, in the Alps, and in Italy.

After returning to the United States, he put his Düsseldorf training to work in 1857, painting the impressive White Mountain region of New England. The next year, he accepted an invitation to join an expedition commanded by General Frederick W. Lander to survey a wagon road from Fort Laramie to the Pacific. Throughout the summer of 1859, Bierstadt sketched in the Wind River range and in Shoshone country, exhibiting his first Rocky Mountain panoramas at the National Academy of Design in New York City the next year. Not only were the works an instant hit with the public, Bierstadt won immediate election to the academy.

In 1863 and 1866, Bierstadt returned to the West, making enough sketches and studies to serve as the foundation for several years of titanic landscapes. With his works bringing prices unparalleled for an American artist, Bierstadt built a suitably majestic studio on the Hudson River at Irvington, New York. In 1872 and 1873, he journeyed to California and lived and worked on the Pacific coast.

The destruction of his Irvington studio by fire in 1882 came as an omen of the imminent decline of Bierstadt's fortunes. With American taste turning toward the French style, the landscapist's work began to seem dated and was soon woefully out of fashion. The American Committee for the 1889 Paris Exposition rejected his *Last of the Buffalo* because it did not represent cur-

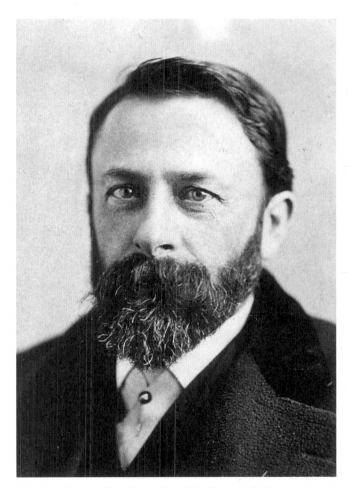

Napoleon Sarony, *Albert Bierstadt*, c. 1870. Photograph. National Portrait Gallery. Smithsonian Institution

rent American painting. Four years later, his *Landing of Columbus* was turned down for display at the World's Columbian Exposition in Chicago. He died in 1902, forgotten by colleagues, connoisseurs, and the public alike. Today, his canvases once again fetch record-breaking prices.

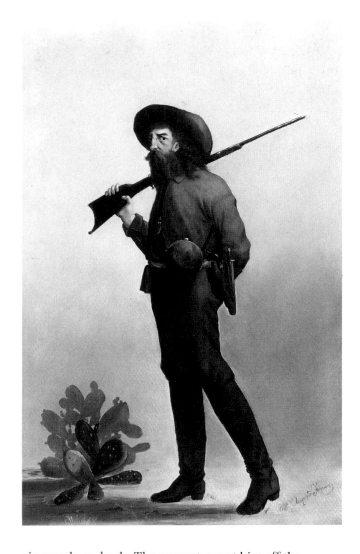

The party put out to sea on September 22, having butchered for food one horse every three days since early August and having lost forty men to disease and at least ten to Indian attack. In all, about two hundred men were distributed among the five improvised vessels, and through the month of October they coasted the Florida gulf, sailing westward and encountering Indian hostility. By the end of the month they reached the mouth of the Mississippi River. At the delta, a violent current drove the barges apart. Cabeza de Vaca counseled Narváez to exert every effort to keep the flotilla together; Narváez abdicated, replying "that it was no longer a time when one should command another; that each must do as he thought best to save himself; that that was what he was doing now. So saying, he pulled away in his barge" and ultimately drifted out to sea. It is unclear whether the drifting away was an accident—the hour was midnight, the gale was strong, and the barge was anchored only by a stone—or deliberate desertion. In either case, Narváez was lost.

Cabeza de Vaca's barge, together with another, sailed farther westward for four days, "each man eating a ration of half a handful of raw corn a day." Then, in a

river on horseback. The current swept him off the saddle; he grabbed the reins and drowned with his mount. This death was just the beginning.

About two days later, the expedition reached the promised land of Apalachen. Narváez dispatched fifty foot soldiers and nine cavalry to invade the village. They found only women and boys and walked about among them. The menfolk appeared suddenly—having returned, apparently, from hunting—discharged a few arrows (one of which killed a horse), and fled. "The village consisted of forty low, small, thatch houses"; the inhabitants wore "poor-quality shawls." It was, they learned, the largest and richest village in the country.

Dispirited, the conquistadors wandered about the Florida Panhandle for the better part of the summer. Malaria complicated by dysentery disabled a third of the men by the beginning of August 1528, pushing the band to a point of extremity that would characterize much of the later western American experience. Concluding they were doomed if they remained in this sickly area, the conquistadors decided to build ships. The trouble was that "this appeared impossible, since none of us knew how to build ships." But as western explorers would do in the future, they *did* the impossible, inventing, improvising, wresting materials from a recalcitrant land. By September 20, five barges, each about thirty feet long, were ready.

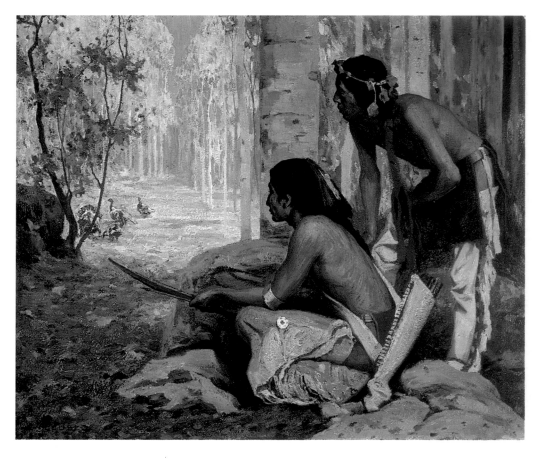

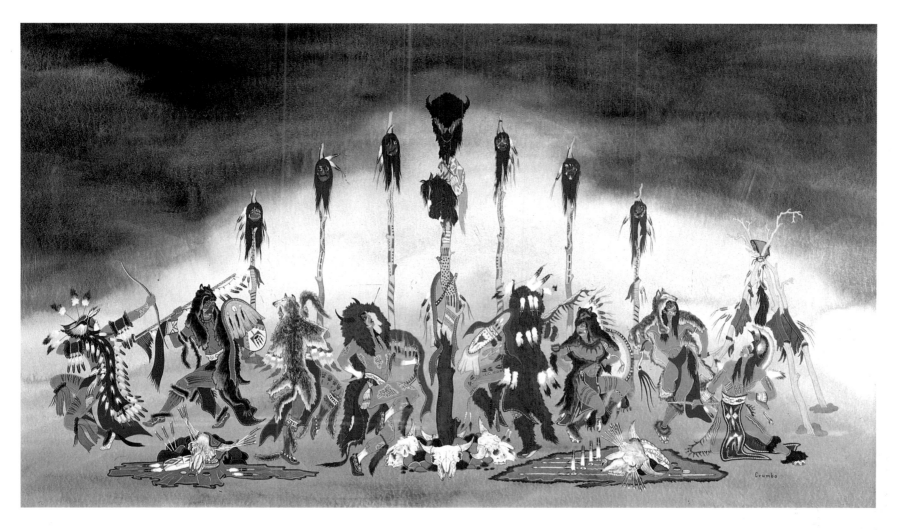

Woodrow Crumbo
(1912–1989)
Animal Dance, n.d.
Tempera on paper, 25 ½ × 44 in.
Gilcrease Museum, Tulsa, Oklahoma

This beautifully realized work is the product of the artist's Creek-Potawatomi heritage and his study with the painter Clayton Staples at Wichita University.

E. Irving Couse (1866–1936)
Taos Turkey Hunters, 1915
Oil on canvas, 24 × 29 in.
Santa Fe Collection of Southwestern Art

The Taos Indians had a long tradition of peaceful coexistence with all of their neighbors, white and red alike.

bitterly cold November storm, the companion barge was lost. The next day, the men on Cabeza de Vaca's vessel began to collapse. "By sunset, all in my barge had fallen over on one another, close to death." At nightfall, only the conquistador and his navigator—two out of the fifty men in the barge—were able to stand. Two hours after dark, the navigator told Cabeza de Vaca to take over; "he believed he was going to die that night." When November 6 dawned, the barge drifted ashore on Galveston Island. There the men found fresh water and were able to parch some of their ration of raw corn. This, together with the succor of friendly Indians, revived them, and they set out again. It was hard work, digging the beached barge out of the sand, so the men stripped naked, stowing their clothes in the craft.

The surf suddenly took up the barge, and the men clambered into it. They rowed "two crossbow shots from shore when a wave inundated us. Being naked and the cold intense, we let our oars go. The next big wave capsized the barge." Several men drowned; the remainder were tossed ashore, alive—and "naked as they were born. . . . in that bitter November cold." Having eaten nothing but corn—and that often raw—since May, the once-proud and proudly clad conquistadors were little more than living skeletons, apparitions that terrified the friendly Indians of these parts.

But the Indians' fear quickly melted into compassion; they fed and clothed the white men and sat down to lament with them—"so loudly they could have been heard a long way off. It was amazing," declared Cabeza de Vaca, "to see these wild, untaught savages howling like brutes in compassion for us." This was the first of many realizations by our prototype westerner concerning the humanity of the Native Americans. Later, as nineteenth-century white men pushed relentlessly toward the setting sun, there would be precious few who would allow themselves the same realization.

The weather turned stormy and colder, freezing the ground so that the Indians could not pull up roots for subsistence. Nor did their cane-made fish traps yield any catch. "Our men," says Cabeza de Vaca, "began to die."

Everyone knows that the Wild West was a dangerous place, but its chief danger, apart from the obvious fact that it could kill you, was also its attraction. The West *changed* you. It changed Hernán Cortés into a sort of king, wealthy and powerful. And this, we shall see, it would do for others in the centuries that followed. For Cabeza de Vaca, the West became the stage for many transformations. Those we have seen so far were unrelentingly traumatic. Soon, his Indian rescuers began to die of dysentery; the survivors blamed the plague on the wicked white men (doubtless, they *were* the source of infection) and determined to kill them. Yet, as in any good western story, the nadir of the hero's fortunes proved to be the turning point. One of the Indians reasoned with

KARL BODMER

—

BORN 1809, RIESBACH, SWITZERLAND

DIED 1893, BARBIZON, FRANCE

—

Trained from an early age in the precise and delicate tradition of the watercolor draftsman, Bodmer became known in Europe for the German valley views he engraved from his own originals. In 1832, Prince Maximillian of Wied Neuwied, an avid amateur naturalist, commissioned Bodmer to tour the western United States with him. The drawings and watercolors Bodmer made on this trip record, with jewellike clarity of detail, the landscape, wildlife, and Indians of the early American West.

Both Maximillian and Bodmer prepared carefully and earnestly for their tour, Bodmer talking to Titian Peale in Philadelphia, studying the paintings he and Samuel Seymour had made when they accompanied Major Stephen Long on his 1819 western expedition. Bodmer and the prince also purchased some Peter Rindisbacher watercolors from the 1820s and examined the more recent work of George Catlin.

After numerous side trips in the East, South, and Middle West, Maximillian and Bodmer boarded the American Fur Company steamer *Yellowstone* at St. Louis in March 1833, bound for Fort Pierre (in present-day South Dakota), some fifteen hundred miles distant. Throughout the seven weeks of this leg of the journey, Bodmer diligently sketched and painted Indians in full costume, taking as much as a full day to execute a single, scrupulously accurate drawing. Leaving the *Yellowstone,* the travelers steamed another five hundred miles up the Missouri aboard the *Assiniboin,* bound for Fort Union (in present-day North Dakota). From there, the keelboat *Flora* carried the pair to Fort McKenzie (in present-day Montana), where they lived for more than a month in the heart of Blackfoot country. Bodmer and Maximillian narrowly escaped death when a band of Cree and Assiniboin Indians attacked the fort—an event the artist had the presence of mind to record. Bodmer also made an extensive record of the Mandans, who were destined to be wiped out within three years by a smallpox epidemic.

After his return to Europe in 1834, where he took up permanent residence at Barbizon, Bodmer used his sketches and 427 watercolors to create etchings as illustrations to Maximillian's *Travels.* In this form, Bodmer's work served other, later artists—including some employed by Currier & Ives—who never saw the West for themselves. The original paintings were forgotten until they were discovered at Neuwied Castle after World War II.

Bodmer never returned to America, but became associated with the Barbizon School of French painters and counted the likes of Rousseau and Millet among his peers.

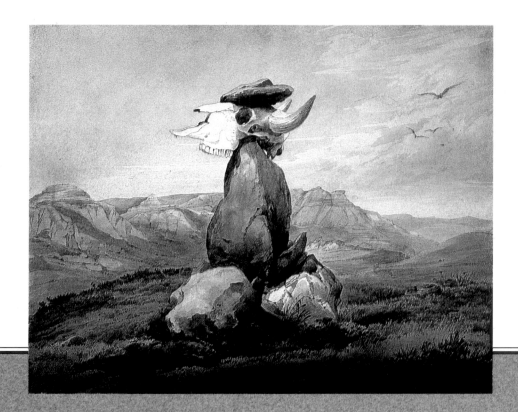

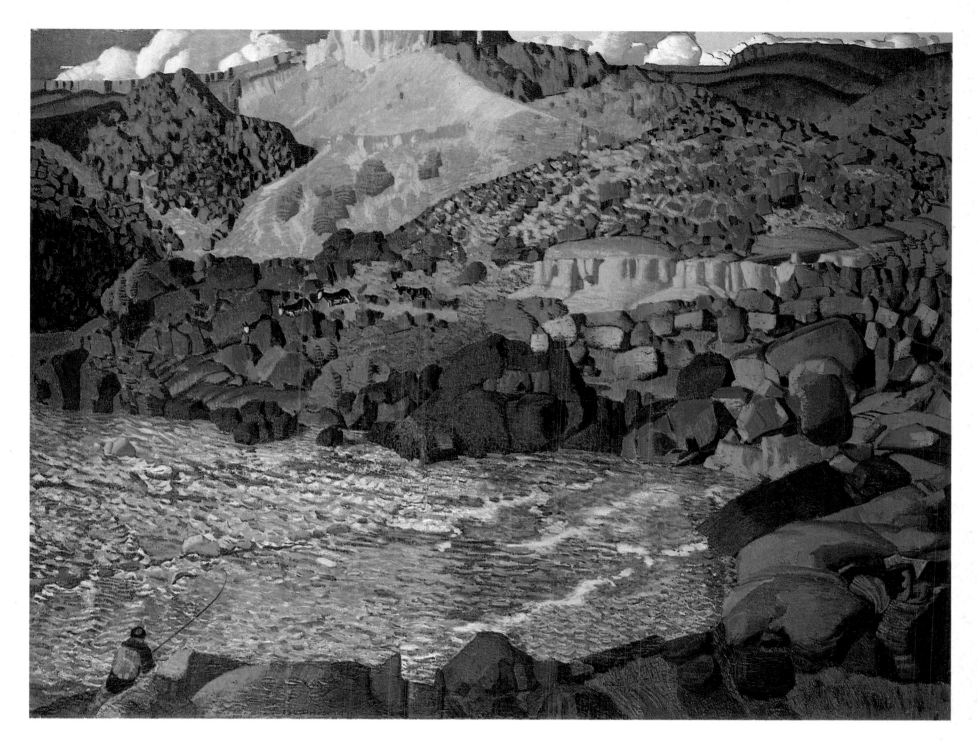

the others that, if the whites were such powerful sorcerers, why would they have allowed to perish all but a few of their own number? "God our Lord be praised," writes Cabeza de Vaca, "they listened and relented." And, as he had done before, Cabeza de Vaca integrated himself into the lives of his hosts. He became a medicine man.

Whereas the Indians themselves treated the sick by making an incision over the point of pain, sucking the wound, and then cauterizing it (Cabeza de Vaca tried this on himself "with good results"), the conquistador confined himself to blessing the sick, breathing upon them, and pronouncing a *Pater Noster* and an *Ave Maria*. It worked; the sick were healed, and the Indians treated the by now greatly reduced band of Europeans with kindness and gratitude.

These happier circumstances prevailed until Cabeza de Vaca himself fell ill, and, though he recovered, the Indians again turned against him, summarily demoting him from honored medicine man to hard-used slave.

Yet, he seized opportunity once more. Finding life intolerable under the yoke of slavery, he escaped and, as he put it "turned to trade." For the next two years, "I did my best to devise ways of making my traffic profitable so I could get food and good treatment. The various Indians would beg me to go from one quarter to another for things they needed; their incessant hostilities made it impossible for them to travel cross-country or make many exchanges. . . . As a neutral merchant I went into the interior as far as I pleased [at least as far as Oklahoma] and along the coast forty or fifty leagues [probably as far north as the Sabine River marshes and as far south as Matagorda Bay—near present-day San Antonio].

Cabeza de Vaca seems to have taken pleasure in his peregrinations up and down the Gulf Coast, until he was enslaved by Mariames. Still, he was faring better than his fellow conquistadors, most of whom had fallen victim to disease, starvation, or Indian attack. The main party had wasted away, partly through cannibalism among themselves and harsh treatment at the hands of Indian captors.

For six more years Cabeza de Vaca wandered the West, experiencing just about everything that later sojourners would encounter, experiencing the stuff of western history that also became the stuff of western lore and myth and art. Among the Mariames there was great cruelty, practiced not only against the white intruders, but against their own offspring: "They cast away their daughters at birth; the dogs eat them." For this tribe is perpetually at war. "All the nations of the region are their enemies . . . if they were to marry off their daughters, the daughters would multiply their enemies." But Cabeza de Vaca also knew kindness and generosity from the Indians, and he himself wandered the West as a combination merchant and healer, bestowing his own care and kindness on all he met. Though he heard tell of gold, of fabulous wealth, Cabeza de Vaca himself found in the West wealth of a different kind. He found people who, unlike the white man, were utterly unconcerned with property and boundaries and ownership. In what is today Texas, near the Pecos River, he found tribes who lived in plenty, the land offering up unending supplies of deer and rabbits and fruit. The people "ever plundered each other, and those who lost were as content as those who gained." In what is today Sonora, Mexico, Pima Indians presented Cabeza de Vaca with emeralds and over six hundred opened deer hearts, "which they kept in great supply for food." The conquistador named the place of this offering Pueblo de los Corazones—the Town of Hearts.

And then there was the land itself. When we read Cabeza de Vaca's history, it is the landscape we imagine most vividly, as we do when we read any western narrative or call to mind paintings of the West.

EMPIRE'S VAST STAGE

Eight years of wandering in the name of the Spanish empire revealed to this first westerner an empire far vaster. For the most part, it is an empire of desert, sparsely grown with cacti—saguaro, fishhooks, pincushions, hedgehogs, prickly pears—and with sage and mesquite, with primrose, wild four-o'clocks, and other wildflowers. An empire whose subjects are animals who never drink, or seem never to: kangaroo rats, ground squirrels, scorpions, peccaries, kit foxes, wood rats, mule deer, white-tailed deer, Gila monsters, rattlesnakes.

Cabeza de Vaca roamed the Guadalupe Mountains of Texas, the high-and-dry remnant of a tropical reef formed when this area was under water in some remote geologic period. They are mountains of sediment, much of it plant and animal remains, crystallized into something like limestone, dramatically stratified and culminating in the rugged Capitan Reef, a massive escarpment overlooking the plains of Texas and New Mexico—plains that call to mind a limitless sea, especially if one is a half-

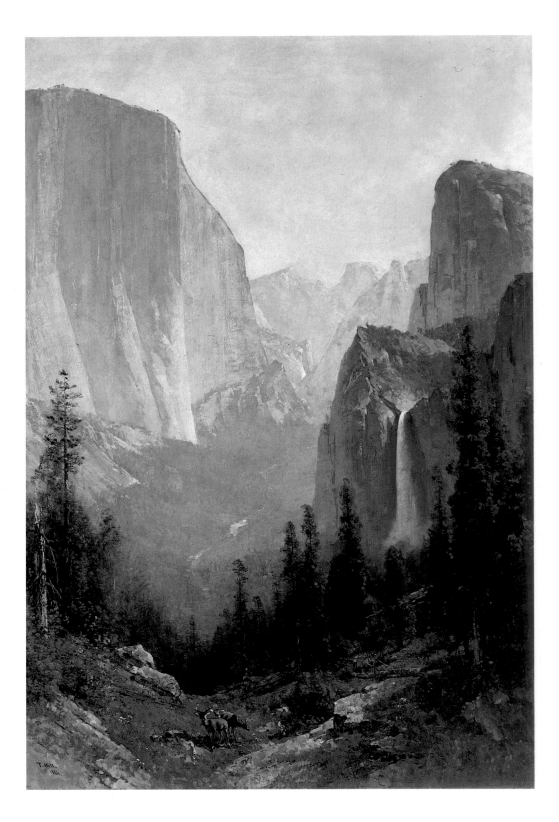

starved, half-naked wanderer swallowed up in them. Mile after mile of wide flats punctuated by brush, arroyos, low hills, and veined with crystals of gypsum and blue salt.

In New Mexico the spectacle included the caverns of Carlsbad, the underground portion of the Capitan Reef. Among the subjects in this nether region of the empire are eighteen species of bats, and if Cabeza de Vaca ventured much into the caverns, perhaps the baroque display of stalactites and stalagmites reminded him of the great cathedrals of Spain.

An empire of deserts, mountains, caverns—and riv-

Thomas Hill (1829–1908)
Early Morning, Yosemite Valley, 1884
Oil on canvas, 53 ½ × 36 in.
The Chrysler Museum, Norfolk, Virginia; Gift of Edward J. Brickhouse

Thomas Moran (1837–1926)
Minerva Terrace, Gardiner's River, 1872
Watercolor on paper, 13 ½ × 9 ⅜ in.
W. Graham Arader III

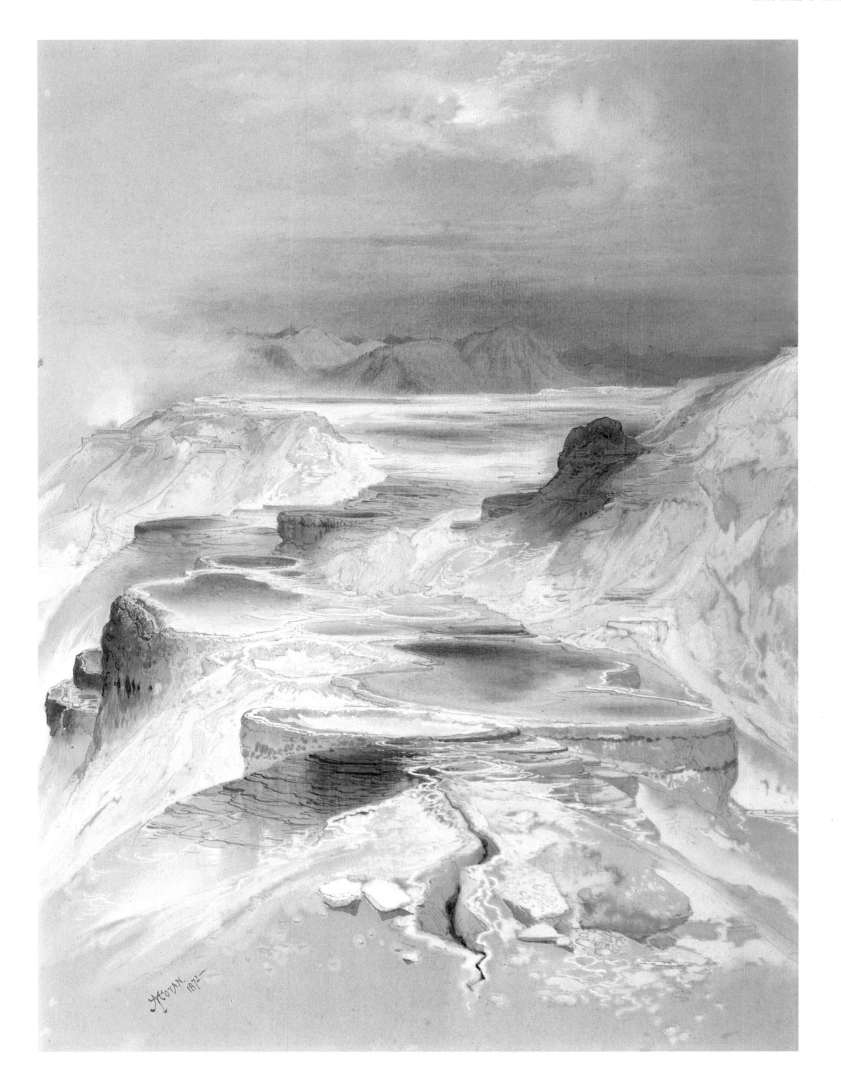

ers. The one the conquistador got to know best was the Rio Grande, especially as he made his way through Texas Big Bend country, where the river turns ninety degrees from southeast to northeast, cutting remote canyons through the soaring Chisos Mountains, a realm of juniper and giant dagger cactus, agaves, catclaw, and mesquite and, at higher elevations, forests of pine and Douglas fir. It is the realm, too, of dinosaur bones, petrified trees, and limestone embedded with fossils.

In the seventh year of his sojourn, having survived through faith, skill, adaptability, respect for his surroundings and for the people he encountered, having been a slave, a healer, a hunter, and an itinerant merchant, Cabeza de Vaca, pressing ever westward—"we concluded that our destiny lay toward the sunset"—reached the town of Redrock, on the present-day Colorado–New Mexico state line. Thence he turned

from his wardrobe. I could not stand to wear any clothes for some time, or to sleep anywhere but on the bare floor."

He had seen, survived, and, in a spiritually significant way, prospered in almost all the western settings millions more would come to know in the centuries that followed. Indeed, the only western environment he did not experience was the prairie, which extends from Indiana to the slopes of the Rocky Mountains and the deserts of the Southwest. As spectacular as are the canyon lands and mountain lands and desert lands through which Cabeza de Vaca passed, perhaps none of these is finally as stupendous as the seemingly boundless prairie—an ocean of man-tall grass navigated, during the mass migrations of the nineteenth century, by wagons called prairie schooners.

The vast western stage was not, of course, void of

Curt Walters (b. 1950)
Chisos Mountains— Big Bend, Texas, 1986
Oil on canvas, 32 × 80 in.
Alterman and Morris Gallery, Houston

Cabeza de Vaca crossed and recrossed the uncompromising landscape of the Big Bend many times.

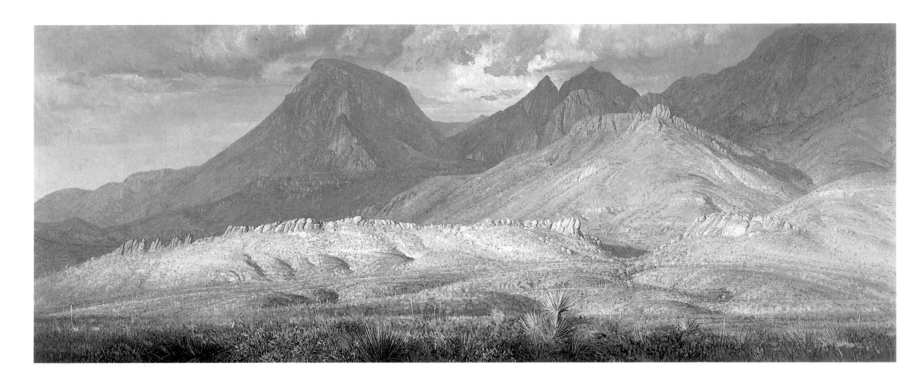

south and made his long, long way down to Mexico City, the principal outpost of the Spanish empire in the New World.

It was at the point of this wide swing round that he must have beheld the western landscape at its most fantastic. For this is a region of red rock—and pink and gray—and red rivers, of striated canyons and blowing sand. It is a region of thirst and hunger, too. On the plains between the Gila River and the massive Chiricahua Mountains, Cabeza de Vaca came upon people who for a third of the year eat nothing but dried desert herbs. A beautiful land that is an anvil, the sun a hammer.

On that anvil, this emissary from a European empire had been forged anew. It was with discomfort and difficulty that he became a European again. When Cabeza de Vaca reached Mexico City some eight months later, on July 24, 1536, "the Governor . . . outfitted us

actors before the entrance of Cabeza de Vaca. During his sojourn, the conquistador encountered some thirty different tribes—or, at least, distinct Indian groups. As we have seen, none of these were empire builders in the European sense or in the manner of the Aztecs; the West of Cabeza de Vaca was wilderness, and many of the peoples Cabeza de Vaca lived among barely survived from day to day.

Nevertheless, the conquistador encountered some formidable groups, beginning with the Apalachee of Florida, the most famous fighters in those parts. Out West, the variety of his encounters is astonishing: the Avavares, with whom he endured perpetual hunger; the Maliacones, with whom he subsisted on berries; and the Arbadaos, who knew even greater hunger than the Avavares. There were the Tularosas, who lived in the foothills of the Sacramento Mountains and who offered

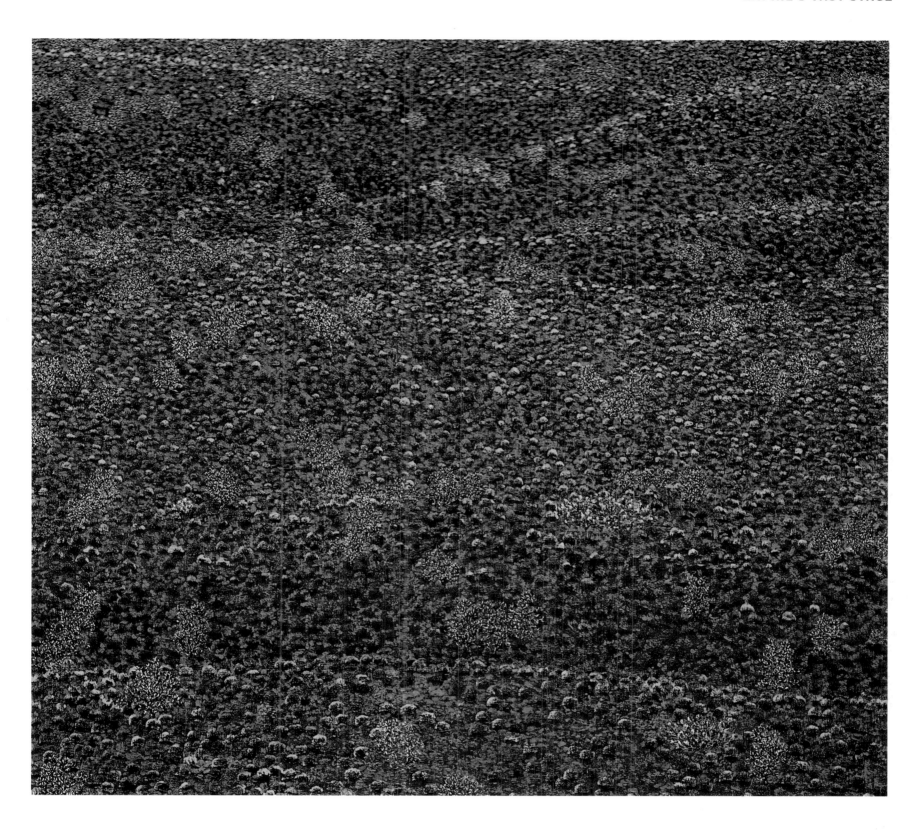

Elmer Schooley (b. 1916)
Hot Country, 1985
Oil on canvas, 80 × 90 in.
Munson Gallery, Santa Fe,
New Mexico

"A beautiful land that is an anvil, the
sun a hammer"—the western
landscape as abstraction, but no less
"real" for it.

the small band of Spaniards everything they had, believing these ragged, half-starved men came from heaven. There was a group identified only as the Cow People, for they preyed upon cows; they, too, looked upon the Spaniards with dread and awe, "sitting in their houses facing the wall with bowed heads, their hair pulled down over their eyes, and all their possessions piled in the middle of the floor."

Along the Texas Gulf coast, Cabeza de Vaca found the Capoques, the Hans, the Charrucos, the Deguenes, the Mendicas, the Quevenes, the Mariames—who enslaved the conquistador band—the Guaycones, and the Yguaces. There were the Atayos, the Decubadaos, the Quitoles, the Chavavares, the Cultalchulches, the Susolas, the Comos, and the "Fig People"—the Camolas.

Cabeza de Vaca found that the Indians of the plains shared one characteristic in common: they "are warlike, and have as much strategy for protection against enemies as if they had been reared in Italy in continual feuds." They employed camouflage of leaves and brush, and thereby advanced upon an enemy unseen. They seemed able to dodge arrows and even musket fire. They fought low to the ground. "I believe," Cabeza de Vaca wrote, "these people see and hear better and have keener senses

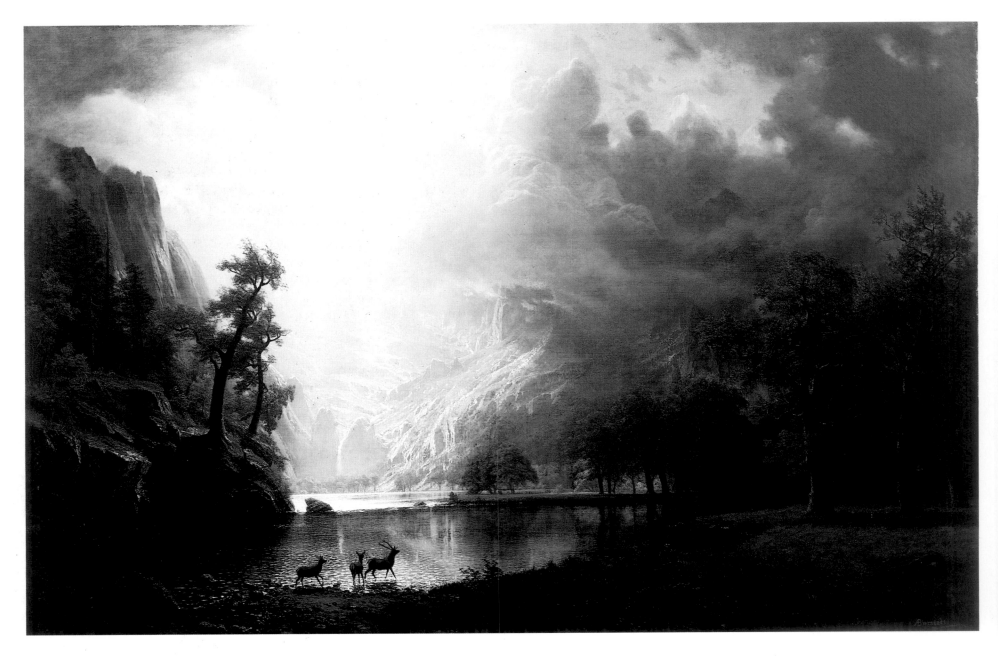

Albert Bierstadt (1830–1902)
Sierra Nevada Morning, c. 1870
Oil on canvas, 54 ½ × 86 ¼ in.
Gilcrease Museum, Tulsa, Oklahoma

A vision of the West as an enchanted
land capable of working magic on all
who venture into it.

in general than any in the world. They know great hunger, thirst, and cold, as if they were made for enduring these more than other men. . ."

The conquistador's observations would be confirmed and reiterated independently by eighteenth- and nineteenth-century Indian fighters and would figure in popular fictional and artistic depictions of Native Americans. Indians—even as Cabeza de Vaca saw them in the early sixteenth century—occupy background and foreground of the western image. But who, exactly, are these people?

The thirty or so tribes Cabeza de Vaca encountered hardly suggest the number of separate tribes or bands that inhabited the Americas at the time of Spanish contact. It has been estimated that between five hundred and a thousand mutually unintelligible languages were spoken in North America (and probably twice as many in South America), which gives some idea of the great diversity among Native American groups. Yet the actual population of North America in the sixteenth century was likely a mere one to two million.

Hardly an empire. Yet thin as their numbers were, the Indians did possess one attribute to which all empires aspire and which few achieve: cultural longevity.

The ancestors of the people Cabeza de Vaca encountered had been in America for at least ten thousand years—more probably, twenty, perhaps even thirty. Almost certainly these ancestors migrated from Asia via the Bering Strait during the glacial epoch. Even today, the strait is at times frozen and can be crossed on the ice; during an earlier geologic age, it might well have been dry land. The migration was no conscious act—nothing like, say, the Conestoga wagon journey of a white homesteader in the nineteenth century. It would have been a movement over many, many lifetimes, perhaps as the inexorable but imperceptible advance of glaciers drove game southward. Sites in Cabeza de Vaca's Southwest—in Texas, New Mexico, and Arizona—have yielded archaeological evidence of habitation eight to twelve thousand years ago.

There would be countless dramas played out on the vast stage of the American West, but the most significant of them enact a single titanic theme: the invasion of a timeless world by time. For, in any practical sense, the world of the Indians was timeless in that it was changeless, geared to nature and wedded to the land. The Europeans who entered that world—and, later, the "Americans" who breached it further—were people com-

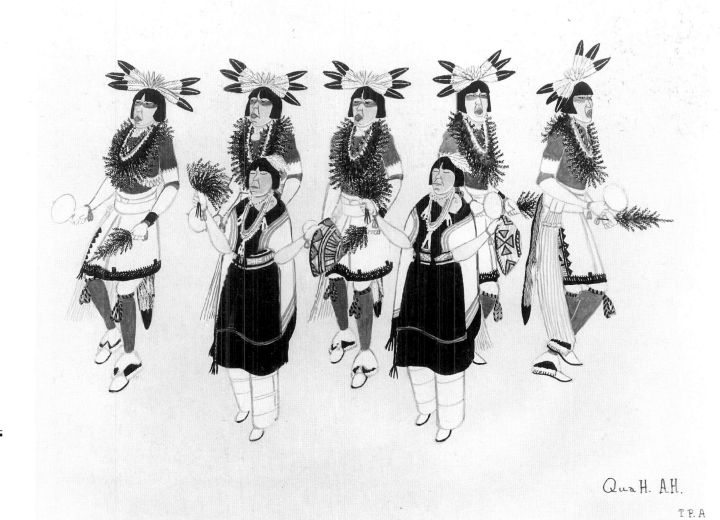

Tonita Pena (1895–1949)
Seven Spring Ceremony Dance,
c. 1920
Gouache on board, 10 ⅞ × 14 in.
Collection of The Newark Museum;
Gift of Miss Amelia E. White, 1937

Born at the San Ildefonso Pueblo, New Mexico, Pena was educated at the pueblo's day school and at St. Catherine's Indian School in Santa Fe. A nationally recognized artist, Pena taught at Indian schools in Santa Fe and Albuquerque.

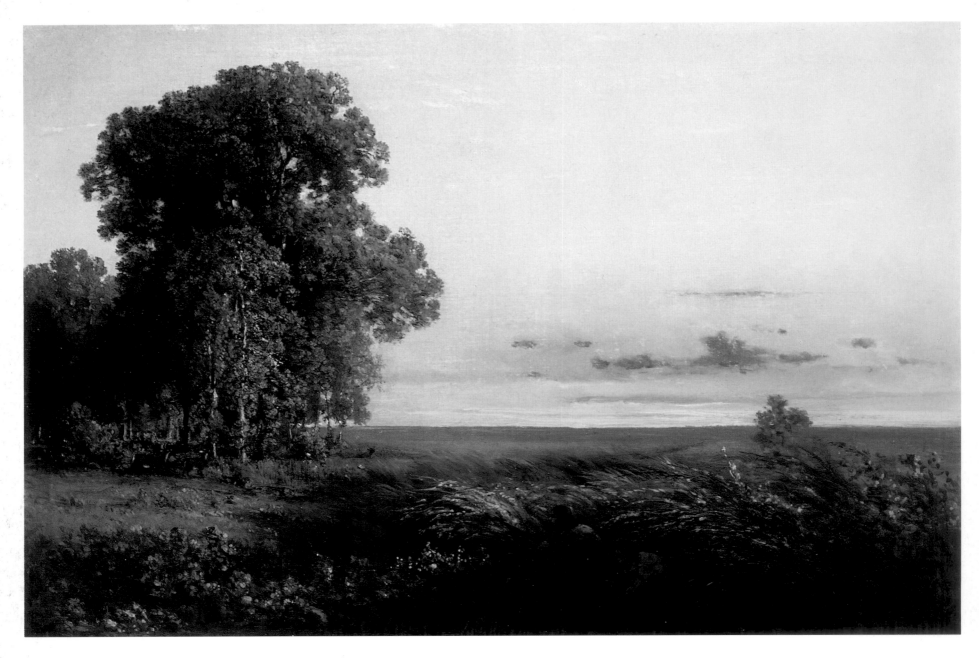

George Inness (1825–1894)
Afterglow on the Prairie, 1856
Oil on canvas, 14 × 21 in.
Courtesy of the Anschutz Collection
(above)

Alfred Jacob Miller (1810–1874)
Approaching Buffalo Under the Disguise of a Wolf, c. 1837
Watercolor, gouache, and pen and ink on pink crayon board, 6 ⅛ × 8 ½ in.
Amon Carter Museum, Fort Worth, Texas *(right)*

Ernest L. Blumenschein (1874–1960)
Evening at Pueblo of Taos, 1913
Oil on canvas, 28 × 41 in.
Santa Fe Collection of Southwestern Art

Pueblos had been standing some five hundred years before Cabeza de Vaca saw them. *(opposite)*

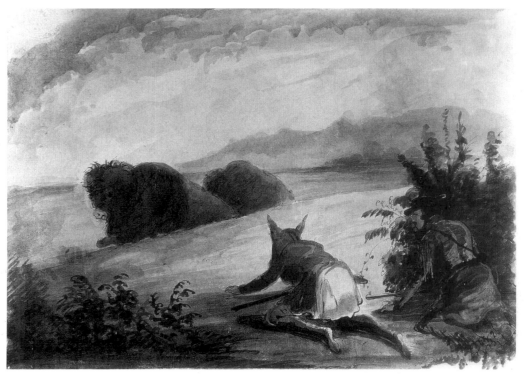

ERNEST LEONARD BLUMENSCHEIN

BORN PITTSBURGH, 1874

DIED 1960, TAOS, NEW MEXICO

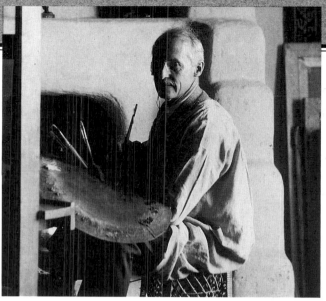

Will Connell, *Ernest Leonard Blumenschein*, 1932
Photograph. The Harwood Foundation Museum, Taos, New Mexico

While he was traveling from Denver to Mexico in 1898 with his friend and fellow artist Bert Phillips, Blumenschein's wagon broke down in the mountain country of New Mexico. The nearest village where they might find a blacksmith to repair a damaged wheel was twenty miles away. It was called Taos, and when Blumenschein gazed at it from atop a towering peak, he was "stirred . . . deeply" and "inspired . . . to a profound degree . . . notwithstanding the painful handicap of the broken wheel I was carrying."

Years later, in 1915, he and Phillips would establish the Taos Society of Artists, which would come to include, besides themselves, Joseph Henry Sharp, Eanger Irving Couse, O. E. Berninghaus, W. Herbert Dunton (Blumenschein's pupil), and others.

The son of a successful musician, Blumenschein almost pursued a musical career himself, studying violin at the Cincinnati Conservatory and playing in a symphony orchestra. However, he soon decided to turn his attention to art and studied at the Cincinnati Art Academy, the Art Students League in New York, and the Académie Julian in Paris, where, in 1895, he met Sharp, who first told him about the remote village of Taos.

The year after he first visited Taos, Blumenschein returned to Paris and stayed, except for one trip home, until 1909. Between 1910 and 1918, he divided his time between New York and Taos, moving there permanently in 1919.

Imbued with the colors and rhythms of the New Mexican landscape and Pueblo Indian life, Blumenschein's vision, shaped by European training, also incorporated strong modernist influences. His Taos colleagues regarded him as the most accomplished member of their group.

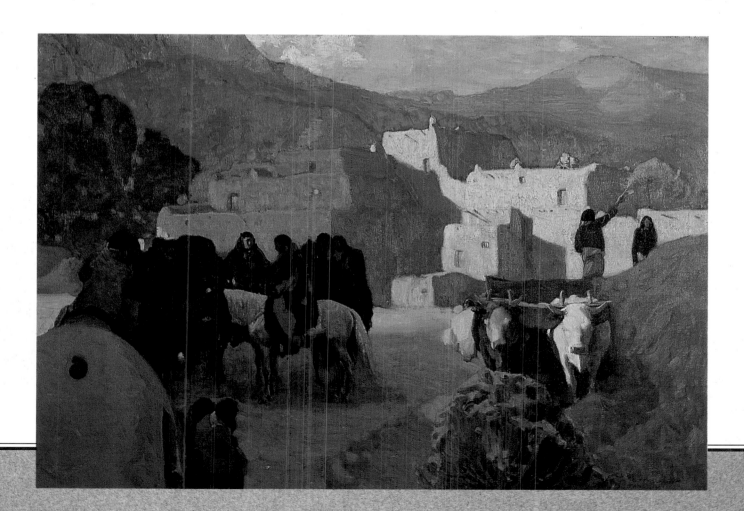

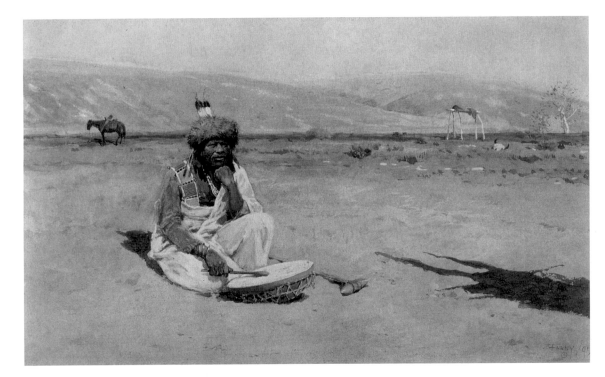

Henry F. Farny (1847–1916)
The Wailer, 1895
Gouache on paper, 8 ⅞ × 14 ⅜ in.
The Rockwell Museum, Corning,
New York

A very popular illustrator, Farny often turned his attention to the more contemplative and spiritual aspects of Indian life.

mitted to time, driven by change and a need to change. The Indians had a place in the world; the Europeans of the later Renaissance were looking for a place. They were spurred on in their search by a rebirth of the spirit of inquiry, which had all but flickered out during the long darkness of the Middle Ages. They were compelled, too, by less abstract motives. In much of Europe, a "place" in the world really was hard to find. Among the noble classes, primogeniture, by which the first son in a family commonly inherited all titles and property upon the death of the father, severely limited opportunities for second, third, and fourth sons. Among the lower classes, opportunities at home were even more limited. And in the seventeenth and eighteenth centuries, the New World would present itself as the only available haven for various religions that could find no "place" in Europe.

As Europeans—and "Americans"—penetrated the West for abstract as well as more immediately practical motives, so the invasion of timelessness by time had its immediate and practical consequences. Except among a few tribes of the Northwest coast, the concept of property was virtually unknown to the Indians. In contrast, without exception, the concept of property was universal among Europeans. As one recent writer, William Brandon, put it: "the Indian world was devoted to living, the European world to getting." The former is possible only in a timeless, changeless world; the latter is predicated on time and change—on movement, a movement west.

THE SPANISH WEST

By European reckoning it was in July 1540 that Don Francisco Vasquez de Coronado rode into the Zuni pueblo of Hawikuh with a band of conquistadors. While Cabeza de Vaca's report to his Spanish sovereign was

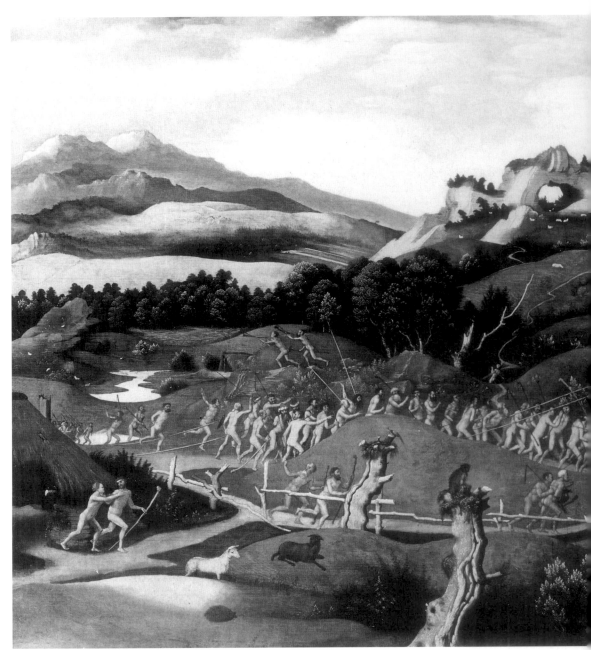

filled with hardships, it did hold out the possibility of frontier gold in amounts comparable to what Cortés had found in Mexico and to what his fellow conquistador Francisco Pizarro had, in 1533, discovered in Peru. To this slim chance, Coronado hitched his expedition. He rode into Hawikuh, demanded its surrender, was attacked with stones and arrows, even knocked unconscious. But he took the town in little more than an hour.

In September the main force of Coronado's army ventured into the pueblo region along the Rio Grande, occupying Zuni and Hopi towns all along the river. The Spaniards seem to have admired the Hopi and Zuni, one soldier—Pedro de Castañeda—remarking on the absence among them of drunkenness, sodomy, sacrifice, cannibalism, larceny, sloth, and chiefs: "They do not have chiefs . . . but are ruled by a council of the oldest men." Nevertheless, the conquistadors compelled the people into slavery, taking from them food, women, and houses. The Indians doggedly resisted, and Coronado pulled up stakes in the summer of 1541, bound for the

Great Plains in fruitless search of the Seven Cities of Gold.

He returned briefly to the pueblos for the winter of 1541–42, then departed, leaving behind two missionaries. It was nearly forty years before any more Spaniards visited the Hopis—a small band of missionaries and soldiers, who learned that the original friars had been martyred. Two more missionaries took up residence in the pueblos. They, too, were killed.

In 1579 Sir Francis Drake entered a central California bay and laid claim to a land he called "New Albion." Hearing of this, the Spanish viceroy in Mexico City expressed his alarm to the court in Madrid. Occupied with European wars, the crown did nothing to protect New Spain's northern frontier for some twenty years. Finally, in 1598, an expedition was dispatched north from Mexico. On April 30, Don Juan de Oñate reached present-day El Paso, Texas, and claimed all of "New Mexico," a province stretching from Texas through California. Oñate marched farther north, colonizing the pueblo country in earnest, with four hundred men, women, and children, seven thousand head of stock, and some eighty wagons. Of all the pueblo towns, only one, Acoma, in western New Mexico, offered serious resistance. Perched atop a steep-walled mesa, it made a formidable objective; yet the soldiers fought their way to the top, killed most of the town's warriors, and took captive five hundred women and children. A few men over the age of twenty-five also had been captured; for their resistance at Acoma, they were sentenced to the loss of one foot and enslavement for a period of twenty years. Women, and children over twelve, kept their extremities but were likewise sentenced to slavery. Children under twelve years of age were entrusted to the care of priests. Two Hopis had been visiting Acoma during the siege; innocent though they were, Oñate returned them to their home pueblo minus their right hands—just as a warning about the consequences of rebellion.

It was Spanish governors like Oñate whose cruelty forged the so-called "Black Legend" of Spain in the New World, particularly in the American West. In part, Oñate had inherited the ruthless conquistador traditions that had animated Cortés and Pizarro. In part, too, he was bitter and probably panic-stricken over all he had failed to find in the frontier lands of New Spain. Son of a rich Mexican mine owner, Oñate had financed the colonization of the pueblo country himself, hoping—as so many had and would—to grow rich from gold and silver. As it was, the country failed even to produce enough food for the colonists. Oñate tried working the Indian populace harder and harder, but to no avail. Fifteen years after he had marched into the province, Don Juan de Oñate was fined and stripped of all honors by a Spanish court on charges of brutality and illegal enslavement.

It was hardly an auspicious opening chapter in the history of Spain in the American West. Indeed, had the

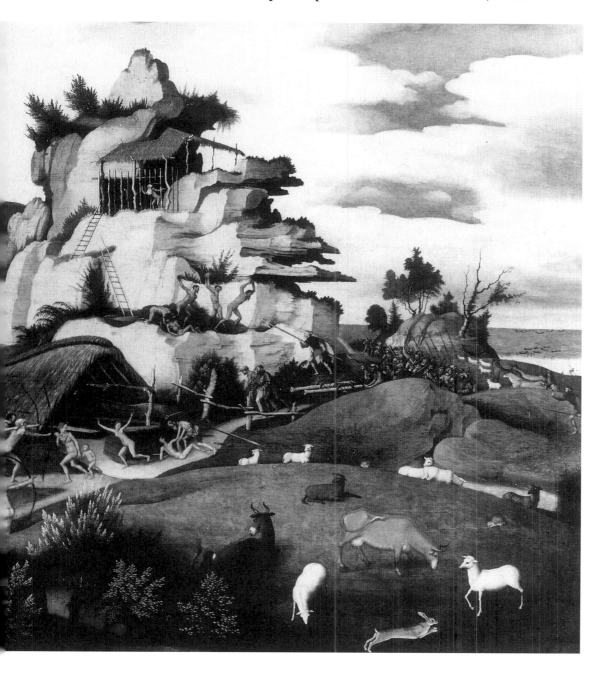

Jan Mostaert (c. 1475–1555 or 1556)
An Episode in the Conquest of America or *West Indian Landscape,*
c. 1542
Oil on panel, 34 × 52 in.
© Rijksdienst Beeldende Kunst, The Hague

Francisco Coronado and his men fall under attack while storming the Zuni pueblo. The landscape of this painting is purely the artist's invention.

PETER MORAN

BORN 1841, BOLTON, ENGLAND

DIED 1914, PHILADELPHIA

Brought to the United States at age three, Peter Moran was raised in Philadelphia, attended the Harrison Grammar School in that city, and, like many other young artistic hopefuls, was apprenticed to a lithographer. As his talent developed, Peter studied under his older brothers Edward and Thomas, concentrating at first on animal subjects rather than the landscapes that made Edward and, even more, Thomas famous.

In 1863, Peter Moran returned to England, intending to study with Edward Henry Landseer, the noted watercolorist. But young Moran had clear notions of what he liked and did not like in art and, on examining Landseer's work, promptly returned to Philadelphia. He kept his studio there for the rest of his life, earning his living principally as an etcher.

Peter Moran journeyed west in 1864, traveling and sketching in New Mexico, and accompanied Thomas on a trip to the Tetons in 1879. In 1881, Peter was attached to an ethnographic expedition to the pueblos of Arizona and New Mexico. Nine years later, he served as special agent to the United States Bureau of the Census (along with Gilbert Gaul and other western artists), assigned to illustrate the bureau's report *Indians Taxed and Indians Not Taxed*. Three sketches of life on the Shoshone agency were published in this work.

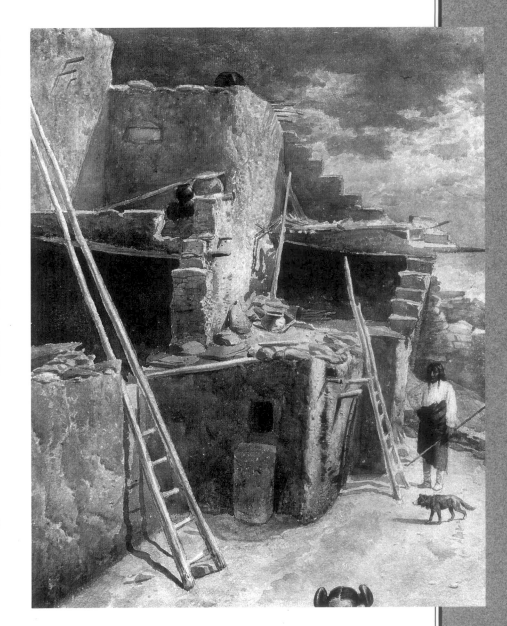

P eter Moran (1841–1914)
Walpi, Arizona, 1881
Watercolor and graphite on paper,
17 ¼ × 13 ¾ in.
Amon Carter Museum, Fort Worth,
Texas

The pueblo buildings of the American Southwest have been dated by tree-ring evidence to at least A.D. 919, and the so-called Classic Age of the great pueblos lasted from A.D. 100 to 1300.

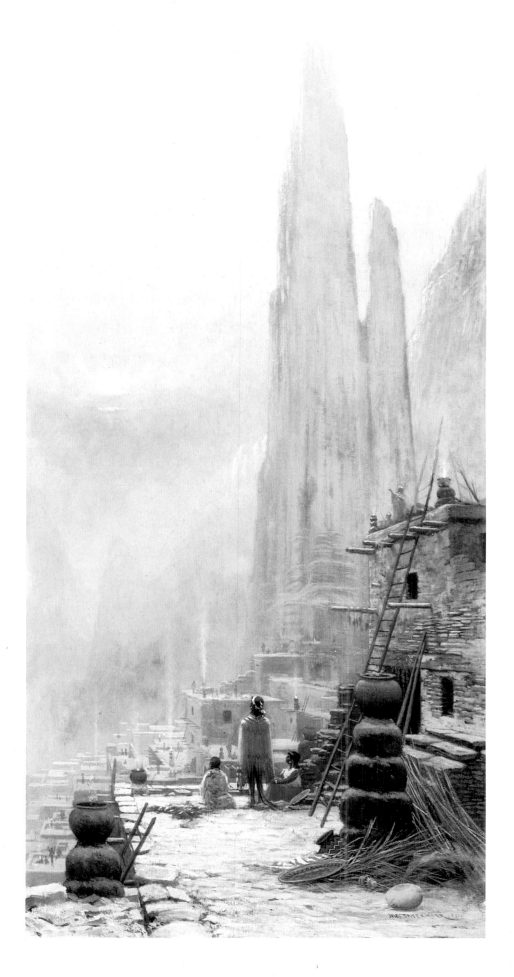

Spanish been motivated entirely by economic motives, it would have been the first and last chapter, and the American West would have been a very different place. But during the fifteen years of Oñate's failing enterprise, a small army of priests had been baptizing thousands of Indians, creating a population of Christian souls who (the padres argued) must not be abandoned. Ironically, this perpetuated in large measure the inhumane conditions for which Oñate had been censured. For, like him, each succeeding governor had to buy the office and then had to devise a way to turn a profit from his investment. This meant relentlessly working the Indians. While the unvarnished species of slavery Oñate had practiced was outlawed, the *encomienda* system, central to the Spanish colonization program, was nothing less than a system of enslavement. In return for services rendered the crown, a colonist was granted designated Indian families—sometimes the inhabitants of several towns—from whom he could exact labor as well as commodity tribute. Technically, the Indians were not held in slavery, but in trust, as wards. After all, while they might be worked to death, they were being saved (whether they liked it or not) from the eternal damnation to which their unbaptized state would otherwise have consigned them.

The *encomenderos* were supposed to facilitate the Christianization of the Indians. However, the missionaries were often at odds with these secular colonists over exploitation of their presumed charges. Not that the Indians always found better treatment at the hands of the missionaries themselves, who meted out public floggings in a vain effort to discourage "pagan" religious dances and other evidence of "devil worship."

By the middle of the seventeenth century, after some fifty years of Spanish tyranny, the Pueblo Indians made alliance with their hereditary enemies, the Apaches. Though they lived in the same arid region, the Pueblos and Apaches illustrate the vast range of American Indian culture. The Pueblos were agricultural, settled in their adobe-built towns, inclined to be peaceful. The Apaches were nomadic hunters, who roamed within a large territory. Fully two centuries before the great Indian wars of the American West, the Apaches had already earned a reputation as avid makers of war.

Even thus allied, the first attempts at Pueblo rebellion were defeated, and at least twenty years passed before the Apaches went on the warpath in earnest, terrorizing the Spanish Southwest. After two years of these guerrilla raids, Governor Antonio de Oterrmin arrested forty-seven Pueblo "medicine men," hanged three,

Jules Tavernier (1844–1889)
Indian Village of Acoma, 1879
Oil on canvas, 64 × 29 ½ in.
Courtesy of The Anschutz Collection

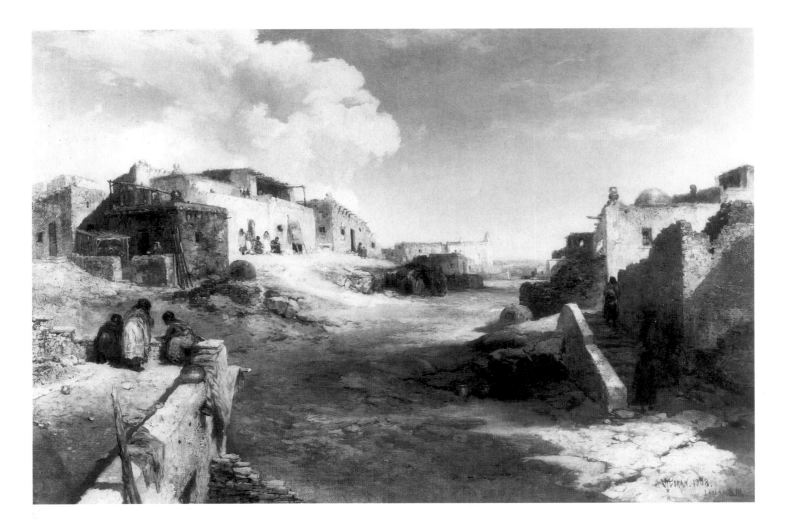

Thomas Moran (1837–1926)
Indian Pueblo, Laguna, New Mexico,
1908
Oil on canvas, 20 × 30 in.
Courtesy of The Anschutz Collection

and imprisoned the remainder in the territorial capital, Santa Fe. Among these was Popé, from the Tewa Pueblo. Released after several bitter years of ill use, he went into hiding in Taos, where he secretly organized a full-scale rebellion. That was no small task, since no action could be taken in any given pueblo without the unanimous decision of that pueblo's council. As it turned out, Popé failed to galvanize only the most remote pueblos far down the Rio Grande.

To coordinate the strike among the pueblos, Popé dispatched runners bearing knotted cords designed so that the last knot would be untied in each pueblo on the day set for the revolt: August 13, 1680. Despite a ruthless effort to keep the revolt secret—Popé killed his brother-in-law because he suspected him of treachery—word got out, and the revolt had to be launched on the tenth. Premature though it was, the action proved devastatingly effective. The major missions at Taos, Pecos, and Acoma were burned and the priests murdered, their bodies piled on the hated altars; lesser missions throughout the frontier province likewise fell; and outlying haciendas were destroyed, their inhabitants slain. Popé and his band moved on Santa Fe, taking the capital after a four-day siege. Popé installed himself in the palace Governor Oterrmin had evacuated. Of the twenty-five hundred Spaniards who had inhabited the province, perhaps a fifth had been killed. The survivors fled far downriver, as far as present-day El Paso, Texas, leaving behind all of their wordly possessions.

Indian triumph would prove rare in the history of the American West, and Popé's conduct after his victory was also highly unusual for an Indian and unheard of for a Pueblo. He set up as a dictator, probably more oppressive than even the Spanish had been. His eight-year reign of plundering taxation and summary execution for any disobedience spawned civil war among the pueblos. In 1692, four years after Popé's death, Governor Don Diego de Vargas laid siege to Santa Fe, cutting off its water and food supply until the inhabitants surrendered. In the course of the succeeding four years, all of the pueblos submitted once again to Spanish rule—except for the Hopis, whom the Spanish somehow overlooked.

The Apaches—and the Navahos to the north of them and the Comanches to the east—the Spanish could hardly overlook. From the time of the reconquest until the Mexican Revolution in 1821, these Indians made war on the colonists, raiding, plundering, and murdering while being raided, plundered, and murdered in return. After the revolution, the warfare continued, albeit now between Mexicans and Indians. And, after the 1846–48 war between Mexico and the United States, the fighting went on for another forty years as a long episode in the American Indian wars.

Not all relations between Spanish and Indians were hostile. As would be the case throughout the history of the American West, alliances were variously formed even with the Apaches and the Comanches to aid in putting down frequent Indian rebellions. In some cases, Indian alliances were sought to act as buffers against the encroachment of other European seekers of empire. By the end of the sixteenth century, England and France, traditional enemies of Spain, were making forays into the New World, as was Holland, newly independent of Spanish subjugation.

For the most part, Spain's monopoly on American settlement was challenged from the East Coast, with the English settlement of much of the seaboard north of Florida and south of present-day Canada, the Dutch settlement of present-day New York, and the French settlement of Canada. France also briefly occupied the

Carolinas and Florida, from which the Spanish handily evicted them in 1565 by taking Fort Caroline and slaughtering its defenders to a man.

Victory in the Carolinas and Florida notwithstanding, by the end of the sixteenth century, Spain was, quite simply, broke, having exhausted its treasure in European wars and, worse, its credit by defaulting on a 14.5 million ducat debt to the Old World's moneylenders. There was little the crown could do to counter a threat from France far more significant than that represented by her brief presence in Florida. In 1685 Robert Cavelier, sieur de La Salle aimed to establish a French colony at the mouth of the Mississippi, but his ships drifted off course in the Gulf of Mexico, and he landed at Matagorda Bay, Texas.

Ernest L. Blumenschein (1874–1960)
Sangre de Christo Mountains, 1925
Oil on canvas, 50 × 60 in.
Courtesy of The Anschutz Collection

These mountains, which shelter the village of Taos, became a favorite subject of several generations of artists, Taos visitors and residents alike.

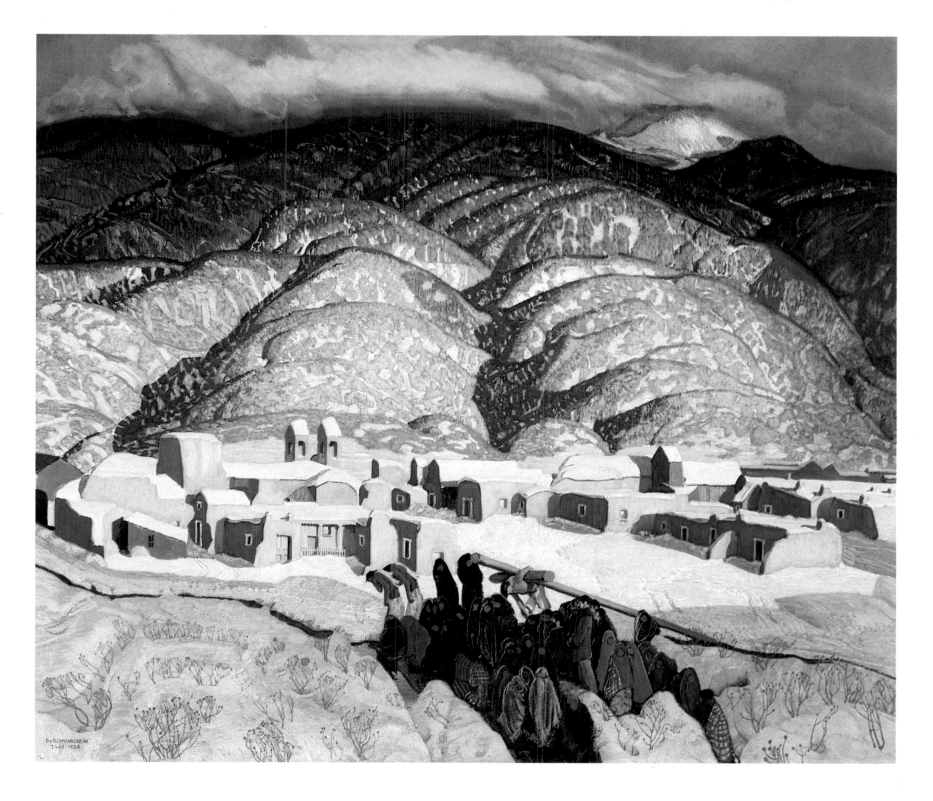

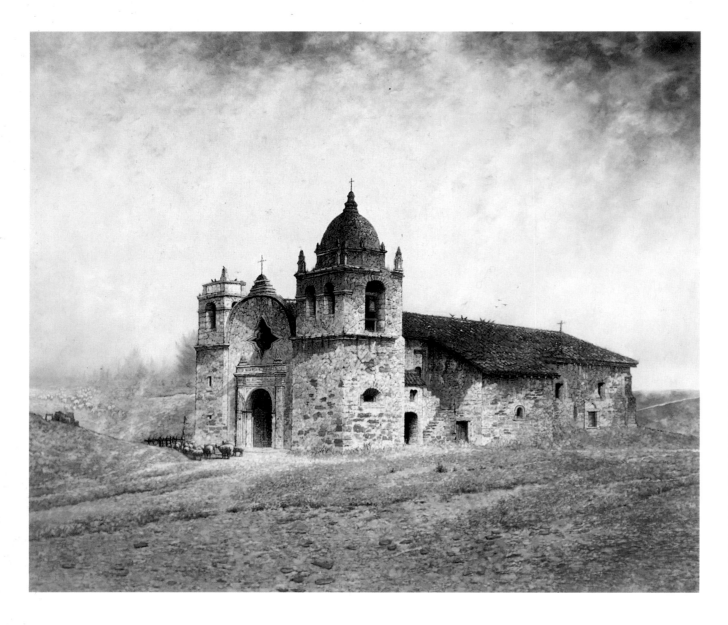

Edwin Deakin (1838–1923)
Mission San Carlos Borromeo, 1895
Oil on canvas, 50 × 60 in.
Seaver Center for Western History
Research, Natural History Museum
of Los Angeles County

The second California mission, San
Carlos Borromeo was established in
1770 at Monterey Bay by Father
Junípero Serra. One year later, the
mission was relocated to Carmel.
The structure seen in this painting
was built in 1793 under the direction
of Father Fermín de Lasuén.

Disease and Indian attack soon wiped out the colony (La Salle himself was killed in a mutiny), but a beachhead of sorts had been secured, and the French established their first lasting Louisiana colony in 1699. When they moved even closer to Spanish Texas by establishing a colony at Natchitoches on the Red River, Mexico City at last lost patience with the inaction of Madrid and authorized a series of Catholic missions, including one only fifteen miles from the Natchitoches colony. In 1718, one of the missions was even fortified with a garrison, or presidio, at Bexar, today's San Antonio. It was called the Alamo.

Thus, in the face of the mother country's near collapse, the Spanish West actually expanded—led no longer by conquistadors, but by black-robed Jesuit and Franciscan friars. By the end of the eighteenth century, Mexico, Texas, Arizona, New Mexico, and, most spectacularly, California were thickly dotted with missions, around which towns often grew and ranches were established.

Some of the mission priests were extraordinary men, vastly different from the small-minded tyrants who had accompanied Oñate in East Texas. Best known are the Jesuit Eusebio Francisco Kino and the Franciscan

Junípero Serra. Kino was born about 1645 near Trent, Italy, but entered a German Jesuit order in 1665 and trained as an astronomer and mathematician. These seemingly esoteric pursuits proved of great practical use when Kino began his missionary work in Mexico, Arizona, and California in the 1680s. For in the course of a quarter-century of missionary travel, during which Kino journeyed some twenty thousand miles—as much as seventy-five miles a day on horseback—and founded twenty-four missions, he drew up the most accurate maps of the Spanish frontier empire, from the Colorado River to the Gulf of Mexico; his map of California proved once and for all that it was not an island, as many had believed.

Described by a contemporary as "merciful to others but cruel to himself," the indefatigable Kino was beloved of the Indians who were settled in his missions. He was, moreover, a benefactor to later generations of southwesterners. At least twenty cities in the region owe their origins to his work, and the band of ranchos he established in conjunction with his missions was the genesis of the cattle industry in the American Southwest; he introduced to the country many varieties of livestock as well as Eu-

Walter Ufer (1876–1936)
Oferta para San Esquipula, 1918
Oil on canvas, 25 × 30 in.
Courtesy of The Anschutz Collection

Many of the old mission churches of
the Southwest are still used today
for worship.

WALTER UFER

BORN 1876, LOUISVILLE, KENTUCKY

DIED 1936, ALBUQUERQUE, NEW MEXICO

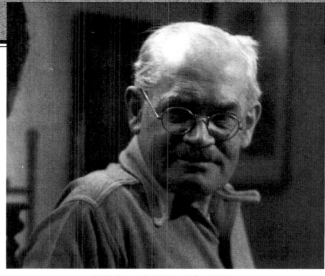

Will Connell, *Walter Ufer*, 1932.
Photograph. The Harwood Foundation Museum, Taos, New Mexico

Son of an engraver from Germany, Ufer was apprenticed to a commercial lithographer in 1892 and was then sent abroad to study at the Royal Applied Art Schools (1895–96) and the Royal Academy (1897–98) in Dresden, Germany. In 1900 he settled in Chicago, where he became a commercial artist and portrait painter, at the same time studying at the Art Institute and the J. Francis Smith Art School. Between 1905 and 1911, he worked as an advertising artist for Armour and Company, the meat packers, and then traveled to Munich for two years of study with Walter Thor. He spent 1913 painting in Italy, Paris, and North Africa.

Back in Chicago in 1914, Ufer found a patron in the city's former mayor Carter Harrison, who financed a trip to Taos. The artist was captivated by the New Mexican light and landscape and gave up studio painting entirely, preferring now to work out of doors and developing a brilliant Impressionist style that some have compared to Cézanne. When one of his paintings won third prize at the Carnegie International, all of the Taos artists benefited from the attention and prestige. Ufer's own success was fairly brief. Although he made as much as $50,000 per year during the early 1920s, bad advice from his dealer resulted in a long series of unsuccessful paintings. Emotionally unstable at best, Ufer gambled and drank. By the onset of the Great Depression, his work was wholly out of vogue, and he died disheartened and largely forgotten.

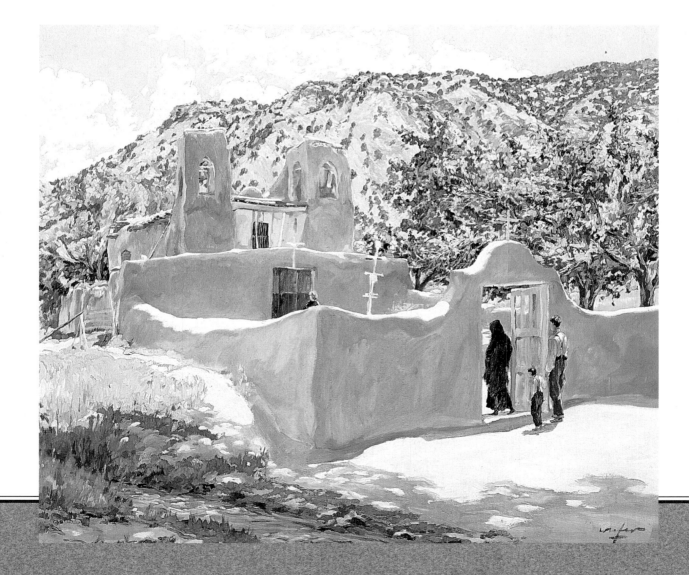

ropean grains and such fruits as grapes and pomegranates.

In 1713, two years after this explorer, cartographer, missionary, rancher, and builder died at his beloved Misión Santa Magdalena, Junípero Serra was born in Majorca. He became a Franciscan and, like his Jesuit counterpart, a scholar. But he eagerly abandoned the secure world of the university for life as a missionary in the New World, declaring that martyrdom was the "true gold of the Indies." After working as a missionary among the Pamé Indians of eastern Mexico and then serving as an itinerant minister, Serra was made president of the Baja California missions in 1768.

Soon thereafter, yet another seeker after empire was making its presence felt perilously near Spanish territory. Russian fur traders were setting up in Northern California. Again, the enfeebled Madrid government turned to the Church as a means of securing Spanish claims. Serra was attached to General José de Gálvez's expedition to occupy Alta California. It would have been a formidable undertaking for any man. Serra was partially lame and suffered from chronic ill health aggravated by his zeal for public self-mortification, which included flogging himself with a chain, beating his breast with a stone, and even burning himself with candles. It is said that, at the outset of the expedition, Serra was so weak that he had to be lifted into the saddle of his mule. As Kino had done in Texas, Arizona, and New Mexico, Serra brought not only religion, but the seeds of new crops—including the flower and vegetable seeds that started California's celebrated mission gardens—and about two hundred head of cattle.

In the course of his work in California, Serra founded nine of the twenty-one Franciscan missions in that country—an ingenious chain of settlement stretching from San Diego to Sonoma, each mission separated by about thirty miles, a day's ride along El Camino Real, the Royal Highway, which was no more than a dusty path at the time. Moreover, Serra's lifelong agitation for improved communication and supply routes between the missions was in large measure responsible for the development of the territory. Serra died in 1784, like Kino, at one of his missions—San Carlos Borromeo in Carmel.

The stated purpose of the missions was to Christianize Indians and train them to become productive citizens of New Spain. As we have seen, sometimes this was attempted through cruelty and hard usage. Sometimes, however, the missions were of positive benefit to the Indians, though even well-treated Indians often bridled under regimentation. In either case, the missions left a lasting mark on the American West, architecturally, culturally, and spiritually. Their mere presence "settled" the Southwest; they were communities and gave rise to satellite ranchos and haciendas. At their best, and perhaps their worst, they brought a certain *order* to the frontier.

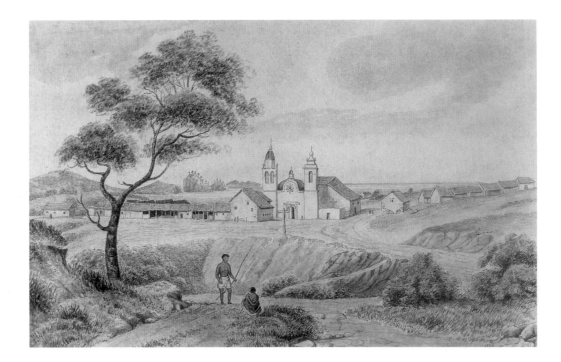

William Smyth (1823–1903)
San Carlos Mission Near Monterey, Sketched in the Autumn of 1827, 1827
Watercolor, 14 × 9½ in.
Peabody Museum, Harvard University

A cruder rendition of the celebrated Misión San Carlos Borromeo by a British naval officer whose ship had touched port at Monterey.

Misión San José, founded in 1720 by Father Antonio Margil de Jesús in Texas, is typical of one of the more successful Spanish missions. To begin with, its Indian inmates, the Coahuiltecans, welcomed the protection the walled mission and its adjacent presidio offered against raiding Apaches and Comanches—though the price of this protection was dawn-to-dusk regulation.

The product of empire, the missions were themselves miniature empires. Farming was the principal industry of San José, with staple crops raised at the mission itself, and animal products—meat, hides, wool—coming from the mission rancho some twenty-five miles away. Within the mission compound was, of course, the church, a graveyard, workshops, a communal oven and well, and a granary. The space between the compound's double walls was divided into Indian apartments. Measuring 11 by 14 or 16½ feet, furnished with bedsteads, buffalo-hide mattresses, cotton sheets, and wool blankets, the accommodations offered a higher standard of living than many Indians might find outside the mission. Even clothes were provided: a workday set and a Sunday set.

The day began at sunup with prayer and hymns, followed by a breakfast of *atole*, roasted corn gruel. Some Indians worked on the church, whose construction typically spanned years, and some fashioned arrows for defense against Apaches and Comanches. Others farmed just outside the mission walls, protected from hostiles by armed guards. Women wove baskets, spun wool, made pottery, and baked bread in the communal oven.

The tolling of Angelus summoned the Indians to prayer and lunch, followed by a siesta. Work was resumed until Vespers, a time for prayer and religious instruction. After an evening meal of roasted corn gruel, there was a brief interval of recreation, and bedtime came at sunset.

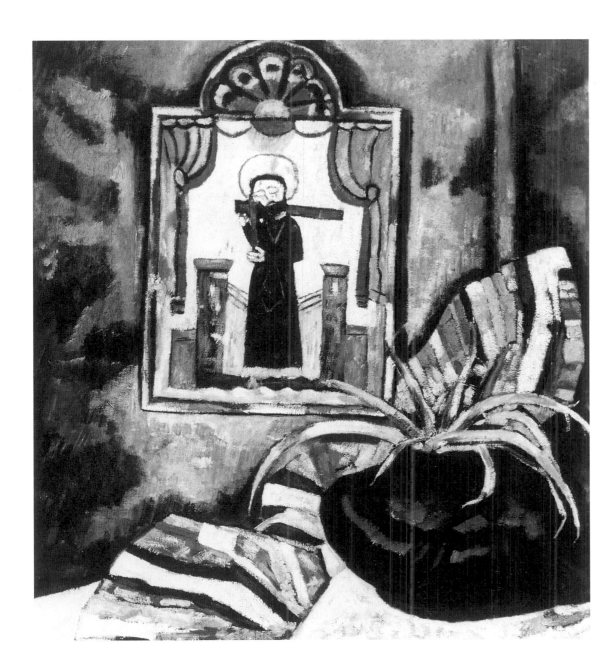

Marsden Hartley (1877–1943)
El Santo, 1919
Oil on canvas, 36 × 32 in.
Museum of Fine Arts, Museum of
New Mexico; Anonymous Gift

This great American Modernist
visited Taos and Santa Fe only
twice—in 1918 and 1919—but the
experience left a lasting impression.
He was especially attracted by the
objects of Hispanic-Indian religious
devotion, such as the *santos*, the
region's sacred folk art.

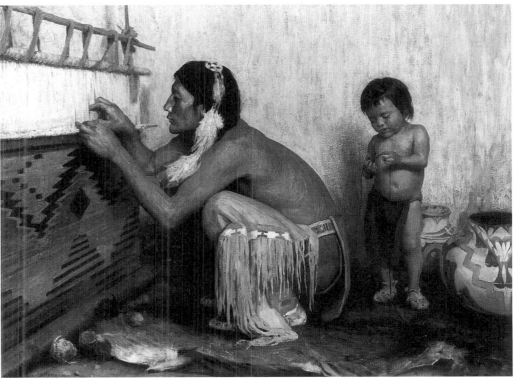

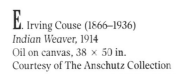 Irving Couse (1866–1936)
Indian Weaver, 1914
Oil on canvas, 38 × 50 in.
Courtesy of The Anschutz Collection

Weaving, traditionally practiced by
the southwestern tribes, supplied
blankets for the Indians' own use as
well as for trade. It was a native
industry the missions encouraged.

Whereas the conquistadors had treated the Indians as essentially a bestial enemy, the padres treated them as children to be supervised and regulated; neither extreme allowed for a full appreciation of their humanity. Yet, with all its inadequacies, the missions endured, many of them, into the nineteenth century, when they were secularized by the Mexican Republic in 1833–34.

BRITISH, FRENCH, AND INDIANS

In 1730, General James Edward Oglethorpe obtained a charter from the British crown to establish Georgia, thereby extending England's colonial empire down from the Carolinas and into the land Spain claimed as part of Florida. While Madrid boldly vowed to extirpate the English from Georgia, Oglethorpe wooed valuable allies among the Indians of the Gulf and the Cherokee of the uplands, neither of whom had any love for the Spanish. In 1738–39, they ceded most of their coastal lands to the Oglethorpe colony. Sporadic warfare between England and Spain ensued for some nine years, between 1739 and 1748, ending without settling the dispute over Georgia's southern border. However, British Georgia was clearly there to stay.

If the British were moving south on Spanish territory, they had also been moving west, threatening Spain and, even more directly, France. As early as 1718, Governor Spotswood of Virginia had led an expedition west, across the Blue Ridge. But it was the organization of the Ohio Company, by president of the Virginia Council Thomas Lee in 1747, that at last provoked vigorous French response. For the Ohio Company proposed to acquire half a million acres on each side of the Ohio River, trade with the Indians, and "extinguish" Indian claims to the land, thereby driving a wedge between French Canada and French Louisiana. To head off the Ohio Company, Celerón de Bienville was dispatched in 1749 with a fleet of bateaux and canoes to take possession of the Ohio Valley for France. Four years later, Governor Duquesne built a chain of French forts on the Allegheny and upper Ohio rivers, claiming the right to all of the West north of the Ohio. Virginia governor Robert Dinwiddie sent twenty-two-year-old George Washington to the forks of the Ohio to protest, but to no avail. Thereupon, Dinwiddie dispatched Washington with a regiment of 150 to the site of what would become Pittsburgh; his mission was to forestall French occupation of the commanding confluence of the Ohio, Monongahela, and Allegheny rivers.

Albert Bierstadt (1830–1902)
Yosemite Valley, 1868
Oil on canvas, 36 × 54 in.
Collection of the Oakland Museum;
Gift of Marguerite Laird

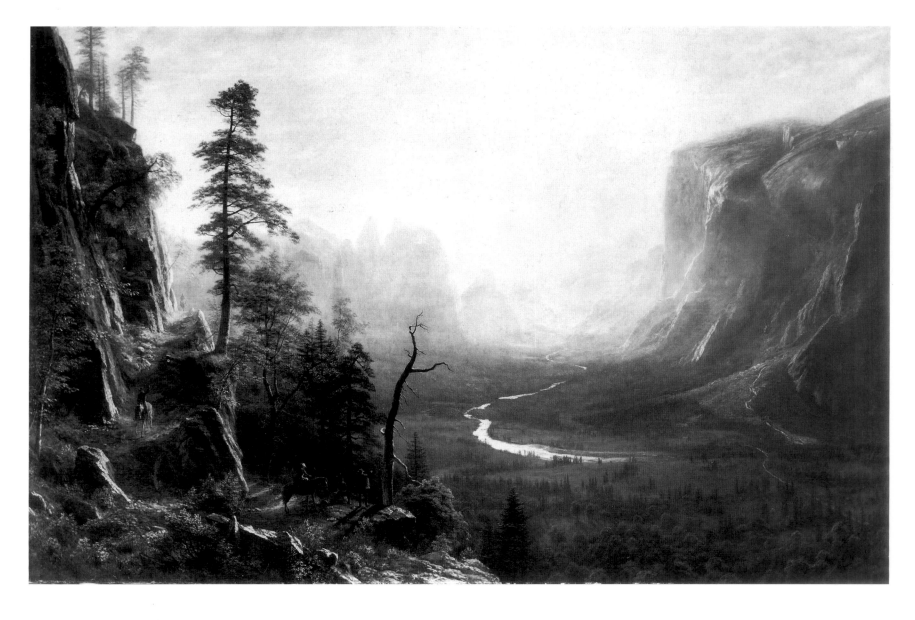

While the issue that had touched off the war was control of the upper Ohio, and while the outcome of the war would be the opening of the trans-Appalachian West and, ultimately, the opening of the entire West to eastern, English-speaking settlers, the conflict was in a larger sense one theater of Europe's Seven Years' War. Indeed, it was part of what might well be called the real first world war: in Europe, France, Austria, Sweden, some small German states, and, later, Spain were squared off against Britain and Prussia; naval forces contended on the Atlantic and Indian oceans and the Mediterranean and Caribbean seas; battles were fought in India and in the Philippines. In America, as had been the case in previous, more localized, colonial disputes, Indians took up sides willingly and unwillingly. As is apparent from the numbers who fought Braddock at Fort Duquesne, Indians often bore the brunt of the fighting. Almost always, they did most of the dying.

At Fort Duquesne the most important of the French Indian allies were the Delawares, who, after Braddock's defeat, freely raided the frontier, effectively pushing back the western borders of Pennsylvania, Maryland, and Virginia some one hundred miles. Indeed, next to the Indians, it was the white settlers of the frontier who suffered most during the nine-year course of the war. Nevertheless, that one-hundred-mile retreat from western expansion was quite temporary. Between Braddock's defeat in 1754 and the summer of 1758, the British suffered many reverses, perhaps the most stunning of which was the defeat on July 1, 1758, of some twelve thousand British troops, sent to take Fort Ticonderoga on Lake George, by a mere three thousand French soldiers. But that was to prove the high-water mark of French fortunes. Later that month, Major General Jeffrey Amherst and Brigadier General James Wolfe took the French fort of Louisbourg, Nova Scotia, at the mouth of the Saint Lawrence, and the next month English troops seized Fort Frontenac near present-day Kingston, Ontario. Such British victories emboldened Conrad Weiser, a western trader employed by the Pennsylvania legislature as a kind of ambassador to the Indians, to approach Tedyuskung, leader of the peaceful Delawares—those who had not moved west and sided with the French—to enlist his influence in securing peace with the western Delawares. In a series of councils held at Easton, Pennsylvania, a tenuous peace was achieved by playing the Delawares off the Iroquois, who were officially neutral in the hostilities between the French and English, but who in fact were unofficially allied with the English. At the October council, the English representatives persuaded the Iroquois to revise a 1754 treaty whereby they had ceded most of western Pennsylvania to the English. The Iroquois now granted the Delawares the right to hunt and live on these western lands, and the English agreed not to settle the territory. In return, the Delawares would cease cooperation with the French.

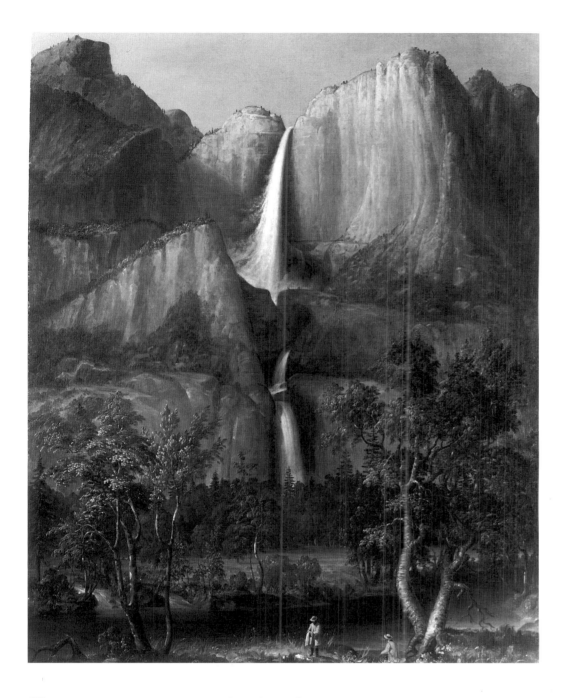

William Smith Jewett (1812–1873)
Yosemite Falls, 1859
Oil on canvas, 52 ⅛ × 42 in.
Collection of The Newark Museum;
Gift of Mrs. Charles W. Engelhard,
1977

The simplified massing of vertical planes here is peculiarly modern in feeling.

The only trouble was that the French had already raised Fort Duquesne there. Washington's small band was defeated at Great Meadows, in western Pennsylvania, taken prisoner, released, and sent home.

Young Washington next served as aide-de-camp to General Edward Braddock, who had been sent from England to America with portions of two regiments to take Fort Duquesne and challenge the French claim to the western territory. Wholly unprepared for a campaign in the wilderness, Braddock insisted on marching his troops in a full column of four through thick woods, their bright red coats offering excellent targets for the sortie—637 French-allied Indians, 150 French Canadian militiamen, 72 French regulars—that issued from Fort Duquesne on July 9, 1754. Of the 1,459 men in Braddock's advance guard, 977 were killed or wounded that day, including Braddock, shot through the lungs, who lived long enough to turn command over to an inept colonel. The French and Indian War had begun.

That was in October. On November 25, English forces closed on Fort Duquesne. A short time before, the French commander approached a Delaware camp with a "war belt," a string of wampum traditionally sent to one's ally before a battle. The Indians treated it like a snake, kicking it from one to another until one of them flung it away with a stick. The British closed on Fort Duquesne, but before they could take it, the French blew it up. Coincident with the advance on the fort—which, rebuilt, became Fort Pitt, around which Pittsburgh grew—was the opening of Forbes's Road, the first of three roads that would traverse western Pennsylvania by the start of the Revolution. To the British colonists, the fall of Fort Duquesne and the opening of Forbes's Road seemed unambiguous license to ignore the month-old Treaty of Easton. The inexorable push west was resumed, and, not incidentally, a pattern of white-Indian promises and betrayal was established.

Though Wolfe's taking Quebec in September of 1759 effectively finished France as a major power in North America, and ended its claims to the West, the war dragged on for another four years, with considerable loss of life on the frontier. Despite the continued Indian attacks and an official proclamation on October 13, 1761, reiterating the terms of the Treaty of Easton, settlers continued to pour into the troubled West.

Meanwhile, Spain was becoming painfully aware that a British victory in North America would be more of a threat to its western settlements and to Florida than would a New World at least divided up among Spain, France, and England. Madrid prepared to join the Seven Years' War—and, perforce, the French and Indian War—on the side of France and her allies. Anticipating attack, Great Britain declared war on Spain on January 2, 1762. The Spanish promptly suffered a series of defeats, including the loss of Cuba. In compensation for these losses to her ally, war-weary France, seeking a quick end to what had become a futile contest, secretly concluded the Treaty of Ildefonso on November 3, 1762, ceding to Spain all her territory west of the Mississippi, including the Isle of Orleans. Thus, when the Treaty of Paris ended both the Seven Years' War and the French and Indian War on February 10, 1763, the Mississippi effectively became a border between English and Spanish America.

Hard upon that treaty came colonial petitions to King George III for land to settle in Illinois and West Virginia, and the colony of Virginia summarily asserted claims to the territory covered by present-day West Virginia, Kentucky, Ohio, Indiana, Illinois, Michigan, Wisconsin, and parts of Minnesota. In September of 1763, the Mississippi Company, led by George Washington, received a royal grant of 2.5 million acres between the Ohio and Wisconsin rivers for settlement by Virginia soldiers who fought in the French and Indian War, but in October the king issued the Proclamation of 1763 otherwise establishing the Appalachian Mountains as the limit of western expansion.

Why debar settlement of territory so hard won?

Three years earlier, on September 8, 1760, the governor of French Canada surrendered to Jeffrey Amherst. Among the prizes taken were the forts built by the French on the western Great Lakes, including Detroit. Among the Indians in the area of the fort were the Ottawas, led by chief Pontiac. At first Pontiac showed great willingness to come to amicable terms with the English, accepting wampum from the British envoy, Robert Rogers (who had commanded Rogers' Rangers during the war), and smoking a peace pipe with him. The fort officially changed hands on November 29, and Captain Donald Campbell was installed as commander. Really, it seemed, little had changed: the French settlers who lived nearby still gathered at the fort to gossip and pass the time of day; trade continued with the Indians; there were even parties, with card games and dancing, late into the evening.

But Lord Amherst had a policy, and one he was particular about enforcing. Whereas the French had maintained the goodwill of the Indians by supplying them with regular gifts of provisions and ammunition, Amherst could "not see why the Crown should be put to that expense. . . . [P]urchasing the good behavior either of Indians or any others . . . I do not understand. When men of whatsoever race behave ill, they must be punished but not bribed." That was one affront. Add to that the victors' open contempt for the Indians, as well as a fear that the English intended to usurp the Indians' land (indeed, Amherst had already attempted to give some Seneca land near Niagara to officers as a reward for war service), and conflict was inevitable.

There appeared among the Indians a prophet—the "Delaware Prophet"—who urged a total break with the whites. They blocked the Indians' path to heaven, and to remove that block, war would undoubtedly be necessary.

Peter Rindisbacher (1806–1834)
A Party of Indians, 1822–26
Watercolor on paper,
8 3/8 × 10 5/8 in.
Denver Art Museum

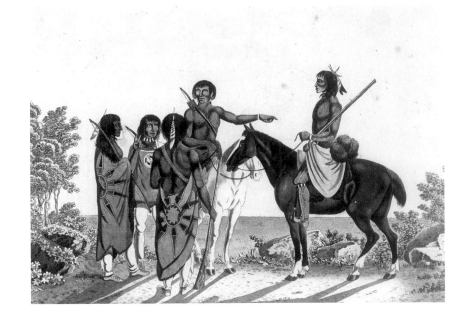

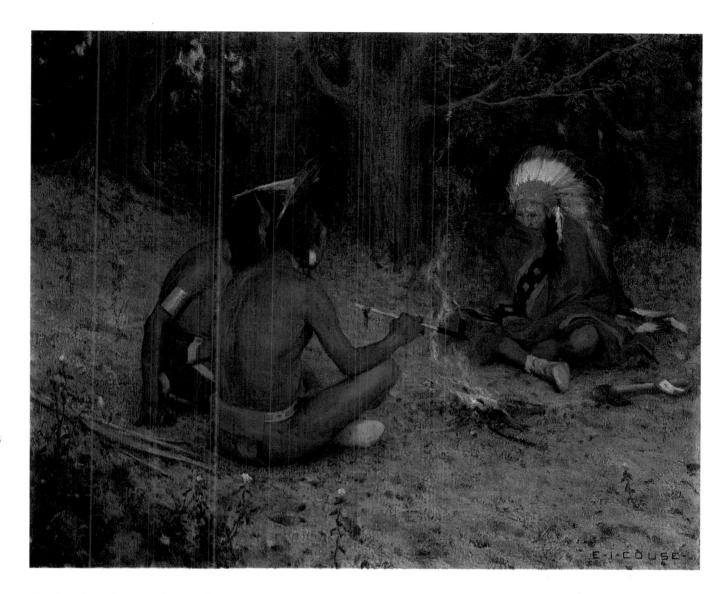

E. Irving Couse (1866–1936)
The Peace Pipe, n.d.
Oil on canvas, 26 × 32 in.
The Metropolitan Museum of Art;
Gift of Mrs. Adolph Obrig in memory of her husband, 1917

The tradition of smoking a "peace pipe"—called a calumet by the white traders in Canada and the Great Lakes region—survived the centuries and was practiced by otherwise culturally and regionally diverse tribes. The Indians Couse depicts here are from the Southwest of the early twentieth century.

Pontiac plotted a surprise attack on Detroit to take place on an ostensibly peaceful visit, but his plan was betrayed—perhaps by an Indian girl in love with the fort's new commander, Major Gladwin—and the garrison received the Ottawa visitors on the appointed day fully armed and with fixed bayonets. Pontiac aborted his scheme, resolved to gain admittance to the fort again, but this time Gladwin would admit only the chiefs, no braves. Pontiac turned at last to the settlements beyond the fort and killed three people.

When Pontiac attempted to rally the local French to support an open attack against the fort, they prevailed on him to make peace with Gladwin. A delegation of chiefs and Frenchmen called on the fort with a request that its former commander, Captain Campbell, be sent out to negotiate directly with Pontiac. Campbell volunteered to do so and was summarily taken hostage. Pontiac demanded the surrender of Detroit, Gladwin refused, and Pontiac went to war. On May 16, 1763, a delegation of Ottawa and Huron chiefs approached the fort at Sandusky, on Lake Erie. The commander, Ensign Christopher Pauli, knew the Indians and admitted them. They seized him, slaughtered his fifteen-man garrison, and spared Pauli himself because an Indian widow adopted him as a replacement for her husband. Less than two weeks later, Pontiac at-

tacked and captured a party from Niagara carrying supplies for Detroit. Next, a fort near present-day Fort Wayne, Indiana, fell when the commander, Ensign Robert Holmes, was lured outside the stockade by his Indian mistress and killed. His eleven-man garrison surrendered. On June 1 an Indian party approached Fort Ouiatenon—at present-day Lafayette, Indiana—and called its commander, Lieutenant Edward Jenkins, to attend a council in a nearby cabin. He came out, entered the cabin, was captured, and his twenty-man command surrendered the fort. At Fort Michilimackinac, Captain George Etherington and thirty-five men, unaware of the hostilities, left the stockade to watch a game of lacrosse between some Chippewas and Sauks. The ball was sent flying into the stockade, the Indians hurtled past the sentries and into the fort, dropped their lacrosse sticks, seized weapons previously smuggled in by their women, and killed twenty men. They then attacked the surrounding countryside.

After Michilimackinac fell, Pontiac turned to targets farther east, in Pennsylvania: Fort Pitt, Fort Ligonier, Fort Bedford. All held out. But then the Senecas attacked Fort Venango, in Franklin, Pennsylvania, killing the entire garrison of fifteen or sixteen men. Next came Fort Le Boeuf, Waterford, Pennsylvania, where a half dozen or

EANGER IRVING COUSE

—

BORN 1866, SAGINAW, MICHIGAN

DIED 1936, ALBUQUERQUE, NEW MEXICO

—

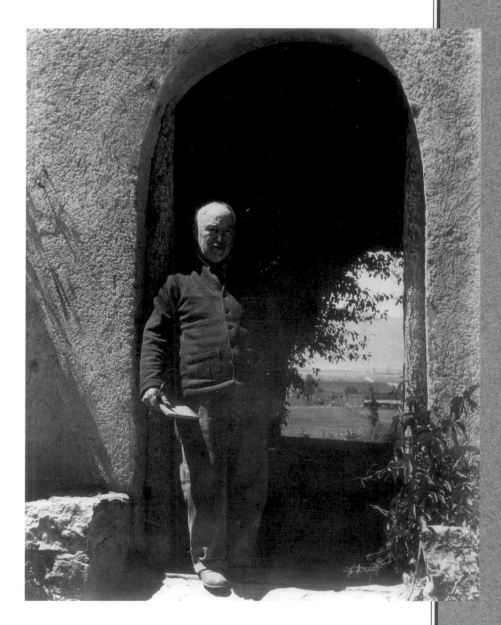

Will Connell, *Eanger Irving Couse*, 1932. Photograph. The Harwood Foundation Museum, Taos, New Mexico.

Growing up in Michigan's Chippewa country, Couse gained an early familiarity with Indians. He painted houses in Saginaw to raise tuition funds for study at the Art Institute of Chicago, which he attended in 1884, subsequently moving to New York for study at the Art Students League and the National Academy of Design. Between 1887 and 1890, he was in Paris at the Académie Julian, studying with Robert Fleury and Adolphe Bouguereau, who was to prove his single most significant influence. In Paris, he met and married a girl from Oregon, and the couple moved to her home state, where Couse set about painting the Indians of the Northwest coast. These early works did not sell, and the Couses left Oregon as well as the United States to settle and paint on the coast of Normandy. The pastorals and marine paintings the artist created there were successful and, after ten years, Couse returned to the States and established a studio in New York City.

In June 1902, Joseph Sharp and Ernest Blumenschein persuaded the painter to visit Taos, which Couse found much to his liking, pointing out that it rhymed with his last name. For the next quarter-century, Couse summered in Taos, until he settled there permanently in 1927.

A prolific painter—his canvases number some 1,500—Couse was praised for his authentic, sensitive, but unsentimental depiction of Indian life. His work gained nationwide popular exposure through publication in calendars distributed by the Santa Fe Railroad.

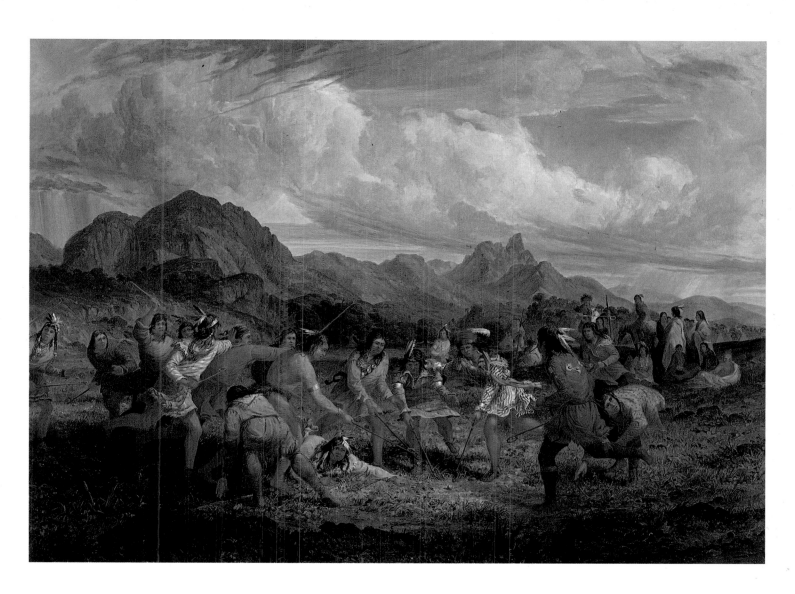

more died. A combined force of Senecas, Ottawas, Hurons, and Chippewas put Fort Presque Isle, at Erie, to the torch. A garrison of thirty surrendered on condition that they be permitted to withdraw to Fort Pitt. The attackers agreed—and then promptly divided the prisoners among the four tribes.

Shortly after this string of Seneca triumphs, a band of Delawares laid siege to Fort Pitt. On June 24, they demanded surrender. The fort would be quite a prize, with its large, 338-man garrison. Simeon Ecuyer, a Swiss mercenary acting as commander in the absence of Colonel Henry Bouquet, refused to surrender, sending the Indians a "present" of two blankets and a handkerchief from the fort's smallpox hospital. The Delawares understood and retreated. (Later, a rescued white captive reported the disease rampant among the tribe.)

Throughout all of this, Detroit held out against continual siege. Periodically, Major Gladwin sent detachments out from the fort to take the offensive. On July 4, two Indians were killed, including the nephew of the chief of the Saginaw Chippewas. The chief demanded that Pontiac turn over Captain Campbell—a prisoner since May 10—to his vengeance. The captain was promptly killed and scalped, his body thrown into the river to float past the fort. In August, Colonel Bouquet led a force of nearly five hundred from Carlisle, Pennsylvania, to Fort Pitt, to relieve the besieged garrison. After a pitched battle at Bushy Run, in which Bouquet man-

aged to outflank and surprise his Delaware, Shawnee, Mingo, and Huron opponents, the column reached the defenders.

In all, perhaps as many as two thousand English settlers died during the spring, summer, and fall of Pontiac's "conspiracy." Such losses, coupled with the exuberant brutality of the Indians in war, provoked a more than equally brutal response from white settlers in the form of vigilantism. A mob from Paxton and Donegal, Pennsylvania, massacred a group of Conestoga Indians in Lancaster County on December 14, 1763. Three men, two women, and a boy were stabbed, hacked, and mutilated. The Indians who survived the attack were taken into protective custody in the Lancaster workhouse, but on December 27 the vigilantes broke in and killed fourteen Indians—again, men, women, and children—as they knelt at prayer.

Not only did the Conestogas have nothing to do with hostilities against the forts and settlers, Pontiac himself had agreed to peace in October. Lord Amherst, for his part, accepted the peace somewhat grudgingly. He advocated extermination of the Indians. He even considered disseminating among them more smallpox-tainted blankets, a plan abandoned for fear of infecting his own people, particularly in the event of close combat.

As to Pontiac, his power had come to an end. He visited the French in the Illinois country, but he did not again embrace them. He was shot in the back by a Peoria

Indian in 1769. Perhaps the English at Fort de Chartres, near Cahokia, Illinois, had put the Peoria up to the deed.

So far as influencing official policy, Pontiac's war making had been effective. With so many outposts threatened or fallen, the king's ministers realized that it was one thing to claim territory and another to hold and defend it. Hence the Proclamation of 1763, and for the next decade, up to the eve of the Revolution, the crown negotiated treaties with the Indians limiting white settlement chiefly to the territory east of the Appalachians. But that was only *official* policy. In reality, Pontiac's defeat and death meant an end to the kind of unity required to halt the British advance west. The king's ministers might legislate, but by the 1770s white settlement had reached western Pennsylvania and Kentucky. When Shawnees attacked settlements established there by veterans of the French and Indian War, Virginia governor Lord Dunmore, who had granted them the land as a reward for war service, called out the militia. The Shawnees appealed to the Iroquois for help in repelling the force, but after a council with the English, the Iroquois refused. The Shawnees were beaten—at the cost of fifty English killed and a hundred wounded.

"Lord Dunmore's War," a brief and ugly affair, was waged not only against the Shawnees in 1774, but against a king who would halt the westward course of empire. The next year a much vaster and longer war against that king would begin, fought in large measure for the same reason.

REVOLUTION

Insofar as the Revolution was fought for the West, it was a war for the future. While most of the battles took place on the eastern seaboard, the West was hardly at peace. As usual, frontiersmen and Indians suffered in a series of raids and counterraids. As, earlier in the century, empires had courted Indian allies in a contest for possession of the continent, so now the British and the Americans vied for the loyalty of the powerful Iroquois. At first they remained neutral—and unified. But by the second year of war, four of the six Iroquois nations—the Mohawks, Cayugas, Senecas, and Onondagas—sided with the British, and two—the Oneidas and Tuscaroras—joined in the Americans' cause.

In the North, the British-Indian alliance threatened to wipe out settlements along the Pennsylvania and New York frontiers. The combined forces of Tory colonel John Butler's Rangers and Mohawks under Chief Thayendanegea—known to the whites as Joseph Brant—raked the Mohawk and Wyoming valleys during 1778 and 1779, until George Washington was able to divert troops from the principal action in the East in order to relieve the West. A force of twenty-five hundred under General John Sullivan combined with a smaller force of fifteen hundred under General James Clinton and

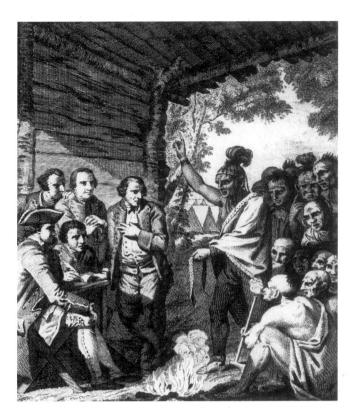

Benjamin West (1738–1820)
Pontiac and Bouquet
New York Public Library, Rare Book Collection

In this print, the famed American expatriate artist depicts the peace parley between the rebellious Pontiac and Colonel Henry Bouquet, who dealt the chief a crushing blow at Bushy Run.

pushed into Iroquois country, destroying some forty Iroquois towns and the Indians' harvest.

And that, General Sullivan assumed, was that. He was wrong. The destruction of their homes and their crops only intensified the Indians' will to fight. The Mohawk Valley remained subject to combined Indian-Tory raids until the autumn of 1781.

In the South, in western Virginia and the Carolinas, as well as west of the Proclamation line, in Tennessee and Kentucky, Cherokees raided the isolated and far-flung settlements. In 1776, John Stuart, the *British* superintendent of Indian affairs in the South, was so appalled by the ferocity of the attacks that he actually warned Tennessee settlers—nominally rebels—of impending raids.

The western situation was not all bad news for the patriots. Between mid 1778 and early 1779, a force of Kentuckians under Colonel George Rogers Clark penetrated the Ohio and Illinois country as far as the Mississippi River, in effect securing American claims to the region bounded on the south by the Ohio River, on the north by Canada, and on the west by the Mississippi.

The conclusion of the Revolution assured the independence of the United States, but it did not end sporadic Indian warfare in the West, and, while the Continental army had secured western New York and George Rogers Clark had at least staked the new nation's claim to the Old Northwest, the Spanish still held the territory west of the Mississippi, and the British still occupied Detroit, a handful of other forts, and the whole of Canada. America's great ally, France, having pushed England out of at least part of the continent, was not eager for the United States to emerge as a potential new rival.

Emanuel Leutze (1816–1868)
Westward the Course of Empire Takes its Way, 1863
Mural, 20 × 30 ft.
Collection of the House of Representatives

Commissioned as a U.S. Capitol mural, Leutze's allegorical masterwork was based on a sketching trip to the Rockies.

EMANUEL GOTTLIEB LEUTZE

BORN 1816, GMÜND, GERMANY

DIED 1868, WASHINGTON, D.C.

The fame of the artist's best-known work, *Washington Crossing the Delaware* (1851), overshadows his single great contribution to western art, the U.S. Capitol mural, *Westward the Course of Empire Takes Its Way* (1859–62). Although it is an allegorical representation of the evolution of civilization from east to west, its realistic details were based on a sketching trip to the Rocky Mountains.

Son of a German political refugee, Leutze was raised in Virginia and Philadelphia, where he studied drawing with John A. Smith and began to paint portraits in 1837. The artist sailed for Düsseldorf in 1840, where he became the pupil of Karl Friedrich Lessing, German master of epic historical painting. Leutze remained in Düsseldorf for almost two decades and even painted *Washington Crossing the Delaware* there, using various American visitors as models, including the sometime western painter Worthington Whittredge, who stood in for Washington. The Rhine, choked with ice, served well for the Delaware.

The artist's return to the United States was occasioned by the Capitol mural commission.

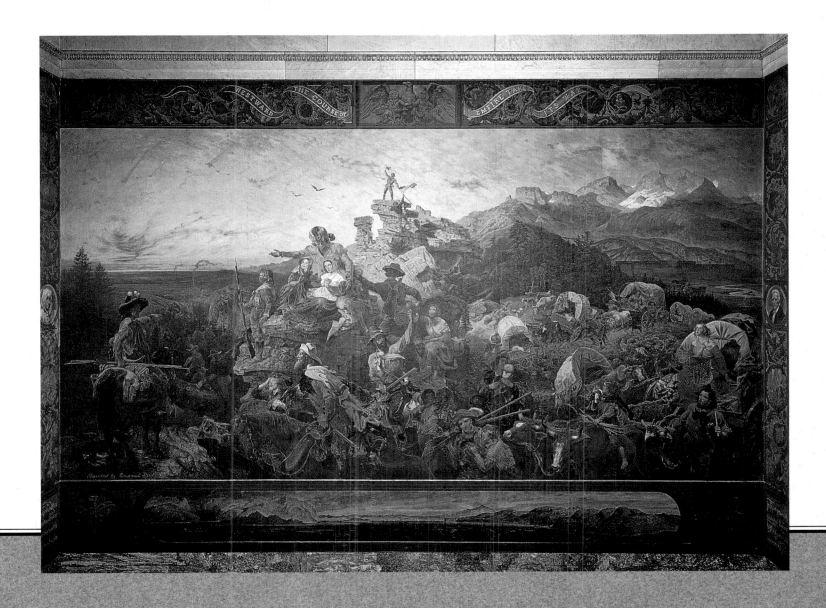

France wanted to see another of her allies, Spain, control Florida, retain sway west of the Mississippi, and hold jointly with the United States most of western Kentucky, Tennessee, and Georgia as a protectorate reserved for Indians and from which the white settlers would be expelled. The Old Northwest would be ceded back to England or divided between England and the United States.

The American peace commissioners outflanked the French and their scheme by soliciting separate talks with the British. Eager to weaken the bond between the two revolutionary allies, the English agreed to the talks and finally yielded the Old Northwest and confirmed American sovereignty over Kentucky and Tennessee. England did cede Florida and its Gulf Coast strip to Spain (a corridor of territory to the north of this, in present-day Mississippi and Alabama, known as the Yazoo Strip, was disputed until Spain ceded it in 1795).

But the problems of control over the West were hardly resolved. By the end of the war, Kentucky had some forty-five thousand settlers and Tennessee ten thousand, both populations pushing toward the Mississippi. Neither territory was a state or even slated for statehood; Kentucky was a region of Virginia, and Tennessee a part of North Carolina. As had been the case since well before the Revolution, the frontiersmen resented government emanating from remote eastern capitals. For that matter, those Tidewater capitals regarded the frontiersmen as a drain on their resources, contributing little in the form of tax revenue and yet demanding costly protection from Indian raids and the like. There was yet another conflict, between the states that claimed western lands and those that did not. The latter refused to sign the Articles of Confederation until all state claims were ceded to the Continental Congress.

Cession was not an orderly process. In 1780, Congress passed a resolution urging cession; only Connecti-

Thomas Moran (1837–1926)
The Grand Canyon, 1913
Oil on canvas, 30 × 40 in.
Gilcrease Museum, Tulsa, Oklahoma

In significant measure, it was for possession of the West—and wonders such as this—that the American Revolution was fought.

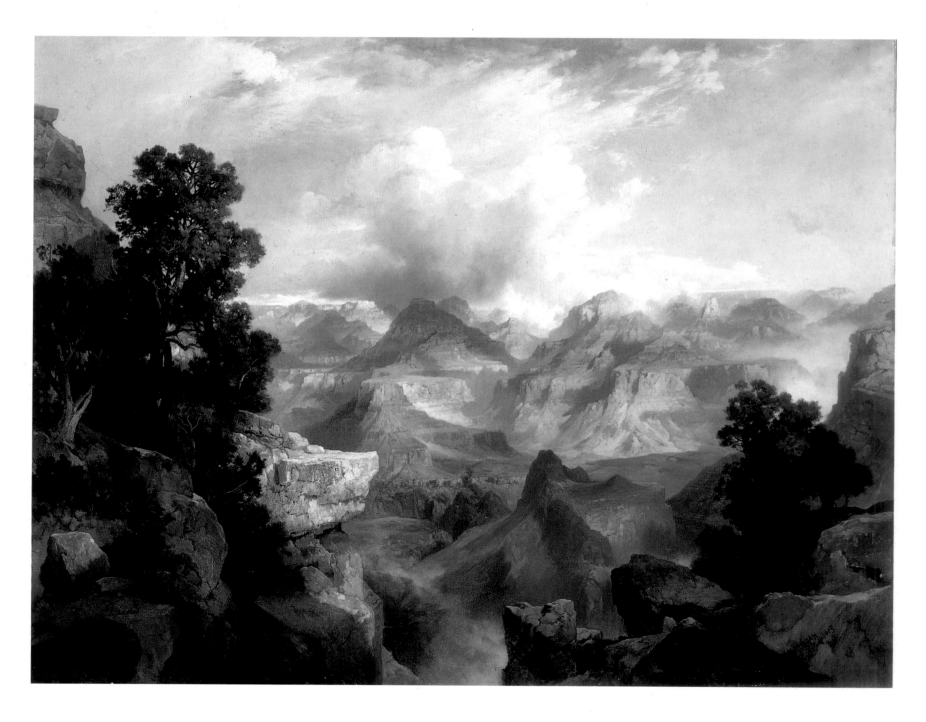

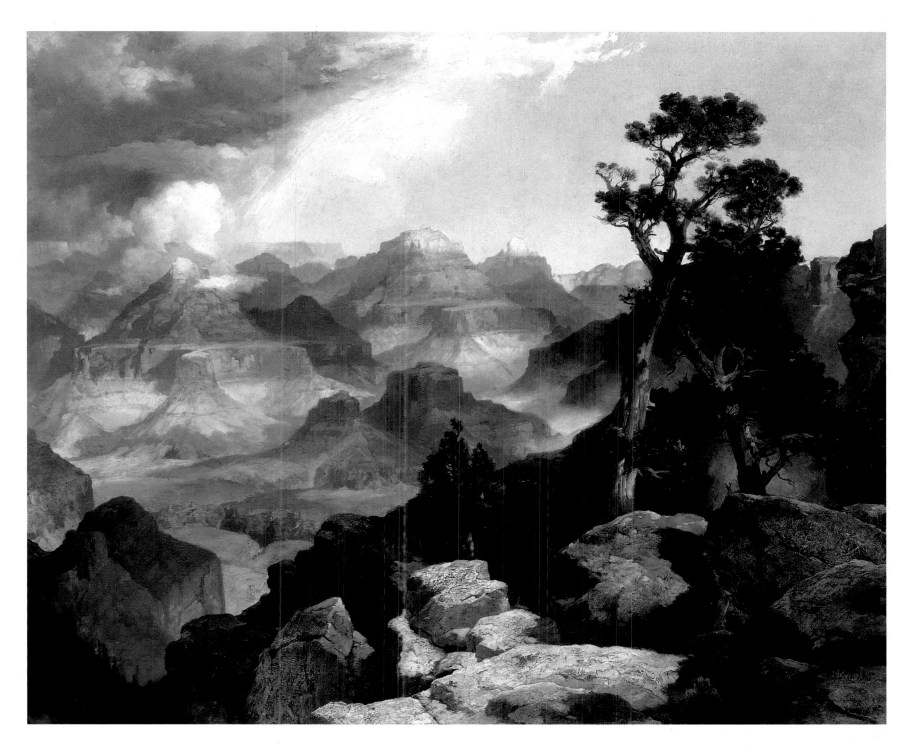

Thomas Moran (1837–1926)
Clouds in the Canyon, 1915
Oil on canvas, 20 × 25 in.
The Rockwell Museum, Corning,
New York

Moran's great gift was a facility for painting—so he made it seem—with light itself.

cut ceded its claims immediately. New York, later in the year, ceded western territory that was actually held by Iroquois Indians. Virginia ceded its claims to land north of the Ohio River in 1781. The other states waited until the conclusion of the Peace of Paris to cede their claims. And in these states, private land speculation ran amok, often to the profit of the state. North Carolina, for example, sold off about four million acres of Tennessee for an average of five cents an acre, pocketed the proceeds, and then ceded the territory to the Continental Congress in 1784. Cession to the central government did not please the frontiersmen of Tennessee, representatives of whom convened at Jonesboro and voted to seek admission to the Union as the sovereign state of Franklin (the name intended to flatter Benjamin Franklin into supporting the endeavor). The application for statehood fell on deaf ears

in Congress, and, in the meantime, North Carolina thought better of its offer to Congress and withdrew it. This unsettled period gave rise to more land speculation (which, if nothing else, further enriched North Carolina), debate over whether to join the territory with American Spain, and even a perfunctory rebellion against North Carolina staged by Franklin's would-be governor, John Sevier. Sevier renounced his gubernatorial claims in 1789, and in 1790 North Carolina again ceded Tennessee to Congress—this time for keeps. Six years later, the territory became the state of Tennessee.

Except for the vacillation of North Carolina and the stubbornness of Georgia (which did not deliver the last portion of its western claim until 1804), all of the states had ceded their claims by 1784. The American West had been carved up by force, fiat, and the divine right of

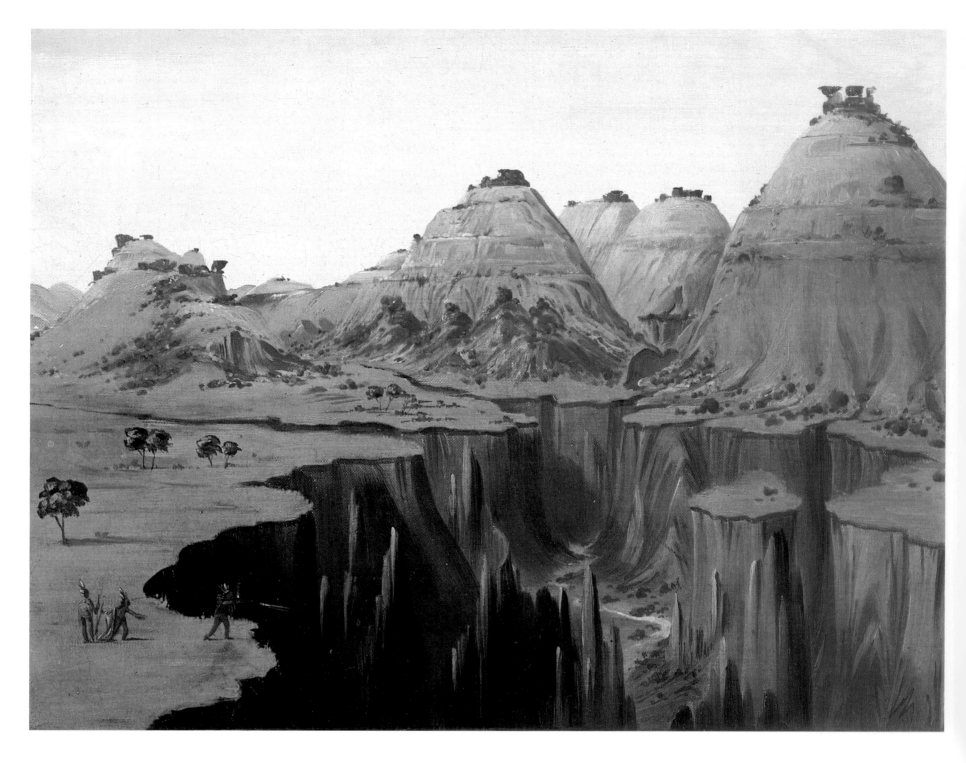

George Catlin (1796–1872)
Brick Kilns, Clay Bluffs, 1,900 Miles above St. Louis, 1832
Oil on canvas, 11 ¼ × 14 ⅜ in.
National Museum of American Art, Smithsonian Institution; Gift of Mrs. Joseph Harrison, Jr.

kings; now Congress proposed survey and legislation. The Land Ordinance of 1785 mandated a massive survey of the West in order to impose on the land a titanic grid of prime meridians and baselines run north and south, east and west without regard for hills, mountains, valleys, or rivers. The grid was to be divided into townships, each six miles square, each containing thirty-six one-mile-square—640-acre—"sections." The surveyed land was to be sold to the highest bidder for at least one dollar an acre. In each township, section 16 was reserved for schools, and sections 8, 11, 26, and 29 were set aside for unspecified future government purposes. A provision of the ordinance to set aside an additional section for the support of the predominant religion of the township narrowly failed to gain congressional approval.

The ordinance was a product of the eighteenth-century passion for rational enlightenment that animated so much of what the founding fathers did. Unfortunately,

the land was not as tidy as the ordinance, and people—especially in restless times—are not so dispassionately rational. Congress and the nation were under pressure. Continental currency, in the years just after the revolution, was so heavily discounted as to be almost worthless, and a substantial corps of retired army officers were not a little disgruntled about being paid in this currency for their revolutionary services. They wanted land. The frontier, meanwhile, was hardly a stable place. Joseph Brant, who had fought so effectively on the side of the British during the Revolution, was proposing a grand confederation of Indian tribes whose object was to hold the territory north of the Ohio against white settlement. And then there were agitators like Daniel Shays, who led a short-lived rebellion against the government of Massachusetts motivated by discontent among debt-ridden farmers who were losing their property to foreclosure. Finally, the land was not selling well. By 1787, the government had netted a mere $117,000. Not that the territory was unpopulated; frontiersmen found it more convenient to squat than to buy.

Despite the government's best efforts, then, the West was ripe for speculation. There unfolded a scheme that might have served as the prototype of the tall tales about consummate sharpers and swindlers that would become so much a part of the lore of the Wild West.

It started with a parson from Ipswich, Massachusetts, one Manasseh Cutler, who, like a Chaucerian cleric, had a healthier appetite for the finer things in life than for the spiritual. "Purchasing lands in a new country," he declared, "appeared to be ye only thing I could do to secure a living to myself and family." He was tapped by the newly formed Ohio Company to act as what may have been the new nation's first lobbyist. His task was to cajole Congress into allowing the company to buy land at the minimum price of one dollar per acre as mandated by the Ordinance of 1785, but to pay that dollar in grossly depreciated Continental currency—in effect securing a price of eight or nine cents an acre. Washington himself approved this plan; it would, after all, enable his loyal army officers to buy land with the devalued currency. But the ordinance also specified that no speculative grants of land were to be made before at least seven ranges had been surveyed, and some congressmen rightly objected that the Ohio Company's petition should be put off until this was done. To this, Cutler replied with a threat to buy lands from individual states, but then added honey to the vinegar: he offered the recalcitrant legislators an opportunity to invest in another land corporation, the Scioto Company, in which the Confederation's secretary of the treasury, William Duer, and Arthur St. Clair, president of Congress, were already principal investors.

That was not all Cutler obtained from Congress. In order to lure settlers to the new lands, he persuaded the law makers to formulate legislation that would guarantee stable government for the West. The result was the famed Ordinance of 1787, also known as the Northwest Ordinance, which provided for territorial governance of the new settlements and established the procedure by which each territory might be admitted to statehood (a population of sixty thousand free inhabitants was the main requisite). Arthur St. Clair became the first governor of the Northwest Territory.

Meanwhile, the Ohio Company founded the communities of Marietta, Columbus, and Cincinnati. The Scioto group obtained an option to purchase five million acres and now required capital to finance the actual purchase. Apparently uneasy about soliciting customers in the United States for land the company did not yet own, Cutler turned to France, sending the well-known Connecticut poet Joel Barlow to Paris to sell stock in the venture. In that city, the callow versifier teamed up with an Englishman named William Playfair.

Playfair took their commission beyond vending stock; he actually sold *land* and organized five boatloads of French men and women who dreamed of building in the Ohio Valley a city to be called Gallipolis.

Playfair and Barlow lured them with a prospectus promising a "climate wholesome and delightful, frost, even in winter, almost entirely unknown." The rivers of this Eden yielded "excellent fish, of a vast size." "Noble forests" consisted of trees "that spontaneously produce sugar . . . and a plant that yields ready made candles." Game abounded "uninterrupted by wolves, foxes, lions, or tygers. A couple of swine will multiply themselves a hundred fold in two or three years." And: no taxes, no military services to perform.

When some five hundred would-be Gallipolitans put into port at Alexandria, Virginia, eager to begin the overland leg of the journey to their new homes in the West, they were told that the Scioto Company had failed to meet its obligations, that the options had expired unexercised, and that, in short, neither the company nor the French immigrant settler-investors owned any land. Duer did not entirely forsake these bewildered people. He secured some land within the Ohio Company tract, hastily built a kind of makeshift barracks, and sent the settlers off to do the best they could. As one observer wrote, contrasting the Scioto Company's prospectus with the realities of the western frontier: "These munificent promisers forgot to say, that these forests must be cut down before corn [wheat] could be raised . . . and they quite forgot to mention, that though there be no bears or tygers in the neighbourhood, there are wild beasts infinitely more cunning and ferocious, in the shape of men, who were at the time at open and cruel war with the whites." Of course, the "promisers" had also failed to note that they didn't own what they were selling.

South of the Ohio River, the West was in similar turmoil. Not only was there the affair of Sevier and his state of Franklin, but the Spanish were doing their best to contain the U.S. presence in the West by offering Americans land if they would become citizens of Spain. Esteban Miró, Spanish governor of Louisiana, also did his best to turn the Indians against the American settlers, and the Creeks, some of whose land had been appropriated by Georgia and North Carolina (when that state opened Tennessee to settlement without consulting the Indians), were ready to cooperate. During 1784 and 1785, Creeks, Choctaws, Chickasaws, and some Cherokee factions raided parts of Georgia and the vicinity of Nashville, Tennessee. In 1784, too, Spain declared the Mississippi River closed to navigation by Americans. In the absence of viable roads, this meant that exports from western Pennsylvania and Kentucky, including tobacco, flour, and whiskey, were virtually embargoed.

The Spanish offered to negotiate: they would reopen the river if the United States would cede to them all of the present states of Mississippi, Alabama, and western Georgia. America's secretary for foreign affairs, John Jay, offered an alternative agreement. In exchange for trading privileges in Spanish ports, the United States would not claim rights to navigate the Mississippi for twenty-five years.

Even though Congress finally rejected Jay's plan, westerners felt themselves betrayed by its having been proposed at all. It inflamed the ever-smoldering distrust and resentment of the East. Some Pennsylvania, Kentucky, and Tennessee settlers—such as Sevier—contemplated secession, not only from their mother state, but from the Confederation itself. While most of these westerners were genuinely and immediately concerned for their survival and that of their settlements, some took advantage of the troubled times to reap profit. Most daring of these was James Wilkinson. Handsome and brave, Wilkinson would have been honored as a hero of the late Revolution had he not been discovered as a participant in the Conway Cabal, a 1777 attempt to unseat George Washington as commander of the Continental army. Arriving in Kentucky in 1784, Wilkinson took a leading position in the agitation for secession from Virginia. He made himself a popular and influential figure among the frontiersmen and determined to peddle this influence to the Spanish in Louisiana by promising to bring the Kentuckians into the Spanish fold.

The single greatest obstacle to Wilkinson's success was George Rogers Clark, the only Virginian who could fully command the respect and loyalty of the Kentuckians. The question was how to discredit Clark. In 1786, fate took a hand when Clark led some Kentucky volunteers in a campaign against Indians along the Wabash. He headquartered at Vincennes, and when three traders, citizens of Spain, arrived from New Orleans, Clark confiscated their vessel and cargo. The traders sued, and Wilkinson used the affair as a means of making points with the Spanish officials. In a secret letter, Wilkinson claimed that Clark's design was to raid and seize Natchez, and Wilkinson further claimed that he had additional information of use to the Spanish. Governor Miró gave permission for Wilkinson to navigate the Mississippi with flatboats and cargo—the only American permitted to do so, a fact that impressed his fellow Kentuckians. In New Orleans, Wilkinson swore allegiance to Spain and promised to foment a rebellion among the already discontented Kentuckians. For this he received money and a monopoly on Mississippi River trade.

Tennessee also flirted with Spain. Pioneer settler James Robertson, of Nashville, saw in the Spanish a means of restraining Indian hostility and saw in Spanish New Orleans a ready market for such Tennessee commodities as cotton and tobacco. To curry Spanish favor, Robertson caused the westernmost judicial district of the territory to be named after the Spanish governor, which he misspelled as Meró. With this western district apparently all but served up to Spain, Robertson apprised

North Carolina of the situation. Like other westerners, Robertson was unhappy with the government of the eastern mother state. He used the Spanish threat to push North Carolina to ratify the new federal constitution so that Tennessee could become a territory of the national government and, eventually, a state. Robertson reasoned that Tennessee would gain a greater degree of self-government as a federal territory than as a western annex to North Carolina. That state did ratify the constitution in 1789 and ceded Tennessee early the next year. In 1796 the territory of Tennessee became a state.

As for Georgia, the West meant little more than a chance for quick profit. Rather than cede all of her western land, Georgia sold over twenty-five million acres of it to three speculative land companies, netting more than two hundred thousand dollars. It was not the state's problem that the three parcels were subject to disputed claims by Indians, the Spanish, and Georgia. The buyers would have to resolve that.

An Irishman by birth, Dr. James O'Fallon, of the South Yazoo Company, was cut from the same "western" cloth as that Englishman William Playfair. When the company secured a deed from Georgia to most of the middle part of present-day Mississippi, O'Fallon enlisted the aid of Wilkinson to persuade Miró to tolerate the settlement and told the governor that his colony would include three to five thousand armed men who would act as a buffer against the Americans. To prospective settlers he promised five hundred acres gratis for the first woman who would land in the colony and another five hundred to "her who shall bring forth the first live child, bastard or legitimate." Despite his hard sell, O'Fallon was not very successful in recruiting settlers for this most unsettled frontier.

Then opportunity seemed to knock from the Far West. By the mid eighteenth century, Spain had pushed the California chain of missions as far north as San Francisco, in large measure a response to the growing Russian fur-trading presence in the Pacific Northwest. At the time of the founding of San Francisco, in 1776, Juan Peréz and Bruno Heceta were leading sea expeditions north of the mission, rather desultorily claiming vast coastal tracts in the name of Spain. In 1778, the English Captain James Cook explored Nootka Sound, on the western side of Vancouver Island. During their lengthy stay there, Cook's crew traded sundry items for otter pelts, which they carried to Canton, China, and sold for extraordinarily high prices. When a group of English traders in Canton heard about this, they took ship for Nootka to get into the fur business. In 1789, two Spanish warships under the command of Esteban José Martínez seized the vessels of an English trader at Nootka, one John Meares, who appealed to London for aid. By May 1790, Spain and England were close to war over the seizure.

The prospect of war between these two powers did

Paul Kane (1810–1871)
Medicine Masks of the Northwest Coast Tribes, 1847
Watercolor on paper, 5 ½ × 8 ¾ in.
Stark Museum of Art, Orange, Texas

The artist was one of the few whites of the period who appreciated the sophistication of Northwest Indian culture. These masks are from the British Columbia coast.

P A U L   K A N E

—

BORN 1810, MALLOW, COUNTY CORK, IRELAND
DIED 1871, TORONTO, CANADA

—

The artist's family moved from Ireland to York (present-day Toronto), Canada, in 1818. At age sixteen, Kane was apprenticed to a furniture decorator and pursued that profession himself for ten years, while also taking drawing lessons from Thomas Drury, drawing master at Upper Canada College, and painting portraits.

Kane left Canada for the United States in 1836, painting portraits in Detroit, Mobile, and New Orleans until he had earned enough money to finance a trip to Europe. From 1841 to 1843, he assiduously studied the Old Masters, after which he re-turned to Mobile and then to Toronto. Between 1845 and 1848, he explored western Canada, journeying overland and by river to Vancouver and back to Toronto, sketching and painting—in oil and watercolor—Indians and Indian life. He is best known for his work in the Pacific Northwest.

By 1856, he had produced one hundred western canvases commissioned by a Mr. George W. Allan. An autobiographical account of his western work, *Wanderings of an Artist among the Indians of North America* appeared in 1859, illustrated with his own paintings. Blindness ended his career in 1866.

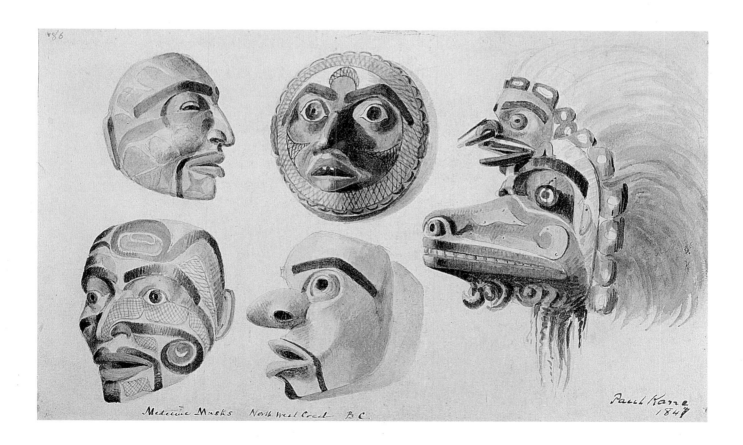

Medicine Masks North West Coast B.C.

Paul Kane
1847

not please President Washington, for the English still occupied territory in the Mississippi Valley, and fighting there between the two empires would further unsettle the West and lay open more vast territories to uncontrolled speculation. The president placated the likes of Sevier, Robertson, and Wilkinson—all of whom had threatened to bring the West into the Spanish camp—with lucrative and influential government appointments. Washington also treated with the chief of the Creek Indians, Alexander McGillvray, a half-breed son of a Scots trader, who had sided with the Spanish against Georgia's interests. Washington made McGillvray a general in the army (at a substantial salary) and convinced him to cede to the United States Creek lands in central Georgia in exchange for those claimed by the Yazoo Company (and Spain!).

In the meantime, the interest of the United States in Nootka Sound became more direct as Robert Gray, the first American captain to circumnavigate the globe, sailed into Boston Harbor. He reported a discovery that both the English and Spanish had failed to make, the existence of a great and navigable western river, which he named after his ship, the *Columbia*. Now the United States had a claim to Pacific Northwest territory, too.

O'Fallon hoped to capitalize on the Nootka affair to garner British support for the Yazoo Company colony by threatening the Spanish, thereby seeming to ally his interests with those of England. He told Miró that Spain must tolerate the colony or it would be taken by force, and he enlisted the desperately debt-ridden George Rogers Clark to lead an army. To cement their partnership, O'Fallon even married Clark's fifteen-year-old sister. But when Washington denounced the Yazoo project and Spain capitulated to England by signing the Nootka Convention, thereby relinquishing most of its Northwest coast claims, O'Fallon was left high and dry. President Washington's denunciation had kept settlers away, and England's agreement with Spain meant that O'Fallon would not be getting any help from Canada if Miró harassed the colony. The Yazoo scheme died. James O'Fallon was certainly not the only pawn in this game of western empire. North of the Ohio River, the Indians were still largely in control, menacing all attempts at settlement. Their power depended in large part on the support of British garrisons in the Northwest. Two American military expeditions failed miserably—indeed, one disastrously—to remove the Indian threat. General Josiah Harmar's force, up from Cincinnati, suffered two hundred casualties, rout, and retreat. Another expedition, commanded by the governor of the Northwest Territory, Arthur St. Clair, met with the worst defeat the U.S. Army was ever destined to suffer in contest with Indians. Six hundred thirty men were killed and 283 wounded when Indians surprised St. Clair's sleeping camp at the headwaters of the Wabash River.

Washington next called on "Mad Anthony" Wayne, hero of the Revolution, to reorganize and command an effective western army. After American negotiators were spurned by British and Indians alike, and after the British built a fort beside the Maumee River, on what was clearly American territory, the president ordered Wayne into action. Defeat would surely have cost the new nation prestige, threatening national sovereignty and any American pretensions to western territory.

As Wayne advanced, the Indians dug in at Fallen Timbers, on the banks of the Maumee. Anticipating an immediate battle, they fasted, as was their custom in preparing for a fight. But Wayne did not attack. Nor did the Indians. After three days, large numbers of them simply left their battle positions to eat. At this point, Wayne attacked, routing the hungry and much-diminished forces, sending them back toward the British fort. But between the time of the Indian victories against Harmar and St. Clair and the battle with Anthony Wayne, the French Revolution changed everything. The British now feared that the Americans would support the French, militarily or by restrictions on British trade, so British commanders were ordered to stop supporting the Indians. The gates of the fort on the Maumee were closed, and the Indian force surrendered to General Wayne. The next year, with the Treaty of Greenville, the Indians ceded to the United States much of southern Ohio and a portion of Indiana, and allowed the establishment of sixteen enclaves, well within Indian territory, where the Americans could establish trading posts and forts.

In 1794, Washington's minister John Jay took advantage of England's concern over a possible alliance between France and the United States in order to negotiate the withdrawal of English garrisons from all United States territory (however, Jay's treaty allowed Canadian fur traders to continue to work south of the border, a provision that angered American traders). The next year, Spain, acknowledging herself too weak to hold out against the expansion of the young nation, concluded the Treaty of San Lorenzo, which relinquished Spanish claims north of the thirty-first parallel and opened the Mississippi to American commerce. And that meant the West was opening.

But France, which had relinquished so much in the French and Indian War, and which had been the United States' revolutionary ally, nevertheless refused to bow out of the continent. The French Revolution, which established a republic in the name of the rights of man, ignited anew a quest for French empire in the West. The plan was to enlist the aid of the United States—by treaty allied to France—in the extirpation of Spain from Florida, the Louisiana country, and Mexico. Once this trans-Mississippi empire was secured, British Canada might fall to France. And the United States? It would be safely confined to the territory east of the Allegheny Mountains.

Implementation of the scheme was to begin with the work of one man, a botanist who, had he traveled through time as well as space and into that western outpost known as Hollywood, would have been cast as Indiana Jones. André Michaux had become a scientist-adventurer shortly after the death of his young wife. He gained the admiration of his government after completing a hazardous botanical expedition to Persia, between the Tigris and Euphrates. In 1785 the French government commissioned him to explore the United States in order to find trees that might be used for constructing naval vessels. Michaux and his son botanized in Florida and the Appalachians, during the period of acute frontier discontent and Spanish plotting, until 1790, when the younger Michaux returned to France in support of the revolutionary cause. The senior Michaux stayed on in America and traveled north to Hudson Bay. In Canada he learned of Alexander Mackenzie's plan of taking an overland expedition clear through the Northwest to the Canadian Pacific. Michaux was bitter: he would make the same trip farther south, along the Missouri River and, ultimately, to the Pacific. The scientist applied to the American Philosophical Society for financial backing and was granted a total of $128.25, including $25 from Washington and $12.50 from Thomas Jefferson, to "find the shortest & most convenient route . . . between the U.S. & the Pacific ocean."

Either an access of patriotism or the realization that $128.25 was not going to get him anywhere near the Pacific led Michaux to the French revolutionists intent on establishing an empire in the American West. The plan was to use the scientific expedition as a cover for a military campaign against the Spanish. George Rogers Clark, by now thoroughly decrepit, offered the French his services, claiming that "by my name alone" he could raise fifteen hundred men at arms and that, beginning with such a core, the French and Americans in Spanish-held Louisiana would "flock to my standard."

At precisely this moment, Edmond Charles Gênet—Citizen Gênet—landed in Charleston, South Carolina, under instructions from the Girondist regime to secure friendship with the United States and to negotiate a trade treaty. Yet directly upon his arrival, he commissioned privateers to harass British shipping along the coast and eagerly embraced the notion of dispatching an expedition against the Spanish. President Washington informed Gênet that the privateers would not be permitted to operate in American waters and that commissioning a military expedition on American soil constituted an infringement of national sovereignty. Though Gênet promised to desist, he armed a captured vessel, *The Little Sarah,* rechristened it *La Petite Démocrate,* and ordered it to sea. When Washington condemned this high-handed act, Gênet threatened to appeal directly to the American people, whereupon Washington demanded Gênet's recall. And that pulled the rug out from under Clark as well as André Michaux and the expedition to reclaim the American West for the Republic of France.

In the meantime, while intrigue was originating from abroad, pressure was building at home. The "West"—that is, the territory between the Appalachians and the Mississippi—was filling fast. Congress enacted legislation to protect the Indians against rapacious settlers and to evict squatters from the territories, but the federal government lacked the muscle to enforce these laws. The answer, it seemed, was more space—either for white settlement or Indian "relocation"—and that space lay across the Mississippi.

There was talk, in high federal circles, of taking Louisiana by force. Doubtless that would have happened at some point, but then Napoleon Bonaparte made his presence felt—if not his person—on the already well-trod stage of western American empire. In a secret treaty concluded on October 1, 1800, Spain ceded Louisiana back to France in exchange for certain territories in Tuscany and a promise that France would maintain the territory as a buffer between the United States and Mexico. Napoleon, however, immediately disappointed his ally by abandoning the war that would have given Spain the Tuscan territory. A dispute developed, and Spain continued to administer Louisiana. In October 1802, the Spanish intendant at New Orleans revoked American traders' right of deposit—license to store goods in New Orleans for loading onto ocean-going vessels—effectively closing the Mississippi to American trade three years after it had been opened. By this time, France's involvement in Louisiana and the Spanish closure of the river was an open secret, and Jefferson realized that a West controlled by Napoleon's France was a far greater threat than that territory administered by a feeble Spain. Even if France—still an ally of the United States—did not threaten the new nation directly and immediately, war between France and England would likely result in England's seizure of the territory. In either case, the United States would be choked off at the Mississippi.

Accordingly, President Jefferson made warlike noises in the direction of France and Spain—even as he sent James Monroe to Paris with an offer to buy the city of New Orleans and Florida. But he was thinking of more than the city. Captain Gray's voyage in the *Columbia* had established a claim to some part of the Northwest coast. Establishing an American presence at the mouth of the Mississippi would imply an American claim to the territory between that river and the Pacific. Of course, it was only proper that the United States learn something about the territory it was about to claim. Jefferson commissioned his private secretary, Meriwether Lewis, to prepare for an expedition to the Pacific, across what was at the time foreign soil.

It would not be foreign soil for long. Napoleon's army, fighting in the West Indies, began to die—not from English bullets, but from yellow fever and guerrilla warfare with the islanders. Napoleon decided to withdraw from the New World, at least for the present. Yet he still feared English usurpation of the Louisiana Territory, and he needed funds to finance his European wars. When he had failed to win Tuscany for Spain, Napoleon abrogated one major provision of the secret Treaty of Ildefonso. Now he reneged on the other major provision: he sold Louisiana to the United States—909,000 square miles of trans-Mississippi territory—for $23,213,567.73, about four cents an acre.

DREAMERS OF EMPIRE

I. LEWIS AND CLARK

A hunter and woodsman since the age of eight, Meriwether Lewis enlisted in the Virginia militia at age twenty in 1794 to help suppress the Whiskey Rebellion in western Pennsylvania. Two years earlier he had volunteered for a western expedition Thomas Jefferson was planning, but was rejected on account of his youth. However, Jefferson remembered the young man in 1801, when, as president-elect, he asked Lewis to serve as his personal secretary. Soon after his appointment, at the president's direction, Lewis began preparing for a western expedition, assembling equipment and supplies, gathering information, and obtaining technical and scientific training at the University of Pennsylvania. For the West was much on Thomas Jefferson's mind. When his father died, the fourteen-year-old Jefferson counted among his guardians Dr. Thomas Walker, the first explorer of Kentucky, who must have had an ample stock of western adventures to relate. President Jefferson was also president of the American Philosophical Society, and his curiosity was hardly to be bounded by the Mississippi River. Ever aware that American settlement was driven by an irresistible westward force, he thought that western exploration might yield even more immediate gains: access to an abundant far western peltry, a Northwest Passage to the Pacific Ocean, and lucrative trade (much of it in furs) with Asia. In 1793, Alexander Mackenzie crossed the continent from Fort Chipewyan on Lake Athabasca, Saskatchewan, to Bella Coola at Dean Channel on the Pacific. Once English traders began exploiting in earnest Mackenzie's Canadian route, they could well dominate the fur trade and the Far West. Furthermore, since he had succeeded in reaching the Pacific via a northern Canadian route, what was to stop Mackenzie or some other Englishman from attempting the crossing farther south, by way of the Missouri River? Such an expedition would seriously compromise whatever claim to the Northwest Robert Gray's discovery of the Columbia River had given the United States. Jefferson wanted Lewis to find a connection between the Missouri and the Columbia rivers as the United States' Northwest Passage to the Pacific, and to secure the nation's claim to territory beyond the bounds of the nine hundred thousand square miles between the Mississippi

and the Rocky Mountains purchased from Napoleon.

The twenty-eight-year-old Lewis invited his friend and comrade-at-arms, William Clark, aged thirty-two, to serve as co-commander of the expedition. If anything, Clark's frontier pedigree was even more impressive than Lewis's, for he was the youngest brother of no less than George Rogers Clark. The pair set about recruiting "good hunters, stout, healthy, unmarried men, accustomed to the woods, and capable of bearing bodily fatigue." In addition to the two captains, the party numbered twenty-nine, including Charles Floyd, nephew of one of Kentucky's first explorers; John Colter, member of another of Kentucky's first families; Patrick Gass, veteran of service on the Pennsylvania frontier; New Hampshireman Alexander Willard, who had run away to the frontier as a boy; master woodsmen Reuben and Joseph Fields, Kentucky brothers; John Shields, invaluable as a gunsmith; George Drouillard, who had been reared by the legendary frontiersman Simon Kenton. The expedition also included a number of Frenchmen, among them Toussaint Charbonneau, recruited when the expedition reached winter camp at a Mandan village in the Dakota country. Hired on as an interpreter, he was to prove far more valuable for the Indian wife he brought with him. Sacajewea was a Shoshone who had been captured by the Minnetarees when she was eleven and eventually sold to Charbonneau as a slave. Sixteen years old when Lewis and Clark encountered her, she was pregnant with Charbonneau's child. The Indian girl would prove a remarkable guide and, in the process, become an American legend.

The expedition needed all the guidance it could get. For the Missouri River was charted only as far above St. Louis—at the time a trading center of perhaps two hundred houses—as the Mandan villages where Lewis and Clark would make their first winter camp. As to the Columbia River, it was charted only at its mouth; nothing was known of its course inland. Of the country between the Dakota region of the Mandans and the Columbia River nothing was known. There were, however, myths aplenty: of a tribe of man-hating Amazon huntresses who amputated their right breasts the better to draw back a bowstring; of a tribe of Welsh-speaking Indians descended from an ancient Celtic wanderer; of a tribe of eighteen-inch-tall devils at a place called Les Côtes Brulées. One of Lewis's tutors during his cram-course preparation for the expedition, none other than the renowned Dr. Benjamin Rush, prepared a list of anthropological queries, including a number aimed at ascertaining affinities between Indians and Jews, since many believed that the red men were descended from one of the Lost Tribes of Israel.

Somewhat more useful than the questions Rush prepared were the pills he supplied. Intended to relieve one bane universal among travelers—constipation—Lewis and Clark used them to treat all manner of ills, including dysentery. In other respects, Lewis saw to it that

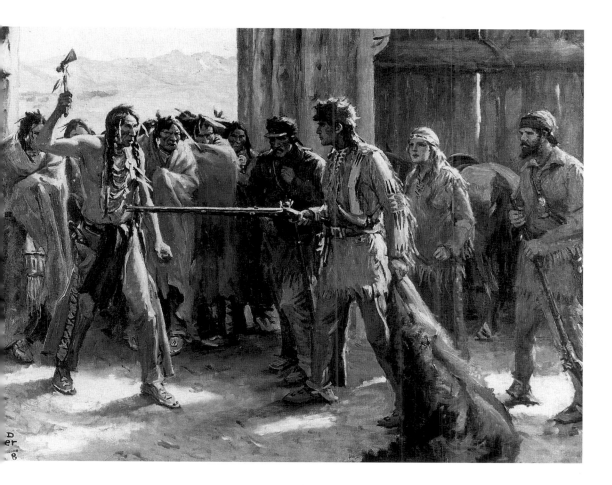

W.H.D. Koerner (1878–1938)
Tomahawk and Long Rifle, 1928
Oil on canvas, 28 × 40 in.
The Rockwell Museum, Corning,
New York

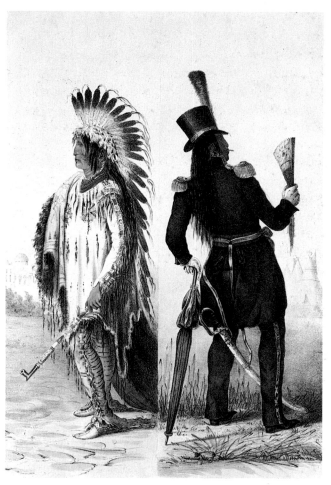

Currier & Ives (after George Catlin)
*Wi-Jun-Jon—the Pigeon's Egg Head/
Going to Washington. Returning to
His Home*, n.d.
Museum of the City of New York

This popular print of a George
Catlin painting depicts an Assiniboin
as he appeared when the artist first
saw him in 1831 and, a year later,
after the Indian had visited the
"Great White Father" in Washington,
D.C. Wi-Jun-Jon was eventually
killed by his own people, who had
either wearied of his ceaseless
boasting about his talks with
Andrew Jackson or believed his
fantastic tales of the white man's
East to be dangerous lies.

known the presence of human beings, tamely approached members of the expedition. In other respects,
that same country was hellish, blighted with mosqui-
toes in such numbers that one couldn't help *breathing*
them in.

It was fully eleven weeks after leaving St. Louis before the expedition encountered Indians, the peaceful
Otos, to whom Lewis distributed gifts and Jefferson
medals. Near present-day Sioux City, Iowa, the expedition suffered its only death, that of Sergeant Charles
Floyd, who succumbed to a ruptured appendix. A force
recruited from among hunters and trappers might be ex-

the expedition was better prepared. Like many another
frontiersman, Lewis admired the Kentucky long rifle. He
recognized, however, that it was too fragile to withstand
the rigors of a protracted expedition, so he went to the
arsenal at Harper's Ferry, where he had gunsmiths re-
design the weapon to his own specifications. For years
thereafter, the "Harper's Ferry Rifle" would serve as
standard issue in the U.S. regular army. Lewis betook
himself next to Pittsburgh to oversee construction of a
fifty-five-foot, twenty-two-oar barge, or keelboat, with a
large square sail. And President Jefferson saw to it that
his explorers were supplied with various gifts with which
to ingratiate themselves among the Indians: beads, calico
shirts, handkerchiefs, mirrors, bells, sheet metal, brass
curtain rings (meant to be worn on Indian fingers), and
specially struck peace medals bearing the likeness of
President Jefferson on one side and hands clasped in
friendship on the other. Between 1804—even before
Lewis and Clark themselves returned east—and 1806,
three Indian delegations traveled to the Great Father in
Washington, D.C., using the medals as passports. At a
cost of $669.50, the various and sundry gifts were the
single largest item on Lewis and Clark's inventory.

The expedition left St. Louis on May 14, 1804, not to
return for two years, four months, and ten days. Early in
the century, even along the lower Missouri, the buffalo
herds were vast, numbering ten thousand animals per
herd, Lewis estimated, figuring that his eye could take in
some three thousand at a glance. In some respects, the
country was Edenic, as elk and antelope, having never

pected to present some problems of discipline. Near
Sioux City, one Moses Reed deserted and fled back to the
Otos. Lewis sent a party after him, with orders to bring
him back dead or alive. He was returned, alive, and sentenced to run the gauntlet, as Clark recorded in his journal, "four times through the Party & that each man with
nine Swichies Should punish him." He was also summarily discharged from "the Party." Some time later, farther
upriver, an army private named John Newman endured
seventy-five lashes and discharge for "malingering." Indians who witnessed the punishment were appalled. The
chief explained to Clark that "his nation never whipped
even their Children." How would you, then, enforce discipline? Clark asked the chief. Kill him, he replied.

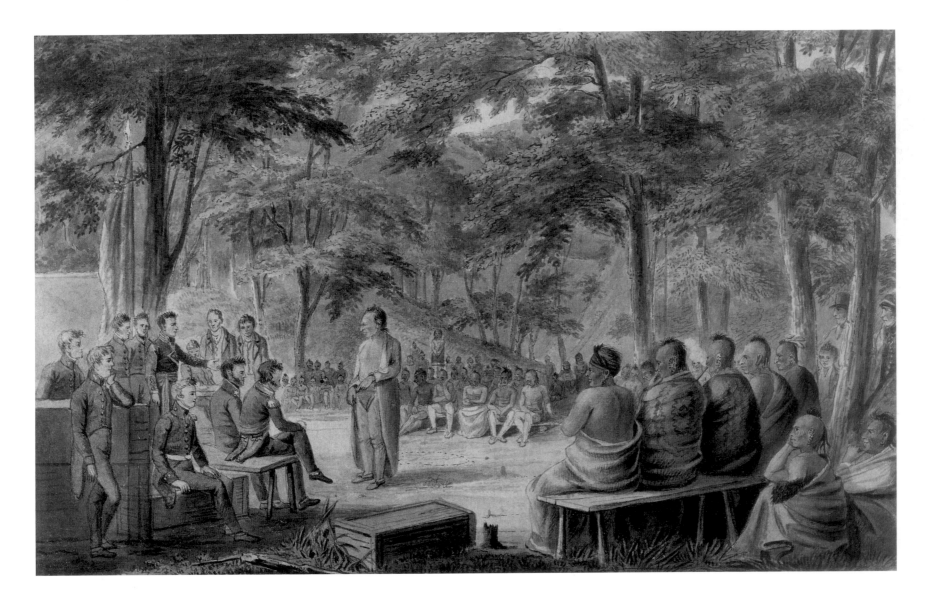

It was not until the party reached the mouth of the Teton River, in present-day South Dakota, that they were seriously challenged by Indians. The pro-English Teton Sioux were known to be hostile, not only to neighboring tribes, but to white traders, from whom they extorted tribute in exchange for safe passage. A formidable band of warriors massed at the riverbank and made it clear that they intended to stop Lewis and Clark's upriver progress. The expedition now numbering forty-two, Clark was hardly backed by a vast army when he ventured ashore to speak to the Indians. The braves attempted to seize him, whereupon Clark drew his sword, and his companions paddled to the rescue; the keelboat's cannon was made ready and aimed. The Americans' spirit—certainly, it could not have been their number—brought the situation to a tense standoff, as Clark recorded:

Most of the Warriers appeared to have their Bows strung and took their arrows from the quiver. as I was not permitted to return [to the keelboat], I Sent all the men except 2 Interpreters to the boat, the perogue [pirogue, a dugout canoe] Soon returned with about 12 of our determined men ready for any event. this movement caused a no: of the Indians to withdraw at a distance.

Clark offered his hand to the number one and number two chiefs, who refused to receive it, but did not prevent Clark and his men from departing in the pirogue. "We proceeded on about 1 Mile & anchored out off a Willow Island placed a guard on Shore . . . I call this Island bad humered Island as we were in a bad humer."

The tension persisted through ten more days of slow upstream progress as Sioux warriors continued to mass along the river, at times menacing the expedition, at other times making gestures of friendship, including offers to share what Clark called their "handsom squars"—pretty squaws. That the greatly outnumbered expedition persisted in the face of all threats not only kept the Indians at bay on this occasion, but broke what was in effect a Sioux blockade of the Missouri—though Sioux hostilities would persist to the end of the century.

After 166 days of travel, the expedition reached the Mandan villages at the mouth of the Knife River, in present-day North Dakota. While the two captains could be bold and brash when the situation demanded, as it had among the Teton Sioux, they were also thoughtful and methodical leaders. At Mandan they took time to build a solid, well-daubed log fort in preparation for winter. It was a good thing; in his journal, Lewis recorded

Samuel Seymour (active 1796–mid 1824)
Oto Indians in Council with the Stephen Long Expedition, 1819
Watercolor, 5 × 8 in.
Library, The Academy of Natural Sciences of Philadelphia

The 1819–20 expedition of Major Stephen Long was commissioned by Secretary of War John C. Calhoun for the purpose of finding the headwaters of the Red River. Long failed to find the river's source, but members of his expedition did succeed in climbing Pikes Peak (which Zebulon Pike, who sighted the mountain in 1806, was unable to do). Long himself reached a fateful conclusion about the "extensive section of country between the Missouri River and the Rocky Mountains." Labeling it "the Great American Desert," he declared the territory "almost wholly unfit for cultivation"—whereupon white policy makers determined that it was a *most* fitting place for Indian "removal."

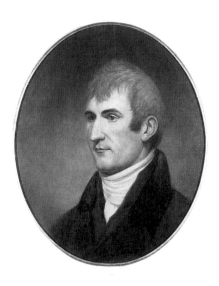

Charles Willson Peale (1741–1827)
Meriwether Lewis, 1807
Oil on panel, 18 ¾ × 23 in.
Independence National Historical
Park Collection

The great American painter,
amateur scientist, and public
showman exhibited in his celebrated
Philadelphia museum many
specimens of flora and fauna Lewis
and Clark brought back from the Far
West.

temperatures as low as forty-five degrees below zero,
and some hard liquor (he noted) froze solid in fifteen
minutes. In all, they wintered five long months at "Fort
Mandan," using the time to recruit two additional adventurers from the nearby village of the Minnetarees—
Toussaint Charbonneau and his wife, Sacajewea—and to
learn all they could about the upper Missouri from the
Mandans. A chief named Big White told them that the
river was navigable nearly to its source and that, as
Lewis recorded in his journal, "at a distance not exceed-
ing half a days march, there is a large river running from
South to North." That river, Lewis reasoned, must be the
south fork of the Columbia. And the Columbia, he well
knew, emptied into the Pacific. It was the promised
Northwest Passage.

In the bitter cold of February, the pregnant Sacajewea underwent the agonies of a difficult first labor. A
visiting trapper recommended rattlesnake rattle as a
drug to hasten the process. Two rings were broken into
small pieces, administered, and a baby boy named Pomp
was delivered ten minutes later—the youngest member
of the expedition.

The first long leg of the journey had been difficult
enough, but it was through country known to trappers
and traders. Travel beyond the Mandan villages was a
progress into territory wholly unknown to whites. What
impressed the men most immediately—hunters and

trappers all—was the abundance of game (buffalo) and
peltry (beavers, which had never been pursued and
which therefore swam tamely in broad daylight). The
prodigious animal life was not all benign. Lewis's journal
entry for April 29, 1805, notes that "about 8 A.M. we fell
in with two brown or yellow bear; both of which we
wounded; one of them made his escape, the other after
my firing on him pursued me seventy or eighty
yards. . . ."

On May 5:

*Capt. Clark and Drewyer killed the largest brown bear
this evening which we have yet seen. it was a most tre-
mendious looking animal, and extremely hard to kill notwithstanding he had five balls through his lungs and five
others in various parts he swam more than half the distance across the river to a sandbar, & it was at least
twenty minutes before he died.*

Add to the menace of Indians and bears the fierce-
ness of western storms, and such were the hazards Lewis
and Clark successfully negotiated for months toiling
upriver. On May 26, the party first saw what the Indians
called the Shining Mountains, the Rockies. A few days
later, they were faced with the greatest hazard of wilderness exploration: getting lost. They came to a fork in the
Missouri, a north branch, silt-filled and muddy, and a

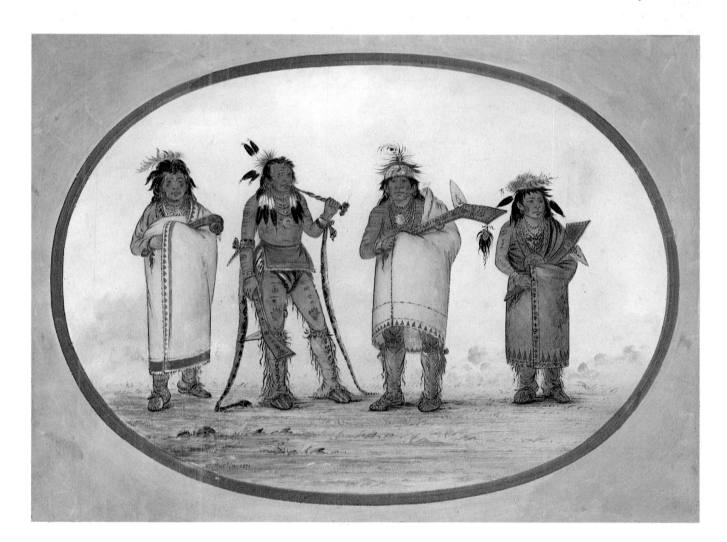

George Catlin (1796–1872)
Mandan Indians, 1871
Oil on paper, mounted on multi-ply
board, 18 × 24 ⅜ in.
The Rockwell Museum, Corning,
New York

These Indians of the upper Missouri
opened trade with the white man—
and paid dearly for it. An 1837
smallpox plague, carried upriver by
an American Fur Company
steamboat, effectively destroyed the
tribe. In 1838 only 130 Mandans
were left alive.

south branch, which ran clear. Which branch was the true Missouri, the way west? The consensus among the party was that the north branch, which looked as muddy as the rest of the river, must be the principal stream. The leaders of the expedition thought differently, however, reasoning that the clarity of the southern branch betokened a high mountain origin. A wrong choice would be disastrous, Lewis and Clark knew, so they divided, each with a small party, to probe both streams. Lewis followed the north stream far enough to convince himself that it indeed led to nothing but bewilderment in Canada. He named the tributary Maria's River, after a girlfriend back east.

Despite lingering doubts among many of the men, the expedition had learned through the long course of their exploration to trust their commanders. They followed the southerly stream without complaint until they reached the Great Falls of the Missouri—a roaring torrent, Lewis noted, three hundred yards wide and eighty feet high. The only way to negotiate it was by means of circuitous portage through eighteen miles of difficult, cactus-grown terrain. Lewis ingeniously set his men to hewing great cart wheels from the twenty-two-inch trunk of a cottonwood in order to transport their river vessels and other heavy gear—though even with ingenuity it took twenty-four days to accomplish the eighteen-mile portage.

Completing the portage meant that the expedition had reached the high country, the country of the Shoshones, the country in which Sacajewea had spent the first eleven years of her life. Her guidance brought the party quickly to the Continental Divide (on August 12, 1805, Hugh McNeal, a member of the expedition, ceremoniously straddled the stream Lewis and Clark mistakenly took for the headwaters of the Missouri), thence to a tributary of the Columbia River and the Pacific slope.

Canoes were of little use in the high country; if the party was to continue its westward push, horses were needed. Accordingly, Lewis was anxious to make contact with Sacajewea's people to trade for mounts. But the Indians were fearful of intruders from the plains and evaded the captain's overtures of friendship. Finally, on August 13, the day after the expedition had crossed the Divide, Lewis came upon an old squaw, who led him to a Shoshone hunting camp. It took two more days of patient persuasion, conducted in sign language, to convince the hunting party to accompany Lewis back to the expedition's main camp. The Indians nervously accompanied him, mistrustful until George Drouillard shot three deer. Game was scarce in the high country, and the Shoshones were hungry; they ate and continued on the journey.

By August 17, the Shoshones had grown restive again; but at that moment, Clark appeared with Charbonneau and his wife, Sacajewea. The chief of the band accompanying Lewis was the Indian girl's brother, and he recognized the long-lost Sacajewea with great joy. The

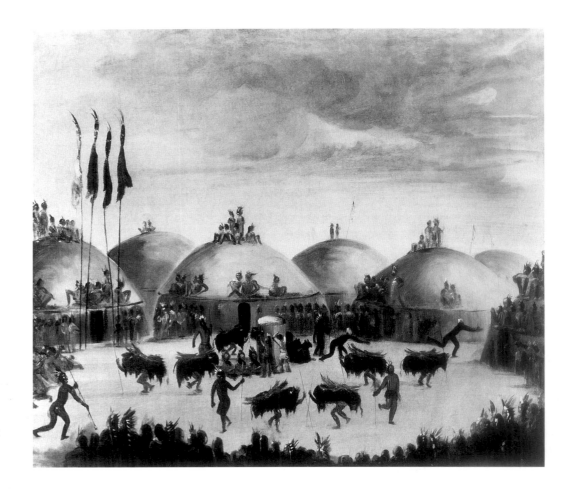

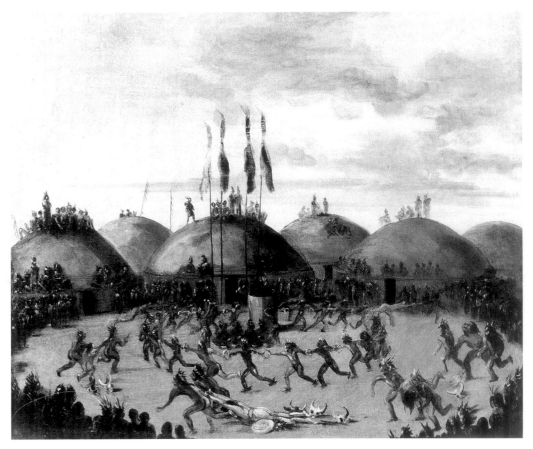

George Catlin (1796–1872)
Mandan Dance, 1832
Oil on canvas, 23 ½ × 28 in.
Courtesy of The Anschutz Collection

George Catlin (1796–1872)
Bull Dance, 1832
Oil on canvas, 23 × 28 in.
Courtesty of The Anschutz Collection

"Every dance has its peculiar step,
and every step has its meaning;
every dance also has its peculiar
song, and that is so intricate and
mysterious oftentimes, that not one
in ten of the young men who are
dancing and singing it, know the
meaning of the song which they are
chanting over."—George Catlin, *The
Manners, Customs and Condition of
the North American Indians.* The
artist was especially intrigued by the
bull dance; part of a four-day
religious ceremony, its purpose was
to propitiate the buffalo for another
season. *(opposite)*

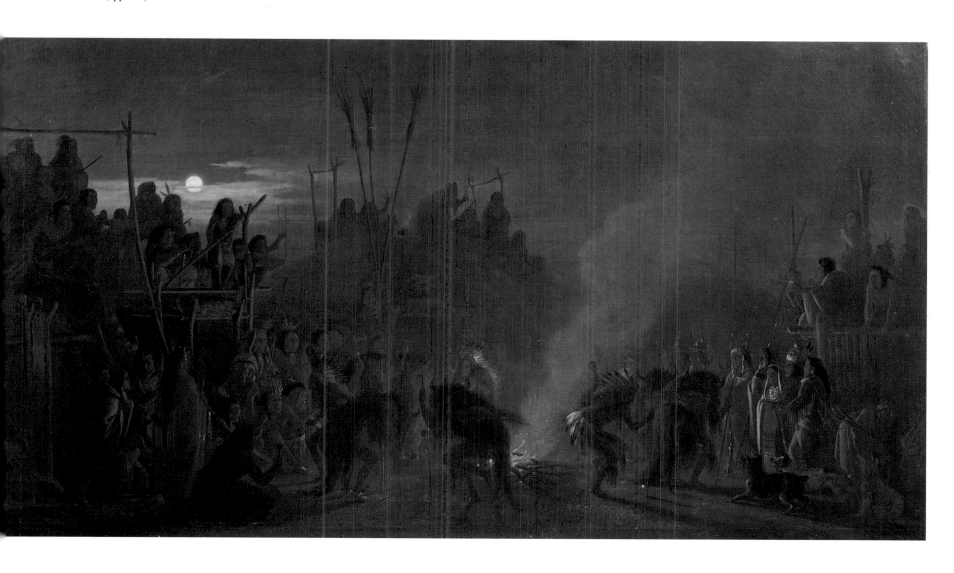

Charles Wimar (1828–1862)
The Buffalo Dance, 1860
Oil on canvas, 24 ⅞ × 49 ⅝ in.
The Saint Louis Art Museum; Gift of
Mrs. John T. David

The ways and rites of Indian culture
were endlessly fascinating to white
men, who, nevertheless, seemed
incapable of understanding them.

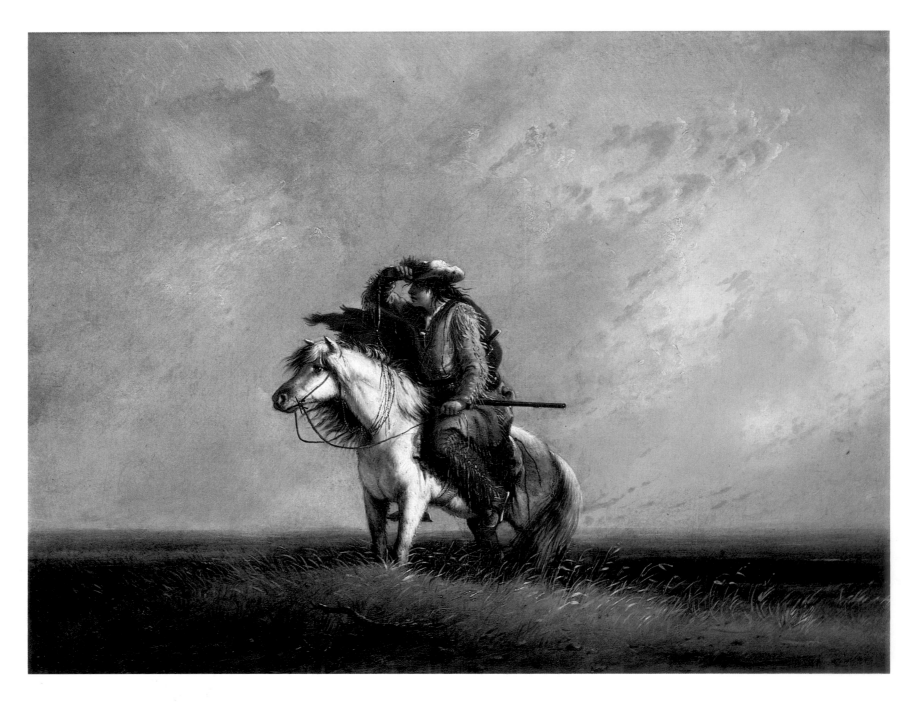

Shoshones would sell horses to Lewis and Clark.

Yet the Indians also had discouraging news. They told the captains that there was no passable route from the Missouri headwaters to the Columbia, at least to any navigable part of it. As usual, Lewis and Clark took nothing secondhand. While Lewis bargained for the necessary horses, Clark led a probe far enough westward to convince himself that the Indians were correct. Nevertheless, late in August, the entire party resumed their journey, intending to penetrate farther north, through tortured mountain passes, in search of *some* way west. Young Sacajewea, so briefly reunited with her people, elected to accompany her husband on the expedition.

The hardships they all endured—snow, starvation, exhaustion, desperation for the elusive passage—demonstrated just how blessed the journey had been up to this point. They did finally reach navigable waters late in the fall, but they had hardly found the fabled Northwest Passage, for it was not there to be found.

On November 7, 1805, they saw the Pacific; a month later, they set up camp near the mouth of the Columbia, a vantage from which they could watch for passing ships. For among their supplies, Lewis and Clark carried a letter of credit from President Jefferson, with which the expedition might purchase supplies or even sea passage home. By the first of the new year, the party had built a stockade fort—Fort Clatsop, they called it—and waited.

And waited, until March 23, 1806. No ship ever showed itself. The trip east, like that west, would be overland and on the river. At the Continental Divide, Lewis and Clark separated in order to make a more thorough search for better passes through the mountains. Clark took the southerly route, eventually descending the Yellowstone River. Lewis traveled northeastward as far as the Great Falls of the Missouri; here he divided his party again in order to explore Maria's River. It was nearly a fatal excursion.

The party of four—Lewis, Drouillard, and the

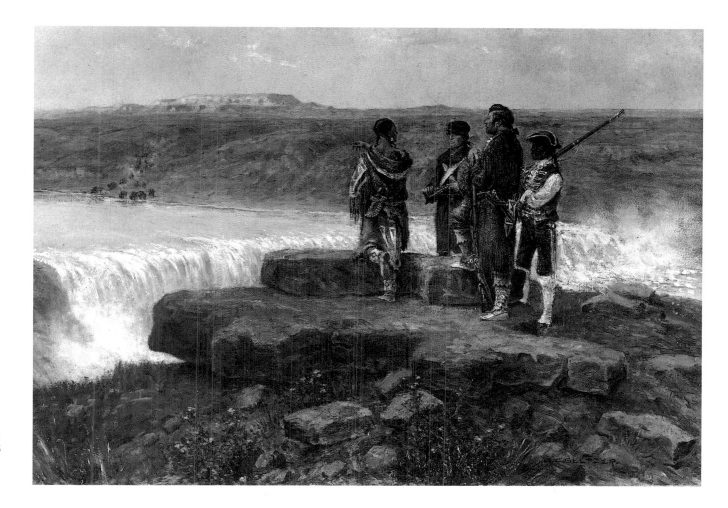

Olaf Carl Seltzer (1877–1957)
Lewis & Clark with Sacajawea at the Great Falls of the Missouri 1804,
1927
Oil on canvas, 11 × 16 in.
Gilcrease Museum, Tulsa, Oklahoma

Sacajawea: first of the West's highly select gallery of heroines.

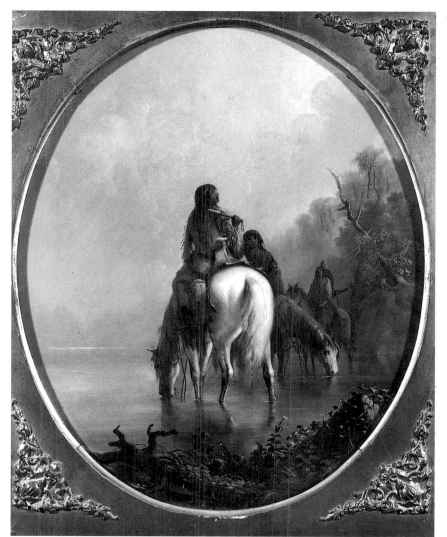

Alfred Jacob Miller (1810–1874)
Shoshone Women Watering Horses,
c. 1850s
Oil on canvas, 24 × 20 in.
Collection of The Newark Museum;
Gift of Mr. and Mrs. A. M. Adler,
1961

Sacajewea was a Shoshone who had been captured by Minnetarees and was subsequently sold by them to a white trader, who took her as his bride.

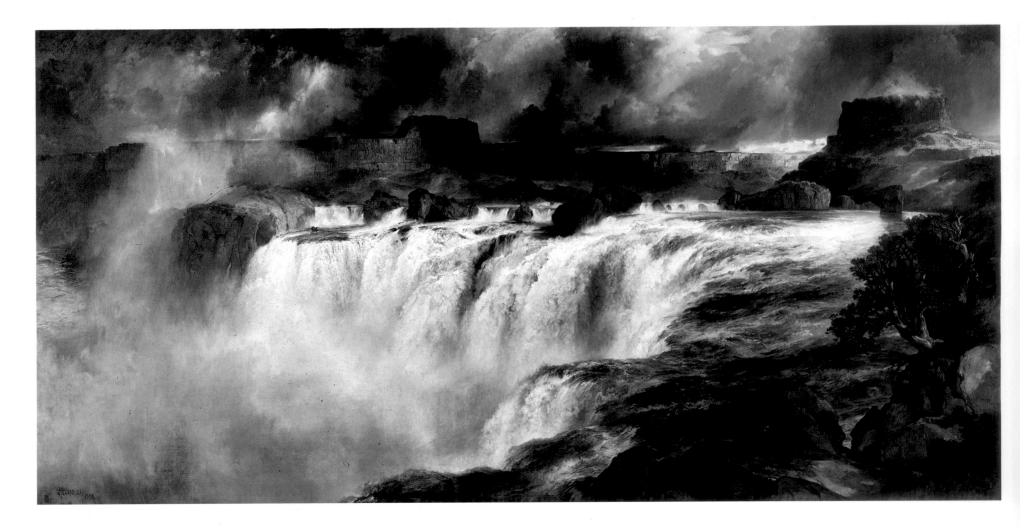

Thomas Moran (1837–1926)
Shoshone Falls on the Snake River,
1900
Oil on canvas, 71 × 132 in.
Gilcrease Museum, Tulsa, Oklahoma

Fields brothers, Joseph and Reuben—was set upon by eight Blackfeet, who attempted to relieve the adventurers of their rifles and horses. In brief battle, two Indians were killed, and it was they, rather than the white men, who lost their guns and mounts. There was little enough time to savor this victory, however, as Lewis realized Blackfoot reinforcements were probably not far behind. The four men aborted their expedition and rode hard to rejoin the northeastward party. Reunited with them, Lewis proceeded downriver to rendezvous with Clark's southeastward division. On the way, Lewis was chasing elk with a one-eyed hunter named Peter Cruzatte—who aimed, fired, and hit the captain in the thigh. It was a serious wound that cost Lewis much pain, but he recovered and met up with Clark on August 12. Just the day before, Clark's party had encountered the first white men they had seen in over a year, two American trappers named Joseph Dickson and Forest Hancock, the latter from Daniel Boone's Kentucky settlement. John Colter, who had been with Lewis and Clark now for more than two years of hard wilderness travel, pleaded with Captain Clark for permission to leave the homeward-bound expedition and join the westering trappers. He was allowed to go, and we shall hear more of him later.

Twenty-eight months and six days after they had left the Mandan villages—thirty-six and a half months after Lewis left Pittsburgh with his custom-built keelboat—the "Corps of Discovery" reached St. Louis on September 23, 1806. They had not accomplished the impossible; they had not found the Northwest Passage. But they had explored 7,689 miles of new United States terri-

tory, supplying invaluable topographical data for the first reliable map of the West. They had catalogued a dazzling array of flora—some 200 new plant species and 122 species and subspecies of birds and animals. They even unearthed the bones of a forty-five-foot dinosaur.

Among the more than fifty Indian tribes with whom they made contact, Lewis and Clark had mostly positive experiences. They brought back numerous artifacts and established cordial relations with many groups—relations not destined, however, to endure. Most important, they solidified America's claim to new western territories and asserted its dominion over the territory of the Louisiana Purchase. Their adventure had the symbolic significance that comes only from very real deeds: they forged the spirit of a vast new nation.

II. AARON BURR

The West was the object of dreams and dreamers. It was also the place for desperation and desperate men.

Aaron Burr's star rose in the Revolution. A young graduate of the College of New Jersey, he survived Benedict Arnold's disastrous Canadian campaign—serving with another rising star, James Wilkinson—and joined George Washington's staff, but was dismissed after antagonizing the general. Admitted to the bar after the war, he was elected to the New York Assembly in 1784, became attorney general of New York in 1789, and a United States senator two years later. When he was defeated for reelection, he served another two-year term in the New York Assembly, but had gained sufficient national prominence to gain the Republican vice-presidential nomina-

Charles M. Russell (1864–1926)
Lewis and Clark on the Lower Columbia, 1905
Watercolor on paper, 18 ⅞ × 23 ⅞ in.
Amon Carter Museum, Fort Worth, Texas

Sacajewea interprets Captain Lewis's peaceful intentions to a potentially hostile Indian. The tribes of the Northwest coast excelled at religiously inspired ornamental woodcarving.

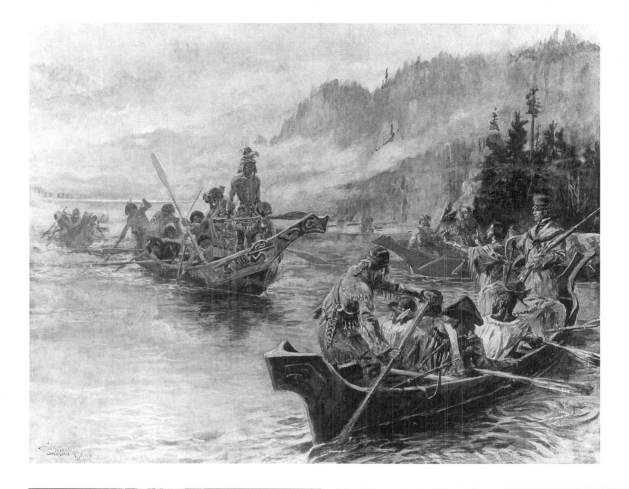

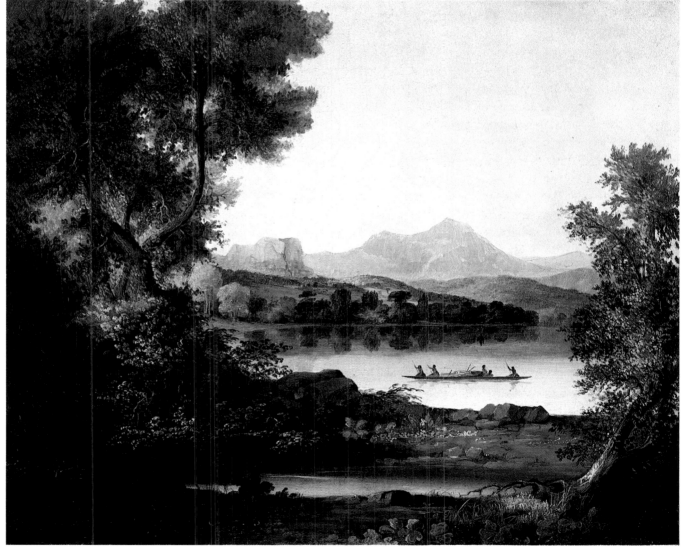

John Mix Stanley (1814–1872)
Scene on the Columbia River, 1852
Oil on canvas, 17 ⅛ × 21 ⅛ in.
Amon Carter Museum, Fort Worth, Texas

Captain Robert Gray's discovery of this river's mouth was the United States' first claim on the Far West.

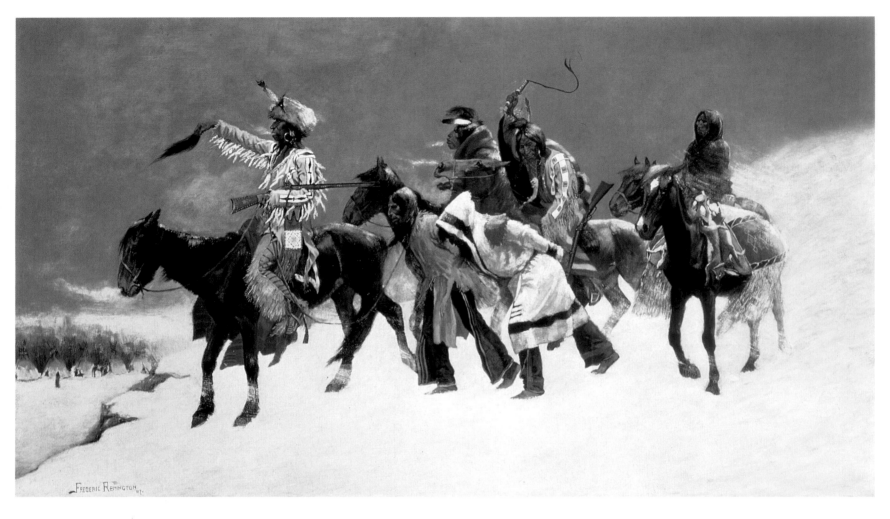

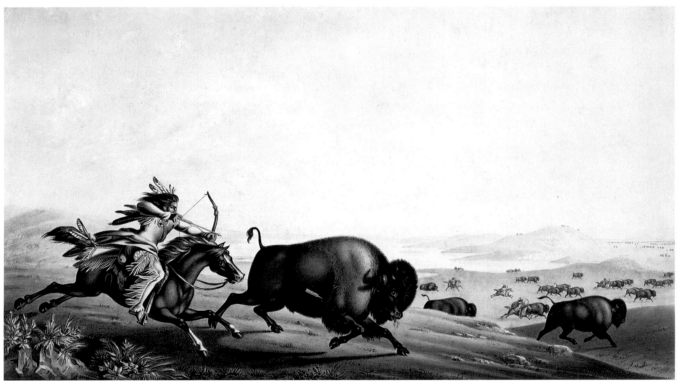

An early white trader who dealt with the Blackfeet reported that "War, women, horses, and buffalo are their delights, and all these they have at their command."

Peter Rindisbacher (1806–1834)
Assiniboin Hunting on Snowshoes,
1833
Watercolor on paper, 9 ¾ ×
16 ⅜ in.
Amon Carter Museum, Fort Worth,
Texas

The Assiniboins were a large tribe
pushed by white settlement from
southern Ontario west onto the
northern plains. They traded in fur
with the Hudson's Bay Company.

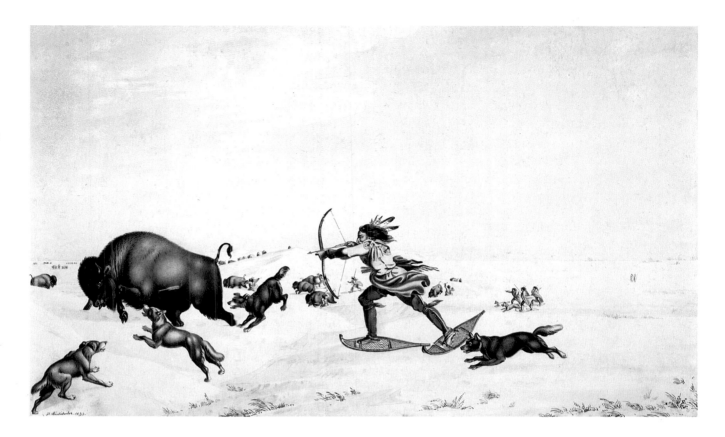

tion in 1800. Under the procedures then prevailing, the electoral college cast its votes for Jefferson and Burr, without indicating which should be president and which vice president. The contest went to the House of Representatives for a decision. Burr's arch political foe, Alexander Hamilton, lobbied against him, and the House elected Jefferson. Aaron Burr became the nation's third vice president. Toward the end of his term, in 1804, he ran for governor of New York. Burr, a Republican, struck a secret deal with a group of hyper-Federalists, who promised to support his candidacy if he would swing New York into a secessionist "Northern Confederacy of New England and New York." Alexander Hamilton, a more orthodox Federalist, caught wind of the apparent conspiracy and advised his Federalist friends to vote against Burr, who was, indeed, defeated. Subsequently, newspapers reported that Hamilton had called Burr "a dangerous man, and one who ought not to be trusted with the reins of government." When Burr demanded a printed retraction of the slur and Hamilton refused, the vice president challenged him to a duel. They met on a hill in Weehawken, New Jersey. Hamilton fired first, apparently discharging his pistol into the air; Burr leveled his piece and shot Hamilton in the chest. He died some thirty hours later.

That Aaron Burr was vice president of the United States and presiding over the Senate did not prevent his being indicted in New Jersey and New York for murder. While he was not finally tried, his political career was ruined.

But he was not entirely an outcast. He had friends in the West. This man who had been prepared to use radical Federalists to make him governor of New York

was regarded by some western Republicans as a hero for having slain a "dangerous" Federalist. Some even suggested that he run for Congress from Tennessee, but the vice president had other ideas. When, late in 1804, a delegation of French residents of New Orleans came to Washington to protest the government Jefferson had instituted there, Burr promptly courted them.

And he courted the British diplomats serving in Washington—to the extent of suggesting that he would facilitate the separation of the West from the United States. Then there were the Spanish: Burr supplied that government with information about American designs on Florida and Texas. Don Carlos Martínez de Yrujó, the Spanish minister to the United States, paid Burr about fifteen hundred dollars for such information.

But he was hardly loyal to Spain. The West was poised on the edge of war with Spain over the boundary between that empire and the United States. Westerners hungered after Spanish territory across the Sabine River in Texas, land that was more fertile and inviting than what was immediately open to them. War—and an American victory—would mean the Spanish forfeiture of Florida and Texas. In April 1805, little more than a month after his vice-presidential term had ended, Burr rode west. He had been in constant communication with his old friend and companion of the Benedict Arnold campaign, the treacherous James Wilkinson, at the time commanding the United States' small western army. The two were formulating a scheme to fan the boundary dispute into a full-scale war, but they would not be content with gaining Florida and Texas for the United States. Burr and Wilkinson would invade Mexico and establish an independent government there; that done, they would encourage the West to break with the Union and form a new empire with their new government in Mexico—all administered from a capital to be established in New Orleans.

Burr canvassed the West, from Pittsburgh to New Orleans, making himself known and garnering support. In New Orleans he solidified his relations with that city's discontented French residents. All of these contacts encouraged Burr in his plans, and he returned to the East, luring backers with promises of power and wealth. To Yrujó he proposed a scheme to seize Washington, D.C., and exploit the confusion that was bound to result in order to appropriate navy ships, sail to New Orleans, capture that city (with the aid of its French residents), and effect the secession of the entire West and its defection to the Spanish camp.

Except for the fifteen hundred dollars from the Spanish, Burr was unable to raise money for his schemes from foreign governments. However, a wealthy Irish immigrant, Harmon Blennerhasset, who lived in a kind of manor house on an island in the Ohio River near Marietta, was sufficiently impressed with Burr to advance him five thousand dollars as a down payment on a 400,000-acre tract on the Ouachita River in Kentucky. The land was adjacent to the Spanish frontier, and Burr recruited men ostensibly to settle the tract, but actually to fight a war against Spain.

These activities did not escape the notice of Joseph Hamilton Daveiss, a United States district attorney, who haled Burr into court and before a grand jury on a charge of preparing to make "war upon the subjects of the King of Spain." The jury was dissolved for lack of witnesses, whereupon Daveiss petitioned for a second grand jury, which again refused to indict Burr. The fact was, as Burr well knew, the West *wanted* war with Spain.

Burr was once again free to press westward, thence down the Mississippi to link up with James Wilkinson and take the city of New Orleans. And Wilkinson led his old friend to believe that he was ready to proceed. But on October 21, 1806, James Wilkinson—who commanded the U.S. Army on the western frontier while he was on the payroll of the Spanish secret service, even while he was also plotting with Burr a war on Spain—sent an urgent dispatch to President Jefferson revealing the entire scheme. The president issued a proclamation denouncing Burr as one who aimed "to place himself on the throne of Montezuma and extend his empire to the Alleghanies, seizing on New Orleans as the instrument of compulsion for our western states." Such was Jefferson's prestige that even Burr's western supporters turned against him. A militia party seized many of the boats he had gathered and even raided Blennerhasset's island. As to Burr himself, he was already on his way to New Orleans.

Wilkinson now spread the alarm in that city; Burr, he said, was about to invade with a vast army. William

Claiborne, the territorial governor, declared martial law, began the construction of fortifications, and got up a military force of his own. Burr's "army," sixty men in thirteen boats, was taken by Natchez militiamen. While a grand jury in Natchez declined to indict Burr—and even denounced Wilkinson and Claiborne for inciting public hysteria—Wilkinson continued to hold him prisoner. The former vice president of the United States put on some worn-out clothes and a floppy white hat and made a run for it.

He stopped at the house of one Nicholas Perkins to ask directions to a plantation where he planned to spend the night. A backwoods lawyer, Perkins had never seen Aaron Burr, not even a picture of him, yet he somehow *knew* that the stranger who had asked directions was Burr. Perkins rode to the sheriff, who refused to intervene, whereupon Perkins rode to Fort Stoddard and persuaded its commander, Lieutenant Edmund P. Gaines, to arrest the conspirator. Once Burr was in custody, Perkins volunteered to deliver him to federal officials in Virginia. It was a long journey—for Perkins was careful to avoid populated areas, which were bound to harbor many sympathizers who might take steps to free the prisoner—but it was a successful journey so far as the young lawyer was concerned. He netted more than three thou-

Alexander Lawson (1773–1846; after Alexander Wilson)
1. Louisiana Tanager. 2. L. Crow. 3. L. Woodpecker, c. 1811
Engraving, hand-colored, 13 ½ × 10 ¼ in.
Library, The Academy of Natural Sciences of Philadelphia

Three bird specimens collected by the Lewis and Clark expedition were exhibited at Charles Willson Peale's Philadelphia museum. There they were sketched by ornithologist/artist Alexander Wilson, whose work was adapted by the engraver Alexander Lawson.

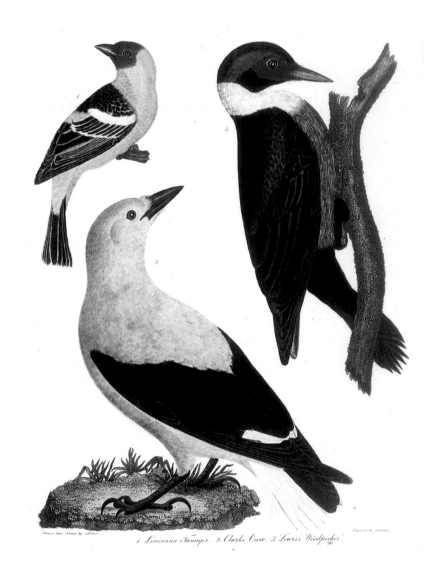

1. Louisiana Tanager. 2. Clarks Crow. 3. Lewis's Woodpecker.

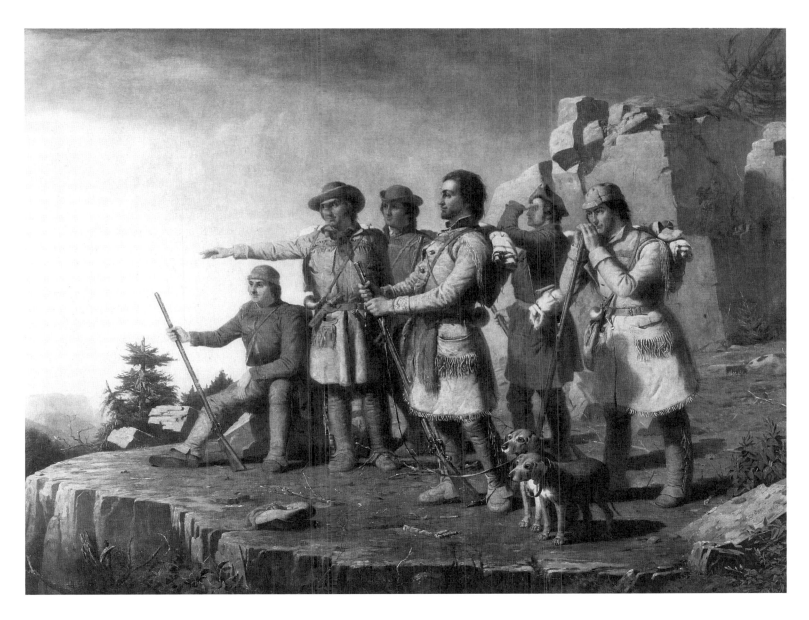

William Tylee Ranney (1813–1857)
Daniel Boone's First View of the Kentucky Valley, n.d.
Oil on canvas, 36 × 52 ½ in.
Gilcrease Museum, Tulsa, Oklahoma

A master at depicting mountain men of the Far West, Ranney portrays Boone and his party rather more as sporting outdoorsmen than authentic frontiersmen.

sand dollars in reward money, along with the thanks of the president.

The plan was to try Aaron Burr for high treason, but Supreme Court Chief Justice John Marshall, brought to Richmond to preside over the proceedings at the federal district court, refused to hold the prisoner on that charge, allowing only the lesser offense of high misdemeanor. Nevertheless, the grand jury indicted Burr for treason on the grounds of levying war against the United States and plotting to take possession of New Orleans. The trial proceeded, but Marshall ruled the prosecution's principal evidence inadmissible. All the government could bring to bear was evidence that Burr *intended* to commit an act of war; indeed, these intentions were thwarted before any act was committed. Marshall ruled that Burr could not be convicted for his intentions, and the jury had no alternative but to find him not guilty.

A free man yet again, Burr left for Europe, where he tried to interest Napoleon Bonaparte in a scheme to conquer Florida. After four impoverished years abroad, Burr returned to New York in 1812 and practiced law for almost a quarter century. He died in 1836.

III. DANIEL BOONE

Daniel Boone was born on November 2, 1734, in Berks County, Pennsylvania, the son of a lapsed Quaker whose given name was Squire, a name he would bestow on Daniel's elder brother as well. That name notwithstanding, the family was hardly aristocratic; they were wilderness folk, truly, and young Daniel, like his father, enjoyed nothing more than roaming the woods and hunting in obscurity. Yet, in the popular mind, Daniel Boone would come to acquire the kind of nobility Aaron Burr sought in vain. He became the archetypal frontiersman, uncrowned king of the wilderness. And not only Americans thought so. No less than Lord Byron celebrated Boone in *Don Juan:*

> The General Boon, back-woodsman of Kentucky,
> Was happiest amongst mortals anywhere . . .
>
> And what's still stranger, left behind a name
> For which men vainly decimate the throng,
> Not only famous, but of that *good* fame,
> Without which glory's but a tavern song—

He got his first rifle at the age of twelve or thirteen, and about that age, too, he had his first recorded run-in with civilization. The story goes that Boone attended a country school whose headmaster—and only teacher— habitually hid a bottle of whiskey in a nearby thicket, the better to punctuate his lessons. Young Boone, in pursuit of a squirrel, found the bottle and, with some school- mates, filled it with an emetic. When the schoolmaster next returned from one of his recesses, he was more than usually out of sorts. Daniel was called on to work sums, made a mistake, and was flogged. But he struck back— and decked the pedagogue.

When Daniel was nineteen, his father was begin- ning to feel crowded in Berks County and moved farther into the wilderness, settling in the Yadkin Valley of North Carolina. That was in 1753; two years later, the young man, in the capacity of wagoner, accompanied General Braddock on his disastrous expedition against the French at Fort Duquesne. He learned two things from that experience: how not to fight Indians (don't ad- vance in drill formation, red-coated), and, from a fellow wagoner, John Finley, he learned of a place called Kentucky.

Boone returned to Yadkin, courted his neighbor's fifteen-year-old daughter, Rebecca Bryan, married her, and built a cabin on his father's property. The idyll was short-lived, interrupted by fierce Indian raids in the Yad-

kin Valley from 1758 to 1760. Squire Boone, the elder, re- treated for a time to Maryland. His son Squire went back to Pennsylvania to learn blacksmithing. Daniel and Re- becca went to Culpepper County, Virginia, where Boone joined General John Forbes's expedition to Fort Du- quesne, this time as wagon master. He killed his first In- dian, hurling him off a bridge across the Juniata River. In 1759 he was back in the Yadkin Valley, having pur- chased 640 wilderness acres from his father for fifty pounds. He made his first trip across the Blue Ridge at this time, in pursuit of game, and he carved into the bark of a Tennessee tree:

> D. BOON
> CILLED A BAR ON TREE
> IN THE
> YEAR
> 1760

But Yadkin life was not all hunting. Boone was be- coming friendly with some influential men in those parts, chief among them Richard Henderson, a lawyer and a justice in the colonial courts. They talked about the steady influx of immigrants, and how the seaboard was becoming crowded, and how men could become wealthy and powerful if they controlled the vast lands to the west. Henderson sent Boone to explore whatever of that

Albert Bierstadt (1830–1902)
Mount Whitney, c. 1875
Oil on canvas, 67 ⅞ × 116 ⅝ in.
The Rockwell Museum, Corning, New York

Boone's bold venture into the Trans- Appalachian West was a first essential step in opening up the Far West.

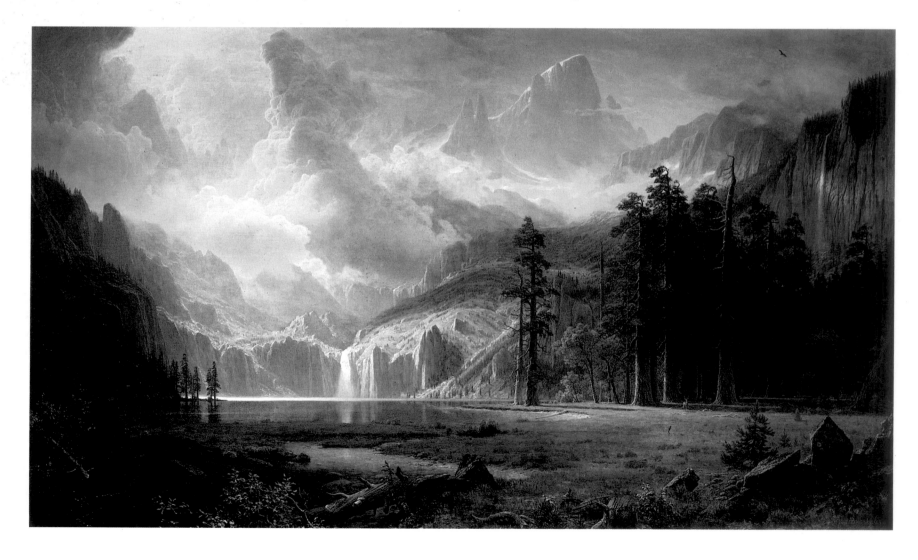

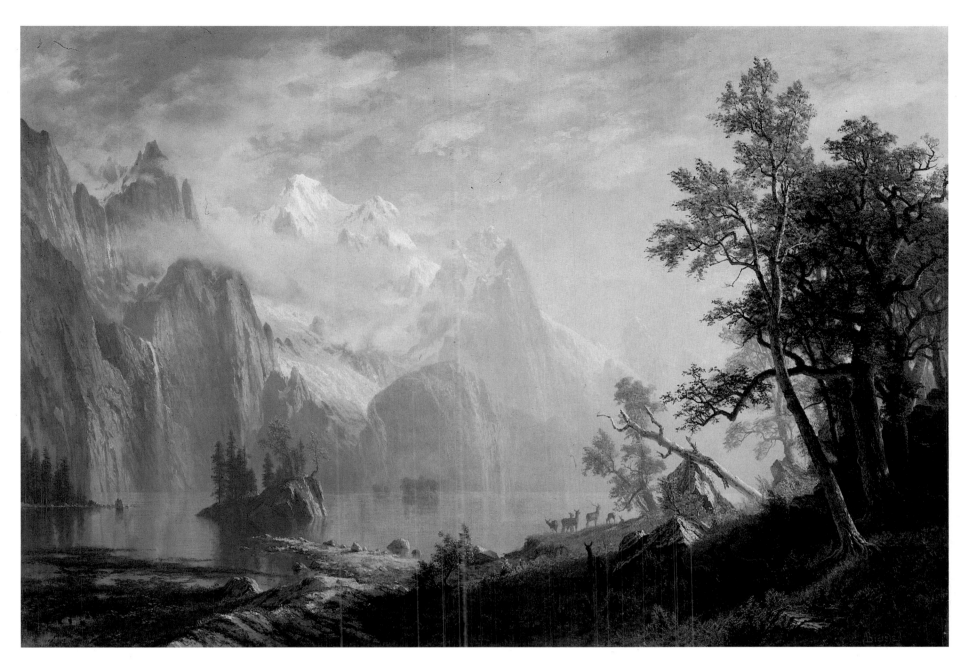

Albert Bierstadt (1830–1902)
Western Landscape, 1869
Oil on canvas, 36 ¼ × 54 ½ in.
Collection of The Newark Museum;
Purchase 1961 The Members' Fund

Although Bierstadt based his titanic depictions of the western landscape on firsthand knowledge of the territory, his romantic vision was shaped by training in the grandiloquent approach taught at Düsseldorf's famed art academy.

territory he could. By 1764, Boone had moved his family upriver, closer to the Kentucky country he had heard John Finley talk about.

As Boone explored, he hunted, struggling to make ends meet; for, like many frontiersmen, he was plagued by debt. Hunting deerskins was potentially quite profitable. A good hunter could expect to gather four or five hundred skins in a season and sell them for anywhere between forty cents to five dollars each. (The average price for a male deerskin was a dollar: one buck.) But hunting was not easy. One had to learn to move noiselessly and stay downwind of the animal, yet one had to get close enough—about a hundred yards—to accommodate the limited range of the rifles of the day.

With the onset of winter, deer became lean and their skins hardly worth taking. The hunter turned trapper, going after beaver and otter, both valuable for their pelts.

But then one had to get the skins and pelts to a trading post—and *that* was a problem. One horse could transport a hundred skins, so Boone managed six to a dozen horses, carrying skins, pelts, and equipment. Negotiating the woods with such a load was hard enough,

but there were also Indians to contend with, who delighted in robbing hunters and trappers. In a single hour, one might well lose an entire season's work, and, if he survived, return home empty-handed.

Indeed, even the resolute Boone seems to have faltered. When east Florida became a British colony after the French and Indian War, its new governor issued a proclamation offering a hundred acres to any Protestant immigrant. Boone secured a house and lot near Pensacola, but Rebecca objected to moving there, the house remained unoccupied, and the Boones were destined to push westward. Throughout the later 1760s and into the early 1770s, Boone probed Kentucky, finding, in 1767, the short route through the Cumberland Gap that he would eventually establish as a major trail of western migration.

On one trip, in 1769, Boone and his brother-in-law, John Stuart, were captured by Shawnees, robbed of seven months' worth of skins, and told to leave Kentucky—or else. Instead of leaving, the pair trailed the Shawnee party and even managed to recapture four or five stolen horses.

They were watering the horses when the same band

fell upon them again, took the pair prisoner again, and, again, they managed to escape. Later, however, John Stuart wandered off to hunt alone and was not heard from thereafter. Five years later, when Boone was cutting the Wilderness Road to Kentucky, one of his band found a skeleton, its left arm broken, smashed by a bullet. Beside the skeleton was a hunting horn bearing Stuart's initials.

After Stuart disappeared, Boone continued hunting with his brother, Squire, both determined now to recoup their losses. They were masters of woodcraft, eluding Indians by cooking only at night to conceal telltale smoke, sheltering the fire itself on all sides to hide the flame. They walked in shallow streambeds to break their trail; they even swung, like colonial Tarzans, from dangling wild grapevines. As ammunition ran low, Squire set off for the settlements with a new store of skins, promising to return with fresh supplies.

This is what it meant to be a frontiersman—to be left in absolute solitude in the forest, without bread, salt, sugar, horse, or dog, and barely enough ammunition to supply oneself with meat and fend off Indians. Boone used his solitude to explore as much of Kentucky as he could. After three months, he was rejoined by Squire on July 27, 1770, and the two continued to hunt and then trap through March of 1771. They headed back to the Yadkin Valley. Near the Cumberland Gap, on the very outskirts of the settlements, they were set upon by Indians who robbed their skins and pelts. Except for the two pack trains Squire had taken back earlier, the frontiersmen were bereft of two years' work.

But Daniel Boone did not return to Yadkin entirely empty-handed. He had seen Kentucky now, and he knew that it was where he wanted to live.

Late in the summer of 1773, Daniel Boone sold his farm and set off for Kentucky with six families, including his own. What was it that impelled him? For it was not only an extraordinarily hazardous move on account of the hostility of Indians (Kentucky would soon be known as that "dark and bloody ground") and the sheer remoteness of the country, it was also illegal. The Proclamation of 1763 forbade settlement that far west, fully acknowledging the Indians' right to the land. True, Boone was hopelessly in debt, and Kentucky was effectively beyond the reach of his creditors. It was doubtless true as well that Henderson's as-yet undeveloped scheme for colonization occupied some part of Boone's thoughts. But it was also true that Daniel Boone shared with certain others who had come before him, and even more who would come after, an elemental need to move into the unknown West.

This first attempt cost him dearly. When the party had reached the Cumberland Gap, Boone realized that they needed more flour and farm tools before they pushed into Kentucky. He sent his son James back to Captain William Russell's house to get the supplies. The

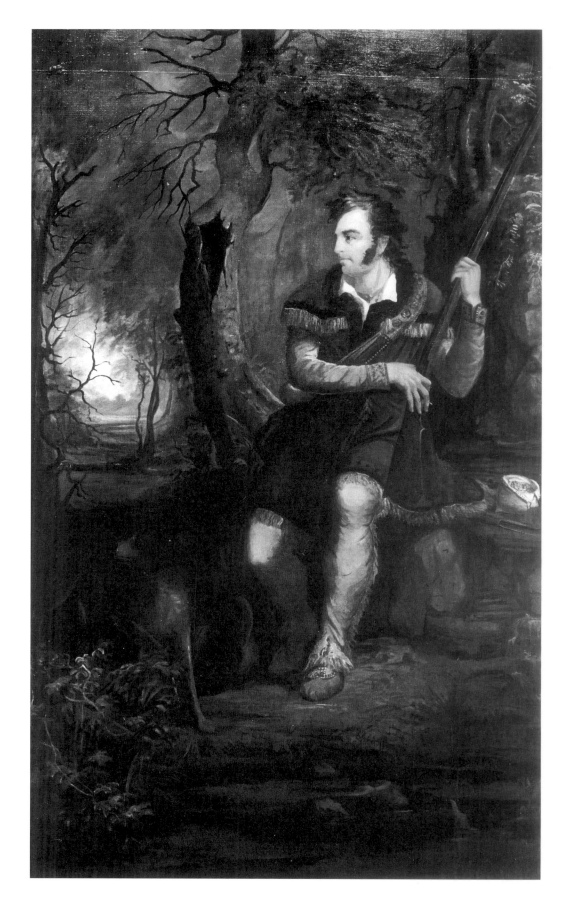

boy reached Russell's and set off, now fully supplied, with the captain's seventeen-year-old son, Henry, two slaves, and some white workmen. They set up camp on Walden's Creek, only three miles behind Boone's group—doubtless, James and Henry did not realize they were close enough to rejoin the main party. It was a fatal error.

William Allen (1849–1924)
Portrait of Daniel Boone, 1830–40
Oil on canvas, 103 × 64 ½ in.
Collection of the Museum of the
Kentucky Historical Society

The "first settler" of Kentucky
dandified by the hand of the artist—
with stylish mutton chops no less.

George Caleb Bingham (1811–1879)
*Daniel Boone Escorting Settlers
through the Cumberland Gap,*
1851–52
Oil on canvas, 36 ½ × 50 ¼ in.
Washington University Gallery of
Art, St. Louis; Gift of Nathaniel Phil-
lips, Boston

This splendid icon of the
frontiersman leading settlers
through the Cumberland Gap—for
many, the gateway to the West—is,
for Bingham, a rare excursion into
the deliberate depiction of heroism.
Nevertheless, nothing pompous
intrudes into this canvas. The man
stooping to tie his shoe is not only a
charming counterpoint to the high
drama of the striding figures, but
allows Bingham to complete one side
of his classic triangular composition.

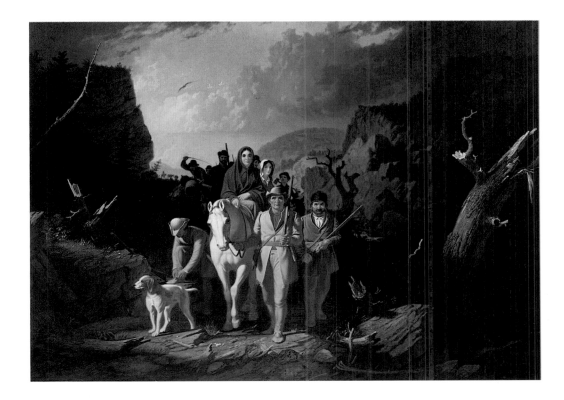

In the profound darkness before dawn, on October 11, 1773, a party of Indians attacked the camp, shooting James and Henry each through the hip and killing the rest outright, except for one white man, who escaped into the woods, never to be seen again (a skeleton was later discovered), and a black slave, who concealed himself in a pile of driftwood near the river and saw how the two boys were finally, slowly killed. James, who could not move because of his shattered hip, recognized one of the Indians as Big Jim, a Shawnee who traded with his father, and begged him to spare their lives. The Indians responded by flaying the helpless boys alive. Soon, James was not pleading to be spared, but simply to be tomahawked instantly.

It was a deserter from Boone's party who first discovered the slaughter. He stood staring at the horrible scene as Captain Russell came up from the east to join Boone. Russell's men began digging graves, and one of their number was sent ahead with the grim tidings and to warn Boone of a probable attack. (Some say that attack never materialized; others say that the Indians did attack, but were driven off.) For the Indians, the mayhem had not been entirely gratuitous. The horror of it succeeded in frightening most among the six families that accompanied Boone; they turned back to North Carolina.

After service in Lord Dunmore's War during 1774—fought against Shawnees in western Pennsylvania and Kentucky—Boone was hired by Richard Henderson, who had now set up the Transylvania Company, to blaze a trail through the Cumberland Gap. The idea was to treat directly with the Indians for some twenty million acres, bypassing colonial authorities completely, and then establish Kentucky as the fourteenth colony. The principals of the company—and this, presumably, would include Boone—would get large tracts for their estates, charge a quit-rent for every acre sold, and have special rights in the new colony's government.

One step ahead of his North Carolina creditors, Boone set off to start work on the Wilderness Road. On March 24, 1775, his camp was attacked by Indians, and three days later he and his men encountered another party who had suffered a similar attack. Many of Henderson's band of would-be settlers turned back. Despite this, enough followed Boone to establish Kentucky's first permanent settlements, Boonesborough, Harrod's Town, and Benjamin Logan's. In August Boone brought his wife and his last unmarried daughter, Jemima, to Boonesborough—perhaps the first white women to come willingly into Kentucky (occasional female captives had preceded them). But Shawnees attacked Boonesborough on December 23, 1775, and the attacks increased in frequency with the commencement of the American Revolution; most Indians in the vicinity of the new settlements sided with the British. With the opening of the Wilderness Road, some five hundred persons had come to settle in Kentucky. By the beginning of 1776, only two hundred were left, among them a mere dozen women. Among those who remained, dissension was rife—for the most part disputes over haphazardly surveyed land claims. Over a ten-year period, Boone himself would lay claim to some ten thousand acres; some say that, at one point, his claims totaled a hundred thousand acres. Virtually all of these claims would be found faulty and ultimately rejected by the courts.

On July 7, 1776, Jemima Boone and Betsey and Fanny Calloway, ages fourteen, sixteen, and fourteen, decided to paddle on the river. It should have been harmless enough recreation, but not in Kentucky in 1776. A band of Shawnees and Cherokees, led by the Cherokee chief Hanging Maw, fell upon the girls and made them captive. The girls were not missed at Boonesborough until late in the day, whereupon Boone and a small party trailed the captors with incredible skill (the feat was celebrated throughout the settlements), and surprised the Indians in their camp.

As rifles sounded, Jemima cried, "That's Daddy!"

Throughout 1776 and 1777, Boonesborough and the other Kentucky settlements were subject to Indian attack. Then, in February 1778, as Boone headed home from hunting, his horse loaded with buffalo meat, he was ambushed by Shawnees. Boone reached for his long knife, intending to cut the thongs that held the buffalo meat on the horse so that he could jump on and escape. But the knife, coated with blood and fat, had frozen solid in its sheath, and the handle was too greasy to grip. Boone footed it, but when an Indian bullet cut through the thong of his powder horn, he knew the game was up, and he surrendered. His captivity would stretch into five months, during which time he was adopted as a son by the Shawnee chief Blackfish. His escape, when it finally

CHARLES WIMAR

—

BORN 1828, SIEGBURG, GERMANY

DIED 1862, ST. LOUIS, MISSOURI

—

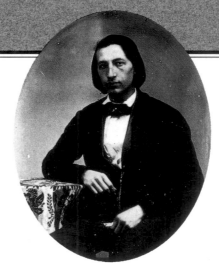

Portrait of Charles Wimar, n.d. Daguerrotype.
The Saint Louis Art Museum

Wimar's father died when the boy was seven years old, his mother remarried, and the stepfather immigrated to the United States. After he had opened a tavern in St. Louis, he sent for Wimar, his mother, and his own sons and daughters, all of whom arrived in 1842. Shy and brooding, speaking little English, young Charles preferred the company of Indians, who camped near his stepfather's tavern while trading furs, to that of the town's white residents.

Wimar was apprenticed to a local house painter and folk artist, Leon de Pomerade, with whom he spent about six years and traveled up the Mississippi, sketching Indians and the western landscape for a panorama he and his mentor intended to exhibit in St. Louis. After completing the panorama, Wimar established a studio in 1851 and, the next year, journeyed to Düsseldorf for study at the academy there under Josef Fay and Emanuel Leutze. Dark complexioned and dark haired, obsessed with Indian themes and their scrupulously accurate depiction

(in, nevertheless, a romantically rendered context), Wimar was called "the Indian painter" by his Düsseldorf colleagues, who thought he was actually part Indian. He sent his Indian work home to his parents, who had no trouble finding buyers; one painting sold for the handsome price of $300.

When he returned to St. Louis in 1856, Wimar immediately set about amassing a large collection of Indian artifacts and worked in a style at once freer and more imaginative than he had been able to achieve in Europe. He took a six-month trip up the Missouri and Yellowstone rivers in 1858, sketching Yankton Sioux, Gros Ventres, and Crows, including exciting buffalo hunting episodes. His *Buffalo Hunt* of 1861 was praised by no less a personage than Buffalo Bill Cody.

The dramatic vigor of Wimar's paintings and his own rugged frontier dress of buckskins and shoulder-length black hair belied his deteriorating health. He died of consumption at age thirty-four.

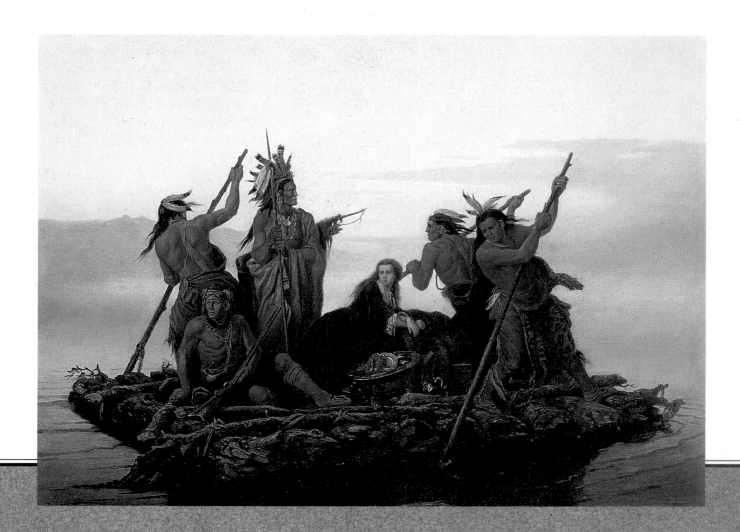

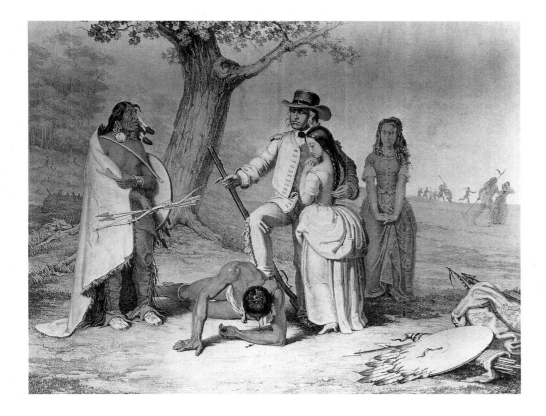

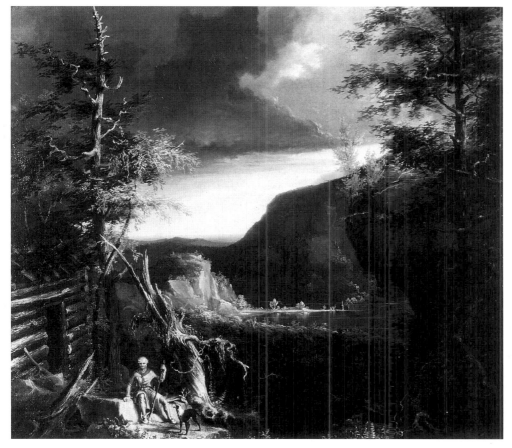

came, was oddly unspectacular. While the braves were out hunting and Boone was left among the squaws, he merely mounted a horse and rode off—in time to warn Boonesborough of the attack Blackfish and the British intended. Because of the warning, Boonesborough withstood a ten-day siege.

Throughout the war, Boonesborough and the other settlements would continue to be threatened and to resist those threats. Boone came to be recognized, even in his own time, as the frontiersman and pioneer par excellence. John James Audubon, in his *Ornithological Biography,* described Boone as he had seen him some time in the eighteen-teens: "The stature and general appearance of this wanderer of the western forests, approached the gigantic. His chest was broad and prominent; his muscular powers displayed themselves in every limb; his countenance gave indication of his great courage, enterprise, and perseverance; and when he spoke, the very motion of his lips brought the impression, that whatever he uttered could not be otherwise than strictly true."

Yet, despite his fame, despite his universally acknowledged role in opening up the West to settlement, Daniel Boone did not prosper. Henderson's scheme collapsed; Kentucky failed to become the fourteenth colony under his feudal rule. It was made a part of Virginia, later ceded to the federal government, and in 1792 became a state of the union. The great majority of Boone's many land claims were nullified in the courts. After the Revolution, Boone worked as a surveyor along the Ohio River. The very year the state of Kentucky named a new county after him, the sheriffs of Mason and Clark counties seized more than ten thousand acres of Boone's land to be sold for delinquent taxes. The next year Boone followed his son Daniel Morgan Boone to Missouri, in what was then Spanish Louisiana Territory, where he continued to hunt and trap, and where he established the town of Missouriton. He was granted some land (the titles to which, as had been the case in Kentucky, later proved faulty), and he was made a citizen and magistrate of Spain.

But the Louisiana Purchase would make him a citizen of the United States again, and while lawyers denied him and his posterity title to those parts of the West he had won from nature and Indians, subsequent legend—as it did with so many westerners—erased all irony and ambiguity.

For most, Daniel Boone is the first western hero.

Charles Wimar (1828–1862)
The Abduction of Boone's Daughter by the Indians, c. 1855
Oil on canvas, 18 ⅝ × 25 ¼ in.
Amon Carter Museum, Fort Worth, Texas *(opposite)*

G. W. Fasel (birth and death dates unknown)
Boone Rescuing His Daughter Jemima in 1776, 1851
Lithograph
Courtesy Library of Congress *(top)*

Thomas Cole (1801–1848)
Daniel Boone and His Cabin on the Great Osage Lake, 1826
Oil on canvas, 38 × 42 ½ in.
Mead Art Museum, Amherst College, *(bottom)*

The celebrated frontiersman is depicted in a pose recalling classical sculpture and in surroundings redolent of the Golden Age.

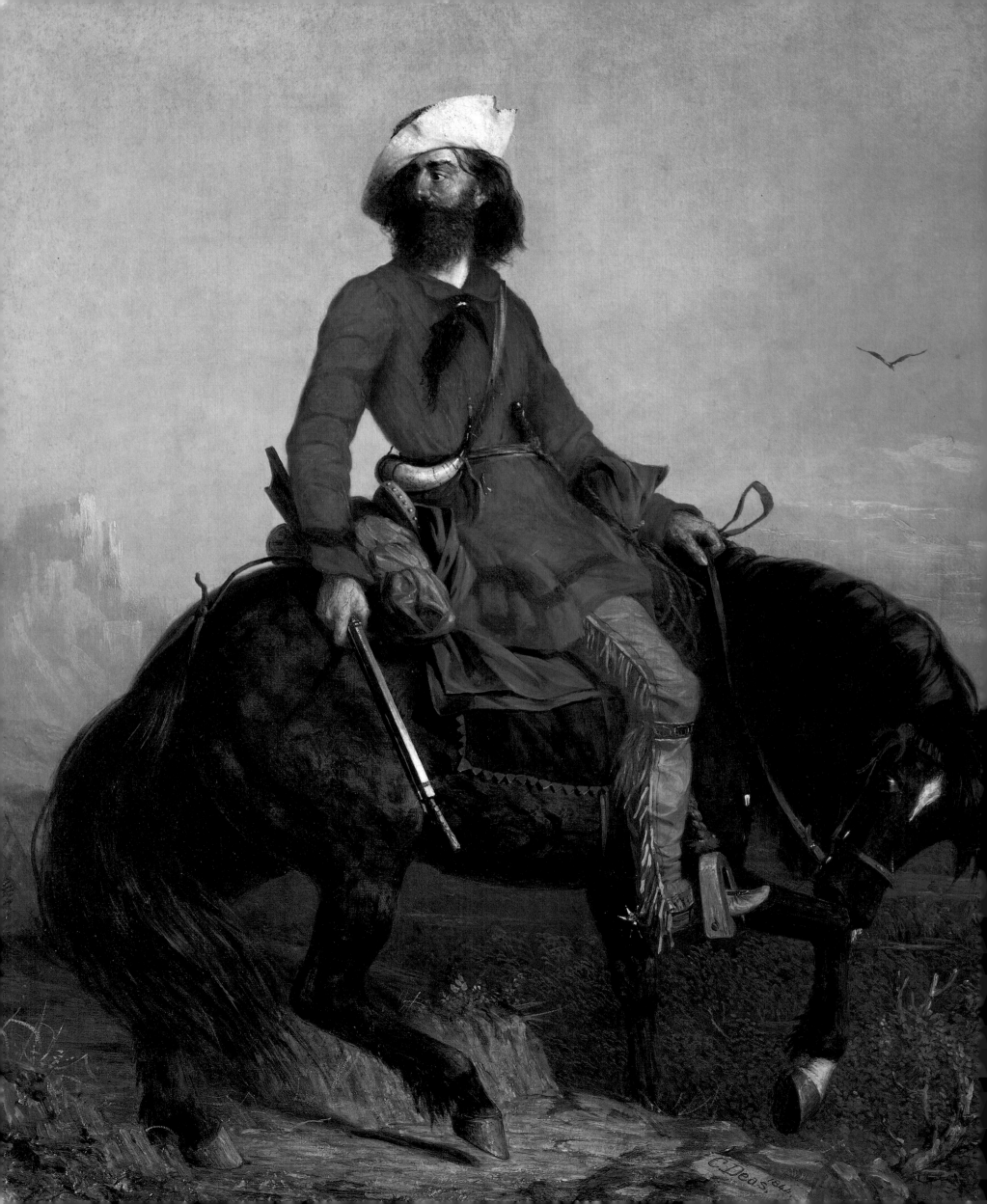

MOUNTAIN MEN AND MANIFEST DESTINY

L egend tells us that Daniel Boone went west because he had to—it was in his nature. We know, as a matter of historical fact, that Daniel Boone was poor and debt-ridden and that he expected to get rich in the West. What pushed America west was never purely "nature" or "destiny" or "opportunity" or "greed," but a complex and variable amalgam of motives. The men who explored the West after Lewis and Clark would not have called themselves explorers. They were fur trappers who, if they referred to themselves as anything in particular, took the name of mountain men. Singly, in small bands, or backed by considerable corporations, they ranged the Rocky Mountains in search of beaver. Fashion—*eastern and* European fashion—through the 1830s decreed the absolute necessity of beaver hats for gentlemen, and beaver trim on collars, cuffs, hems, bonnets, and boots for both sexes. Other pelts—marten, fox, and otter—were also in great demand. Thus, in the service of high fashion, the mountain men were launched into the Far West, and so the Far West was opened.

FUR

As far back as 1600, French *coureurs de bois* trapped or traded for furs with the Indians. After the British took Canada as a prize in the French and Indian War, the peltries of that nation were open to exploitation by two giants, the North West Company and the Hudson's Bay Company. But it was not until Lewis and Clark's expedition that Americans began trapping in any number. When John Colter, returning east with Lewis and Clark in 1806, ran into Joseph Dickson and Forrest Hancock, the two trappers were on their way up the Missouri to take beaver near the Yellowstone. As soon as his commanders granted his petition for discharge, Colter, by then a two-year veteran of the far western wilderness, turned back west with the trappers.

At six feet, John Colter, like Daniel Boone, was a tall man for his time. Before he joined the Lewis and Clark expedition, he had been fighting Indians in Virginia country, west of the Alleghenies. With Dickson and Hancock he trapped successfully for a full season along the Yellowstone and, as he had done abortively with Lewis and Clark, set out for home. On the upper Missouri, he encountered Manuel Lisa with a party of sixty men in keelboats. Lisa persuaded Colter to turn westward yet again as his guide.

Manuel Lisa was an entrepreneur among mountain men. Born in New Orleans, a Spaniard of ob-

Charles Deas, *Long Jakes (Long Jakes, The Rocky Mountain Man)*, 1844. Detail; see page 85

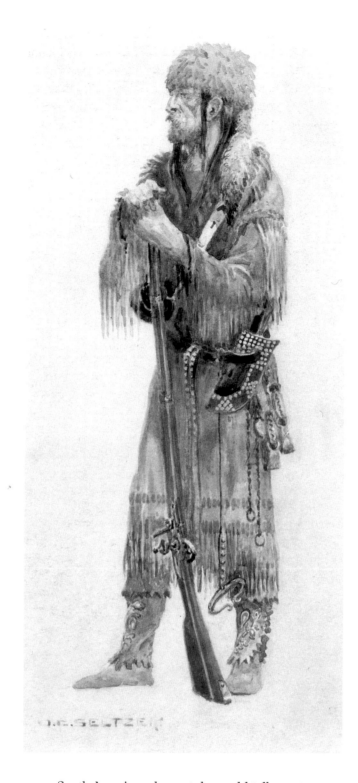

Olaf Carl Seltzer (1877–1957)
Trapper, n.d.
Watercolor on paper, 12 × 7 in.
Gilcrease Museum, Tulsa, Oklahoma

The Hudson's Bay Company trapper in full regalia, including beaver traps suspended from his belt.

was leading an expedition from St. Louis that had gotten a head start on three other fur parties. Those three expeditions, led by Auguste Pierre Chouteau, Pierre Dorion, and Lieutenant Joseph Kimball with Ensign Nathaniel Pryor, a Lewis and Clark alumnus, had delayed their departure from St. Louis in order to join forces for greater safety. The acting governor of the Upper Louisiana Territory asked Lisa to do the same, but the wily Manuel merely took the request as an invitation to get a jump on the others.

With similar high-handedness, Lisa managed the party's first encounter with Indian hostility. When Arikaras refused him permission to pass, he made a show of force (which, as with Lewis and Clark, included an intimidating display of cannon) but simultaneously offered the bribe of trade goods and promised that a much larger expedition was in his wake with even more. By November 21, 1807, he began building a fort on the Yellowstone at the mouth of the Bighorn River. He called it Fort Raymond, but it was soon to be known as Fort Lisa or even Fort Manuel and was the westernmost American outpost at the time.

Meanwhile, the combined Kimball-Pryor-Chouteau-Dorion expedition failed where Lisa had succeeded. Not only did the Arikaras refuse them passage, they attacked the party, killing four and wounding nine. Since Kimball and Pryor were army officers and their men soldiers, this was the first encounter west of the Mississippi between the U.S. Army and Indians. The army retreated, and the Indians won. This time.

Manuel Lisa's fur-gathering strategy was twofold. His trappers, as well as "free" trappers who signed on with him, would take all the pelts they could while Lisa hoped to trade with Indians for even more. This far west, however, the Indians were unacquainted with white traders, and it became John Colter's mission to range in advance of the main party in search of Indians with whom to trade. Traveling alone, he made a circuit through present-day Wyoming, Montana, and Idaho; he was the first white man to see Wind River, the Absaroka Mountains, Jackson Lake, the Tetons, Pierre's Hole, and the hot springs and geysers of Yellowstone Park. Returning to Fort Manuel, he led hundreds of Crows and Flatheads interested in establishing a trading relationship with Lisa. The column was attacked by Blackfeet, and Colter was wounded in the ensuing battle.

After recovering, he again set off from Fort Manuel in the fall of 1808, determined to make peace with the Blackfeet. He took with him only one companion, John Potts—another veteran of the Lewis and Clark expedition—figuring that the Blackfeet would not interpret the presence of just two men as an act of war. While trapping near the Jefferson River, the pair was captured, which was pretty much according to plan, for, in captivity, Colter could open negotiations. Potts, however, panicked, attempted to escape, and was shot full of arrows. Colter

scure South American descent, he could talk most anybody into anything. A smuggler and a mercenary spy, he had served as a supplier to the Lewis and Clark expedition but, whether by design or accident, had failed his customers sufficiently to earn a "Damn Manuel" from Meriwether Lewis. Yet, in 1808, after squirming out from under a murder rap (he had ordered the death of a member of his trapping party, claiming the man was a deserter; the court believed him, and the murder was excused on that account), he persuaded a group of St. Louis investors to back what he proposed to call the Missouri Fur Company. The investors included William Clark and Lewis's brother Reuben.

In 1807, when he persuaded Colter to join him, Lisa

was stripped naked and tortured while his captors debated the means by which they would end his life. Finally, one of the chiefs asked him how fast he could run. Colter replied that he was very slow indeed. That decided it. He was told to run for his life.

Actually, John Colter had a considerable reputation for speed. Naked as he was, the mountain man tore off toward the Jefferson River. After three miles at top speed, only one of his pursuers had gained on him. Colter wheeled about, tripped him, and ran him through with his own lance. When Colter reached the river, he hid under some driftwood as Blackfeet searched the shore. After swimming downstream some five miles, he resumed running. Seven days later, naked, blistered, and flayed, he reached Fort Manuel, two hundred miles distant from where he had been captured.

While Colter and Lisa's other employees continued trapping operations from their base at Fort Manuel, Lisa returned to St. Louis to organize the Missouri Fur Company. The new company would not depend on Indian trade; instead, furs would be gathered by hired white trappers who would bring their catch to a central point, Fort Manuel, for shipment back east. This consolidation of operations would mean increased efficiency and, therefore, increased profits. It also foreshadowed what would become a trapping institution, the annual "rendezvous," a riotous convocation of mountain men who came from all parts to trade their furs and to enjoy what was for them the rare pleasures of society.

Unfortunately, the Missouri Fur Company was doomed to failure from the start. Three hundred fifty men was a titanic force for a trapping party, but half that number deserted or were discharged during the first leg of the journey up the Missouri. Part of the party, guided by John Colter, traveled to Three Forks—site of much Blackfoot trouble—in the bitter weather of early spring. The thought was to defy the Indians by a show of white numbers. The Blackfeet, however, were unimpressed and killed eight trappers, including the redoubtable George Drouillard, veteran mountain man and companion of Lewis and Clark. Even worse than the Blackfeet were the grizzly bears of the region, the most ferocious

Alfred Jacob Miller (1810–1874)
The Indian Guide, n.d.
Pen, ink, gray wash on paper,
8 7/8 × 10 7/8 in.
Denver Art Museum

The artist made this sketch of his patron, the Scottish hunter and amateur explorer Captain William Drummond Stewart, who commissioned Miller to document his tour of the West.

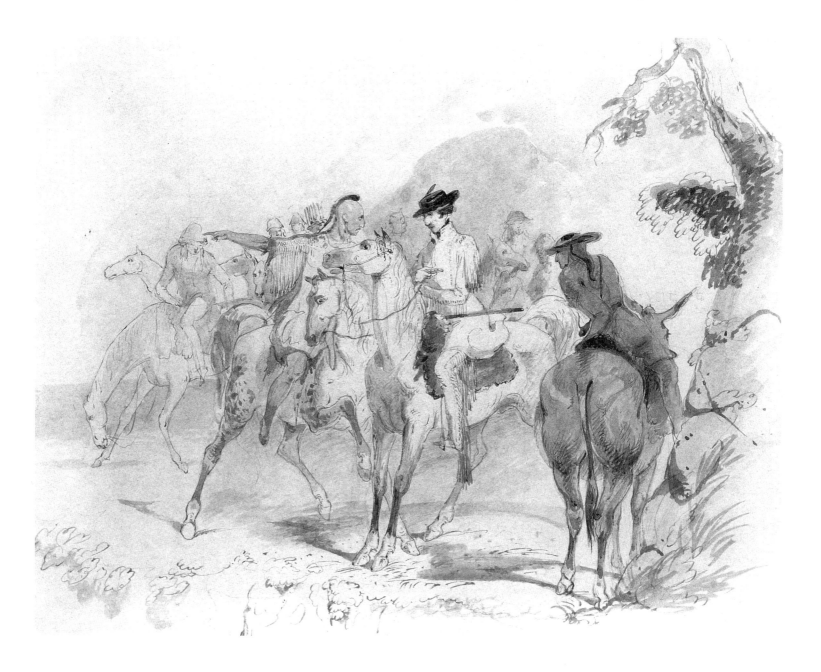

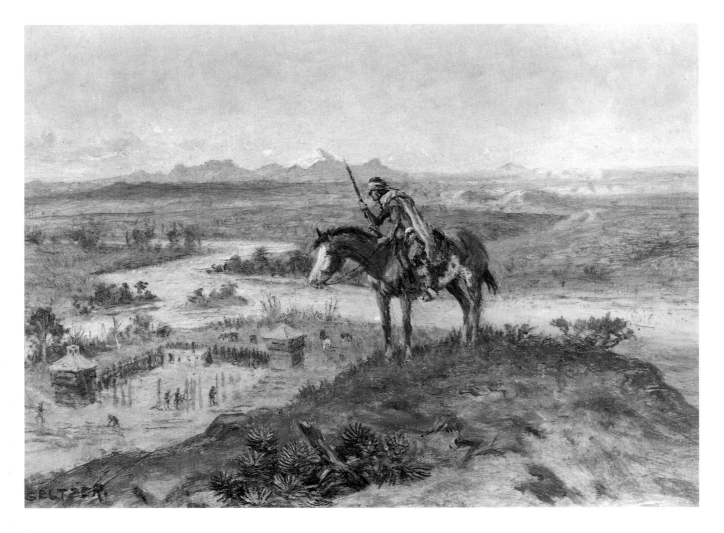

Olaf Carl Seltzer (1877–1957)
*Manuel Lisa 1807, Watching the
Construction of Fort Lisa*, 1934
Oil on board, 4 ¼ × 6 ⅛ in.
Gilcrease Museum, Tulsa, Oklahoma

The wily fur entrepreneur built this
fort at the mouth of the Big Horn
River in 1807 as an outpost for
gathering and trading pelts.

that trappers had encountered anywhere.

Colter returned to Fort Manuel, where, reportedly, he threw his hat down and declared, "If God will only forgive me this time and let me off I will leave the country day after tomorrow—and be damned if I ever come into it again!" Indeed, the entire Missouri Fur Company expedition withdrew, and the firm folded.

True to his word, Colter retired from mountain life. Though his company had dissolved, Lisa continued profitably to work the fur trade until he died—in bed—in 1820.

John Colter was by any measure an extraordinary man, but he was, on the whole, a typical *mountain* man. Between 1806, when Colter followed Dickson and Hancock, and the 1830s, when fickle fashion began to crave far less in the way of fur, perhaps two thousand men essayed a trapper's life. It required months, even years of work in the wilderness. Usually, it was solitary labor, and if one wanted to get the best and most abundant pelts, it was solitary labor in unexplored country. Grizzly bears were an ever-present hazard, always aggressive and monstrously powerful. When you tangled with one, you either killed it or it killed you. To wound a grizzly only incited it to more devastating attacks. And there were the Blackfeet, hostile since Meriwether Lewis had killed two of a party of eight who were attempting to steal horses and rifles. Perhaps five hundred mountain men fell victim to the Blackfeet—a mortality rate of

about 25 percent. Even friendly Indians could be a problem, since they often stole horses and looted pelts.

Then there was the process of trapping itself, as Hiram Chittendon describes it in his three-volume *American Fur Trade of the Far West*:

The universal mode of taking beaver was with the steel trap . . . a strong one of about five pounds' weight. The chain attached to the trap is about five feet long, with a swivel near the end to keep it from kinking. The trapper, in setting the trap, wades into the stream so that his tracks may not be apparent; plants his trap in three or four inches of water a little way from the bank, and fastens the chain to a strong stick, which he drives into the bed of the stream at the full chain length from the trap. Immediately over the trap a little twig is set so that one end shall be about four inches above the surface of the water. On this is put a peculiar bait, supplied by the animal itself, castor, castorum, or musk, the odor of which has a great attraction for the beaver. To reach the bait he raises his mouth toward it and in this act brings his feet directly under it. He thus treads on the trap, springs it and is caught. In his fright he seeks concealment by his usual method of diving into deep water, but finds himself held by the chain which he cannot gnaw in two, and after an ineffectual struggle, he sinks to the bottom and is drowned.

John Mix Stanley (1814–1872)
Scouts in the Tetons, n.d.
Oil on canvas, 24 × 34 ⅛ in.
Gilcrease Museum, Tulsa, Oklahoma

After the market for fur dwindled by
the mid nineteenth century, many
mountain men traded on their
intimate knowledge of the far
western wilderness and hired on as
civilian scouts for the army—which
usually needed all the help it could
get.

JOHN MIX STANLEY

BORN 1814, CANANDAIGUA, NEW YORK
DIED 1872, DETROIT

Stanley's earliest experience of Indian life came in his father's tavern, located in New York's Iroquois country. According to possibly credible legend, even the war chief Red Jacket patronized the tavern. After six years as apprentice to a coachmaker in Naples, New York, Stanley moved to Detroit, where he became a house and sign painter. James Bowman, an itinerant painter who had studied in Italy, admired the young man's sign work and offered to instruct him in portraiture.

Between 1836 and 1838, Stanley and Bowman went into partnership painting portraits in and around Chicago. After this venture, Stanley traveled throughout the Old Northwest, visiting Galena, Illinois, Fort Snelling (present-day Minneapolis), and Green Bay, Wisconsin, painting Indian scenes, which he could not sell. He returned to the East for a time, painting portraits in New York, Philadelphia, and Baltimore. By 1841 he was in Troy, New York, where he entered into partnership with Caleb Sumner Dickerman, a young clerk with artistic leanings, to set up an Indian gallery similar to those of George Catlin and the U.S. War Department. While in Troy, Stanley also learned daguerreotype techniques and always carried a camera on his sketching tours;

he was one of the first photographers of the Indian.

The artist set up a studio in Fort Gibson, Indian Territory (present-day Oklahoma), painting Indians through 1845, and was present at the Cherokee capital of Tahlequah when a great council drew some ten thousand Indians from more than a dozen tribes. By 1846, Stanley was displaying his work in Cincinnati. That year he also joined a wagon train bound for Santa Fe and offered his services to Stephen Watts Kearny as topographical draftsman on Kearny's expedition to aid in the conquest of California during the Mexican War. From San Diego, Stanley traveled to San Francisco and then to Oregon territory, where he nearly met his end in the midst of the Indian uprising that followed the Marcus Whitman massacre at Wailatpu.

From Oregon, the peripatetic artist sailed to Hawaii, where he painted Polynesian portraits during 1848–49 before returning to Troy and taking the now-expanded Indian gallery on a tour of eastern cities. In 1852, the artist put his gallery on display at the Smithsonian Institution and repeatedly petitioned Congress to purchase it from him. Not only were these petitions unsuccessful, but in 1865 almost all of the paintings were destroyed in a catastrophic fire that gutted the Smithsonian. (Other paintings would be destroyed by a later fire in P. T. Barnum's American Museum in New York City.)

Stanley was commissioned in 1853 as official artist for Isaac Stevens's survey of a northern route for a transcontinental railway, and the next year he prepared a giant panoramic painting of scenes along the survey route, which required two hours for viewing. No trace of this immense work survives.

Despite the indifferent success of his Indian gallery, the refusal of Congress to buy his work, and the loss of so many of his paintings, Stanley spent the latter part of his career comfortably and successfully as a studio artist in Detroit.

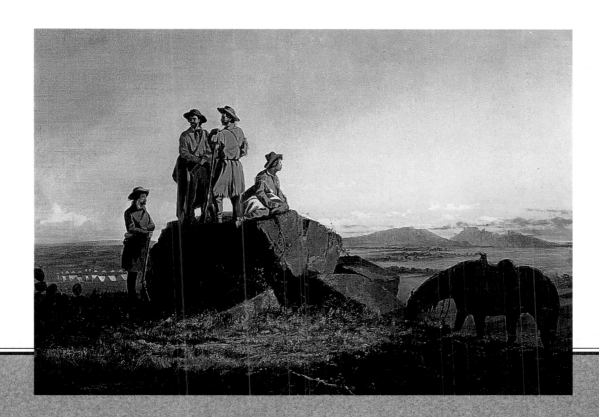

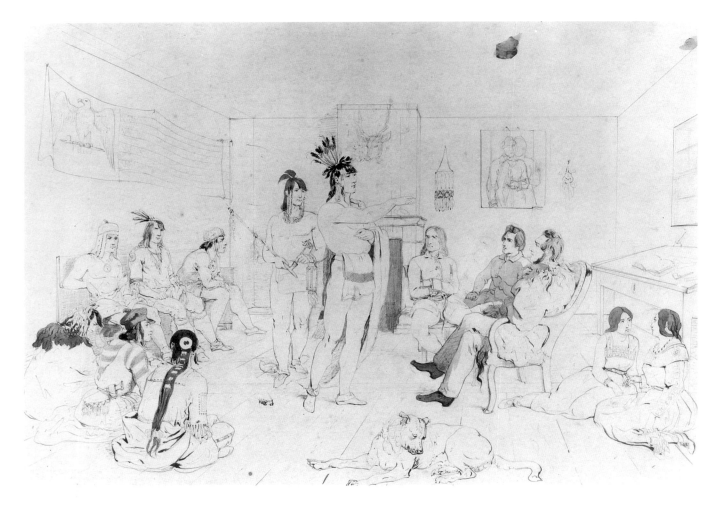

Rudolph Friedrich Kurz (1818–1871)
*Cree Chief Le Tout Pique and Fur
Company Agents at Fort Union*, 1851
Ink and wash drawing on paper,
14 × 20 in.
Gilcrease Museum, Tulsa, Oklahoma

This Swiss artist documented an
American sojourn spanning 1846 to
1852 in journals, sketches, and
paintings. This sketch, made at Fort
Union on the upper Missouri River,
shows an October 19, 1851,
conference between Crees and
American Fur Company agents. The
artist is pictured seated between an
interpreter, Battiste (arms folded),
and chief agent Edwin T. Denig. The
women seated on the floor are
probably Denig's two Indian wives.

Since the pelts were valuable only when they had thick-
ened during the fall, winter, and early spring, a trapper
spent his days wading in ice-cold water, with no prospect
of a change of dry clothes.

It wasn't that the mountain man was a masochist.
For the life had its rewards. If you survived, and if you
successfully husbanded your pelts home or to the annual
"rendezvous" at which they were traded, you could make
a fortune. But there was more. For all its hazards and
hardships, a trapper's life was one of manly self-
indulgence, of continual hunting and fishing, of absolute
freedom from the demands and constraints of civilization—taxes, mortgages, wives, the law. As to sex, that
was available, too, as many mountain men took Indian
wives or, at least, companions. Indeed, the mountain
man became something of a white Indian himself, as
Washington Irving observed in 1837, discarding "everything that may bear the stamp of civilized life," adopting
"the manners, habits, dress, gesture and even walk of the
Indian," plaiting his greater-than-shoulder-length hair
and tying it with otter skins or "parti-colored ribands."
His knee-length hunting shirt was of ruffled calico
brightly dyed, or of ornamented leather, and his legs
were wrapped in leggings "ornamented with strings,
fringes, and a profusion of hawks' bells," while his feet
were shod in "a costly pair of moccasons of the finest Indian fabric, richly embroidered with beads." A scarlet
blanket hung from his shoulders, "girt around his waist
with a red sash, in which he bestows his pistols, knife,

and the stem of his Indian pipe." As to the mountain
man's horse—"selected for his speed and spirit, and
prancing gait"—it was decked out as fantastically as its
rider, with beaded and embossed bridles and crupper,
the head, mane, and tail "interwoven with abundance of
eagles' plumes," and its coat "bestreaked and bespotted
with vermillion, or with white clay, whichever presents
the most glaring contrast to his real color."

As Lisa's abortive Missouri Fur Company demonstrated, organizing mountain men into a disciplined,
businesslike body was a formidable task and perhaps a
forlorn hope. Still, the British seemed to have accomplished it with the North West Company and Hudson's
Bay Company, and there was an American willing to try
again.

John Jacob Astor had been born in Germany and
came to America one year after the close of the Revolution. Like many who would come after him, Astor saw
the United States as a land of opportunity. He was determined to make his fortune—but how? It sounds like the
plot point in a bad Hollywood movie, but the answer
came to him on board ship during the voyage to America.
He had long talks with a fellow passenger, a furrier by
trade, and, in the course of conversation, John Jacob Astor decided to deal in furs. Within twenty years of landing in America, he was the richest man in the nation.

But he had made his fortune marketing, rather than
producing, furs. In 1810 he decided to change that with
his new American Fur Company. His aim, which was

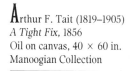

Alfred Jacob Miller (1810–1874)
Setting Traps for Beaver, n.d.
Watercolor, gouache and ink on
paper, 8 × 10 in.
Joslyn Art Museum, Omaha,
Nebraska

This vivid sketch suggests the chief
misery of the trapper's life: standing
in the cold air, knee deep in icy
water, performing the tedious work
of setting traps.

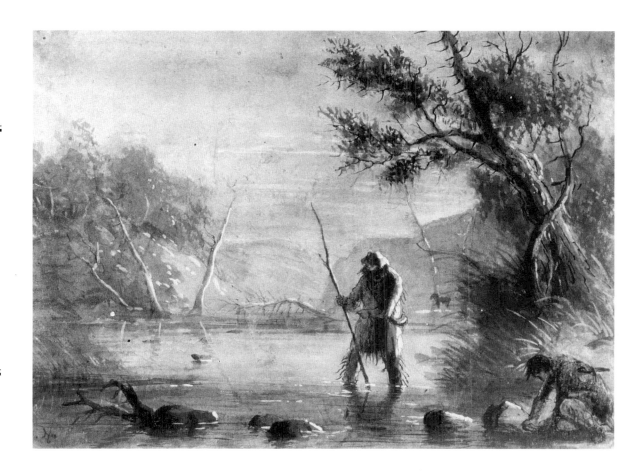

Arthur F. Tait (1819–1905)
A Tight Fix, 1856
Oil on canvas, 40 × 60 in.
Manoogian Collection

Tait combined the outdoor genre
painter's mastery of brilliant detail
with an instinct for drama to become
Currier & Ives's most popular
western painter.

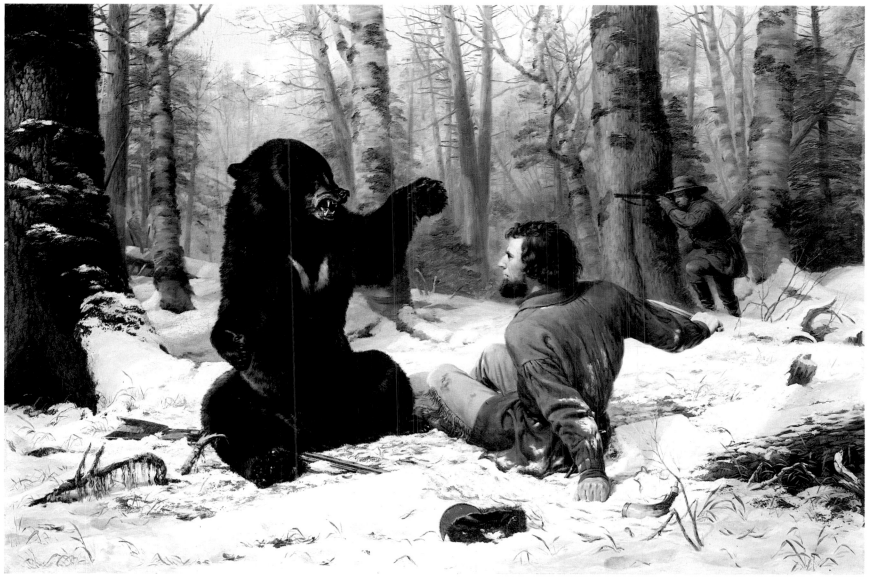

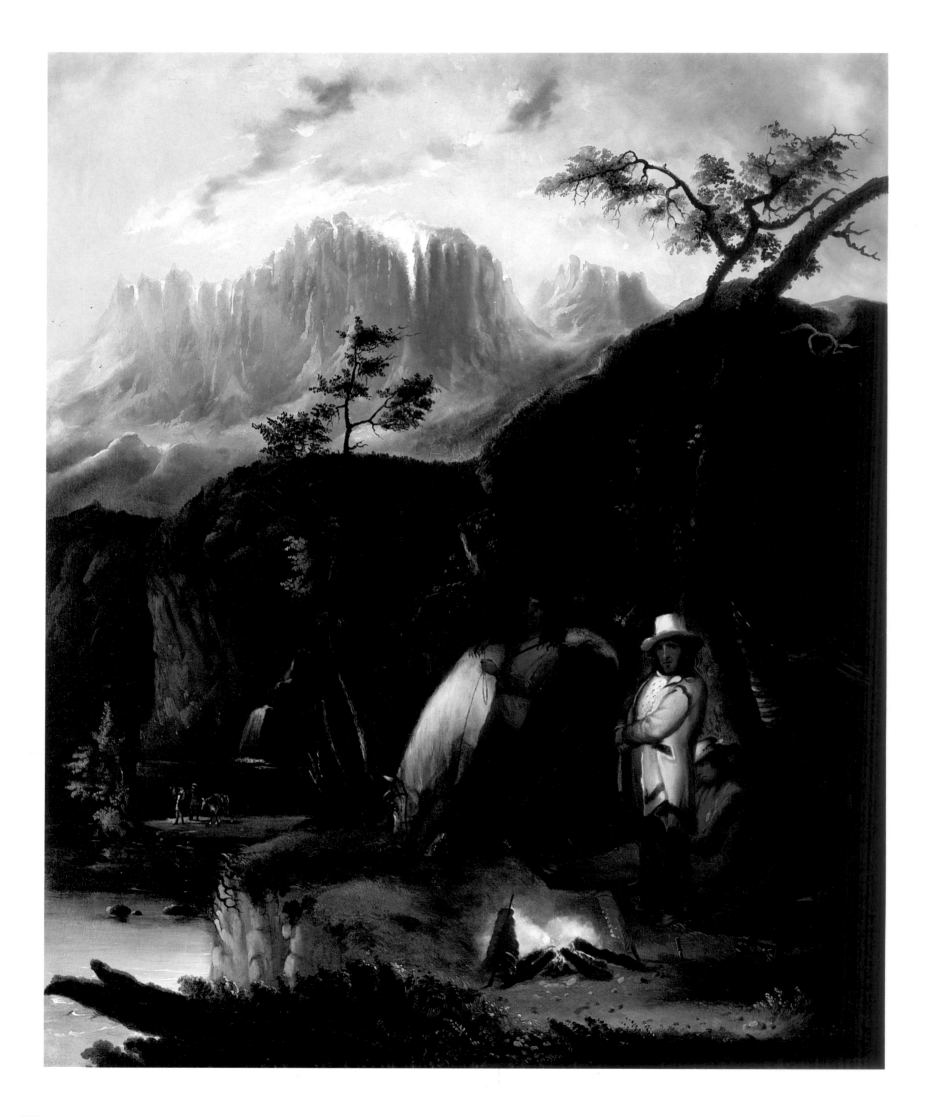

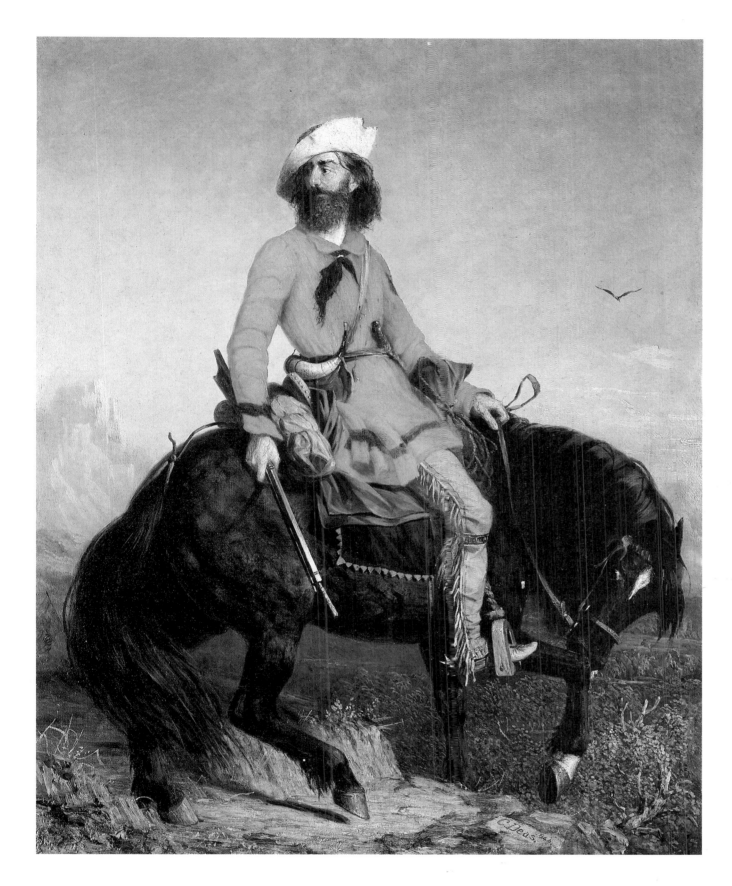

Charles Deas (1818–1867)
*Long Jakes (Long Jakes, The Rocky
Mountain Man)*, 1844
Oil on canvas, 30 × 25 in.
Manoogian Collection

Preserved for all time: the
archetypal image of an all-but-
superhuman western character—the
mountain man.

Alfred Jacob Miller (1810–1874)
Trappers Around a Campfire, 1838
Oil on canvas, 38 ¼ × 32 ⅛ in.
The Warner Collection of Gulf States
Paper Corporation, Tuscaloosa,
Alabama

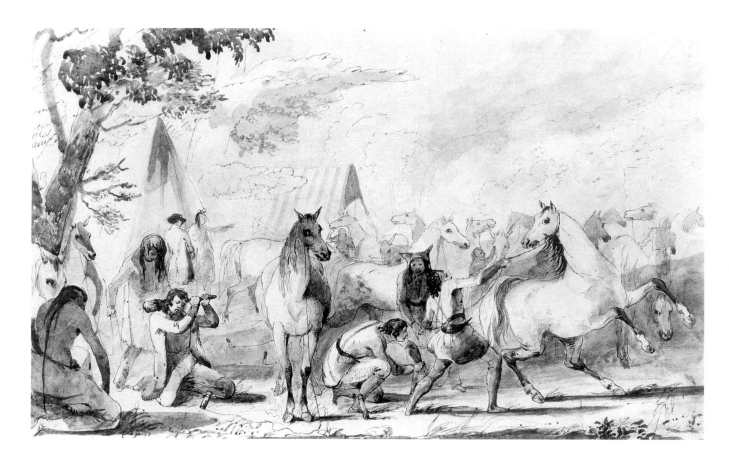

Travelers in the western wilderness
learned to secure their horses at
night—lest they wander off, often
into the hands of Indians.

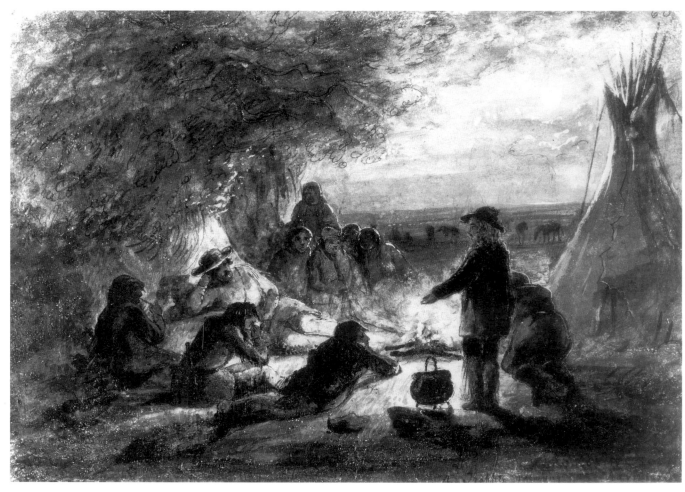

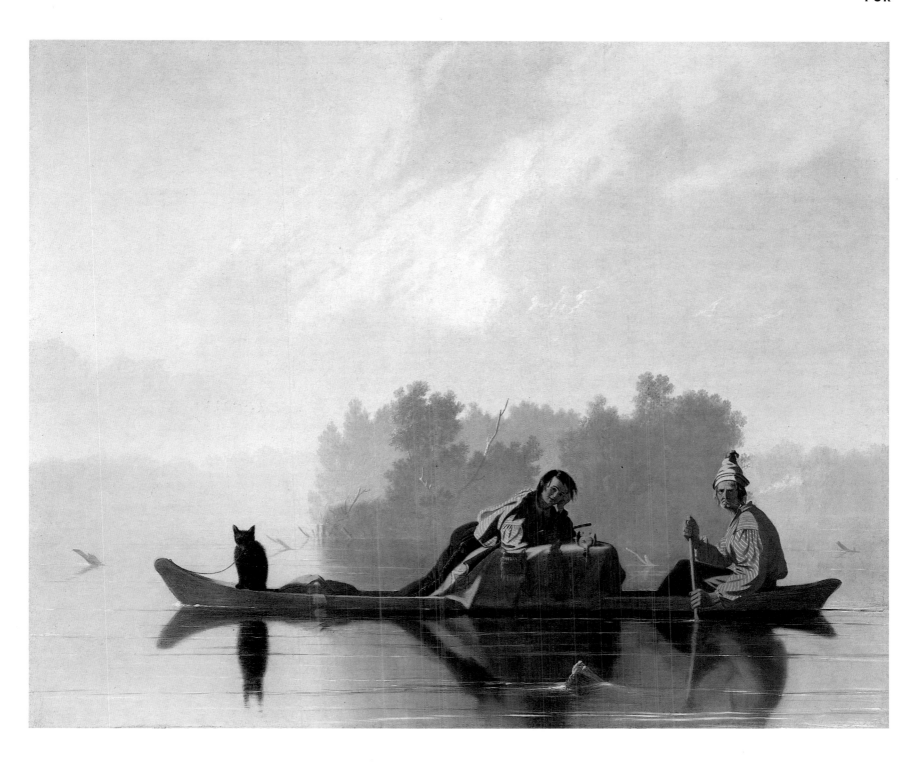

George Caleb Bingham (1811–1879)
*Fur Traders Descending the
Missouri,* c. 1845
Oil on canvas, 29 × 36 ½ in.
The Metropolitan Museum of Art;
Morris K. Jesup Fund, 1933.

At his best, Bingham imbues his
western compositions with the grace
of a classical frieze. The fox tethered
at the prow of the canoe is often
misidentified as a cat.

heartily approved by Thomas Jefferson himself, was to establish his company in the region of the Columbia River before the two British companies became absolute masters of that territory. Nothing in Astor's plan was to be left to chance. Posts would be established on the Columbia and on the Pacific, continually maintained and supplied via an overland route as well as by sea. The overland route would insure that British sea power could not effect a total blockade, while Astor's ships could unload their supplies, pick up furs, and sail directly on to China, where the import fur business was especially lucrative.

The enterprise was conceived at a make-or-break time. The North West Company's David Thompson had already penetrated very far west in Canada and in the present states of Montana and Idaho. There were also the Russians to contend with. As early as 1805, Nikolai Rezanov had attempted to plant the Russian flag at the mouth of the Columbia and, in 1811, would succeed in establishing a base on the California coast. Even the Spanish continued to be troublesome, as they asserted claims to the Pacific Northwest based on prior discovery.

In keeping with his logical, methodical approach to the project, Astor reasoned that relatively inexperienced American fur men stood little chance in competition with the seasoned professionals engaged by the North West Company. He therefore hired ex-Northwesters and French Canadians. Among the Northwesters were Alexander McKay, who had accompanied the great Alexander Mackenzie on his two Canadian transcontinental expeditions, Duncan McDougal, Donald McKenzie, David Stuart, and Robert Stuart, all of whom Astor made part-

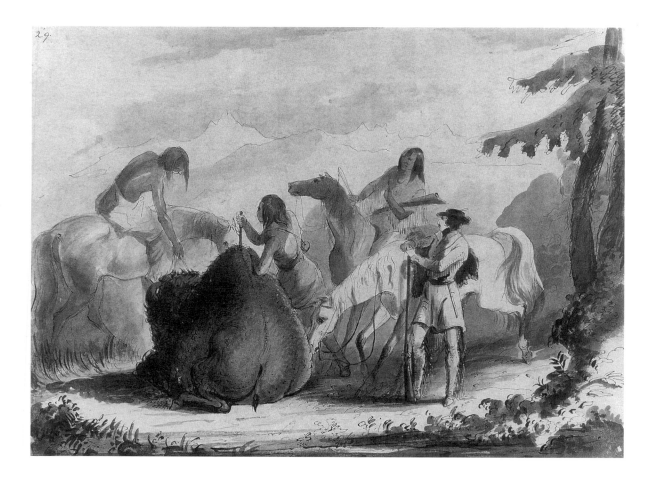

Alfred Jacob Miller (1810–1874)
Taking the "Hump Rib," c. 1837
Pen and ink, ink wash, and graphite on gray card, 8 ⅛ × 10 ⅞ in.
Amon Carter Museum, Fort Worth, Texas

This artist paid careful attention to detail. Here he documents an Indian method of butchering a buffalo. The hide was slit along the backbone, peeled off, and spread out on the ground where it served as a "blanket" on which chunks of the animal's meat were laid.

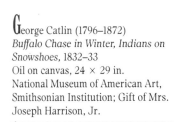eorge Catlin (1796–1872)
Buffalo Chase in Winter, Indians on Snowshoes, 1832–33
Oil on canvas, 24 × 29 in.
National Museum of American Art, Smithsonian Institution; Gift of Mrs. Joseph Harrison, Jr.

"The Indians generally kill and dry meat enough in the fall . . . to last them through the winter; so that they have little other object for this unlimited slaughter, amid the drifts of snow, other than that of procuring their robes for traffic with their Traders. The snow shoes are made in a great many forms, of two and three feet in length, and one foot or more in width, of a hoop or hoops bent around for a frame, with a netting or web woven across with strings of rawhide. . . ."—George Catlin, *The Manners, Customs and Condition of the North American Indians,* 1841

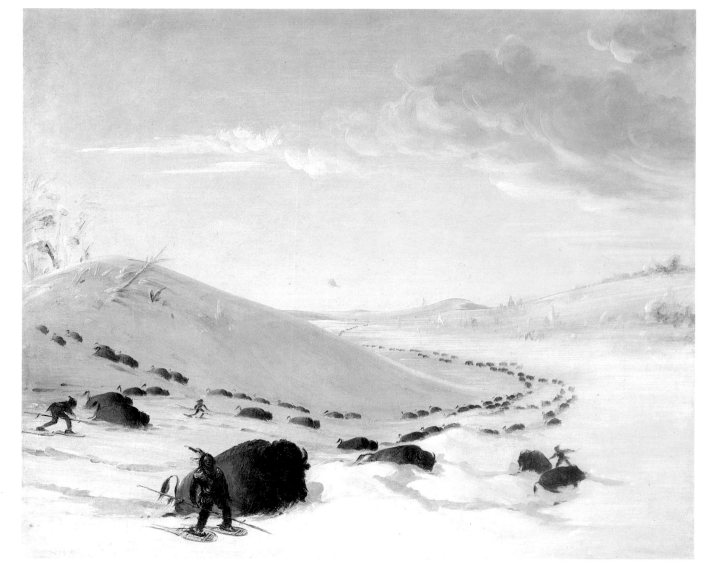

John Mix Stanley (1814–1872)
Camp of the Red River Hunters,
1857
Oil on canvas, 13 ¾ × 21 ⅛ in.
Amon Carter Museum, Fort Worth,
Texas

White hunters on the plains adopted
the Indians' highly practical—and
highly portable—form of housing.

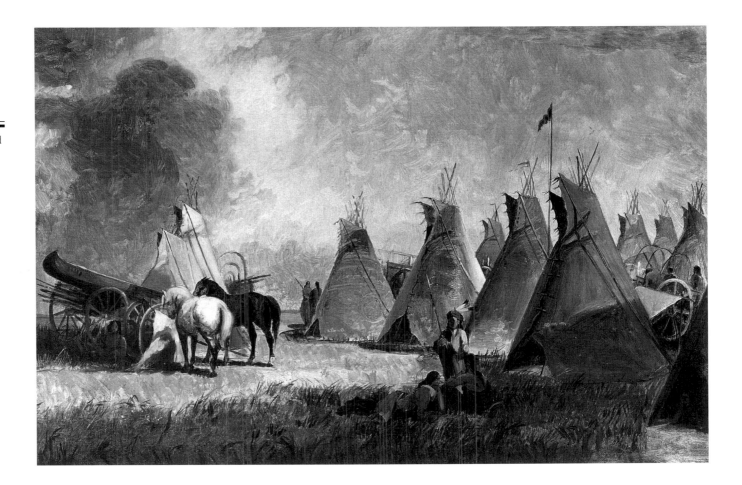

ners in the enterprise. Only one American served similarly, Wilson Price Hunt. Together with McKenzie, he
oversaw the overland division of the expedition while the
others journeyed by sea.

Although the ex-Northwesters certainly had experience with furs, they had no experience with the *American* wilderness and, of course, though they stood to
profit as partners, they lacked any patriotic motive for
making the enterprise succeed.

Astor fitted out a 290-ton, ten-gun schooner, the
Tonquin, for the voyage round the Horn to the mouth of
the Columbia. Under the command of Jonathan Thorn,
as courageous as he was harsh, abrasive, and self-willed,
she sailed with a crew of twenty on September 8, 1810.
The treacherous passage round the Horn was accomplished without incident, but, within sight of the Columbia, Captain Thorn ordered his first mate, Ebenezer Fox,
to take a crew in a whaleboat to make soundings of the
shallows in order to guide the *Tonquin* across the bar.
The weather, Fox protested, was "boisterous," this was
"the most dangerous part of the northwest coast," and,
even worse, Captain Thorn allowed Fox but one trained
seaman to man the boat; the other three members of
Fox's crew were French Canadians who were making
their very first ocean voyage. Thorn cut short all protest.
"Mr. Fox," he said, "if you are afraid of water, you should
have remained in Boston." The first mate turned to Astor's appointed partners. "My uncle was lost a few years
ago on this same bar," he declared, "and I am now going
to lay my bones alongside of his."

The boat was lowered, and, as Washington Irving
relates in his history of the Astoria enterprise, "All eyes
were strained after the little bark as it pulled for shore,
rising and sinking with the huge rolling waves, until it
entered, a mere speck, among the foaming breakers, and
was soon lost to view." Neither the boat nor its crew was
ever seen again.

Astoria was founded April 12, 1811, a mere three
months before the North West Company's David Thompson paddled his canoe down the Columbia. But for the
loss of the whaleboat crew, so far, so good. The *Tonquin*
discharged a party under David Stuart to trap upriver as
she coasted northward to trade with Indians. While anchored in Nootka Sound, Thorn attempted to barter
items from the ship's cargo of trade goods for otter skins.
But the Indians drove so hard a bargain that Thorn became frustrated and insulted one of the band by snatch-
ing up a proffered otter skin, rubbing an old Indian's face
in it, and then sending all the would-be traders off his
vessel. Alexander McKay, who had been ashore during
this episode, urged Thorn to weigh anchor; he knew that
the Indians would brook no insult. Not only did Thorn
make light of the warning, but the very next morning admitted a canoe-full of some twenty Indians on board to
resume trading. John Jacob Astor himself had cautioned
against allowing more than a few Indians on the ship.

Then another canoe approached, and another, and
still more. Indians were clambering aboard from all
sides. McKay, noticing that many of them wore "short
mantles of skins," realized that they were probably con-

cealing weapons. He urged Thorn to clear the ship and get under way. Thorn delayed, but then made ready to depart; whereupon the Indians suddenly gave in to the terms of trade they had rejected the day before. What they traded for were knives.

At last ready to set sail, the captain ordered the decks cleared. That is when one of the Indians shouted a signal. "It was echoed on every side," Irving writes, "knives and war-clubs were brandished in every direction, and the savages rushed upon their marked victims."

Thorn and McKay were among the first slain. In all, eighteen of the twenty-three men aboard ship were killed on deck. Five seamen had been in the rigging during the attack and managed to secure muskets, with which they drove the Indians off ship. Using the *Tonquin*'s cannon, they even sunk some of the retreating canoes.

One of the five survivors, James Lewis, ship's clerk, was severely wounded. When the other four men, deciding that they were too few to handle the ship, elected to set off in a small boat under cover of darkness, Lewis resigned himself to remaining on board. The other four attempted their escape but were captured, tortured, and killed. With morning, the Indians returned to the ship to loot whatever they had missed on the first go-around. Suddenly, the powder magazine exploded—evidently the work of the doomed Lewis—destroying the *Tonquin* and killing hundreds of Indians.

Astoria was now dependent for resupply on the overland contingent of the expedition. Astor had placed the American, Wilson Price Hunt, in command of the party. Brave and well-meaning, Hunt was wholly inexperienced as a frontiersman, having been a St. Louis storekeeper for some five years. He was so slow to get moving that the party was able to travel a mere 450 miles up the Missouri before it was forced to make winter camp at the mouth of the Nadowa River in November of 1810. It was not until April 21, 1811, that the expedition began its trek in earnest. At one point, Astor's men even engaged in a race with Manuel Lisa's party, which was en route to relieve the Missouri Fur Company's beleaguered Bighorn–Three Forks operation. The race was broken off when Hunt, fearful of Blackfeet, abandoned the route Lewis and Clark had established and decided to travel due west, forsaking the river for land travel. The party traded for horses among the Arikaras and Mandans, a process that consumed a month.

Hunt's was the first substantial expedition to attempt to cross the plains. In addition to the usual hardships and hazards posed by the terrain, climate, and Indians, there were logistical problems to overcome. The goods that had been transported in the four forty-foot keelboats had now to be carried by eighty pack-saddled horses, which needed to be expertly handled and, in country where forage was often scarce, fed. It was a formidable undertaking for a St. Louis storekeeper.

With great good luck, however, they made surpris-ingly swift progress across the increasingly arid plains and into the Rockies. When they reached the Snake River, knowing that it eventually joined the Columbia, they decided to resume water travel and built canoes. Five men stayed behind in the mountains to trap, while the main party embarked downriver. For some three hundred miles, their progress was gratifyingly smooth. Then, on October 28, 1811, the lead canoe was wrecked in a vortex rapids, drowning the best boatman among them, Antoine Clappine.

Albert Bierstadt (1830–1902)
Rocky Mountain Waterfall, 1898
Oil on canvas, 60 × 38 in.
Courtesy of The Anschutz Collection

It was such magnificence that the solitary mountain man claimed as his domain.

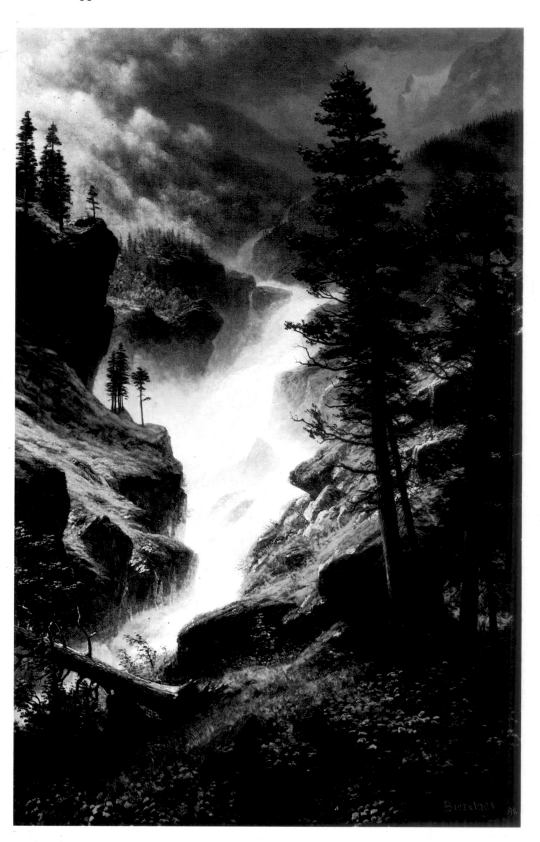

CHARLES DEAS

—

BORN 1818, PHILADELPHIA

DIED 1867, NEW YORK

—

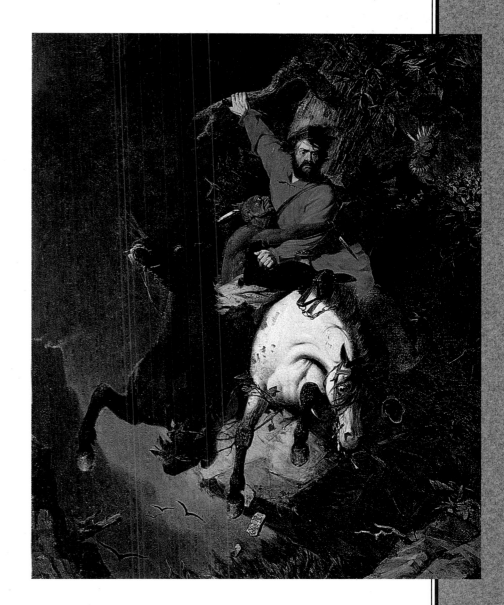

Deas's earliest ambition was to enroll at West Point and become a U.S. Army officer. He failed to gain admission, however, possibly because he already exhibited the acutely nervous temperament that presaged the insanity in which he ended his days. Indeed, the artist's most characteristic works are charged with a vivid, almost nightmare quality, as in the terrifying *Death Struggle* (ca. 1845) and *Prairie Fire* (1847). But Deas should also be remembered for his calmer genre depictions of Sioux and Winnebagos as well as trappers and hunters. *Long Jakes (Long Jakes, The Rocky Mountain Man)* (1844) was regarded even by contemporaries as *the* image of the half-wild, half-civilized mountain man.

A frequent childhood visitor to the Pennsylvania Academy of the Fine Arts and the Philadelphia studio of the highly successful portraitist and landscapist Thomas Sully, Deas spent two years at the National Academy in New York. Returning for a visit to Philadelphia in 1838, he was deeply moved by Catlin's Indian paintings on exhibit there. Two years later, he journeyed to Fort Crawford, Prairie du Chien, Wisconsin, to visit his brother, and in 1841 he visited Fort Winnebago. The next year, he toured the Sioux country of the upper Mississippi.

In 1841, the artist established his studio in St. Louis, where he could be closer to his western subjects and, in 1844, traveled to the country of the Pawnees.

Deas enjoyed success with public and critics alike, but in 1847 or 1848, he suffered an emotional breakdown that ended his career. *A Vision,* exhibited in 1849 at the National Academy of Design (but, like a great many of Deas's paintings, now lost), was described by one admiring critic as the very embodiment of "Despair and Death . . . . Frenzy glares from the blood red sockets of the victims." Deas spent the last two decades of his life confined in New York's Bloomingdale Asylum for the Insane, where he died "of apoplexy."

Charles Deas, *Self-Portrait,* 1840. Graphite on paper, 9 ½ × 6 ¾ in. National Academy of Design, New York City.

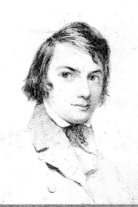

Charles Deas (1818–1867)
The Death Struggle, c. 1845
Oil on canvas, 30 × 25 in.
Shelburne Museum, Shelburne, Vermont

———

The realism in this remarkable painting is not of incident or surfaces, but of deep emotion. Deas, who ended his days in a New York asylum for the insane, was a master at distilling into vivid nightmare vision the potential terrors of western life. The trapper clutches a dead branch, the attacking Indian embraces the trapper in a death grip, the trapper clutches the beaver, the trap has caught the beaver, and the beaver sinks his teeth into the Indian's arm.

It was a disaster. Hunt sent a detachment by land to reconnoiter the river ahead. The conclusion: the Snake was unnavigable. And they had come too far into the mountains to return for their horses. It was almost November; a fierce Rocky Mountain winter was already threatening. There was only one course of action open to them. March. March to the Columbia before the full onslaught of winter, through a region barren and virtually devoid of game.

It turned out to be an epic of suffering. The party first divided in two and then, finally, broke up into smaller, disorganized groups. With one of these were the trapper Pierre Dorion and his wife, Marie, who, pregnant, gave birth on December 30. The child died during a frozen, snowy crossing of the Blue Mountains ten days later—a melancholy contrast to the joyous wilderness birth of Sacajewea's son on the outward leg of the Lewis and Clark expedition. Miraculously, however, the newborn and two French Canadians were the only fatalities. Most of the scattered party straggled into Astoria during January and February of 1812. Others failed to arrive until May. And seven individuals showed up in Astoria on January 15—*1813!*

To be sure, the Astorians were happy enough to see their comrades. However, these pathetic refugees from the winter were hardly the relief expedition anticipated.

The Astorians huddled together, short on food and fearful of Indian attack, throughout the winter. Finally, early in May, a second supply ship, *Beaver,* arrived. Robert Stuart was sent on an overland trek back east to apprise John Jacob Astor of the status of his enterprise—that conditions were difficult, but that Astoria was established and in active competition with the North West Company. It proved to be a valuable journey, for Stuart probed southward and found the easier routes that had eluded Lewis and Clark. Much of the trail he blazed would become the Oregon Trail, principal highway of the far western immigrant.

Astor was gratified by Stuart's report. "I have hit the nail on the head," he declared.

That conclusion was premature. On August 4, 1812, Wilson Price Hunt left Astoria on the *Beaver* to trade for furs with the Russians in Alaska. Two months earlier, on June 19, President James Madison proclaimed a state of war between England and the United States. John George McTavish, of the North West Company, journeyed to Astoria to announce the imminent British naval capture of the outpost and its cache of furs. He offered to buy Astoria and its inventory and, after months of negotiations, did just that, paying forty thousand dollars for furs and other property valued at two hundred thousand. Likely, had Hunt—the only American among Astor's

Arthur F. Tait (1819–1905)
Trappers at Fault, Looking for the Trail, 1852
Oil on canvas, 36 × 50 in.
Denver Art Museum *(opposite)*

This artist, an Englishman transplanted to New Jersey, never journeyed west. He did, however, amass a collection of authentic western gear and costume (some of it borrowed from William Tylee Ranney), which he delighted in portraying.

Albert Bierstadt (1830–1902)
Rocky Mountains, "Lander's" Peak, 1863
Oil on canvas, 44 ⅜ × 36 ½ in.
The Metropolitan Museum of Art; Rogers Fund, 1907

The Indian camp in the foreground, overborne by the majesty of the mountains, may be taken as the artist's statement of man's place in the natural order of the West.

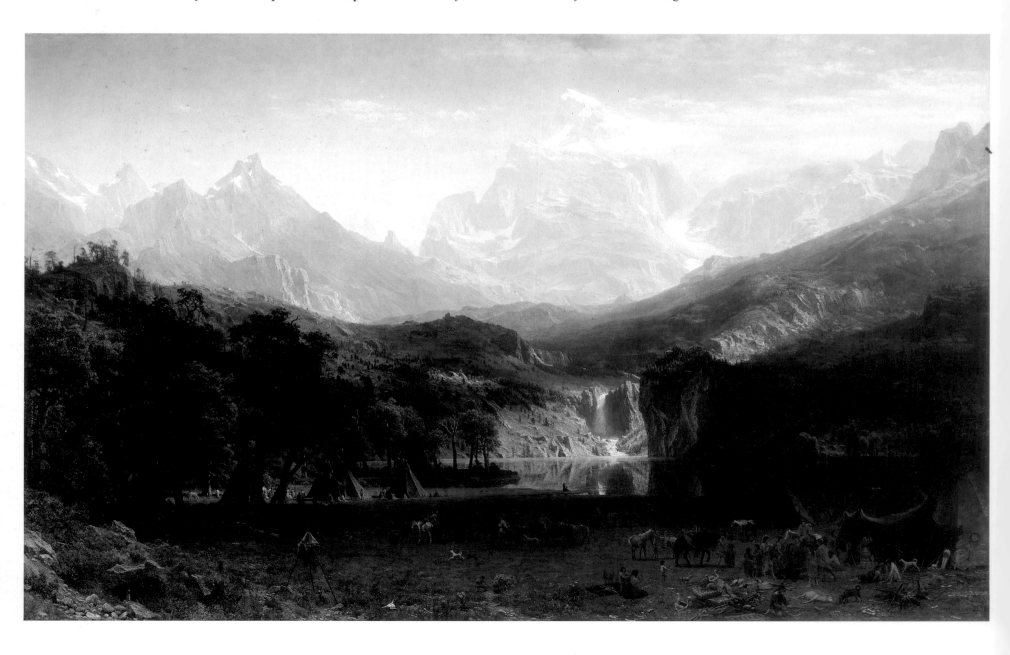

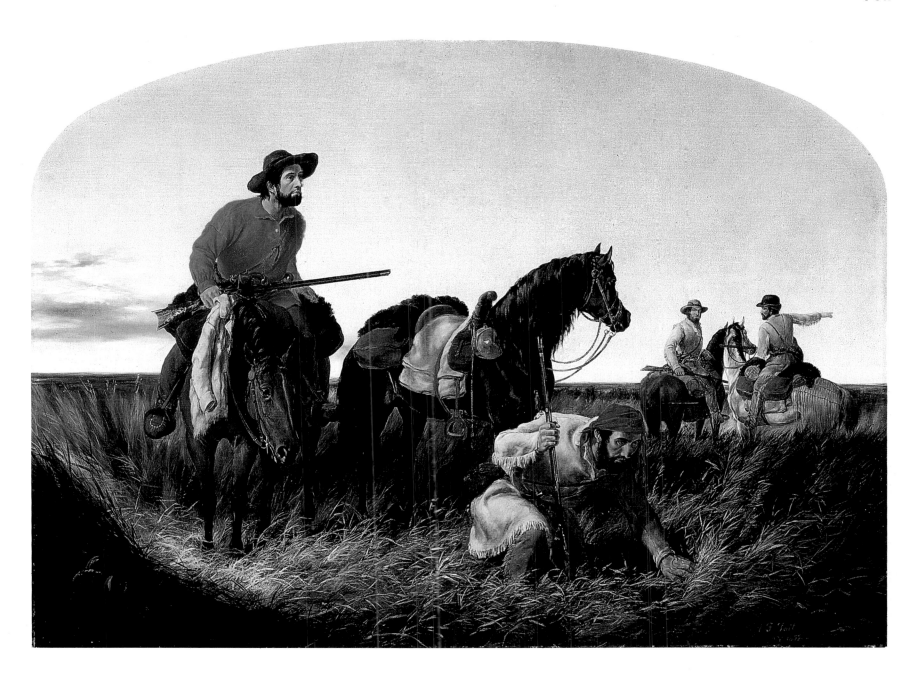

Arthur F. Tait (1819–1905)
The Check, 1854
Oil on canvas, 30 × 44 in.
Gilcrease Museum, Tulsa, Oklahoma
(right)

In *American Frontier Life: Early
Western Paintings and Prints,*
Warder H. Cadbury quotes Captain
Randolph B. Marcy, a veteran of
early western exploration, on the
life-saving technique depicted here.
When Indians approach on the
plains, Marcy advises, signal them to
keep their distance. If they do not
obey, head for the nearest timber. If
they follow, point your gun at
them—but don't pull the trigger
unless you are convinced that your
life depends on that shot; you won't
have time to reload.

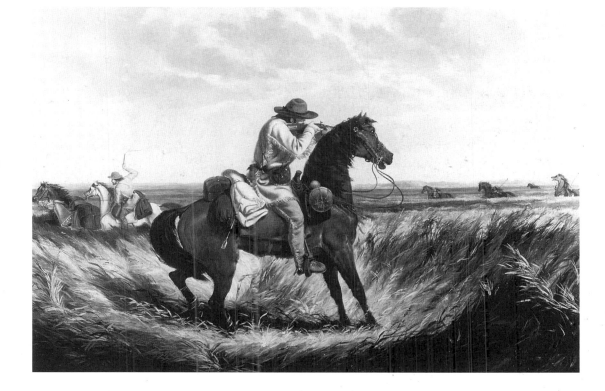

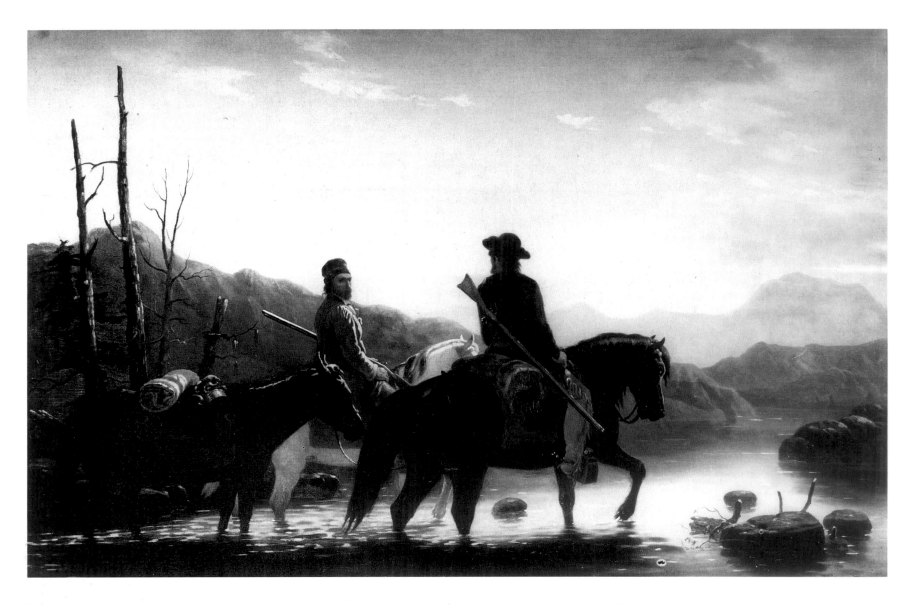

William Tylee Ranney (1813–1857)
The Trappers, 1856
Oil on canvas, 23 ½ × 36 in.
Gene Autry Western Heritage
Museum, Los Angeles

Ranney not only shared subject matter with Arthur Fitzwilliam Tait, he was equally generous with his collection of western gear, which he lent to the Englishman for use as studio props. While Tait enjoyed tremendous popularity for his work reproduced by Currier & Ives, Ranney (also reproduced by those lithographers) was more admired by critics and connoisseurs.

field partners—been present, some other strategy would have been adopted; the outpost and goods could have been moved inland, safe from naval attack. But the partners with whom McTavish negotiated were all ex-Northwesters and, indeed, loyal to the British crown. True, the partners held out for months before they finally sold. Had luck been with Astor just this once, the American would have returned to Astoria in good time. However, *Beaver* had been battered by storms in Alaska, and its captain, Cornelius Sowles, an overcautious seaman, determined that his ship had been made unseaworthy by the heavy weather and made for Hawaii (then called the Sandwich Islands) to effect repairs. From Hawaii, Sowles set off for Canton to trade his cargo of Alaskan furs for nankeen cloth. Hunt was stranded for more than a year, and Astoria was lost. Even so, had Sowles carried out his Canton trading with resolution and dispatch, Astor could have profited handsomely. In China, the captain was offered $150,000 for a cargo that had cost $25,000 in trade goods. That $150,000 would have bought a quantity of nankeen worth $300,000 in New York. But Sowle held out for a higher price at precisely the moment when the fur market began to suffer a decline; the offers became successively lower rather than

higher, and Sowle, borrowing heavily on Astor's account, laid up the ship to await the conclusion of the war, when he could sail the furs back to New York.

It would seem that no greater disaster could have resulted had the calamities been deliberately orchestrated. But even after the demise of Astoria proper, there were still inland outposts to be run. One such operation, on the Boise River, was set upon by Shoshones or Nez Percés who were out to avenge the hanging of one of their number for theft. Some nine or ten trappers were killed, including Pierre Dorion. His wife, Marie, and their two children escaped on horseback, the children wrapped in a buffalo robe. They survived for two winter months in the Blue Mountains, living off the meat of the horse they had ridden out on. Eventually, they reached the safety of a friendly Indian town on the Columbia River.

John Jacob Astor lost four hundred thousand 1813 dollars in the debacle of Astoria. Sixty-one men perished. Yet the failure was not total. No sooner had John George McTavish purchased the enterprise at a fire-sale price than *H.M.S. Raccoon* put in at the mouth of the Columbia and its captain changed the outpost's name to Fort George, making it a possession of the king. The War of 1812, we shall see, was largely a dangerous and futile affair as far as the West was concerned. One mark of that futility was the article in the Treaty of Ghent that simply called for the return of any territory taken during the war—nothing gained and nothing (except human lives) lost. But in taking Astoria, the captain of *H.M.S. Raccoon* had actually legitimated the U.S. claim to Oregon, and the United States rightfully demanded its return at the end of the war. More difficult to calculate, but even more important, was the knowledge of the Far West gained through the wanderings of the trappers attached to Astor's scheme. As soon as the War of 1812 ended, the fur trade resumed with renewed profit, and immigration to the farther western frontiers began in earnest.

THE WAR THE WEST WANTED

Grade-school history teaches that the War of 1812 was fought largely because the British, at war with Napoleon and in need of sailors, claimed the right to intercept neutral vessels, including those of the United States, and, on the flimsiest of pretexts, impress seamen into his majesty's service. That is only partially correct. Indeed, the American declaration of war, on June 19, 1812, virtually coincided with Great Britain's suspension of its policy of interference with commerce on the high seas, in an agreement concluded on June 16 and to take effect on June 23.

Actually, the War of 1812 was brewed in the West. There was, to begin with, the region's insatiable hunger for new territory, the most readily available of which was in Spanish Florida, which then extended as far west as the Mississippi. In 1812, Spain was allied with Britain against Napoleon. War with Britain would mean war with Spain, and victory in such a war would mean the acquisition of Florida. And there was, as the West saw it, ample reason to fight with England. The question of freedom of seaborne commerce was not just a matter of national sovereignty and pride. Disruption of commerce on the high seas had not only damaged the coastal economy, but had brought on a bad depression in the West, whose abundant produce could be exported only if the sea lanes were open. Finally, there was a widespread belief that the English in Canada were arming Indians south of the border and inciting them to harass western American settlers.

While the British government formally disavowed any official sanction of Indian hostility against Americans, private English traders did supply arms and ammunition, and there could be no doubt that, as the white settlement line pushed farther westward, the Indians were becoming an increasing menace. The great Shawnee chief Tecumseh ranged from the Ohio country to the Rockies, attempting to unite the scattered tribes into a confederacy that could effectively oppose white en-

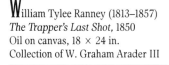

William Tylee Ranney (1813–1857)
The Trapper's Last Shot, 1850
Oil on canvas, 18 × 24 in.
Collection of W. Graham Arader III

This dramatic canvas was made into a Currier & Ives lithograph some time after 1855.

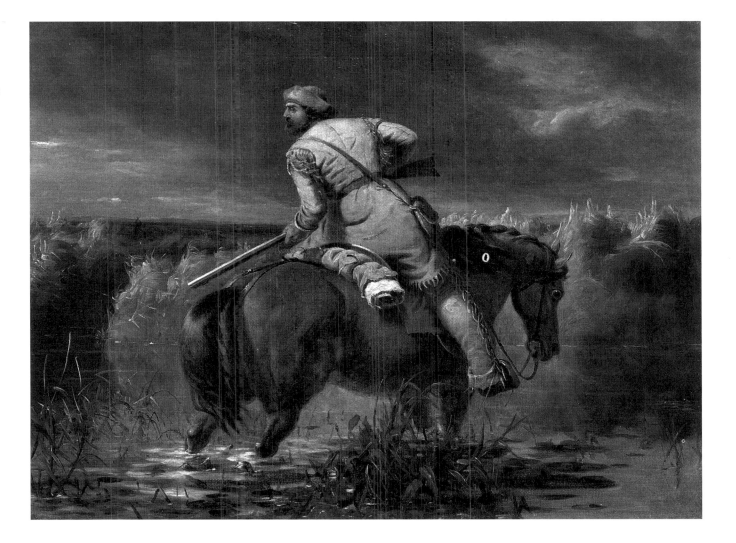

PETER
RINDISBACHER

—

**BORN 1806, UPPER EMMENTHAL,
SWITZERLAND
DIED 1834, ST. LOUIS, MISSOURI**

—

Short-lived, all but untrained as an artist, Peter Rindisbacher was nevertheless an important painter of the Canadian wilderness and that of northern Minnesota and North Dakota. Son of a veterinarian, he was brought by his parents to the Earl of Selkirk's Red River Colony, near present-day Winnepeg, in 1821. The fifteen-year-old Rindisbacher sketched the Indians and landscape he encountered enroute to the colony. Once settled, the young man continued to draw and paint the scenes around him, selling his work to help support his family.

After five years, the colony was generally abandoned, and the Rindisbachers moved south, settling briefly in Wisconsin and finally in St. Louis. The artist sold Indian portraits to the U.S. commissioner of Indian affairs, which were subsequently pub-

lished in Thomas L. McKenney and James Hall's *History of the Indian Tribes of North America* (1837). Other works were published during the artist's lifetime in *The American Turf Register and Sporting Magazine,* and a lithographed portfolio was issued in England as *Views in Hudson's Bay.*

By 1829, when he opened a studio in St. Louis, Rindisbacher was making himself well known locally as a portraitist and as an artist of the frontier. His reputation was beginning to reach the rest of the nation when he died, aged twenty-eight. Approximately one hundred of his engagingly primitive works survive, including forty scenes of Hudson's Bay and the Red River colony preserved at the Public Archives in Canada.

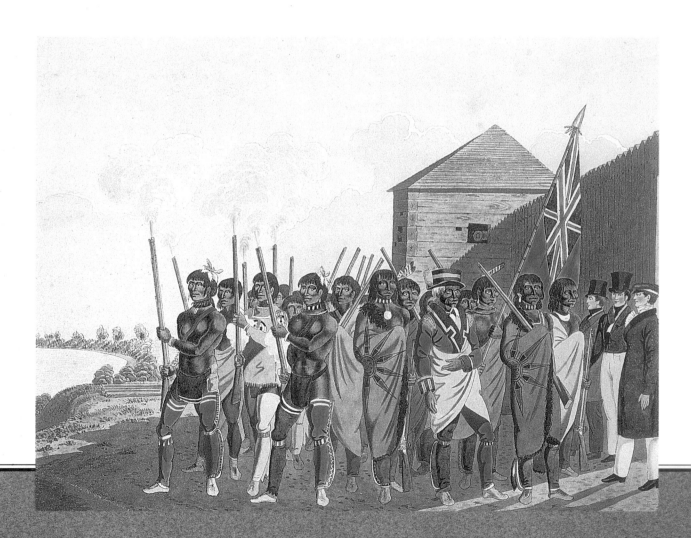

croachment on their lands. Soon, Tecumseh was accompanied by his brother, Tenskwatawa, better known as the Prophet.

Tecumseh aimed his campaign of unification squarely against the governor of Indiana Territory, William Henry Harrison, who had wheedled from various tribes and factions numerous treaties ceding to the

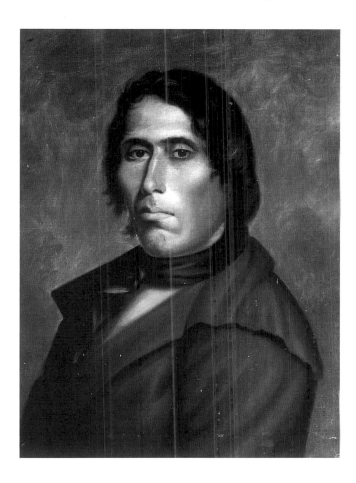

Anonymous
Portrait of Tecumseh, no later than 1813
Oil on canvas, 28 × 23 in.
Field Museum of Natural History, Chicago

The subject of this painting has never been positively identified, but it is believed to be Tecumseh. The portrait was once owned by the grandniece of William Clark, the western explorer, and by General George Rogers Clark. Both men fought against the great chief in the Ohio Valley.

Peter Rindisbacher (1806–1834)
War Party at Fort Douglas Discharging Their Guns in the Air as a Token of Their Peacable Intention, c. 1823
Watercolor and pen and ink,
10 7/16 × 12 7/8 in.
Royal Ontario Museum, Toronto; Sigmund Samuel Collection

British, French, and American interests formed many uneasy alliances with various Indian groups during the early years of the nineteenth century.

United States vast tracts of land. Tecumseh held that such cessions, granted by Indian minorities, were invalid. As Tecumseh sought to unite the tribes on this point, his brother preached a doctrine of abstinence from contact with white men and the cultivation of a purity that would endow the Indians with a supernatural invincibility.

Governor Harrison met with Tecumseh in Vincennes, Indiana Territory, on August 15, 1811. Both men were intractable; Tecumseh set out to rally the Creeks, Cherokees, and Choctaws to the cause of unity; Harrison exploited his absence by provoking the Indians to a premature attack. He marched a force of 900 to a spot just outside the town in which the Prophet lived, on the Tippecanoe Creek. The Prophet told the assembled braves that his powers rendered them all impervious to bullets, and, just before dawn on November 7, 700 Indians attacked Harrison's camp. It was a close fight. Harrison lost 62 men killed and another 126 wounded. The Indians suffered similar casualties, but, far worse, they were utterly dispirited inasmuch as the Prophet's medicine had failed to protect them.

The Battle of Tippecanoe heated up the war fever in the West, as it seemed clear that the Indians had been incited to fight by the British. When war came, westerners were eager to take the offensive by invading Canada. William Hull, a superannuated hero of the Revolutionary War, now governor of Michigan Territory, was placed in command of American forces north of the Ohio, which consisted of three hundred regulars and twelve hundred Kentucky and Ohio militiamen. His mission was to advance on Fort Malden, guarding the entrance to Lake Erie. On the way to this objective, a good many of the Ohio militiamen deserted, though their numbers were almost made up for by Michigan militia. On July 12, Hull crossed the Detroit River into Canada, but the old man, feeling he was outnumbered, had no stomach for a fight. Repeatedly, he delayed the assault on Fort Malden—long enough for the British commanders to reinforce their positions.

Meanwhile, on July 16, Captain Charles Roberts, commander of the British garrison at St. Joseph's Island, in the St. Mary's River between Lake Huron and Lake Superior, assembled a force of Indians and North West Company traders to invade the strategically crucial Mackinac Island. The invaders, over five hundred strong, complete with two six-pounder cannon, landed on the island undetected about three o'clock on the morning of July 17. The American garrison of sixty-one men, hopelessly surrounded, surrendered without a fight.

In August, General Hull finally withdrew his troops from Sandwich—present-day Windsor—Ontario and returned to Detroit. A week later, on August 16, Hull surrendered Fort Detroit and his fourteen hundred men without firing a shot. Just the day before, the garrison at Fort Dearborn—present-day Chicago—had surrendered. As the troops, together with settlers, their wives, and children, were withdrawing, Indians attacked, killing thirty-five, many by torture.

These humiliating American defeats lured Tecumseh to the side of the victorious British, and what had started as an American assault on Canada became a desperate scramble for survival. The West was laid open to Indian massacre and British invasion. Every Indian nation between the Great Lakes and the Rocky Mountains was poised against the American settlers.

Yet neither the British nor their Indian allies were able to capitalize on their advantages. The coordinated assault never materialized, and in 1813 Benjamin Howard, governor of the Missouri Territory, led a successful invasion of the Illinois country. William Clark, who succeeded him as governor, mounted an offensive against Prairie du Chien (in present-day Wisconsin) the next year.

Meanwhile, William Henry Harrison, the "hero of Tippecanoe," was given command of the western forces. He, too, was determined to take the offensive and cap-

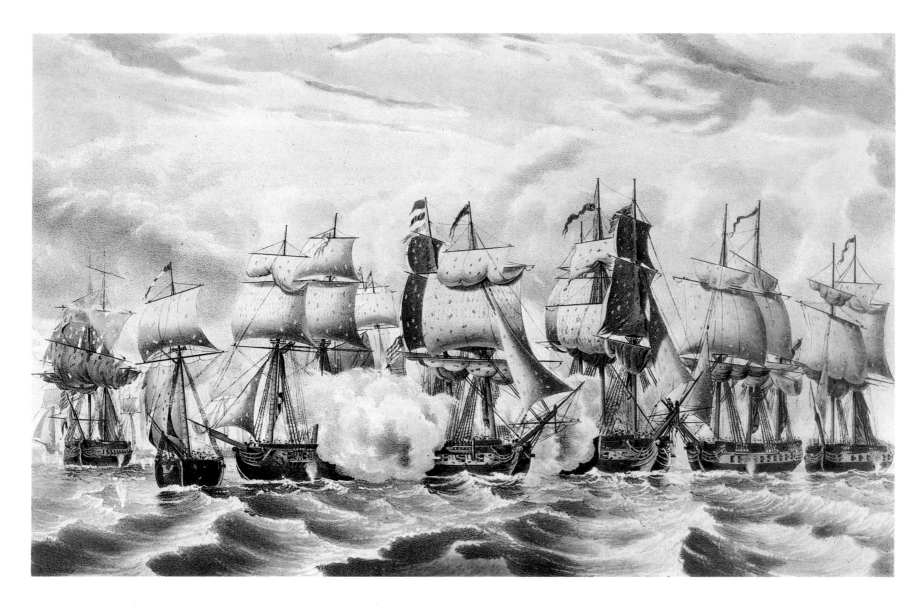

Nathaniel Currier (after Napoleon Sarony)
Perry's Victory on Lake Erie/Fought Sept. 10th, 1813, n.d.
Museum of the City of New York

On September 10, 1813, twenty-seven-year-old Oliver Hazard Perry did battle with the British navy on Lake Erie. This American victory turned the tide of what had been a disastrous war.

ture Fort Malden, as General Hull had failed to do. It was January of 1813, and Harrison decided to move against the fort by advancing across the frozen Lake Erie. Perhaps the bold scheme would have succeeded, but Harrison never had the opportunity to find out. One of his generals, James Winchester, took it upon himself to advance, ill-prepared and unsupported, to the Raisin River, just south of Detroit. British forces under Henry Proctor attacked Winchester's unguarded encampment and annihilated it. Only thirty-three men escaped. One-third of the American army of eight hundred were killed.

As a result of this fiasco, Harrison lost the initiative, and, once again, what had started out as an offensive campaign became a desperate effort to defend positions already held. British General Henry Proctor laid a two-week siege against Fort Meigs at the Maumee Rapids of the Ohio River during April and May of 1813, which Harrison successfully defended—at a cost. In one relief column, 650 were killed or captured. In the summer, Proctor, fielding an army of 3,000, attacked Harrison's principal supply depot on the Sandusky River and was held off by Major George Croghan and 150 men.

The American resistance was heroic, but wars are not won by defense alone. Fort Malden, the British

stronghold on Lake Erie, had to be taken. But how?

Since the end of March 1813, twenty-seven-year-old Captain Oliver Hazard Perry had been supervising the construction of an armed flotilla at Presque Isle, Pennsylvania. By August, the shallow-draft vessels were ready, and Perry moved them out onto Lake Erie. On September 10 he engaged the British fleet and sent to General Harrison a message, as stirring as it was laconic: "We have met the enemy and they are ours." It was the first real American victory of the war.

With his waterborne support defeated, General Proctor abandoned Fort Malden. Harrison, now with an army of three thousand, pursued the retreating British and the Indians, who were led by Tecumseh. That chief persuaded General Proctor to take a stand at the Thames River, where Harrison defeated him on October 5, 1813. Tecumseh died that day, and with him died the last real hope any group of American Indians had to stop the northwestward rush of settlement.

While the Battle of the Thames reversed the course of the War of 1812, hostilities were by no means ended. In the South, the Creek Indians of Georgia, Tennessee, and the Mississippi Territory were engaged in civil war between those who advocated cooperation with the white man, and those bent on driving the whites out of their land. On August 30, 1813, the latter faction, known as the Red Sticks, attacked Fort Mims, on the lower Alabama River, killing almost five hundred, Indians, mixed-bloods, whites, and blacks. It was to be the last Indian attack on a settlement east of the Mississippi, and it provoked a terrible vengeance executed by Andrew Jackson, who marched into Red Stick country with an army of five thousand Tennessee militiamen, nineteen companies of Cherokee warriors, and two hundred non–Red Stick Creeks. Jackson destroyed every Red Stick town in his path, so that by August of 1814, the Indians were begging for peace. Jackson exacted from the Creek Nation—Red Sticks and even those opposed to them—two-thirds of its territory, thereby extending the theater of American settlement from the Tennessee River to the Gulf of Mex-

ico, that is, to the border of Spanish settlement.

Meanwhile, also in August of 1814, American and English commissioners began peace negotiations in Ghent, Belgium—during which, as the war continued, General Robert Ross burned Washington, D.C. The Treaty of Ghent was signed on Christmas Eve.

On the face of it, nothing had been settled by the war. The treaty returned the two nations to the "status quo ante bellum." Yet, so far as the West is concerned, this is misleading. As a result of the war, we have seen, the United States' claim on the Far Northwest was strengthened. The collateral war with the Red Stick Creeks pushed American settlement to the Spanish border. The withdrawal of the British from United States territory meant the collapse of various alliances with western Indian tribes, most notably the Sioux, who

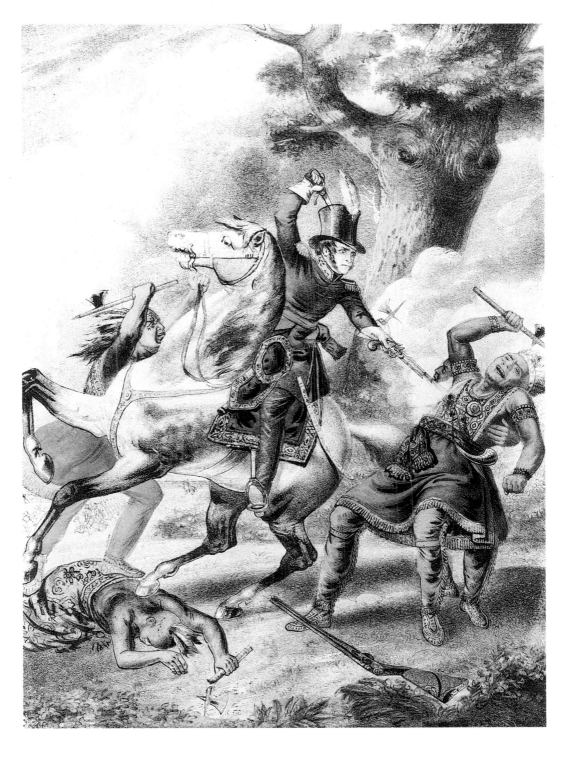

Nathaniel Currier
*Death of Tecumseh/Battle of the
Thames, Oct. 18, 1813,* 1841
Museum of the City of New York

The great chief, one of a very small handful in the course of American Indian history who attempted to forge a strategic confederacy among diverse tribes, met his death at the Battle of the Thames, October 5, 1813.

agreed by treaty to recognize the sovereignty of the United States over the Missouri Territory.

The war's most glorious battle, so far as the United States is concerned, was fought after the Peace of Ghent was concluded, when forty-five hundred British troops stormed New Orleans. The city was defended by Andrew Jackson, who mustered an army of ten thousand Tennessee volunteers. The English commander, Edward Pakenham, lost two thousand of his force in a mere twenty minutes—all victims of frontier sharpshooting—and Pakenham himself was killed. The American victory not only insured that its hero, Andrew Jackson, would become the nation's first western president (William Henry Harrison would be its second), it restored much of the self-confidence and arrogance the West had lost in the humiliating series of defeats it had suffered during most of the war. The war also fostered a new patriotism and forged a sense of national identity and national purpose that would mean much in propelling the country westward.

THE RECEDING FRONTIER

Immediately following the War of 1812, the westward movement resumed its wonted momentum. By 1815, some fifty wagons were being ferried across the Mississippi to St. Louis every day. Along the Missouri, settlement was pushing back the frontier at a rate of thirty or forty miles each year. Directly after the war, the Arkansas River valley and the Red River valley were flooded with hunters and trappers as well as squatters—though "legal" settlers soon followed as well.

For the American fur trade, the War of 1812 was a crippling disruption; for Astor's grandiose Astoria, it was downright fatal. Only Manuel Lisa somehow managed to continue operating during the hostilities, though his Missouri Fur Company had been greatly diminished and was now known simply as "Manuel Lisa's company." In 1819, determined to revive U.S. commercial interests in the Far West, Congress commissioned Colonel Henry Atkinson to journey up the Missouri to the Mandan villages and establish military posts there. His force of eleven hundred soldiers, carried upriver in six newfangled steamboats, was calculated to impress upon the Indians of the region, as well as any British traders illegally present, that the United States held sway over the territory and had the might to enforce its sovereignty.

Five of the steamboats broke down early on; one got as far as Council Bluffs. A hundred soldiers died of scurvy. Congress, discouraged, all but canceled the expedition, save for a nineteen-man party led by Major Stephen Long, who was charged with finding the origin of the Red River. While he failed to find that river's headwaters, and while his tiny expedition could not have impressed anyone with the majesty of the republic, Long did extensively explore the eastern slopes of the Rocky

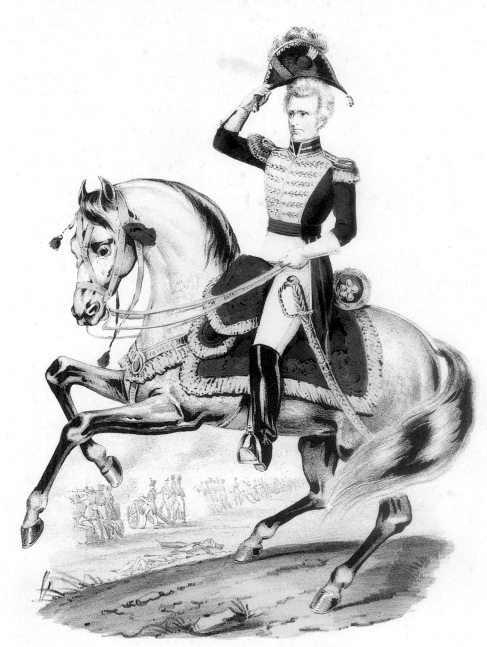

GEN: ANDREW JACKSON.
THE HERO OF NEW-ORLEANS.
Lith. & Pub. by N.Currier 2 Spruce St.N.Y.

Mountains and succeeded in climbing Pikes Peak, as Zebulon Pike had failed to do.

Like Pike, though, Long reported that the great southern and central plains were largely uninhabitable. This was not greeted by the federal government as bad news. True, there was great anxiety to assert control over the Far West, but there was also a strong urge to limit western expansion. In 1819, wild land speculation—something to which the West all too often fell victim—had triggered a severe financial panic, which the govern-

Nathaniel Currier
General Andrew Jackson/The Hero of New Orleans, 1837
Museum of the City of New York

Jackson's gallant defense of New Orleans, probably the best-remembered American victory of the war, came *after* the War of 1812 had been officially ended by the Treaty of Ghent.

ment sought to contain in part by limiting expansion. Besides, the "uninhabitable" land could be put to a better use than as territory for white settlement; it could serve as a repository for Indians *displaced* by white settlement. By 1825, the limit to westward expansion seemingly imposed by nature would be codified into law. In January of that year, President James Monroe would approve a new frontier line running through present-day Kansas and Oklahoma, beyond which settlement was forbidden.

But fur trappers had little patience with limitation and, in any event, were not interested in settling the country they explored. When Manuel Lisa died in 1820, the Lieutenant Governor of the brand-new state of Missouri, William Ashley, decided to take over where Manuel had left off. He teamed up with Andrew Henry, Lisa's former partner, and organized the Rocky Mountain Fur Company. Early in 1822 he was recruiting young men as trappers, promising to pay them "$200 per annum." The group he assembled included men destined to be remembered as some of the West's boldest and most colorful ex-

plorers, including Jedediah Strong Smith, Jim Bridger, Tom Fitzpatrick, Edward Rose, Hugh Glass, James Clyman, and Milton and William Sublette.

In the spring of 1822, Andrew Henry set out with some of the recruits to the mouth of the Yellowstone, where they built a fort. The next year, Ashley himself led a party of seventy up the Missouri, intent on following it up into Yellowstone country, where they would commence trapping.

On May 30, the party arrived at two Arikara Indian villages near the present North and South Dakota state line. The villages, which consisted of earthen houses contained within palisaded walls and ditches, were fortresses, and the Arikaras were generally known to be hostile. Yet they were willing to sell badly needed horses to the Ashley party, and Jedediah Strong Smith was dispatched with a party of forty men to camp near one of the villages and negotiate the purchases. The first day, he was successful, buying some twenty mounts.

The night that followed was stormy, but, despite the weather, one of Smith's men ventured into one of the

William Tylee Ranney (1813–1857)
Completed by William Sidney Mount
The Pipe of Friendship, 1857–59
Oil on canvas, 23 × 36 in.
Collection of The Newark Museum;
Gift of J. Ackerman Coles, 1920

Fellowship, hard to come by on the lonely prairie, was a commodity highly prized.

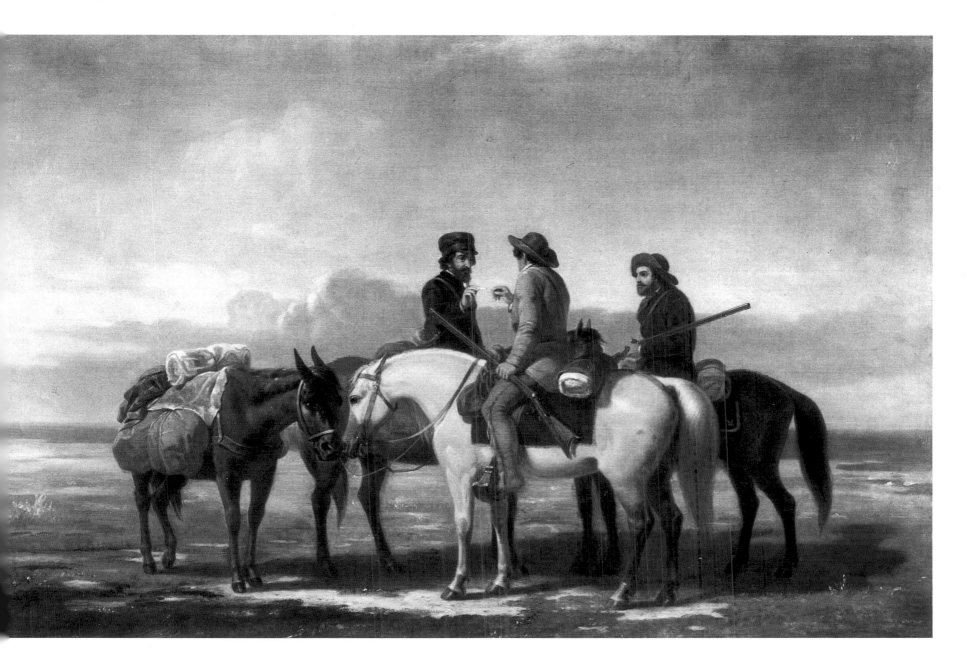

Arikara villages, seeking female companionship, a commodity often available from the Arikaras.

What happened is a mystery. Shortly before dawn the next morning, June 2, Edward Rose, Smith's interpreter, frantically reported that the young man out for a good time had been killed. At dawn the Arikaras began firing on Smith's party from behind their palisade. The trappers fought desperately, often using the carcasses of their newly purchased horses as cover. It was no use. Fourteen men died, and nine were wounded, including Hugh Glass. The French Canadian in charge of Ashley's keelboat refused to risk his neck attempting a rescue. Some men got away in smaller boats; some swam for it.

The attack broke the spirit of some of Ashley's men, who accompanied the wounded in a keelboat sent down the Missouri to Council Bluffs, the location of the nearest army outpost, Fort Atkinson. But there were others willing to go on, including Jed Smith, who volunteered to dash overland to the mouth of the Yellowstone, where Henry's party was camped, and bring the trapper and his men downriver to unite with Ashley's survivors, who, thus strengthened, could regain control of the upper river.

Smith's mission was a success. But Henry had his own bad news for Ashley: Blackfeet had attacked, killing four of his men. With hostile Indians ruling the Missouri, the river route was—for now, at least—closed to the trappers. With the northern trapping grounds usurped by Hudson's Bay Company men and the revived American Fur Company of John Jacob Astor, there was only one course open: due west, overland.

Even as Ashley had made the decision to abandon the river route, Colonel Henry Leavenworth, commander of Fort Atkinson, was mulling the news of the Arikara and Blackfoot attacks upriver. He decided that the United States could not brook such an insult to its sovereignty and, on June 22, 1823, set out with six companies of infantry and an artillery detachment: 223 soldiers, joined by some 800 Sioux allies and 120 trappers.

When the column reached the Arikara villages, the Sioux took the point and engaged the Arikaras first, killing thirteen (two Sioux died). Leavenworth was less bold. He positioned his forces around the villages, but declined to attack until his artillery—two six-pound cannon, some swivel guns, and a 5½-inch howitzer—could be brought to bear. The colonel exhausted his ammunition on the earthen towns, delayed attacking with the balance of his forces, and was deserted by his Sioux allies—from whom he now feared a rear attack. He therefore opened negotiations with the Arikaras, who promised to return horses they had stolen from Ashley and to fight no more.

That night, the Arikaras slipped out of the two villages. They did return one horse.

The U.S. Army had once again lost face. Failure to punish the Arikaras meant that the river was still, for all

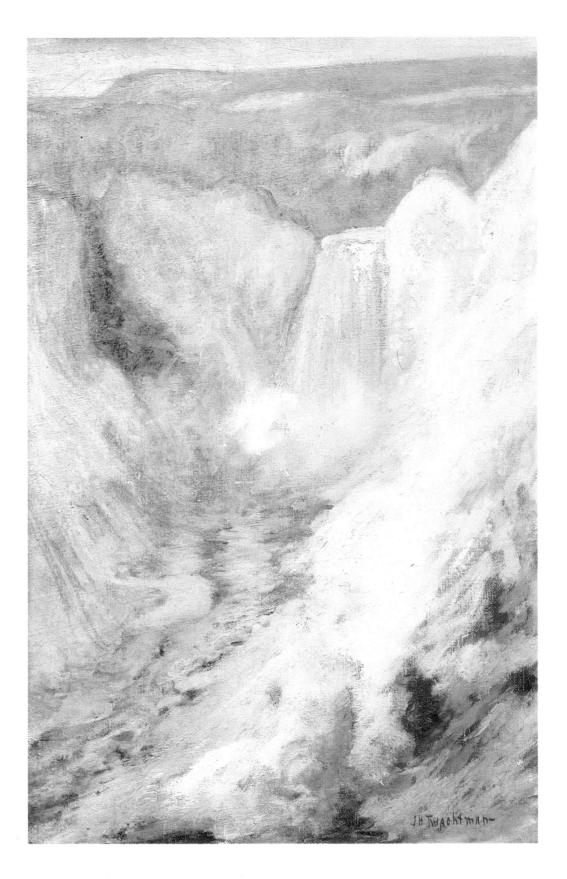

practical purposes, closed. Ashley's man, Jedediah Strong Smith, therefore began an *overland* exploration of the Far West that would consume seven years of virtually continuous travel.

Smith had been born in Bainbridge, New York, in 1799, the son of deeply religious New Englanders, and he himself would remain of a staunchly spiritual turn, quite literate (in sharp contrast to most who called themselves mountain men), and a gentleman. After serving as a clerk

John H. Twachtman (1853–1902)
Waterfall in the Yellowstone, c. 1895
Oil on canvas, 23 ⅜ × 16 ½ in.
Buffalo Bill Historical Center, Cody, Wyoming

A western landmark interpreted by a genteel master of American Impressionism.

on a Lake Erie vessel, he went to St. Louis, where he answered Ashley's call for recruits. Before his western career was cut short in 1831, he traveled some sixteen thousand miles, most of it in previously unexplored wilderness.

With him on the expedition he undertook for Ashley were twenty men, including those other archetypal mountain men, William Sublette, Thomas Fitzpatrick, James Clyman, and Edward Rose. In the Dakota Badlands, the party nearly died of thirst; Smith saved two men by burying them up to their necks in order to conserve body moisture until he could search out a waterhole. Beyond the Badlands, into the Black Hills, Smith encountered one of the two scourges mountain men most dreaded: not a Blackfoot Indian, but a grizzly bear—and a wounded one at that. He was severely mauled, the animal having clamped his head in its jaws. Jim Clyman took up the role of impromptu surgeon and stitched the trapper's eyebrow, ear, and scalp back in place. After ten days' rest, Smith was on the move again.

In a similar incident, one of Smith's most illustrious colleagues, the legendary Hugh Glass (who was traveling overland with Ashley's partner, Andrew Henry) had not been so lucky. He was so badly mangled that he could not be moved. Henry's eighty-man party had to press on to the upper Missouri before winter set in, so Henry offered a reward to two volunteers who would stay with Glass, presumably to preside over his imminent demise. The men were John S. Fitzgerald and nineteen-year-old Jim Bridger, the latter destined to discover the Great Salt Lake, to marry three Indian women (a Flathead, a Ute, and a Snake), and to serve forty years as the West's most renowned scout and guide.

But on this occasion, Bridger, with Fitzgerald, betrayed his trust. After five days, the two men determined that Glass would not recover. They took his rifle, knife, and other belongings, rejoined Henry, and reported that Glass had died.

He hadn't. The mountain man crawled to a spring where he found wild cherries. These, coupled with the

Thomas Moran (1837–1926)
Giant Blue Spring, Yellowstone, 1873
Watercolor on paper, 9 ½ × 13 ½ in.
Museum of Western Art, Denver

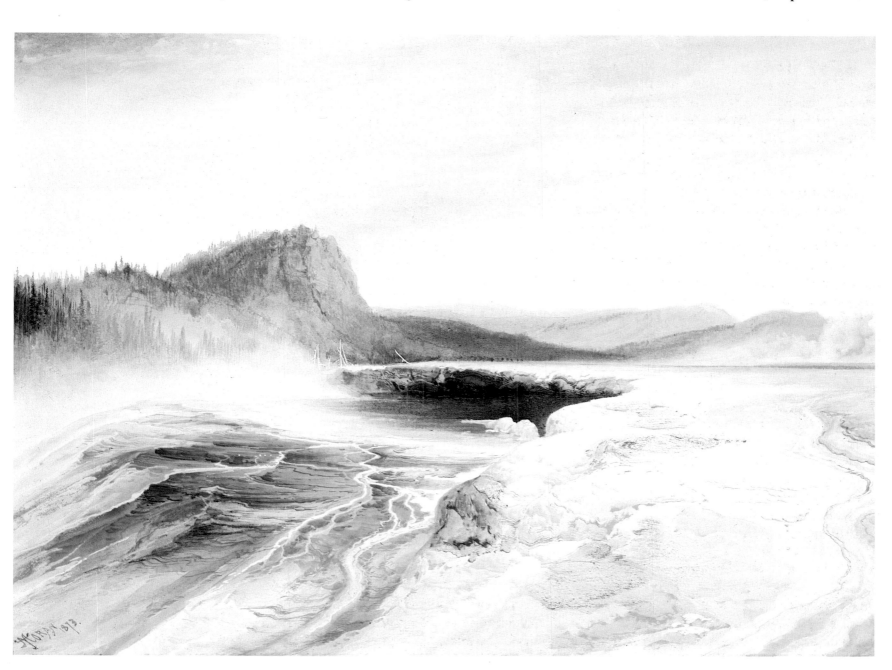

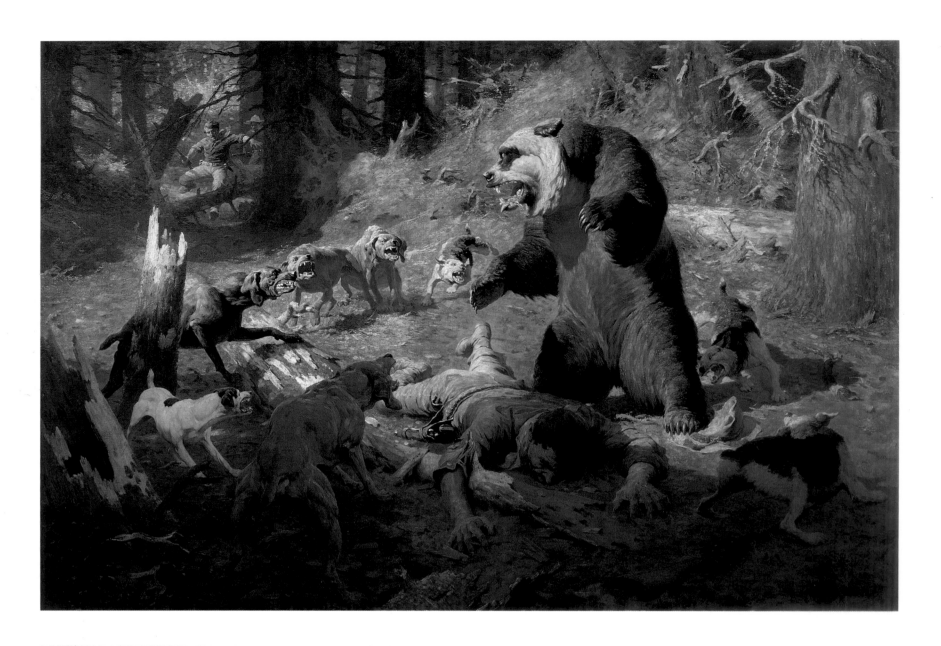

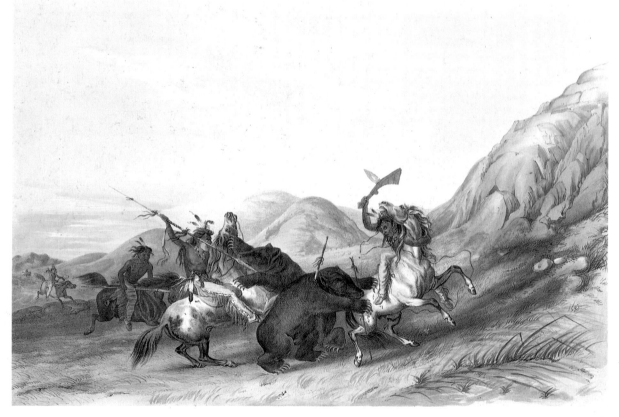

George Catlin (1796–1872)
Indians and Grizzlies, n.d.
Oil on canvas, 18 ⅝ × 26 ³/₁₆ in.
Royal Ontario Museum, Toronto

"It is a well-known fact, that man and beast, upon their feet, are sure to be attacked when they cross the path of this grizzly and grim monster, which is the terror of all this country. . . ."—George Catlin, *The Manners, Customs and Condition of the North American Indians*, 1841

William Robinson Leigh (1866–1955)
A Close Call, 1914
Oil on canvas, 40 × 60 in.
Gilcrease Museum, Tulsa, Oklahoma

Since the early days of the mountain man, frontiersmen feared savaging by a grizzly bear more than they did an Indian attack.

energy generated by the rage he must have felt at having been abandoned, recruited his strength sufficiently so that, after ten days, he began a painful progress back to Fort Kiowa, a hundred miles distant. Too weak to hunt, and quite without weapons in any case, Glass saw a pack of wolves drag down a buffalo calf. Reports differ as to whether Glass simply waited for the wolves to gorge themselves so that he could consume the remains, or whether Bridger and Fitzgerald, in their haste, had overlooked Glass's razor, with which he struck a spark to ignite a grass fire that sent the wolves running.

In any event, the meat brought him more strength and bought him more time for his injuries to mend. It took Glass six weeks to reach Fort Kiowa.

Even before his injuries were fully healed, Glass was eager to rejoin Henry and find Fitzpatrick and Bridger. He embarked from Fort Kiowa with a party of six and headed upriver to attempt a run past the Arikara blockade. Ironically, the party actually passed three men in a canoe coming downriver; one of them was Fitzgerald.

Near the Mandan towns, Glass left the canoe to hunt. No sooner had he done so than the Arikara attacked the tiny vessel, killing everyone except the venerable Toussaint Charbonneau, Sacajewea's husband, who

had decided to make his way overland. Glass was also attacked on land, but was saved by some friendly Mandans. Alone again, still suffering the lingering and painful effects of his encounter with the bear, Hugh Glass set off for the old Fort Henry at the mouth of the Yellowstone. He was on foot. The season was deep winter. The distance was 260 miles.

When he got there, he found that it had been abandoned.

So it was another 220 winter miles up the Yellowstone to the new Fort Henry at the mouth of the Bighorn River. He received welcome and succor, and he even found Jim Bridger there, whom he promptly forgave, ascribing his faithlessness to youth. But Fitzgerald was not at Fort Henry, and Fitzgerald, who was older and should have known better, was not to be forgiven.

Glass volunteered to carry a dispatch from Andrew Henry at Fort Henry to Ashley, 750 miles east at Fort Atkinson, hoping to encounter Fitzgerald along the way or at the Fort Atkinson headquarters. He set out with four other men. Exhausted by the overland leg of the trip and then by a difficult winter descent of the North Platte River ("a mile wide and a foot deep," as mountain men despairingly described it), they reached the open plains and sighted Indians they took for friendly Pawnees.

Alfred Jacob Miller (1810–1874)
Captain Joseph Reddeford Walker and His Indian Wife, n.d.
Watercolor on paper, 7 × 9 ¼ in.
Joslyn Art Museum, Omaha, Nebraska

It was common for a mountain man to take an Indian wife—often more than one.

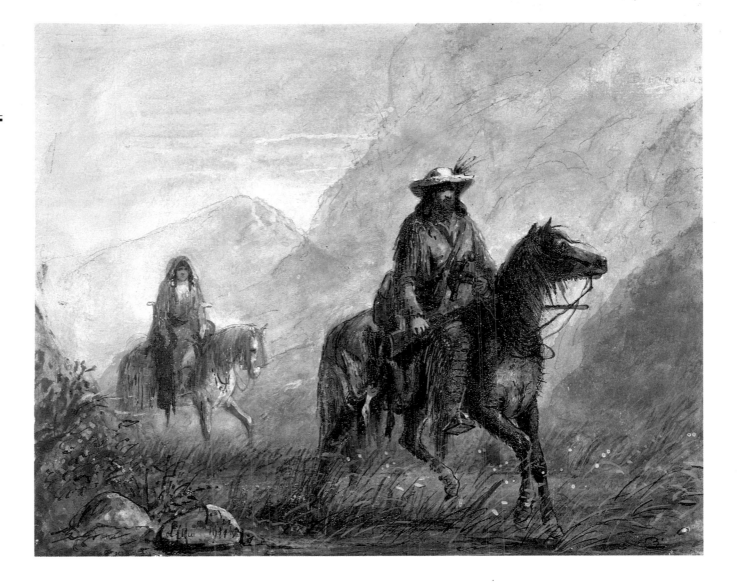

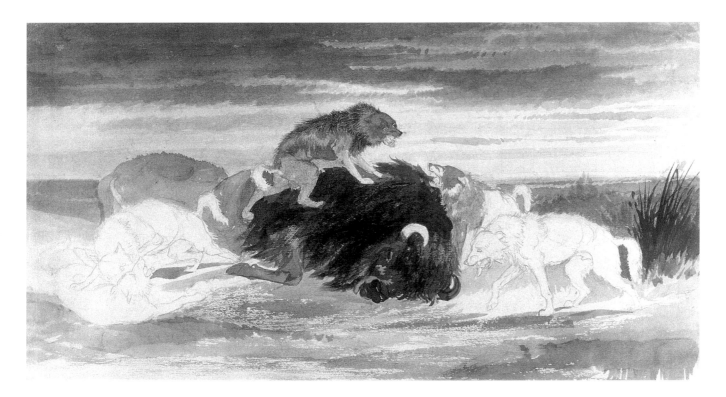

Peter Moran (1841–1914)
Greedy Wolves over Dead Buffalo,
1890
Ink wash and graphite on paper,
7 ⅜ × 14 ¼ in.
Amon Carter Museum, Fort Worth,
Texas

It turned out they were Arikaras. In the ensuing hand-to-hand struggle, two of Glass's companions were killed. Glass escaped, but he was separated from the other two survivors and bereft of his rifle. He had three hundred miles of winter travel on foot, alone, without weapons, to Fort Kiowa. He reached it in two weeks, and set out again, with a traders' party, still in search of Fitzgerald.

Glass discovered John S. Fitzgerald at Fort Atkinson. A soldier now, Sixth Regiment, U.S. Army, he was safe from any revenge Glass may have contemplated. The mountain man decided to join a caravan bound for Taos.

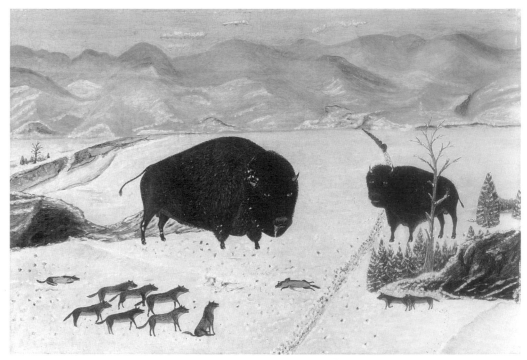

Anonymous
Fight on the Plains, c. 1860
Oil on canvas, 20 ⅛ × 30 ⅛ in.
Amon Carter Museum, Fort Worth,
Texas

Human beings were hardly alone as combatants on the battlefield of the Great Plains.

More fortunate in his encounter with a grizzly, Jed Smith wintered with his party at the site of modern-day Dubois, Wyoming, where he learned about an easy pass through the Rockies. It was almost the very route young Robert Stuart had taken in 1812 with the eastward-bound Astorians, but whereas Stuart had crossed the pass from north to south, thereby missing its full significance as *the* gateway to the Far West, Smith crossed it east to west and was able to report that he had found a means by which wagons could cross the Rockies. Located on the Continental Divide in the Central Rockies (present-day Fremont County, Wyoming), the South Pass became for the Far West what the Cumberland Gap had been for the trans-Appalachian West. It would first provide trappers with access to their quarry and a means of getting their catch to market; more important, it would become the basis of the Oregon Trail, principal highway of immigration to the West beyond the Rocky Mountains.

In October 1824 Smith came upon the camp of Iroquois Indians who were trapping along the Snake River in the employ of the Hudson's Bay Company and under the command of Alexander Ross, a former Astorian. Short of food and ammunition, the Iroquois were in a bad way—terrified, too, of lurking Blackfeet. Smith offered to buy their cache of furs at a bargain price in return for his protection.

It was a good haul. But there was much more. Ashley had sent the mountain man on a mission to explore the Columbia country for profitable trapping grounds. Smith escorted the Iroquois back to Ross's camp and then shadowed the veteran British trappers across some of the richest fur country on the continent. This reconnaisance laid the foundation of the American trappers' ascendency over their British rivals, and in 1825 Smith became Ashley's full partner. That year, too, Ashley established what Manuel Lisa had earlier made a preliminary essay toward: the rendezvous system. Beginning in 1825, mountain men would converge annually at a prearranged place to deliver their furs, receive their pay, and reoutfit themselves. They also caroused, socialized, and swapped the fantastic tales that, judging from the experience of men like Smith and Glass, could not have been all that far from actual fact.

At the rendezvous of 1826, Smith, with David E. Jackson and William Sublette, bought out Ashley's interest in the Rocky Mountain Fur Company. That fall, Jed Smith set out for the Southwest in search of new trapping grounds.

California, New Mexico, Arizona, and Texas, the Mexican borderlands destined to become the American Southwest, were drifting from their mother country during the first quarter of the nineteenth century. The first Mexican revolution removed Spain from the Southwest in 1821, but, isolated and thinly populated, the frontier territories had no more in common with Mexico City than they had had with Madrid. They were strikingly different even from one another.

California, the most established territory, was the richest. Its chain of twenty-one missions, which stretched from San Diego to San Francisco, harbored thirty thousand Indians by 1830, all converted to Christianity and all engaged in massive farming and stock operations. In 1834, the missions held 400,000 cattle, 60,000 horses, 300,000 sheep and swine. At the San Gabriel Mission alone, the Indian converts tended 150,000 cattle, 20,000 horses, and 40,000 sheep. In that year, a Mexican law that had been enacted in 1833 was put into effect: all of the holdings of all of the missions were secularized, the lands thrown open to occupation. As with most sudden property bonanzas in the West, greed and anarchy triumphed as speculators rushed in and grabbed. The Indians, liberated in a single stroke, looted the missions and, with ritualistic abandon, slaughtered vast numbers of mission cattle—30,000 at the San Gabriel Mission, for example. The animals' sun-bleached bones provided settlers with fence material for years to come.

After the immediate effects of secularization subsided, Mexican California entered a brief golden age. Mexican citizens were granted vast tracts of land—from 4,428 to 48,708 acres—for "ranchos." The proprietor of each rancho, the *ranchero*, presided over a small kingdom. His adobe home, with its terra-cotta tiled roof, was

Henry C. Eno
(birth and death dates unknown)
S. E. Hollister, The Great American Hunter & Trapper, n.d.
Lithograph, 13 ⅛ × 19 ⅝ in.
The Bancroft Library, University of California, Berkeley

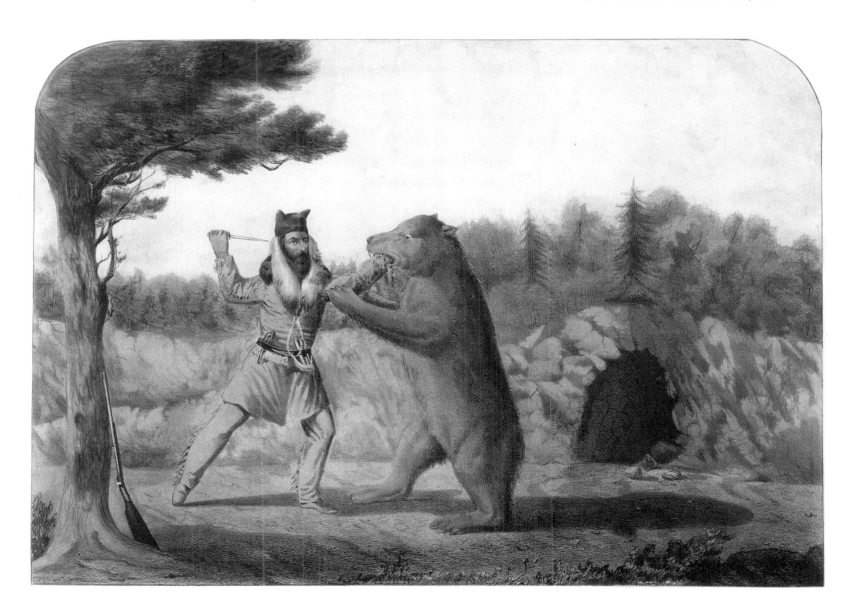

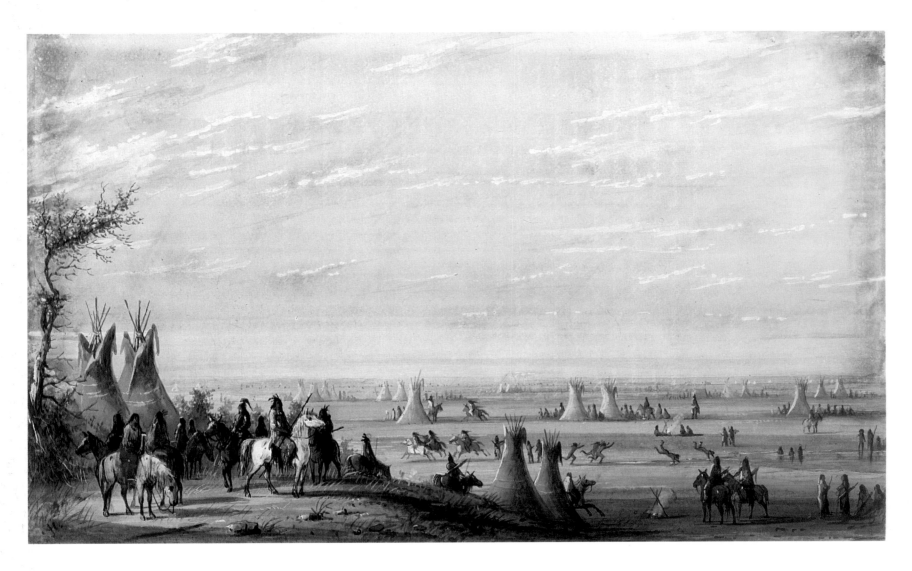

ample, a simplified imitation of the great country houses of Spain. Families were huge, and rancheros loved nothing more than visiting one another, despite the considerable distances that often separated them. Amusements were plentiful: horse racing, lassoing bears, bullfighting, staging fights between bulls and bears, cockfighting—all accompanied by incessant betting. Travelers reported that even small children laid wagers, staking their shirt buttons.

The golden California life was one of indolence and ease. Unless you were an Indian. Many of them, having been turned loose from the missions, now labored on the ranchos in exchange for food and shelter. These men, technically and legally free, were in fact slaves, and they included in their number the *vaqueros,* the first cowboys—an irony for those of us who see in the cowboy an incarnation of freedom itself.

Life in Arizona country offered a harsh contrast with that in California. The missions had been for the most part abandoned under continual attack from Apache and Yuma Indians. There were ranchos and mines near the fortified outposts of Tubac and Tucson, but, for the most part, poverty reigned in the region, and Indians were dominant.

New Mexico fared better. With forty-four thousand inhabitants at the end of the 1820s, it was far more popu-

lous even than California. Sheep raising and mining were predominant in the region's economy, activities that tended to concentrate wealth in the hands of the very few, and of all the Mexican frontier provinces, this was the most corrupt and ineptly governed.

While New Mexico's population hovered in the mid five figures during this period, Texas harbored a mere four thousand settlers in 1820. Its most desperate need was for people.

The government of the Mexican Republic saw that California was faring quite well, that Arizona was a lost cause, and that New Mexico and Texas might be made to prosper. Throughout the eighteenth and early nineteenth centuries, royal New Spain had been hostile to the United States and attempted to restrict trade and prohibit settlement. American traders were repeatedly turned back or imprisoned by Spanish authorities. The Hildago Revolt, a prerevolutionary movement in Mexico, brought rumors that restrictions would be lifted and prompted a party of ten Americans to set off for Santa Fe in 1812, hoping to get the jump on other traders. Arriving in town, the party found that the Spanish government was still in control, and their initiative was rewarded by imprisonment. Later efforts by others resulted similarly in prison terms and confiscation of goods, until 1822, when a newly independent Mexico sought to revitalize

Alfred Jacob Miller (1810–1874)
Trappers' Rendezvous, 1837
Watercolor on paper, 9 ¾ × 15 ¼ in.
Gilcrease Museum, Tulsa, Oklahoma

White fur traders bargained for the Indians' harvest of pelts at these annual gatherings.

James Walker (1819–1889)
Gauchos Lassoing a Bear, 1877
Oil on canvas, 29 × 50 in.
Gilcrease Museum, Tulsa, Oklahoma

While the grizzly was feared even by the most intrepid of mountain men, bear roping was considered great sport by California cowboys, who are called "gauchos" here, but who were usually known as vaqueros— from which the American word *buckaroo* is derived.

JAMES WALKER

—

BORN 1819, NORTHAMPTONSHIRE, ENGLAND

DIED 1889, WATSONVILLE, CALIFORNIA

—

Walker specialized in two western subjects: military scenes and the world of the vaquero, the traditional name for the California cowboy.

His family settled in Albany, New York, when he was five, and the boy grew up in New York City, where he may have studied painting. He lived for a time in New Orleans before moving to Mexico, first to Tampico and then to Mexico City. He was interned as a hostile alien in Mexico City at the outbreak of the Mexican War, but managed to escape and volunteered his services to General Winfield Scott as an interpreter. The experience gave him the opportunity to sketch the war's major battles and to record the capture of Mexico City.

At the conclusion of the war, in 1848, Walker returned to New York City and then toured South America. In 1850 he established a studio in New York and specialized in military commissions. Between 1857 and 1862, he painted *The Battle of Chapultepec* in Washington, D.C., and thereafter worked on a series of Civil War studies, which he later developed into popular battle panoramas.

After the war, Walker moved to San Francisco and, during 1876–77, sketched and painted the vaqueros, lavishing great attention on details of dress and gear, establishing the pattern for such later cowboy artists as Charles M. Russell and Olaf Seltzer.

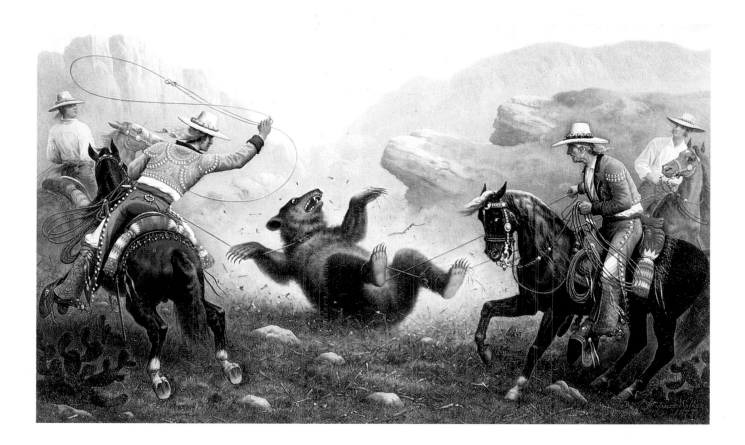

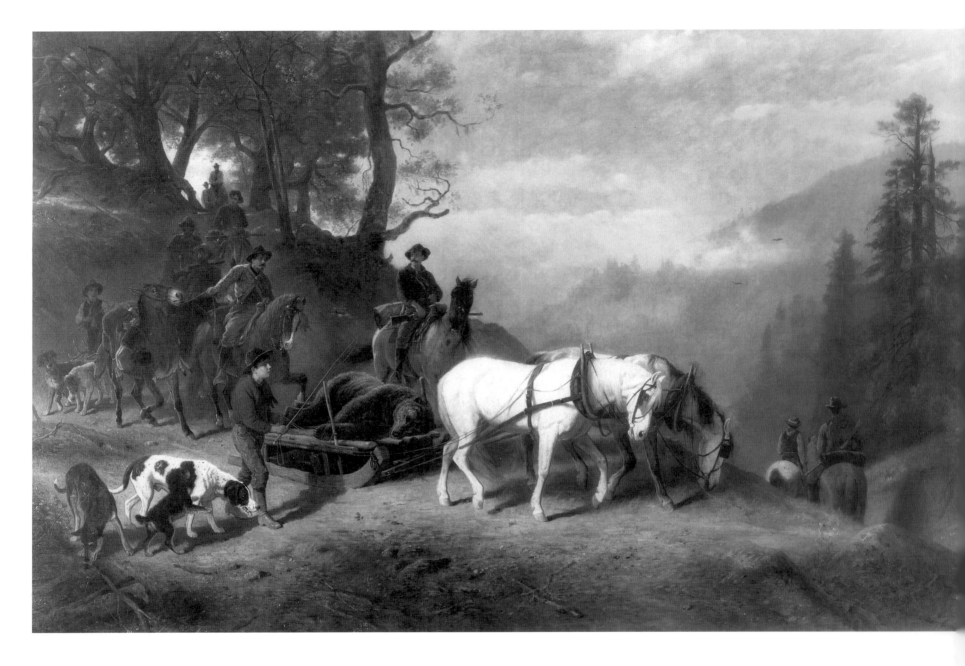

New Mexico by actually inviting trade between the province and the United States—though settlement was still illegal.

In Texas, the new government was taking an even bolder step.

Moses Austin was born in Durham, Connecticut, in 1761. With his brother, he set up in Philadelphia as a merchant, opened up a branch of the business in Virginia, and moved there. In 1798, he began mining lead in what was then Spanish Missouri, becoming a Spanish citizen in order to obtain the land for this enterprise. For more than a decade he prospered, but, like many westerners, he fell victim to the depression brought on by the War of 1812. In bad financial straits, he began to formulate a plan for making a new start in a new country. In 1820 he traveled to San Antonio de Bexar, provincial capital of Texas, and asked the governor for permission to bring three hundred families into Texas, all pledged to become Mexican citizens. The plan was approved early the next year, and a jubilant Moses returned to Missouri to recruit colonists. On the way, he fell ill and died.

His son, Stephen Fuller Austin, was twenty-seven years old at the time. He was a slight and delicate young man, of a scholarly and introspective turn. He played the flute. Few would have bet on his successfully leading rough-and-ready frontiersmen to a new land, let alone establishing and governing a colony there. But immediately on learning of Moses Austin's death, he set out for Texas, saw the governor, who confirmed the authorization he had given his father, and began to explore the country for a felicitous settlement site. He found what he liked in the green country of the Brazos and Colorado river valleys and embarked next for New Orleans to recruit his three hundred families.

Austin loaded a first group aboard the ship *Lively,* which was supposed to sail to the mouth of the Colorado and discharge its passengers, who would build a fort and plant a crop of corn. Meanwhile, Austin himself journeyed to Natchitoches to lead a group of 150 overland to the site of the new fort. But when he arrived with his followers in December 1821, neither the *Lively* nor its passengers were to be found. (It turned out, Austin later

Carl William Hahn (1829–1887)
The Return from the Bear Hunt,
1882
Oil on canvas, 59 ½ × 92 ¼ in.
Collection of The Oakland Museum;
Kahn Collection

Another way to deal with grizzlies was to organize a hunting party and take one down.

discovered, that the ship had mistakenly landed at the mouth of the Brazos.) With great difficulty, the settlers survived their first winter.

Nor did spring 1822 bring an end to Stephen Austin's troubles. It seemed that, in granting Moses Austin authority to establish a colony, the Texas governor had acted without the full approval of his superiors, and Stephen Austin had to travel to Mexico City to clear up the matter. He arrived in August 1822, in the midst of post-revolutionary infighting that kept his case in limbo for nearly a year before the grant was finally confirmed on April 14, 1823.

The colony to which he returned, however, was in disarray, suffering the consequences of a summer drought and Indian attacks. Undaunted, Austin negotiated terms with the hostile Indians and recruited more settlers. Three hundred families were well established by the summer of 1823, and during the next year more came, prompting Austin to petition the Mexican government for additional land and permission to settle more families. Other entrepreneurs began to imitate Austin's effort, hoping to achieve similar success. They were encouraged by a National Colonization Law passed in the summer of 1824, effectively opening all of Texas to foreign immigration in return for an oath of allegiance to Mexico. As usual, a great many of the new speculators lacked the morals—let alone the skill and determination—to establish successful colonies. Yet a good number did succeed, so that, by 1830, some nine thousand settlers had colonized Texas. As the Mexican government had hoped, the provincial economy was revitalized, but officials were beginning to worry. The new settlers called themselves citizens of Mexico; to look at them, however, they were still Americanos.

When New Mexico was opened to American trade, the timing was just right for William Becknell. Born about 1790, probably somewhere in Kentucky, Becknell was a small merchant in Franklin, Missouri, by 1821. That year he advertised for men to join an expedition "for the purpose of trading Horses and Mules and catching Wild Animals of every description." Some twenty or thirty plainsmen set off with Becknell in August or September for the southern Rockies. They became lost in the Raton Pass, where they encountered an encampment of Mexican soldiers—hardly a welcome sight to a trader familiar with the fate of American merchants in Mexican territory. To Becknell's surprise and delight, the soldiers greeted his party warmly, informing them that Mexico was now an independent republic. Becknell determined to be the first United States trader in the lively southwestern marketplace of Santa Fe.

And so he was. From this and subsequent expeditions he made great profits and inaugurated profitable trade for others as well. He also established the famed Santa Fe Trail between Missouri and the New Mexican capital, the effect of which reached even beyond lucrative trade and the American infiltration of New Mexico; it demonstrated that wagon travel across the arid plains was possible, which meant that immigration into this part of the West was also feasible.

The town of Franklin, from which the Santa Fe trade had begun, was entirely washed away by a Missouri River flood in 1828. Independence, Missouri, became headquarters for traders, who loaded their goods on Murphy wagons—built in St. Louis by the Murphy firm—three feet wide and sixteen feet long, with rear wheels five feet in diameter and shod with four-inch-thick iron tires. The wagons were pulled by three or four yokes of oxen or by mules, a team of as many as a dozen, which fared better in the desert than oxen.

The first stop on the westward journey was Council Grove, some 150 miles distant. It was here that the traders would pause to organize into larger caravans. For beyond this point, Indian attacks and natural hazards made individual travel foolhardy. A caravan captain was elected by the assembled traders, together with four lieutenants in charge of the four columns into which the wagons were commonly divided. Sergeants of the guard, whose job it was to oversee the nightly watches, were also appointed. The caravan then proceeded west from Council Grove at the rate of ten to fifteen miles a day, the men living off the austere rations they carried until they hit buffalo country, where it was an easy matter to shoot a feast from among the vast herds. If Indians were present, the four wagon columns formed themselves into a hollow square and proceeded thus, a moving stockade fort. Rivers had to be forded, sheer cliffs negotiated, and quicksand—endemic to Arkansas River country—had to be crossed. If the water was high in these areas of quagmire, the unwieldy wagons had to be caulked and floated across.

Then there was the dreaded Cimarron Desert, fifty miles of waterless, treeless, lifeless sand that had to be traversed at the agonizing ten- or fifteen-mile-a-day rate. The expanse was navigated in much the same way as a seafarer navigates the trackless ocean, by the compass. (In 1834, a caravan crossed in torrential rain, leaving wheel ruts that baked in the sun and lasted for years—an indelible trail marker.) Past the Cimarron River, the going got easier all the way into Santa Fe, where the caravans encountered obstacles of a different sort. Mexican customs officials were, at best, whimsical, and it was entirely up to them to assess import duties. Shrewd merchants smuggled in as much as possible, duty-free, but even the shrewdest had to pay on the bulk of their goods. The art was in figuring how much to bribe in order to avoid injury to profits. Customs negotiations often consumed weeks.

Despite the hardships and Mexican tariffs and Mexican graft, the trade was extraordinarily profitable at first, until tariffs grew higher and Indian attacks increased in number and ferocity. It was Pawnee and Co-

(T H O M A S)
W O R T H I N G T O N
W H I T T R E D G E

—

BORN 1820, SPRINGFIELD, OHIO

DIED 1910, SUMMIT, NEW JERSEY

—

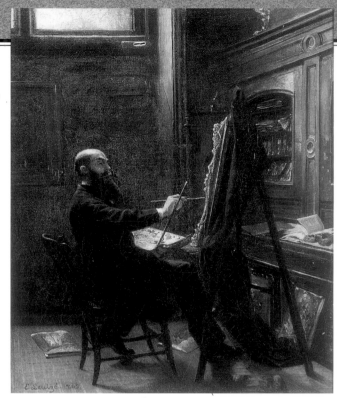

Emanuel Leutze, *Worthington Whittredge in His Tenth Street Studio,*
1865. Oil on canvas, 15 × 12 in.
Reynolda House, Museum of American Art; gift of Barbara B. Millhouse

Known primarily as a painter of the Hudson River School, Whittredge made two, possibly three, western tours, accompanying General John Pope from Fort Leavenworth, Kansas, to Denver, south along the Rocky Mountains, and into New Mexico in 1866, and again in the Rockies, with fellow painters Sanford Gifford and J. F. Kensett, in 1870. He may have made a third western trip in 1877.

A farmer's son, Whittredge set up in Cincinnati as a house and sign painter while he studied fine art. By twenty, he was making daguerreotype as well as painted portraits in Cincinnati, then turned to landscapes within a few years. These early works sold well locally, and in 1849 he was commissioned to paint a series of European scenes. While abroad, Whittredge studied with Andreas Aschenbach in Düsseldorf and was befriended by

Albert Bierstadt and Emanuel Leutze—even serving the latter as a model for *Washington Crossing the Delaware.*

Returning to the United States in 1859, Whittredge established his studio in New York City and prospered as a landscapist. While his western scenes lack the grandiloquence of Bierstadt's work or the breathtaking, luminous poetry of Thomas Moran's, they are sensitive and beautifully crafted. During the artist's lifetime, his western paintings commanded as much as $10,000 each.

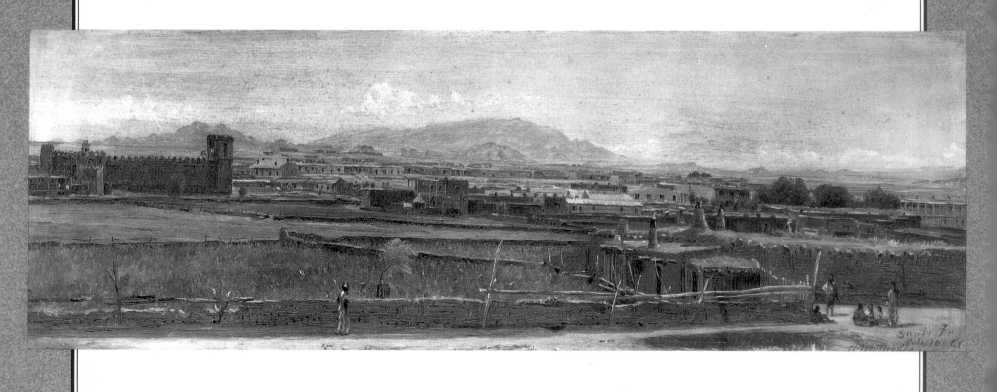

Worthington Whittredge
(1820–1910)
Santa Fe, 1866
Oil on canvas, 8 × 23 ⅛ in.
Yale University Art Gallery; Gift
from the estate of William W. Far-
nam, B.A. 1866, M.A. 1869, to the
Peabody Museum of Natural History
(opposite below)

In 1866, when this oil was painted,
Santa Fe was still a squat, dusty
center of trade.

Currier & Ives (after John Cameron)
*Taking the Back Track/A Dangerous
Neighborhood,* 1866
Museum of the City of New York
(below)

manche attacks on the Santa Fe caravans that first
touched off demands for aggressive military intervention
against the Indians of the Far West. In 1829, 170 infantrymen were dispatched under the command of Captain
Bennet Riley to accompany the Santa Fe caravan to the
Mexican border. When, six miles beyond the border, the
caravan was attacked by Comanches, Riley charged
across the boundary, but by then the men of the caravan
had beaten off the attack themselves. Riley's men rode
escort for two more days before returning to the American side of the Arkansas River to await the return of the
Santa Fe traders.

The wait was not pleasant. Indians kept the encampment under continual siege; foot soldiers were easy
pickings for mounted warriors. The beleaguered troops
greeted the return of the caravan with jubilation, for it
was escorted by five companies of Mexican cavalry. It
was not until 1832 that the War Department despatched
mounted troops to escort the caravans, but by then the
trade's days were already numbered as Mexican-
American relations became increasingly strained.

Despite the Santa Fe Trail, most of the Southwest
was unknown to white men in 1826 when Jedediah

Strong Smith set out to explore the country south and
southwest of the Great Salt Lake in search of peltries for
the company he and his partners had just acquired. His
meandering route ran from the Salt Lake, southward
onto the Colorado Plateau, and along the Colorado River
into the Mojave Desert, where Smith and his party of
seventeen were reduced to eating their dying horses.
Crossing into California, the men ascended the San Bernardino Mountains and crossed them, arriving at the San
Gabriel Mission on November 27, 1826. There the pious
Jedediah charmed the fathers, who were astounded that
anyone could have reached them overland.

Governor José Echeandia was by no means
charmed, however. Mexico had its reasons for admitting
Americanos into Texas and opening the Santa Fe trade to
them, but California was doing marvelously well without
foreign interference or intrusion. The governor ordered
Smith and his party to San Diego, intending to send them
on to Mexico City to stand trial for illegal entry. Fortunately for the trapper, California was not entirely closed
off to American trade—as long as it was seaborne; ships
could touch port, unload, load, and leave. New England
shoe factories were creating a demand for an article of

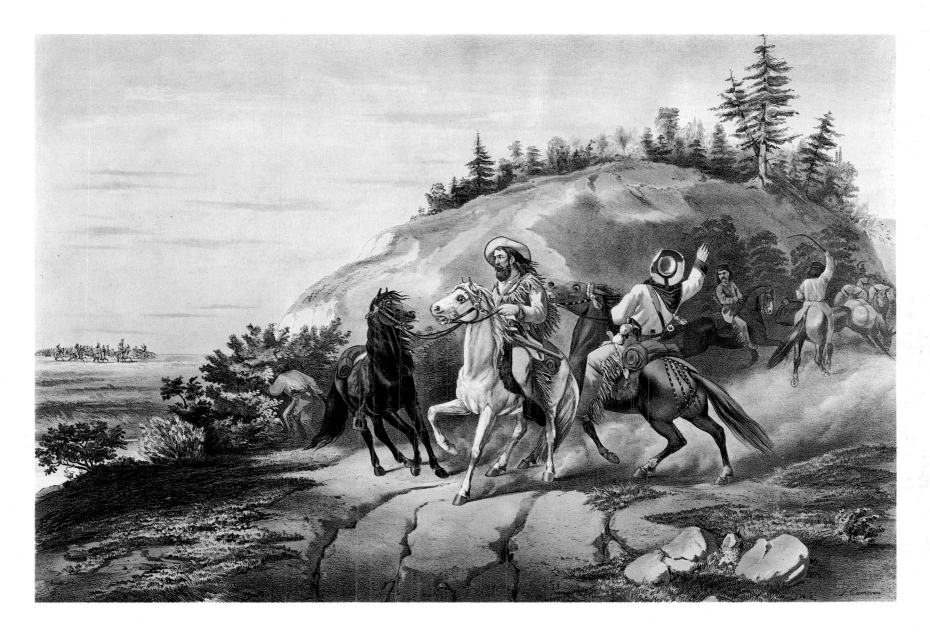

western produce even more abundant than beaver fur—leather—and California was abundant in hides. Captain William Cunningham of the *Courier,* trading in hides, persuaded the governor that Smith and his men were simply trappers who had lost their way, that they were certainly not spies or invaders. Echeandia relented, releasing Smith and his men on condition that they return by the way they had come.

Smith and company sailed in the *Courier* to San Pedro Bay and left San Gabriel on January 18, 1827. But the mountain man did not honor his pledge to the governor. Instead, he headed due north through the San Joaquin Valley, where the trapping, he discovered, was very good. In May, Smith departed the Sierra Nevada foothills with two men—leaving the others behind to continue trapping—in order to make the rendezvous of 1827. The deserts of central Nevada and northeastern Utah almost finished the three. As Smith recorded in his journal: "we dug holes in the sand and laid down in them for the purpose of cooling our heated bodies. . . . Our sleep was not repose, for tormented nature made us dream of things we had not and for the want of which it then seemed possible, and even probable, that we might perish in the desert unheard of and unpitied." But they made Bear Lake and the rendezvous just in time.

Ten days after he had arrived at the rendezvous, Smith, sixteen men, and two Indian women set out on a return journey to California to collect the trappers and their furs. When they reached the Colorado River, the men built cane rafts to ferry themselves and their goods across. They thought nothing of the Mojave Indians who were watching them; the Mojaves had always been friendly enough. But, unknown to Smith, just a few months earlier, a number of Mojaves had been killed in a dispute with other trappers. They were out for revenge now—and took it, clubbing to death ten men and making captives of the two women.

Smith had eight men left, one of whom was wounded, and between them they had five guns. He was on the west bank of the Colorado, the Indians on the east. "We took our position in a cluster of small Cotton Wood trees," Smith recorded in his journal. "With our knives we lopped down the small trees in such a manner as to clear a place in which to stand, while the fallen poles formed a slight breastwork. We then fastened our Butcher knives with cords to the end of light poles so as to form a tolerable lance. . . . Some of the men asked me if I thought we would be able to defend ourselves. I told them I thought we would. But that was not my opinion." The Indians were coming closer, but they kept under cover. Finally, when a few Indians appeared within range, Smith "directed two good marksmen to fire they did so and two indians fell and another was wounded. Upon this the indians ran off like frightened sheep and we were released from the apprehension of immediate death."

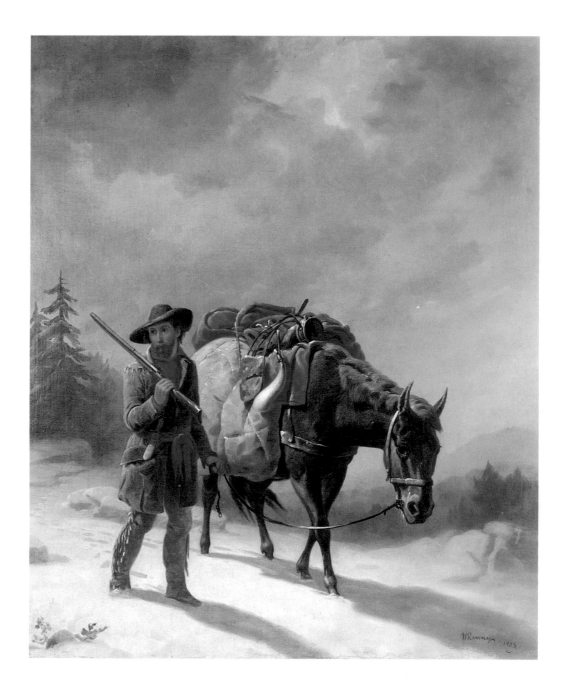

After another cross-desert march, Smith and the survivors of the attack reached the trappers' camp—on schedule, remarkably enough, but without the supplies they had had to abandon in the Colorado. Smith would have to resupply his men, and that meant contacting the Mexicans. Governor Echeandia was not pleased that Smith was still trespassing on Mexican territory. He had the trapper imprisoned and once again threatened to send him to Mexico City. Two sea captains, an American and an Englishman, spent months negotiating with the governor for Smith's release. At last it was won, and Smith sold fifteen hundred pounds of fur to Captain John Bradshaw of the American ship *Franklin.*

Still he pressed northward. In Oregon he encountered terrain that made driving his herd of horses all but impossible. On July 14, 1828, Smith took two men to scout out easier routes. Seventeen were left behind to make camp at the Umpqua River to await Smith's return. The men were cautioned not to allow Indians into the

William Tylee Ranney (1813–1857)
Trapper Crossing the Mountains,
1853
Oil on canvas, 29 × 24 in.
Collection of the J. B. Speed Art Museum, Louisville, Kentucky

Although Ranney spent three or four years in the West, serving with the army of the Texas republic, he painted his western works in his New Jersey studio, a decade later.

Louis Choris (1795–1828)
Indian of California, c. 1816
Watercolor on paper, 5 ⅜ × 4 ⅞ in.
Collection of The Oakland Museum;
Museum Donor's Acquisition Fund

Born in Russia, Choris served as
official artist attached to a South
Seas expedition, led by Captain Otto
de Kotzebue, from 1815 to 1818. His
California watercolors date from
1816.

Samuel Colman (1832–1920)
Colorado Canyon, n.d.
Oil on board, 9 × 23 ¾ in.
Courtesy of The Anschutz Collection

A pupil of Asher B. Durand, Colman
was identified with the Hudson
River School of American landscape
painters. After European study, he
decided, in 1870, to tour the West by
train. Although his acquaintance
with the country was superficial, he
produced a number of creditable
landscapes.

camp—for there had been an argument over a stolen axe, and Smith was all too aware of the Indian passion for settling scores.

One of the many miseries of the journey through Northern California and southern Oregon was continual and unrelenting rain. The men in camp were trying to dry out their weapons when the Indians descended on them, killing all but one, Arthur Black, who ran into the forest and eventually turned up at Fort Vancouver on the Columbia River, where Hudson's Bay trappers took him in. Smith and his two companions were also attacked when they returned to the camp, but fled and also made their way to Fort Vancouver. There, Hudson's Bay factor John McLoughlin generously provided Smith with an armed party to recover as much fur and supplies as possible. That turned out to be thirty-eight horses, 635 skins, and some other equipment.

For all his peregrinations, Smith had not added greatly to his company's profits. He did make one last dangerous and triumphant sortie into the very heart of Blackfoot country on the Missouri, securing a handsome haul of furs, but the experience at Fort Vancouver had been a sobering one. The Hudson's Bay Company facility there consisted of a seemingly impregnable stockade surrounded by warehouses and other company buildings, including an impressive house for the factor. There were fields of grain, there was plenty of livestock, and there was a fine dock for loading and unloading ocean-going vessels. And what Hudson's Bay didn't grab, Astor's wholly recovered American Fur Company surely would. It was the desperate pressure of overwhelming competition, rather than the hardships and disasters endemic to the life of a mountain man, that led Smith and his partners, David Jackson and William Sublette, to take their profit (the last year's gross was $84,499.14) and pack it in.

Smith bought a house in St. Louis, bought two

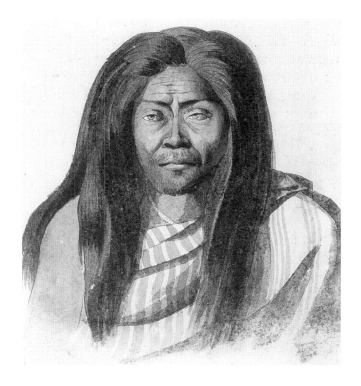

slaves to keep it for him, and invited his four brothers to share his domestic bliss.

But he had been settled for only six months when the Santa Fe trade beckoned; New Mexico was, after all, the only part of the Far West he hadn't seen. With his two fur partners, Jackson and Sublette, he organized a caravan of twenty-four wagons and eighty-four men—the most substantial force the mountain man had ever journeyed with—and set out from Independence.

In the Cimarron Desert, always a trial by thirst, Smith scouted out ahead in search of water. It was May 19, 1831. He found water. And Comanches found him.

"Though he fell under the spears of savages," the *Illinois Magazine* eulogized in June 1832, "and his body has glutted the prairie wolf, and none can tell where his bones are bleaching, he must not be forgotten."

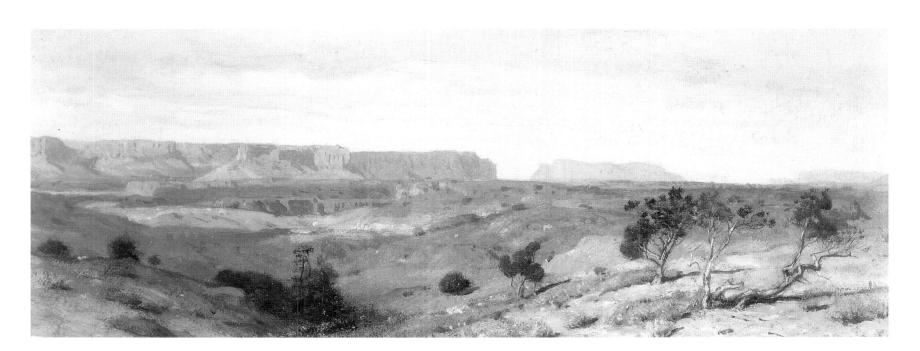

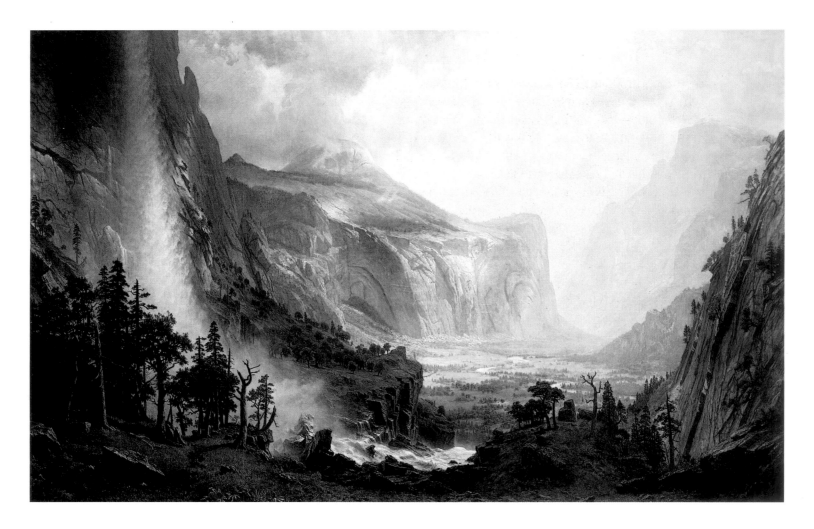

SETTLING AND UNSETTLING

Jedediah Strong Smith left the fur trade when he felt himself squeezed out by the competition. Indeed, Astor's American Fur Company was becoming increasingly dominant in the early 1830s, partly because of the introduction of steam navigation on the Yellowstone River in 1832. Supply was surer, swifter, and more economical, as was transportation of the collected furs. Sanctioned by the federal government and working in part for Astor, Captain Benjamin Bonneville set out in 1832 with 110 men and twenty-eight wagons on a two-year exploration of the Rocky Mountains. His wagon train was the first to cross the Continental Divide by way of the South Pass Smith had rediscovered. It was a route that many would follow—and very soon—not in search of beaver, but of homes.

During the 1830s and well into the 1840s, the plains, known as the Great Desert, remained largely unsettled. It was the Far West that first drew the focus of manifest destiny. By the early 1830s, Americans were beginning to settle in California, many of them mountain men who turned from that profession to ranching and even mercantile pursuits. Until 1833, these settlers wandered into the territory by way of the southwestern deserts and posed little threat to Mexican sovereignty. But in 1833, Joe Walker, a mountain man from Tennessee, marched due west from Missouri, took the South Pass through the Great Divide, went east to west across the Great Basin, climbed the Sierra Nevada Mountains, and entered California. In short, he blazed the California fork of what

would come to be called the Overland Trail, thereby opening California to the United States.

In this, he behaved like a typical mountain man. He was serving under Benjamin Bonneville, who was reconnoitering the Green River region, ostensibly in search of fur, though it seems certain that his explorations served a military purpose as well. Bonneville dispatched Walker to explore the vicinity of Salt Lake. Walker decided to head for California instead. He remained in that Mexican province for two months, but six of his party decided to settle there. By 1840, 117 mountain men had decided likewise, bringing the American population to about 400.

The same year that Bonneville embarked on his expedition, Nathaniel J. Wyeth, a Boston ice merchant, inspired by the tireless western propagandizing of another rank easterner, Boston schoolmaster Hall Jackson Kelley, decided to organize an expedition to Oregon and the mouth of the Columbia. His purpose was twofold. With Kelley, he proposed to found a colony; he also planned a more immediate business venture as victualer and general supplier to the Northwest trappers.

It soon became apparent that Kelley had more zeal than sense, and Wyeth split with him, leaving Boston with twenty followers. He got as far as Independence, Missouri, when it dawned on all involved that his group was ill-prepared for travel across the mountains. But all was not lost, as William Sublette allowed Wyeth (whose company had lost two discouraged members) to accompany him westward. At Pierre's Hole, site of the 1832 rendezvous, seven more men turned back. But Wyeth and eleven remaining followers pressed on, this time in company with William Sublette's brother, Milton. Together, they survived an Indian fight—the Battle of Pierre's Hole—and continued as far as the Snake River. There Sublette had to leave the Wyeth group. With difficulty, the eastern greenhorns negotiated the Snake and the Columbia and reached Fort Vancouver on October 29, 1832, only to discover that the all-important supply ship Wyeth had dispatched from Boston had been lost at sea. "I am now afloat on the great sea of life without stay or support," Wyeth wrote in his journal, and returned to Boston empty-handed.

He would organize a second expedition in 1834. But that, too, was destined to fail when fur men reneged on a trading contract and when the vessel Wyeth had planned to use to catch salmon for packing and shipping back east was damaged by lightning and so delayed by repairs that it missed the salmon run.

Nevertheless, Wyeth's venture signaled the beginning of a transition for Americans in the Far West. Wyeth's journey was the first continuous overland trek from coast to coast. News of it fired the imagination of

many. The beaver had been trapped virtually to extinction in the mountains, and fur, which had started it all, was beginning to fall out of fashion back east. In 1834 John Jacob Astor sold his company. Soon, the mountain men would be supplanted by fishermen, merchants, farmers, and other settlers.

Down in Texas, settlement was reaching a new, distinctly *unsettling* stage. Stephen Austin had written, in an 1823 proclamation, of the "bountiful . . . favors and privileges" Mexico had bestowed on his colony. Nevertheless, conflict between Texans and Mexicans had taken root from the very beginning. Most of the Texas settlers were southern Protestants; the Mexican government sanctioned Catholicism as a matter of national policy and prohibited public worship by any non-Catholic sect. The Texas settlers brought slaves with them to work the land, and they would require more; the Mexican government proposed gradual but absolute emancipation in Texas and had already abolished slavery throughout the rest of Mexico.

The colonists succeeded by the end of 1829 in per-

Karl Bodmer (1809–1893)
Fort MacKenzie, August 28, 1833
Lithograph
Courtesy of the Library of Congress

This fur-trading outpost on Marias River was the scene of a battle between Blackfeet and Assiniboins. Bodmer, best known for his meticulous delineation of landscapes and carefully posed portraits of Indians, was on hand to document this scene of violent action.

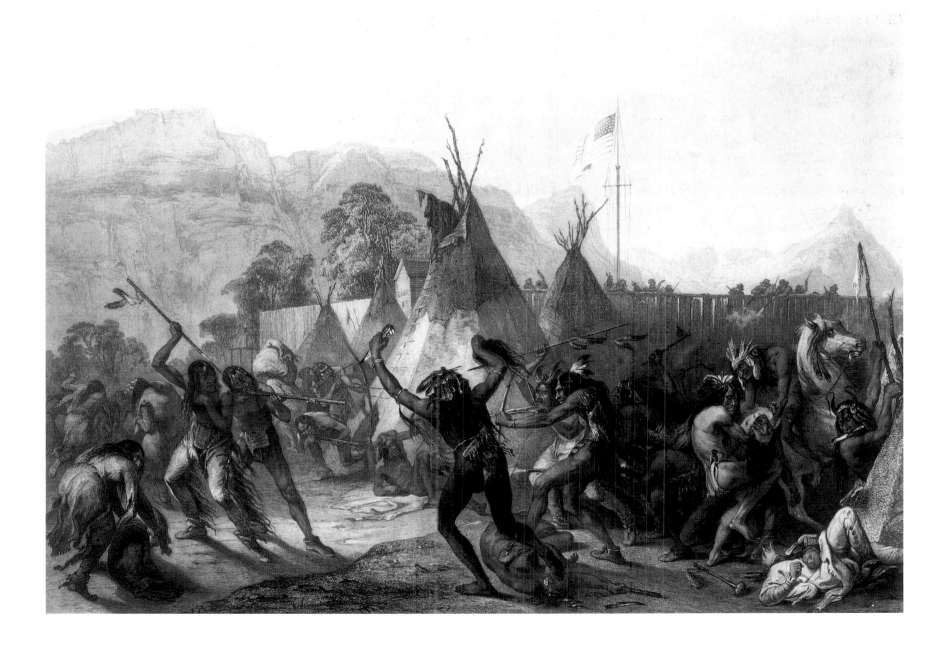

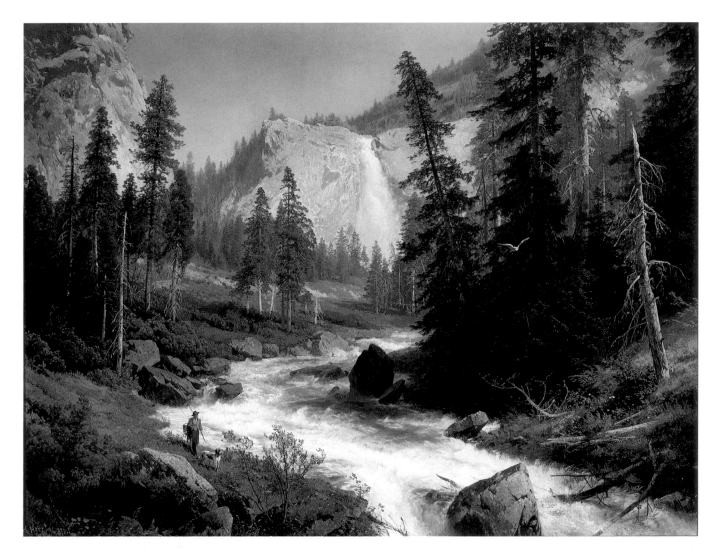

Hermann Herzog (1831–1932)
Sentinel Rock, Yosemite, 1875
Oil on canvas, 34 × 44 in.
Courtesy of The Anschutz Collection

Born in Bremen, Germany, Herzog
studied at Düsseldorf. He painted
landscapes throughout Europe until
1869, when he immigrated to
Philadelphia. He worked in the
Pennsylvania countryside and along
the Hudson River in addition to
California's Yosemite Valley and
Sierra Nevada.

John Russell Bartlett (1805–1886)
Crossing the Pecos, c. 1851
Pencil and sepia wash on paper,
9 × 12 in.
Courtesy of the John Carter Brown
Library at Brown University

By profession, Bartlett was a bank
cashier and a book importer. By
avocation, he was a historian,
ethnologist, and artist. At the age of
forty-five, he was appointed
commissioner for the U.S.–Mexico
boundary survey of 1850–53. It was
during this service that he sketched
the difficulties of fording the deep
and swift Pecos River.

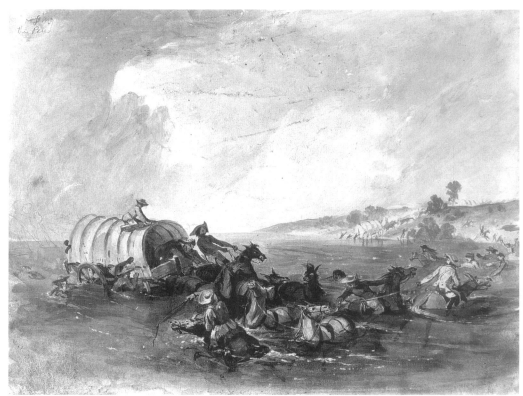

suading the Coahuila-Texas state legislature to declare that "labor contracts" made outside of the state were binding, and secured for Texas a presidential exemption from the decree abolishing slavery. But these concessions did not assuage the growing ill will between the Texas settlers and the nation to whom they had pledged their loyalty. For the bad feelings ran deeper than unpopular legislation. The Texans simply saw themselves as superior to the Mexicans, whom they regarded as stupid, indolent, and immoral. There smoldered within the settlers a powerful resentment at having to answer to the authority of such people.

In December 1826 and January 1827 a farcical rebellion sounded a comic-opera prelude to the bloody conflict yet to come. Like Stephen Austin, Haden Edwards was an *empresario,* a colonizing entrepreneur granted land by the Mexican government. But with that fact ended all similarity between the two men. Whereas Austin was sincere, dedicated, and wise, Edwards was shady, opportunistic, and rash. Granted three hundred thousand acres near Nacogdoches in East Texas, Edwards planned to settle eight hundred families. His vast grant included, however, some parcels of land occupied by American squatters and by Mexicans—some of whom actually held legitimate titles under original Spanish land grants that the Mexican government had pledged to honor. Rather than accommodate prior claimants (who, after all, held a minuscule fraction of the grant), Edwards issued a high-handed ultimatum demanding that the pretenders to "his" property prove their title to *his* satisfaction or forfeit their lands, which "will be sold to the first person who occupies them." Thus threatened, the original settlers protested to the Mexican government.

Edwards had settled some fifty families on his grant when he returned to the United States in June 1826 to conduct some other business. He left his hotheaded brother, Benjamin, to take charge of the colony during his absence. It was Benjamin who received word that, in response to protests, the Mexican government had revoked the Edwards grant. Now the original settlers started reclaiming the land on which Haden Edwards's first fifty families had just settled. Benjamin Edwards called for a revolt against Mexico. On December 16, 1826, he led thirty colonists into Nacogdoches, occupied an old fort, raised a red-and-white banner emblazoned with the motto "Independence, Liberty and Justice," and proclaimed the Republic of Fredonia.

The revolution was "backed" by a treaty with Cherokee Indians (to whom the Mexicans refused to grant land) promising them half of Texas. But the treaty had been signed without any tribal authority, and the tribal council summarily disavowed the document. On January 28, 1827, a detachment of 250 Mexican soldiers, augmented by 100 members of Austin's colony who were fearful that reprisals against Edwards would turn Mexico against all American settlers, marched into Nacogdoches; but they found no one at the fort. Deserted by the Cherokees, the thirty would-be Fredonians had come to their senses and decamped for the safety of the United States.

Neither Texans nor Mexicans laughed off the laughable six-week history of the Republic of Fredonia. The Texans learned that the Mexican government was capable of revoking grants without notice, let alone debate. The Mexicans saw the Fredonian Revolt as the first gesture in a scheme to take its northern provinces. This impression was confirmed when President John Quincy Adams offered to buy Texas—all of it—for a million dollars. The offer was declined. When Andrew Jackson took office he upped the ante to five million, and when that met with refusal, the president replaced his negotiator and minister to Mexico, Joel R. Poinsett, with someone considerably less scrupulous. On behalf of President Jackson, Anthony Butler attempted bribery, usury (foisting on the Mexicans an unpayable loan with Texas as collateral), and advocated the use of force, all of which fostered more ill will between the two nations.

Seeking to stave off the American menace, Mexico enacted legislation in 1830 augmenting the number and size of garrisons in the province and aimed at stopping U.S. immigration into Texas while increasing immigration from European countries. The new laws failed miserably. They halted *legal* immigration—immigration by families who had been screened and certified as sober and law-abiding by the empresarios—but anybody else could cross the long border illegally and at will. As for the Europeans, they simply were not interested in coming, so, in 1833, Mexico again began admitting Americans, and Texas fever raged. By 1835, Texas had a population of thirty-five hundred Mexicans and some thirty thousand Americans.

They readily chafed under Mexican rule. As so often happened in western affairs, frontiersmen and settlers felt themselves underrepresented by a central government based hundreds of miles away. Saltillo, capital of Coahuila-Texas, was seven hundred miles distant from any Texan, and the province had little voice in the election of representatives. Then, in 1831, open conflict erupted between settlers and the beefed-up garrisons, many of which were commanded by mercenary and cynical Americans. When Colonel John Davis Bradburn, commander of the Anahuac garrison, illegally and arbitrarily barred the issuance of government-authorized land grants to squatters living east of the San Jacinto River, "borrowed" settlers' slaves to work on the garrison fort, generally gave his soldiers license to behave as they wished, and then jailed two Americans—without trial—for protesting his actions, 160 settlers laid siege to the fort, which, after much bloodshed, surrendered.

Stephen Austin and the majority of Texans were not prepared for out-and-out rebellion. Austin negotiated peace between both sides, pledging Texan support for

General Antonio López de Santa Anna, who was at the time leading one of Mexico's many revolutions. When Santa Anna emerged victorious, Texas was much in his favor for having supported his cause. It seemed a good time to present to the new president the grievances of the province, which included a petition for separate statehood.

The grievances and petition went unanswered, save that the "Committees of Safety" organized in each settler community were ordered dissolved.

The next year, 1833, another Texas convention was convened, the grievances reiterated, and a state constitution drafted. Austin himself carried these documents to Mexico City, where for some five months he attempted, without success, to see Santa Anna. When he finally did gain an audience, the president expressed willingness to remedy all grievances except for the statehood demand. Still, it was more than Austin had expected, and he began his journey back to Texas—only to be arrested at Saltillo, returned to Mexico City, and imprisoned. It seems that, during his long wait to see the president, he wrote an impatient letter to a friend, urging the immediate formation of a state government. The letter had been intercepted by the police, and Stephen Austin spent the next two years in jail.

He returned to Texas in 1835, an embittered man broken in health. While the two years of his absence actually saw some improvement in the province's political situation, Santa Anna repudiated all of his previous liberal gestures when he abolished *all* state governments and proclaimed himself dictator of a wholly centralized Mexico. He reestablished all garrisons, and his customs collectors demanded bribes and exorbitant fees; it became clear that Santa Anna would soon abolish all local government in Texas. When Texans intercepted one of Santa Anna's couriers carrying word of the impending arrival of reinforcements for the Anahuac garrison, William B. Travis and a force of forty men forced the surrender of the garrison before additional troops could arrive. Santa Anna ordered the arrest of Travis and three others. That at last galvanized the revolutionary spirit in Texas. And this time, Stephen Austin was in no mood to mediate. He, too, counseled revolt.

It began on October 2, 1835, as Mexican cavalry crossed the Rio Grande and demanded the surrender of a cannon in the town of Gonzales. The Americans quickly forged a small army and chased the Mexican force southward. Next, Austin himself led a force of five hundred against San Antonio, where most of the retreating Mexican army, under General Martín Perfecto de Cós, had taken refuge. The Texans dug in for a long siege in November. That same month representatives of the twelve American communities of Texas convened to decide just what the territory was fighting for: Independence? Or a return to Mexico under the 1824 constitution? The vote was solidly against independence. A

provisional government was created, but with the object of appealing to Mexican liberals to unite against Santa Anna so that Texas might rejoin a constitutionally governed Mexico.

Meanwhile, life for the ragtag army of siege was becoming increasingly miserable during a bitter East Texas winter. Discipline and resolve began to crumble. Some officers proposed to withdraw their men. Then Ben Milam, a Texas settler from Kentucky, drew a line in the cold earth. "Who will go with old Ben Milam to San Antonio? Who will follow old Ben Milam?"

On December 5, Milam and Francis W. Johnson led three hundred Texans into San Antonio. They fought the Mexican troops in the town's streets, and when Milam was felled by a bullet in the head, the Texans fought yet more fiercely. General Cós retreated with some eleven hundred troops into the garrison's barracks and armory.

It was an abandoned mission, built by Franciscans in the mid 1700s across the river from what was then the village of San Antonio de Bexar. The church was a ruin, towers and dome collapsed, a stone wall skeleton remaining. There was a two-story "Long Barracks" and a one-story "Low Barracks." There were also officers' quarters. The whole area—about 250 by 450 feet—was enclosed by formidable stone walls, twelve feet high in some places. While the compound held twenty cannon, there were no firing platforms behind the walls, nor were there embrasures; the cannon could neither fire over nor through the walls.

The name of the abandoned mission was San Antonio de Valero, but almost from the beginning it was known as the Alamo, after a grove of cottonwood—*alamo*—trees nearby.

The Texans brought their cannon to bear against the Alamo's walls, and Cós finally surrendered his eleven hundred men to three hundred Texas volunteers.

After the taking of the Alamo, Green Jameson, a twenty-nine-year-old lawyer originally from Kentucky, began to repair the fort and to build usable gun positions and firing platforms so that the converted mission could be effectively defended. But this work proceeded amid political chaos, as Texans could not decide whether to declare independence or attempt to reestablish the constitutional republic of Mexico and seek statehood within it. Sam Houston and Henry Smith, the elected governor of Texas, urged independence, warning that reprisal from Santa Anna himself was inevitable. But a legislative council decided to dispatch a force to Matamoros, a Mexican town at the mouth of the Rio Grande that was known as a stronghold of liberals opposed to Santa Anna, and unite with them to reestablish the republic. Led by James Fannin, the expedition got as far as Goliad, Texas, where Sam Houston convinced the small army to pause and reconsider the dangers Texas faced. Reasoning that Santa Anna was gathering his forces and would have to enter Texas through San Antonio, Houston

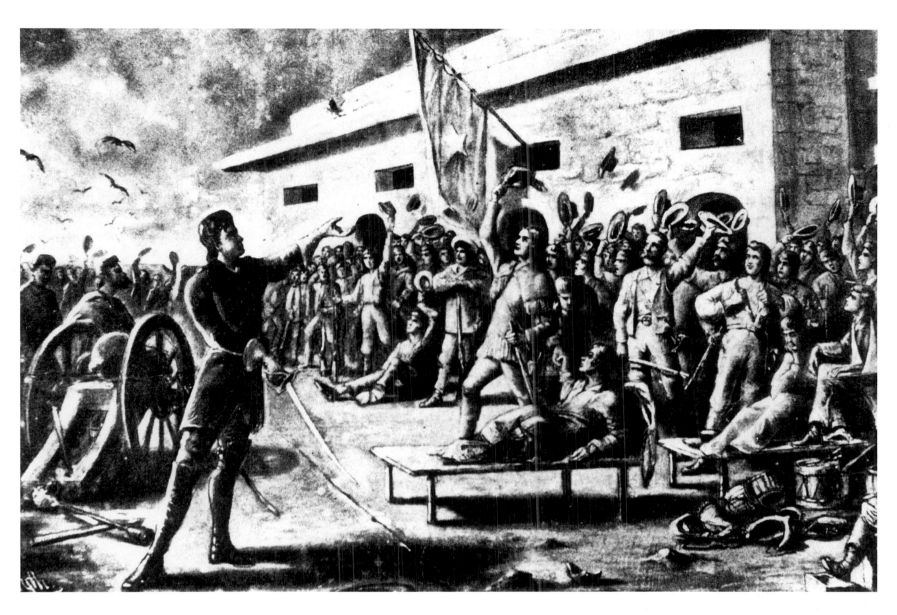

Louis Eyth (1838–1889)
The Speech of Travis to His Men at the Alamo, 1870s
Oil on canvas, dim. unknown
(original lost)
Daughters of the Republic of Texas
Library at the Alamo, San Antonio

In this fanciful depiction of an apocryphal Alamo incident, William Travis warns his men that they can expect no aid in defending the fortress. Drawing a line with his saber, he asks those who would join him to step across—presumably to a certain, albeit glorious, death. In actuality, Travis dispatched several appeals for aid during the seige of the Alamo, all in vain except for one sent to the little Texas town of Gonzales, which drew a twenty-five-man militia reinforcement.

wanted to raise an army of his own—now.

But the one place he did not wish to fight was the Alamo. Even repaired and modified with firing platforms, it was a poor excuse for a fortress. Far better for the outnumbered Texans to fight a guerrilla war against Santa Anna out in the open, in the countryside familiar to the volunteers. Houston dispatched Jim Bowie to Colonel James C. Neill, in command at San Antonio, with orders to remove the Alamo's guns, blow up the "fortress," and abandon it utterly.

Bowie reached San Antonio but did not enforce Houston's orders. Quite the contrary, he, Neill, and Jameson decided that the Alamo was *the* major obstacle to any Mexican advance and resolved never to "be driven from the post of honor" in defending it.

By February 1836, General Santa Anna was leading two infantry brigades, one cavalry brigade, artillery, and sappers toward the Rio Grande, where they would join with a force under the command of General Joaquín Ramírez y Sesma. In the meantime, Neill and Bowie, with 134 men, were appealing for reinforcements. Fannin turned a deaf ear to these pleas, as he was still contemplating the Matamoros objective from his loosely orga-

nized camp at Goliad. Another commander did bring aid, however, in the form of 25 men. He was a twenty-six-year-old native of South Carolina who had a reputation as a ladies' man, was addicted to the romantic adventure novels of Sir Walter Scott, and was rumored to have killed his estranged wife's lover. He was none other than William B. Travis, who had started it all at Anahuac.

On February 8 another volunteer arrived, leading a dozen Tennessee sharpshooters. Davy Crockett, fifty years old, was already a western legend. As a marksman, he was known to have shot the wick off a candle at three hundred feet. As a hunter, he once killed forty-seven bears in the space of a month. He was a hero of the War of 1812. He was the hero of *Davy Crockett's Almanac,* published by a Nashville entrepreneur beginning in 1835 and continuing for two decades following Crockett's death. And he was elected three times to the Congress of the United States. Defeated in a bid for a fourth term, he cursed his faithless constituents, saying that *he* was going to Texas and *they* could go to hell.

On February 11, Neill had to leave the Alamo because of illness in his family. He turned over command to Travis, which touched off a dispute among the Alamo garrison that was a microcosm of the disorder and contentiousness characteristic of all Texas affairs. The majority of the Alamo defenders wanted to serve under Bowie, to whom Travis finally conceded command. But Bowie was critically ill with tuberculosis and typhoid-pneumonia; he was given to heavy drinking and caroused through the streets of San Antonio even as Santa Anna's main force reached the Rio Grande. By February 14, Bowie agreed to share command with Travis.

On the sixteenth, Santa Anna began a forced march up from the Rio Grande in the cold of a brutal winter. He commanded 5,400 soldiers, equipped with 21 cannon, 1,800 mules, 33 wagons, and 200 carts.

There were about 150 men defending the Alamo.

Travis had ample warning of the Mexicans' advance, but he couldn't believe that anyone would march an army through the barren country south of San Antonio in the dead of winter; surely, Santa Anna would wait until spring, and by that time Texas and the world would have answered Travis's repeated pleas for aid. But, so far, Fannin, still encamped at Goliad, a mere ninety-five miles away, failed to respond.

The attack came not in spring, but on February 25, when the van of Santa Anna's army entered San Antonio. Some twenty-five noncombatants, mostly women and children, took refuge in the Alamo, and the siege began as a red flag was raised from a church steeple. It signified Santa Anna's intention to show no mercy, to take no prisoners. Travis let fly a volley from an eighteen-pounder.

But his co-commander was not *all* defiance. Hearing a cavalry bugle, he took it as a signal that the Mexicans wished to parley. Bowie sent a messenger to Santa Anna offering surrender on condition that the defenders be granted what the Texans had allowed General Cós and his men: freedom to return to their homes unharmed.

Santa Anna demanded unconditional surrender. Bowie, for his part, became increasingly ill and was confined to his cot, unable to stand. Travis, during a lull after the first twenty-four hours of bombardment, wrote a dispatch "To the People of Texas & all Americans in the world," appealing again for reinforcements and promising "Victory or Death." The letter secured little relief for the Alamo's defenders. Fannin at last mustered his 320 men for a march to the beleaguered fortress. They left on the 26th, proceeding a short distance before their supply wagon broke. Its team of oxen got loose and had to be gathered. Fully a day was lost and, with it, momentum. Fannin reconsidered, and he returned to Goliad. The only reinforcements that finally materialized was a band of twenty-five men who were the militia of the town of Gonzales.

After a week of unrelenting Mexican bombardment, not a single Texan had been killed, while Texas grapeshot and sharpshooters took their toll on Santa Anna's troops—though his army was augmented daily by the arrival of additional units. Within the walls of the Alamo, the defenders busied themselves with the endless task of shoring up walls crumbling under cannon fire. Jim Bowie had his cot carried about the compound and rallied his troops. It was reported that Davy Crockett fiddled to keep spirits up. On March 3, Travis got off another letter: "At least two hundred shells have fallen inside of our works without having injured a single man. . . . I look to the [Texas] colonies alone for aid; unless it arrives soon, I shall have to fight the enemy on his own terms."

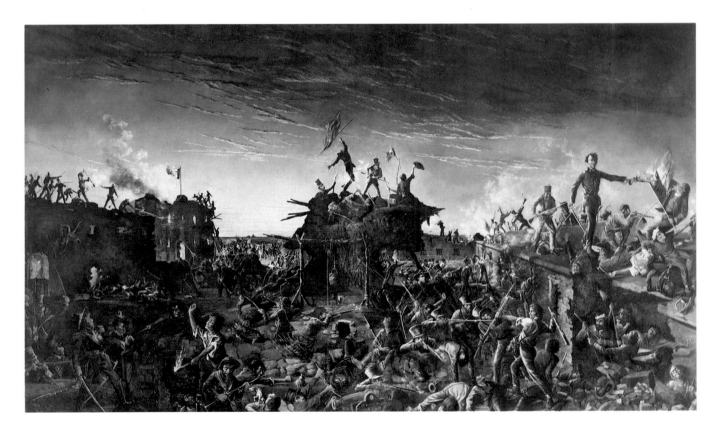

Henry McArdle (1836–1908)
Dawn at the Alamo, c. 1905
Oil on canvas, 84 × 144 in.
Archives Division, Texas State Library

This Irish-born artist was a meticulous craftsman, lavishing detailed attention on uniforms and likenesses. Each of the many figures in his battle scenes is a clearly delineated individual. Although the State of Texas hung *Dawn at the Alamo* in the legislature's senate chamber, the painting was not paid for until almost twenty years after the impoverished artist had died.

Santa Anna's forces drew ever closer. "I think we had better march out and die in the open air," Davy Crockett declared on March 5. "I don't like to be hemmed up." That same day, the eternally optimistic Travis at last faced reality. They could surrender, he told his men, attempt to escape, or die fighting. One man, Louis Rose, a mercenary, veteran of the Napoleonic Wars, took the option of escape, slipping through the Mexican lines in the dark of night.

The bombardment stopped. The Texans waited. Santa Anna deployed some four thousand of his soldiers for the final attack. They rushed the fortress just before daybreak on March 6, a Sunday.

It was a clumsy assault. The column approaching from the east was effectively pinned by Texas grapeshot. The southern column was picked apart by Crockett and his sharpshooters. The northern column failed to seize the initiative.

Travis, directing the defense from the parapet, was among the first Texans to fall, shot through the head. Still facing the Texans' withering fire, the Mexican commanders had to whip their men forward with the flats of their sabers. The carefully planned approaches from east, south, and north deteriorated in a chaos of panic, and soon the columns merged into a single advancing mass stopped by the Alamo's wall, beneath which the men huddled, close-range targets for Texas rifles. Santa Anna threw in his reserves, who fired from behind the first units, catching them in a crossfire. They were being killed by Mexican as well as Texan bullets.

But sheer numbers prevailed as, in a frenzy, Santa Anna's army began to pour over the Alamo walls. The fighting was hand to hand in the open plaza of the compound. The Texans retreated to the Long Barracks, and the light gun mounted atop that building was brought to bear on the Mexicans. From other guns, too, grapeshot—which the defenders had made by chopping up iron horseshoes—rained down on Santa Anna's troops.

The Mexican general would lose perhaps fifteen hundred men—a third of his forces—fighting fewer than two hundred. But numbers prevailed. Like the other Texans, who survived eleven days of fierce bombardment, Davy Crockett seemed invincible, as a Mexican sergeant, Felix Nuñez, recalled: "Of the many soldiers who took deliberate aim and fired, not one ever hit him. On the contrary, he never missed a shot. He killed at least eight of our men, besides wounding several others." But, like the rest, Davy Crockett died. A lieutenant "sprang at him and dealt him a deadly blow with his sword, just above the right eye, which felled him to the ground, and in an instant he was pierced by not less than 20 bayonets."

The survivors made a desperate last stand in the Long Barracks, but were dispatched by musket fire and bayonets. Jim Bowie, bedridden, helpless, was "tossed . . . on their bayonets until his blood covered their clothes and dyed them red." A few defenders in the church remained; they were soon killed, including Almeron Dickerson, but not before he had taken leave of his wife, Susannah, who was hiding with her baby in a room of the church: "Great God, Sue, the Mexicans are inside our walls! If they spare you, save my child!"

The massacre had taken ninety minutes, but Santa Anna did indeed spare Susannah Dickerson, charging her with the task of telling all of Texas what had happened at the Alamo and warning that the same would befall any others who crossed Santa Anna. Then the general commanded that the bodies of the defenders—183 in all—be arranged on a pyre of branches and wood and set ablaze. His own dead he buried as quickly as possible, and when the cemetery filled up, he dumped the remainder in the river.

In his butchery at the Alamo and in his sending Susannah Dickerson to tell of it in detail, Santa Anna made the error all tyrants sooner or later make. He gave his enemies martyrs. The cry went up all over Texas—and beyond: Remember the Alamo! In winning that abandoned and tumbled-down Franciscan mission, Santa Anna lost Texas.

But not before the Mexican general had committed an additional act of barbarity. A force of 1,400 under General José Urrea surrounded the ever-vacillating Colonel James Fannin and his force (now about 400 men) on an open plain some six miles outside Goliad. Fannin adopted the tactic of the Santa Fe caravans and pulled his wagons into a hollow rectangle, from behind which his men stood off the Mexicans for two days, killing 250, losing 7 killed and 60 wounded—Fannin among the latter. On March 20, they surrendered on condition that they be sent "on parole" to the United States. General Urrea agreed and treated his captives well, until orders came from Santa Anna: execute them all.

On Palm Sunday, March 27, the prisoners were marched out of Goliad and told that they were to be sent to New Orleans. Near the San Antonio River, the Mexican escort column wheeled about and formed a line facing the prisoners. A command was shouted to kneel, and the shooting began. More than three hundred unarmed Texans died.

Even as the Alamo was under siege, a convention at San Felipe de Austin had finally resolved to declare independence, adopting a declaration on March 3. The ensuing events of that month produced a mixture of panic and a burning passion to resist the Mexican advance. Sam Houston understood how to prevail during the panic and how to use the heat of passion to forge an army. Like George Washington, Houston knew the value of strategic retreat, playing for time in order to build strength and train an effective fighting force. It was a hard strategy to sustain as Texas settlers—men, women, and children—fled before the advancing Mexicans, and the provisional government fled with them.

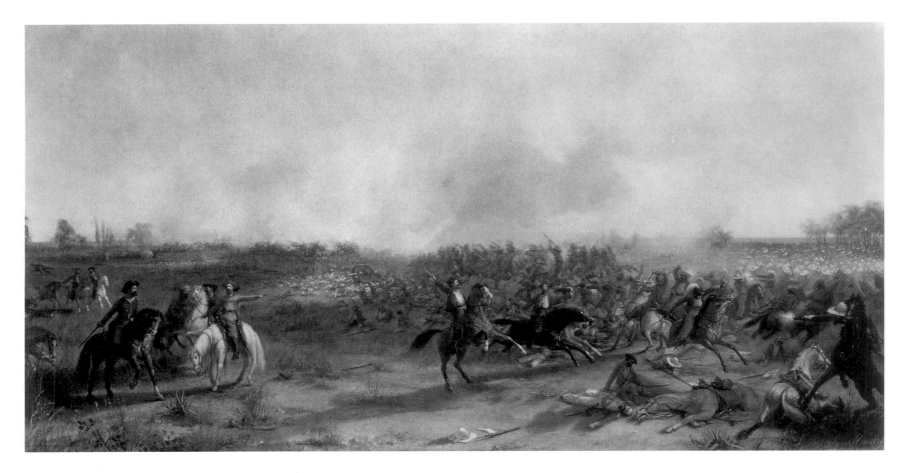

Louis Mathieu Didier Guillaume (1816–1892)
Battle of San Jacinto, c. 1892
Oil on canvas, 24 ¼ × 48 in.
Courtesty of The R. W. Norton Art Gallery, Shreveport, Louisiana

A Frenchman by birth, Guillaume became a polite portraitist in Richmond, Virginia, and witnessed the surrender of Robert E. Lee at Appomatox. He was not present at the Battle of San Jacinto, but painted it years after the event, in 1892, while he was living in Washington, D.C. It was his last work.

It was not until April 20, with an army grown to some 800 now well-disciplined men, that Houston felt ready to turn and make a stand. Santa Anna was camped with about 700 men on an open prairie west of the San Jacinto River just off Galveston Bay. Houston took up a position and set the next day for his attack. At the last minute, Santa Anna was joined by reinforcements that swelled his ranks to 1,250.

It did not matter. Houston moved his 800 men forward in three columns just as the Mexicans were settling down for their afternoon siesta. As usual, Houston combined infectious zeal with nerveless restraint. "Victory is certain," he exhorted. "Trust in God and fear not!" And as his columns advanced, he was equally explicit: "Hold your fire! God damn you, hold your fire!" It was not until his front lines were a mere sixty yards from the Mexicans that Houston finally gave the order to start shooting and then to charge. "Remember the Alamo!" was the battle cry.

And the battle ended in a quarter of an hour. Six hundred thirty Mexican soldiers were dead; 730 were prisoners. The Texans counted 9 killed and 34 wounded, including Sam Houston, who had had two horses shot from under him and who had taken a musket ball in his right leg.

Victory won, the Texans lost all discipline, and many went about the field bayoneting the wounded. Houston realized that madmen made for a vulnerable army. He also knew that Santa Anna himself had escaped, and that some twenty-five hundred Mexican troops were waiting only forty-five miles away. The battle won, all could yet be lost. But, by twilight, the madness had subsided, and the thirst for blood was quenched. Houston dispatched search parties to find Santa Anna, who was located near Buffalo Bayou. He had gotten lost trying to find the road to Fort Bend and the fresh Mexican troops quartered there. He had disguised himself with an old cotton jacket he had found, but had neglected to remove his linen shirt and jeweled studs. By these, the search party recognized him as an officer; then one of the Mexican prisoners shouted, "El Presidente!" And the search party knew just whom they had found.

He was brought to Sam Houston, who was suffering the agony of his shattered leg. Santa Anna requested his medicine box, which was brought to him. The general partook of opium and addressed Houston: "That man may consider himself born to no common destiny who has conquered the Napoleon of the West. And now it remains for him to be generous to the vanquished."

"You should have remembered that at the Alamo," said Houston.

Santa Anna replied that such were "the usages of war" when the enemy refuses surrender. To which Houston responded vehemently: "You have not the same excuse for the massacre of Colonel Fannin's command. They had capitulated on terms offered by your general. And yet after the capitulation they were all perfidiously massacred."

Santa Anna assumed he was a dead man. But Houston, as always, declined to act rashly. In exchange for his life, Houston secured from the dictator an order to remove all Mexican soldiers from Texas and an acknowledgment of Texas's independence. (Santa Anna was held prisoner for some eight months before he was returned to Mexico. He lay low in his Veracruz hacienda until his country's perpetually unsettled political situation presented a critical moment, and he returned to Mexico City, reestablished himself as dictator, and continued sporadic fighting with Texas over the next ten years. But he never attempted to retake his former province.)

Houston was elected president of the new Texas republic. The task of instituting orderly government was Herculean, especially under the burden of crushing debt brought by the war. It was imperative to gain annexation to the United States, but that was also a formidable task. Annexation would bring war with Mexico, which the United States did not want, and many of the American people were opposed to admitting into the Union another slave state. At most, Houston's agent, William H. Wharton, was able to wrest from the United States a grudging official recognition of the new republic on March 2, 1837.

However, the financial panic that gripped the United States in 1837 was a stroke of luck for Texas, which offered all newcomers who were heads of families 1,280 acres free (single men got 640 acres) as well as the right to purchase additional land at fifty cents an acre. Thousands of debt-ridden Americans accepted the haven offered by the new republic. In 1836 the population of Texas was 30,000; ten years later it stood at 146,000.

In 1838 Sam Houston's term as president ended, and the Texas constitution forbade his succeeding himself. Mirabeau B. Lamar, vice president under Houston, was elected, bringing to office expansionist policies that mirrored those of the United States. Lamar's ambition was to push the western border of Texas all the way to the Pacific. His first objective was the annexation of New Mexico, population 150,000 in 1841, which had already staged several revolts against Mexican rule. Lamar organized a trading caravan to Santa Fe, which would impress on the New Mexicans the vast economic benefits of annexation. The expedition set off from Austin on June 21, 1841, with 303 men. By September, an advance detachment of some 100 men had reached Mora, about a hundred miles from Santa Fe; the rest of the party was camped at Palo Duro. An army under New Mexico governor Manuel Armijo took both the main group and the advance group by surprise; both surrendered without firing a shot.

They were bound with rope and rawhide and marched two thousand miles to Mexico City. Many fell along the way; those who could not continue were shot; the survivors reached Mexico City in December 1841 and were thrown into prison or pressed into forced labor. Worse, the "invasion" rekindled hostilities between Texas and Mexico. Mexican soldiers attacked San Antonio twice and Corpus Christi. Sam Houston, reelected president after Lamar's term ended in 1841, launched three retaliatory campaigns. One, commanded by General Alexander Somervell, scouted the Rio Grande in November and December of 1842, but was ordered back to San Antonio when it failed to engage any of the enemy. The men, however, being Texans, refused to obey orders, elected their own officers, and crossed the Rio Grande into Mexico. They briefly occupied the town of

William H. Huddle (1847–1892)
Surrender of Santa Anna, completed 1886
Oil on canvas, 71 ½ × 114 in.
Archives Division, Texas State Library

Sam Houston, his foot painfully wounded, invites the defeated Mexican general to sit as Battle of San Jacinto hero Deaf Smith strains to hear the parley.

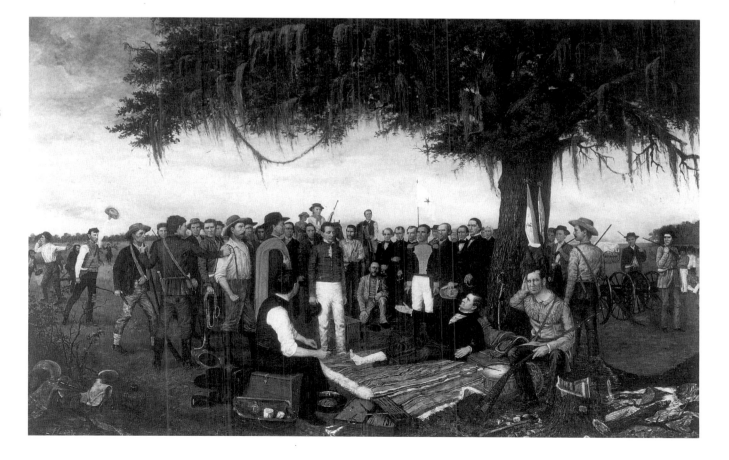

Mier, until a vastly superior Mexican force captured them and sent them marching to Mexico City. On the way, they overpowered their guards and escaped—very briefly. Recaptured, they were forced to draw beans from a mug. One in every ten beans was black, and those who drew them were executed.

Another retaliatory expedition, under Colonel Charles Warfield, failed as well, both militarily and diplomatically. A premature attack on the village of Mora resulted in a rout, and the wanton murder of a Mexican Santa Fe trader outraged sentiment in the United States, something the annexation-minded Houston wanted most to avoid. A third expedition, commanded by Major Jacob Snively, was charged with raiding Mexican Santa Fe caravans. When one appeared under strong army escort, Snively and his men surrendered and returned, much abashed, to Texas.

Far more successful were the Texas campaigns against the Cherokees and the Comanches. Lamar's policy was expulsion. In the summer of 1839, Texas militia and rangers drove the Cherokees across the border into Arkansas. At the same time, in the western borderlands, warfare against the Comanches was conducted so mercilessly that the Indians ceded land and pledged themselves to peace.

MANIFEST DESTINY

In the United States, Indian "removal" became official policy in 1830 with the passage of the Indian Removal bill. On the face of it, the new law seemed fair enough, not authorizing removal by fiat and force, but by land exchanges. In practice, however, Andrew Jackson's government was ruthless and devious. The Indians Jackson proposed to move west of the Mississippi were primarily the Choctaws, Chickasaws, Cherokees, and Creeks living in Georgia, Alabama, and Mississippi. These states passed legislation abolishing tribal government and placing Indians under state jurisdiction. When the Indians protested to the federal government that such state legislation violated treaties made with the United States, Jackson replied that he was unable to enforce these provisions on the states—even as he tried to persuade the tribes to make *new* treaties agreeing to removal to "Indian Territory" in present-day Oklahoma. Meanwhile, the states systematically violated what today would be called the civil rights of the Indians, prosecuting them under state laws but barring in court Indian testimony against white men, including testimony presented in defense of charges brought against Indians by whites. In addition, squatters and land speculators invaded Indian lands and often swindled Indians out of their property. At all times the federal government looked the other way, protesting that it lacked the power to enforce federal regulation. Jackson "answered" Indian protest by urging them to accept removal.

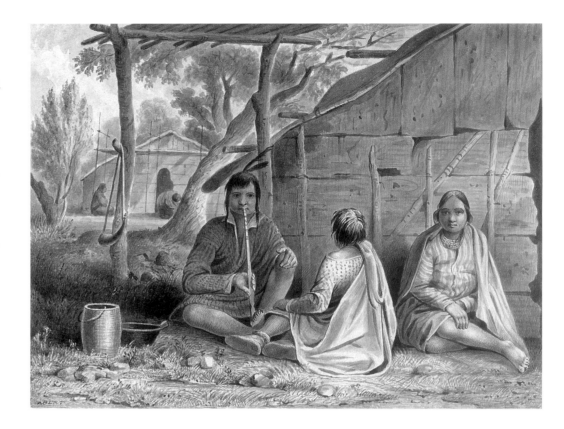

James William Abert (1820–1871)
Eastern Sioux on the Upper Missouri, c. 1845
Pen and ink, wash and graphite on paper, 8 ⅜ × 10 ½ in.
Amon Carter Museum, Fort Worth, Texas

Abert made this sketch while serving with John Charles Frémont on an expedition to South Pass. A West Point graduate, Abert illustrated various army expedition reports. After being wounded during the Civil War, he retired from the army with the rank of colonel and became professor of mathematics and drawing at the University of Missouri.

The Choctaws left for the West in 1831, suffering through a terrible winter and the corrupt inefficiencies that would characterize the government's handling of Indian affairs throughout the nineteenth century.

The Chickasaws assented to removal treaties in 1832 and 1834 that provided for the federal government to *sell* the lands vacated and hold the proceeds in trust for Chickasaw use. Sometimes this was actually done.

The Creeks had a longer history of removal. William MacIntosh, a tribal chief, made treaties in 1821, 1823, and 1825 that ceded to Georgia some twenty-five million acres. The overwhelming majority of Creeks, including a council of thirty-six chiefs, repudiated the MacIntosh treaties as illegal. The tribal council, acting upon Creek law, condemned MacIntosh to death; accordingly, a party of Creek soldiers led by Menewa shot him and his son-in-law, and Menewa went to Washington to conclude a new treaty securing the Creeks in the territory that remained to them. Georgia's governor, George Troup, cousin of William MacIntosh, was bent on driving the Creeks out of the state, federal treaty or no. He encouraged squatters, speculators, and bootleggers—whose concoctions had a dangerous and debilitating effect on the Indians—to move in. Appealed to, Jackson, as usual, replied that he lacked the power to enforce the provisions of the treaty and that relief could be gained by moving west of the Mississippi. After staging a brief war in 1836, the Creeks at last complied with removal, amid fraud, theft of land, and impoverishment.

The Cherokees resisted unrelenting pressure from the government of the state of Georgia, including seizure of property and grossly unjust treatment in state and local courts. The tribal council finally laid their case before the United States Supreme Court. Chief Justice John Marshall found in favor of the Cherokees, declaring Georgia's persecution of the Indians unconstitutional. President Jackson refused to enforce the decision of the court and, worse, used the provisions of a corrupt treaty to remove the Cherokees from Georgia by force. Except for a handful who hid in the mountains, they were penned into concentration camps during a long, hot summer. Then, during the fall and winter of 1838–39, they were marched westward along what came to be called the Trail of Tears. Fifteen thousand followed that twelve-hundred-mile trail, always cold, always short of food and other supplies. Four thousand died along the way.

Finally, there were the Seminoles of Florida. Efforts at removal began in 1835 and touched off a war that dragged on until 1842 at a cost of fifteen hundred soldiers and some twenty million dollars. Seminole resistance was so fierce that women were known to kill their own children in order to free themselves to fight beside their men. The army resorted to repeated violations of truce to effect capture of prisoners, including the famed chief Osceola. He set up a conference—requested by the army—under the white flag of truce, only to be captured and sent to prison, where he died within three months. Neither side won this long guerrilla war fought in the Ev-

erglades When peace finally came, most of the Seminoles were persuaded to seek new homes in the Indian Territory, but many remained in Florida.

In all, some fifty thousand southeastern Indians were "removed."

In the Northeast, removal was for the most part less dramatic. Most tribes accepted the policy with little resistance. Two exceptions were the Sauk and Fox Indians, who fought the Black Hawk War—named for the chief who led them—in 1832. The year before, white settlers encroached on Indian land near present-day Rock Island, Illinois. Black Hawk moved his band to the west bank of the Mississippi, but then, on April 5, 1832, he recrossed the river to unite with his Winnebago allies led by White Cloud. General Henry Atkinson pursued Black Hawk's band, and the chief attempted to surrender. But when one of his truce bearers was killed, Black Hawk went to war, winning his first battle on May 14 and temporarily demoralizing the white settlers. On August 2, however, a battle fought at the mouth of the Bad Axe River in Wisconsin proved decisive. Perhaps as many as six hundred Indians were killed in a frenzy of clubbing, stabbing, and shooting. And so the Sauks and Fox accepted their fate.

It takes little moral sensitivity today to decry the enormity of a policy that sent so many traveling so many

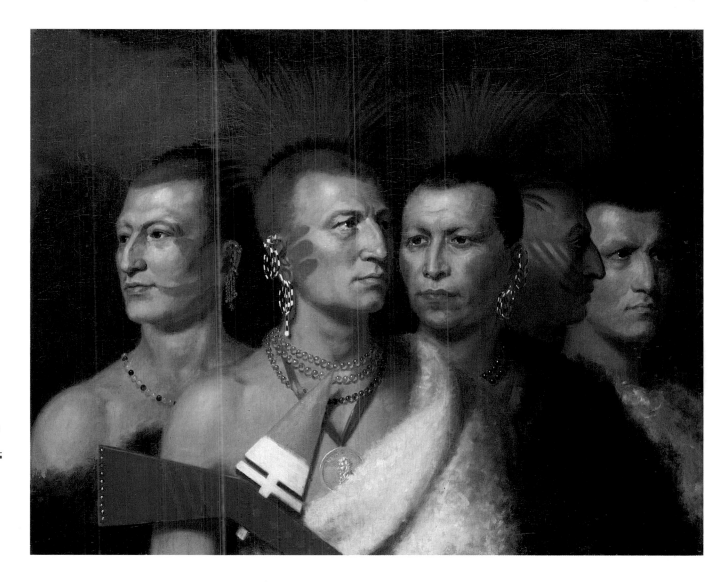

Charles Bird King (1785–1862)
Young Omawhaw, War Eagle, Little Missouri, and Pawnees, 1821
Oil on canvas, 36 ⅛ × 28 in.
National Museum of American Art, Smithsonian Institution; Gift of Miss Helen Barlow

These distinguished chiefs were painted by the artist during their visit to Washington, D.C. Like so many others, they and their people were then being "removed" from eastern homelands to western reservations.

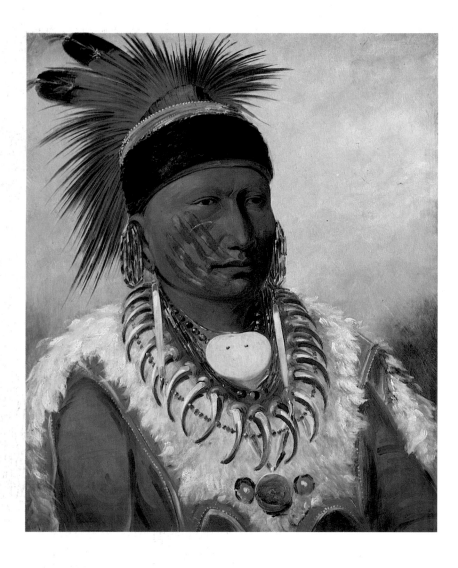

George Catlin (1796–1872)
The White Cloud, Head Chief of the Iowas, c. 1845
Oil on canvas, 27 ¾ × 22 ¾ in.
National Gallery of Art, Washington, D.C.; Paul Mellon Collection

This Iowa chief agreed to a major land cession when he surrendered claims to northern Missouri.

Charles Bird King (1785–1862)
Makataimeshekiakiah (Black Hawk), Sac, 1833
Oil on panel, 29 × 19 ¾ in.
The Warner Collection of Gulf States Paper Corporation, Tuscaloosa, Alabama

This Sauk (or Sac) leader allied his people with British forces during the War of 1812 and unsuccessfully resisted "removal" west of the Mississippi in 1832. King painted him when the chief visited the "Great White Father" in Washington, D.C.

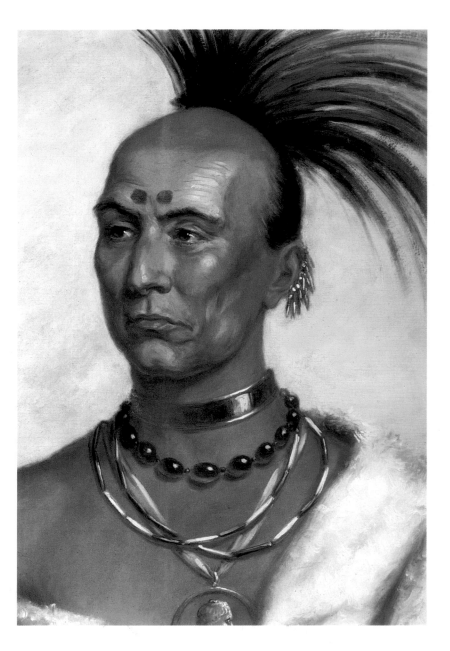

trails of tears. Worse, the Indians sent west would hardly find peace there. Disputes with Plains Indians indigenous to the region often arose, and soon the tide of white immigration would encroach even on the lands to which the eastern Indians had been exiled. Yet these horrors and privations seemed to many Americans at the time incidental to a force as impersonal and unstoppable as fate. In 1845 the editor of the New York *Morning News,* John L. O'Sullivan, gave it a name. "It is our manifest destiny," he wrote, "to overspread and to possess the whole of the continent which Providence has given us for the development of the great experiment of liberty and federated self-government entrusted to us." Even without a label, the westward movement would have pulsed onward, heedless as any natural process. As "manifest destiny," that force, movement, and process took on the moral trappings of divine ordination, with which Indians and the government of Mexico, or that of any other nation, were powerless to interfere.

Despite the isolationist policies of Mexican governors, California had been opened to American immigration by Joseph Walker, who blazed the California fork of the Overland Trail in 1833. Oregon, dominated by the British Hudson's Bay Company, had been intruded upon by Nathaniel Wyeth, first in 1832 and then in 1834. With him on the second expedition were Jason and Daniel

CHARLES BIRD KING

BORN 1785, NEWPORT, RHODE ISLAND
DIED 1862, WASHINGTON, D.C.

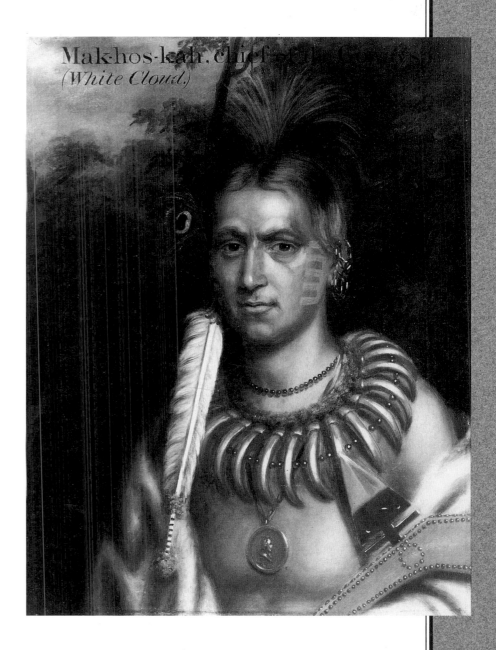

Although his Indian portraits are among the finest and most significant works in the genre, King was not really a western artist. He executed the Indian paintings in Washington, D.C., initially at the behest of Thomas L. McKenney, head of the Bureau of Indian Affairs, who commissioned likenesses of eight chiefs visiting the president. The artist went on to paint about ninety more, all depicting members of Indian delegations to the capital.

King's earliest training came from a local Newport artist, Samuel King (no relation), followed by study with Edward Savage in New York and the great early American expatriate artist Benjamin West in London. Returning to the United States in 1812, King began painting portraits first in Philadelphia and then in Washington, where he earned a reputation as a pleasant, if mediocre, society portraitist. His breakthrough as an artist came with the Indian portrait commissions in 1820.

Indian bureau chief McKenney saw King's work as the core of a National Indian Portrait Gallery, a collection subsequently transferred to the Smithsonian Institution. Three years after the artist's death, a fire at the Smithsonian destroyed virtually all of King's work included in the McKenney project. Fortunately, King had made some copies for his own collection, and many of the lost portraits had been reproduced as lithographs in McKenney and James Hall's *History of the Indian Tribes of North America* (1837).

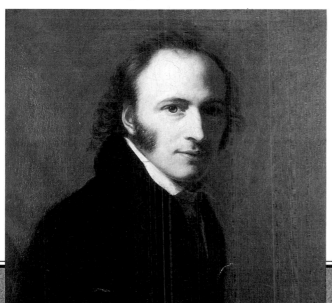

Charles Bird King, *Self-Portrait*, 1825.
Oil on canvas, 30 × 25 in.
Redwood Library and Athenaeum,
Newport, Rhode Island

Charles Bird King (1785–1862)
Mak-Hos-Hah, Chief of the Gowyas,
1824
Oil on panel, 17 × 14 in.
Gilcrease Museum, Tulsa, Oklahoma

A few days before he sat for this portrait, Mak-Hos-Hah—White Cloud—quarreled with one of his seven wives. The chief was staying with her at a Washington, D.C., hotel, and when the Indian agent in the next room heard the ruckus, he barged in. White Cloud made a hasty exit through a window. Unfortunately, the room was on a second floor, and the chief broke his arm in the fall.

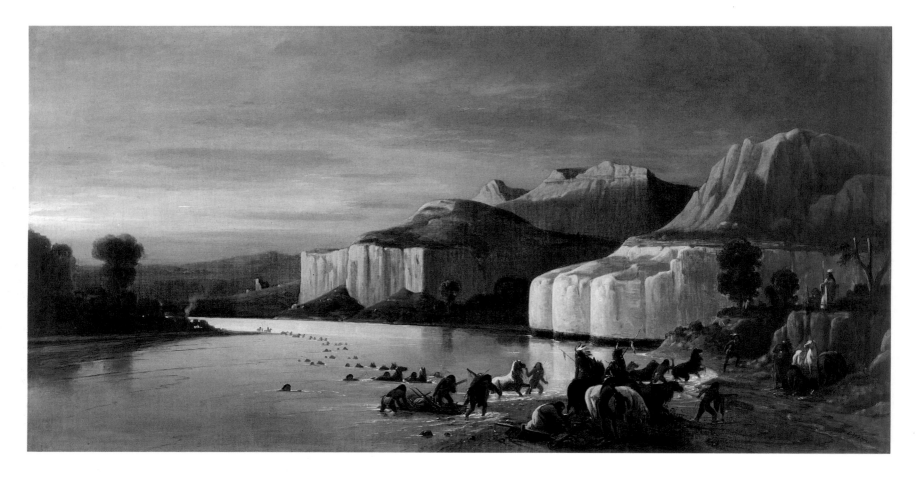

Charles Wimar (1828–1862)
Indian Crossing the Upper Missouri,
(c. 1859–60)
Oil on canvas, 24 ¼ × 48 ⅛ in.
Amon Carter Museum, Fort Worth,
Texas

Broad and shallow, the Missouri was
easy enough to ford in many places,
but difficult to navigate.

Lee, Methodist ministers from Massachusetts. Their intention was to found a mission; but their arrival was actually the first step toward American annexation of the territory.

The story really begins with the Hudson's Bay Company, which brought Iroquois Indians—employed as trappers—across the Rockies to Columbia River country shortly before the War of 1812. The Iroquois, who had been converted to Catholicism in Canada, introduced some aspects of the religion to the Nez Percés and Flatheads, and in particular talked up the "black robes," who had great and powerful wisdom to impart—a knowledge, the implication ran, that would make an Indian as powerful as a white man. But it was not until 1831 that the Nez Percés and Flatheads sent a party east to seek missionaries. They reached St. Louis, where they met with William Clark, superintendent of Indian affairs. With difficulty, he deciphered their talk of "black robes" and sent the delegation to a group of St. Louis Catholics, who, as it turned out, had neither the authority nor the resources to organize a missionary venture. Meanwhile, as so often happened when Indians ventured into white settlements, two of the delegates fell ill and died—though not before having been baptized. The other two delegates set off for home aboard the steamboat *Yellowstone*—an embodiment of powerful white magic that must have dejected them the more for their having failed to secure "black robes." But even worse was to come: one of the delegates died on board the *Yellowstone* and the other was ambushed and killed by Blackfeet as he was making his way through the mountains.

Prospects for an Oregon mission were dim, if they existed at all, when William Walker, a chief of the northern Ohio Wyandots, visited St. Louis. Born of a white father, who had been adopted into the Wyandot tribe, and a mother who was one-quarter Indian, Walker had been educated at the Methodist Kenyon College academy and even served Michigan's territorial governor as private secretary. Shortly after the Nez Percé–Flathead delegation had left St. Louis, Walker arrived in that city to discuss with Superintendent of Indian Affairs William Clark suitable tracts of Indian Territory on which his tribe—like the other eastern tribes, subject to "removal"—might settle. He had little success on this head (the Wyandots finally moved west, though not until 1842), but from Clark he did learn of the recent delegation in search of missionaries. Walker dashed off a letter to Methodist churchmen in Ohio, a letter zealous to the point of fabrication, Walker reporting that he had interviewed the Nez Percé and Flathead representatives himself. He even invented dialogue to prove it. The letter was published in the March 1833 number of the *Christian Advocate and Journal,* creating a sensation. Here were wretched savages yearning for the light of religion! Walker, who had never seen a Flathead, even made reference to what he imagined was the tribe's characteristic deformity. Though, in fact, the tribe did not flatten their heads, anymore than the Nez Percés pierced their noses, Walker's inclusion of this detail served to make the Indians' plight seem that much more poignant. The Wyandot's letter launched a generation of Oregon missionaries.

Jason Lee and his nephew Daniel were the first.

They set out with Nathaniel Wyeth in 1834, along with three lay assistants. But when they reached Flatheads and Nez Percés by the hundreds at Ham's Fork, Jason Lee decided not to accompany them back to their settlements. He chose instead, quite contrary to the mandate of his mission, to continue with Wyeth to Fort Vancouver.

Headquarters of the Hudson's Bay Company, Fort Vancouver was presided over by Dr. John McLoughlin, whose role had become a particularly delicate one since 1818, when the United States and Great Britain agreed to a convention allowing both nations free movement in the Northwest While honoring this agreement, McLoughlin had also to maintain the Hudson Bay Company's dominance of the northwest fur trade, thereby also serving the interests of Great Britain, which sought to delay American access to the Pacific as long as possible. So when Jason Lee sought McLoughlin's advice on where to establish a mission, McLoughlin, who wanted to keep the

newcomers as far as possible from Fort Vancouver, steered Lee to the Willamette Valley, which was at a remove from Hudson's Bay Company trapping grounds. However, the valley was also far more fertile and inviting than the more arid region of the Flatheads and Nez Percés. McLoughlin failed to realize that he had recommended more than a mission site. He had inadvertently shown Jason Lee where to plant an American colony.

At about this time, Hall Kelley, the Boston schoolmaster whose propagandizing had sent Nathaniel Wyeth off to Oregon in the first place, decided at last to see the country for himself. After a long and circuitous trek southwestward, he reached San Diego, where he met Ewing Young and converted him to the Oregon cause. Young gathered sixteen fellow mountain men and a good stock of horses and mules (intended for sale to what Kelley described as a flourishing American colony in Oregon) and accompanied Kelley up the coast. But the governor of California, resentful of yet more American intrusions,

George Catlin (1796–1872)
St. Louis from the River Below,
1832–33
Oil on canvas, 19 ⅜ × 26 ⅞ in.
National Museum of American Art,
Smithsonian Institution; Gift of Mrs.
Joseph Harrison, Jr.

A grand view of the steamboat
Yellowstone—a vessel famous
throughout the West.

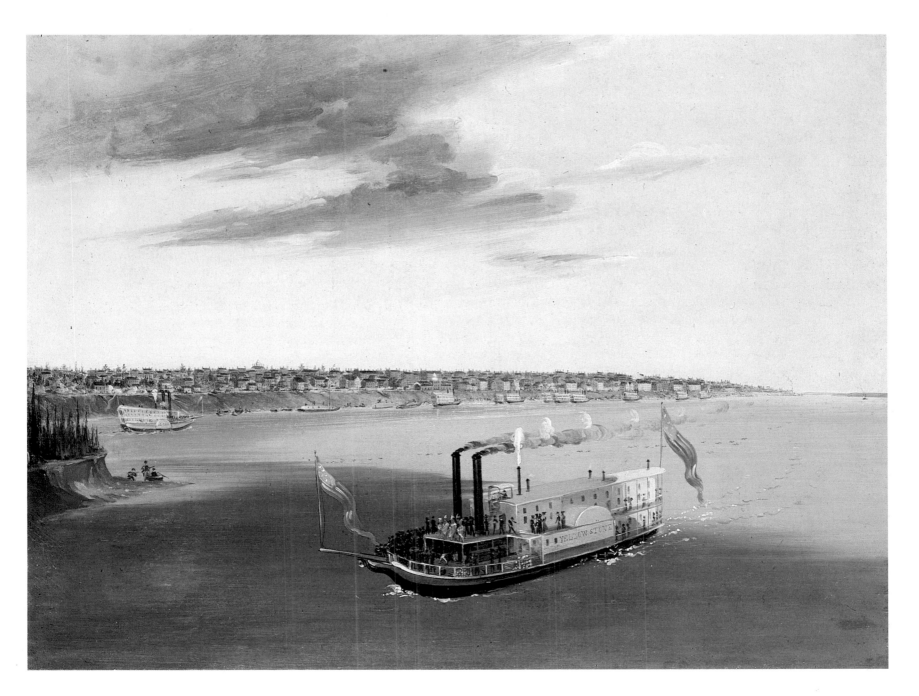

G E O R G E   C A T L I N

—

BORN 1796, WILKES BARRE, PENNSYLVANIA

DIED 1872, JERSEY CITY, NEW JERSEY

—

Destined to be regarded as the first great visual chronicler of the western American Indians, Catlin grew up in a household that was steeped in Indian legend and lore. The boy's mother had been captured by Indians when she was only eight years old, and the family hosted numerous frontier guests who must have shared many stories. Young Catlin often busied himself collecting Indian relics in the vicinity of Wilkes Barre.

Catlin studied law in Litchfield, Connecticut, and practiced in Luzerene, Pennsylvania, until 1823. All along, however, he had been teaching himself the fundamentals of portraiture and, in 1823, left Luzerene for Philadelphia to make a living as a painter. Likely, Catlin could have done quite nicely depicting New York and Washington politicians—his large historical canvas *Constitutional Convention,* completed in 1829, contains no fewer than 115 figures. But the year after he moved to Philadelphia, Catlin encountered "a delegation of dignified Indians from the wilds of the West, tinted and tassled off exactly for the painter's palette," who were visiting Charles Willson Peale's celebrated museum of natural history.

Catlin knew immediately that he had found his great subject—or, rather, it had found him—and he declared his determination to rescue "from oblivion the looks and customs of the vanishing races of native man in America."

In 1830, he began to paint the tribes of the lower Missouri, beginning in the vicinity of St. Louis. The next year, he traveled up the Platte River, and then, in 1832, up the Missouri to Fort Union, as a passenger on the *Yellowstone,* which was making its maiden voyage. In 1834, he crossed the prairies west of Leavenworth, Kansas, to accompany a detachment of dragoons out of Fort Gibson, Indian Territory, on an expedition into the land of the Pawnees and Comanches. Later, he traveled extensively in Wisconsin and Minnesota territory.

Between 1834 and 1836, Catlin painted Indians in the summer and returned east in the fall and winter in order to earn the funds necessary to finance his Indian expeditions. During 1829–38, he executed some six hundred Indian portraits and other sketches depicting their customs and mode of life. The artist attempted to sell his vast work to Congress, but was turned down. He exhibited his paintings widely in the United States as well as

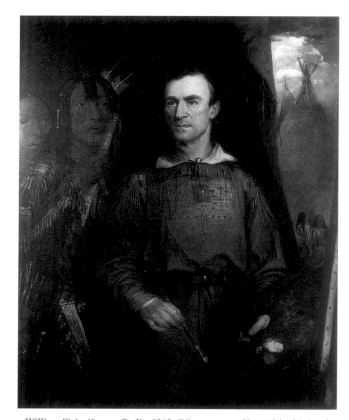

William Fisk, *George Catlin,* 1849. Oil on canvas, 50 × 40 in. National Portrait Gallery, Smithsonian Institution.

Europe during 1837–52, but fell increasingly into debt. Although his precarious finances compelled him to part with much of the collection, he did publish a number of his paintings in his *Letters and Notes on the Manners, Customs, and Conditions of the North American Indians* (1841) and, much more spectacularly, in the *North American Indian Portfolio* (English edition, 1844; American, 1845).

Toward the end of his life, Catlin copied many of his earlier works, adding some new Indian portraits created during trips to South America. Despite his dedication, industry, and achievement, the artist died a financial failure. It was for later generations fully to appreciate all he had accomplished.

wrote to John McLoughlin, warning of the party's approach and claiming that Young's horses and mules were stolen. As a result of the letter, Kelley and Young did not get anything like the hospitality McLoughlin had extended to Jason Lee. Moreover, Young quarreled bitterly with the colonists of Lee's settlement. (Nevertheless, he and his men joined the community and, as skilled frontiersmen, were valuable to it. By his trek up from California, Young had also established what was to become the principal avenue of American migration from that region to Oregon.) Kelley, impatient with the quarrelsome circumstances prevailing in Oregon country, headed home by sea and vented his frustration in charges that the British were obviously using the Hudson's Bay Company to foil American interests in Oregon.

One who took these charges most seriously was President Andrew Jackson. He sent Lieutenant William Slacum, U.S.N., to Oregon on a tour of inspection. Slacum assured the American colonists that the United States intended to press its claims on the Columbia country—discovered by the American captain Robert Gray, after all, and explored by Lewis and Clark as well as the Astorians—and he also successfully mediated disputes among them, so that, in the lieutenant's wake, the colony actually did begin to prosper. Young drove 630 head of cattle from California to Oregon, and another Methodist mission—the "First Reinforcement"—arrived, which in-

cluded women who would marry into the colony. Most important of all, Slacum's report to the president stirred in Congress and the nation at large a growing passion for the West.

Like most passions, the craving after western expansion was made more urgent by the thought that others craved the same object. In the case of Oregon, both Great Britain and the United States asserted claims. The territory was bounded on the south by the forty-second parallel and on the north by a line of fifty-four degrees, forty minutes. The British were actually willing to settle on a boundary that followed the Columbia River to the sea, thereby reserving to itself only that territory north of the Columbia, where the Hudson's Bay Company was profitably dominant. But the platform of the Democrats' presidential candidate of 1844, James K. Polk, was uncompromisingly expansionist. "All of Oregon or None" was the party's battle cry, and "Fifty-four Forty or Fight!"

While Polk's 1845 inaugural address struck a belligerant note on the Oregon question—"Our title to the country . . . is 'clear and unquestionable,' and already are our people preparing to perfect that title by occupying it with their wives and children"—he actually was inclined to compromise on a northern boundary at the forty-ninth parallel. When the British rejected this proposed boundary, Polk asked Congress for authority to

Albert Bierstadt (1830–1902)
*A Storm in the Rocky Mountains—
Mount Rosalie*, 1866
Oil on canvas, 83 × 142 ½ in.
The Brooklyn Museum

It is on account of such canvases that the work of this Düsseldorf-trained artist is often described as "Wagnerian."

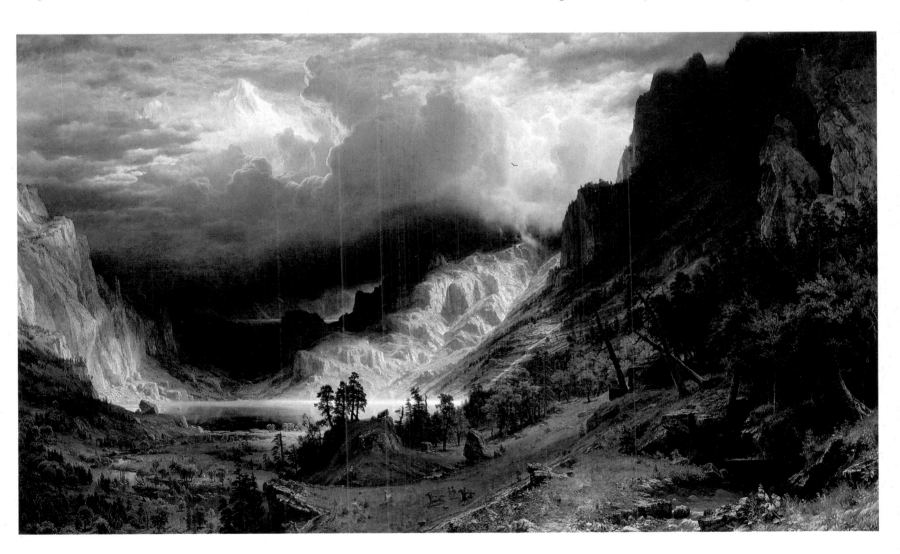

abrogate the treaty of joint occupation. Recognizing this as a prelude to war, the British offered to negotiate. This time, it was Polk who declined.

It was then that Dr. John McLoughlin and the Hudson's Bay Company intervened. By 1845 the American population of Oregon numbered about five thousand while fewer than a thousand British subjects lived in the area. Beginning with Jason Lee, McLoughlin had engineered the influx of American settlers such that they occupied the Willamette Valley, well south of Fort Vancouver. But now McLoughlin recognized that, united in the cause of nationalism, the five thousand Americans posed a serious threat to the fort and to the company. Moreover, the spread of settlement had driven fur animals northward. On McLoughlin's advice, the Hudson's Bay Company informed Sir Robert Peel, prime minister of Great Britain, that it had no objection to a boundary at the forty-ninth parallel. On June 15, 1846, that boundary was formally agreed upon by the two nations, and a vast tract of the Pacific Northwest was added to the territory of the United States.

About the time that the Oregon question was being settled, the matter of annexing Texas was also becoming more urgent, as both France and England worked to block U.S. expansion in that quarter. Both nations saw an independent Texas as a profitable market for export goods. England also envisioned Texas as a potential ally against the United States, should some future conflict develop. Although the French foreign minister in Washington was instructed to do all he could to oppose annexation, he could, in fact, do very little. If anything, rumors of his government's opposition merely served to heighten the expansionists' fervor. The British foreign secretary, Lord Aberdeen, proposed an alliance of Britain, France, Mexico, and Texas to guarantee the independence of Texas (Mexico would benefit by the allies' promise to protect its boundaries "forever"). France immediately demurred, not wishing to fight a war to defend the independence of a country so remote. At this, Lord Aberdeen retreated, although he did get Mexico to recognize its former territory's independence, a gesture he thought might somehow discourage annexation.

But the retreat was too late. News of an impending Anglo-French alliance against the the United States prompted outgoing President John Tyler to urge Congress to adopt an annexation resolution. Three days before the expiration of his term, Tyler signed the resolution. On June 16, 1845, the Congress of the Republic of Texas accepted, and President Polk admitted Texas to the Union on December 29.

England and France seemed also to have designs on California, held so feebly by Mexico that it looked to be ripe and ready to fall into the hands of whoever was there to catch it. In 1839, the Mexican Congress and a swarm of the nation's British creditors agreed on a plan to settle half the debt by land grants of some 125 million California acres. The scheme failed to go forward, but in that same year a British official posted in Mexico published a widely read history and promotional tract depicting California as an ideal place for "receiving and cherishing the superfluous population of Great Britain." Two years later, Sir Richard Pakenham, England's minister in Mexico City, went so far as to urge the planting of a British colony in California. Private colonization schemes were also proposed, one by an Englishman and another by an Irish priest. The French presence in California consisted of a diplomatic agent, Duflot de Mofras, who was stationed there after some Frenchmen had been killed during Mexican revolutionary activity in 1840. Mofras openly urged the French government to take steps to acquire the country.

Once again, in the face of perceived interest from abroad, the president was prompted to action. James

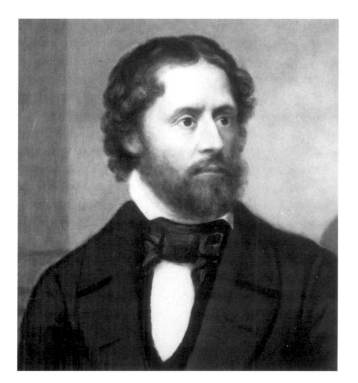

Bass Otis (1784–1861)
John Charles Frémont, 1856
Oil on canvas, 48 ¼ × 42 ½ in.
The University of Michigan Museum of Art; Bequest of Henry C. Lewis

Intrepid but inept, Frémont was an important California explorer and brash participant in the Bear Flag Rebellion. His later career as a Civil War commander was brief and disastrous.

Polk is often depicted as a war-mongering expansionist. Expansionist he was, and a war he would finally fight. But when he wanted California, he was willing to make a cash offer first: forty million dollars. He sent John Slidell to Mexico City to negotiate the purchase, but Mexican President Herrera refused to see him. Thereupon Polk commissioned the U.S. consul at Monterey, Thomas O. Larkin, to organize—albeit quietly—California's small but powerful American community into a separatist movement sympathetic to annexation. Larkin might have succeeded in this had Polk given him sufficient time, but the president had heard rumors that the English vice-consul in San Francisco was successfully wooing Southern California's governor, Pío Pico, over to the notion of a British protectorate. Polk became impatient.

In the meantime, John Charles Frémont, intrepid

western explorer surveying potential transcontinental railroad routes for the U.S. Bureau of Topographical Engineers, was camped with sixty armed men near the fort John A. Sutter had built in Northern California. Their presence sufficiently disturbed José Castro, governor of Northern California, that he ordered them to leave California. Frémont responded by moving his men to a hilltop, Hawk's Peak, and raising the Stars and Stripes. Before Castro could dispatch a military force to counter this act of defiance, Thomas Larkin intervened and defused the situation. Frémont and his band retired to the lower Sacramento Valley and then started for Oregon.

En route they were met by a messenger, Lieutenant Archibald Gillespie, who brought letters from Frémont's father-in-law, Missouri senator Thomas Hart Benton, as well as news that war between the United States and Mexico was imminent, that the U.S. warship *Portsmouth* was anchored in San Francisco Bay, that the rest of the Pacific fleet was anchored off Mazatlán, primed for attack, and that U.S. and Mexican troops faced each other across the Texas border. According to Frémont's later account, Gillespie delivered one additional item: secret orders from James K. Polk authorizing him to take action to bring about rebellion in California.

Most historians do not believe Frémont. He turned back to California, they say, on his own, and on his own he assumed command of the Bear Flag Revolt.

Like so much that happened in the West, the revolt itself was enacted by a few men and on a small scale, but its consequences were far-reaching. Frémont set up his camp close to the American settlements near Sutter's Fort. Many of the settlers, fired up by rumors of impending Mexican attack, gathered at the camp for protection and to formulate a plan of action.

Settlers were not the only Anglos attracted to Frémont's camp. A motley group of hunters, trappers, and ship-jumping sailors, all under the loose leadership of one Ezekiel Merritt, came to Frémont with rumors that a herd of horses was being driven to the Mexican militia for use in a campaign against the settlers. With Frémont's blessing, Merritt and his crew intercepted the horses and diverted them to the Anglo camp. Having committed this act, Merritt anticipated Mexican reprisals and therefore determined to continue the offensive. In company with another Anglo-Californian leader, William B. Ide, Merritt took thirty followers to Sonoma on June 14, 1846, intent on capturing this, the chief settlement in the area. The party surrounded the home of Mariano G. Vallejo, a retired Mexican army colonel and the town's leading citizen, and informed him that he was a prisoner of war. The colonel was, in fact, a staunch supporter of annexation to the United States, and his reaction to "capture" was to invite three of Merritt's party inside to negotiate "surrender" terms while the remainder of the band was provided with breakfast in the form of a freshly killed bull.

When the three negotiators failed after some time to emerge from the house, another man was sent in. He, too, disappeared. At that point, Ide ventured inside himself—and found the original three negotiators snoring in a drunken stupor while the fourth struggled with consciousness and the unfinished instrument of surrender.

Yet the die was cast. Ide completed the surrender document, which Vallejo signed, after which he was sent to Fort Sutter, the rebellion's first prisoner. Twenty-five men remained in Sonoma as a garrison, Ide's followers named him president of the California Republic, and a flag emblazoned with the image of a grizzly bear was raised over the town plaza on June 15.

On June 24, in an engagement known as the Battle of Olompali, Ide drove off the small force Governor Castro had mounted against the Bear Flaggers. Two American lives were lost. Meanwhile, by receiving Vallejo as a prisoner, Frémont had dropped any pretense to neutrality in the California Rebellion. On June 25 he marched his small force into Sonoma, high-handedly and summarily took over command from Ide, and set out with 134 men to avenge the two deaths suffered at Olompali. Three Mexicans encountered along Frémont's march south were made to expiate the American casualties, while the body of Castro's army simply fled before Frémont's approach. On July 1, Frémont took the Presidio at San Francisco—an easy victory, inasmuch as the fortress had been without garrison for many years. He took the precaution of spiking a Spanish cannon there—but, then, that rusted-out thing hadn't been fired in half a century.

MR. POLK'S WAR

The Republic of California was destined to a much briefer existence than the Republic of Texas. On July 7, 1846, Commodore John D. Sloat, U.S.N., landed at Monterey, took the harbor and the town without firing a shot, raised the Stars and Stripes, and claimed possession of California in the name of the United States. Frémont was named commander of the California Battalion and would fight in the larger war into which the Bear Flag Rebellion had suddenly dissolved.

War with Mexico was the inevitable result of the United States' westward push. For many Americans, war was justified on the grounds that the Mexican government had failed to make restitution for losses suffered by United States citizens during Mexico's innumerable uprisings and civil conflicts. Furthermore, as the massacres at the Alamo and Goliad had demonstrated, Mexico was a nation of barbarians who needed to be subdued and who were deserving of punishment. Finally, President Herrera's refusal to receive John Slidell and negotiate the sale of California was a diplomatic insult that could not go unchastised.

There were some Americans, in the Northeast particularly, who saw these causes as mere pretenses for stealing territory from a weak neighbor. They called it "Mr. Polk's War." In the South, Middle West, and West, however, enthusiasm for the conflict quickly mounted into a raging fever. Once the official declaration of war was made on May 13, 1846, "it soon became difficult even to *purchase* a place in the ranks," as one Tennessee volunteer recalled. In that state, thirty thousand men drew lots for the three thousand places available. Four regiments had been called for from Illinois; fourteen were formed. In Kentucky, recruitment was stopped after ten days. And so on.

As to the Mexicans, they, too, were spoiling for a fight. Texas was gone. California was going. National honor alone dictated that the Americanos had to be halted, defeated, humiliated.

Texas provided the immediate occasion for battle. When it was part of Mexico, Texas had been bounded on the south by the Nueces River. Independent Texas claimed the Rio Grande as its southern boundary, a claim the United States chose to enforce when the Republic entered the Union. By the end of July 1845, fifteen hundred American troops commanded by General Zachary Taylor occupied the country south of the Nueces. After Slidell's mission was rebuffed, in January 1846, President Polk ordered Taylor to march all the way to the north bank of the Rio Grande. By the end of March, Taylor's force had been increased to four thousand men. In April some fifty-seven hundred Mexican troops under General Pedro de Ampudía were quartered across the river at Matamoros.

The powder was packed in the keg, and Mexican General Mariano Arista (who had replaced Ampudía) lit the fuse. Under orders, he sent his cavalry upriver and crossed to the north bank. Sixty-three of Taylor's dragoons encountered the vastly superior force of sixteen hundred, trading fire with it. Eleven dragoons were killed, five wounded, and most of the remainder captured. Those who escaped rode back to the general with news that the Mexicans had invaded American territory. On April 26, Taylor sent Polk the message that "Hostilities may now be considered as commenced."

On May 1, Mexican forces laid siege against Fort Texas, present-day Brownsville. Taylor, marching south with a force of two thousand to relieve Fort Texas, encountered some six thousand Mexican troops at a waterhole called Palo Alto on May 8. Fortunately for the Americans, the engagement began as an artillery duel; for the Mexicans' powder was so unreliable that their cannonballs fell short or merely bounced behind the American lines and could readily be dodged. There was nothing wrong with the Americans' powder; Taylor's fire was withering. When General Arista attempted to change the mode of battle by rallying for a charge, his troops got bogged down in a morass, panicked, and retreated—whereupon Taylor resumed cannon fire.

At battle's end, four hundred Mexicans lay dead, while only nine American lives were lost. But Taylor, who was repeatedly to prove himself an overcautious commander, failed to capitalize on his victory. Instead of charging the Mexican ranks, he continued to cannonade them until nightfall, when he broke off the engagement. By daybreak the Mexican force had disappeared. However, later in the day, the Americans engaged the Mexicans at Resaca de la Palma, a dry riverbed just north of the Rio Grande. In mostly hand-to-hand combat, 547 Mexicans were killed or wounded, while American casualties numbered 122. But again Taylor failed to pursue the routed enemy. It was not until May 18 that he crossed the Rio Grande and occupied the now-undefended town of Matamoros.

Early in June, action commenced against the Mexicans in California. Stephen Watts Kearny, already a popular western leader, was put in command of the "Army of the West," which mustered at Fort Leavenworth, Kansas, and began moving westward at the end of July. The various units of Kearny's force made their rendezvous at Bent's Fort on the Arkansas River and escorted the annual caravan to Santa Fe.

As Kearny's army approached, New Mexico's governor, Manuel Armijo, at first attempted to rally resistance. Kearny sent word to the citizens of Santa Fe—via captured Mexican spies—that those who surrendered would be protected. He also sent emissaries to Armijo in order to convince him to surrender the entire province. The talks that ensued were most cordial, but Armijo led an army of three thousand out of Santa Fe on August 16 and took up a position at steep-walled Apache Canyon, through which Kearny's columns would have to pass on their way to Santa Fe. It was an ideal point from which to defend the town. The trouble was that Armijo's ill-disciplined and ill-equipped troops panicked at the approach of the Americans, the governor loudly quarreled with his officers, and finally commanded the entire army to disperse. Kearny passed through the canyon unopposed, Santa Fe was taken, and, on August 15, New Mexico was annexed, all without firing a shot.

Kearny pressed on to California, but was intercepted en route by a band of frontiersmen led by Kit Carson, who told him that victory had already been achieved there; for on August 17, Commodore Robert F. Stockton had announced the annexation of California. Commodore Sloat had taken Monterey, but, due to retire from the navy, he was replaced by Stockton. It was he who sent Frémont and his California Battalion south to San Diego in pursuit of the retreating forces of Mexican governors Pico and Castro, and it was he who took possession of Santa Barbara and Los Angeles.

The victories in California and New Mexico did not go unchallenged. Frémont was charged with defending the northern half of California, while the southern portion was administered by Lieutenant Archibald Gillespie,

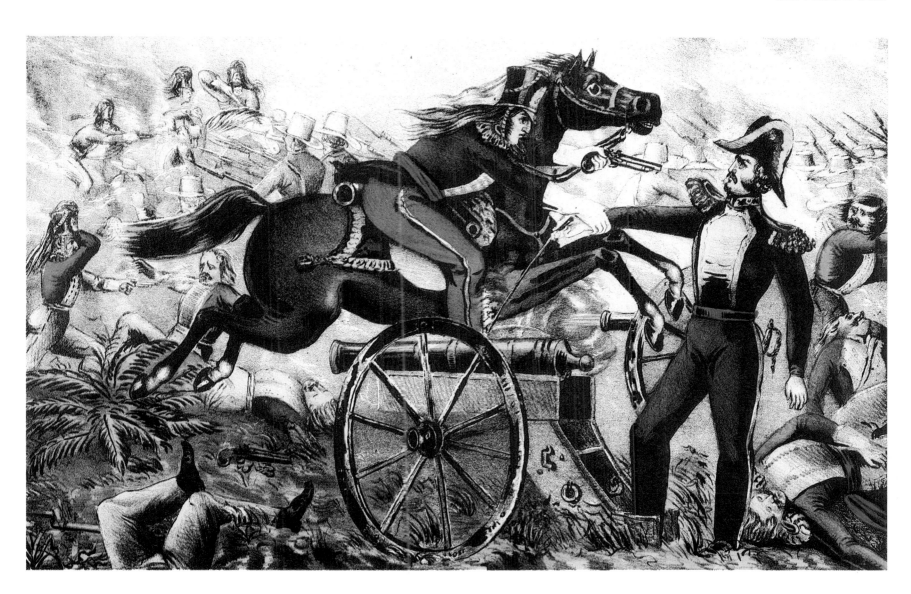

Nathaniel Currier
Battle of Resaca de la Palma, May 9th 1846, 1846
Museum of the City of New York

Fought even before General Zachary Taylor had word of the declaration of war, the Battle of Resaca de la Palma was a stunning American victory. At the cost of 122 dead, Taylor's forces killed 547 Mexican troops. Ever cautious, Taylor failed to capitalize on his gains, allowing the enemy to retreat across the Rio Grande.

with a force of only fifty men. On the night of September 22, 1846, rebels—poorer Californians and Mexicanized Indians led by one José María Flores—attacked Gillespie's small troop, which surrendered and fled north to Monterey. During the fall, Flores would retake from the Americans Santa Barbara, Los Angeles, and San Diego. In December, Kearny and 100 dragoons, reinforced by 38 men under Archibald Gillespie, engaged a force of 80 rebels at San Pasqual and were defeated with the loss of 18 dead and 15 wounded, including both Kearny and Gillespie. Commodore Stockton, anchored off San Diego, had been awaiting the arrival of Frémont's overland force of 428 men. At the news of Kearny's defeat, Stockton decided not to wait, but to land his sailors immediately. Four hundred of them attacked and overran the rebel position on the San Gabriel River near Los Angeles. Stockton retook Los Angeles on January 10 and was at last joined by the recently arrived Frémont. The Americans granted the insurgents such generous surrender terms that resistance simply evaporated. California was secure.

In New Mexico, the winter of 1846–47 also brought rebellion. The army of occupation often abused citizens and indulged in drunken brawling as well as general looting. Citizens began plotting revolt in December and made their move in Taos on the night of January 19,

1847, killing the sheriff and a deputy, then Governor Charles Bent (whose body was paraded through the town), and finally any other Americans they could find; in all, 15 were killed. Colonel Sterling Price responded with five companies of soldiers. On their way to Taos, Price's men engaged and dispersed rebels at La Cañada and elsewhere. In Taos itself, the Americans had to face a rebel force barricaded behind the adobe walls of the seven-story-high Taos Pueblo. When artillery proved useless against the pueblo, Price ordered a charge. His men breached the wall with axes, engaged the enemy within, killed 150 of them, and the Taos Rebellion was quelled.

While the "Army of the West" was engaged in securing what had been Mexico's northern provinces, Zachary Taylor's "Army of the Center" had secured the borderlands, and now his "Army of Occupation" was thrusting deep into Mexico itself. His object was the capital, Mexico City, but first he would have to take the Mexican towns of Monterrey and Buena Vista. Two smaller forces, one commanded by Brigadier General J. E. Wool and the other by Colonel A. W. Doniphan, guarded Taylor's right flank. Wool succeeded in taking the city of Monclova without firing a shot and then rejoined Taylor's main force. The career of Doniphan's First Missouri

OLAF CARL SELTZER

**BORN 1877 OR 1881,
COPENHAGEN, DENMARK
DIED 1957, GREAT FALLS, MONTANA**

Recognized today as one of the great western painters and illustrators, during most of his career Seltzer was consigned to the shadow cast by his neighbor, sometime painting partner, and wholehearted booster, Charles Russell, with whom he shared a similar style and subject matter.

Seltzer studied art at the Danish Art School and the Polytechnic Institute in Copenhagen until, at age fourteen, he immigrated with his mother to Great Falls, Montana. There he worked briefly as a cowboy and a railroadman, serving as a machinist and locomotive mechanic for the Great Northern Railroad. During this period he made pen-and-ink drawings and, encouraged by friends, including Russell, began to paint in oils.

It was not until he was laid off by the railroad, at age forty-four, that Seltzer took up painting full time. His success was immediate, since there was great demand for work in the manner of Charles Russell. In 1926, Seltzer even went to New York to complete some commissions Russell was too busy to finish himself. In 1930, Dr. Philip Cole, a wealthy Montana physician turned New York industrialist, commissioned one hundred miniatures depicting episodes and characters from Montana history. The project amounted to a small gallery of western types. The strenuous work of painting the miniatures, which required long hours of painstaking labor with a magnifying glass, apparently damaged the artist's eyesight, so that he always had to work in very bright light thereafter. This, however, hardly curtailed his output, which amounts to some 2,500 paintings.

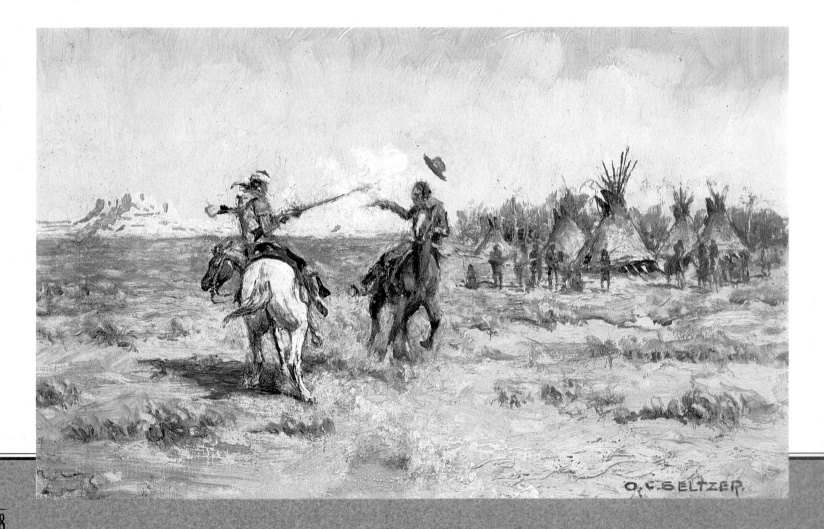

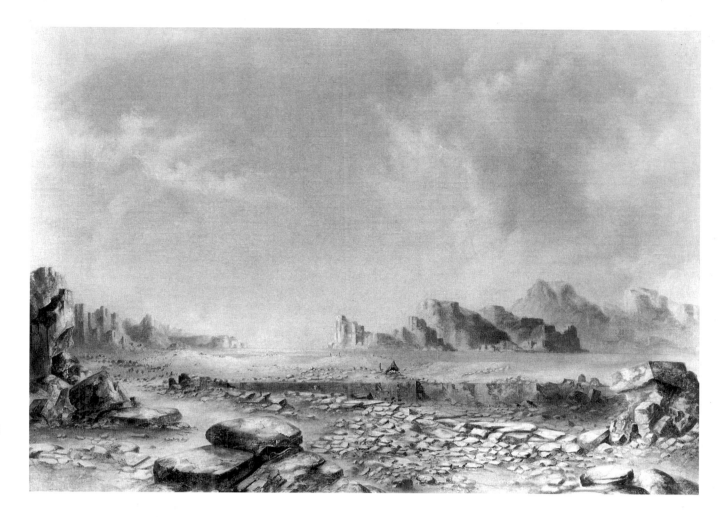

George D. Brewerton (1827–1901)
Jornada del Muerte, 1853
Oil on canvas, 30 × 44 in.
Collection of The Oakland Museum;
Kahn Collection

The dreaded desert through which
Santa Fe caravans had to pass was
depicted by this army lieutenant
who served with Kit Carson.

Olaf Carl Seltzer (1877–1957)
*Duel Between Kit Carson and Capt.
Shunar—August 1835 on the Banks
of the Green River*, 1934
Oil on board, 4 × 6 in.
Gilcrease Museum, Tulsa, Oklahoma

Trapping with the legendary
mountain man Jim Bridger in 1835,
Carson attended the fur-trading
"rendezvous" convened on the Green
River that year and fought Captain
Shunar, a belligerent French
trapper, in a "duel" long celebrated.

Regiment—"ring-tailed roarers," these backwoodsmen called themselves—was more interesting.

Doniphan set off from Santa Fe in November 1846 with 856 men accompanied by a 315-wagon caravan of Santa Fe traders seeking to sell their wares, war or no war. After crossing the Jornado del Muerto, the desert expanse dreaded by those who plied the Santa Fe trade, marching three days without water, they encountered 1,200 Mexican soldiers near El Paso. The gorgeously outfitted Mexican regulars summarily demanded the surrender of Doniphan's ragtag army. "Charge and be damned," Doniphan replied. Charge they did—and, with devastating calm and accuracy, the First Missouri picked off rank after charging rank.

Doniphan's jubilation was short-lived, however, as he next learned that the rebellion at Taos had cut off his supplies. The men pressed on, foraging for what they needed. On February 27, 1847, they reached Chihuahua, where Doniphan received his next piece of distressing news. The town was defended by twenty-seven hundred Mexican regulars and an additional thousand rancheros. They were perched on a rise of land where the Sacramento River joins a canyon called the Arroyo Seco and were certain of victory, in anticipation of which they were preparing short lengths of rope to bind their prisoners and were already dividing the anticipated spoils of the Santa Fe traders.

Attacking such a force head on, Doniphan knew, would indeed assure a Mexican triumph. Instead, he or-

dered his Missourians to cross the arroyo and labor up a steep bank beyond it so that they could face the Mexican force in the open. The engagement began with an artillery duel, and, yet again, the Mexicans' powder failed them. As had Taylor's men at the battle of Palo Alto, Doniphan's ring-tailed roarers simply dodged slow-moving cannonballs while they returned fire with devastating chain shot. The epitome of the dry, drawling westerner, Doniphan directed the battle from his horse, whittling all the while; as the cannonballs rolled in, he paused to remark, "Well, they're giving us hell now, boys."

When the Mexicans began their retreat, Doniphan ordered a charge. The Battle of Sacramento had begun at three in the afternoon; by five it was over. The First Missouri's eight hundred had defeated a force of four thousand, killing at least three hundred. One of Doniphan's men died; five were wounded. The roarers, deep behind the enemy lines now, marched a thousand miles across completely unfamiliar country to rendezvous with Taylor's main force at Saltillo. When they arrived on May 21, 1847, Taylor had already moved on. The First Missouri caught up with him at Monterrey, some sixty miles distant. In one year, the ring-tailed roarers had traveled six thousand miles and defeated two armies. It was an extraordinary military feat—but the kind of thing one came almost to expect from determined westerners.

Taylor's far more conventional army had attacked Monterrey on September 20, 1846, driving the Mexican defenders, under General Pedro de Ampudia, deeper

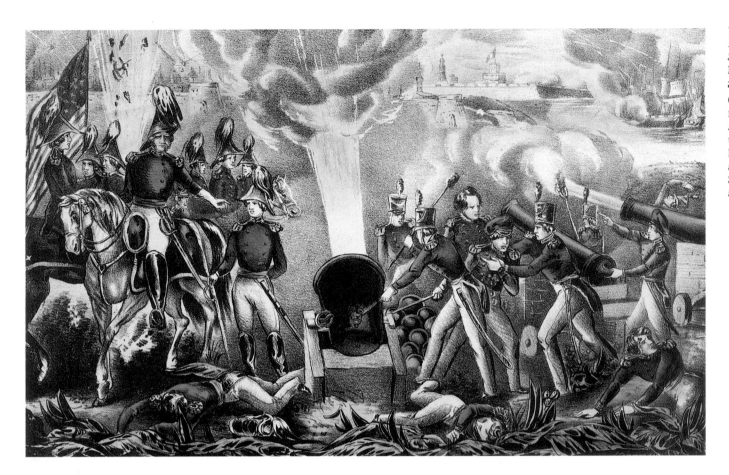

General Winfield Scott mounted the first amphibious assault in U.S. Army history when he landed some twelve thousand men near Veracruz. He laid siege, took the town, and advanced inland. By the middle of September, Mexico City had fallen, and the war was over.

and deeper into the town. After a four-day siege, Ampudía, fearful that American artillery would touch off his own powder magazines, surrendered. Yet again Taylor declined to capitalize on what he had gained. He allowed Ampudía's forces to withdraw—armed—and promised not to advance deeper into Mexico for two months!

In July 1846 the ever-resiliant Antonio López de Santa Anna, exiled in Cuba, made a proposal to the government of the United States, pledging to help it win the war, to establish a Rio Grande boundary for Texas, and to secure a California boundary through San Francisco Bay. His price was thirty million dollars and safe passage to Mexico. The United States was prudent enough not to pay him, but Santa Anna was allowed to return to his homeland—whereupon he began to organize an army to defeat Zachary Taylor, making especially good use of the eight-week armistice the general had imposed on himself. By January 1847, Santa Anna had gathered eighteen thousand men, about fifteen thousand of whom he hurled against Taylor's forty-eight hundred men at Buena Vista after the American declined a demand for unconditional surrender. Two days of bloody battle ensued, in which the Mississippi Rifles, commanded by Jefferson Davis, particularly distinguished themselves. And when at last it seemed certain that the far more numerous Mexicans would break through the American lines, Taylor brought up his highly mobile artillery, which fired on Santa Anna's troops at point-blank range and forced their withdrawal on February 23.

President Polk was well aware that the trouble with victorious generals is that they become heroes, and heroes sometimes become presidents. Polk was a Democrat; Taylor, a Whig. It would not do for "Old Rough and Ready" to capture the glory of final victory. True, the only other distinguished general available for that honor was Winfield Scott, also a Whig, but "Old Fuss and Feathers," as he was called, fell short of Taylor's popularity. Citing Taylor's overcautious approach to the war, including his truce after Monterrey and a letter the general published in January 1847, proposing that the war could be won by simply holding the present line, Polk replaced Taylor with Scott as supreme commander and ordered his new man to invade Veracruz from the sea and advance thence to Mexico City. On March 9 Scott's army landed—the first amphibious assault in U.S. military history—and laid siege against the fortress at Veracruz for eighteen days.

Santa Anna next withdrew to the steep Cerro Gordo canyon with eight thousand of his best troops. Like Doniphan at the Battle of Sacramento, Scott declined the frontal attack the Mexicans expected. Instead, he sent part of his force to cut paths up either side of Cerro Gordo and attacked pincer-style. Panic gripped Santa Anna's troops, who, skirmishing all the way, retreated to Mexico City. Scott boldly severed his rapidly pursuing army from its slower-moving supply lines. Hearing this, no less an authority than the duke of Wellington, vanquisher of Napoleon Bonaparte, pronounced the Americans' doom: "Scott is lost—he cannot capture the city and he cannot fall back upon his base."

After three months of pursuit, engagement, and pursuit, the army of Winfield Scott was at the gates of the

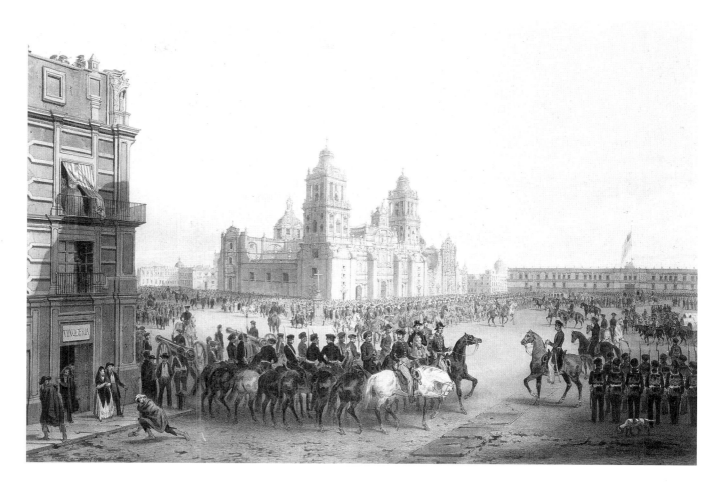

Anonymous
*General Scott's Entrance into
Mexico City*, 1851
Courtesy of the Library of Congress

Mexican capital. On September 13, Chapultepec Palace, the seemingly impregnable fortress outside Mexico City, now defended by a force that included teenage cadets from the Mexican Military College, fell to Scott. Hand-to-hand combat followed in the streets of the city itself until, on September 17, Santa Anna surrendered. Mr. Polk's War had been won.

Peace talks, which had been commenced before the invasion of Mexico City, on August 27, and which were broken off by the Mexicans on September 7, resumed on November 22. Nicholas P. Trist was charged by President Polk with the task of negotiating a treaty that would secure California, New Mexico, and a Rio Grande boundary for Texas in return for a payment of no more than fifteen million dollars. But just before the talks recommenced, Polk had second thoughts about Trist's abilities—which were, indeed, mediocre—and, even more, about the relatively modest extent of the demands to be made of Mexico, even as the president's constituency, flush with victory, was clamoring for "All Mexico."

On November 16, Trist received Polk's order recall-

ing him to Washington. General Scott, however, convinced Trist to proceed with the treaty; the bellicose Santa Anna had fled the country, but the present government was tottering, and *now,* Scott argued, was the time to legitimate the spoils of the war, before the other side lost all power to legitimate anything.

Trist presented the Treaty of Guadalupe Hildago to Polk in February. Despite misgivings, the president could not repudiate a treaty that did, after all, embody everything he had actually asked for—though in the interim he had decided that he wanted even more. On March 10, 1848, the treaty was ratified—38 yeas, 14 nays—by the Senate, or, as one Whig summed up the process: "The treaty negotiated by an unauthorized agent, with an unacknowledged government, submitted by an accidental President to a dissatisfied Senate, has . . . been confirmed."

Manifest Destiny had been served, politically, at least. Now the West had *really* to be won—from nature, from the Indians, and from land-grabbing greed and self-defeating anarchy.

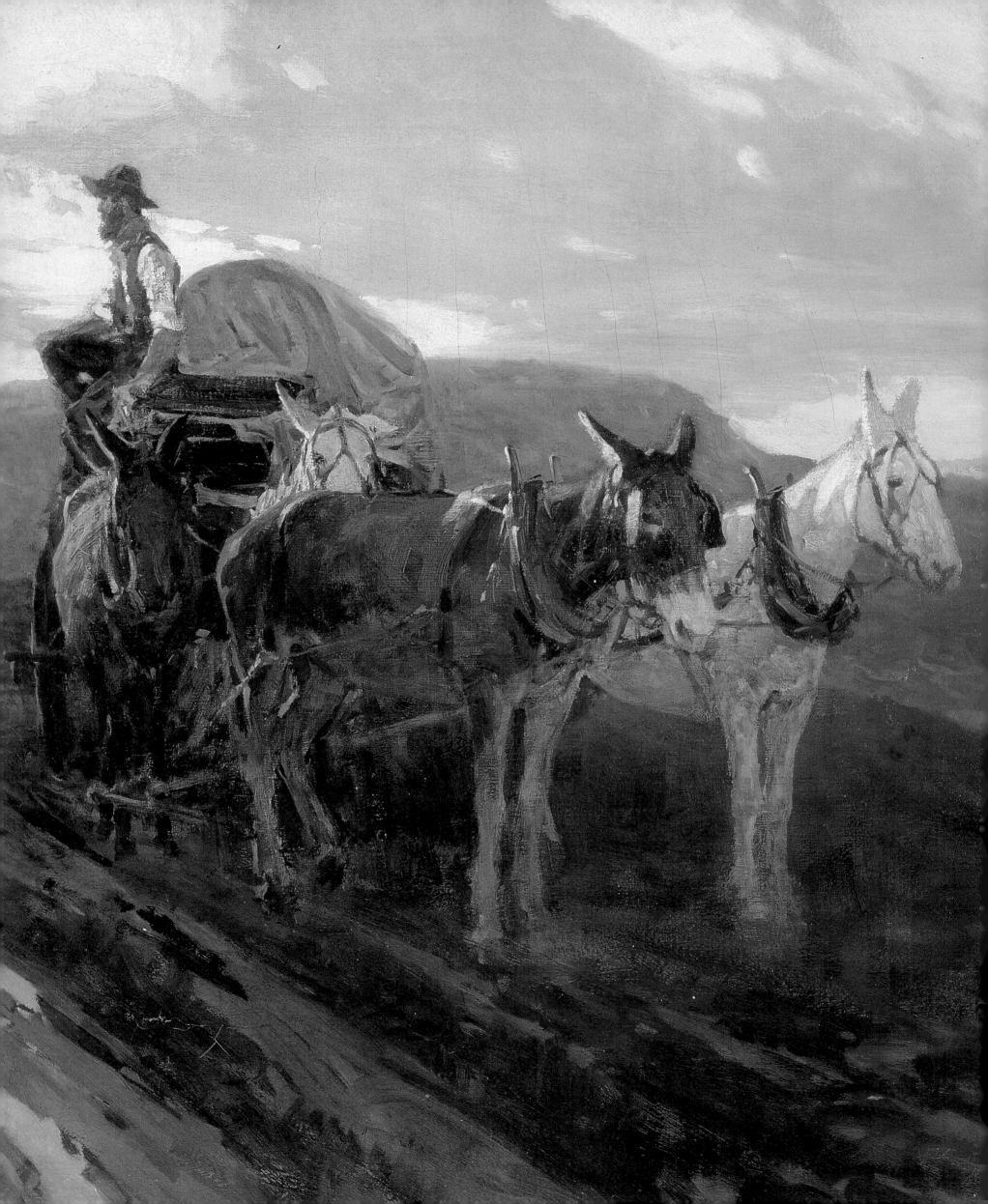

GOD AND GOLD

The Spaniards of the sixteenth and seventeenth centuries were drawn to the New World and the American West by motives of God and Gold. While the Spanish missionaries did, in fact, make a lasting impression on the country—doing much good and no little harm, as well—the quest for gold proved chimerical. In the mid nineteenth century, as the West was rapidly annexed onto the United States, these two motives for exploration and settlement reemerged.

We have seen how God—at least the Methodist version of Him—came to Oregon country, via expeditions inspired by an eccentric Boston schoolmaster and by a Methodist Indian chief from the Middle West. The small colony Jason Lee established sent its founder to Washington, D.C., in 1838 to petition Congress for protection under the laws of the United States. While Congress failed to act, Lee did acquire more converts, the fifty-one new colonists of the "Great Reinforcement" of 1840, which included four women teachers, six ministers, a physician, and others with skills useful to civilized life. That same year, Joel Walker, a mountain man and brother of the more famous mountain man, Joe Walker, moved his family to Oregon by wagon. His was the first *family* to immigrate to the region.

Many more wagons followed the Overland Trail to Oregon and California. On February 1, 1841, fifty-eight men, settlers in Jackson County, Missouri, met in Independence to plan the first organized immigrant wagon train to California. By the time the company had assembled at Sapling Grove, the traditional rendezvous point for Santa Fe caravans, the party had increased to sixty-nine, fully one-third of whom were women and children, under the captaincy of John Bartleson. Just before departure, the train was joined by a Catholic missionary, Father Pierre-Jean de Smet, and his guide, the mountain man Thomas Fitzpatrick. In all there were fifteen wagons and four carts. The journey was marked by a death, a birth, and a marriage, and by hunger, fatigue, and despair: a trek of five months, three weeks, and four days—two of those weeks spent starving and struggling across the Rockies.

The wagon trains that followed were larger. In 1842 there were about 20 wagons carrying well over a hundred persons. In 1843, the train consisted of 120 wagons carrying two hundred families and accompanied by two thousand head of cattle. It was called the Great Emigration and would be followed by others year after year, until the completion of the transcontinental railroad in 1869. The wagon trains were mobile communities, which elected leaders and assigned tasks according to the skills of each emigrant. The wagons themselves varied from farm equipment hastily modified, to specially built

Frank Tenney Johnson,
California or Oregon, 1926.
Detail; see page 184

143

prairie schooners, the "covered wagon" that has become an icon of western migration. A development of the Conestoga wagons (so named because they were originally developed in the Conestoga River valley of Lancaster County, Pennsylvania), which had been carrying freight and settlers since the eighteenth century, prairie schooners could carry a ton and a half, but were light enough to be pulled efficiently by a yoke of oxen. Constructed of hardwoods with some iron reinforcement and iron "tires" fitted to the wooden wheels, the prairie schooner was hardly built for comfort; there were no springs, and the wagon bed, ten to twelve feet long, was a simple box without seats or other comforts. Hickory bows, over which a canvas or cotton cover was stretched, were fitted to the sides of the box, affording minimal protection for cargo and passengers.

On the trail, reveille—the discharge of sentinels' rifles—was at four in the morning. The stock, which had been set out to graze, was gathered, and teamsters selected their teams of oxen and drove them into a corral, formed by the circled wagons, to be yoked. By seven, the train was on the move, led by a mounted pilot and his guards. At nightfall the wagons circled up to form a stockade; the teams were unyoked and driven out to pasture. Evening meals were prepared, and by eight there was time for some diversion—fiddle music, a flute, dancing—then sleep. Reveille would be at four in the morning.

Emigrants may have grumbled about the regimen-

tation of the wagon train and, from time to time, may have challenged the authority of a punctilious wagon master, but the order, preparedness, and discipline of a well-conducted wagon train could well mean the difference between reaching California and dying in the attempt. There were untold scores of emigrants who, unwise or unfortunate in their choice of leadership, ended their journeys in hastily made and rudely marked graves along a trail through some nameless prairie or hostile mountain pass. Many of the dead had no graves at all.

The best known among the ranks of the doomed was the Donner party. Their horrific odyssey began when two wealthy brothers from Springfield, Illinois, Jacob and George Donner, read a book by Lansford W. Hastings, a lawyer turned emigrant advisor, who outlined a shortcut to the Promised Land of California. Hastings even set up shop at Fort Bridger, the point at which the shortcut began, offering his services as guide. The Donners organized a party of eighty-nine emigrants, who headed west in the summer of 1846. When they arrived at Fort Bridger on August 3, they discovered that Hastings had already left to lead another party, but—not to worry—he had marked a trail for the Donners. They began to trek southwest.

At Weber Canyon they found, in a forked stick, a note from Hastings instructing them to wait until he could show them the best route through the Wasatch Range.

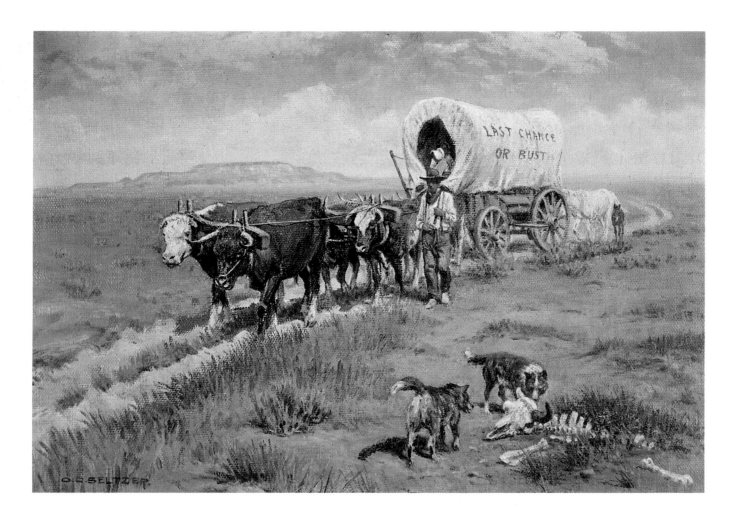

Olaf Carl Seltzer (1877–1957)
The Prairie Schooner, 1932
Oil on canvas, 11 × 16 in.
Gilcrease Museum, Tulsa, Oklahoma

The classic vehicle of western migration.

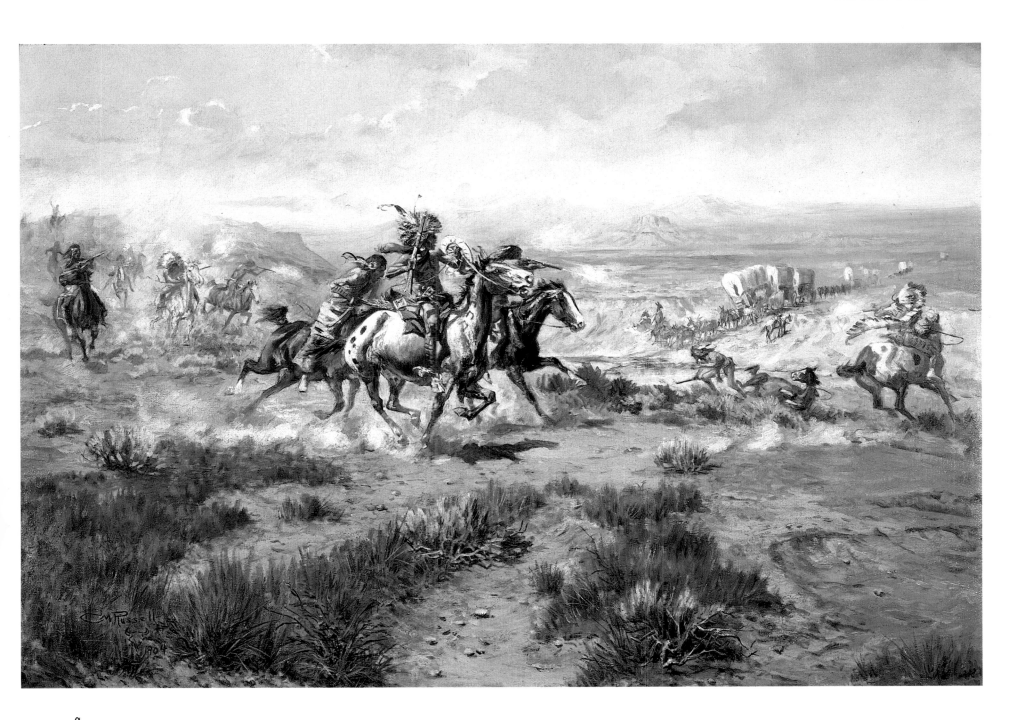

Charles M. Russell (1864–1926)
The Attack on the Wagon Train,
1904
Oil on canvas, 24 ¼ × 36 in.
Gilcrease Museum, Tulsa, Oklahoma

While Indian attacks on emigrant
wagon trains were less common
than is popularly thought, lone
stagecoaches were at greater risk. In
1859 alone, the Butterfield stage line
lost ten drivers to Indian attack.

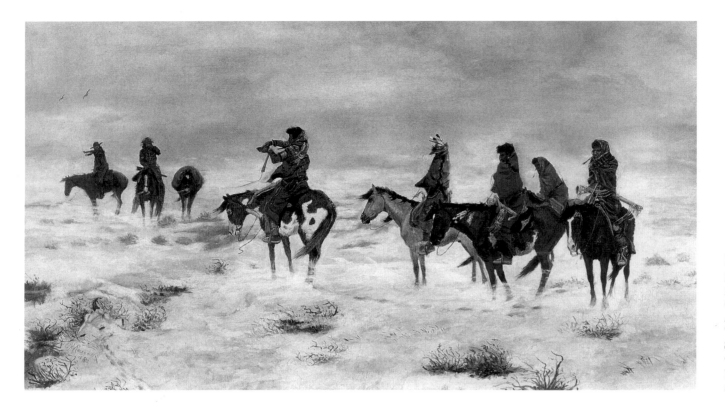

Charles M. Russell (1864–1926)
Lost in a Snowstorm—We Are Friends, 1888
Oil on canvas, 24 × 43 ⅛ in.
Amon Carter Museum, Fort Worth, Texas

The exigencies of the elements could be a more effective peacemaker than any treaty.

After eight days of waiting, the Donner party sent a messenger in search of Hastings. The messenger returned with instructions to follow a trail through the Wasatch; it proved virtually impassable. For twenty-one days the emigrants rolled massive boulder after boulder, often progressing no more than a mile a day. By the time they finally broke through to the valley of the Great Salt Lake, they were in every sense exhausted. How could they cross that sterile, saline desert? And yet, how could they turn back, back through the mountain range that had all but killed them?

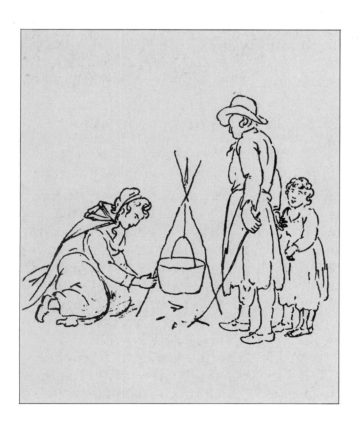

Cross the desert they did—in six terrible days (Hastings said it would take two)—their livestock, thirst-crazed, stampeding off, their yoked oxen collapsing. Indians shot or rustled what animals remained to them. Not all of the Donner party's trouble came from the outside. One James Reed quarreled with another man and stabbed him to death. Another man was abandoned when he could no longer keep up. A third was murdered. A fourth died from an accidental gunshot.

At last, two of the party were sent ahead to Sutter's Fort, California, to secure food. They succeeded, returning with two Indian helpers and five or seven mules (sources conflict) loaded with provisions. But by then it was October in the Sierra; even so, the first snow wasn't due until November.

This year it came early, falling—heavily—on the night of October 28. The Donner party was cut off through November and half of December. They ate hides, bones, twigs, and the bark of trees. One man went insane; four others died. At last, on December 16, fifteen of the strongest survivors—eight men, five women, two Indian guides—ventured to scale the peak in search of help. And that's when it happened.

The small expeditionary party had set out on starvation rations meant to last at most six days. By Christmas Day they had gone without food for four days, and they were far from any sign of civilization. They drew lots to decide who would die that the others might live. But no one had the heart to do in the one who had drawn the short stick. That night, they were engulfed by a fierce storm that lasted two days and left four of the party dead. The survivors stripped the flesh from their bones (according to one of them), "roasted and ate it, averting their faces from each other, and weeping." Thus they

Joshua Shaw (1776–1860)
Sketch of a Family by a Fire along the Wilderness Road, n.d.
Museum of Science and Industry, Chicago

A Britisher, Shaw came to the United States in 1817 and traveled widely through the country, compiling sketches for "Picturesque Views of American Scenery," a series of etchings he published in 1819. The Wilderness Road, which extended westward across Kentucky from the Cumberland Gap, was blazed by none other than Daniel Boone. It became an early "highway" of immigration in the Trans-Appalachian West.

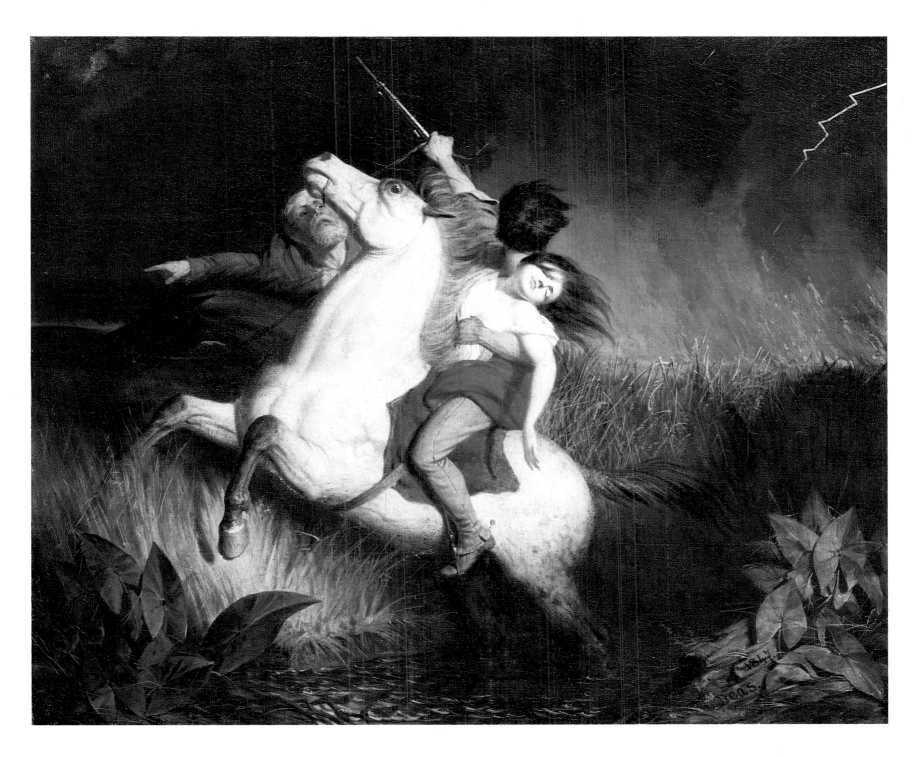

Charles Deas (1818–1867)
Prairie Fire, 1847
Oil on canvas, 28 ⅞ × 36 1⁄16 in.
The Brooklyn Museum; Gift of Mr.
and Mrs. Alistair Bradley

Lightning—or hunters flushing out game—often set an autumn-dry prairie ablaze. Deas transforms the phenomenon into a scene of romantic nightmare.

subsisted, in camp, for another two days.

Their strength recruited, they carefully packed what flesh remained, labeling each fragment so that no one would eat his own kin, and set off again. Their supply of flesh was soon exhausted, however, and they resorted to boiling the strings of moccasins and snowshoes. Once, they were fortunate enough to kill a stray deer.

All along, the two Indian guides had refused to eat human flesh. Presumably, cannibalism horrified them more than starvation. When these abstemious guides, who, after all, had eaten far less than the whites, collapsed on the trail, they were shot—and eaten.

On January 10, 1847, seven of the fifteen who had set out in mid December reached an Indian village; the first of several relief parties reached the rest of the Donner party on February 19. As in the expeditionary party,

those who survived to greet their rescuers had become cannibals.

Disease, the ruthless elements, and the hostility of Indians were hazards of the trail; often, they were also hazards of the settlement at the end of the trail. In 1835, Marcus Whitman, a physician and Presbyterian minister, toured the Pacific Northwest with Samuel Parker, scouting a location for an Oregon mission. After finding a site, he returned east briefly, marrying Narcissa Prentiss, whose blonde, buxom, wide-eyed beauty would be celebrated among the small fraternity of mountain men who wandered into Whitman's Cayuse Indian mission near Walla Walla in present-day Washington. Whitman was indefatigable, having to fight his own mission board to continue his work, while ministering both spiritually and as a physician to Indians and whites alike. In a short time, his mission became a vital way station for mountain men and incoming settlers, who came to rely on his courage and medical skill. Legendary mountain man Jim Bridger, who had taken a Gros Ventre arrow in the back during a fight at Pierre's Hole in 1832, came to Dr. Whitman in 1835 to have the long-imbedded arrowhead removed.

A zealous missionary, Marcus Whitman was no anthropologist. He insisted that his Cayuse converts sever themselves utterly and completely from their former beliefs. When, in 1847, the Cayuses were devastated by an epidemic of measles—half the tribe died—many among the Indians attributed the origin of the disease to the new white settlers, and to the evil influence of Marcus Whitman. A French Canadian from Maine named Joe Lewis sought to direct the Indians' growing resentment of whites away from himself and exclusively against Whitman. He let it be known that the epidemic was a plot to steal the Indians' land. But, some pointed out, didn't the doctor try to heal the sick Indians? Yes, replied Lewis, and the whites, too. The difference was that the whites recovered from the measles, while the Cayuses all died.

On November 28, 1847, Whitman traveled thirty miles south of his mission at Waiilatpu to treat sick Indians in the Umatilla Valley. He ministered to them and returned directly home—for eleven of the forty-two mission children were ill with measles—reaching his house about midnight. There Narcissa was watching two girls, Helen Meek and Louise Sager (one of the Whitmans' adopted daughters), both very ill. Although he had been traveling and working all day and night, Whitman

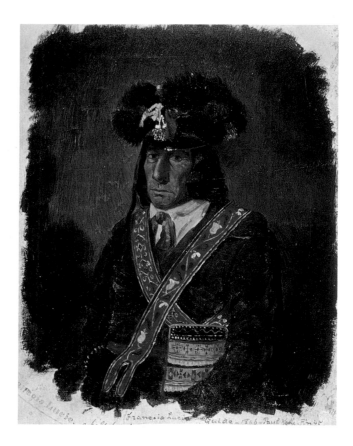

Paul Kane (1810–1871)
François Lucie, A Cree Half-Breed Guide, 1846
Oil on paper, 10 ⅞ × 3 ¾ in.
Stark Museum of Art, Orange, Texas

The Hudson's Bay Company, like other fur-trapping enterprises, employed Indians and half-breeds as guides.

sent his wife to bed while he continued to watch the two sick girls. After breakfast on a foggy, dark morning, he supervised the butchering of some beef. He returned to the kitchen, where seventeen-year-old John Sager was winding twine. Whitman sat reading and, for a time, dozed.

About noon, an Indian came to tell Whitman of three more measles deaths among his tribe. The mission-

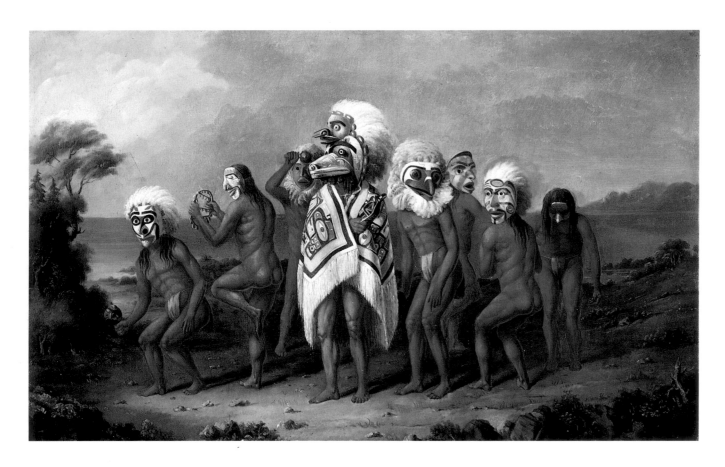

Paul Kane (1810–1871)
Medicine Mask Dance, c. 1850
Oil on canvas, 18 × 29 in.
Royal Ontario Museum, Toronto

The Indians of the Northwest developed a complex culture in which religious ceremonies such as this played a central role. Missionaries like Marcus Whitman sought to replace Native American religion with Christianity, but Whitman's heavy-handed zeal turned many Indians against him, creating the emotional climate in which he was murdered.

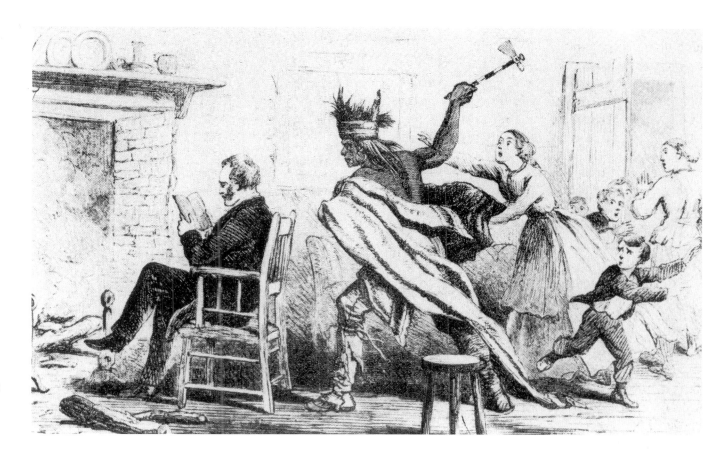

Anonymous
Massacre of the Whitmans, n.d.
Historical Picture Service, Chicago

A fanciful depiction of the missionary's demise: it must have been a very absorbing book indeed.

ary left to officiate at the burial.

Later in the afternoon, when Whitman had returned home, two more Indians, Tomahas and Tiloukaikt (whose daughter had been among those who had died that day), came to the doctor's door. Tiloukaikt spoke to Whitman, and, as he did, Tomahas struck him from behind with a bronze tomahawk and hacked his face. Another Indian entered, pressed a rifle against Whitman's neck, and fired. When young John Sager leaped up to get a gun that was hanging on the wall, he, too, was shot—dead. The sturdy preacher, still breathing, was dragged outside to die.

Narcissa, who had been in another room, ran to the window. A bullet hit either her arm or lodged in her breast. She apparently staggered upstairs to the attic bedroom, where (it is said) she prayed for the children—and the Indians.

More Indians attacked the mission's miller, teacher, tailor, and the three men who had been butchering the beef, but other whites in the Whitman house held off a final assault. At last, one Indian, an old friend of the Whitmans, warned those inside that the house was about to be put to the torch. He promised them safe conduct out. Narcissa, unconscious from loss of blood, was put on a wooden settee and carried out the door. Whereupon the Cayuses opened fire.

The missionary's wife, riddled by bullets, rolled off the settee. An Indian seized her by her long, blonde hair and beat her across her face with a quirt.

Accounts vary as to the final death toll. Either twelve men in addition to Whitman were massacred, or eleven men and one woman in addition to Narcissa.

Louise Sager, Helen Meek, and probably another sick girl died from lack of care. It is known that at least one brave raped some of the women and girls. Six other settlers escaped, though one of them subsequently drowned in the Columbia River. Thirty-four children, eight women, and five men were captured and held hostage until Peter Skene Ogden, of the Hudson's Bay Company, ransomed them for five hundred dollars' worth of trade goods: shirts, firearms, blankets, tobacco.

As it turned out, this tragedy only hastened the displacement of the Indians by white settlement. The mountain man Joe Meek led a party of Oregon settlers all the way east to Washington, D.C., to petition his cousin-in-law, President Polk himself, to make Oregon, at last, a territory of the United States, entitled to the full protection of the federal government. Meek saw Polk on May 28; on August 14, the Oregon Territory was formed.

SAINTS

If the West meant enduring loneliness, misery, disease, and even unspeakable horror, it also represented adventure, opportunity, freedom, and virtually unlimited self-fullfilment. In the epic of the Mormons, the very hardships of life in the West were embraced as opportunity and the means of religious survival.

In 1820, a fifteen-year-old boy named Joseph Smith, Jr., was visited by God the Father and Jesus Christ near his family's farm in upstate New York. Three years later, the angel Moroni told Smith to dig in a certain place on a hill near his home. There he found thin golden plates bound with wire rings. It was a history written by Mo-

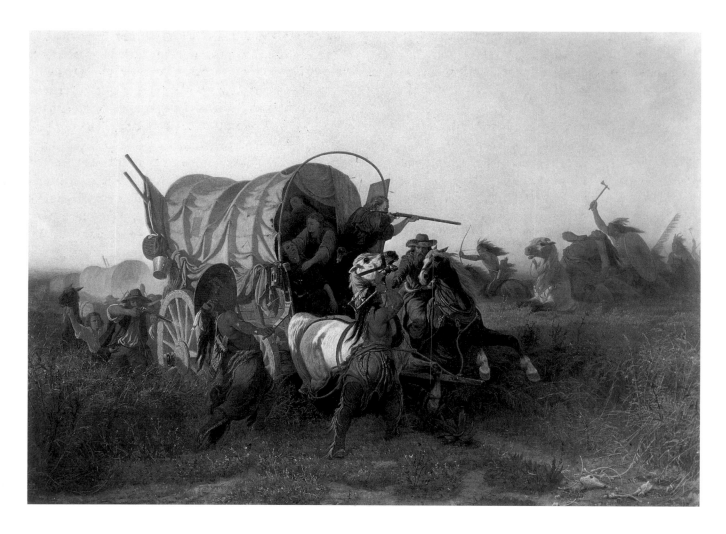

Charles Wimar (1828–1862)
The Attack on the Emigrant Train,
1856
Oil on canvas, 55 ⅛ × 79 ⅛ in.
The University of Michigan Museum
of Art; Bequest of Henry C. Lewis

This canvas, inspired by a book
Wimar had read—Gabriel Ferry's
*Impressions des voyages et
aventures dans le Mexique, la haute
Californie et les régions de l'or*—was
painted in Düsseldorf.

roni's father, Mormon, telling of an ancient struggle between two tribes that lived in the New World long before
Columbus discovered it, a light-skinned "delightsome
people" and a "bloodthirsty people," whose skin God had
turned reddish brown as a mark of their savage nature.
Moroni, sole survivor of the final battle between the two
peoples, had buried the history. Whoever dug it up again
was commanded to restore in the world the true Church
of Christ.

But Moroni forbade removing the plates for four
years after Smith found them, so that the youth might be
instructed in prophethood. Finally, in 1827, Moroni permitted Smith to dig up the plates, which bore "Reformed
Egyptian" hieroglyphics. In the hole with the plates, however, were crystal spectacles through which the hieroglyphics miraculously appeared as King James biblical
English. In 1829, Smith announced the forthcoming publication of a new volume of Scripture. That year, three
other men reported that Moroni had appeared to them
and had shown him the holy plates. Eight other men tes-
tified that Smith had let them handle the plates. Under
authority from John the Baptist and the apostles Peter,
James, and John, Joseph Smith published the Book of
Mormon in March 1830 and founded a church with six
members in April of that year.

Smith made converts rapidly, but just as rapidly he
made enemies. To escape the hostility of his New York
neighbors, he moved his fledgling church to Kirtland,

Ohio. When he and his followers were persecuted there,
they moved to northwestern Missouri. And when the
governor of that state declared them "public enemies"
who must either be "exterminated or driven from the
State," they moved back east, to Illinois, to start the Mormon city of Nauvoo (from a Hebrew word connoting a
beautiful and restful place). They built an enviable frontier town, mostly in brick, each house possessing a garden. In the center of the village, they raised a tall and
ornate temple. By 1844, Nauvoo was the largest town in
Illinois, with fifteen thousand residents, a little less than
half of the total number of Mormons at the time. The
prosperity—as well as the arrogance—of Nauvoo's citizens aroused the jealous ire of its neighbors. Yet, united,
the Mormons were a formidable body now and not easily
intimidated.

In 1843, Joseph Smith informed the church elders
of a revelation he had received some years earlier,
through which God gave permission for certain Mormons
to take more than one wife. The issue and practice of
polygamy (which Smith called "celestial marriage") split
the church, as some believers denounced their spiritual
leader not only among themselves, but to the Gentiles as
well, using a newly founded opposition newspaper called
the *Nauvoo Expositor.* Smith dispatched the Nauvoo
marshal to destroy the paper's presses. The owners
brought in outside authorities to arrest Smith, who was
jailed in Carthage, Illinois, on charges of having violated

the United States Constitution. There, on June 27, 1844, he and his brother were lynched by a mob of two hundred anti-Mormons. The killing, in turn, triggered a riot, as more mobs roamed the countryside, bent on destroying Nauvoo.

The threats were not carried out; indeed, Nauvoo went about its business peacefully for another year. Brigham Young, a house painter, carpenter, and glazier at the time of his conversion to Mormonism during 1830 to 1832, assumed leadership of the church after Smith's death. He realized that Nauvoo, despite appearances, was no longer secure. When, in 1845, the village's Gentile neighbors again agitated for the Mormons' removal, Young saw in the West a haven for his people, a new Promised Land—but not one of Milk and Honey. He wanted a place that no other people would ever covet. Based on his reading of various western narratives and journals of exploration, he chose the country beside the Great Salt Lake precisely because it was isolated, lonely, and hostile (though, Young gathered from John C. Frémont's published journal, well-watered). No one would molest the Mormons there.

During the winter of 1845–46, all Nauvoo turned to building wagons and other necessities of travel. Facing a fourteen-hundred-mile overland journey, Brigham Young planned the mass migration with the precision and brilliance of a great general preparing for a titanic battle. Young set off first with a pioneer party to build in Iowa a rendezvous point and staging area for the remainder of the emigrants. It was called Camp of Israel. When all had gathered there in the spring of 1846, Young began deploying the Mormons westward in parties of a few hundred. The first group built way stations at various intervals—small settlements, really, with crops planted for food, gristmills, and shops built to serve the main body of pilgrims. Winter Quarters, near present-day Council Bluffs, Iowa, included a meetinghouse, mill, shops, and about a thousand cabins.

Travel by wagon train was becoming increasingly routine and better organized during the 1840s and 1850s; Young's trains made even the best-conducted secular outfits look like a rabble. He sent his pilgrims off in carefully staggered waves, so that no single way station would be overburdened. Every train was divided into "hundreds" or "fifties," each commanded by a captain and each subdivided further into "tens" commanded by lieutenants. Despite hunger and disease—a plague killed some six hundred Mormons during the winter of 1846–

Albert Bierstadt (1830–1902)
The Oregon Trail, 1869
Oil on canvas, 31 × 49 in.
The Butler Institute of American Art, Youngstown, Ohio

The most popular "highway" of western migration depicted by one of the most popular of western landscapists.

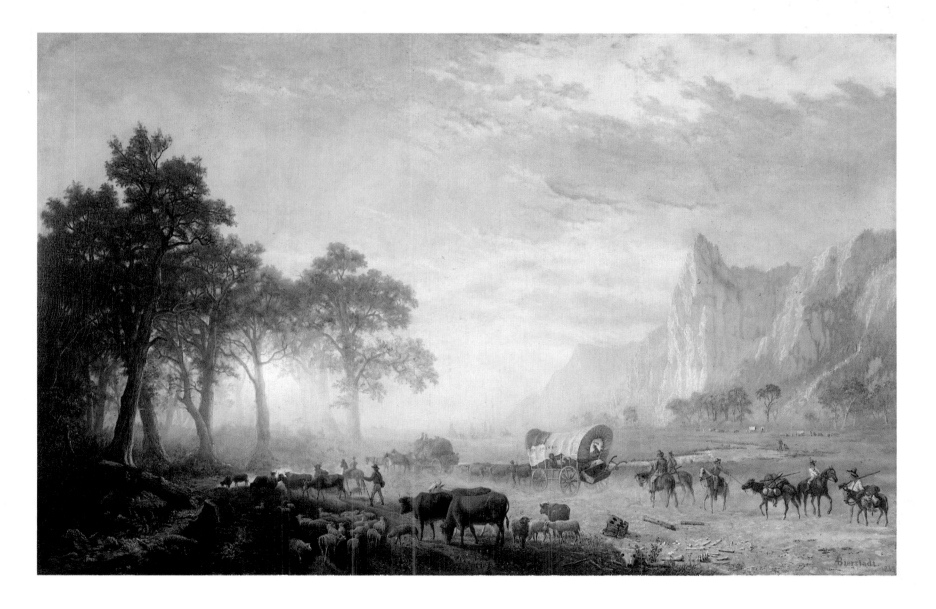

WILLIAM SMITH JEWETT

BORN 1812, SOUTH DOVER, NEW YORK
DIED 1873, SPRINGFIELD, MASSACHUSETTS

After study at the National Academy, Jewett practiced successfully as a New York City portrait painter from 1833 to 1849, when he was caught up in the California gold fever. Joining the Hope Company gold expedition, he netted all of $20 in nuggets and dust. "It is difficult to say what predominates here," he wrote, "mud or gold." Discouraged by 1850, he settled in San Francisco and opened portrait studios in that city as well as in Sacramento, churning out landscapes and two or three portraits every week, getting between $200 and $300 apiece. In 1855 the State of California commissioned a full-length portrait of John Augustus Sutter, paying Jewett $2,500 for it. Jewett wisely invested his painting profits in San Francisco real estate, amassing a fortune sufficient to buy, among many other things, a castle in the Pyrenees.

Despite the profusion of Jewett's output, little of his work was identified until a twenty-year cache of his California letters was discovered in 1942. Today, over one hundred Jewetts have been authenticated. He is best remembered as California's first professional painter.

William Smith Jewett (1812–1873), *The Promised Land—The Grayson Family,* 1850. Oil on canvas, 50 ⅞ × 65 in. Berry-Hill Galleries, New York

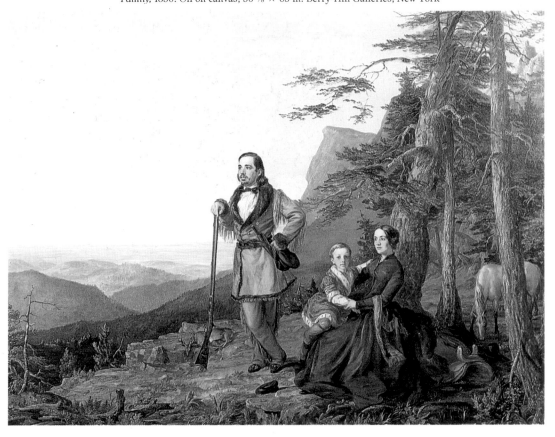

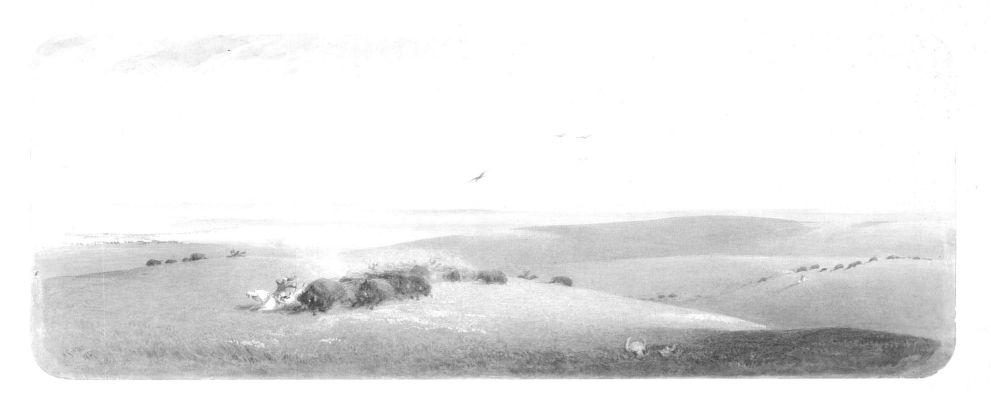

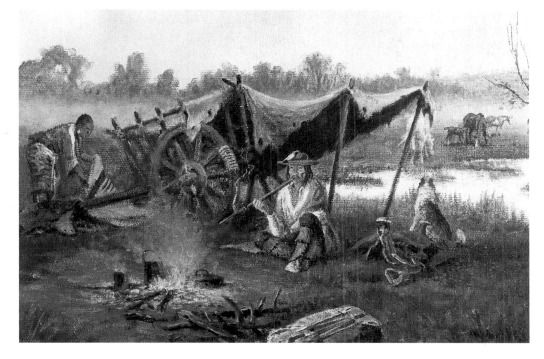

Henry George Hine (1811–1895)
Buffalo Hunt on the Prairies, 1847
Watercolor with gouache,
8 ¼ × 22 ⅜ in.
Royal Ontario Museum, Toronto;
Sigmund Samuel Collection *(top)*

Olaf Carl Seltzer (1877–1957)
The Red River Cart, 1932
Oil on canvas, 11 × 16 in.
Gilcrease Museum, Tulsa, Oklahoma

Western transportation at the low
end: note that the traveler is a "half-
blood," a condition guaranteed to
place one at the bottom of the
socioeconomic ladder. *(bottom)*

47—discipline prevailed.

Led by Brigham Young, a "Pioneer Band" left Winter Quarters on April 9, 1847—143 men, 3 women, 2 children. At the North Platte River, they paused to build a ferry, not only for themselves, but for later comers. The Pioneer Band even ferried another, non-Mormon emigrant group, bartering the service for much-needed food and supplies. However, not all encounters along the trail boded well. Coming through the South Pass, the Pioneer Band was met by the old mountain man Jim Bridger, who told them that the valley of the Great Salt Lake was so arid and alkaline that it could never support farming. He told Young he'd give him a thousand dollars for the first bushel of corn grown there. Undaunted, the band pressed on. Near the Green River, they met Samuel Brannan, another Mormon elder, who had led 238 of the faithful to California, by sea, the year before. He tried to persuade Young to join him in the San Joaquin Valley. But Young knew that a settlement there would be no more secure than Nauvoo had been. If any of the Pioneers was tempted, none of them let on.

In July the advance party skirted the Wasatch Mountains, exploring the canyons for a passage into the valley that would be their home. The first sight of Salt Lake country revealed a barren plain scorched by the sun, without meadow or forest. When all of the Pioneer Band reached the valley on July 24, 1847, they set about immediately planting potatoes and building a dam across the nearby creek in order to quench the hard-parched soil. That very night a heavy rain fell—surely a sign from God. By autumn, 1,800 Saints lived in the valley, and Young set off with 108 men to return to Winter Quarters to lead the next year's migration.

Yet that first winter was a time of famine, as the Mormons had arrived too late to assure a good harvest before the onset of cold weather. Brigham Young's brother, Lorenzo, boiled ox hides for soup; "glue soup," he called it. With spring, hope revived as they planted a good crop early. Then the crickets descended upon them, devouring the crop—until sea gulls, which lived around the Salt Lake, descended upon the crickets and began devouring *them.* Surely, the Saints agreed, another sign from the Lord.

The true import of Joseph Smith's revelation concerning multiple wives was certainly not (as many Gentiles thought) a ploy to gratify the carnal lusts of Mormon men. Rather, it was a means of rapidly increasing the Mormon population. While Brigham Young had established his people in a spot isolated from the Gentile world, he also dispatched missionaries throughout the United States, England, and northern Europe who were converting thousands (32,894 in England alone by the end of 1851), almost exclusively among the hard-working

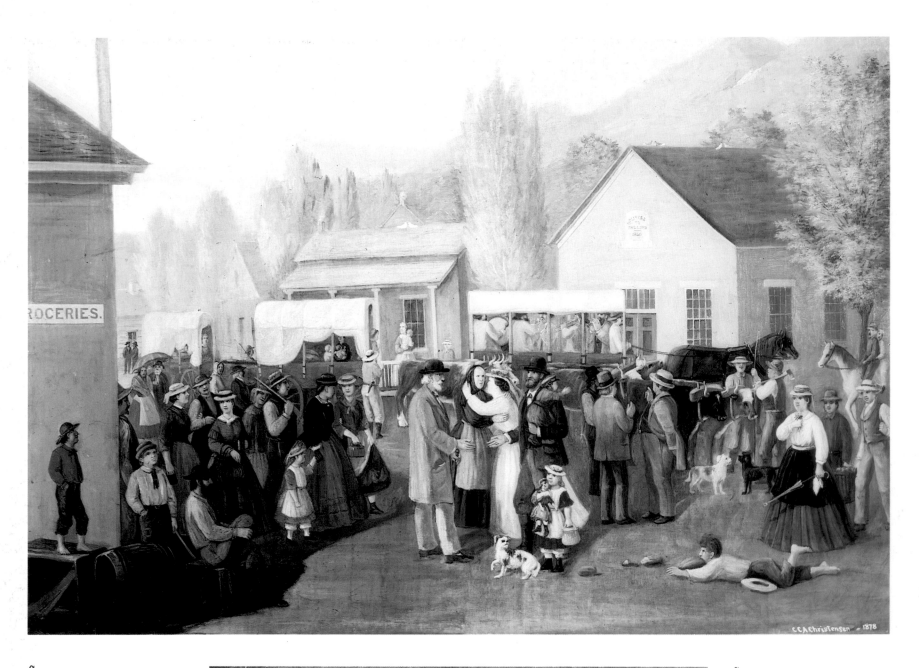

C. C. A. Christensen (1831–1912)
Emigration of the Saints, 1878
Oil on canvas, 34 ⅛ × 50 in.
Daughters of Utah Pioneers
Museum, Salt Lake City

An arrival in the Promised Land.
(above)

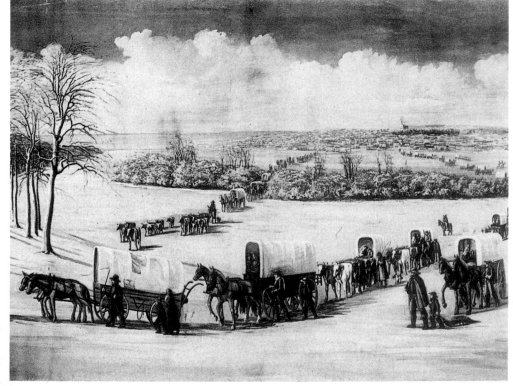

C. C. A. Christensen (1831–1912)
Crossing the Mississippi on Ice,
c. 1878
Mural: tempera on canvas, 78 × 117 in.
Brigham Young University Fine Arts
Collection, Provo

This episode of the epic Mormon
Trek was painted by a Danish-born
convert to Mormonism who served
as a missionary in Denmark before
immigrating to the United States in
1857. He was among the Mormon
"Handcart Brigade," which made its
way to Utah on foot, carrving
belongings and supplies in handcarts.
(left)

William Tylee Ranney (1813–1857)
*Crossing the Ferry (Pennsylvania
Teamster)*, 1846
Oil on canvas, 29 ½ × 40 in.
Gilcrease Museum, Tulsa, Oklahoma

Apparently, this wagoner has chosen
to ford the ferry rather than pay the
ferryman. *(opposite)*

WILLIAM TYLEE RANNEY

—

BORN 1813, MIDDLETOWN, CONNECTICUT

DIED 1857, WEST HOBOKEN, NEW JERSEY

—

Son of a sea captain who plied the West Indian trade, Ranney lived in Connecticut until 1826, when he moved to Fayetteville, North Carolina, where he lived with his uncle and was apprenticed to a tinsmith. During the six years he spent in the South, the youth learned to sketch the natural scenes around him. In 1833 or 1834, Ranney moved to Brooklyn, New York, where he studied painting and worked for an architect. In 1836 he answered a call for volunteers to enlist in the Texan Army and avenge the massacre at the Alamo. During the year that he spent in Texas—as paymaster for Captain C. A. W. Fowler's First Regiment of Volunteers—he sketched prodigiously, amassing a stock of studies and memories that he would later develop into great western paintings.

Returned to Brooklyn in 1837, Ranney became a portrait painter by the next year, and in 1843 opened a studio in Manhattan. Five years later he moved across the Hudson to Weehawken,

New Jersey, and in 1853 settled in West Hoboken (today part of Jersey City), where he built a studio in imitation of a "pioneer's cabin or border chieftain's hut."

It was not until 1846, ten years after his return from Texas, that Ranney began painting western subjects, concentrating on romantic views of trappers and prairie life, favoring the intimate, anecdotal, and dramatic genre approach rather than the breathtaking panorama. The western phase of Ranney's career was cut short by consumption. So respected was his work, however, that ninety-five artists, among them Frederick Church, Albert Bierstadt, Arthur Fitzwilliam Tait, John Frederick Kensett, and George Inness, donated paintings to a benefit auction for the artist's widow. The great Long Island painter, William Sidney Mount, a close friend, completed several canvases Ranney had left unfinished in his studio.

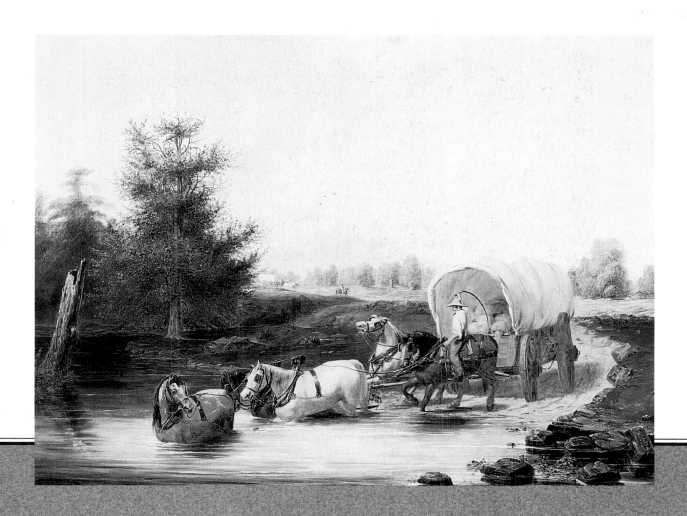

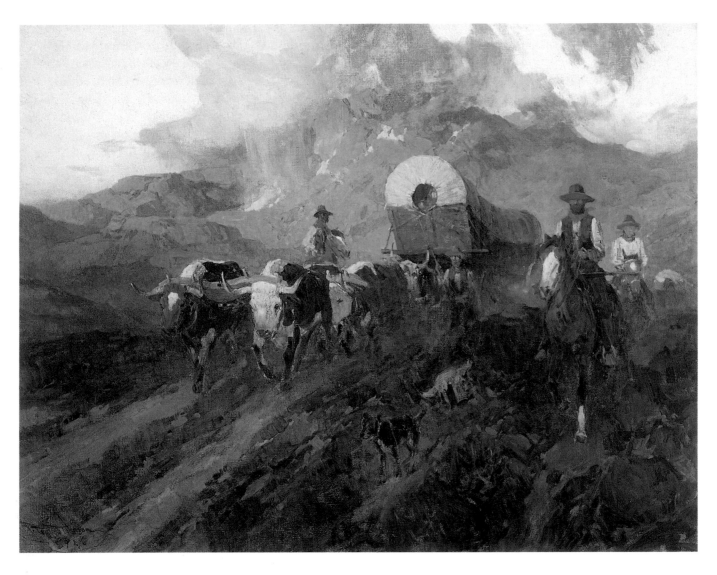

Frank Tenney Johnson (1874–1939)
The Overland Trail, 1926
Oil on canvas, 28 × 36 in.
Gilcrease Museum, Tulsa, Oklahoma

Along with the Oregon and Santa Fe
trails, the Overland was, by the mid
nineteenth century, a principal
avenue of far western immigration.

poor and disadvantaged classes. Throughout the 1850s, they came pouring into the Salt Lake country. Meanwhile, Young had announced the building of a great city centered on a ten-acre Temple Square (originally it was to have been forty acres!) with broad streets laid out in a grid, and ample, regular lots for houses with gardens. Young also designed an extraordinary irrigation system, which allotted farmers adequate water in strictly regulated rotation—this at a time when systematic irrigation was virtually unknown in American farming. By 1865, 277 irrigation canals had been dug, totaling 1,043 miles in combined length and irrigating 154,000 acres of previously arid land.

Government was engineered with similar precision. Young, as president, presided over what he called a Theo-Democracy, which also included the Quorum of Twelve Apostles, who supervised spiritual matters, and the Presiding Bishopric, which regulated temporal affairs. Geographically, the settlement was divided into "stakes," which were further divided into "wards" presided over by a bishop responsible for providing rule and guidance in all matters, from the most consequential to the most minute. While all church officers were elected by the people at large, they had been nominated by higher officials, which usually meant that they had

been chosen ultimately by Brigham Young. Few dared vote against his choice.

With the California gold rush of 1849 came both new prosperity (after all, the Forty-Niners had to be supplied with food and equipment, at premium prices) and a new challenge, as some of the westward-bound gold seekers decided to settle among the Saints. Young realized that church government was inadequate to meet the needs of this newly integrated population. Accordingly, in March 1849, the Mormons of Salt Lake decided to organize a secular state, patterning its constitution after those of states back east, providing for a governor (elected to a four-year term), bicameral legislature, manhood suffrage, and religious toleration. The issue of slavery was not addressed. Deseret, a word meaning "honeybee" in the Book of Mormon, was the name they chose for their state, and in July the legislature voted to petition the United States Congress to admit Deseret as a state of the Union.

The petition came at a fortuitous moment, as Henry Clay and Stephen A. Douglas were fashioning the Compromise of 1850. The acquisition of territories following the Mexican War presented the United States with an urgent crisis. The Wilmot Proviso of 1846, endorsed by every northern state legislature (except that of Iowa), prohibited slavery forever in any territory to be ceded by Mexico to the United States. Southern states, led by John C. Calhoun, threatened to secede from the Union rather than submit to the Proviso. Adding to the urgency of the crisis was the situation in Texas and California. In 1849, Texas, a slave state, attempted to claim as part of its territory a large portion of New Mexico, including Santa Fe, thereby extending slavery deep into territory ceded by Mexico. The federal government denied the claim, and Texas militia threatened to march against U.S. troops. In California, the gold rush had brought an overwhelming increase in population that demanded rapid organization of a civil government, lest the situation degenerate into complete anarchy. Southerners, however, blocked California's admission to the Union because, entering as a free state, it would upset the delicate balance between free and slave states. The Compromise adjusted the Texas–New Mexico boundary in accordance with federal wishes, but Texas was compensated by a payment of ten million dollars, which effectively discharged debts incurred during its difficult days as a republic. California was admitted as a free state (in return for which Congress enacted the much harsher fugitive slave laws demanded by the South), and New Mexico and Utah territories were organized in abrogation of the Wilmot

Proviso, as the South had desired. The people of the new territories would vote for or against slavery within their boundaries. Thus the territory of Utah—which encompassed present-day Utah, Nevada, and half of Arizona and Colorado—provided a valuable bargaining chip that forestalled Civil War for a decade. Brigham Young was named territorial governor, with four Mormon officials under him and four Gentiles. In effect, then, little had changed; Mormons held sway over Utah (for Congress had rejected the name of Deseret), and Brigham Young held sway over the Mormons, except that the Mormons had secured official U.S. sanction for their new Zion, even though territorial status fell short of statehood and the large measure of independence that statehood entailed.

In 1849 the Mormons had established a Perpetual Emigrating Fund to loan funds to the many who could not provide for their own way to Utah. By 1855, it had become apparent that the kind of fully equipped wagon trains that had brought the first settlers to the Salt Lake valley were too expensive for the Saints to finance. That year, Young directed Mormon carpenters in Iowa to build handcarts as cheap substitutes for the traditional prairie schooners. Pushing these, immigrants could still make fifteen miles a day, which meant that they could

Albert Bierstadt (1830–1902)
Overland Trail, c. 1871
Oil on paper mounted on board,
7 ½ × 11 ½ in.
Courtesy of The Anschutz Collection

The spectacular prairie sunset allows no mistake: these wagons are headed west.

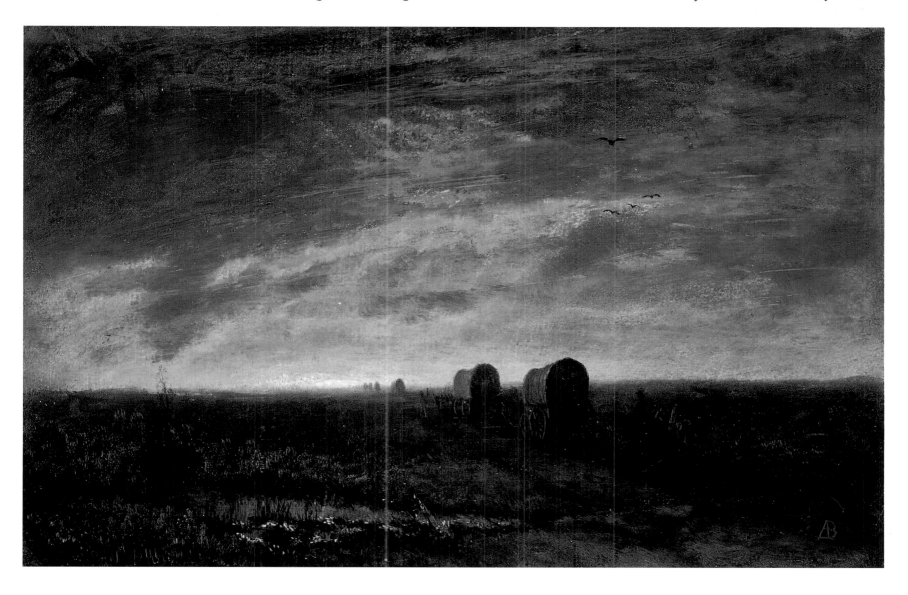

WILLIAM DE LA MONTAGNE CARY

BORN 1840, TAPPAN, NEW YORK

DIED 1922, BROOKLINE, MASSACHUSETTS

A successful illustrator for *Harper's* and other popular magazines, Cary profitably indulged a wanderlust that sent him and two other young men on a leisurely tour of the West in 1860–61. He traveled by riverboat on the upper Missouri, and when the vessel caught fire—a distressingly common occurrence aboard western steamers—he continued his journey on a homemade flatboat, later joining a wagon train for an overland trek. Among the young artist's adventures was a brief captivity among the Crow Indians. After this, joining a railway survey team, Cary and his friends got as far as Portland, Oregon, and San Francisco, from which Cary took a boat to the Isthmus of Panama and thence back to New York. He carried with him a rich cargo of sketches, which, on the eve of Civil War, proved to be the last record of the forts of the upper Missouri before they were abandoned. Moreover, Cary's sketches and keen visual memory provided material for three decades of western painting and illustration.

Cary returned to the West once more, in 1874, when he was invited to accompany a government survey of the U.S.–Canada boundary. The artist arrived in time to accompany the party on their return to Bismarck, North Dakota. Years later, he painted *Return of the Northern Boundary Survey Party,* a major canvas by an artist perhaps even better remembered for his extraordinary sketches.

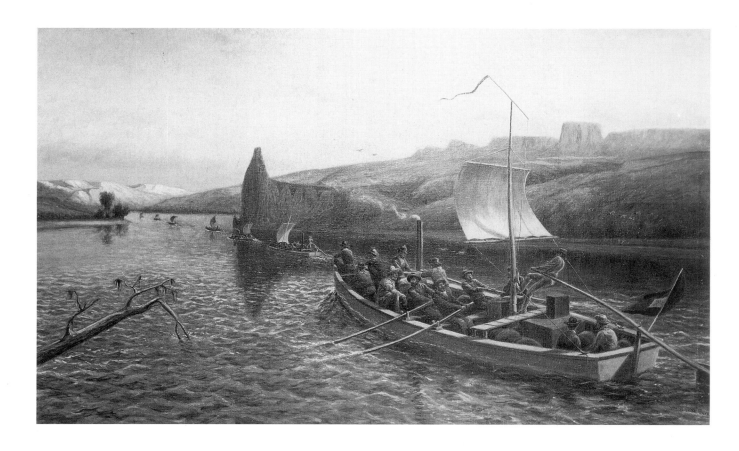

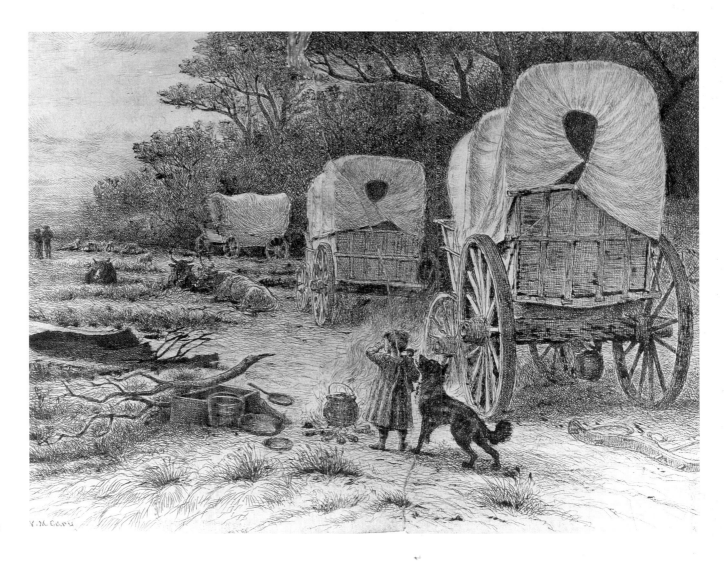

William de la Montagne Cary (1840–1922)
Untitled (Settlers Moving), n.d.
Pencil and wash drawing, 14 × 11 in.
Gilcrease Museum, Tulsa, Oklahoma
(right)

William de la Montagne Cary (1840–1922)
Mormon Haymakers, n.d.
Pencil sketch on paper, 8 × 8 in.
Gilcrease Museum, Tulsa, Oklahoma
(left)

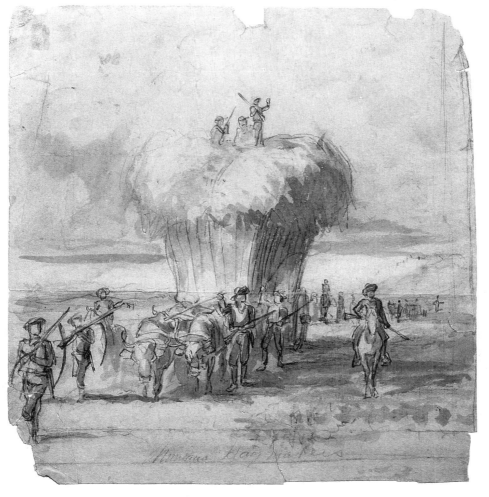

William de la Montagne Cary (1840–1922)
The Return of the Northern Boundary Survey Party, n.d.
Oil on canvas, 44 × 84 in.
Gilcrease Museum, Tulsa, Oklahoma
(opposite)

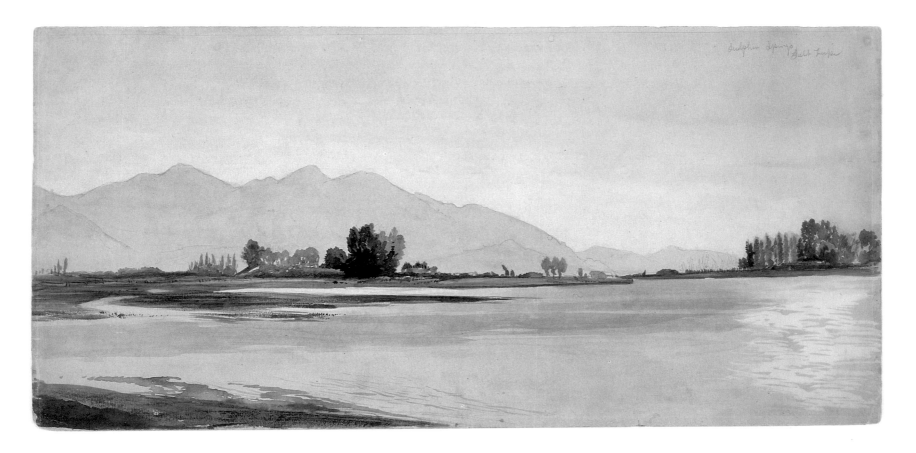

cross the plains in a little over two months. Some five hundred Saints, pushing a hundred carts, left Iowa City on June 9 and 11, 1856, arriving in Salt Lake City late in September.

Departure of the next two "Handcart Brigades" was delayed until August, as carpenters rushed to build the required number of carts. The delays were compounded by frequent breakdowns; for many of the carts were built of green lumber, which shrank in the hot, dry air of the plains. Overloaded, they simply fell apart. With few carts to carry provisions, the emigrants made do on short rations, expecting to lay in fresh supplies at Fort Laramie. But, when they reached the fort, they discovered that the supplies had been exhausted. In a state of semistarvation, they were caught by fierce winter storms, which stranded them in the South Pass. In all, of a thousand Saints, 225 died before they were rescued by a relief wagon train from Salt Lake City.

The tragedy of the second Handcart Brigade was an exceptional episode in the otherwise remarkably successful program of Mormon settlement. As early as 1847, the community expanded northward with the purchase of lands in the Weber River valley, where the Saints founded the town of Ogden. In 1849 the valley of Lake Utah was settled, and Provo and Fort Utah were founded. That same year, twenty-six other towns were laid out. Brigham Young wanted to establish a Mormon corridor clear to the Pacific. By 1855, settlements reached the San Bernardino valley in Southern California. Farming, milling, and mining prospered.

With prosperity came, unavoidably, national attention, and, as in Illinois, the focus narrowed to the issue of

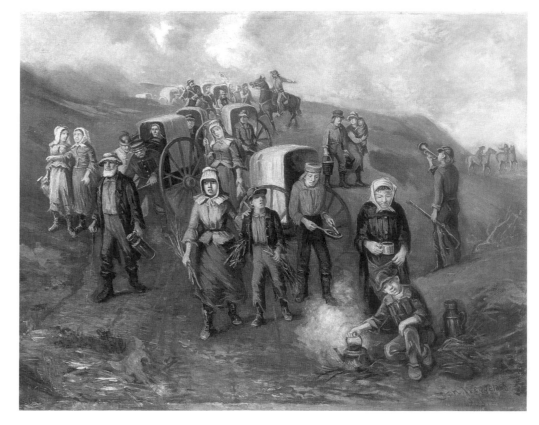

Peter Moran (1841–1914)
Sulphur Springs, Salt Lake, 1879
Watercolor on paper,
9 ¼ × 19 ¾ in.
Amon Carter Museum, Fort Worth,
Texas

Mormon country. *(opposite)*

polygamy. It was a fact that fewer than 20 percent of Mormons engaged in plural marriage; however, Brigham Young himself had twenty-seven wives (who bore him fifty-six children), and the popular image among Gentiles was that of a communal harem—not only a morally obnoxious institution, but one that would result in the alarming multiplication of Mormons. A Mormon newspaper in England published a calculation demonstrating just what a dutiful Mormon could accomplish if he married forty wives. By age seventy-eight, he would have been responsible for having produced 3,508,441 Saints, assuming all of his descendants were as dutiful as he. (A monogamous Gentile could hope to produce a mere 152 descendants by age seventy-eight.) In response to growing public outrage, President James Buchanan decided it was time to clip the Saints' wings. In 1857 he removed Brigham Young from the office of territorial governor, appointing in his stead a former mayor of Augusta, Georgia, Alfred Cumming, and dispatching twenty-five hundred soldiers from Fort Leavenworth, Kansas, to promote a smooth transition.

Young responded by addressing a congregation in Temple Square: "Woe, woe to those men who came here to unlawfully meddle with me and this people. . . . I swore in Nauvoo, when my enemies were looking me in the face, that I would send them to hell . . . and I ask no more odds of all hell today." Young mobilized the Mor-

mon militia even as he made plans for the evacuation and burning of Salt Lake City.

The inflammatory atmosphere was bound to breed tragedy. It came in September 1857, and it was called the Mountain Meadow Massacre. In a remote part of southern Utah, where the Mormon settlement had recently been swept by a wave of fanaticism, the Saints were visited by a band of 137 Gentile pioneers bound for California. While most of this group consisted of the usual decent and respectable farmers looking for a new life in the Far West, a gang of so-called Missouri Wild Cats had tagged along, who (it was said) sold poisoned beef to some Indians and fouled an Indian well. They swore, committed various acts of theft and vandalism against Mormon farms, and loudly denounced Mormon women as whores. Finally, on September 7, some two hundred Indians attacked the emigrant band, killing seven before the whites were able to retreat behind a barricade of circled wagons.

Three emigrants attempted to sneak out and through the Indian lines in search of aid. Two were killed by Indians; the third, William Aiden, was slain by a Mormon fanatic who was participating with the Indians in their attack. The Indians also sent a delegation in search of aid—for the Mormons had always treated them well—and called on John D. Lee, who had worked as a missionary among them. Lee gathered fifty Mormon rein-

April Gornik (b. 1953)
The West, 1986
Oil on canvas, 72 × 98 in.
Private collection, Courtesy of
Edward Thorp Gallery, New York
(right)

Dan Weggeland (1827–1918)
Handcart Pioneers, 1908
Oil on canvas, 32 × 41 in.
Museum of Church History and Art,
Salt Lake City

By 1855, the volume of Mormon immigration to Utah had become so great that the Church could no longer afford to finance fully outfitted wagon trains. Brigham Young hit on the idea of supplying would-be immigrants with handcarts, which they pushed from Iowa to Utah at an average rate of fifteen miles a day. Two of these so-called Handcart Brigades were caught in early winter snows through the South Pass during 1856. Two hundred twenty-five persons died in that disaster. *(opposite)*

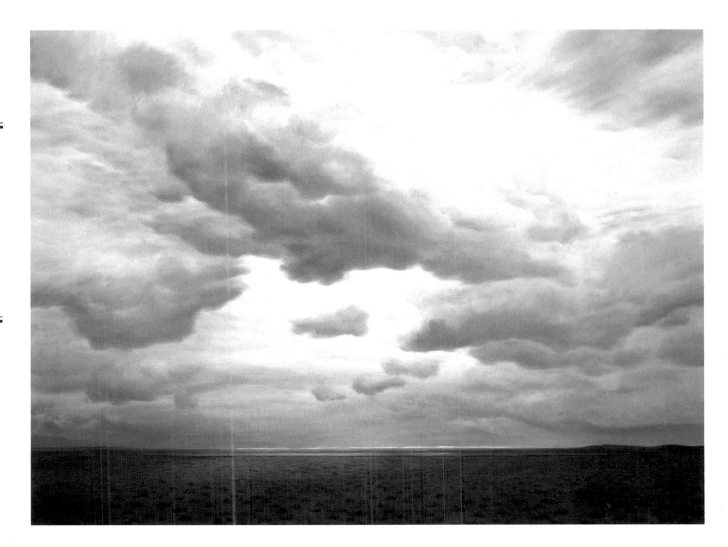

forcements, who held a meeting to decide whether they should intercede on the part of the emigrants or help the Indians. Fearing reprisals for the murder of Aiden, they decided that every emigrant had to be killed to keep news of the murder from reaching California.

John Lee rode to the scene of the siege, entered the emigrants' camp, and told them that he had arranged safe conduct out. As the emigrants marched out, the Mormons began killing the men, leaving the women and children to the Indians. Except for seventeen children (judged too young to give an account of events), all of the emigrant party was killed. The Mormon band spread the word that they had been the victims of Indian massacre, but the Gentile world laid the blame solely on the Mormons. President Buchanan labeled it a rebellion. During the fall of 1857, Mormons engaged in a guerrilla war against the column of troops Buchanan had dispatched to aid in the installation of the new governor. The soldiers

were forced to hole up for the winter at Fort Bridger. Meanwhile, the Mormons had made preparations to destroy all they had built in order "to disappoint our enemies."

By spring, in the face of repeated demonstrations of the strength of Mormon faith, public opinion was coming to favor the Saints. President Buchanan "forgave" the "rebellion," and Brigham Young, in turn, accepted Albert Cumming as territorial governor. Far more warily, Young agreed to allow Buchanan's twenty-five hundred soldiers to enter the Salt Lake valley, but on strict condition that they not stop in Salt Lake City itself. If they did so, Young warned, he would raze the city personally. To make his point, he ordered all thirty thousand Mormon residents to evacuate, save for those few who had the responsibility of applying the torches. When, on June 26, 1858, the soldiers marched into town, they found it eerily empty. The Saints waited in suspense, camped near

William W. Major (1804–1854)
Brigham Young and Family, 1851
Oil on canvas, 25 × 33 in.
Museum of Church History and Art,
Salt Lake City

An Englishman, this artist converted to Mormonism in 1842 and immigrated to the Mormon village of Nauvoo, Illinois, in 1844. He was part of the 1848 trek to Salt Lake City in 1848. Major died in England, to which he had returned on a mission for the Church.

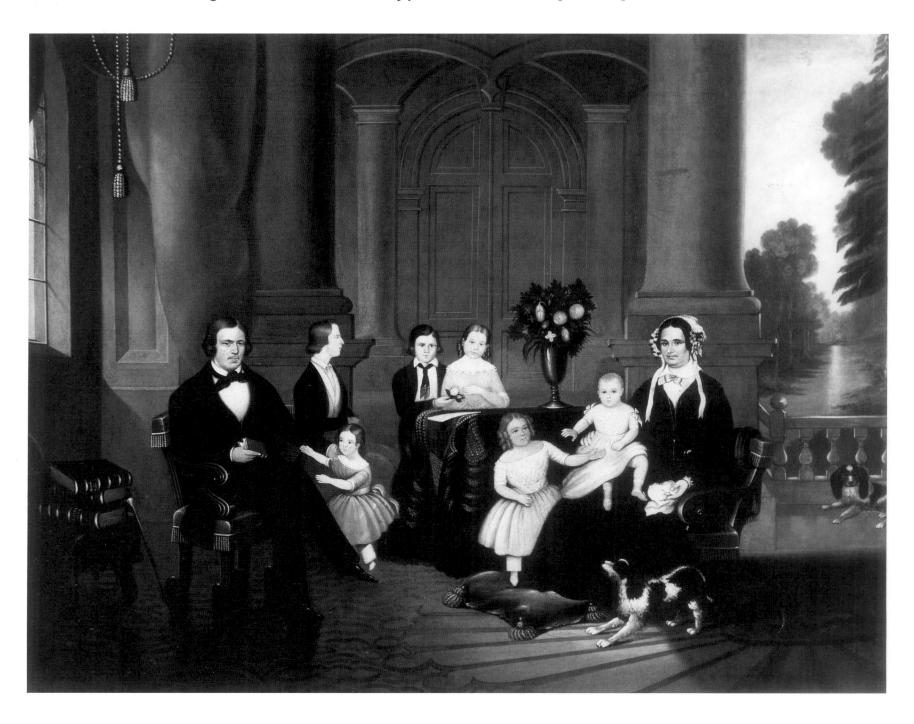

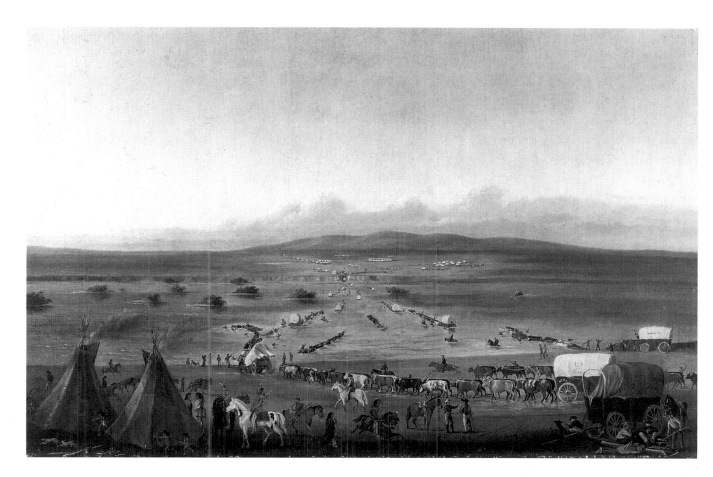

William Henry Jackson (1843–1942)
California Crossing, South Platte River, 1867
Oil on canvas, 22 × 34 in.
Gilcrease Museum, Tulsa, Oklahoma

At the age of twenty-three, Jackson paid for his passage west by working as an apprentice bullwhacker. This painting records the wagon train's crossing of the South Platte River at a spot then known as the California Crossing (present-day Julesburg, Colorado). Jackson is better known as a western photographer than as a painter.

Provo. Had the troops come to destroy the Mormon Church? And would they, the Saints themselves, be forced to destroy the city they had built and move yet again—to Canada, to Mexico?

The troops marched through and set up camp, which they would occupy for the next three years, forty-four miles from the city. The Saints did not want the soldiers there, though they did manage to profit handsomely from supplying the garrison until it left in 1861, needed to fight the Civil War. When, during that war, T.B.H. Stenhouse, the Mormons' representative in Washington, asked President Lincoln what *he* intended to do with the Saints, the embattled chief executive told him a story. "When I was a boy on the farm in Illinois," he said, "there was a great deal of timber which we had to clear away. Occasionally we would come to a log which had fallen down. It was too hard to split, too wet to burn, and too heavy to move, so we plowed around it. That's what I intend to do with the Mormons." As to polygamy, Congress and the Supreme Court attempted now and then to act against it, but to little avail. The issue became moot in 1890, when the Mormon Church itself revoked its endorsement of the practice.

RUSH TO EL DORADO

Almost simultaneously with the Mormon Trek another great magnet began to attract western voyagers, this one as temporal as the object of the Mormons' quest was eternal. But, as the Mormons themselves would quickly learn, both Gold and God could stake a claim in the heart of a westerner, Saint and Gentile alike.

The story does not begin in the American West, but in Switzerland and the city of Berne, where John Augustus Sutter was living miserably in a bad marriage and the hopeless abyss of bad debts. In 1834, aged thirty-two, he left both wife and creditors, came to the United States, and wandered in and out of a series of mercantile ventures in New York, St. Louis, Santa Fe, Oregon, and Honolulu, suffering in the process one more bankruptcy. In July 1839 he came to Mexican California and, using letters he had secured from the always-helpful Dr. John McLoughlin of the Hudson's Bay Company at Fort Vancouver, persuaded Governor Alvarado to grant him fifty thousand acres in the Sacramento Valley at the confluence of the Sacramento and American rivers. Although, as part of the deal, Sutter had renounced his Swiss citizenship for Mexican, he named his fort and stockade New Helvetia.

Everyone else called it Sutter's Fort, and the expatriate Switzer enjoyed what was to all appearances a brisk business supplying settlers, mountain men, and other travelers. In fact, still and always in debt, he saw salvation in the American settlement that was growing up in the vicinity of his fort and decided to build a sawmill to serve its building needs. In 1847 he took as partner James Wilson Marshall, a man as inclined to financial mischance as he himself was. The thirty-five-year-old carpenter from New Jersey had already lost, through illness, a homestead in Kansas; another, in California, had been looted by thieves. Marshall found a good mill site for Sutter on the south fork of the American River, about

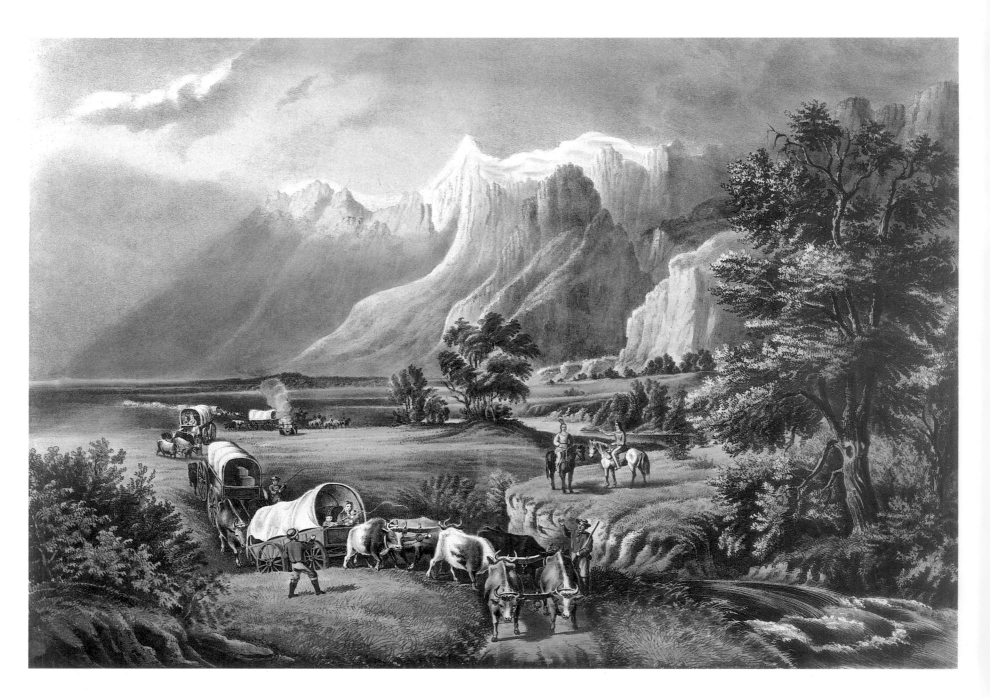

Currier & Ives (after Frances Flora Palmer)
The Rocky Mountains/ Emigrants Crossing the Plains, 1866
Museum of the City of New York

The West for popular consumption in the East: a lush and picturesque Eden.

fifty miles northeast of the fort. Both Marshall and Sutter pointedly ignored the fact that the land belonged to the Coloma Indians.

After building the mill, Marshall laid out a millrace to bring water from the river. He would open the sluice gates from time to time so that the river flow would widen and deepen the race channel. Each day Marshall inspected the mud and gravel the current had carried down to the end of the race. On Monday, January 24, 1848, "upon the rock about six inches beneath the water I discovered the gold."

Marshall examined the nuggets as carefully as he had inspected the progress of the millrace. He pounded a piece against a nearby rock "and found that it could be beaten into a different shape but not broken." Then he tried hammering a nugget on an anvil; it flattened, where fool's gold would have shattered. He had the mill crew's cook, Mrs. Jenny Wimmer, toss a piece of the gold in the lye solution she was boiling for soap; it emerged unchanged. Four days later he rode back to Sutter's Fort and showed his partner what he had found. The two men consulted an encyclopedia and tested the nugget further.

Sutter accompanied Marshall back to the mill. He was less elated by the thought of a rich strike than he was apprehensive about what a gold rush might do to his substantial agricultural operation: twelve thousand head of cattle, ten thousand sheep, two thousand horses and mules, a thousand hogs. In preparation for his partner's visit to the site, Marshall had told the mill hands to gather all the gold they could and plant it along the millrace, so that the find would be obvious to Sutter. But even before Sutter reached the race, Mrs. Wimmer's son greeted him with several nuggets. "By Jo, it is rich!" Sutter exclaimed, and fell to picking up some pieces the boy had overlooked.

He admonished the mill hands to keep the find secret as he and Marshall pondered the fact that neither of them had any formal title to the land. Unaware of the outcome of the Mexican War in a land of few roads and vast distances, Sutter could turn neither to Mexican officials to authenticate his claim to the land nor to Americans. He needed to act quickly, however, and therefore turned to the only people he thought had legitimate connection with the land. In exchange for clothing and other supplies, he purchased a lease from the Coloma Indians for the mill land and vicinity.

In the meantime, one of Sutter's mill hands, a Mormon named Henry Bigler, became California's first prospector. He took every opportunity, including Sundays, to search for gold, telling the Gentiles that he was going hunting, but sharing the news of the gold strike with other Mormons, who, like him, had marched West to fight Mexicans as part of the so-called Mormon Battalion, but had reached California after hostilities there had ended.

Other people around Sutter's mill broadcast the secret as well. When Colonel R. B. Mason was appointed military governor of California, Sutter indiscreetly sent a messenger to him in Monterey to confirm the lease he had negotiated with the Coloma Indians. The messenger, a man named Charles Bennett, carried with him a small pouch of gold he had collected, which he showed to various and sundry along the way to Monterey. Despite admonishing others to keep the strike secret, Sutter himself boasted of it. Yet, oddly, the fever for gold did not rise until the word was spread by another Mormon, Sam Brannan—the man who had led 238 fellow Saints to California in 1846 and then tried to persuade Brigham Young's group to follow him back to his settlement.

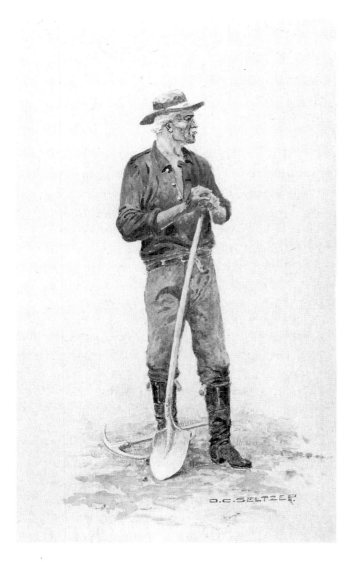

Brannan visited what had become known locally as the "Mormon Diggings," decided to open a store to serve prospectors near Sutter's mill, filled a quinine bottle full of gold dust, and ran through the streets of San Francisco (then called Yerba Buena) shouting "Gold! Gold! Gold from the American River!" *That,* he reasoned, should bring plenty of business to his store.

Coupled with a well-timed story in his own newspaper, the San Francisco *Star,* Brannan's announcement induced San Franciscans to abandon their work, close up shop, walk off the fields, drop their tools, and seek gold. The shrewd Mormon, in the meantime, had bought up all the prospectors' supplies locally available. An iron pan—used in "panning" gold out of riverbeds—which could have been bought for twenty cents before anyone had heard of Sutter's mill, now sold for as much as sixteen dollars. Soon, flour would go for four hundred dollars a barrel, whiskey for twenty dollars a quart, and so on. By the end of 1848, some ten thousand prospectors were at work in California and had already extracted a quarter million dollars' worth of the yellow metal. Two men extracted seventeen thousand dollars in gold dust and nuggets from a single canyon. Five men at Mormon Diggings split a profit of eighteen hundred dollars, garnered from five days' work. A solo prospector earned over five thousand dollars in two months of work. More usual, however, was an average take of twenty dollars a day—still a handsome return in an era when a day of manual labor earned one dollar.

And it was merely a prelude.

In the summer of 1848, Colonel Mason—who had declared Sutter's lease invalid, since the United States did not recognize the Indians' right to the land—toured the gold fields. He purchased samples of the gold, a little over 230 ounces of it, packed it in a tea caddy, and put it in the care of Lieutenant Lucien Loeser for delivery to Washington, D.C. Loeser's sea voyage via Panama was necessarily a lengthy one. There was no canal in 1848; you landed and left ship, crossed the Isthmus via a jungle river and a jungle march, and then you waited, sometimes many weeks, for another ship. He touched port at New Orleans, whence he took a stagecoach to the capital. By the time of his arrival it was late in the year, but telegraphed news of the tea caddy reached President Polk in time for his opening message to the Thirtieth Congress. "The accounts of the abundance of gold in that territory," the president declared, "are of such extraordinary character as would scarcely command belief were they not corroborated by the authentic reports of officers in the public service." The caddy itself arrived two days after the address, on December 7, and was put on public display.

Overnight, gold was the subject of countless newspaper articles and popular lectures, all touting the ease with which a thousand dollars a day could be washed from rivers or plucked from the ground. Typical of the small library of gold seeker's "guidebooks" almost instantly composed and printed was the *Emigrant's Guide to the Gold Mines,* which reported riverbeds "paved with gold to the thickness of a hand," promising that "twenty to fifty thousand dollars of gold" could be "picked out almost instantly." Indeed, while yields fell far short of the editors' and lyceum orators' figures, prospecting really was quite an easy activity—for the firstcomers. The Mother Lode in Northern California presented a good deal of gold close to the surface. In earlier geological times, volcanic activity had pushed magma up from the interior to the surface, where the molten magma gradually hardened into rocks veined with gold and other ores. Over the eons, erosion carried the metals into rivers and streams, depositing heavier pieces farther upstream than the lighter bits. The farther upstream a prospector went, the more gold he could find. The dust and nuggets, there for the taking, were called placer gold. At first, all you needed was to work the dry gulches and ravines—places where the water had deposited gold in superficial crevices that could be excavated with nothing more elaborate than a knife or spoon. If you dug deeper, you might find larger pockets of gold. Heaps of promising earth were shoveled onto a blanket and tossed, winnowing away the dirt and leaving the heavier gold dust behind—or, at least, some of it. In those early days, when the Mother Lode appeared to be limitless, losing some gold dust to the wind did not seem overly wasteful.

Even before the end of 1848, before the onset of the rush, some prospectors were doing more than digging and scraping for surface deposits in dry creek- and riverbeds. They began panning near active rivers and creeks as well. Again, the basic tool could not have been simpler: a tin or iron pan, the same one a prospector might fry his bacon in. The prospector would dredge up some dirt in the pan, swirl it underwater, lift it out of the water and swirl it some more, reimmerse it occasionally, and, at the end of the process, have washed away the dirt and left the gold.

It seemed easy. Actually, like that earlier way of seeking a western fortune, fur trapping, it meant backbreaking hours of squatting in ice-cold water, bent over the pan, swirling and immersing it day after tedious day. Soon, Isaac Humphrey, a miner from Georgia, introduced the "cradle" to California. It was an oblong wooden box, about three feet long and mounted on rockers. At its open lower end, bars—called "riffles"—were nailed, and at its upper end, an "apron"—canvas stretched across a frame—was fitted at a slant, above which a perforated hopper was fixed. Paydirt, as the gold-bearing earth was called, was put into the hopper and water poured over it as the cradle was rocked back and forth. The apron strained out most of the dirt, and the riffles collected the gold-laden sediment. The work was still torture, but at least it proceeded more efficiently.

But even "wet digging," as the panning and cradle methods were called, would yield less and less as 1849

E. Hall Martin (1818–1851)
Mountain Jack and a Wandering Miner, c. 1850
Oil on canvas, 39 ½ × 72 in.
Collection of The Oakland Museum; Gift of Concours d'Antiques, Art Guild

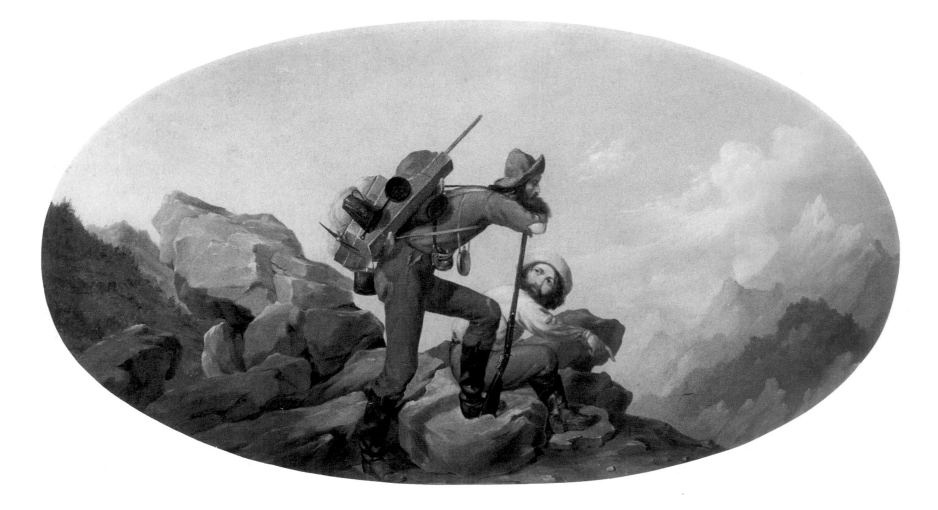

Albertus del Orient Browere (1814–1887)
Trail of the 49'ers, c. 1858
Oil on canvas, 33 × 48 in.
Collection of The Newark Museum;
Purchase 1956 Edward F. Weston
Bequest Fund

A lesser-known member of the so-called Hudson River School of landscape painters, Browere caught gold fever in 1852 and sailed for California via Cape Horn. He made a second trip to gold country in 1858, when he painted this retrospective landscape.

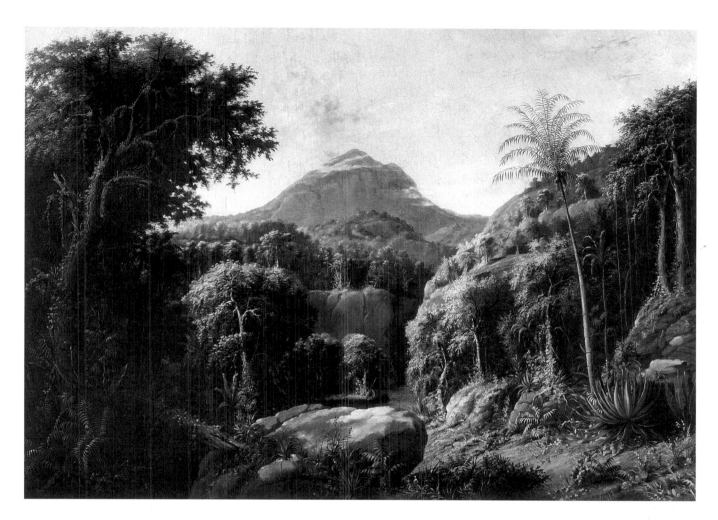

crowded in more than a hundred thousand prospectors to work the beleaguered Mother Lode. A far more certain way to wealth was to set up as a merchant, as Brannan had done. Collis P. Huntington, for example, had been an itinerant peddlar of watches and watch parts and then a small store owner in upstate New York before he left to join the 1849 rush. He prospected for just one day. Then he opened up a miners' supply store in Sacramento, built a fortune, and became one of the principal financiers of the Central Pacific portion of the transcontinental railroad.

No one—even in the flush early days of the gold rush—said *getting* to California was easy. There were four choices, two by sea, one combining river travel with an overland trek, and one that was strictly overland.

By sea, a Forty-Niner could choose the Panama Route or the Cape Horn Route. The Panama Route was, geographically, the shorter, as one sailed from New York to Chagres, on the east coast of Panama. Sometimes, depending on what one could afford to pay, the ocean passage could be made comfortably enough. Often, however, condemned vessels were pressed into service and were overcrowded at that. But it was at Chagres that real hardship began. One had to bargain with the inhabitants of the mud-hut town for canoe transportation up the Chagres River to a point in the middle of the jungle, where the gold seeker then began a two-day tropical march to Panama City, there to await Pacific transportation to California. It was always a long wait, as hundreds

of travelers clamored for limited space on a limited number of ships. And waiting in a disease-infested tropical city was no picnic. Bribes of a thousand dollars for steerage passage were not unheard of.

The far longer—at least in terms of miles—Cape Horn Route held the promise of greater comfort, unless, as was usually the case, the ship was old and overcrowded. The voyage south took many weeks; then perhaps another two or three months might be consumed rounding the treacherous Horn itself. Finally, there was the long voyage north to California. Often, miners banded together into mutual associations in order to finance the journey, either purchasing blocks of tickets or chartering entire ships.

Perhaps twenty-five thousand Forty-Niners chose the two sea routes. Far more—some seventy-five or eighty thousand—went overland. For those with the price of passage, the first leg of the journey could be made by steamboat sailing down the Ohio and up the Mississippi and Missouri rivers as far as St. Joseph, Missouri, the staging point for the arduous overland portion of the odyssey. Not that western steamboats were very comfortable, either. The vessels that plied the Missouri were not the floating palaces—or bordellos—that navigated the Mississippi. Those who could afford cabin passage slept on corncob mattresses, *if* they could sleep at all for the incessant din of the engines, the choking wood smoke, and the relentless vibration of the paddle wheel. Those who could not afford a cabin were immured below

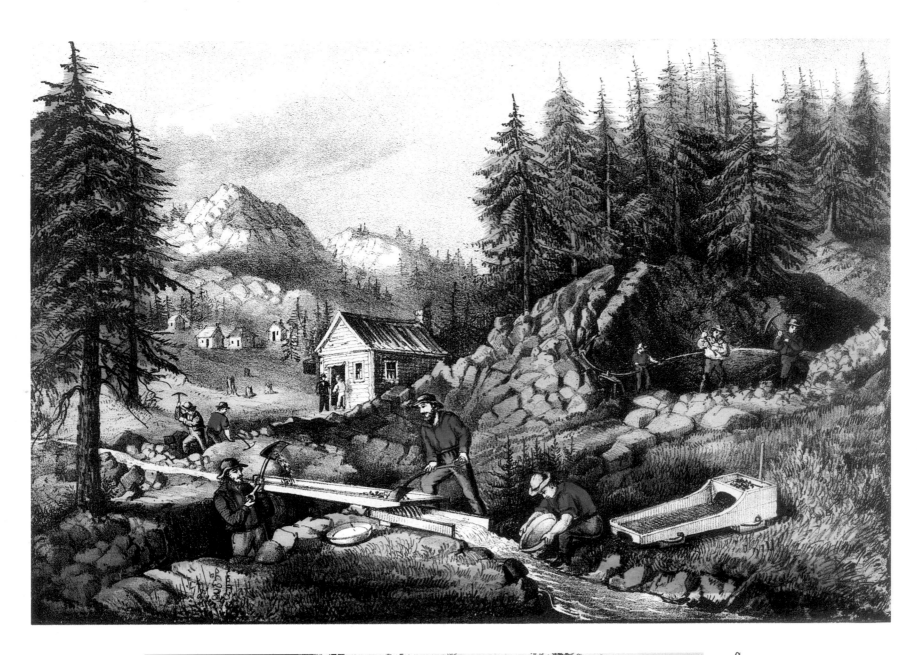

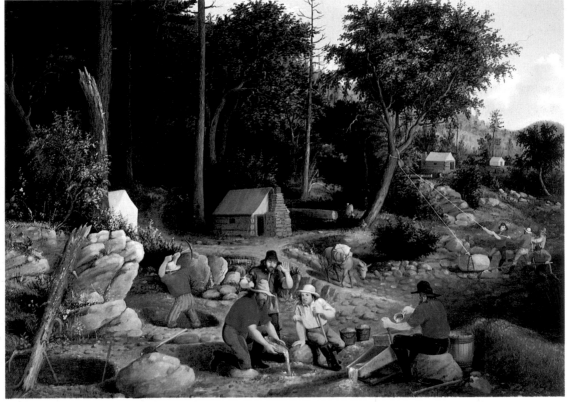

Currier & Ives
Gold Mining in California, 1871
Museum of the City of New York

Four methods of prospecting are illustrated here: sluice, pan, cradle (the device is idle, pictured at the right), and hydraulic (the water hose in the upper right background).

Albertus del Orient Browere (1814–1887)
The Mines of Placerville, 1855
Oil on canvas, 26 × 36 in.
National Cowboy Hall of Fame and Western Heritage

This painting is similar enough to the later Currier & Ives print to suggest that it may have served the lithographers' anonymous artist as source material.

decks and had to find a place to sleep between piles of cargo in stifling darkness. Drinking water for cabin and steerage passengers alike came from the Missouri—the river nicknamed "Old Muddy"—and, on better vessels, was available from barrels stored on deck. On less deluxe boats, passengers were given a bucket tied to a rope and told to fetch up their own refreshment.

Nor was the trip fast. The Missouri is a shallow river well endowed with sandbars. All steamboats carried two enormous spars that could be lowered to the river bottom at a forty-five-degree angle if the boat ran aground. The spars were driven down and back, like crutches, using a steam-powered "nigger engine." The boat then slid, or "grasshoppered," several yards ahead. The process was repeated until the vessel floated free of the bar. But, in especially shallow water, even grasshoppering was to no avail. In these cases, the captain had to lighten ship by unloading a portion of the cargo, steam over the bar, and then reload.

Nor were crew members models of refinement. There were roustabouts, also called roosters, who served as stokers and deckhands. Some were black slaves,

leased out by their onshore owners. Some were immigrants, mostly German and Irish. ("Oh, hell," one pilot was reported to have exclaimed when he did not stop to rescue a man overboard, "it's only an Irishman!") Some were Missouri farm lads. The roosters were overseen by steamboat mates, who coaxed and regulated their charges with fists, clubs, and guns.

Nor was a Missouri steamboat even remotely safe. If Mississippi riverboats were notorious for boiler explosions—the engineer operated his boiler without benefit of a pressure gauge, even as the captain demanded more steam for more speed—those vessels were fortresses compared to the far flimsier and more cheaply built Missouri craft. Running against the current, engineers had a habit of disabling the vessel's single concession to life and limb by tying down the safety valve. Rapids, frequently encountered along the Missouri, posed a particular hazard to the fragile steamboat. Bucking rapids upstream required the setting of a "dead man"—planting a timber onshore, fastening a cable to it, and reeling the cable in with the vessel's steam-driven capstan. Not infrequently, this simply tore out the front of the boat. If

Olaf Carl Seltzer (1877–1957)
The Smoke Boat, 1930
Oil on canvas, 11 × 16 in.
Gilcrease Museum, Tulsa, Oklahoma

Many Indians saw the ramshackle riverboats that plied the waters of the West as evidence of the white man's godlike powers.

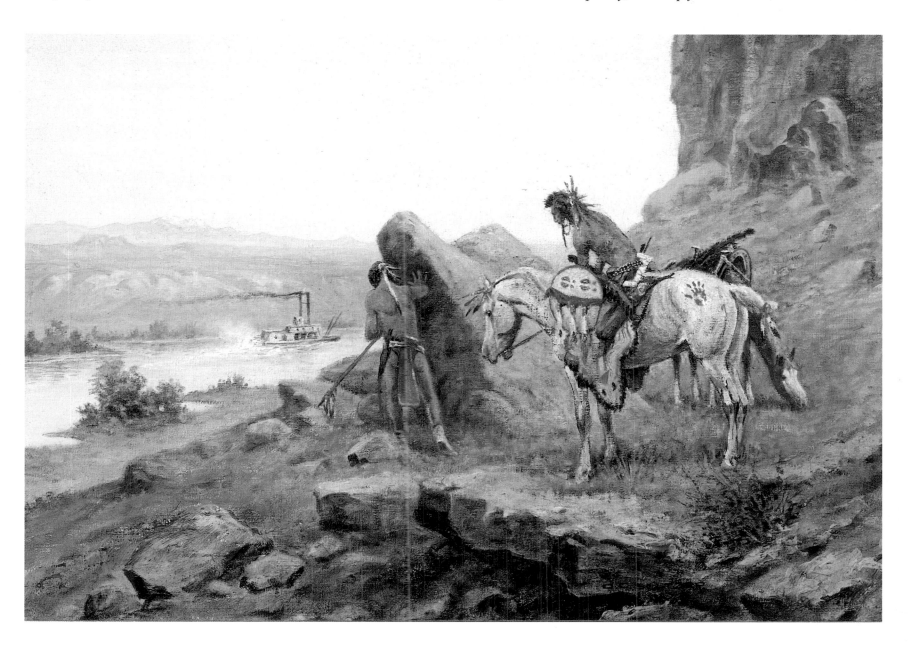

NATHANIEL CURRIER

BORN 1813, ROXBURY, MASSACHUSETTS

DIED 1888, NEW YORK

JAMES MERRITT IVES

BORN 1824, NEW YORK CITY

DIED 1895, RYE, NEW YORK

The paintings of western artists were widely reproduced during the nineteenth and twentieth centuries in magazines, books, and as individual prints. Beginning in the 1850s and practically to the end of the century, no firm reached a greater popular audience with inexpensive, high-quality hand-colored lithographs of such western artists as Arthur Fitzwilliam Tait, George Catlin, Frances (Fanny) Palmer, and J. Cameron than Currier & Ives—although Western scenes represented only a fraction of the more than seven thousand lithographs the company published in its seventy-two-year history.

Apprenticed to the Boston lithographers William and John Pendleton in 1828, Currier worked for M. E. D. Brown in Philadelphia during 1833 before moving to New York, where he began a lithography partnership with Adam Stodart in 1834. The two parted company the next year, and Currier operated the business under his own name, achieving his first local success with *Ruins of the Merchant Exchange . . .* , the first in a genre of disaster prints that Currier would develop masterfully. Six years later, *Awful Conflagration of the Steamboat* Lexington *in Long Island Sound* put the firm on the national map.

Currier hired James Merritt Ives, a self-trained artist, as a bookkeeper in 1852; five years later, Ives was a full partner.

With few exceptions, most notably Palmer, Currier & Ives employed no well-known full-time "staff" artists. They did, however, commission work from a host of America's better professional painters. Doubtless, in those days of loose copyright laws, they also reproduced some paintings without troubling themselves to secure the artist's permission.

The work of Currier & Ives survived even after the technology of reproduction had overtaken the laborious methods of stone lithography and hand coloring. Photography, an increasing presence after the Civil War, could not achieve the vividness of a good hand-colored print. Chromolithography, a process by which color was actually printed rather than added to the finished print by hand, was more expensive and generally less beautiful than the work produced by Currier & Ives. Toward the end of the century, however, improved photographic methods and the ascendency of the illustrated magazine were edging the company out of business. By 1907, the firm, which for some years had been run by the partners' sons, Edward West Currier and Chauncey Ives, was liquidated. Its obsolescent lithographic stones were sold by the pound, and its out-of-favor prints were sold by the bundle. Today, collectors pay five-figure prices for some of Currier & Ives's lithographs.

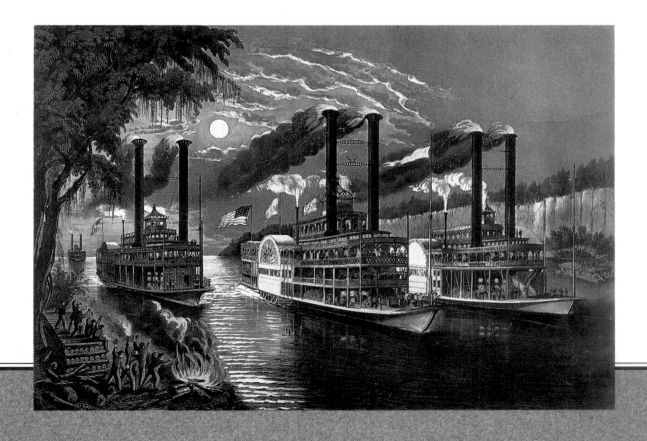

the cable broke, the steamer might be carried off by the rapids and smashed to matchwood against rocks. Snags—underwater obstructions—could do even worse, tearing out the bottom of the hull and sinking the boat in seconds. The hazards, and the tedium, drove roustabouts, mates, and pilots to drink, and, indeed, a well-stocked bar was often also the only gesture toward *passenger* comfort to be found on a steamboat.

The overland trek was the same long, hard, hazardous push, whether one began where the steamboat trip ended or somewhere back east of the Missouri. The Forty-Niner could take a southwestern route to Santa Fe, then turn northward along the Old Spanish Trail or work his way south, along the Gila River, into Southern California and travel north in comparative comfort along the well-worn El Camino Real. He could even venture into Mexico from Santa Fe and proceed overland or take a San Francisco–bound ship from Mazatlán. But more popular than any of these southerly routes was the one that cut due west, from the Missouri River, along the Platte and Sweetwater to South Pass, around the Great Salt Lake, along the Humboldt River, across the desert, over the Sierra, and into California. As we have seen, the popularity of this route both enriched the Mormons of Salt Lake, who did a thriving business in victualing and equipping the emigrants, and also ended the Saints' cherished isolation. It was the gold rush that ultimately herded Deseret into the American territorial fold.

In the overland journey, the Forty-Niners faced the same perils as the Mormons had. Some did so in wagon trains almost as well organized as those of the Mormons. Others attempted the trek solo. The Missouri embarkation towns developed into raucous western metropolises: Independence, St. Joseph, Westport, Kanesville. Merchants in these places fattened nightly, and gambling halls and saloons sprouted like weeds. For those who had begun the trip overland east of the Missouri, that river had to be crossed. Ferryboatmen accumulated fortunes as men sometimes killed for a place in the boat. The traffic jam was backed up for many miles, and delays of two weeks waiting to cross the river were not unheard of. Some idea of the volume of traffic can be gathered from the soldiers at Fort Childs, on the south bank of the Platte River, who could count as many as 460 wagons passing through *each day* by May 1849.

Once across the Missouri, there were the plains to be traversed. The spring and summer of 1849 was a poor time for travel, as rain fell almost ceaselessly, turning the rutted trails into sloughs of mud and bringing dysentery and the dreaded Asiatic cholera. Epidemics raged among the wagon trains; some five thousand emigrants died, their graves left to mark the high plains portion of the trail. Not that traveling alone was any insurance against disease—or worse. The journal of one Forty-Niner records finding the body of such a wayfarer beside the trail, his throat cut, the knife still clutched in his hand.

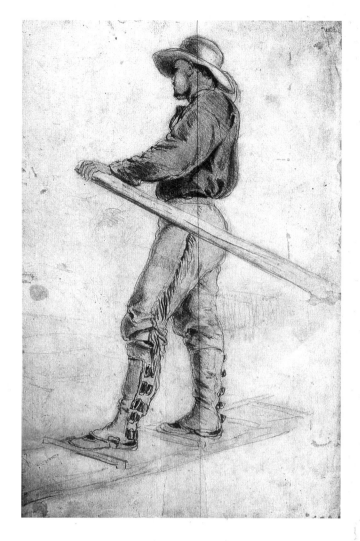

Beyond Salt Lake, the emigrants crossed the Forty-Mile Desert, "the *worst desert* you ever saw," according to one who had made the trip. When the sand and dust of their own passing settled, Forty-Niners found the trail easy enough to follow; for it was marked by the bones of dead stock and dead men. Once the desert was crossed, there were the mountains, the Sierra Nevada, to climb. Loads were lightened; supplies that had been bought at grossly inflated prices in Missouri or in Salt Lake City were discarded, as miners drove their battered wagons up the steep trails. The critical importance of having carefully timed one's departure now became urgently apparent. Those who had left points east too late might well be snowed in, cut off, frozen, and starved. (Of course, those who had left too *early* failed to find sufficient spring grass along the plains portion of the trail to feed their livestock.) Nor was the journey down the Sierra's western face much of a relief, as wagons had to be lowered on ropes down trails more vertical than horizontal.

The miners found their way to camps with names like Poverty Bar, Angels Camp, Coyote Diggings, Cuteye Foster's, Drunkards Bar, Dead Man's Bar, Gouge Eye, Mad Mule Gulch, Rough and Ready, Murderers Bar, Whiskytown, Rattlesnake Bar. There was Dry Bar, which boasted twenty-six saloons. In such mining towns—none was more than a camp, really—newcomers heard stories about a man who dug down four feet and found gold in large hunks, including one fourteen-pound nugget. Or about a southerner and his slave who both had a dream one night about finding gold under a cabin in Old Dry Diggings; the master bought the cabin, and, working alongside his slave, dug up the dirt floor, finding twenty thousand dollars in gold. Or the Frenchmen who up-rooted a stump and found five thousand dollars in gold. Or the man who, in a fit of anger, kicked a rock and found a large nugget beneath it. Or the hunter who shot a bear: the bear fell over the edge of a canyon, the hunter pursued, and found a ledge of gold-veined quartz. Or the solemn burial of a dead miner: the preacher preached, the mourners knelt by the graveside, the sermon became tedious, and the mourners began fingering the grave dirt. "Color!" one of them yelled; the dirt had traces of gold in it. "Congregation dismissed!" shouted the preacher. The body was chucked out of the hole, and all—mourners and clergy—began to dig.

Some of the stories were actually true, more or less. There were prospectors who, indeed, struck it rich, and with little effort. But they were few. By the time most of the Forty-Niners had arrived, the easy pickings and the

rich claims had all been staked and were being worked. For some, there was still a living to be made, but it was hard labor for niggardly wages—a few ounces of gold worth a few dollars a day at most, and even that was ir-regular. Working a mine near Hangtown, one group of prospectors averaged three dollars a day; another netted a penny a day.

For those who did not simply give up in discourage-ment, it was obvious that their fortunes would not be made quickly. They would have to find a claim, stake it, work it, and live from day to day, week to week, month to month. At first, a claim consisted of whatever area a man could work. He proved possession by keeping his tools on the site and by continually working it. Soon, in-dividual camps established bylaws governing claims more formally. Limits to size were established; in rich camps, a claim might be as small as a hundred square feet—the size of a modern bathroom—and the principal of one man, one claim prevailed. Disputes were settled by ad hoc juries. As to living, the camps offered food at inflated prices (potatoes for a dollar a pound; an egg for fifty cents; a chicken, four dollars; apples, two for

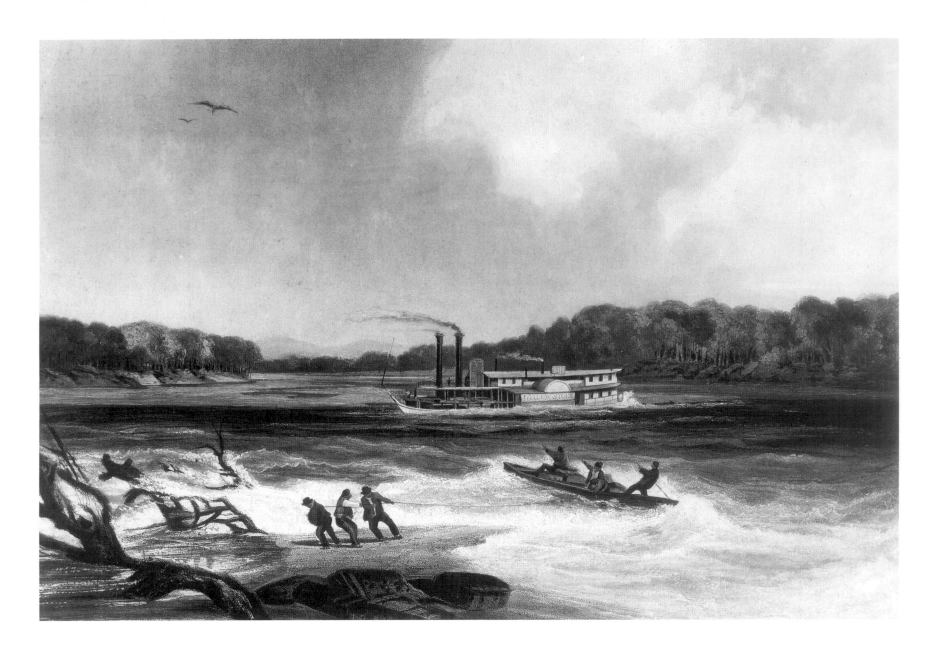

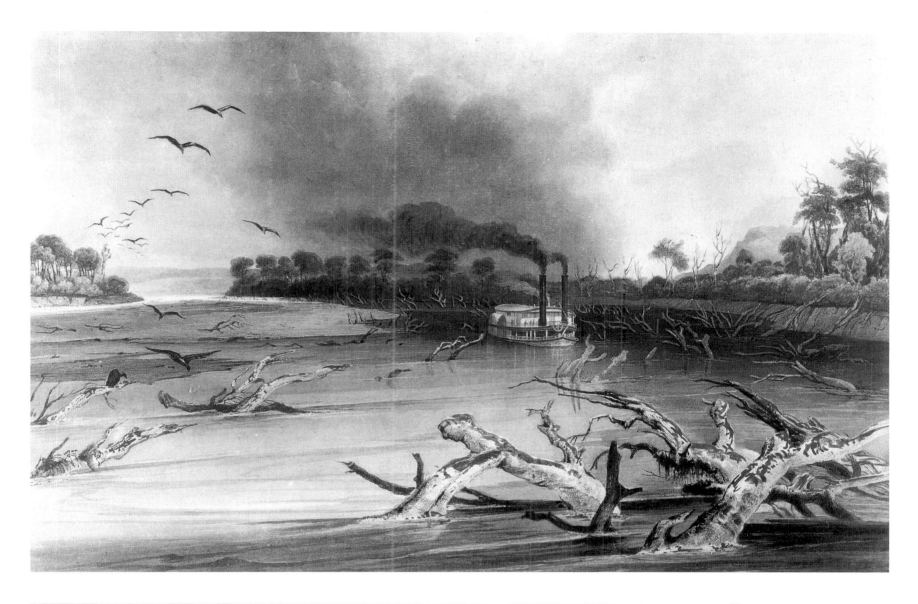

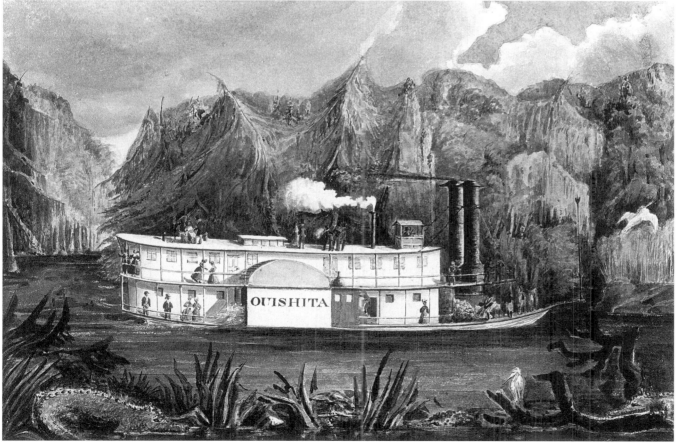

Karl Bodmer (1809–1893)
Snags (Sunken Trees) on the Missouri, 1833
Lithograph
New York Public Library

Travelers frequently described the Missouri as a mile wide and a foot deep. Even the extremely shallow-draft riverboats found navigation hazardous. A snag could easily rip out the bottom of one of these fragile craft.

Sir Richard George Augustus Levinge
The Paddle Steamer "Ouishita" on the Red River, Louisiana Territory, c. 1836
Watercolor and sepia wash on paper, 8 ⅜ × 12 ½ in.
Amon Carter Museum, Fort Worth, Texas

Shallow draft, high center of gravity, crudely cobbled wooden construction, a boiler without gauges, rivers beset with shallows, sand bars, and snags—travel by western steam vessel was yet another hazard of the frontier.

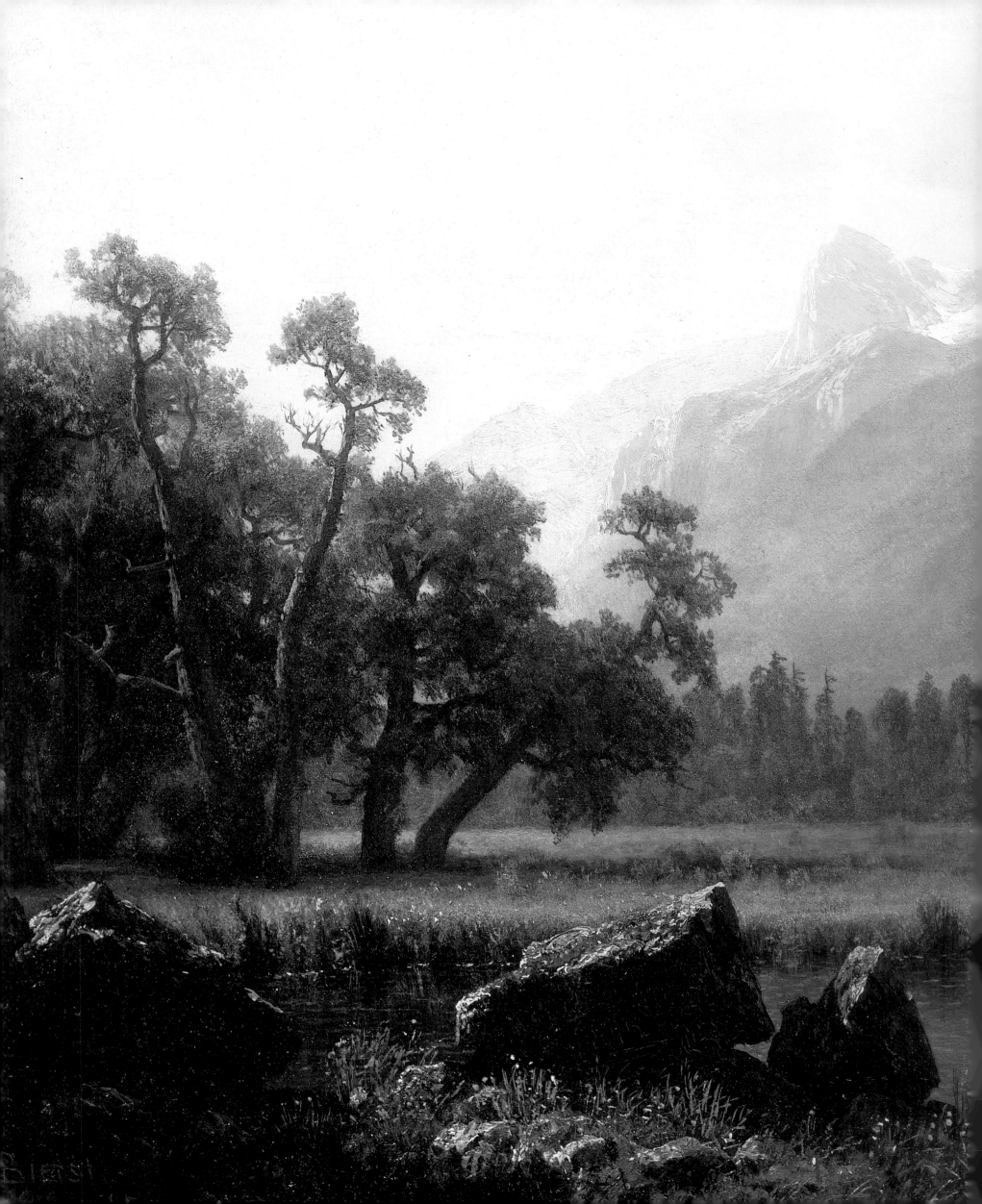

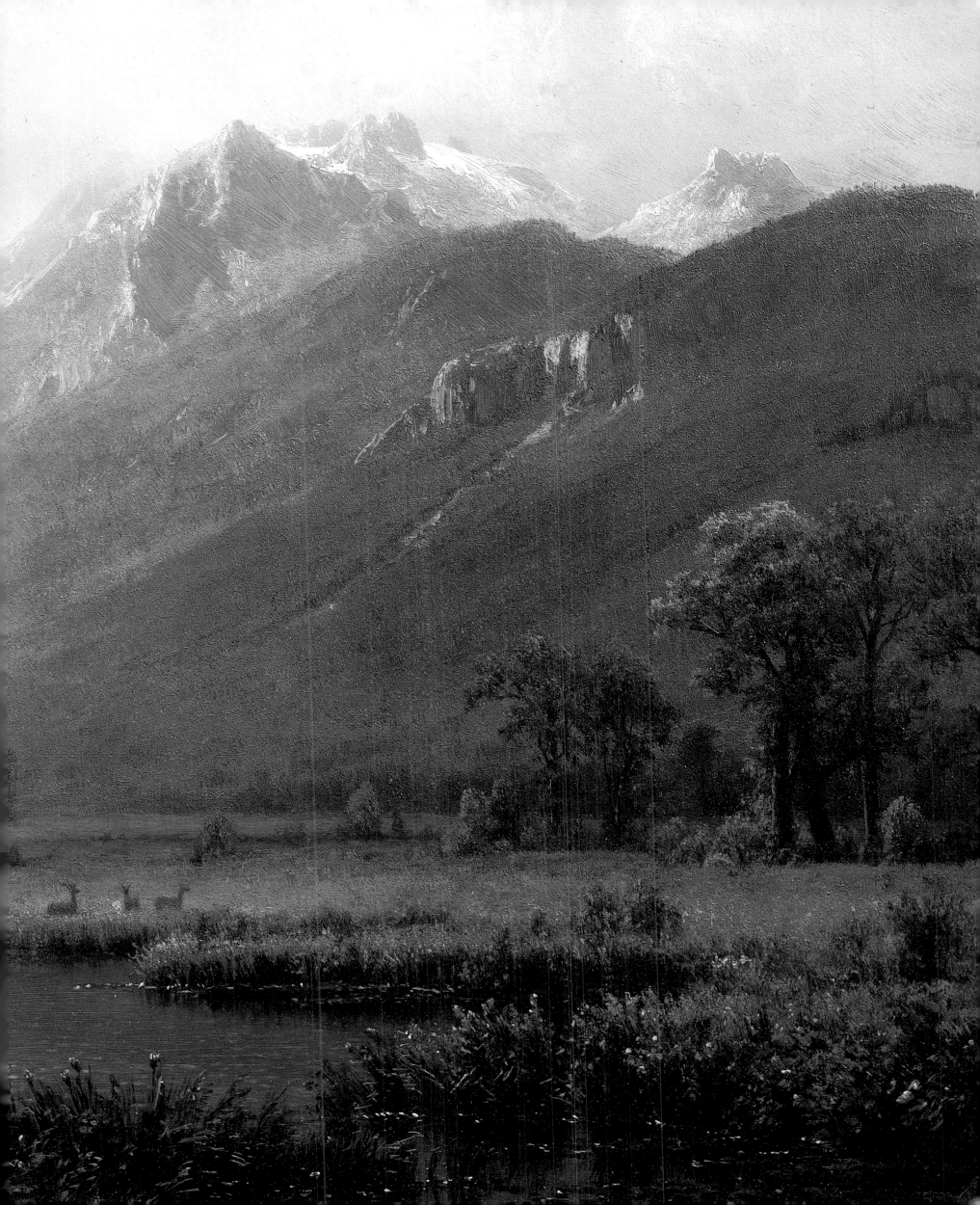

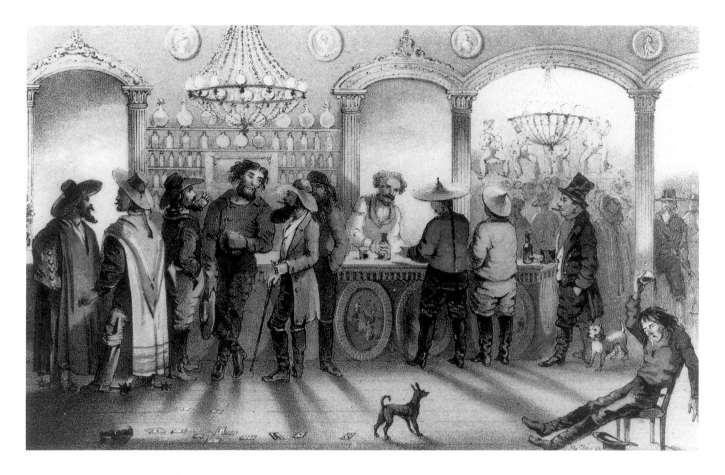

Frank Marryat (1826–1855)
The Bar of a Gambling Saloon (in San Francisco), c. 1850
Lithograph, book page size:
5 ⅜ × 8 ½ in.
Courtesy of The New-York Historical Society, New York City

Son of the popular British writer Captain Frederick Marryat, Francis Samuel Marryat settled in San Francisco in 1850 and worked as a miner, innkeeper, actor, and author. He was also an amateur watercolorist. Marryat died at age twenty-nine, the result of yellow fever contracted during his honeymoon.

seventy-five cents), liquor, gambling (a shrewd three-card monte dealer made more in a night than most miners made in a month of heartbreaking work), and laundry service (eight dollars to wash a dozen shirts—some miners actually sent their shirts to China for washing; it was cheaper). The camps also purveyed disease, including dysentery and scurvy. Women were, it seemed, a million miles away. One camp entrepreneur offered a peek at a lady's bonnet and boots for the admission price of one dollar.

Something like more civilized institutions were hurriedly established in the larger camps. Legal institutions executed justice—as well as those judged guilty—with lightning dispatch. The rule of the twelve-man jury prevailed, and sentences included banishment, flogging, and hanging. Women were recruited for the camps; to be sure, the first were not Sunday school teachers:

> Hangtown gals are plump and rosy,
> Hair in ringlets, mighty cozy,
> Painted cheeks and jossy bonnets—
> Touch 'em and they'll sting like hornets!

While some eastern employment agencies scouted professional prostitutes for the camps, calling them "domestics," other women did come with more honorable intentions. Early in 1849, Mrs. Eliza W. Farnham, widow of an Oregon Trail pioneer and formerly a matron at New York's Sing Sing prison, attempted to recruit "100 to 130 intelligent, virtuous and efficient" women for marrying into the camps. She managed actually to find a grand to-

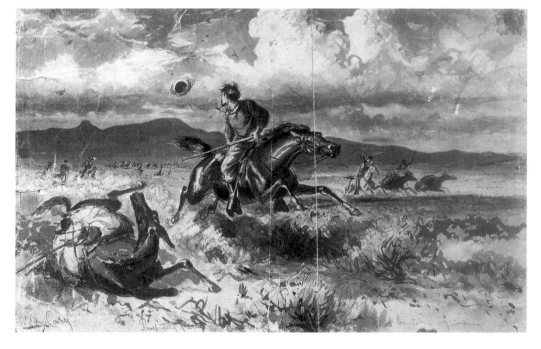

William de la Montagne Cary (1840–1922)
Prospecting Party on Their Way to the Black Hills Overtaken by Indians, n.d.
Wash sketch on paper, 9 × 13 in.
Gilcrease Museum, Tulsa, Oklahoma

The discovery of gold in the Black Hills brought unwelcome whites into this most sacred of Sioux lands.

tal of three. Later, a Miss Pellet attempted to recruit five thousand. She, too, had few takers. By 1850, less than 8 percent of California's population was female. Nevertheless, mining camps were quick to establish schools, lacking only teachers and students.

The camps also supported an astounding wealth of newspapers, more per capita than anywhere else in the United States. A greater surprise was the early presence and tremendous popularity of the theater, with Shakespearean companies in particular favor. The great Booth dynasty—in the persons of Junius Brutus, father and son, and Edwin—performed regularly in the camps. Actresses, of course, were even more in demand, the most famous of whom was Lola Montez. Born in Limerick, Ireland, in 1818 and christened Marie Dolores Eliza Rosanna Gilbert (she took "Lola" as a diminutive of

Dolores, and she took "Montez" as better suited to a Spanish dancer than Gilbert), Montez was celebrated in Europe for her extraordinary figure and numerous liaisons with the rich and famous, including Franz Liszt, Alexandre Dumas, King Ludwig I of Bavaria, and others. As an actress, she met with failure after failure, both in Europe and the American East Coast. She sought a more appreciative audience in San Francisco, and she did make a hit there—though less for her acting than for "La Tarantula," the "Spider Dance," in which fake spiders made of cork, rubber, and whalebone "invaded" her skirts, which she shook out in most edifying ways. But even in the entertainment-starved Far West, her success was brief. A performance in Sacramento was rewarded with a barrage of rotten eggs and apples. The actress at last retired to Grass Valley, west of Lake Tahoe, where

Albertus del Orient Browere (1814–1887)
Goldminers, 1858
Oil on canvas, 29 × 36 in.
Courtesy of The Anschutz Collection

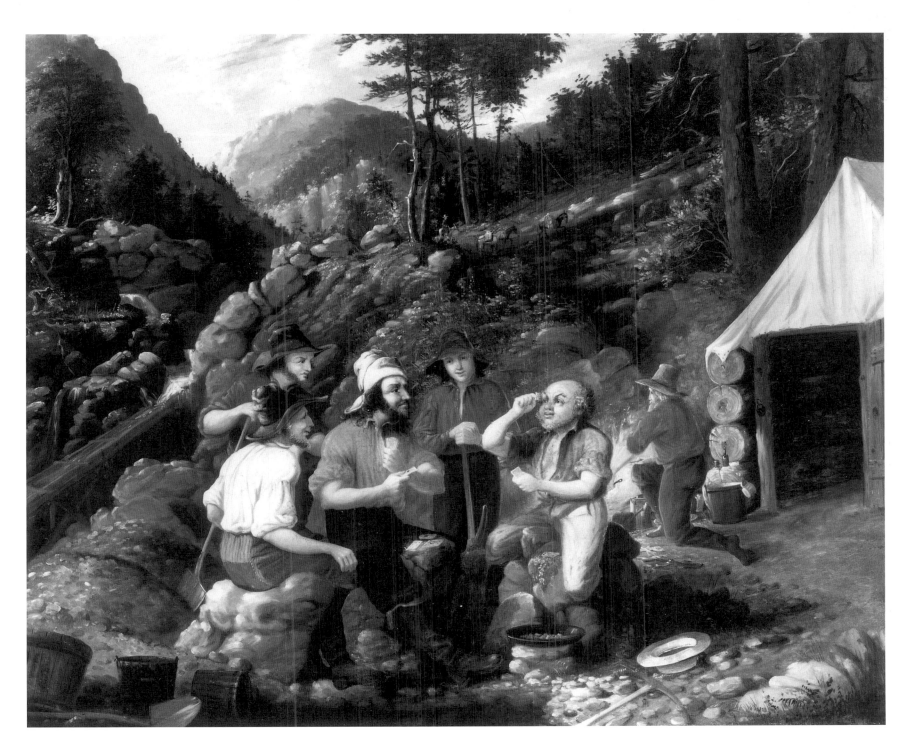

she befriended Mrs. Mary Ann Crabtree. Boardinghouse keeper and wife of a failed prospector, Mrs. Crabtree had theatrical ambitions for her daughter, Lotta, and Lola obligingly taught the girl a repertoire of songs and dances. It so happened that, about this time, child performers were enjoying a tremendous vogue in the mining camps—Fairy Stars, they were called—and Lotta debuted, with great success, in a camp named Rabbit Creek. *She,* at least, struck it rich, earning more money that night than her father had in four years of prospecting. As an adult, she became the nation's most celebrated comedienne.

The existence of such luxuries is the more amazing when one considers the moral and physical squalor of the mining camps. Much of the time spent "in town" was spent drunk. "Town" usually consisted of a collection of tents and a few ramshackle wooden structures. Mrs. Louise Amelia Knapp Smith Clappe, who came to the gold fields with her husband (he wisely set up not as a prospector, but as a physician), described the town of Rich Bar in 1851. She wrote under the nom de plume "Dame Shirley" and published a regular column in a California magazine. Rich Bar, she wrote, had only one street, which was lined with "round tents, square tents, plank hovels, log cabins &c, varying in elegance from the palatial splendor of 'The Empire' down to a 'local habitation' formed of pine boughs and covered with old calico shirts." The Empire was a quintessential mining town saloon/dance hall/general store. Its two stories made it the tallest building in town, and its glass-paned windows were the town's only specimens of the glazier's art. Part of the interior was "fitted up as a bar-room. A really elegant mirror is set off by a back-ground of decanters, cigar vases and jars of brandied fruit." On a table covered with a green cloth was deployed the ubiquitous pack of monte cards. "The remainder of the room does as a shop where velveteen and leather, flannel shirts and calico— the latter starched to an appalling state of stiffness—lie cheek by jowl with hams, preserved meats, oysters and other groceries in hopeless confusion." Four steps up from the barroom/store was the hotel parlor, "carpeted in straw matting and draped with purple calico." Another four steps led to four eight-by-ten bedrooms. "It is," concluded Dame Shirley, "just such a piece of carpentering as a child two years old, gifted with the strength of a man, would produce. . . . And yet this impertinent apology for a house cost its original owners more than eight thousand dollars."

Another feature of mining towns was crime and punishment, and a good deal of both. Drunken brawling was routine and, as the placer gold disappeared and fortunes proved increasingly elusive, thievery also became a fixture of life. Most mining towns lacked a jail, so penalties included banishment and whipping. Grand larceny—theft of more than a hundred dollars in gold, cash, or goods—was punishable by hanging.

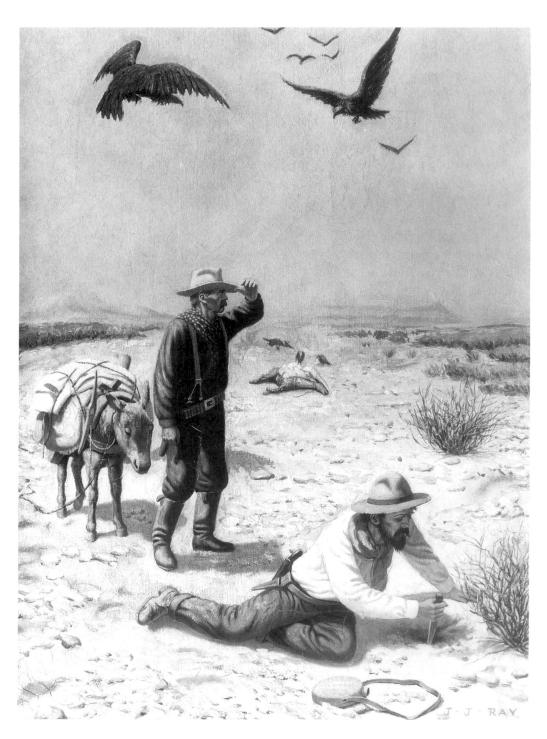

J. J. Ray (active 1906–1908) *Gold Mining in California,* n.d. Oil on canvas, 16 ¼ × 12 ¼ in. Gilcrease Museum, Tulsa, Oklahoma

In California's desert country, prospecting could rapidly turn from digging for gold to scratching for water.

Often, sentence was passed without benefit of trial. Malefactors were captured, accused, found guilty, and executed by informally assembled vigilante bands. These groups frequently extended their ad hoc jurisdiction beyond the prosecution of criminals by indulging themselves in the persecution of "foreigners." Germans, Irish, and Chinese were the principal immigrant victims.

Anglo miners thought of Mexicans as foreigners, too, including those who were *native* Californians. Seven years before James Marshall discovered gold in Sutter's millrace, Francisco López struck a far smaller lode on his rancho in the hills of Los Angeles. Mexican miners from the state of Sonora came up to work in those gold fields and, after the 1848 strike, came up north to work in the vicinity of Sutter's mill. Vigilantes relentlessly harassed the Sonorans, ejecting them from their claims, evicting them from the camps, even lynching them. In this they were abetted by the California legislature, which passed in 1850 the Greaser Act—the law's official title—and a tax on "foreign" miners.

While the Irish and Germans were often anxious to integrate themselves into California's American mainstream, the Chinese tended to keep apart (indeed, the Caucasians gave them little choice), maintaining the dress and traditions of the old country, including allegiance to 'tongs," fraternal organizations ordained by the customs of their homeland. Sometimes rival tongs went to war. When Weaverville's two tongs decided to fight, two thousand Caucasian townspeople came out to watch. The opposing forces were unequally matched—150 versus 400—though both sides had armed themselves with fifteen-foot pikes, great swords, and pitchforklike spears, most all of their weaponry having been commissioned from local blacksmiths.

The battle began with a series of charges and feints, made to the accompaniment of gongs and drums. One spectator, a Swede, grew tired of this bloodless choreography and fired a pistol shot into the ranks of the would-be combatants.

That did it. A ten-minute fight ensued. And—to the spectators' astonishment—the smaller tong was victo-

rious, forcing the four hundred to retreat. It turned out that the smaller group had cheated by engaging white spectators to cover its rear as its members charged, thereby preventing the larger group from closing ranks behind them. Eight Chinese died in the skirmish, and six were wounded. The only Caucasian casualty was the Swede whose gun had induced the brief spasm of violence. Somebody shot him—dead.

If the Chinese tended to practice violence only among themselves, there were Mexicans and native Californians who, cast out by mining-town society, became outlaws against the community at large. The most famous was Joaquín Murieta, the first of the West's gallery of legendary desperadoes.

Murieta had been born about 1830 in Sonora. To grow up in that state was to receive intensive instruction in guerrilla warfare; for Sonora was in continual revolt against Mexico. Murieta married the daughter of a mule skinner working for the mines, and in 1848, the couple joined the march to the gold fields of Alta California. Murieta did not set up as a miner, but worked as a ranch hand near Stockton until 1850, when he was arrested on suspicion of robbery, jailed, and then released as innocent. He left Stockton, lived for a time in the California town of Sonora—named for its population of Murieta's

Ernest Narjot (1827–1898)
The Gold Rush Camp (Miners—Moment at Rest), 1882
Oil on canvas, 50 ¼ × 40 ¼ in.
The Los Angeles Athletic Club Collection

Most depictions of the gold rush are full of color, romance, and excitement. This is a rare quotidian view of the goldminer's existence.

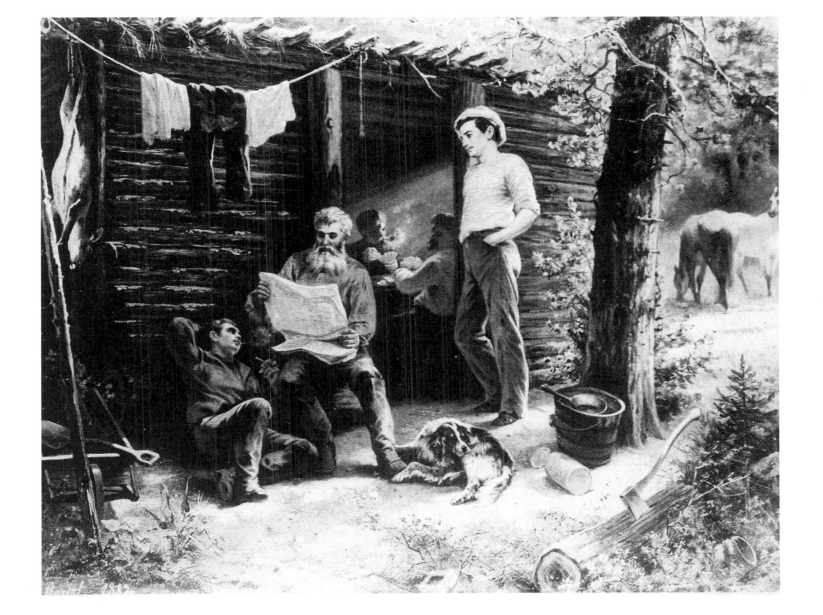

fellow countrymen—built a cabin for his family at Saw Mill Flat, and staked a prospecting claim. As the most prevalent story goes, a band of Anglo miners raped Murieta's wife and horsewhipped him off his claim. Other stories add further depredations, including cattle rustling and the murder of Joaquín's brother.

To avenge the insults and injuries he had suffered, Joaquín waged guerrilla warfare against the mines, killing Anglos and, in the manner of Robin Hood, robbing the rich to give to the poor. That such crimes were committed is beyond dispute. However, whether all of them were the work of the Ghost of Sonora, as the elusive Joaquín was called, or of several disgruntled Sonorans is open to question. In 1853, the state legislature hurriedly established the California Rangers and ordered them to capture *five* men named Joaquín: Valenzuela, Ocomorenia, Carillo, Botellier, and a Joaquín Muriati.

Led by Harry Love, twenty rangers spent two months combing the gold country in search of Murieta. In Tulare Valley, at the Panoche Pass, they encountered what they took to be a bandit gang, summarily decapi-

tated its leader, pickled the head in a jar of spirits, and exhibited it as the head of Joaquín Murieta. (The rangers also dispatched another member of the supposed gang whom, inasmuch as his hand was deformed, they identified as the infamous Three-Fingered Jack, second only to Joaquín as a scourge of the mining camps. His amputated hand was also preserved in a jar and exhibited.)

It is true that raids attributable to Joaquín stopped at this time. However, a woman who claimed to be Murieta's sister examined the pickled head and declared that it was absolutely not that of her brother. A story in a local newspaper, the *Alta California,* reported that the "bandit gang" the rangers had attacked (killing four) was a group of seven native Californians and Mexicans rounding up mustangs. Joaquín was reported alive and well and ranching in northern Sonora, Mexico, late in the 1870s.

Reviled by Anglos as a cutthroat, Murieta was seen very differently by native Californians and Mexicans. Robert Richards—né Rodríguez—who claimed to be Murieta's second cousin, eulogized him in 1932 as "a great

Albert Bierstadt (1830–1902)
Sunrise, Yosemite Valley, c. 1870
Oil on canvas, 36 ⅜ × 52 ⅜ in.
Amon Carter Museum, Fort Worth, Texas

An unsullied morning in the nation's own Eden.

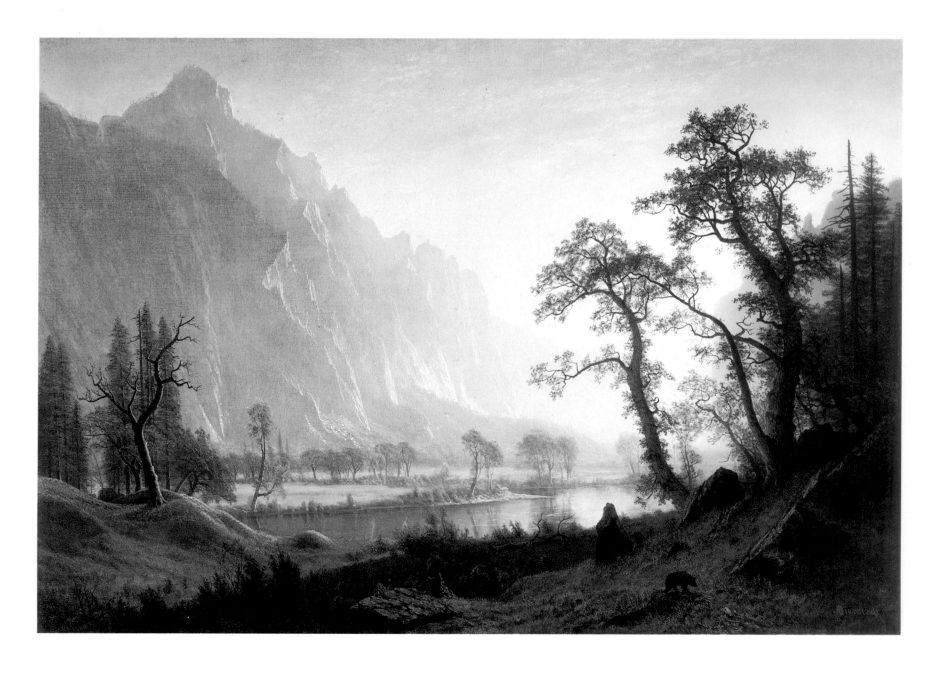

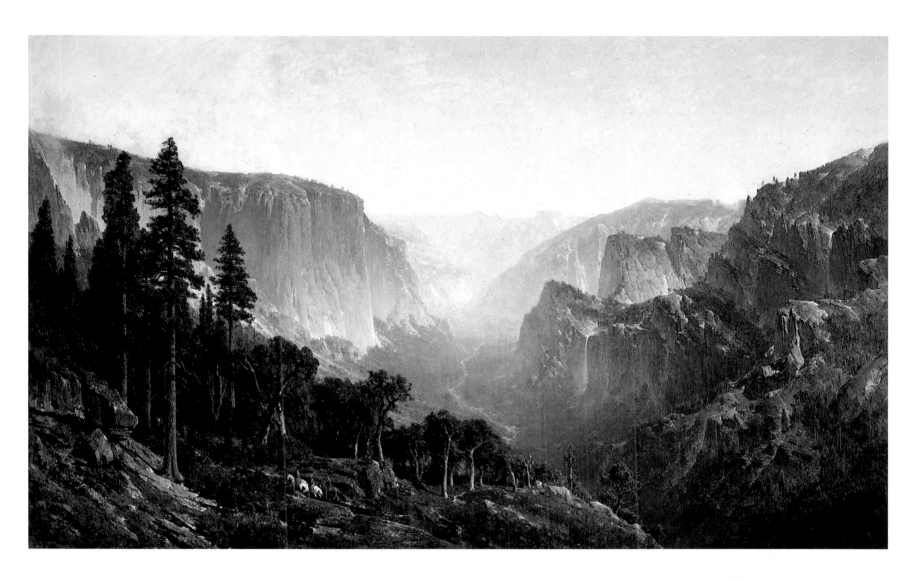

Thomas Hill (1829–1908)
Yosemite Valley, 1876
Oil on canvas, 72 × 120 in.
Collection of The Oakland Museum;
Kahn Collection

Not far from the squalor of the gold camps, this, too, was California gold country.

liberator, come out of Mexico to take California back from the hands of the gringos. They did not call his 'looting' and 'killing' banditry. They called it war."

The formation of the California Rangers was, in effect, legitimation of vigilantism: the rangers apprehended, judged, and executed sentence in a single motion. In San Francisco—a sleepy little village before the gold rush, now a boisterous, albeit ramshackle, metropolis—vigilantism began and developed as a legitimate institution.

The San Francisco Committee of Vigilance had its origin in fire. Matchwood-built San Francisco was plagued by disastrous conflagrations, the first reported as early as 1849, its source traceable to violence—violence directed at yet another minority group that worked the gold fields. In the better saloons, black men were traditionally treated to one drink on the house and then expected to leave. On Christmas Eve, 1849, a black man put down his own money to buy a second round. For his temerity, the bartender stabbed him; he fell, knocking over a lantern, which set ablaze the cloth ceiling of the saloon. The fire quickly spread to adjacent buildings.

As even more catastrophic blazes followed every few months, evidence mounted pointing to chronic arson. Indeed, the city was besieged by crime of all kinds, much of it the work of organized gangs. The most famous

of these, the Sydney Ducks, were composed of Australians, many of them convicts—for Australia then harbored a notorious penal colony. The Ducks, who had been robbing sundry miners and merchants, boasted of their plans to burn down the entire city. Arson was good revenge for arrests and provided a fine opportunity for looting. Sure enough, on May 3, 1850, fire broke out in a paint shop; just before the blaze became evident, a man was seen sneaking out of the building. The conflagration consumed eighteen blocks of the city, some two thousand buildings, and all during the fire, Sydney Ducks were seen looting. Citizens caught several of them, and summarily executed sentence—in their zeal also killing an unfortunate bystander, a sailor who stooped to pick up a burning brand to light his pipe.

Such incendiary episodes spawned a host of colorful, if tragically inefficient, volunteer fire companies, among which rivalries quickly developed, so that volunteers often spent more time fighting each other than they did fighting fires. Arson and other crimes also prompted the Mormon leader and entrepreneur Sam Brannan and other prominent San Franciscans (including future governor Leland Stanford) to organize the Committee of Vigilance. By this time, San Francisco did have a police department and courts of law, but both were notoriously inept and thoroughly corrupt. One hundred three citi-

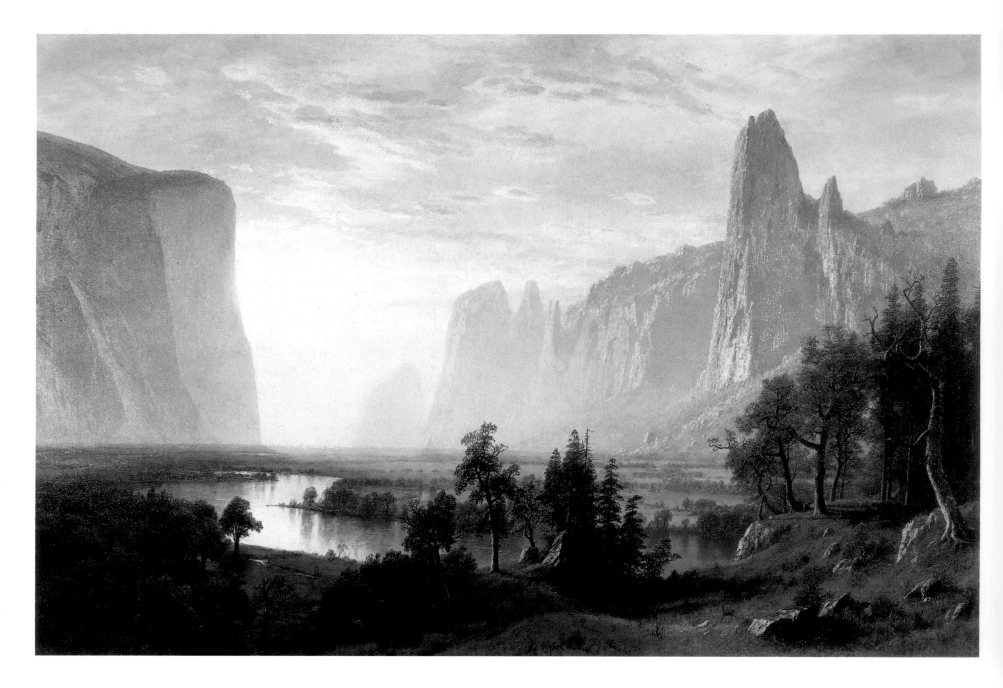

Albert Bierstadt (1830–1902)
Sunset in the Yosemite Valley, 1868
Oil on canvas, 35 ¾ × 52 in.
Haggin Collection, The Haggin
Museum, Stockton, California

It was romantic scenes like this that
showed the West as enchanted ground.

zens of prominence were invited to join the committee; within a year their ranks swelled to six hundred. Typical of their mode of operation was the action they took against a man named Simpton, an Australian who stole a cashbox from a shipping agent.

Simpton was seen rowing off the wharf with his prize. Boatmen gave chase and apprehended him. Instead of turning the man over to the police, however, they summoned the vigilantes by sounding double taps on the fire bell. Eighty committee members "tried" Simpton at the group's headquarters, ignoring police demands that the prisoner be turned over to them. Simpton was found guilty and sentenced to be hanged. As one English visitor to San Francisco observed, the town's citizenry "seemed to cluster like bees on a tree branch . . . and for the purpose of seeing a criminal convulsed and writhing in the agonies of violent death!" Often, the vigilantes buried their man with the rope around his neck, the loose end left above ground as a warning to would-be miscreants. In the case of Simpton, the entire process, from apprehension to execution, took five hours. San Francisco's Committee of Vigilance plied its trade until 1856,

when it voluntarily disbanded, satisfied that it had established law and order in the city.

By the mid 1850s, the lone prospector was rapidly becoming history in California. Placer gold had been thoroughly exhausted by then, and the remaining ore ran much deeper. Getting it required massive mining operations, which called for the capital of big business. Feats of engineering were impressive. In 1851, most of the thirty-mile-long American River was diverted through a system of dams and flumes in order to expose the riverbed for more efficient mining. Along the ten-mile length of the Mother Lode in Amador County, 700-foot-deep shafts were sunk in order to get at gold-laced quartz deposits. Most astonishing technologically was the practice of hydraulic mining. In North Bloomfield, miners dug a forty-five-mile canal to supply water, which was fed through eight-inch-wide nozzles directed against the walls of a gold-bearing cliff. The sixty million gallons of water that were shot against the cliff carried away fifty thousand tons of gravel per day. By the time the lode was mined out, a 550-foot-deep canyon had been created. While such big-time mining wreaked havoc on the natu-

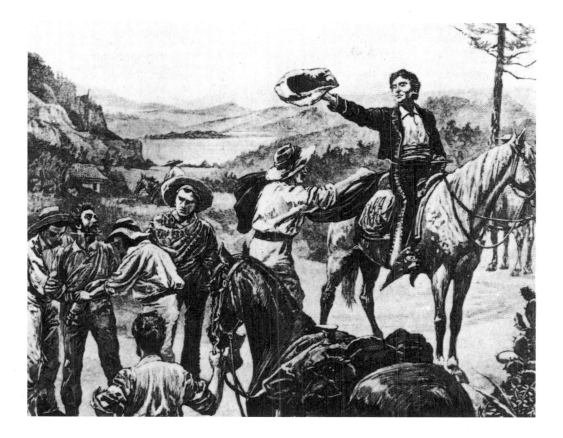

Anonymous
Joaquin Murieta, n.d.
Historical Picture Service, Chicago

Americans considered Murieta a
bandit, the scourge of the mines.
Mexicans saw him as a
revolutionary.

Olaf Carl Seltzer (1877–1957)
Vigilante, n.d.
Watercolor on paper, 12 × 7 in.
Gilcrease Museum, Tulsa, Oklahoma

Commissioned to paint a series of
miniatures depicting Montana
history, Seltzer could hardly have
left out vigilantism—for which the
state was justly infamous.

ral environment, it did build relatively stable towns. By
mid decade, as boom towns and mining camps supported
by deposits of placer gold died out, settlements adjacent
to the deep veins of gold-bearing quartz prospered.

FROM WEST TO EAST

The gold rush had suddenly populated California, and
the presence of population catapulted the territory into
statehood. The exhaustion of placer gold and the subsequent displacement of the lone prospector by big-
business mining operations brought stability to what otherwise would have been a boom-and-bust agglomeration
of mining camps. Quartz mining, the process of working
quartz veins to get at the gold often deposited there, was
an industry run on major capital and involving, like any
other industry, hierarchies of executives, managers, and
laborers. Such complexity required communities—merchants, bankers, farmers, doctors, lawyers, teachers—
and thus California began to be truly *settled*.

But, like the mountain men almost half a century
earlier, the lone prospectors were often loath to join the
civilization for which they had, in effect, blazed a trail.
Few struck it rich, but fewer still would content themselves with laboring for a big mining company. When the
placer gold had all been plucked from California's hills
and riverbeds, many of the Forty-Niners scattered for
points north and east.

In the fall of 1854 a servant at Fort Colville, an outpost of the Hudson's Bay Company in Washington Territory, discovered gold in the Columbia River. Miners
came up from California in the spring of the following

year, but an Indian uprising cut short the rush, and it
was not until the summer of 1858 that troops from Fort
Walla Walla defeated the hostiles. In October, the army
felt confident enough to declare the area open to settlement. That was too late in the season for travel, so the
rush did not resume until spring 1859. The Fort Colville
strike was short-lived, and of the two thousand or so
miners who had come up from California, most were disappointed. But there was soon word of gold strikes farther north, near Bellingham, Washington, and in British
Columbia, along the Fraser River. Some thirty thousand
Californians made the trek to these northern diggings.

The region proved to be rich with gold, but few prospectors became wealthy from it. Prices for supplies and
provisions were even more exorbitant than they had
been in California, and James Douglas, chief factor for
the Hudson's Bay Company, levied a stiff tax on miners.
The mass of those who had made their way up from California returned to that state; but some decided to probe
even farther north, beyond Douglas's ken. In Cariboo
country, at the northern end of the Fraser River, they
struck it rich, and a three-year-long rush commenced,
petering out in 1863. About that time, more gold was discovered on the Kootenai River, only fifty miles from the
U.S. border, and while this rush lasted two years, more

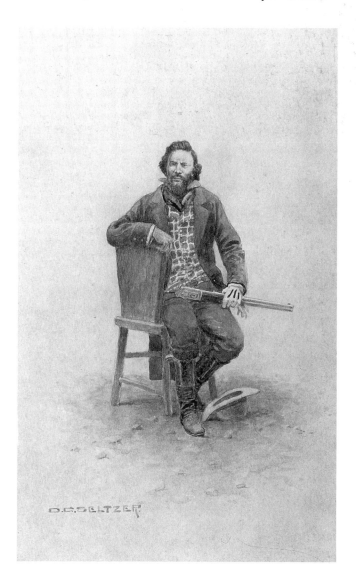

FRANK TENNEY JOHNSON

—

BORN 1874, BIG GROVE, IOWA

DIED 1939, LOS ANGELES

—

A highly successful traditional western illustrator, Johnson was particularly admired for the moonlight scenes in which he specialized. He was born on a ranch near Council Bluffs, Iowa, and was sent to school in Oconomowoc, Wisconsin. He ran away at age fourteen, apprenticing himself to F. W. Heinie, a panorama painter in Milwaukee. The next year, he studied with Texas Ranger–turned–artist Richard Lorenz and began painting portraits as well as doing illustration work for a local newspaper.

By 1902, Johnson had acquired wider ambitions and moved to New York for study at the Art Students League with Robert Henri, William Merritt Chase, Kenneth Hayes Miller, and Joseph Jacinto Mora, a sculptor and painter of southwestern subjects.

After a stint as a newspaper illustrator and fashion artist, Johnson spent the summer of 1904 on a ranch in Colorado, where he perfected his repertoire of western themes. He illustrated numerous Zane Grey western novels. In 1920, he shared a studio in Alhambra, California, outside of Los Angeles, with Clyde Forsythe, a western desert painter and sculptor. The studio became a favorite meeting place not only for western artists like Charles Russell and Edward Borein, but for such popular illustrators as Norman Rockwell and Dean Cornwell.

Johnson died of meningitis at the height of his success.

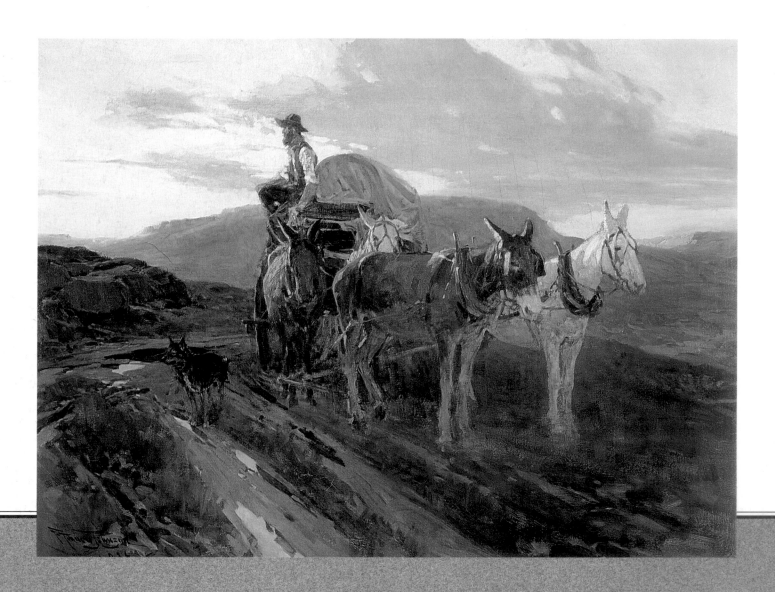

This was the classic prospector—not
a sophisticated professional miner,
but a grizzled amateur in search of
"placer" gold, ore deposited near the
surface of the soil, which could be
readily dug out, winnowed out by
tossing earth in a blanket, or panned
out in a stream.

sustained mining continued for several years afterward.

Late in the summer of 1860, gold was discovered in
the Oro Fino Creek on the western slope of the Bitter
Root Mountains in Idaho (then part of Washington Territory), triggering a stampede from California. Among the
many who came were honest, hard-working miners—
boisterous and colorful, to be sure, and resistant to regulation, but solid and brave men. But there was also a far
more desperate element among these gold seekers, who
were destined to make Montana notorious for lawlessness and for its response to lawlessness in the form of a
particularly ruthless vigilantism.

Henry Plummer is typical of the worst that the gold
rush culture produced. As a teenager, in 1852, Plummer
arrived in Nevada City, a mining camp in the California
High Sierra. He started off uprightly enough, becoming a
partner in a bakery and then, after a few years, the
town's marshal. While serving in that office he killed the
husband of a woman with whom he was conducting a li-
aison. Tried and convicted, Plummer was sent to the
penitentiary, only to be paroled within a few months. Returning to Nevada City, he again became partner in a
bakery, but was soon forced to flee when he seriously injured a man in a whorehouse brawl.

Plummer joined a band of "road agents"—trail robbers—and, with them, unsuccessfully attempted to rob a
bullion express. He returned to Nevada City and to the

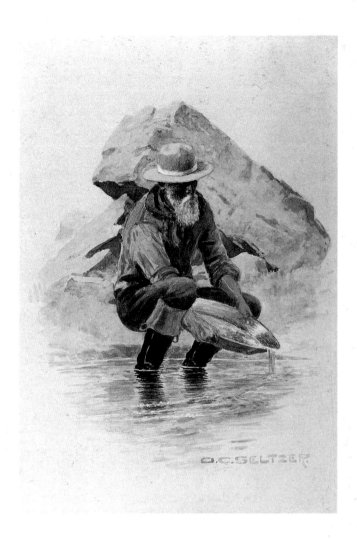

Mormons as well as miners had to
make this decision. *(opposite)*

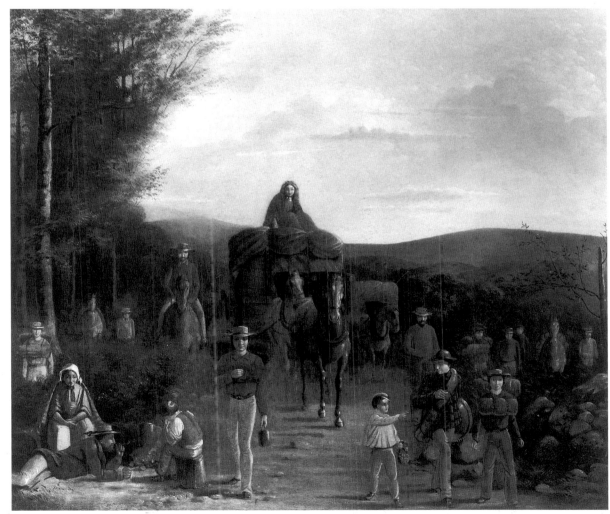

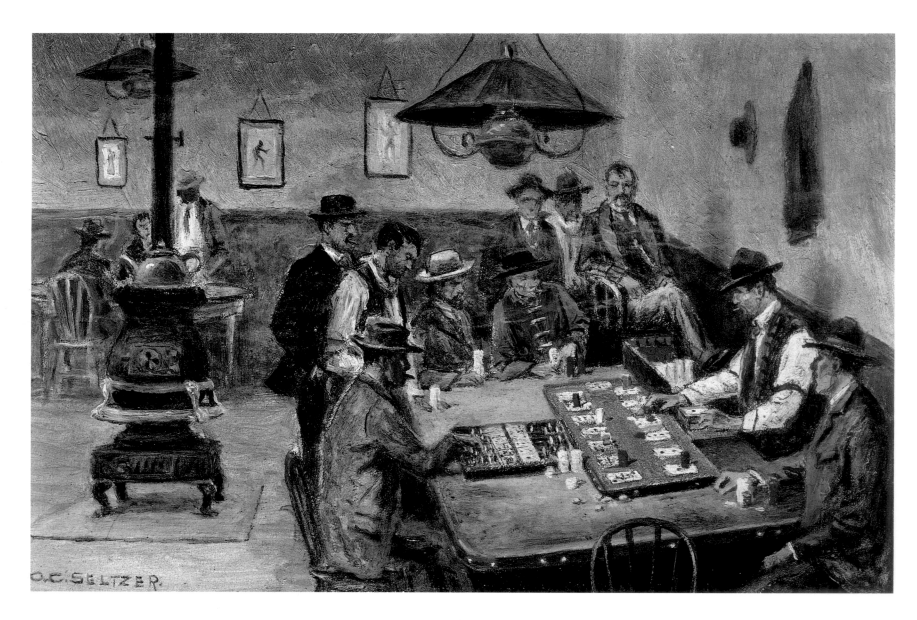

Olaf Carl Seltzer (1877–1957)
The Faro Layout in the Mint Saloon, Great Falls, Montana, 1934
Oil on board, 4 ¼ × 6 ¼ in.
Gilcrease Museum, Tulsa, Oklahoma

Gambling was a fixture of frontier town life—especially in the mining camps.

diversions afforded by a brothel, which included, in addition to the principal activity, brawling. Plummer picked a fight with a man in a bawdy house and killed him. Apprehended, tried, and convicted, he was jailed.

In short order, Plummer bribed his way out of prison and traveled first to Walla Walla (in company with another inmate, who had been incarcerated for killing a sheriff) and then to Lewiston, Idaho (at the time part of Washington Territory), an important supply depot for the Oro Fino miners. Arriving in the spring of 1861 with a woman who had abandoned her husband and children in Walla Walla, he set up as a professional gambler—a reasonably respectable vocation in the frontier West. For Plummer, however, it was merely a front, for he was now secret chief of a band of road agents who preyed on the gold camps.

In October 1862 Lewiston vigilantes captured and hanged some bandits who had robbed a pack train of fourteen pounds of gold. This seems to have prompted Plummer to take his leave of Lewiston; in November he was in the newly founded town of Bannack, Montana (like Idaho, then part of Washington Territory), which had sprung up almost immediately after John White

found gold at Grasshopper Creek on July 28, 1862. (White was murdered in December of the following year.) Professor Thomas J. Dimsdale, a consumptive Englishman who came to the Montana mining country for the salubrious effect of the mountain air, wrote fondly of Bannack: "It is probable that there never was a mining town of the same size that contained more desperadoes and lawless characters."

It was not just that miners and merchants were robbed and killed; citizens of Bannack shot each other routinely, as a means of settling arguments, of redressing injuries to honor, or simply of expressing anger. Two men named George—Carrhart and Ives—were talking together in the street one day. The discussion became heated, and Ives shouted to Carrhart, "You damned son of a bitch, I'll shoot you," whereupon he retired to his grocery store to fetch his revolver. Carrhart ducked into his cabin for his own pistol and was back on the street before Ives. When Ives at last came out, he looked for his opponent in the wrong direction, thus giving Carrhart a chance to shoot him in the back. This he did not do, however. Ives spun around, leveled his weapon, fired—and, as was regularly the case with the notoriously inaccurate six-shooter, missed. Carrhart's first shot was a misfire. Ives's next shot hit the ground. Carrhart returned with a round that whizzed past Ives's face. Carrhart jumped into his house, reached his hand out the window, and fired. Ives also retreated into a building and fired until his ammunition was spent. Carrhart, who had one shot left, used it as Ives tried to slip away. He hit his man in the back, the bullet passing through Ives's body and kicking up the dust in front of him.

But Ives wasn't dead, and he wasn't ready to give up. He shouted for another revolver as Carrhart ran off down the street, pursued only by his opponent's curses for having shot him, coward-fashion, in the back.

As quick as they were to quarrel, Messrs. Ives and Carrhart, it seems, were eager to make up. Ives lived on Carrhart's ranch for the balance of the winter of 1863.

Or there was the evening that a Dr. Biddle and his wife, newly arrived from Minnesota together with a Mr. and Mrs. Short and a hired man were enjoying their campfire on Grasshopper Creek. A citizen of Bannack, J. M. Castner, approached the Biddles and, seeing the lady was pregnant, offered the shelter of his house. As they talked, a shot rang out from the saloon, the bullet coming so close to Castner's ear that it stung for two or three days. Mrs. Biddle all but fainted. Castner sauntered into the saloon and found Cyrus Skinner just then putting his revolver on the table. Skinner asked a card-player to count the bullets remaining in the chamber. "I nearly frightened the hell out of fellow over there," he boasted to the cardplayer. Castner, laying his hand on Skinner's shoulder, said, "My friend, you nearly shot Mrs. Biddle." Skinner didn't exactly apologize, but did swear that he wouldn't shoot a woman "for the world" and excused his casual target practice with the explanation that he thought he was firing in the direction of an Indian camp.

Henry Plummer entered this delightful town in company with a fellow criminal named Jack Cleveland. The pair were in Goodrich's saloon when a dispute arose between Cleveland and a certain Jeff Perkins over some money Perkins owed. At length, Plummer grew weary of listening to the quarrel, which continued even after Cleveland conceded that Perkins had settled the debt. Plummer warned Cleveland to shut up and behave. Perkins went home to fetch his revolvers. Cleveland, in his cups, declared that he was afraid neither of Perkins nor Plummer, whereupon Plummer jumped to his feet, muttered, "You damned son of a bitch, I am tired of this," drew his pistol, and opened fire. The first shot hit a ceiling beam. The second hit Cleveland below the belt. "Plummer," he implored, "you won't shoot me when I'm down?"

"No, you damned son of a bitch, get up." Which, remarkably, Cleveland did. Plummer shot him just above the heart, then in the face, just below the eye. A final shot missed.

Cleveland lived for three hours after the shooting. He sent Hank Crawford to fetch his blankets from Plummer, and Plummer asked Crawford what Cleveland had said about him. "Nothing," was the reply. "It is well for him," said Plummer, "or I would have killed the damned son of a bitch in his bed."

The postscript to this incident tells us even more about life in a Montana mining town. Plummer was tried, acquitted, and subsequently elected sheriff, from which office he masterminded a band of road agents responsible for 102 murders before they themselves—twenty, including Plummer—fell victim to vigilante justice. Unlike California, where sustained mining operations brought some degree of civilized stability, Montana endured many years of ruthless crime and equally ruthless vigilante reprisal. One of the first successful Montana prospectors, Granville Stuart, whose discovery of gold in Deer Lodge valley in 1858 is often credited with starting the rush to the region, became a distinguished territorial politician, even serving as territorial council president. In 1884, while in that capacity, Stuart organized what quickly became the nation's most notorious vigilante movement. He and his men stretched the necks of no fewer than thirty-five horse and cattle thieves. (Stuart's last public office was as United States minister to Uruguay and Paraguay from 1894 to 1899. He died, aged eighty-four, in 1918.)

The Southwest also attracted seekers of gold, many of whom were drawn by tales of "lost mines" abandoned by the Spanish in Arizona. The hostile presence of Apaches kept prospectors away until the early 1850s, when Fort Yuma was built at the confluence of the Colorado and Gila rivers. In 1853, when Jacob Snively panned out gold on the Gila, some twelve hundred prospectors rushed to the spot and set up the mining camp of Gila City, which quickly acquired a lurid reputation as a sinkhole of depravity. Within ten years, Gila City became a ghost, its mines picked clean, having yielded some two million dollars in ore.

In 1853, the Gadsden Purchase added 29,142,400 acres to the United States (price: ten million dollars), including the Tucson area of southern Arizona. Three years later, Fort Buchanan was built to supress Apache attacks there, and prospectors moved in from California. A San Francisco–based venture, the Arizona Mining and Trading Company, located the Planchas de la Plata Mine, abandoned by the Spanish but rumored to have yielded to its former owners a lump of silver weighing twenty-seven hundred pounds. The prospectors were confronted by Mexican troops, who told them they were in Mexican territory. That was untrue, but the Arizona Mining and Trading Company abandoned the site. The next year, the Sonora Exploring and Mining Company, headed by Charles D. Poston and Hermann Ehrenberg, operated eight productive mines in Gadsden country. But shipping the ore out of this remote region proved

WILLIAM HERBERT DUNTON

—

BORN 1878, AUGUSTA, MAINE
DIED 1936, ALBUQUERQUE, NEW MEXICO

—

Although he was born and raised in Maine, Dunton wandered the West as a young man, taking odd jobs as a ranch hand and cowboy—and picking up the appropriate western nickname "Buck." *Harper's, Collier's,* and *Scribner's* magazines all commissioned illustration work from him, as did publishers of western novels, who relished his blend of realistic detail and simple nostalgia.

Already a successful illustrator, Dunton enrolled in New York's Art Students League to study with Joseph DeCamp and Ernest Blumenschein, who told him about Taos. Later that year, Dunton opened up a summer studio there and subsequently participated in the founding of the Taos Society of Artists. He settled permanently in Taos in 1921.

The Great Depression hit Dunton hard, and, like many other artists, he found financial relief in commissions from the WPA's Public Works of Art Project, executing murals. More than any of the other Taos-based artists of the early twentieth century, Dunton was concerned with preserving on canvas the rapidly vanishing Old West.

Will Connell, *William Herbert Dunton,* 1932. Photograph. The Harwood Foundation Museum, Taos, New Mexico.

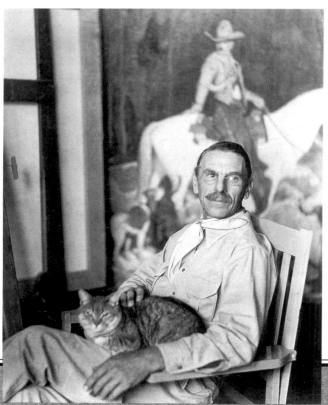

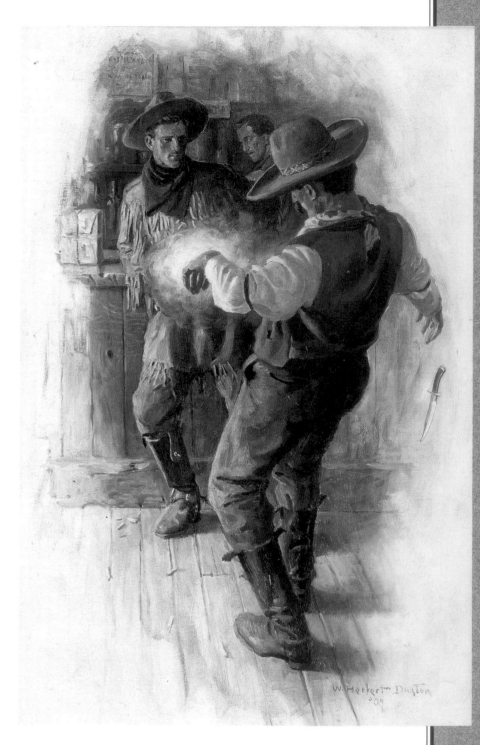

W. Herbert Dunton (1878–1936)
Barroom Scene, 1909
Oil on board, 28 ½ × 19 in.
Stark Museum of Art, Orange, Texas

Bad whiskey, hot tempers, and loaded guns at the required close range: recreation in a mining town bar.

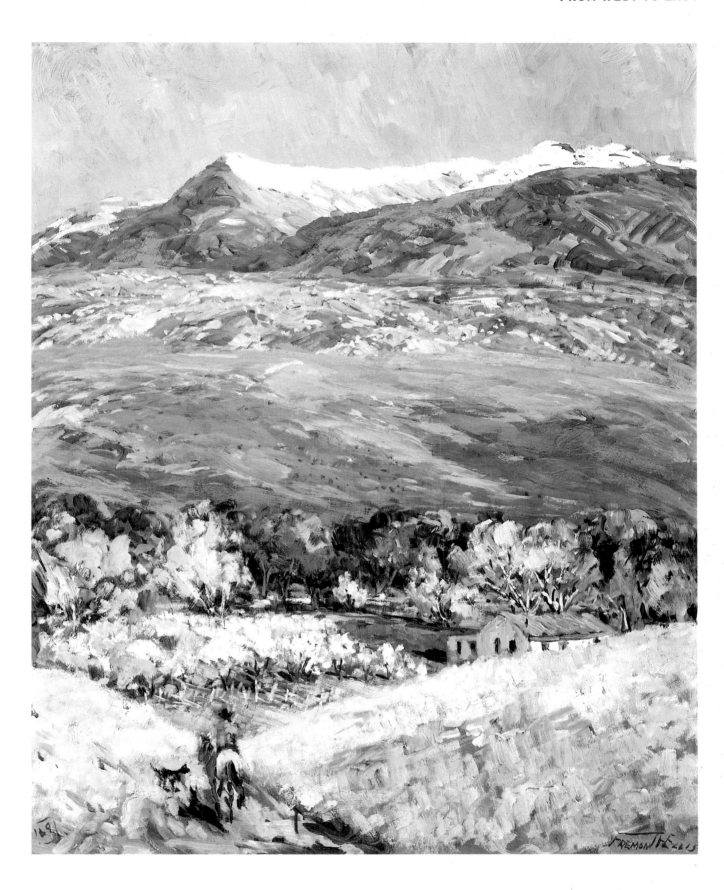

Fremont F. Ellis (1897–1985)
New Mexico Spring, 1969
Oil on canvas, 36 × 30 in.
Courtesy of The Anschutz Collection

prohibitively expensive, and when the Civil War brought the withdrawal of troops from Fort Buchanan, renewed Apache attacks made mining impossible.

Such ventures had produced another frontier hell-hole, however, in the form of Tucson. In 1860, the town's cemetery had only two graves sheltering the remains of men who had died of natural causes. The remainder had been shot. (Like the rest of the region, Tucson was deserted during the Civil War, when no troops could be spared to defend white settlements against Apaches.)

Placer gold had been found in the Washoe Mountains of present-day Nevada as early as 1848, but petered out by the late 1850s. Then, in January 1859, came James "Old Virginny" Finny. He had two talents: a limitless capacity for alcohol and an uncanny eye for paydirt. In a spot they called Gold Hill, Old Virginny and three friends first panned placer gold and then struck a rich quartz deposit. The worthy citizens of nearby Johntown, a shanty settlement built around Dutch Nick's saloon, inspected Old Virginny's claim, but returned to their cabins unimpressed.

Old Virginny and his partners worked the claim in peace and seclusion until Peter O'Riley and Patrick Mc-Laughlin started poking around Six Mile Canyon, hoping to pan out a hundred dollars' worth of dust to finance a trip to more promising diggings elsewhere. They set up their cradle in a spot called Old Man Caldwell's. At first, the yield was disappointing, as the spring they panned produced about four dollars a day. Divided two ways, that was still twice as much as the wage for common labor, so the pair persisted, digging a reservoir to collect the spring water in order to make the tedious work of rocking the cradle move along faster. As the pair dug, on June 10, 1859, they hit soil they recognized as similar to that of Gold Hill. They took a pan of the dirt, washed it in the spring, and were rewarded by a thick deposit of gold dust and flakes. The vein O'Riley and McLaughlin had exposed would be called the Ophir—a single vein of what proved to be the richest mother lode of gold and silver ever discovered.

Henry T. P. Comstock, citizen of Johntown, was so lazy that he never bothered—as did even the most shiftless of miners—to bake bread, so they called him Old Pancake. When he saw the three hundred dollars in gold O'Riley and McLaughlin had to show for a single day's work, he declared that he, Old Virginny, and Manny

Penrod owned Old Man Caldwell's, having purchased the property from that gentleman the previous winter. Rather than waste time fighting Comstock's claim, O'Riley and McLaughlin cut in Old Pancake, Old Virginny, and Penrod for equal shares. Comstock promptly bought out Old Virginny for the price of a blind horse and a bottle of whiskey. Subsequently, Joseph D. Winters joined the partnership. Because Old Pancake talked up the mine to anyone who would listen—while, presumably, the other partners did the actual work of digging—the deposit came to be called the Comstock Lode.

It was the stuff of fairy tale and fable. Soon the mine was yielding three hundred dollars not for a day's work, but for every cradleful of paydirt washed. After a time, a heavy bluish quartz soil was struck, which gummed up the cradle. The miners cursed—but Manny Penrod argued that the material might be valuable, and the partners staked a quartz claim of six hundred feet, this in addition to the several placer claims they had registered. The blue dirt, assay confirmed, was three-quarters pure silver and one-quarter gold.

The rush commenced. Thousands left California for Nevada, jamming the narrow trail over the Sierra in a race to reach Washoe before all the placer claims were taken. There was but one inn along the route, which slept eight to a bed. But the inconveniences of the trail were nothing compared to conditions in Comstock country. There was no housing. A town, Virginia City, was

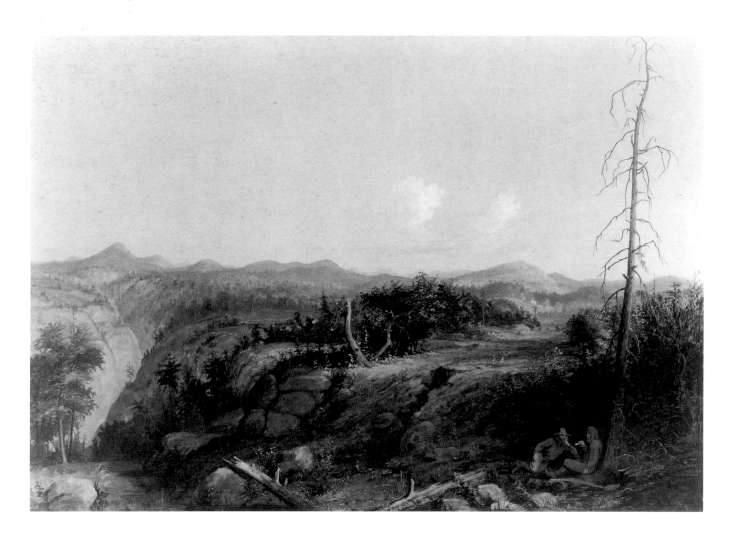

Albertus del Orient Browere (1814–1887)
South of Tuolumne City, 1861
Oil on canvas, 30 × 44 in.
Collection of The Oakland Museum; Kahn Collection

By the time Browere painted this landscape, many prospectors were leaving California mining country for gold and silver fields farther east.

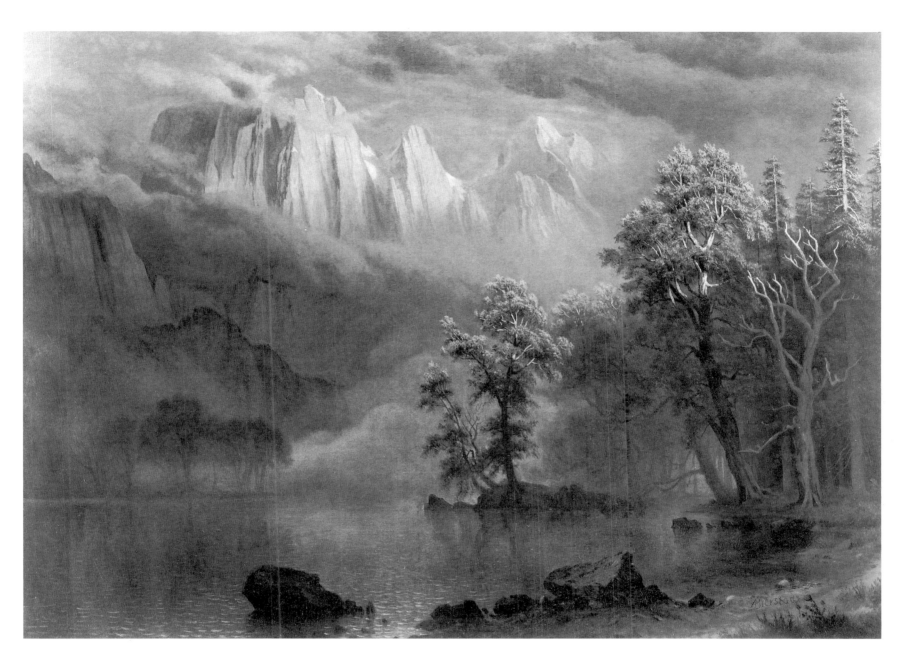

Albert Bierstadt (1830–1902)
Moonlight in the Sierras, 1870–75
Oil on canvas, 25 × 36 in.
Private collection; Courtesy Berry-
Hill Galleries, New York

hastily built of tents and shanties cobbled together from junk—brush, shirts, potato sacks. Soon, Dutch Nick moved his bar from Johntown to Virginia City, purveying "tarantula juice" ("when the boys were well charged . . . it made the snakes and tarantulas that bit them very sick"). Two hundred men paid a dollar a night to sleep on a floor in one of the town's few permanent buildings; another dollar rented a blanket for the night. Yet, within a year of its founding, Virginia City had a theater, thirty-eight stores, eight hotels, nine restaurants, and *twenty-five* saloons.

The town fattened less on gold and silver as such than on speculation *involving* gold and silver. The easy diggings, the placer deposits, were quickly exhausted. While it is true that the quartz veins were rich beyond parallel, advanced mining techniques were required to work such claims. And Comstock country was so remote from anything resembling civilization—so far from any-place where one might convert the gold to cash—that transporting ore presented a very costly logistical prob-lem. For some time, Virginia City's economy operated on

trade in shares of claims—"feet"—bartered for grocer-ies, whiskey, lodging, and the like. Well-capitalized men, like Judge James Walsh or George Hearst (father of fu-ture newspaper tycoon William Randolph Hearst), read-ily bought out the original Comstock partners: McLaughlin for $3,500, Comstock for $10,000, O'Riley for $40,000. (All three of whom quickly dissipated their profits and died in poverty.) To the few capitalists, the Comstock Lode paid out about $300 million over the next two decades, with those "feet" that had been traded for general-store goods leaping in value from $1,225 per foot in April 1861 to $3,800 in October.

Whereas Idaho, Montana, and Nevada diggings drew prospectors primarily from California, news of gold strikes in Colorado country, "only" six or seven hun-dred miles west of the Mississippi Valley, attracted east-erners, especially the restless settlers of the Mississippi Valley region, who were hard hit by an economic depres-sion in 1857. The fact was that prospectors in the Pikes Peak region had actually unearthed only a few ounces of gold. Seizing on these meager discoveries, speculators

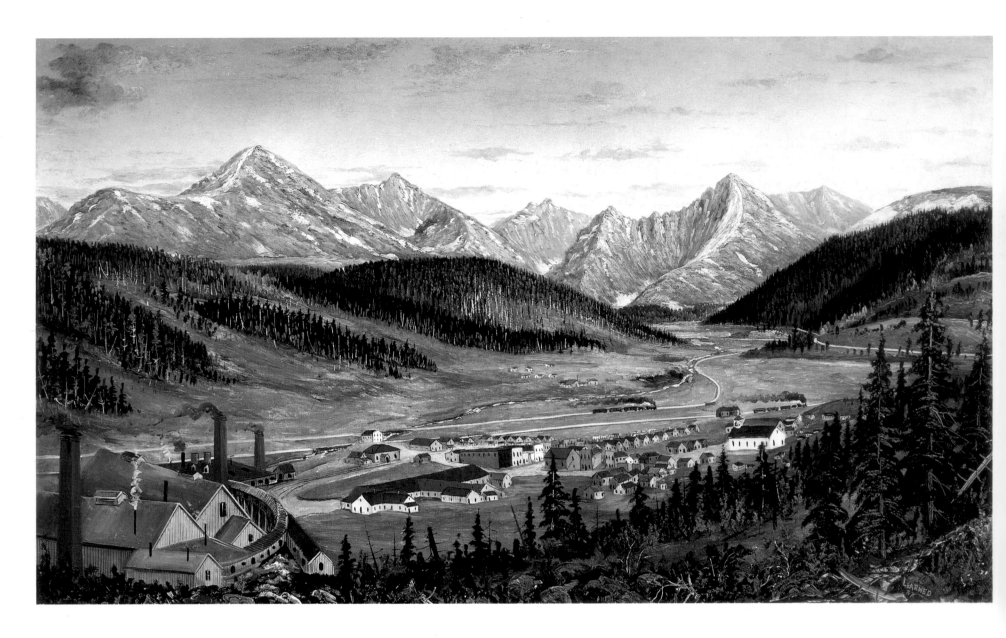

Harry Learned (active 1874–1896)
Robinson, Colorado, 1887
Oil on canvas, 18 ⅛ × 30 ½ in.
Amon Carter Museum, Fort Worth,
Texas

A Colorado mining town as depicted
by an artist who made his living
painting backdrops for theaters.

invaded the region, laying out and building Denver in the expectation of a rush. To the speculators, it mattered little that the vast lode anticipated failed, at least at first, to materialize. They let it be known that gold was there, and in unheard of abundance. Perhaps fifty thousand "Fifty-Niners" took the bait. Many started west in March, too early for sufficient growth of plains grass to feed their animals, so man and beast starved on the trail: There were three brothers named Blue. One reached the diggings. He had eaten the other two.

Sorely disappointed when they arrived in Pikes Peak country, most of the Fifty-Niners turned back immediately. But, as in Nevada, those who stayed and searched and worked did find gold—lots of it. The Rockies proved to be rich with ore, and the town of Denver, founded on humbug and puffery, prospered through the rest of the century.

The gold and silver strikes of mid century started to fill in the vast blank between the Mississippi Valley and the Pacific coast. Where the ore held out, supporting large mining operations, gold camps developed into genuine towns and cities, attracting merchants and tradesmen, as well as farmers.

Nevada would see more gold rushes in the 1860s and 1870s. In Leadville, Colorado, an abandoned gold camp was found to be rich with silver, and a rush commenced in 1877. Also in 1877, Tombstone, Arizona, later made infamous by the Earp brothers' shootout with the Clanton family at the O.K. Corral, became the focus of a rush when Ed Schieffelin discovered silver in the region. In 1883, the Northern Pacific Railroad increased its ridership by trumpeting a gold discovery in the Coeur d'Alene region of northern Idaho.

Colonel George Armstrong Custer, on a military reconnaissance in 1874, discovered gold in the Black Hills of Dakota Territory. The Sioux revered the hills as the dwelling place of their gods and had entered into a treaty with the United States reserving the region in perpetuity. The army did make a perfunctory effort to ward off prospectors, but by 1875 a full-scale rush was on. As we shall see in a later chapter, this violation of the Indians' sacred ground led to war and the tragic entrance of Custer and his Seventh Cavalry into history and legend along a creek called the Little Bighorn.

The last gold rush was sparked in the late 1890s, when Ed Schieffelin, who had stirred things up in Tombstone, found gold along Bonanza Creek, a tributary of Canada's Klondike River. This led to exploration of the Yukon Valley in Alaska, U.S. territory, where more rich deposits were discovered. But the remoteness of the region and the rigors of its climate discouraged the kind of rush that had occurred a half-century earlier.

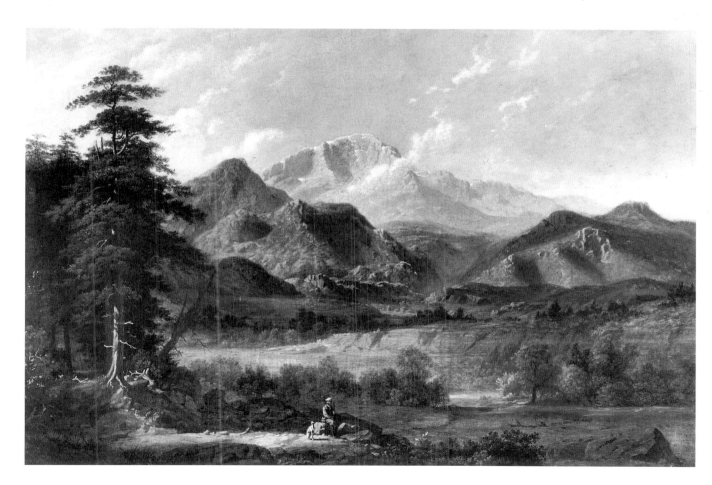

George Caleb Bingham (1811–1879)
View of Pike's Peak, 1872
Oil on canvas, 28 ⅛ × 42 ¼ in.
Amon Carter Museum, Fort Worth, Texas

An impressive landscape by an artist far better known for his genre scenes of small-town and river life.

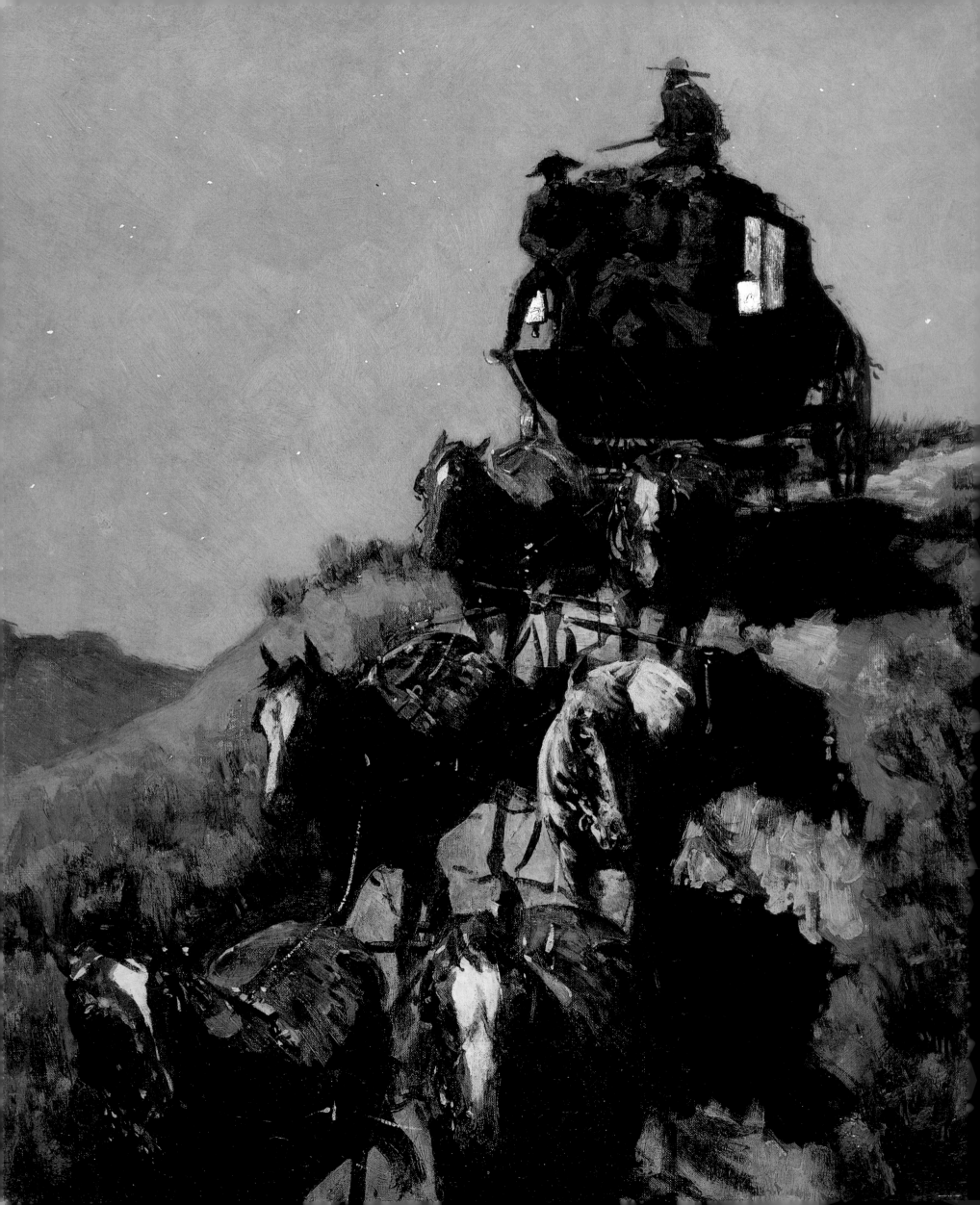

PULLING TOGETHER

The worship of God and of gold sent settlers to the Far West and the coastal West; then rumors and news of more gold sent many of them inland, to scattered points in Montana, Idaho, Colorado, Nevada, New Mexico, and Arizona. Potentially an inland empire, the settlements were few and far between. The great task was to join them one to another and, even more important in a nation on the eve of civil war, to join them to the cities of the Northeast.

We have seen how the Forty-Niners could choose one of two ocean routes, an overland journey, or a combination of river and land travel to reach the gold fields. As early as 1847, the United States government let contracts for mail service between New York and San Francisco via the United States Mail Steamship Company to Panama, where the mail was unloaded and laboriously transported across the Isthmus for shipment to California via the Pacific Mail Steamship Company. (Actual operations did not get under way until 1849.) Service on the Atlantic leg was poor, and the company never was financially successful, although construction of the Panama Railroad across the Isthmus in 1855 was an improvement. In 1853, the government secured a right of transit across the Isthmus of Tehuantepec in Mexico, hoping to reduce the excruciatingly long ocean journey. Service did not begin until 1858 and quickly proved unsatisfactory.

As we have seen, the Mississippi and Missouri rivers served as highways to the West. By the time of the gold rush, steamboats had largely replaced the muscle-powered keelboats for hauling passengers and freight on the Missouri. Keelboats did persist, however, into the 1870s; the so-called Mackinaw could haul fifteen tons of freight and could be hired for as little as two dollars a day. As long as the trip was downstream, the keelboat was hard to beat for efficiency. Poling against the current, however, was another matter. But whether traveling or shipping by flatboat or steamboat, one was limited by a single immutable fact: the course of the river. You and your goods went where the river flowed, or you made costly arrangements for transferring yourself or your cargo to some overland means of transportation. By the 1850s, it was clear that a regular, dependable overland system of transportation was what the far-flung settlements of the West required. Only in Arizona, on the Colorado River, would shallow-draft steamboats and barges serve in preference to stagecoach and wagon well into the 1880s, the era of the railroads. The hostility of the desert and of the Mojave and Apache Indians made overland travel extraordinarily difficult in Arizona country. It was safer, more practical, and far cheaper to ship people and goods from California to the Colorado River delta town of Port Isabel and transfer the

Frederic Remington, *The Old Stage Coach of the Plains*, 1901. Detail; see page 204

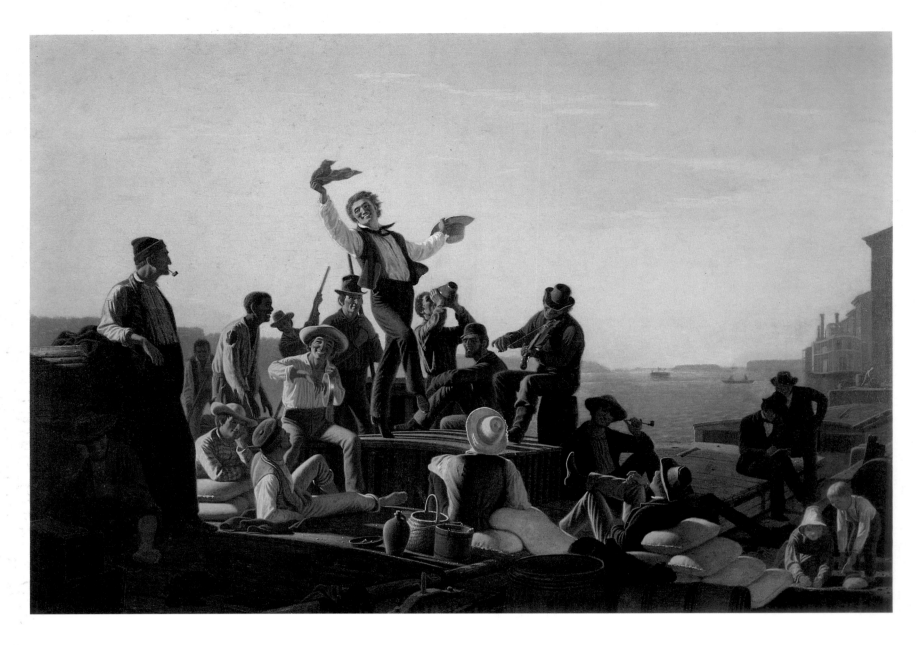

cargo to steamboats or barges (which were pulled by manpower) for transportation to points in southeastern California, Arizona, and southwestern Utah.

WHEELS AND RUTS

While it was clear to westerners that ocean and river transportation were not workable alternatives to reliable overland routes, the operation of the United States Mail Steamship Company and the Pacific Mail Steamship Company did provide a crucial precedent, the subsidy of private companies by federal mail contracts. If steamship companies could be subsidized, why not overland operators as well? Stagecoach lines could be granted contracts to deliver mail, and freight lines could supply the widely dispersed army posts that defended the scattered settlements of the Far West.

Where population was sufficiently dense, of course, no such subsidies were required. Already by the early 1850s, the rapidly growing network of railroad lines was pushing stagecoach and freight operations into the western frontier, regions not yet sufficiently populated to support a railroad, but thickly enough settled to return a profit on expenditures for building decent roads, purchasing a fleet of coaches and wagons, and maintaining stables of horses. In California, the situation was similar. The gold rush had almost instantly populated the Mother Lode country, so that a dozen small stagecoach lines were operating there by 1853. In 1854, these lines merged into the California Stage Company, which operated a total of 2,690 miles of routes in California and parts of Oregon. About the same time, a would-be miner named Alexander Todd, discovering that the back-breaking, soul-saddening work of panning freezing rivers for gold did not agree with his delicate health, realized that money was to be made delivering mail for lonely prospectors far from home. In 1849, he inaugurated a mail posting and delivery service. For $2.50 he would carry a miner's letter to San Francisco for posting; for an ounce of gold dust—at the time worth about $16—he would search through piles of unsorted and unclaimed mail in San Francisco, find letters addressed to his miner clients, and return to the gold fields to deliver them. He also carried gold dust from the lawless claims to places

George Caleb Bingham (1811–1879)
The Jolly Flatboatmen in Port, 1857
Oil on canvas, 46 ¼ × 69 in.
The Saint Louis Art Museum;
Museum Purchase

In several extraordinary canvases, Bingham developed the theme of a free-and-easy life fostered by working on the Missouri.

George Caleb Bingham (1811–1879)
The Jolly Flatboatmen, 1846
Oil on canvas, 38 ⅛ × 48 ½ in.
The Manoogian Collection

Perhaps Bingham's most celebrated canvas, *The Jolly Flatboatmen* enjoyed wide distribution as an excellent American Art-Union mezzotint print. *(opposite)*

GEORGE CALEB BINGHAM

BORN AUGUSTA COUNTY, VIRGINIA, 1811

DIED KANSAS CITY, MISSOURI, 1879

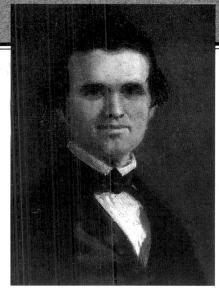

George Caleb Bingham, *Self-Portrait*, 1849–50. Oil on copper, 3 × 2 ½ in. National Portrait Gallery, Smithsonian Institution

Bingham's family left their Virginia plantation in 1819 to take up residence in the Missouri frontier settlement of Boon's Lick. Eight years later, the artist's father died, and young George was apprenticed to a cabinetmaker. He quickly decided, however, that painting was more to his liking and, on the advice of the popular artist Chester Harding (best known for his portrait of Daniel Boone, painted "on a fragment of tablecloth in place of a canvas"), taught himself art by copying engravings with homemade pigments. As early as 1835, he was selling portraits to the burghers of St. Louis for $20 each. When he moved to Natchez in 1836, he found that his work could command twice that amount. His earnings financed three months of training at the Pennsylvania Academy of the Fine Arts in 1837.

A master of western genre scenes—classically composed moments in the lives of trappers, rivermen, and townsfolk—Bingham enjoyed his first national success with *The Jolly Flatboatmen* in 1845, which received wide distribution in the form of an engraving offered by the American Art-Union. Throughout Bingham's career as a painter, his works would reach a large audience through popular print versions, as he had an unerring eye for the universally appealing, homely but timeless aspects of western life. Eschewing the epic and heroic, Bingham elevated the anecdotal to the level of deathless western myth.

Beginning in 1848, Bingham became increasingly involved in Missouri politics, which inspired *The County Election* (1851–52), *Canvassing for a Vote* (1852), *Stump Speaking* (1854), and *Verdict of the People* (1854–55), but which soon left him less and less time for painting—although he did manage intermittent study at the academy in Düsseldorf during European travels between 1856 and 1859.

Late in his career, Bingham returned to painting, producing *View of Pike's Peak* after an 1872 trip to Colorado. Two years before his death, he was made professor of painting at the University of Missouri.

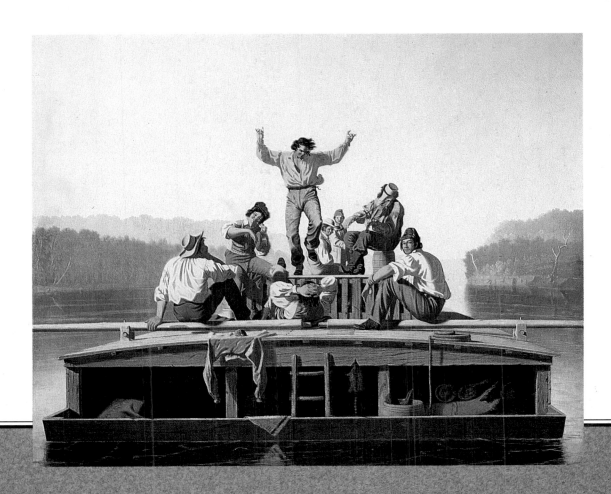

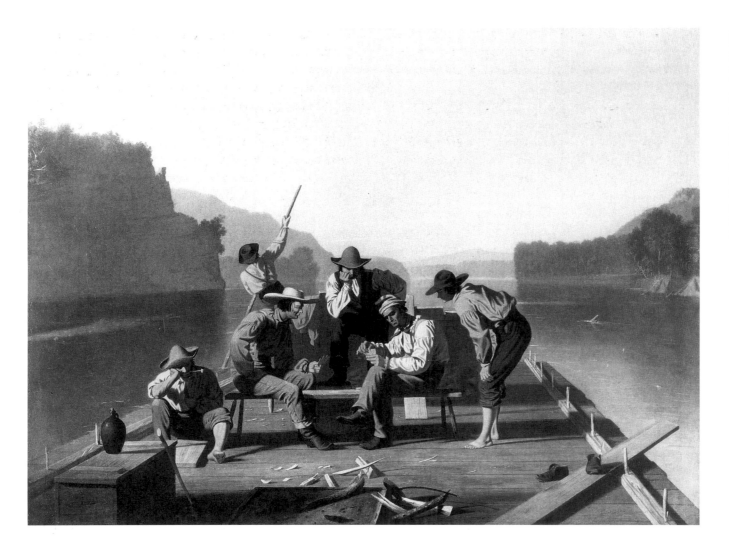

George Caleb Bingham (1811–1879)
Raftsmen Playing Cards, 1847
Oil on canvas, 28 × 38 in.
The Saint Louis Art Museum;
Purchase: Ezra H. Linley Fund

Another of Bingham's lovely river-life genre scenes composed with a classical grace that endows mundane activity with heroic repose—despite such homey touches as the jug of corn liquor, the figure at the left reaching inside his shirt to scratch his belly, and the rude shoes on the right.

of safekeeping in the city, taking as his fee 5 percent of the gold's value. Other such one-man operations quickly proliferated until they were consolidated and bought out in 1852 by the Adams Express Company, a venerable eastern firm. Almost immediately, Wells, Fargo & Company, the western arm of the American Express Company, began cutthroat competition with Adams Express, forcing it into bankruptcy by 1855.

The success of California coaching and express operations served only to intensify the desire in the Far West for similarly efficient and permanent links to the East. As early as 1848, the federal government had contracted with a private carrier for delivery of supplies to the army. During the Mexican War, the military had tried to supply General Kearny's troops itself, but with miserable results. A contract was let to James Brown, a freighter based in Independence, Missouri, for delivery of two hundred thousand pounds of supplies to Santa Fe at $11.75 per hundred weight. Brown succeeded so handsomely that additional contracts were awarded during the next two years, Brown having taken on William H. Russell as a partner. The freighter had little time to savor his success, however, as he died in 1850 of typhus, a disease endemic to the unsanitary conditions of trail life. Russell took William B. Waddell as a partner, and in 1854 approached their principal competitor, Alexander Majors, with an offer of merger. In this way, a charming

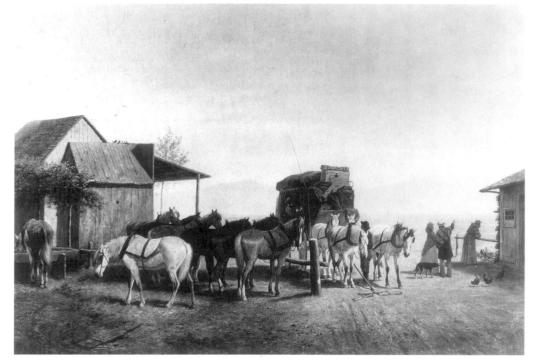

Carl William Hahn (1829–1887)
California Stage Coach Halt, 1875
Oil on canvas, 28 × 40 in.
Courtesy of The Anschutz Collection

Stagecoach service developed early in the settled parts of California.

and somewhat dandified New Englander, a tight-fisted Virginian of Scots descent, and a Missouri plainsman joined forces to create a freighting empire that would endure until the Civil War.

And it *was* an empire. After the crusading editor of the New York *Tribune*, Horace Greeley, toured the company's Leavenworth, Kansas, headquarters depot, he wrote breathlessly: "Such acres of wagons! such pyramids of extra axletrees! such herds of oxen! such regiments of drivers!" In 1855 alone, Russell, Majors & Waddell carried 2.5 million pounds of freight across the plains in five hundred wagons organized into twenty separate trains. Seventeen hundred men were employed as wagon masters, drivers, stock tenders, and the like. Seventy-five hundred oxen supplied the motive force for the firm's five hundred wagons—wagons built to Alexan-

Each outfit also included a "herder," who drove forty or fifty oxen for use as replacements, and a "night herder," who tended the animals at night. Routines were strictly prescribed, including rest periods for the animals, meal periods for the humans (there were only two meals a day), and an admonition to "observe the Sabbath." Majors admired oxen and admired the disciplined manner in which his men worked them. Oxen "did good daily work," he wrote in his *Seventy Years on the Frontier;* they "gathered their own living" from prairie grass.

If properly driven [they] would travel two thousand miles in a season [April to November]. . . . However, the distance traveled depended much on the skill of the wagon-masters who had them in charge. . . . To make everything work expeditiously, thorough discipline was required. . . .

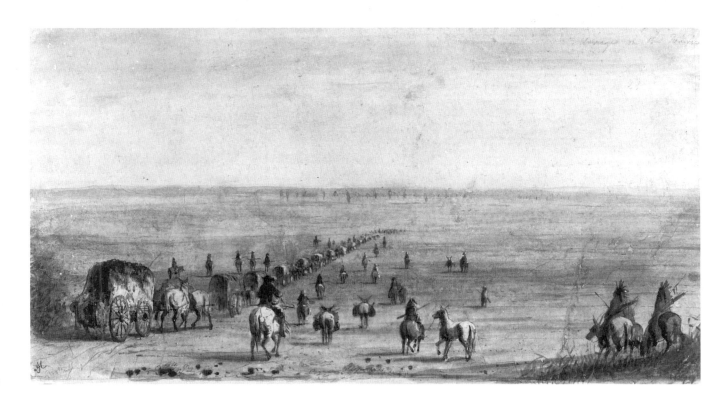

Alfred Jacob Miller (1810–1874)
Mirage on the Prairie (Trader's Caravan), 1837
Watercolor on paper, 7 × 13 ½ in.
Gilcrease Museum, Tulsa, Oklahoma

der Majors's exclusive specifications, using carefully seasoned wood, the wagon boxes built to flare outward in order to prevent five thousand pounds of cargo from shifting; the wagons' front ends were curved like a ship's prow, their rears square in order to make loading and unloading easier.

With a talent for military-style organization similar to Brigham Young's, Majors divided his forces into "outfits" of twenty-six wagons under the command of a wagon master and an assistant. Each wagon was pulled by a team of twelve oxen driven by a "bullwhacker" at an average steady but lumbering rate of fifteen miles a day. The crack of the bullwhacker's eighteen-foot-long whip, which was tipped with special rawhide poppers, could be heard for a distance of two miles across the plains. The dust of a twenty-six wagon train could be seen for twenty miles.

I remember once of timing my teamsters when they commenced to yoke their teams after the cattle had been driven into their corral and allowed to stand long enough to become quiet. I gave the word to the men to commence yoking, and held my watch in my hand as they did so, and in sixteen minutes from the time they commenced, each man had yoked six pairs of oxen and had them hitched to their wagons ready to move.

Westerners were gratified to have efficient, regular, and affordable freight service. But they wanted more. Freighters were dependable, but slow—far too slow to carry mail or passengers. Long-distance stagecoach service was needed, if the West were truly to be joined to the East. But that presented enormous problems. Freighting caravans, because of their very size, were largely self-sufficient, carrying all supplies necessary for

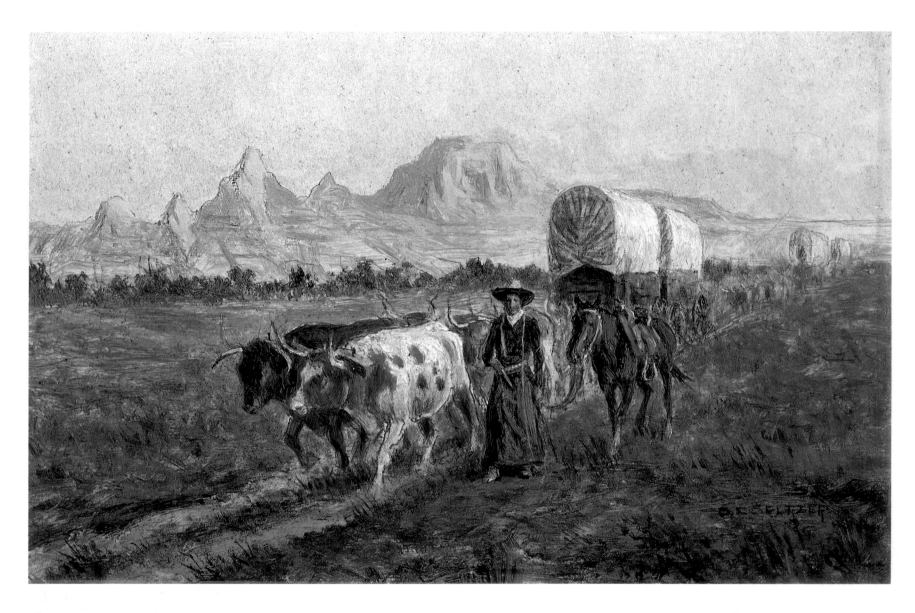

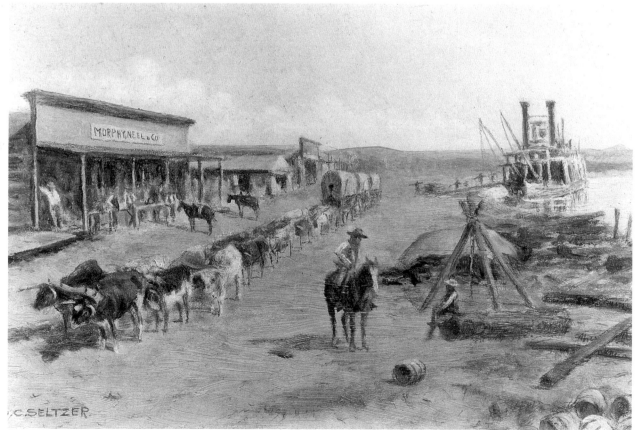

Olaf Carl Seltzer (1877–1957)
Calamity Jane Bullwhacking in the Neighborhood of Townsend, Montana, 1934
Oil on board, 4 × 6 in.
Gilcrease Museum, Tulsa, Oklahoma

Born Martha Canary in 1852, Calamity Jane may or may not have been a construction worker on the Union Pacific, a scout for George Armstrong Custer, and a "bullwhacker" who freighted supplies to Montana and Dakota mining camps. What is certain was her knack for histrionic self-promotion, which secured her a place in western lore and legend.

Olaf Carl Seltzer (1877–1957)
Freighting from Fort Benton, n.d.
Oil on board, 4 × 5 ¾ in.
Gilcrease Museum, Tulsa, Oklahoma

In the 1860s, Fort Benton, Montana, functioned as the freight-handling center for much of the Northwest.

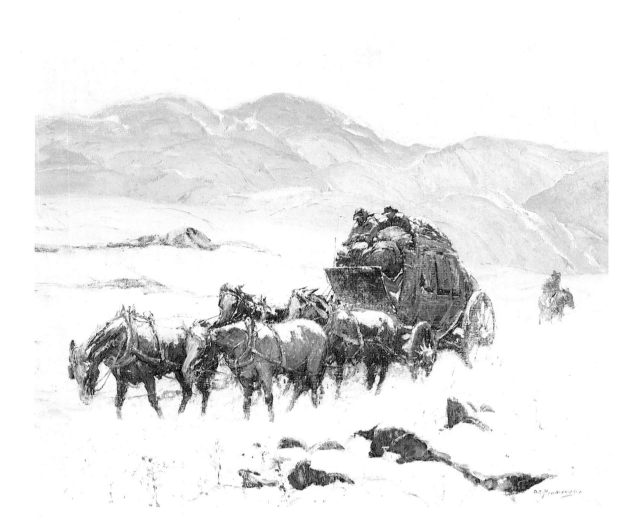

Snow was a costly—sometimes deadly—hazard of stagecoach travel.

At its worst, weather in the great West was an enemy more formidable than any other.

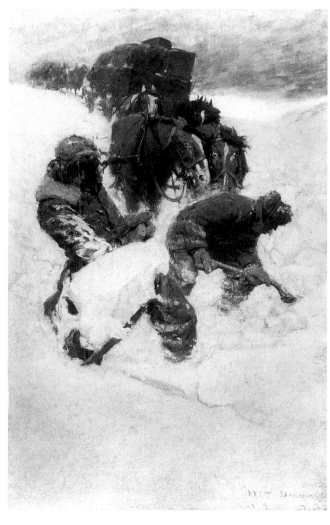

the trail and sufficiently manned to ward off dangers from Indians and other hazards. Slow and heavy, the caravans did not require highly maintained roads, and as Alexander Majors had observed, oxen likewise required little maintenance. In contrast, a stagecoach was a solitary vehicle, horse drawn, and meant for speed. It required something at least approaching decent roads, as well as stations at frequent intervals to supply the needs of passengers, to provide fresh horses, and to help manage the varied hazards of the trail. All of this was expensive.

The government let two modest contracts for overland mail, one to Salt Lake City and one to Santa Fe, in 1849. Almond W. Babbitt attempted the Salt Lake City run in his light wagon. His maiden voyage was also his last; he quit. As for service to Santa Fe, it was thoroughly irregular, carried by the long-established traders' caravans rather than by special coaches. In 1851, George Chorpenning and Absalom Woodward secured a contract to carry mail from Sacramento to Salt Lake City once a month for $14,000 per year. The pair had no fancy stagecoaches, not even wagons. They threw the mail sacks on a mule and made the first run in fifty-three days. In November 1851, Woodward was killed by Indians on the Malad River in northern Utah. Chorpenning persisted, but was defeated by the winter of 1851–52, when snow and bitter weather made it impossible to meet his monthly schedule. The government canceled his contract for failure to perform, but instead of meekly accepting the cancellation, Chorpenning issued a statement detailing the hardships he and his men faced. On one trip, the travelers had to beat down the snow with mauls in order to make a trail that would support the mules. When mules and horses froze to death in the Goose Creek mountains of Utah, the men strapped the mail pouches to their own backs and walked two hundred miles to Salt Lake City, surviving on frozen mule meat. When that gave out, they went six days without food. Chorpenning demanded not only that his contract be reinstated, but that his compensation be raised to $30,000 a year. His demands were met; moreover, between 1854 and 1858 he was granted contracts for weekly mail service at a rate of $130,000 per year. Yet his losses outpaced his profits. Congress at one point approved a payment of $443,010 to cover those losses incurred between 1851 and 1860. A treasury warrant was issued, but then payment was disputed, stopped, and Chorpenning received nothing, dying a poor man in 1894.

The experience of Chorpenning and other contractors and the undependable service even the most heroic of them could deliver resulted finally in a petition to Congress, signed by seventy-five thousand Californians, demanding sufficient government funds to subsidize regular stagecoach service, with way stations and improved roads. Congress was responsive, but, in the tense years immediately preceding the Civil War, the lawmakers were faced with a vexing sectional issue: Should the government subsidize the "Central Route" through the time-tested South Pass, or a "Southern Route" by way of El Paso and Fort Yuma? The North demanded the Central Route; the South, of course, would settle only for the Southern Route. Congress at last sidestepped the issue by specifying that service be established between the Missouri River and San Francisco over any route selected by the successful bidder, provided the trip be made in twenty-five days or less using coaches or spring wagons suitable for passengers as well as mail.

The award of the contract was put in the hands of Postmaster General Aaron V. Brown, a southerner from Tennessee who found a prominent coach operator, John Butterfield, willing to defer to him in the matter of choosing a route. Brown specified a run from St. Louis and Memphis to Fort Smith, Arkansas, to El Paso and Fort Yuma, then to Los Angeles and up to San Francisco. Butterfield promised semiweekly service, each trip to take twenty-five days or less, for an annual subsidy of six hundred thousand dollars. When northerners protested the eccentrically roundabout nature of what they called the "oxbow route," Brown ingeniously countered that it was the only "all-the-year route between the Mississippi and the Pacific."

John Butterfield had been born in 1801 near Albany, New York. From boyhood, he had a feel for horses and an aptitude for handling stagecoaches. He started out at age nineteen driving a coach, earning enough money to buy a small stable and start his own livery business. When he married in 1822, he and his bride opened a boardinghouse in conjunction with the livery stable, profiting sufficiently to invest in, and eventually control, the major mail and passenger lines in northern and western New York. In 1849 he organized the Butterfield and Wasson Express Company and the next year merged it with Wells and Company and Livingston, Fargo and Company to form the American Express Company, giant among eastern freight handlers. He designated Tipton, Missouri, the western terminus of the railroad line out of St. Louis, as the *eastern* terminus of the Overland Mail Company's 2,812-mile-long route to San Francisco, and he divided the route into large but manageable "divisions," each overseen by a superintendent responsible for recruiting crews to create a passable road, remove boulders, uproot stumps, bridge streams, prepare fords, and build "stations." There would be two hundred of these along the route, twenty to eighty miles apart; some were "home stations," complete with stationmaster, herders, harness makers, and blacksmiths; others were smaller "swing stations," where the coaches would stop only long enough to hitch a team of fresh horses. Home stations in remote areas were sod-roofed log structures or adobes with a stable for fifteen horses, space for the stationmaster, his wife, and the other employees. Some stations were equipped with escape tunnels in case of Indian attack.

Butterfield acquired two types of vehicles for his company. In the most remote and desolate portion of the route, from Fort Smith to Los Angeles, he used so-called celerity wagons, lightweight covered wagons built low to the ground to reduce the chances of rolling over on rough roads. At either end of the line, however, Butterfield ran 250 "Concord coaches" made by J. Stephens Abbott in Concord, New Hampshire. They were beautifully crafted and brightly finished vehicles, costing fourteen hundred dollars each, typically weighing a full twenty-five hundred pounds, measuring 8½ feet in length, the same in height, and 5 feet wide. Nine passengers could crowd onto the leather-upholstered benches inside—though, in truth, even more were sometimes jammed in—and a dozen could perch precariously on the roof, along with the passengers' baggage. Mail was carried in a leather "boot" at the rear of the coach. Despite the elaborate construction and thoroughbrace suspension—3½-inch oxhide strips on which the coach body rested—the ride was bone-shattering.

It was also expensive. Through passengers paid two hundred dollars each; those stopping at intermediate points were charged ten cents a mile. The coaches, equipped with oil headlamps, traveled day and night, which meant many days of fatigue and discomfort. One could choose to stop over at a station, but accommodations in these were miserable, filthy, and often scarcely

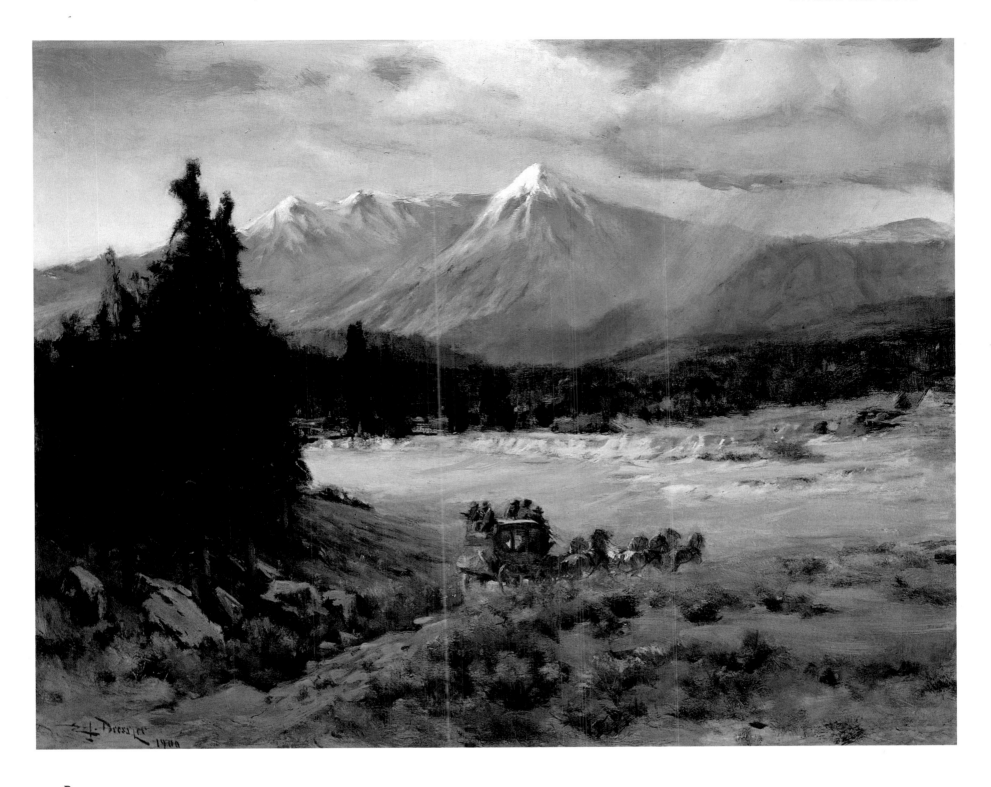

Bertha Menzler Dressler
(1871–1947)
San Francisco Peaks, 1900
Oil on canvas, 30 × 40 in.
Santa Fe Collection of Southwestern
Art

A Concord coach in action.

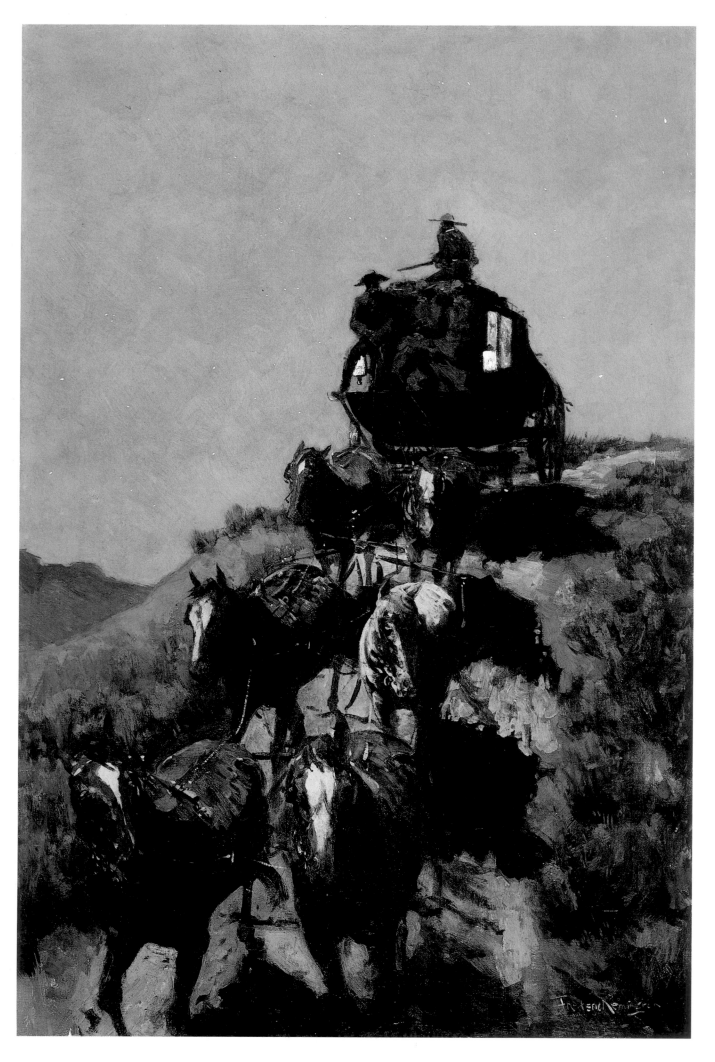

Frederic Remington (1861–1909)
The Old Stage Coach of the Plains,
1901
Oil on canvas, 40 ¼ × 27 ¼ in.
Amon Carter Museum, Fort Worth,
Texas

Stagecoaches traveled day and night
over trails that were more rut than
road.

less cramped than the coaches themselves. Worse, there was a chance of getting marooned for many days waiting for another coach with space to spare. In 1860, for example, passengers typically waited ten days for a seat.

Butterfield recruited his "jehus," or drivers, carefully; their job was to handle a team of six semiwild horses with reins and a twelve-foot-long bullwhip at an average speed of nine miles per hour over roads that, more often than not, were hardly worthy of the name. A conductor or messenger-guard sat beside the jehu, "riding shotgun" to provide protection against Indians and road agents. In western Texas and Arizona, Indian attack was an ever-present danger; ten Butterfield drivers were killed in 1859. Probably because the Butterfield stages carried no gold shipments (as did the line's later competitor, Wells Fargo), they were never stopped by highwaymen. Nevertheless, robbery on the trail was a coaching hazard. Montana's infamous Plummer gang preyed on the Salt Lake City mail coach during the 1860s. At eleven o'clock on one November morning in 1863, the coach approached three riders, each of whom had a shotgun lying across his left arm; they looked like hunters. Before the coach overtook them, the three wheeled their horses about. Whiskey Bill Graves drew a bead on the stagecoach driver, Tom Caldwell. George Ives covered Leroy

Southmayde, a passenger. And Bob Zachary watched another passenger—Captain Moore—and a discharged driver named Billy. Thomas J. Dimsdale, author of *The Vigilantes of Montana* (1866), got the story firsthand from Southmayde:

Southmayde had the opportunity of looking down the barrels of Ives' gun, and could almost see the buckshot getting ready for a jump. As a matter of taste, he thinks such a sight anything but agreeable and edifying, and if his luck should bring him in the vicinity of road agents in pursuit of their calling, he confidentially informs us that he would prefer a side view of the operation, as he would then be able to speak dispassionately of the affair. To report without "fear, favor, or affection" is rather hard when the view is taken in front, at short range. Without "favor or affection" can be managed; but the observance of the first condition would necessitate an indifference to a shower of "cold pewter," possessed only by despairing lovers of the red-cover novelette class, and these men never visit the mountains. . . . Ives called out, "Halt! Throw up your hands," and then bade Zachary "Get down and look after those fellows."

Accordingly, Bob dismounted, and leaving his horse, he walked, gun in hand, up to Southmayde. While

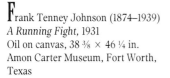

Frank Tenney Johnson (1874–1939)
A Running Fight, 1931
Oil on canvas, 38 ⅜ × 46 ¼ in.
Amon Carter Museum, Fort Worth,
Texas

Stagecoaches were occasionally attacked by Indians—though less frequently than popular fiction and the movies would lead us to believe.

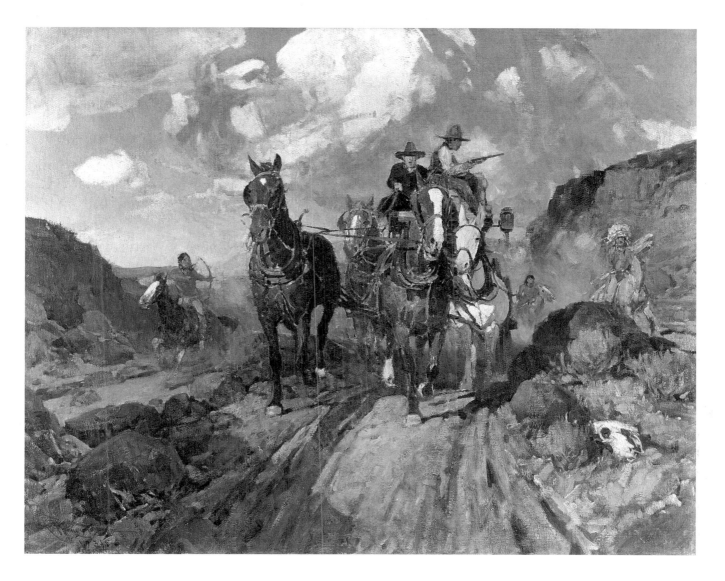

engaged in panning out Southmayde's [gold] dust, he trembled from head to foot (and that not with cold).

The appearance of the road agents, at this moment, was striking. . . . Each man had on a green and blue blanket, covering the body entirely. Whiskey Bill wore a "plug" hat (the antitype of the muff on a soup-plate usually worn in the East). His sleeves were rolled up above the elbow; he had a black silk handkerchief over his face, with holes for sight and air, and he rode a gray horse, covered from the ears to the tail with a blanket, which, however, left the head and legs exposed to view. George Ives' horse was blanketed in the same way. It was a dappled gray, with a roached mane. He himself was masked with a piece of gray blanket, with the necessary perforations. Zachary rode a blue-gray horse, belonging to Bob Dempsey ("all the country" was their stable)—blanketed like the others—and his mask was a piece of Jersey shirt.

Ives was off to the side of the driver, and Graves on the near side. When Zachary walked up to Southmayde, he said, "Shut your eyes." This Southmayde respectfully declined, and the matter was not pressed. Bob then took Leroy's pistol and money, and threw them down.

While Southmayde was being robbed, Billy, feeling tired, put down his hands, upon which Ives instantly roared out, "Throw them up, you ———." It is recorded that Billy obeyed with alacrity, though not with cheerfulness.

Zachary walked up to Captain Moore and made a similar request. The Captain declared, with great solemnity, as he handed him his purse, that it was "all he had in the world"; but it afterwards appeared that a sum of $25 was not included in that estimate of his terrestrial assets, for he produced this money when the road agents had disappeared.

Continuing his search, the relieving officer came to Billy, and demanded his pistol, which was immediately handed over. Ives asked, "Is it loaded" and being answered in the negative, told Bob to give it back to the owner. Tom Caldwell's turn came next. He had several small sums belonging to different parties, which he was carrying for them to their friends, and he had also been commissioned to make some purchases. As Bob approached him he exclaimed, "My God! what do you want with me? I have nothing." Graves told Zachary to let him alone, and inquired if there was anything in the mail that they wanted. Tom said he did not think there was. Zachary stepped up to the brake bar and commenced an

Charles M. Russell (1864–1926)
The Hold Up (Holding Up the Stage), 1899
Oil on canvas, 30 ⅜ × 48 ¼ in.
Amon Carter Museum, Fort Worth, Texas

The sign on the tree offers a one-thousand-dollar reward for the capture of these "road agents," but none of the passengers is in a position to collect.

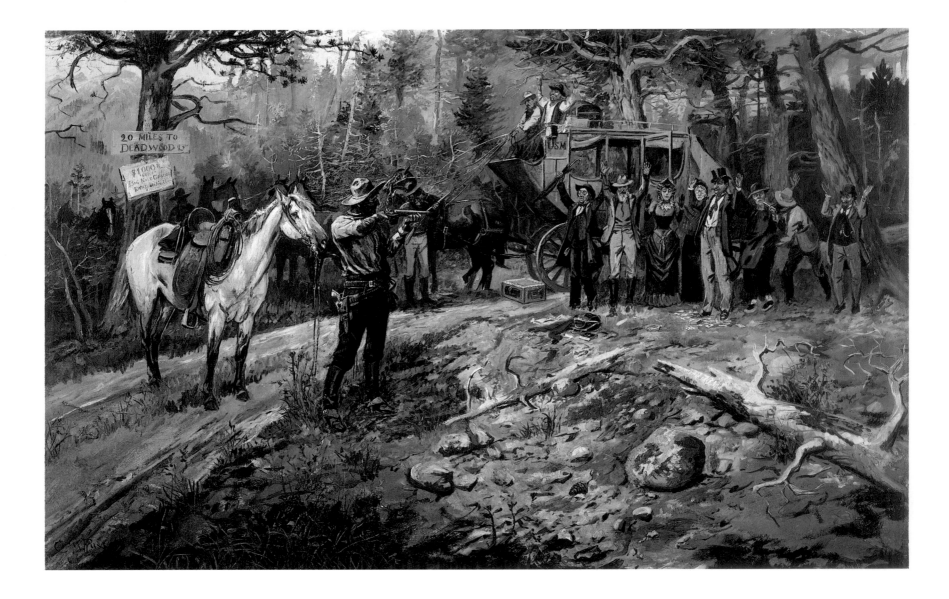

Frederic Remington (1861–1909)
"The Right of the Road"—A Hazardous Rencounter on a Rocky Mountain Trail, 1900
Oil on canvas (black and white),
27 ¼ × 40 ¼ in.
Amon Carter Museum, Fort Worth,
Texas

Not all hazards of the trail involved bandits and Indians.

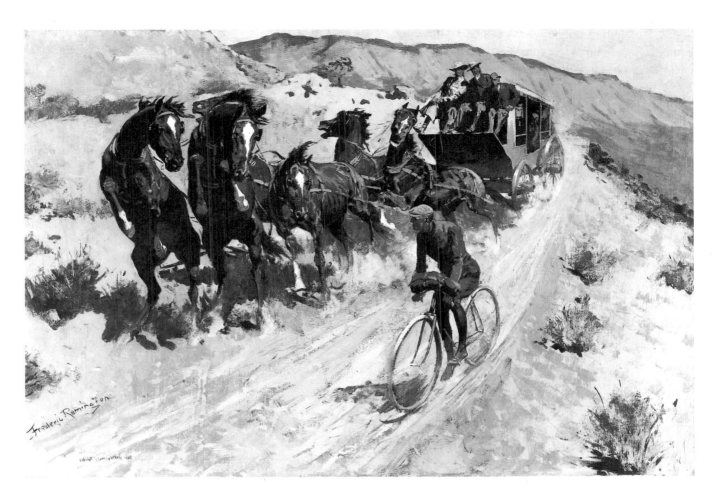

examination, but found nothing. As Caldwell looked at Zachary while he was thus occupied, Ives ordered him not to do that. Tom turned and asked if he might look at him. Ives nodded.

Having finished his search, Zachary picked up his gun, and stepped back. Ives dismissed the "parade" with the laconic command, "Get up and 'skedaddle.'"

The horses were somewhat restive, but Tom held them fast, and Southmayde, with a view to reconnoitering, said in a whisper, "Tom, drive slow." Ives called out, "Drive on." Leroy turned round on his seat, determined to find out who the robbers were and looked carefully at them for nearly a minute, which, Ives at last observing, he yelled out, "If you don't turn round, and mind your business, I'll shoot the top of your head off." . . .

Leroy Southmayde lost $400 in gold, and Captain Moore delivered up $100 in Treasury notes, belonging to another man.

The gentility of this robbery seems almost comic to a late twentieth-century reader bred on contemporary urban mayhem. Yet, Ives, Whiskey Bill, and Zachary were members of a road gang that, in the space of little more than a year, would kill 102 persons. And not all stage robberies went so smoothly. In 1876, Joel Collins, Jack Davis, Bill Heffridge, Jim Berry, and Tom Nixon joined forces with a soon-to-be-infamous bandit named Sam Bass in the town of Deadwood, Idaho Territory, to rob stagecoaches. "They stopped and went through a number of stage coaches and robbed several travelers on

the highway," reports Charles L. Martin in *A Sketch of Sam Bass the Bandit* (1878), "but in all their ventures they made only about $100. Finally they attempted to stop a stage, one day, when the driver not being complacent, put the whip to his horses and started on the run. Collins and Heffridge fired on the driver with their Winchester rifles, and he fell from his seat dead."

Despite all hazards, the Overland Mail operated with extraordinary efficiency, rarely missing a scheduled arrival or departure by more than a few hours. Then, in 1859, Butterfield's governmental benefactor, Postmaster General Brown, died. Judge Joseph Holt assumed his office, determined to run the Post Office Department according to a strict economy. When he discovered that the federal government was actually subsidizing six western mail routes—the sea route via Panama, another via Tehuantepec, Mexico, overland routes including Butterfield's, a San Antonio to San Diego run, Kansas City to Stockton, and St. Joseph to Placerville—he canceled the Stockton and the Tehuantepec contracts, curtailed service between San Antonio and San Diego and between St. Joseph and Placerville, and reduced the Panama subsidy. Butterfield's oxbow route remained untouched, but the new postmaster's action had radically reduced competition and, as William H. Russell saw it, provided what was literally a golden opportunity.

Opportunity was precisely what the freighter needed at this moment in the history of Russell, Majors & Waddell. The year 1857 had promised to be a great one for the company. Its contract called for transporting five

FREDERIC SACKRIDER REMINGTON

—

BORN 1861, CANTON, NEW YORK

DIED 1909, RIDGEFIELD, CONNECTICUT

—

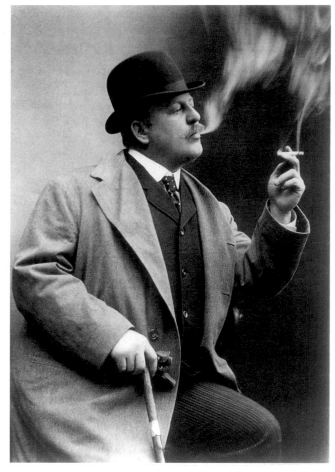

Frederic Remington smoking a cigarette, c. 1909. Photograph. Frederic Remington Art Museum, Ogdensburg, New York

Son of a Civil War hero who published a newspaper in rural upstate New York, Remington grew up with a close knowledge of military gallantry and the outdoors. When, in 1873, the artist's father teamed up with a local harness driver to breed and race trotters, young Remington's intimate acquaintance with horses and riding began. It was not until 1880, when his father died, that Remington took his first trip west, to Montana. One of the sketches made on this excursion was published, two years later, in *Harper's Weekly.*

Prior to his father's death, Remington had been educated at the Vermont Episcopal Institute and had studied one year, 1878–79, at the art school of Yale University. He and a Yale classmate set up as gentlemen ranchers in Kansas during 1883, but poor wool prices and other difficulties prompted Remington to sell his 160 acres the next year. However, he did not leave the West; instead, he traveled Southwest, sketching Indians and Mexican vaqueros. That year, 1884, the artist sold his first paintings, through W. W. Findlay's art store in Kansas City, Missouri. He also sold *Harper's Weekly* a second sketch—this one for the front cover of the March 28, 1885, issue.

After further sketching trips in Arizona, Texas, and Oklahoma during 1885, Remington returned to New York, where he studied briefly at the Art Students League. By 1885–86, he was regularly contributing illustrations to a number of popular magazines, and in 1888 he illustrated Theodore Roosevelt's *Ranch Life and the Hunting Trail,* which brought the artist a great deal of national attention.

Enjoying great success as an illustrator throughout the 1880s and 1890s, Remington held his first one-man show in 1893, in New York City, and began modeling works to be cast in bronze in 1895—the first of which was *Bronco Buster.* That same year, Remington wrote and illustrated his own first book, *Pony Tracks,* which was followed by others, including *Crooked Trails* (1898), *Sundown LeFlare* (1899), and *John Ermine of Yellowstone* (1902). In all, Remington produced some 2,700 paintings and drawings; his illustrations appeared in 41 different periodicals and 142 books. His 24 sculptures appeared in many cast bronze editions and are still widely purchased in the form of reproductions.

The artist was also widely sought-after as an illustrator-reporter, traveling in this capacity to Russia, North Africa, Germany, England, Mexico, and Cuba. Dispatched to the latter in 1896 by newspaper magnate William Randolph Hearst to cover the slowly brewing Spanish-American War, Remington became bored by a lack of action. "Everything quiet," he wired Hearst. "There is no trouble. There will be no war. I wish to return." Hearst reportedly cabled back: "Please remain. You furnish the pictures and I'll furnish the war."

Prickly, racially prejudiced, and generally intolerant, Remington immortalized the uncompromisingly masculine world of the West, especially the activity of soldiers and cowboys, and enjoyed great public and critical acclaim during his lifetime. On December 23, 1909, the artist underwent an emergency appendectomy. Three days later, he was dead.

million pounds of goods. The original five hundred wagons grew to eight hundred, and the firm was scouring the West for bullwhackers and other personnel. Then came the "Mormon War" as President Buchanan dispatched twenty-five hundred federal troops to insure the safe reception of the new territorial governor. Three million additional pounds of supplies had to be transported for the soldiers. Russell, Majors & Waddell paid premium prices to find the necessary oxen and drivers, but the partners had every reason to believe that their greater fortune was in the making.

What they didn't reckon on was the guerrilla-style belligerence of the Mormons, who burned three entire wagon trains. This mischance was compounded by a severe winter with crippling snowfall. By the end of 1857, the firm was out half a million dollars, and the War Department simply informed the partners that, because it had exhausted its appropriation, it was defaulting on payment to them. To add insult to injury, the public's perception of the Mormon War had rapidly come about 180 degrees; what had started as a universal sentiment to put these upstart bigamists in their place became admiration for a people willing to sacrifice everything to defend what they believed in. Russell, Majors & Waddell found they had hitched their wagons not only to a profitless star, but an unpopular one.

William H. Russell saw coaching as his company's salvation and, he reasoned, the time was ripe. Postmaster Holt had fortuitously removed some competition from the field, Butterfield was committed to the roundabout oxbow route, leaving the more direct Central Route, via South Pass, unserved, and rumors of a major gold strike were flying out of Pikes Peak country. Now was the time to profit from coach service between the Mississippi Valley and Denver. When his partners failed to share his enthusiastic confidence, Russell teamed up with John S. Jones to form the Leavenworth and Pikes Peak Express Company, and he pressed on full speed ahead. Stations were built, roads established (after the customary makeshift fashion), fifty Concord coaches were purchased, along with a thousand mules—better suited than horses to the arid territory the new company would serve.

Pikes Peak Express cost a thousand dollars a day to run. The vaunted gold rush failed to materialize; at least, it failed to begin on schedule, and many discouraged prospectors deserted the brand-new city of Denver. When that happened, the firm's revenues evaporated. What Russell needed was that old standby, a government subsidy. To get one quickly, he decided to buy out a company that already had a mail contract, the John M. Hockaday Stage Line, which ran between Independence and Salt Lake City. The franchise was worth $130,000 in subsidy money. Russell had to pay $144,000 to acquire the company. Service began on July 2, 1859, and travelers were delighted.

But it had already cost too much. With the specter

of bankruptcy looming large, Russell's freighting partners, Majors and Waddell, fearful that Russell's collapse would finish off the original firm, took over Russell's company and renamed it the Central Overland, California & Pikes Peak Express. They were taking a desperate gamble. Beginning with a relatively modest contract to carry mail between Placerville and Salt Lake City, they had to prove quickly and dramatically that the Central Route was superior to Butterfield's oxbow. As usual, William Russell supplied the drama.

He proposed to deliver mail from St. Joseph, Missouri, to Sacramento, California—a distance forty-four miles shy of an even two thousand—in ten days. There would be no passengers on this run. Indeed, there would be no stagecoaches and no wagons. Just ponies, a relay of them stretching across the continent, and a lone rider on each: the Pony Express.

Billy Richardson was the first rider, riding out of St. Joseph on April 3, 1860, carrying forty-nine letters and some special-edition newspapers. He would ride the first seventy-five miles or so at full gallop, until he hit the first of twenty-five "home stations" constructed along the route. There another rider would relieve him. At intermediate "relay stations"—there were 165 in all, ten to fifteen miles apart—he would change horses. Russell had purchased five hundred horses, semiwild "outlaw" animals, some having fetched as much as $200. He had eighty riders continuously en route, forty westbound, forty east. They had each answered ads calling for "daring young men, preferably orphans." They were young men, most of them about nineteen, though Buffalo Bill was only fifteen when he joined up, and a boy named David Jay became a rider at thirteen. They were wiry men, none over 135 pounds in weight. They were well paid; in an age when a common laborer earned a dollar a day, Pony Express riders were paid $100 to $150 a month, in addition to room and board.

They earned their pay. When, one day, Buffalo Bill Cody reached the home station at the end of his seventy-six mile route and found that his relief had been killed, he remounted and rode another eighty-five miles. Then he turned around and made the return trip, for a total of 322 miles. The continent's most hostile climate and most punishing terrain challenged the riders. Indians, too, were a constant hazard to a lone horseman. Bob Haslan was attacked by Paiutes and took an arrow through the arm and another through the jaw, resulting in an excruciating fracture. He rode on, making 120 miles in eight hours, ten minutes, using thirteen horses. In the nineteen months of its operation, representing 650,000 miles of travel, the Pony Express lost only one mail.

The Pony Express captured the nation's imagination. In *Roughing It,* Mark Twain recalled how he and his fellow coach passengers longed to catch sight of a rider. "Away across the endless dead level of the prairie a black speck appears against the sky, and it is plain that it moves. . . . In a second or two it becomes a horse and

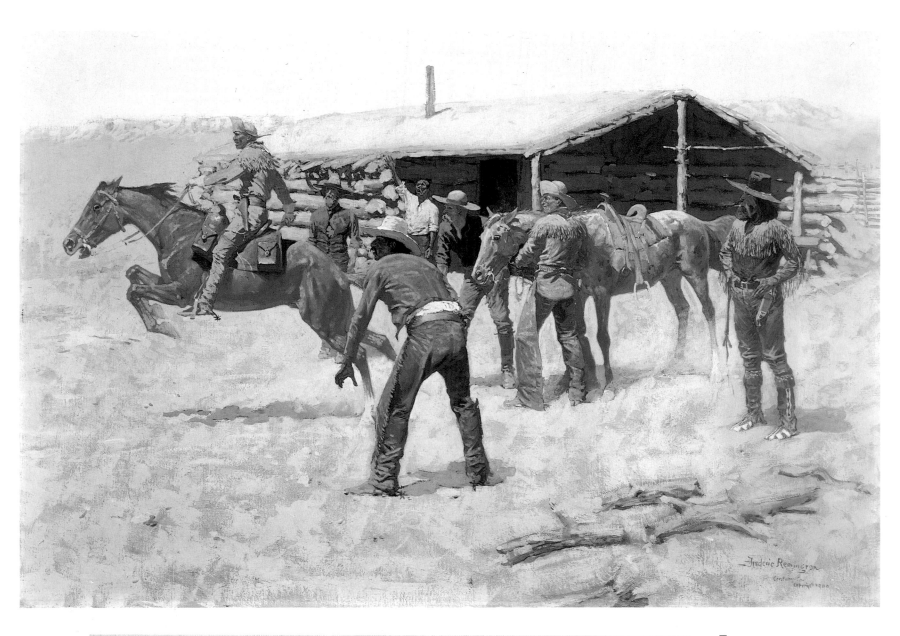

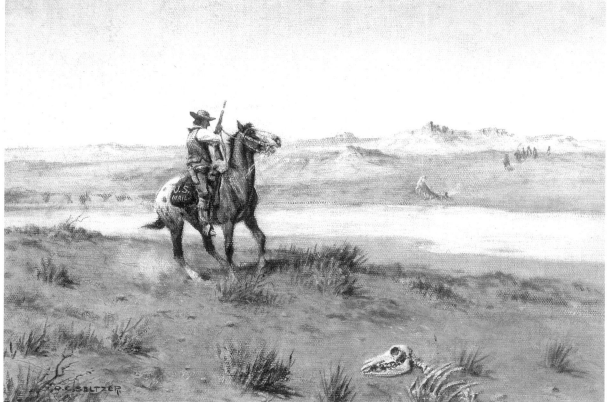

Frederic Remington (1861–1909)
The Coming and Going of the Pony Express, 1900
Oil on canvas, 26 × 39 in.
Gilcrease Museum, Tulsa, Oklahoma

Few western institutions have appealed to the popular imagination more than this short-lived, hazardous, and wholly impractical method of delivering the mail.

Olaf Carl Seltzer (1877–1957)
The Pony Express, n.d.
Oil on canvas, 11 × 14 in.
Gilcrease Museum, Tulsa, Oklahoma

Indian attack was a particular hazard for lone Pony Express riders.

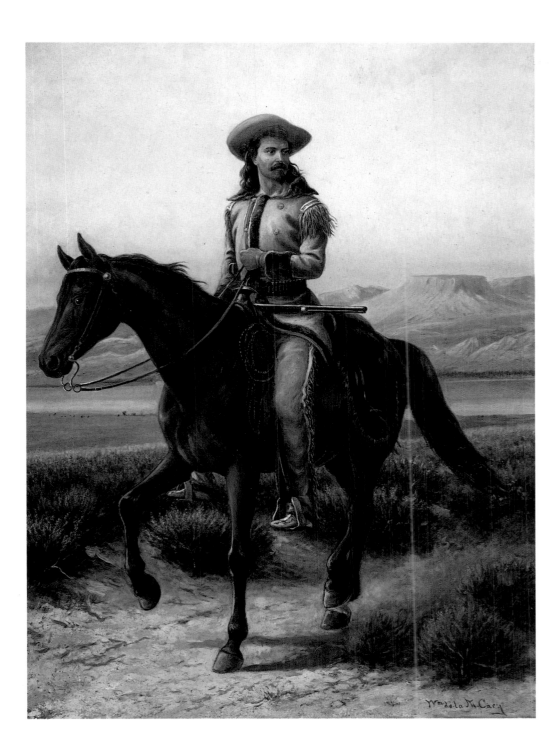

William de la Montagne Cary (1840–1922)
Buffalo Bill on Charlie, n.d.
Oil on canvas, 30 × 40 in.
Gilcrease Museum, Tulsa, Oklahoma

The consummate westerner on his favorite horse.

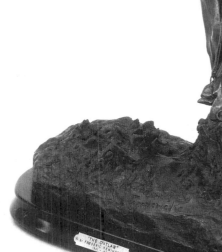

Frederic S. Remington (1861–1909)
The Outlaw, 1906
Bronze, H 23 ¾ in.
The Rockwell Museum, Corning, New York

The title refers to the beast, not the man.

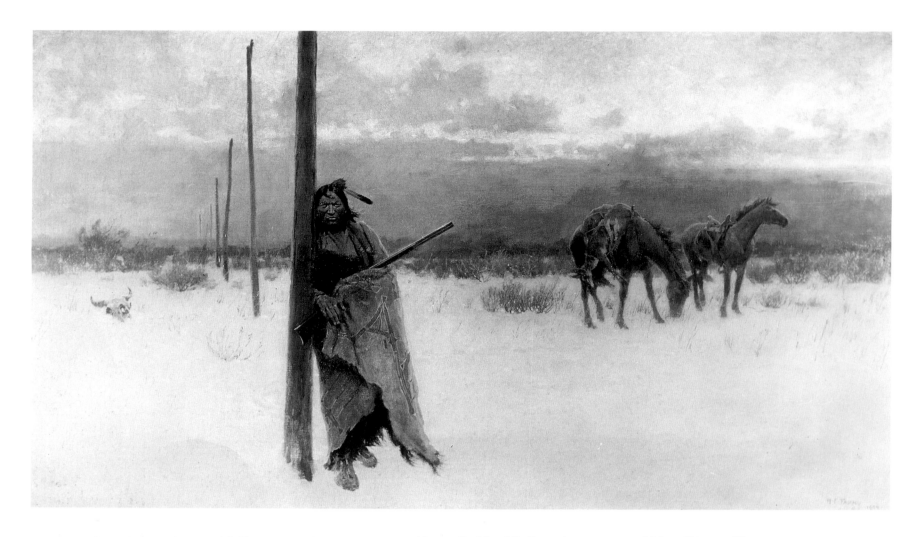

Henry F. Farny (1847–1916)
The Song of the Talking Wire, 1904
Oil on canvas, 22 1/16 × 40 in.
The Taft Museum, Cincinnati, Ohio;
Bequest of Mr. and Mrs. Charles
Phelps Taft

The telegraph not only represented
the incursion of white man's ways
into Indian life, it spelled the end of
the short-lived Pony Express.

rider, rising and falling, rising and falling—sweeping toward us nearer and nearer . . . and the flutter of the hoofs comes faintly to the ear—another instant a whoop and a hurrah from our upper deck, a wave of the rider's hand . . . and man and horse burst past our excited faces, and go winging away like a belated fragment of a storm!" Riders carried the text of Abraham Lincoln's inaugural address from St. Joseph to Sacramento not in the promised ten days, but in the incredible time of seven days, seventeen hours.

Pony Express mail commanded a rate of five dollars per half-ounce—soon lowered to two dollars—and did, indeed, attract business to the Russell, Majors & Waddell's Central Overland route as well as dramatize to Congress, which was debating an Overland Mail Bill during the summer of 1860, the virtues of the Central Route. But the Pony Express lost money—it cost the company sixteen dollars to deliver a letter that returned three dollars in revenue—and southerners in Congress kept the major government mail contract in the hands of Butterfield and his southerly oxbow route. Then, on October 24, 1861, a telegraph line from the East was joined to one from the West, and communication became a matter of seconds rather than days. The Pony Express was out of business, but even before the fatal day in October, it was apparent that Russell, Majors & Waddell were riding toward bankruptcy.

Russell went to Washington, D.C., late in 1860 and met with one Goddard Bailey, who represented himself as a dealer in government bonds. Just what happened next is not entirely clear. Apparently, however, Russell sought to borrow through Bailey $150,000 in state securities, which the freighter would use as collateral with which to raise cash. Bailey delivered the bonds, and Russell asked for another loan, whereupon Bailey revealed that he was not a bond dealer at all, but a Department of the Interior clerk. He had "borrowed" (the courts would say *embezzled*) the bonds himself from the department's Indian Trust Fund. Russell's desperate response to this revelation was to get Bailey to "borrow" yet more, until some $870,000 in securities had changed hands.

So black was the financial pit into which the freighter had slid, that even this enormous sum could not save Russell, Majors & Waddell. Bailey, in abject despair, sent a letter of confession directly to President Buchanan. That was on December 22, 1860; on the twenty-third, William H. Russell was in jail.

Ironically, had Russell not succumbed to temptation, his company might have been saved. The outbreak of the Civil War meant that the United States could no longer subsidize the southerly Butterfield route. The Central Route via South Pass was now in favor, and a one-million-dollar annual subsidy was in the offing. But awarding a major contract to a firm tainted by criminal fraud was out of the question. The Butterfield Overland Mail got the prize, while the role of the beleaguered Central Overland Mail was reduced to operating coaches and the doomed Pony Express east of Salt Lake City.

By this time, John Butterfield had retired, leaving his company in the hands of men who lacked his vision and determination. They sold the firm to Wells Fargo. Russell, Majors & Waddell, as usual seeking cash, mortgaged the Central Overland to Ben Holladay, whom a rival described as "energetic, untiring, unconscionable, unscrupulous, and wholly destitute of honesty, morality or common decency." Late in 1861 Holladay called in his mortgagee's notes, forcing the firm into bankruptcy. Holladay was able to purchase the assets of Russell, Majors & Waddell for a mere half-million dollars and enjoyed a near-monopoly on freight and passenger service between Salt Lake City and the Missouri River. At the height of his operations, he employed fifteen thousand and owned twenty thousand coaches and wagons. There seemed to be no stopping this "Napoleon of the Plains."

But by 1866, Holladay knew it was time to get out of the wagon and stagecoach business. In 1862, Congress had passed the Pacific Railway Act, authorizing the Union Pacific Company and the Central Pacific Company to build a transcontinental railroad. Construction did not begin until the summer of 1863 and, at first, progressed slowly. But progress it did, and Holladay sold his Holladay Overland Mail & Express Company to arch-rival Wells Fargo. The directors of that company were not unmindful of the coming of the railroad, either, but they saw a way to adapt to the changing circumstances of transportation in the West. Wells Fargo relinquished its long-distance service and came to specialize in feeder lines terminating at various western railheads. The firm,

which had for years transported gold dust for mining companies, used its expertise to provide special security cars for transporting bullion and other precious cargo by rail.

TRAIL OF IRON

The first American railroad, the Baltimore and Ohio, was chartered in 1828 and began operating two years later. It was not until 1852 that its tracks reached Wheeling, West Virginia, on the Ohio River. By that time, railroads were already being constructed in the Midwest, and the Chicago and Rock Island (later called the Chicago, Rock Island and Pacific—the Rock Island Line) reached the Mississippi at Rock Island, Illinois, in 1854. Two years later, it had crossed the river, as had the Chicago, Burlington and Quincy, the Chicago and Northwestern, and the Chicago, Milwaukee and St. Paul (later to add "Pacific" to its name).

As early as 1832, a Dr. Hartwell Carver, native of Rochester, New York, published some articles in the *New York Courier & Enquirer* proposing a transcontinental railroad to be built on eight million acres of government land from Lake Michigan to Oregon—at the time the only coastal territory to which the United States had anything like a reasonable claim. Carver presented his ideas to Congress, including the notion of passenger cars one hundred feet in length, containing dining and sleeping facilities. The precocity of Carver's proposal can best be appreciated by recalling that mountain man Joe Walker blazed what would become known as the Overland Trail as late as 1833.

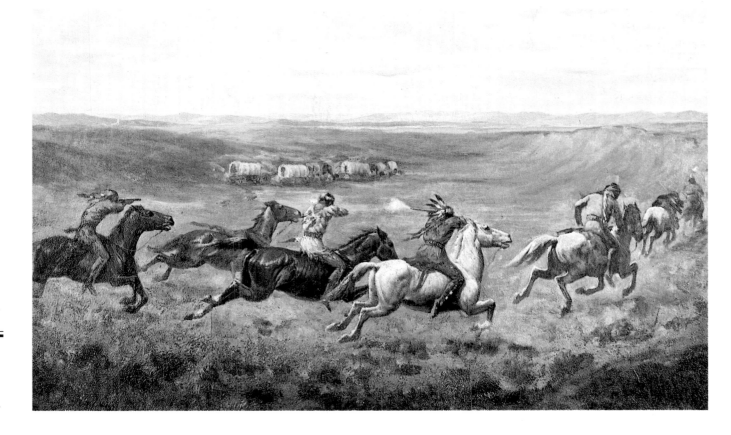

Charles Craig (1846–1931)
Indians Attacking Overland Train,
1887
Oil on canvas, 21 ¼ × 35 ⅜ in.
Santa Fe Collection of Southwestern Art

The painting accurately suggests the Plains Indian's skill at horsemanship, but that expertise was more often applied to hunting buffalo than harassing wagon trains.

The first serious scheme came ten years later. Asa Whitney, a New Yorker engaged in the highly profitable China trade, proposed to Congress that the United States sell him nearly eighty million acres, from Lake Michigan to the Columbia River, crossing the Rockies over Joe Walker's South Pass, at the price of sixteen cents per acre. Whitney, in truth, would sell parcels of the land to settlers and farmers, using the proceeds to push the railroad farther and farther West. It would be pay as you go, and no additional financing would be required. The plan caught the public fancy, and, in the course of five years of lobbying, Whitney gained the endorsement of seventeen state legislatures. Then, in Congress, he butted up against an immovable obstacle in the form of Missouri Senator Thomas Hart Benton.

Benton and a group of his constituents also had been thinking about a transcontinental railroad, but one that would have as its eastern terminus St. Louis—chief city of the senator's home state—rather than Chicago. Benton attacked Whitney's proposal on the grounds of private ownership, protesting government subsidy of a scheme to enrich an individual. Benton and his faction managed to get the proposal tabled. That, perhaps, was just as well. It gave railroad experts the opportunity to point out the logistical and engineering difficulties Whitney had barely acknowledged in the process of promoting his plan. No systematic survey of potential routes existed, but everybody was aware that the western landscape was formidable. Engineers knew that locomotives could not pull a train over a grade that rises any steeper than 116 feet per mile and that a train could not round a curve less than 300 feet in radius. In the mountains of the West, nature did not provide gentle slopes and wide room for rounding bends.

In 1848, Benton persuaded Congress to fund a railroad survey led by his son-in-law, John C. Frémont. Although Frémont had experience as a railroad surveyor—for a line from Charleston to Cincinnati—his conviction that he could find a pass over the Continental Divide by approximately following the thirty-eighth parallel was more wishful thinking than the result of careful consideration. Acting on a foolhardy notion that crossing the Divide in winter would dramatically demonstrate the virtues of the route as an all-weather trail, Frémont stranded himself and his party of thirty-five in a Rocky Mountain blizzard. Ten men froze or starved to death before Ute Indians rescued the party. Nevertheless, Frémont blithely reported that the "result was entirely satis-

Currier & Ives (after Frances Flora Palmer)
American Express Train, 1864
Museum of the City of New York

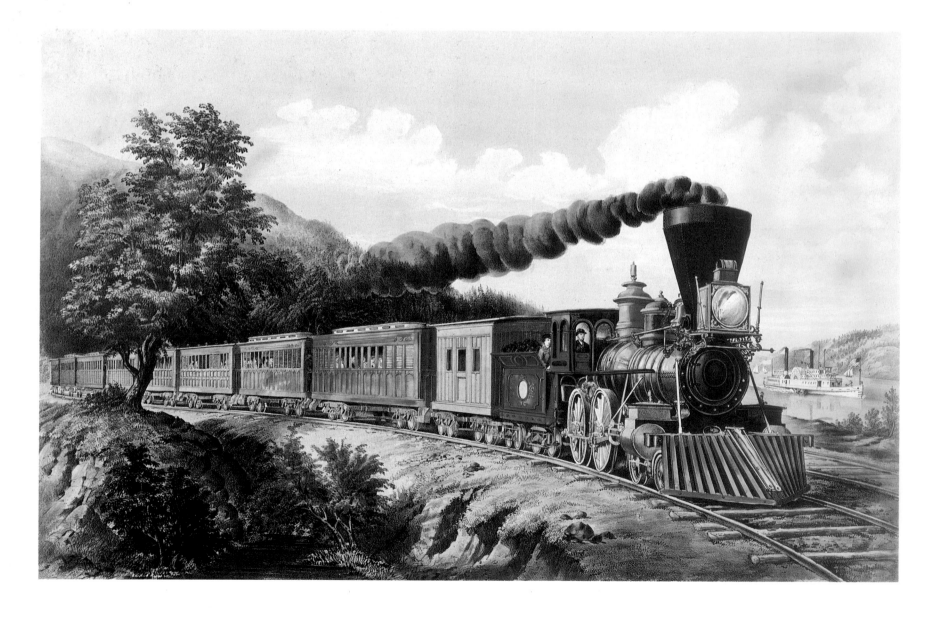

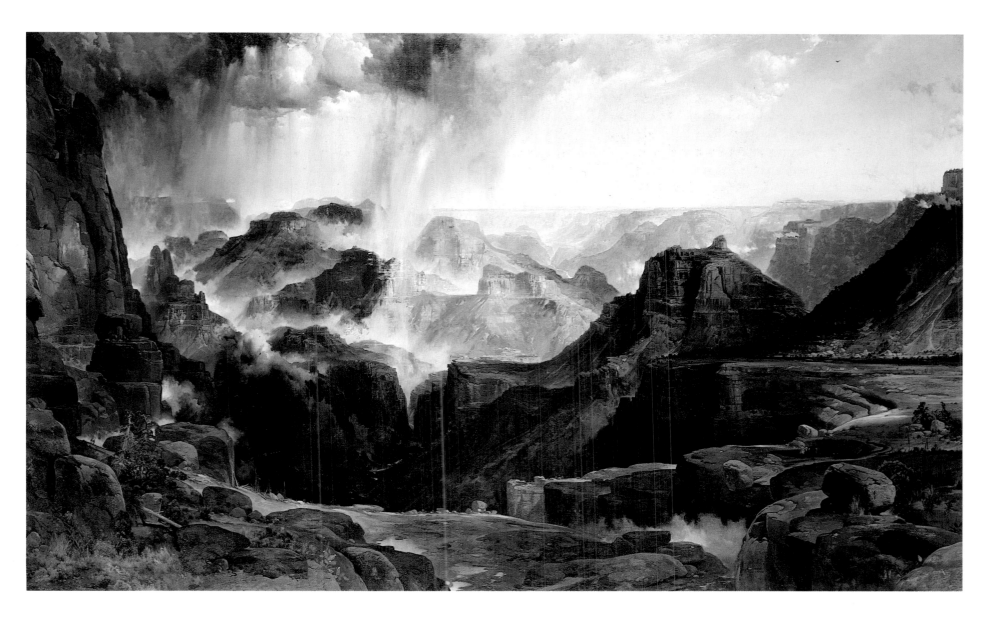

Thomas Moran (1837–1926)
Chasm of the Colorado, 1873–74
Oil on canvas, 84 ⅜ × 144 ¾ in.
National Museum of American Art,
Smithsonian Institution; Lent by the
U.S. Department of the Interior, Office of the Secretary

The western landscape presented no
end of topographical obstacles to the
laying of railroad track.

factory . . . neither the snow of winter nor the mountain ranges were obstacles in the way of a road." Armed with his son-in-law's optimism, Benton proposed the route to the Senate. But he lacked the hard information concerning grades and curves that engineers needed. Besides, the army was now proposing its own route, roughly along the thirty-eighth parallel, through the territory newly won from Mexico.

While argument over routes raged fruitlessly, the means of actually financing a transcontinental railroad were being developed. The one indisputable and, apparently, limitless asset the United States government controlled was land. Railroad lobbyists proposed a system whereby the government would grant expanding railroads large sections of land alternating north and south of the right-of-way. The railroads would sell their land in order to finance construction, and the presence of the railroad would greatly increase the value not only of the purchasers' land, but of the alternate sections retained by the government. President Millard Fillmore signed the first such grant in 1850, apportioning 2.6 million acres to the Illinois Central and a comparable amount to a southern railroad out of Mobile, Alabama. During the next decade, the land-grant policy rolled on like a juggernaut, as 20 million acres of public lands were given to the railroads by 1860.

At last, in 1853, Congress authorized Secretary of War Jefferson Davis to conduct detailed surveys of the "principal routes to the Pacific." In a climate of growing North-South sectionalism, the task presented as many political difficulties as topographical problems. A northerly route would insure the economic superiority of the North; a southerly route would greatly strengthen the South. Davis, the future president of the Confederacy, was hoping to tip the balance in favor of the Southern Trail by omitting it from the survey. For he was counting on obtaining results from surveying the other routes that would be as inconclusive as the results obtained by Frémont, and his proposal would win by default. Accordingly, Davis dispatched parties to survey between the forty-ninth and forty-seventh parallels, from the Great Lakes to Puget Sound; south of that, to survey the route Benton favored; farther south, a trail along the thirty-fifth parallel, from Fort Smith, Arkansas, to Albuquerque, to the region of present-day Los Angeles. Another party would survey California's San Joaquin Valley for passes that could join the thirty-fifth parallel route with the Southern Trail. After these surveys were under way, Davis was compelled to answer critics of the Southern Trail, who claimed that it lacked timber for construction and did not lead to a viable pass through the Rocky Mountains. He was forced to include his pet route among

THOMAS MORAN

—

BORN 1837, BOLTON, ENGLAND
DIED 1926, SANTA BARBARA, CALIFORNIA

—

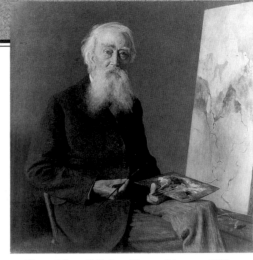

Howard Russell Butler, *Thomas Moran*, c. 1922.
Oil on canvas, 39 ¼ × 36 in. National Portrait Gallery, Smithsonian
Institution, Washington, D.C.

The greatest of the three Moran artist-brothers, Thomas Moran was one of the greatest of all western landscape painters. Born of parents who immigrated to Philadelphia in 1844, Moran was apprenticed in 1853 to a wood engraver. He also studied etching and painting with his older brother, Edward.

In 1860, the artist made his first westward sketching journey, to Lake Superior, and the next year he went to England with Edward. There Thomas discovered what would be the seminal influence on his art, the work of the great atmospheric British land- and seascapist J. M. W. Turner. When, in 1866–67, Moran toured the European continent, he encountered a second great influence in the work of Jean-Baptiste-Camille Corot.

It was Moran's genius to translate the lessons of Turner and Corot into terms of the American western landscape. In 1871, the artist accompanied F. V. Hayden, a geologist who was sur-

veying the Grand Canyon. Moran sketched assiduously, returning east and opening a studio in Newark, New Jersey, where he began transforming his sketches into large western canvases. In 1872, Moran traveled to Yosemite and the next year painted the Grand Canyon. The U.S. Congress bought the Yosemite and Grand Canyon works, paying the artist the handsome fee of $10,000 each.

Moran painted the Mountain of the Holy Cross in 1874, and in 1879 sketched in the Tetons with his younger brother Peter. For the next two decades, Moran traveled widely, especially in the West. His atmospheric, emotionally charged landscapes, one more luminous than the next, sold well, and the artist enjoyed a prosperous living. His energy and inspiration unflagging, Moran painted until the very end of his life. It was reported that on his deathbed, at age ninety, he stared at the ceiling, envisioning landscapes yet to be realized.

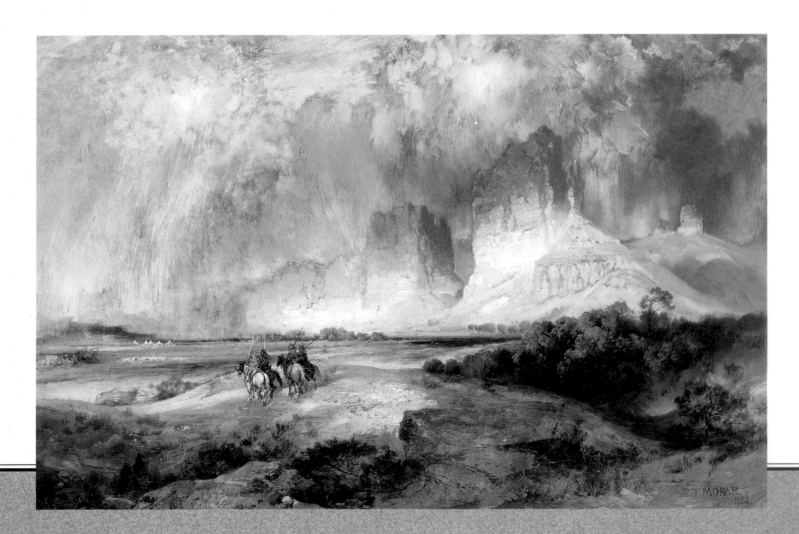

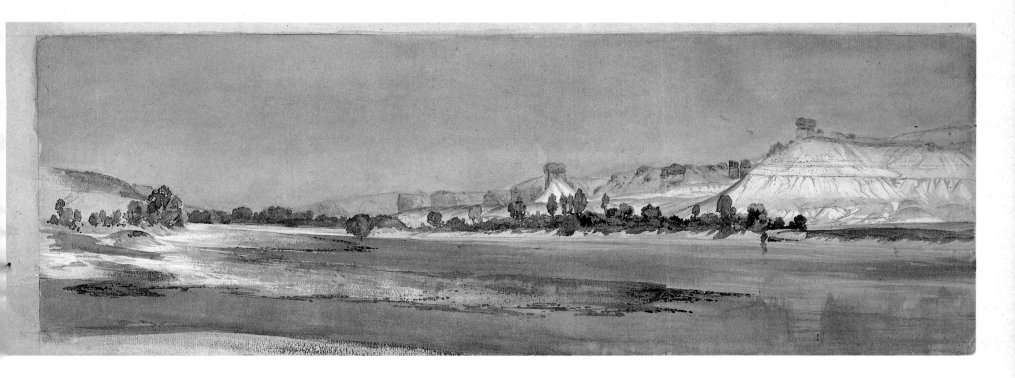

Peter Moran (1841–1914)
Cliffs Along the Green River, c. 1879
Watercolor on paper, 6 ½ × 19 in.
Amon Carter Museum, Fort Worth,
Texas *(above)*

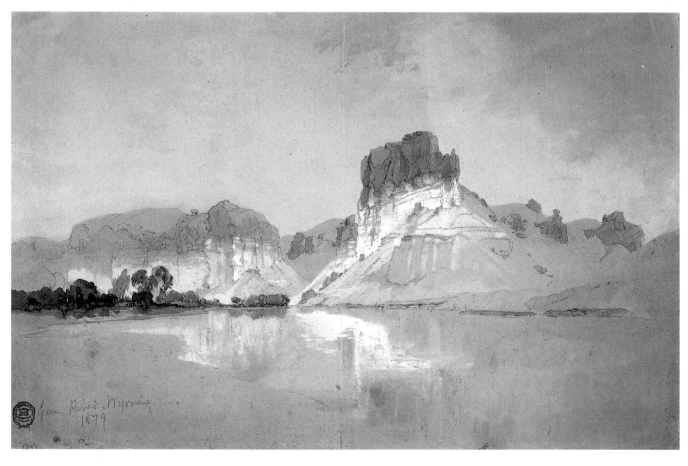

Thomas Moran (1837–1926)
Green River, Wyoming, 1879
Watercolor on paper, 12 ⅝ × 18 in.
Cooper-Hewitt Museum/
Art Resource, New York
(right)

Thomas Moran (1837–1926)
*Cliffs of the Upper Colorado River,
Wyoming Territory*, 1882
Oil on canvas, 16 × 24 in.
National Museum of American Art,
Smithsonian Institution; Bequest of
Henry Ward Ranger through the Na-
tional Academy of Design
(opposite)

those to be surveyed.

Congress had imposed on the surveys a ten-month deadline that insured their superficiality. As with Frémont's survey, no precise data on grades and curves was reported

Isaac Stevens, territorial governor of Washington and leader of the Great Lakes–to–Puget Sound survey, sang the praises of the northern route. A railroad, he said, could be built for ninety-six million dollars, and the prospect of winter snow he dismissed as not presenting "the slightest impediment to the passage of railroad trains." As a governor in the Pacific Northwest, Stevens was hardly an impartial surveyor. His findings were met with grave doubts.

The survey of Benton's favorite route presented far more conclusive results. The survey party was attacked by Paiutes on the Sevier River in Utah, with the loss of eight men. At the time, it was the worst defeat the U.S. Army had suffered in the West, and many thought the Mormons had instigated it. More likely, it was an act meant to avenge a Paiute killed the previous month. Whatever the motive, it convinced politicians that Indian hostility along the so-called Buffalo Trail presented a hazard too great for building and running a railroad.

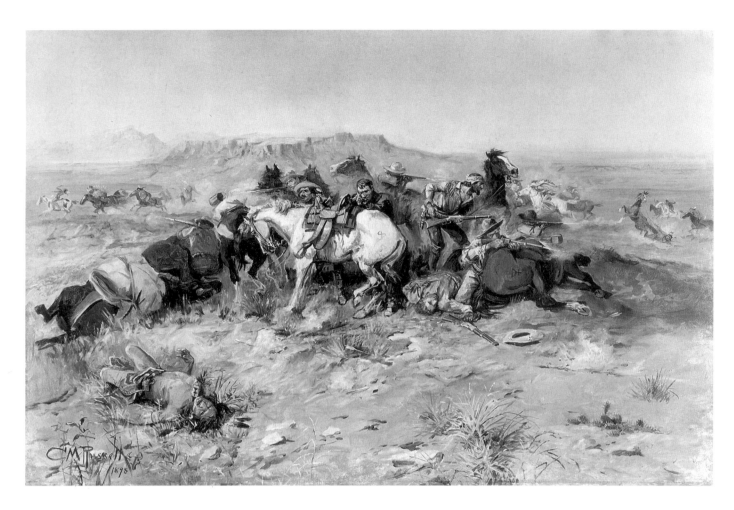

The result of the thirty-fifth parallel survey seemed equally, if less tragically, conclusive, as the party's chief surveyor, Lieutenant Amiel Weeks Whipple, concluded that building a railroad along that trail would cost $169,210,265. Later, it would be discovered that the lieutenant was a better surveyor than accountant, for he had made an error in addition. The true cost was closer to the estimate Isaac Stevens had submitted for the Northern Trail.

Citing all of these problems, Jefferson Davis recommended to Congress the Southern Trail. That it, too, suffered from a serious drawback—part of it lay below the Mexican border!—did not deter Davis, who urged the Gadsden Purchase to readjust the international boundary. The purchase was made, but the transcontinental railroad remained a pawn in the dangerous game of sectional politics the North and South were playing out.

As is true of many momentous events in the West, it took a single remarkable man to accomplish what Congress, bureaucrats, the army, and others could not. Theodore Dehone Judah was the son of an Episcopal clergyman in Bridgeport, Connecticut, but the young man's interests were sharply focused on this world rather than the next. He became a civil engineer, directing work on five railroads in the East, including the spectacular Niagara Gorge line. He had not yet turned thirty when, in 1854, Colonel Charles Wilson, president of the Sacramento Valley Railroad, commissioned him to survey a right-of-way. Judah surveyed the first twenty-two miles of the railroad, from Sacramento to the gold mining town of Fulsom, telling his employers that this could well be the Pacific end of a transcontinental railroad.

So might it have been, if the gold hadn't run out. But Fulsom shrank almost to nothing, and the rail line went no farther. But Judah would not stop. He published a pamphlet called "A Practical Plan for Building the Pacific Railroad" and criticized the Jefferson Davis surveys for their paucity of hard, useful data. He became a transcontinental railroad lobbyist, journeying to Washington, D.C., on numerous occasions. In 1860, after searching the region north of Lake Tahoe for a pass across the mountains, he received a letter from a pharmacist and amateur surveyor named Daniel "Doc" Strong. Strong had read Judah's pamphlet and had also, some years earlier, charted a wagon route through a relatively easy corridor in the Sierra to Dutch Flat, the mining town in which he lived. The pharmacist led the engineer over the route. Later, in Strong's drugstore, Judah worked up his survey maps and concluded, with Strong, an agreement to incorporate a Pacific railroad association.

Judah found seven backers, including four whose fortunes were destined to be made by the railroad: Collis P. Huntington and Mark Hopkins, partners in a hardware store; Leland Stanford, wholesale grocer; and Charles Crocker, dry goods merchant. The railroad, Judah said, would secure for them a trade monopoly in the mining camps of Nevada. When the rail line was laid over the mountains, Judah declared it the first western

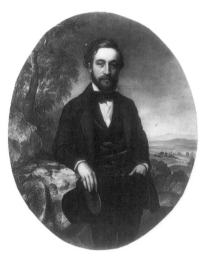

link in a transcontinental railroad. Back in Washington, D.C., he successfully lobbied for passage of the Pacific Railway Act of 1862, authorizing the Central Pacific and the Union Pacific railroads to begin construction of a transcontinental railroad.

Passage of the act was spurred by two factors. In the middle 1850s, Grenville Mellen Dodge, native of Danvers, Massachusetts, and an able civil and military engineer, was working for the Rock Island Line as a surveyor. He came to the attention of Thomas Durant, a Rock Island executive, who commissioned him to survey a rail route from Council Bluffs, Iowa, to the Rocky Mountains. Dodge spent some five years exploring the vast region, returning to Council Bluffs at the end of the decade. There, in 1859, he met presidential candidate Abraham Lincoln, who was inspecting some property he had been offered as collateral for a loan and had been directed to Dodge as an expert on conditions in the region. Dodge took the opportunity to discuss plans for a transcontinental railroad.

When Civil War broke out, Dodge and Durant were ready with a proposed route from the East, and Judah was ready with one from the West. Jefferson Davis, as president of the Confederate States of America, was well out of the picture, and Thomas Hart Benton was dead. It now seemed imperative to build a railroad that would strengthen the Union's hold on the Far West, and the 1862 act was signed into law. For every mile of railroad constructed, the Central Pacific would receive ten miles

of land, in alternate sections—one south of the tracks followed by one north of the tracks. Across the level plains, the railroad would be further assisted by a loan of sixteen thousand dollars per mile; through the harsher climate and more rugged landscape of the Great Basin, the loan was increased to thirty-two thousand dollars per mile; and through the formidable Rockies and Sierra, the amount was further increased to forty-eight thousand dollars for each hard-won mile. The Union Pacific was granted similar terms.

Yet, with authorization and funding in place, the grand project did not leap boldly ahead. Judah's Big Four—Huntington, Hopkins, Stanford, and Crocker—wanted to halt construction of the Central Pacific at the Nevada line, indefinitely—or, at least, until settlement caught up with the tracks and insured maximum profitability. After bitter argument with the men, Theodore Judah decided to journey back to Washington, D.C., in search of new backers. He traveled by way of the Isthmus of Panama, there contracted yellow fever, and died. He was thirty-seven years old.

Nor did the Union Pacific move. To begin with, the company had lost its ramrod, Grenville Dodge, to war service. However, Dodge was hardly idle. He rose to the rank of major general and served with such skill and gallantry that he won the respect and friendship of Grant, Sherman, and Sheridan. To Lincoln he was already known, and the president summoned him to Washington in 1863 to advise him on where to establish the eastern

Albert Bierstadt (1830–1902)
Emigrants Crossing the Plains, 1867
Oil on canvas, 67 × 102 in.
National Cowboy Hall of Fame and
Western Heritage Center

Compare this with the artist's
Oregon Trail (page 151), a later
version of the same scene. Using
sketches made in the field, Bierstadt
developed his finished canvases in
the studio—often years later.

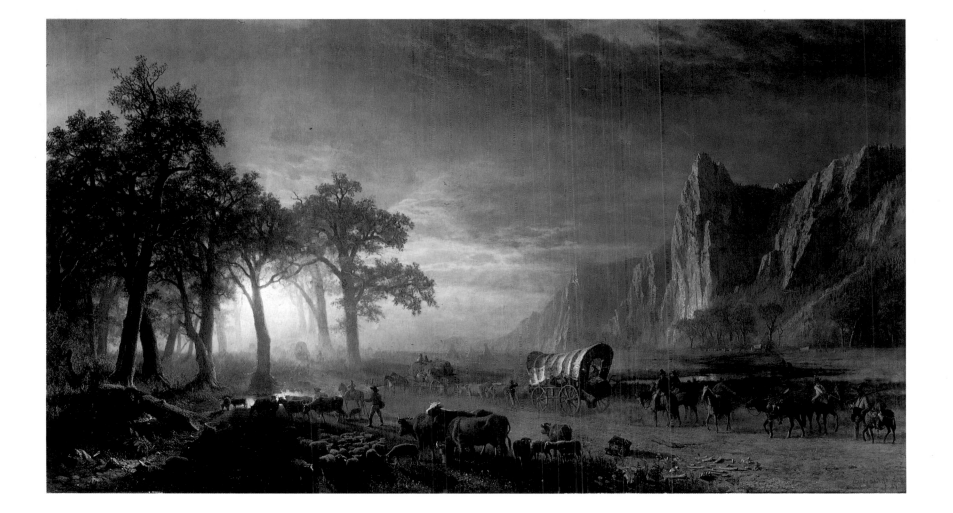

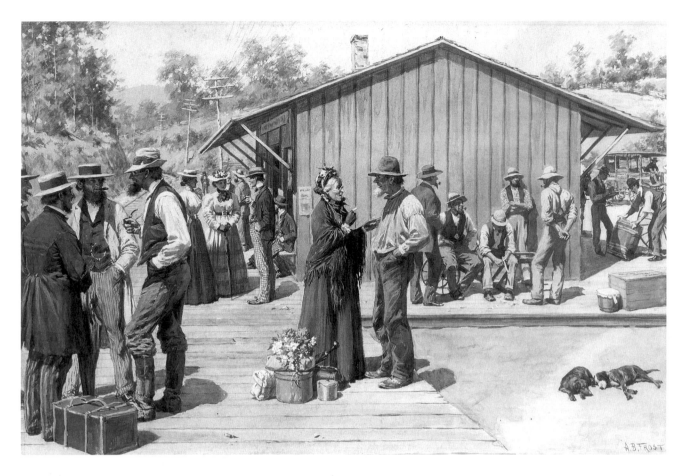

Arthur Burdett Frost (1851–1928)
Railroad station, n.d.
Lithograph
Arthur J. Phelan, Jr., Collection

With Howard Pyle, A. B. Frost was one of the turn of the century's most popular illustrators. Born in Philadelphia, he studied briefly with Thomas Eakins and went on to a long career as an illustrator. His specialty was humorous rural and folksy scenes, such as those he produced for Joel Chandler Harris's *Uncle Remus.* Frost illustrated Theodore Roosevelt's western classic *Hunting Trips of a Ranchman.*

Currier & Ives (after James M. Ives and Frances Flora Palmer)
Across the Continent/
"Westward the Course of Empire
Takes Its Way," 1868
Museum of the City of New York

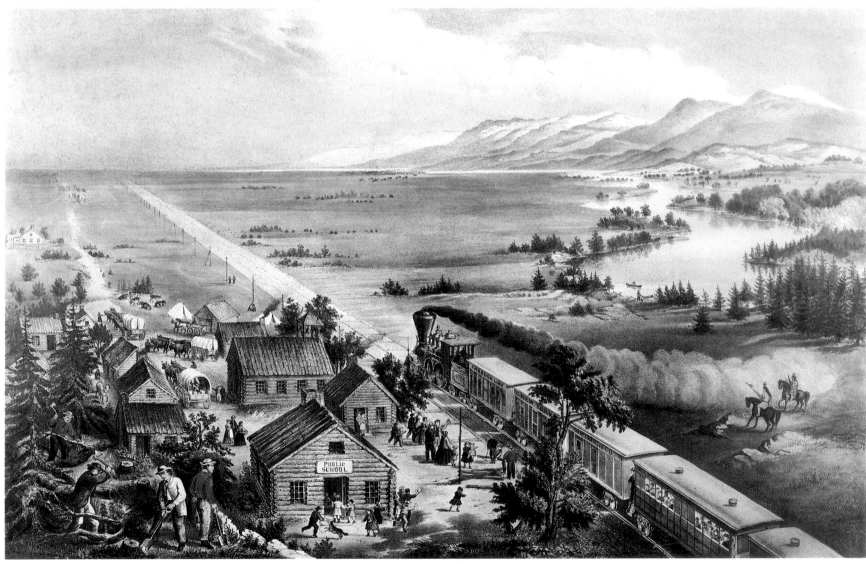

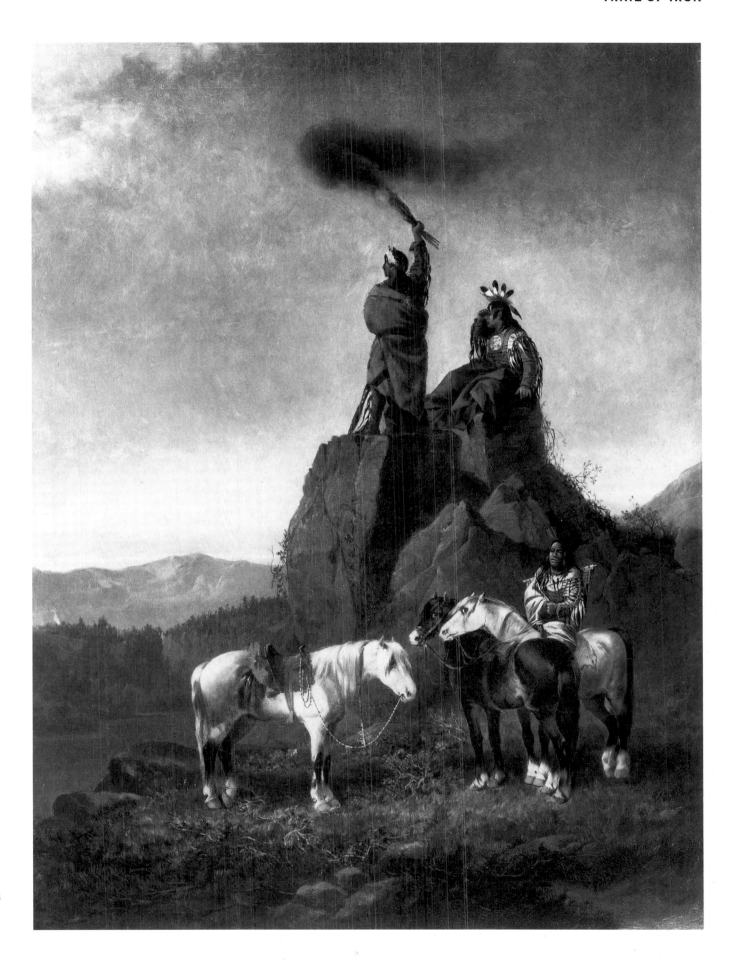

John Mix Stanley (1814–1872)
The Smoke Signal, 1868
Oil on canvas, 29 ⅜ × 22 ½ in.
The Rockwell Museum, Corning,
New York

The classic means of communication
among the Plains Indians.

terminus of the line. Dodge recommended Omaha, and the Union Pacific at last broke ground in December. A new Pacific railroad act was passed in 1864, doubling the land grants from ten square miles to twenty and releasing loan money even before track was laid. Then, shortly before his fatal visit to Ford's Theater, Abraham Lincoln summoned to his office a multimillionaire congressman known as the King of Spades. Oakes Ames had built his family's shovel works into one of the largest and most successful industrial concerns in the United States. The president, referring to the hopelessly stalled Union Pacific, told him, "Ames, take hold of this."

Ames and his brother, Oliver, invested and attracted others to invest, contributing not directly to the Union Pacific, but to a corporation created by Union Pacific vice president Thomas Durant. It was named after the company that had successfully financed the French railway system ten years earlier, Crédit Mobilier, and worked like this: The corporation, run by the directors of the Union Pacific, was paid by the Union Pacific to build the Union Pacific, the directors (the major investors) making a profit on the railroad as well as the cost of building it. The scheme, wholly precedented by railway construction financing practice in the East, was praiseworthy in that it did, at last, attract the investors needed to get the railroad under way. However, it was also an open door to fraud. Construction bills were padded, with some sections of track being paid for two or three times.

Peter Dey, the Union Pacific's chief engineer, resigned in protest.

When the army transferred Dodge to the western plains, the general used the opportunity to further the Union Pacific by fighting Indians with an eye toward removing them as a menace to track laying. In the terrible winter of 1865, Cheyennes and Arapahos were already attacking forts and sabotaging telegraph lines. Acting on his own authority, Dodge led his soldiers on a sweep through the Platte River valley. His Eleventh Cavalry mutinied, refusing to ride in the bitterly cold weather. Dodge had the regiment's officers arrested, sent the regiment marching the next day, and lost thirteen men, who froze to death. After waging unrelenting war on the Indians through the winter, spring, and summer, Dodge was bitterly disappointed when, in the fall of 1866, Washington, weary of all war and wishing to make peace with the Indians, ordered the general to break off the attack. He promptly resigned his commission and signed on for the post that had been vacated by Peter Dey, chief engineer of the Union Pacific.

Under the leadership of Dodge and another ex-army general, John Stephen Casement, who was in charge of forging the titanic work force needed to build the railroad, the Union Pacific began laying prodigious lengths of track, 266 miles in 1866. Surveyors were in the lead, followed by a battalion of "roustabouts" who graded the roadbed, working as much as 300 miles

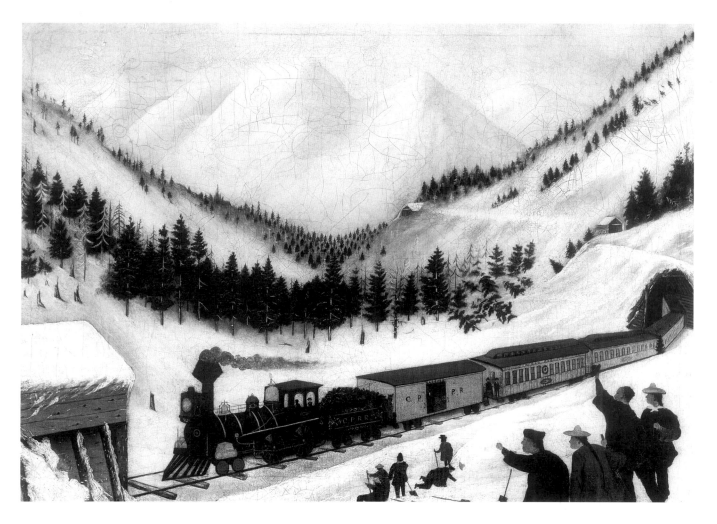

Joseph Becker (1841–1910)
Snowsheds on the Central Pacific Railroad in the Sierra Nevada Mountains, 1869
Oil on canvas, 19 × 26 in.
Gilcrease Museum, Tulsa, Oklahoma

These wooden structures were built in areas subject to heavy snowfall and high drifts, either of which could stop a locomotive—even several locomotives ganged behind a plow. Note the presence of Chinese workers.

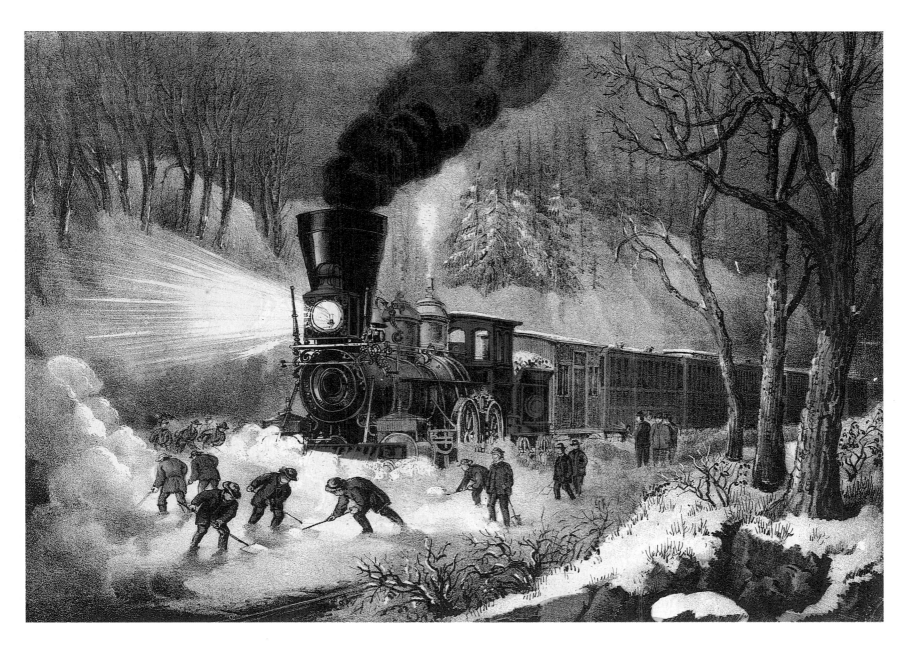

Currier & Ives
American Railroad Scene/Snowbound, 1871
Museum of the City of New York

Even the massive horsepower of a great locomotive was no match for a Rockies or Sierra snowstorm.

ahead of the 'end of track." About 20 miles in advance of the track layers were the "bridge monkeys" who quickly—even hastily and none too carefully—erected trestles over rivers and streams, using vast amounts of timber cut in Minnesota, floated down the Mississippi, and brought by Missouri River barge to Union Pacific headquarters in Omaha, where it was cut to size and transported by mule-drawn wagons to the site of construction. Next came the wagons bearing ties, set down by crews working only a few miles in advance of the actual work train, which carried provisions, equipment, track-laying crews, and the rails they laid. The work train was pushed, not pulled, by a locomotive. At the head of the train were flatcars bearing rails and tools and a blacksmith shop; behind these were boxcars, eighty-five feet long and three stories high, barracks on wheels capable of housing a hundred or more workmen each; a commissary car came next, accommodating 125 men for meals; and finally a combination kitchen, storeroom, and office car was coupled just in front of the locomotive. It was a mobile factory town, and laborers earned thirty-five dollars a month. The Union Pacific hired mostly un-

skilled Irish immigrants, who received, in addition to their pay, room and board. The Chinese laborers on the Central Pacific were paid at about the same rate, but had to furnish their own tent accommodations and their own food.

Laying and spiking five-hundred-pound sections of rail was hard enough, but these men faced perils unknown to any factory worker. On the plains, weather was a formidable enemy, flooding out track and workers during the summer and burying them in snow during the winter. In the Sierra, where the Central Pacific was working during the winter of 1866, conditions were even worse. Forty-four blizzards were counted, one lasting thirteen days straight and dumping ten feet of snow. A thirty-foot-long snowplow, its blade constructed like the prow of a ship, was pushed by twelve locomotives—and still could not get through. Crews boring the Summit Tunnel were cut off from all supplies for weeks. Twenty Chinese laborers were killed in a single avalanche during one of the snowstorms, and nobody knows how many were killed in lesser disasters.

The Union Pacific men on the plains faced a human

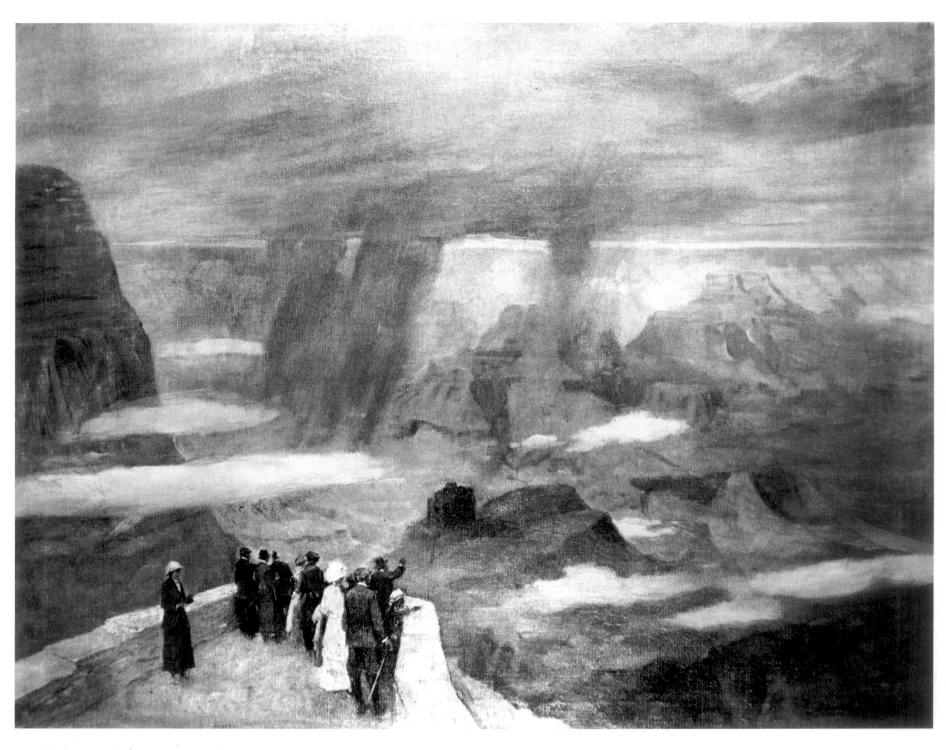

O. E. Berninghaus (1874–1952)
A Showery Day, Grand Canyon, 1915
Oil on canvas, 30 × 40 in.
Santa Fe Collection of Southwestern
Art

One commodity the railroads
brought to the West in abundance
was tourists eager to see in person
the natural wonders they had
glimpsed in paintings and popular
prints.

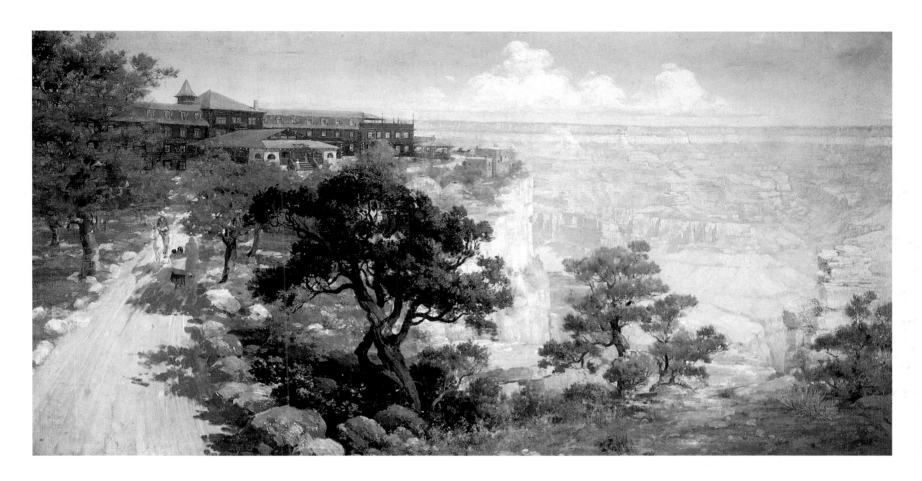

Louis Akin (1868–1913)
El Tovar Hotel, Grand Canyon, 1904
Oil on canvas, 25 × 50 in.
Santa Fe Collection of Southwestern
Art

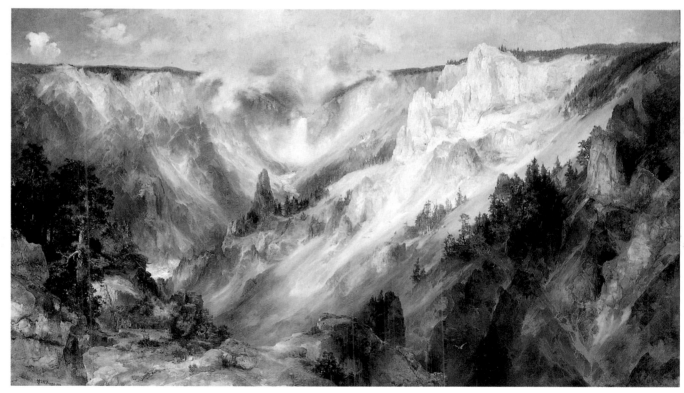

Thomas Moran (1837–1926)
The Grand Canyon of the Yellow-stone, 1872
Oil on canvas, 96 ½ × 168 ⅜ in.
National Museum of American Art,
Smithsonian Institution; Gift of
George D. Pratt

enemy as well. As the rails penetrated Sioux and Cheyenne hunting grounds in western Nebraska and southeastern Wyoming, advance work crews fell under attack. A party of Cheyennes decided to sabotage some Union Pacific track by piling loose ties on it and lashing them down with telegraph wire torn down from the line overhead. The telegrapher at the Plum Creek, Nebraska, station, William Thompson, an English immigrant, discovered that the line had gone dead and set out on a handcar with five men, wire, tools, and a rifle to investigate. It was night, and the crew did not see the pile of ties ahead. They hit it and were derailed, whereupon the Indians attacked, rapidly dispatching all but Thompson, who was brutally clubbed and, though he was still semiconscious, scalped.

The Indians walked back to the tracks, one of them inadvertently dropping Thompson's bloody scalp. Dazed and badly injured, the young Englishman crawled to where the scalp had been dropped and recovered it, stuffing it into his pocket. Unnoticed by the Cheyennes, he inched away.

Meanwhile, the attackers worked further on the rails, unbolting and bending them. A freight train barreled into the barricade and derailed, catapulting the fireman into the boiler's blazing firebox and severely injuring the engineer, who was dragged out of the wrecked cab and killed by the Indian war party. The caboose crew managed to escape and warn the following train.

As for poor Thompson, he reached Plum Creek near dawn and was taken by special train back to Omaha, 250 miles east, accompanied by his scalp, which had been placed in a bucket of water. Dr. C. P. Moore, an Omaha physician, judged the scalp too badly damaged to try to sew back onto its owner's head, but his ministrations did pull Thompson through alive. Out of gratitude, the young telegrapher had the scalp tanned and presented it to the good doctor as a memento.

By 1868, five thousand soldiers were patrolling the Union Pacific tracks, and Indians ceased to be a serious threat.

While the Central Pacific and Union Pacific crews were separated by two thousand miles, work proceeded with one outfit giving little or no thought to the other. The Railroad Act of 1864 had set no meeting point for the two lines and had specified only that the Central Pacific was to build beyond the eastern face of the Sierras. As late as 1868 and 1869, both the C.P. and the U.P. were pressing ahead on the assumption that whichever company laid the most rail would subsequently own and profit from the most railroad, collecting more government money and more government land. To pile up mileage, temporary trestles often stood in for permanent ones, and, when snow was heavy, rails were even laid on top of it—which sometimes actually worked, until the spring thaw. Roadbed construction was accelerated many miles beyond track work, on the theory that he

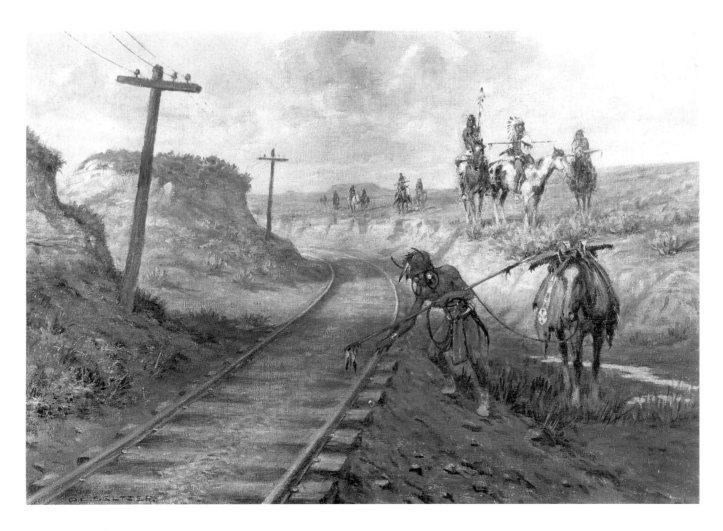

Olaf Carl Seltzer (1877–1957)
The Iron Trail, 1931
Oil on canvas, 11 × 16 in.
Gilcrease Museum, Tulsa, Oklahoma

The "iron horse" was yet another white invasion of Indian lives. Tracks were the frequent object of sabotage—sometimes with deadly results.

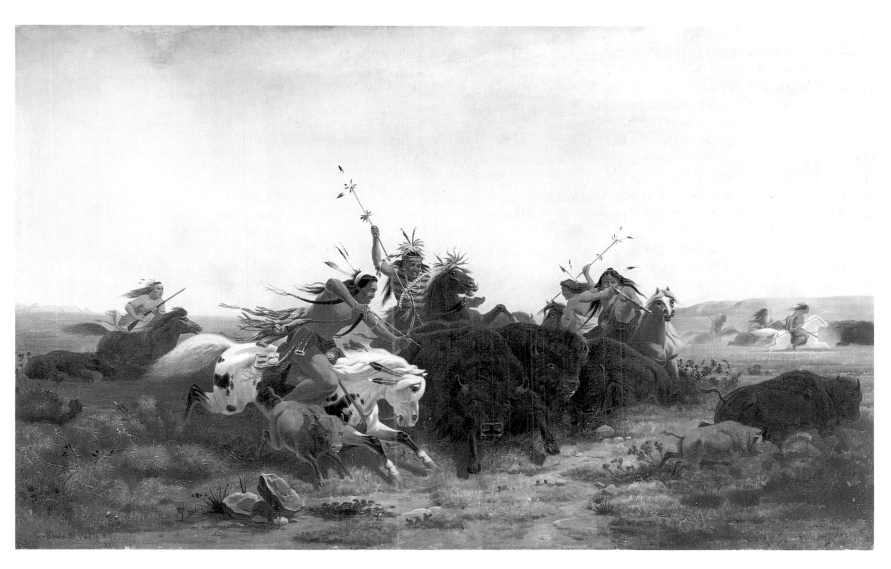

Charles Wimar (1828–1862)
Buffalo Hunt, 1861
Oil on canvas, 36 × 61 in.
Gilcrease Museum, Tulsa, Oklahoma

Like many of the white man's
incursions into the Indian's West,
the railroad menaced the buffalo.
Not only did the tracks divide the
animal's grazing range, but easy
transportation meant an influx of
"sportsmen," some of whom shot at
herds without even bothering to
leave the train.

who graded a bed was entitled to lay track on it. When
the U.P. discovered that it had to dig four tunnels (the
C.P.'s more demanding terrain had called for no fewer
than fifteen), it put off boring the longest of these—772
feet at the head of Echo Canyon, Utah—by building temporary track in a meandering loop around Echo Summit.

By this time, the C.P. and U.P. roadbed crews had
met. Indeed, in the absence of an official point of meeting, survey parties had already laid out some two hundred miles of overlapping, parallel right of way. After
grading parties passed each other—blasting away at recalcitrant rocks and almost blasting away at one another—U.S. Secretary of the Interior Orville H.
Browning commissioned a group of civil engineers to decide on the place at which the two lines would be joined.
It was to be Promontory Summit, fifty-six miles west of
Ogden, Utah.

Now, with a definite limit set to either side's track-
age, the last lap of the race was run for sport rather than
money. And perhaps to prove a point. Back in 1865,
when the Central Pacific was suffering from an acute
shortage of labor (company president Charles Crocker
had advertised throughout California for five thousand
men and got eight hundred) James Harvey Strobridge,
the company's slave-driving chief of staff, reluctantly began hiring Chinese laborers. Like many Americans of the

nineteenth century, Strobridge was a racist, and, in fact,
it *was* hard to believe that these oddly dressed little men
(average weight: 110 pounds) in pigtails, who subsisted
on rice, mushrooms, and bamboo shoots, could do the
work of burly, beef-eating Irishmen.

The Chinese proved to be extraordinary workers.
Soon, Strobridge couldn't get enough of them, hiring
agents to "import" more directly from China. By 1866,
over six thousand were working on the Central Pacific.
Not that their feats of labor and endurance earned their
employers' respect. If anything, part of their value as laborers derived from a perception of them as expendable
assets. No records of injuries or deaths were kept, and
when Strobridge came upon a suicidal construction job,
it was the Chinese he sent to do it. When C.P. surveyors
determined that the railroad had to negotiate a flank of
the Sierra, a sheer shale face fourteen hundred feet
above the American River, with nary a toehold in it,
Strobridge dispatched Chinese workers to cut a ledge for
the tracks. He lowered them down in wicker baskets so
that they could place explosive charges, which were set
off after the baskets had been raised "safely" above the
blast. Astoundingly, the work was handled with such
skill that not a single life was lost. Perhaps, then, it was
racial pride that spurred the Chinese crew of the Central
Pacific to spike ten miles and fifty-six feet of track in

THOMAS HILL

—

BORN 1829, BIRMINGHAM, ENGLAND

DIED 1908, RAYMOND, CALIFORNIA

—

Called the "Artist of the Yosemite" because of his devotion to that seemingly inexhaustible subject, Hill grew up in Massachusetts, where he was apprenticed to a coach painter until, at age fifteen, he went to work in Boston as an ornamental painter. After study at the Pennsylvania Academy of the Fine Arts, Hill won a prize in 1853 for an allegorical canvas. His precarious health sent him west, and in 1861 he settled in San Francisco, where he set up as a portrait painter until he sailed for Paris in 1866 to study with Paul Mayerheim.

Returning to Boston in 1867, Hill abandoned portraiture for landscape painting. His *Yosemite Valley* was well received, both as an original and as reproduced in a popular Prang chromolithograph.

The artist returned to Yosemite in 1871, after which he spent all his summers there until 1888, when he established a permanent studio in the area. His largest canvas is the 98-by-138-inch *The Last Spike,* executed between 1887 and 1891, depicting the completion of the Union Pacific. Using contemporary photographs of the 1869 event, Hill included in the painting about four hundred carefully delineated figures, taking the liberty of inserting Collis Huntington, Mark Hopkins, Charles Crocker, and engineering mastermind Theodore Dehone Judah, who were not present at the event.

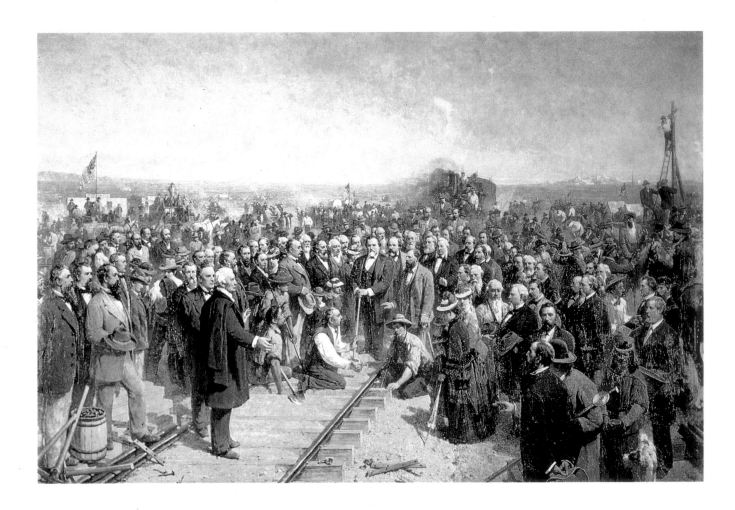

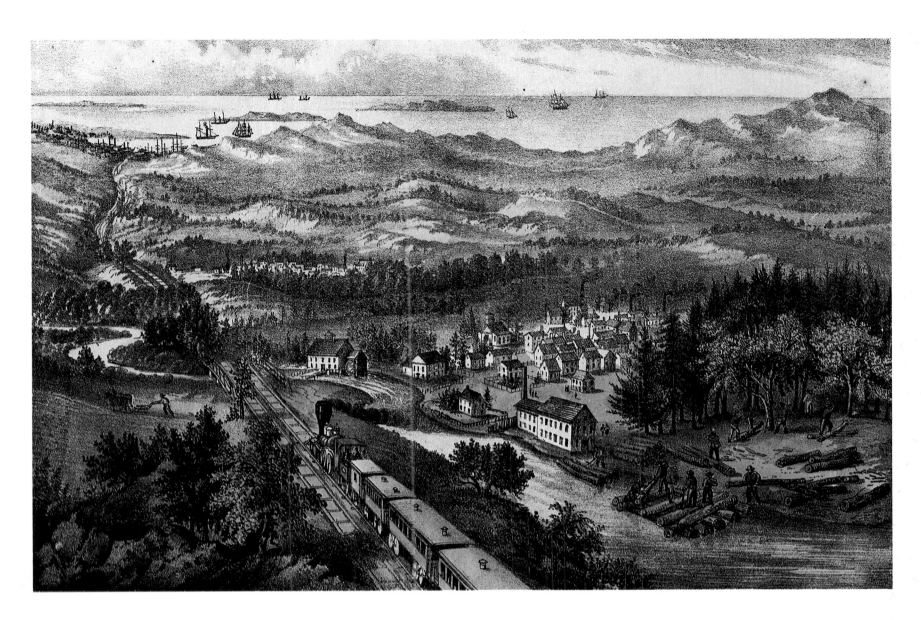

Currier & Ives
Through to the Pacific, 1870
Museum of the City of New York

A continent spanned.

Thomas Hill (1829–1908)
The Last Spike, 1878
Oil on canvas, 10 × 13 ft. (30 × 39 in.)
California State Railroad Museum

Hill wasn't above stretching the truth for the sake of this commemorative canvas. Leland Stanford, posed with the hammer, was indeed present at the driving of the spike, but his partners Collis Huntington (behind Stanford, just to our right), Mark Hopkins (the bearded man behind the two women), and Charles Crocker (turned full profile, holding his hat) were not. Theodore Judah, the engineering mastermind behind the transcontinental railroad, is facing us, just to the right of Crocker. Judah died a half dozen years before the Golden Spike was driven home.

twelve hours on April 28, 1869—a record the Union Pacific could not equal.

The ceremonial union of the two lines at Promontory Summit was set for May 8, 1869. Leland Stanford of the Central Pacific set off from Sacramento—though he almost failed to reach the rendezvous because a plummeting tree, just felled by a Chinese crew, slipped down a slope and lodged in the tracks below, where Stanford's train collided with it. No one was seriously injured, but the president's train had to be hitched to a new locomotive. Thomas C. Durant of the Union Pacific had his own problems, as he had been kidnapped at Piedmont, Wyoming, by tie cutters his company had not paid since January. Durant telegraphed for money and was released, delaying the ceremony by two days. On May 10, then, workers and executives alike were prepared to savor their finest moment. Chinese workmen, apparently all too aware of how Caucasions felt about them, were lowering the last rail in place when a photographer hollered, "Shoot!" They dropped the five-hundred-pound rail and fled.

Then came the truly great moment, when Leland Stanford would drive the Golden Spike—wired to the telegraph, so that each blow would be transmitted across the country—and unite a continent. He swung, and he missed.

But the deed got done, and over the next two decades four more railroads would bind together East and West: the Southern Pacific and the Northern Pacific in 1883; the Atchinson, Topeka and Santa Fe in 1885; and the Great Northern in 1893. The transcontinental journey, which had taken almost a month by stagecoach and many months by wagon train, could now be accomplished in less than a week, on trains equipped with such luxuries as Pullman Palace sleeping cars and dining cars. Massive railroad advertising campaigns insured a steady flood of emigrants, both from the East and from Europe, who not only provided the new lines with passengers but with purchasers of the land the federal government had so prodigally granted along the rights-of-way. As the American West grew in population, providing markets for eastern goods and producing food and mineral wealth for the East as well as itself, no longer could the interests of one part of the nation be separated from those of the other.

The interests of the American Indian were as always—but now even more so—another matter.

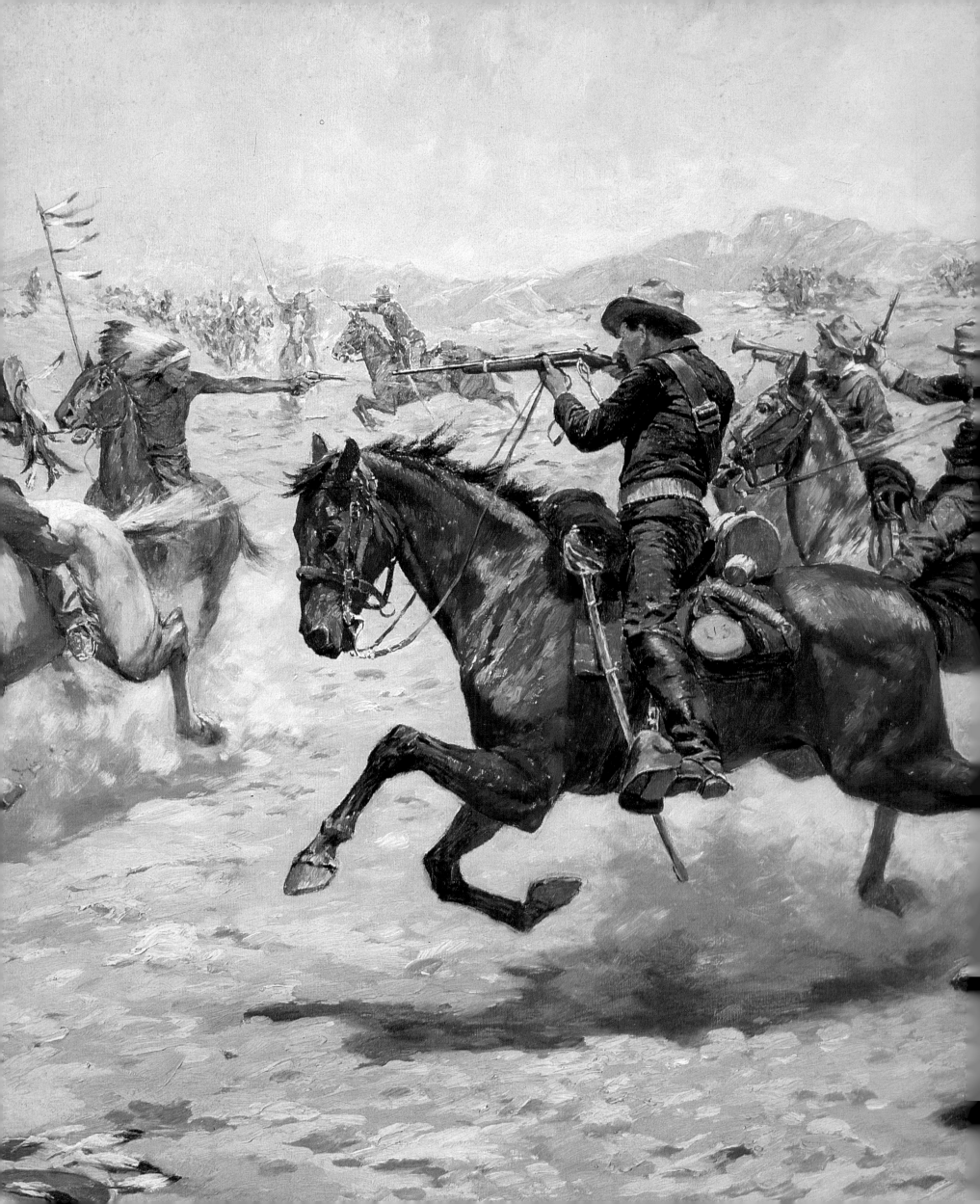

TEARING APART

William Tecumseh Sherman, one of the Union's most able and ruthless Civil War generals, commanded the army's Division of Missouri from 1866 to 1869, waging war against the Indians of the plains. He who had advocated total war during the contest between the states—"War is hell," he declared, and burned a highway through the South to prove it—gave no quarter to his new enemies. Yet, like many Americans, he had a keen awareness of the Indians' plight, which he summed up with all the laconic austerity of his more celebrated utterance. "The poor Indian finds himself hemmed in," Sherman reported to the second session of the Thirty-ninth Congress in 1866.

When Thomas Jefferson made the Louisiana Purchase at the opening of the century, it was in large part with the purpose of acquiring space—seemingly endless space—into which white settlement, inexorably and always moving from east to west, could push the Indian. When Andrew Jackson signed into law the Indian Removal Bill in 1830, it was still a matter of pushing tribes from east to west. But with the settlement of Oregon country, the annexation of Texas, and the sudden acquisition of California, New Mexico, and Arizona from Mexico, Indians in all parts of the West were indeed "hemmed in," caught in a great pincers of white settlement. Maine's Senator Lot Morrill summarized the situation in a speech before the Fortieth Congress in 1867: "As population has approached the Indian we have removed him beyond population. But population now encounters him on both sides of the continent, and there is no place on the continent to which he can be removed beyond the progress of population."

The enveloping net of white settlement, with its ramifying systems of trails, then roads, then railroads, caught up both Indian and white in two-thirds of a century of war. The result—the defeat of the Indian—was probably inevitable. By the end of the Civil War, the white population of the West outnumbered the Indian population by a factor of ten. Yet the Indians did not, as some later historians have claimed, suffer genocide; the Indian population in the area encompassed by the United States is greater today than it has ever been. This is not to deny that any number of white racists, some highly placed, advocated extermination of various Indian populations. But such was never the policy of the United States government. If any single approach to the Indian can be identified as the nation's official policy, it was "concentration," the gathering together and installation of Indians on lands "reserved" for them. Theoretically, once consigned to a reservation, Indians became wards of the federal government, which pledged to provide rations and other necessary goods. In practice, one of the many tragedies

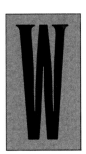

Charles Schreyvogel, *A Sharp Encounter*, 1901. Detail; see page 307

that beset United States Indian policy was the almost universal corruption among the agents entrusted with the administration of the reservations. Many reservation Indians suffered varying degrees of starvation and abuse.

Corruption and calculated deceit were only two evils in what the crusading nineteenth-century novelist Helen Hunt Jackson called "A Century of Dishonor." Even when treaties between the United States and Indians were drawn up in good faith—even when, in good conscience, good men attempted to preserve the peace and welfare of all parties involved—war, dispossession, and death were frequently the result. Cultural barriers were often insurmountable, and treaties were signed without comprehension and without authority. The American government sought to treat with the various tribes as if they were sovereign foreign powers, but tribal organization was far too loose and too organic for such an approach to have real meaning. Tribal decisions were reached by highly democratic means, often through innumerable meetings—councils—which rarely came to a unanimous conclusion. While those charged by the government with concluding treaties insisted on investing tribal "chiefs" with the absolute authority of monarchs, the Indian people themselves did no such thing.

The cultural differences between the westering civilization of the whites and that of the Indians ran even deeper. While the whites waged war principally to acquire and control territory, the Indians often fought from more diverse motives: for the honors of war—which carried religious significance—or for plunder—a way of life for some tribes—or for revenge. Or, because of white aggression, to defend home and family.

Finally, of course, not all Indians were hostile, and not all hostile Indians were hostile all of the time. As to fighting, the culturally diverse tribes warred with one another far more frequently than they fought against whites. Distinguishing enemies from allies, enemies from neutrals, and neutrals from allies was commonly a matter of hopeless confusion.

Even if the United States had wanted to wage a war of extermination against the Indian, it could hardly have done so with the military forces available to it. Before the Civil War, most campaigning against Indians was conducted by locally organized bands of settlers or, what is much the same thing, locally raised bands of militia. Some of these groups were more effective than others. After the Civil War, the regular army took on most of the responsibility for what amounted to policing hostile Indians, impressing upon them the invincible majesty of the government of the United States of America.

To accomplish this task a less majestic instrument than the mid nineteenth-century U.S. Army could hardly have been found. Following the Civil War, the army rapidly mustered out men—almost a million of them—leaving about 30,000 regular troops in 1866. Congress did act

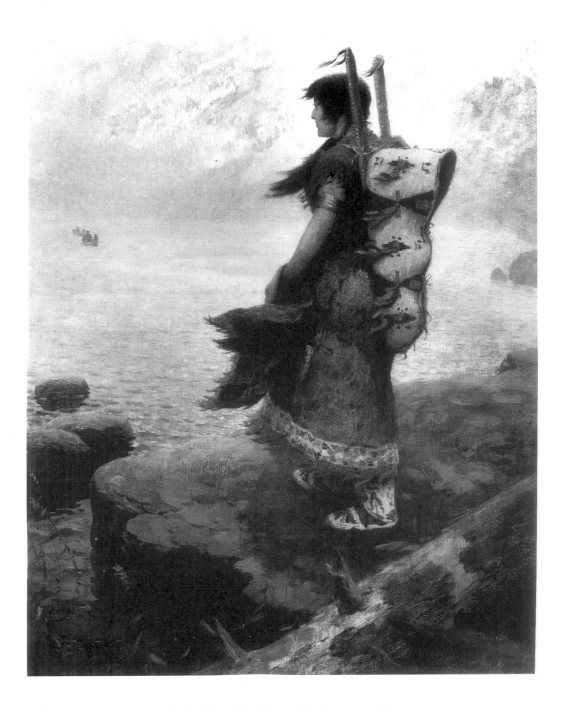

to increase manpower, and the size of the "peacetime" army peaked at 56,815 in September 1867. But fully one-third of these troops were needed in the South to conduct the work of Reconstruction, and as this was completed, a war-weary and economy-minded Congress put into effect a series of cutbacks. In 1869, troop strength was reduced to 37,313; in 1870 the limit was set at 30,000; in 1874 a ceiling of 25,000 enlisted men was set (with officers, the total came to 27,000). As these mandated limits included casualties, deserters, even dead men who had not yet been officially discharged, the actual strength of the army throughout much of the 1870s was closer to 19,000. These forces were apportioned into 430 companies to man about two hundred posts—more than one hundred of which were widely dispersed and isolated western forts—which meant that companies were often ludicrously undermanned. An officer of the Twenty-fourth Infantry, an all-black regiment posted in the West, com-

William Robinson Leigh (1866–1955)
Return of the War Canoes, 1920
Oil on canvas, 28 × 22 in.
The Rockwell Museum, Corning, New York

A cliché, to be sure, but no less moving for it: a woman, with papoose, gazes toward the distant canoes. Whom do they carry?

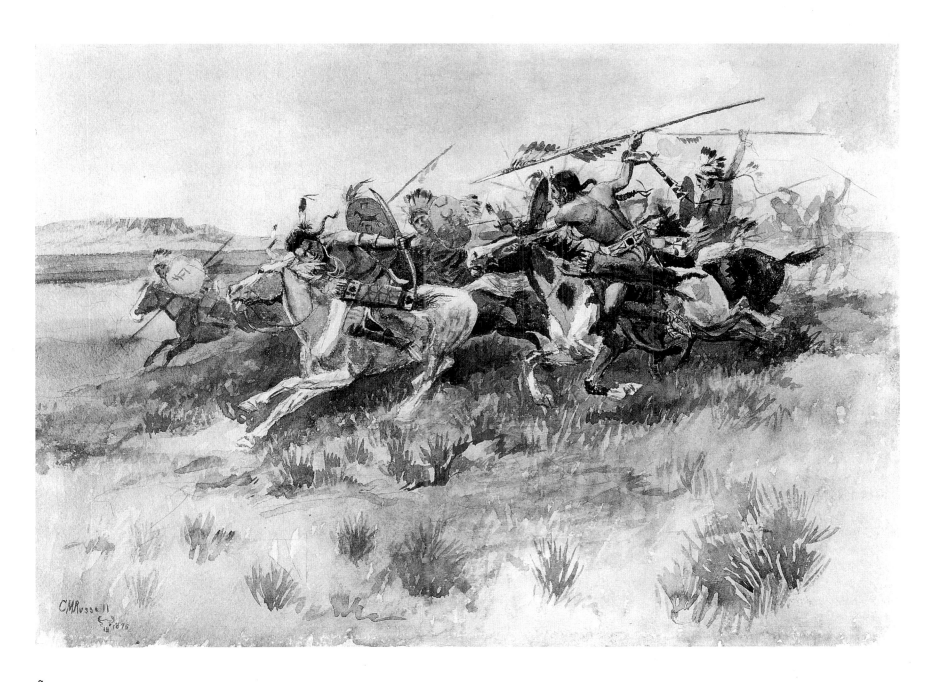

Charles M. Russell (1864–1926)
*Running Fight Between Crees &
Blackfeet (Indians Attacking)*, 1895
Watercolor on paper, 13 ⅞ × 19 ¾ in.
Amon Carter Museum, Fort Worth,
Texas

For most Plains tribes, warfare was
a way of life; sometimes it was
combat with white settlers and
soldiers, but more often it was one
tribe or group against another.

plained that the largest company he could muster consisted of seven men. "It is rather stupid work for an officer to go out and drill four men," he reported to the secretary of war. "I have seen a captain go on parade with only a sergeant," he continued, "the captain forming the front line and the sergeant the rear."

Nor did the small size of the army mean that it attracted a select group of recruits. Pay was miserable—thirteen dollars a month for privates, twenty-two dollars for sergeants—and was made in currency, quite useless on the frontier, which demanded specie. Converting one to the other slashed the paltry salary even further. Food was terrible and poorly prepared, not by trained commissary personnel but by men detailed to ten-day tours as cooks. Tainted rations were common, as was scurvy. The few officers who tried to supplement their men's monotonous meals of hash, stew, salt pork, beans, rice, and hardtack with fresh vegetables grown on the fort were often frustrated. One officer recalled the Darwinian cycle of nature at Fort Rice, Dakota Territory, in 1873: "The damn hoppers came along, by God, and ate my garden,

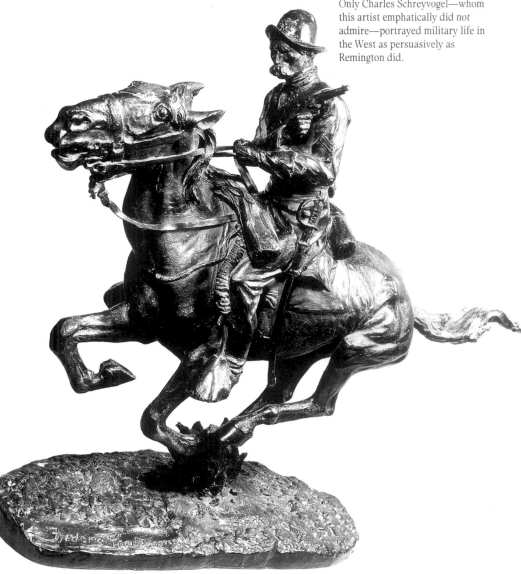

Only Charles Schreyvogel—whom this artist emphatically did *not* admire—portrayed military life in the West as persuasively as Remington did.

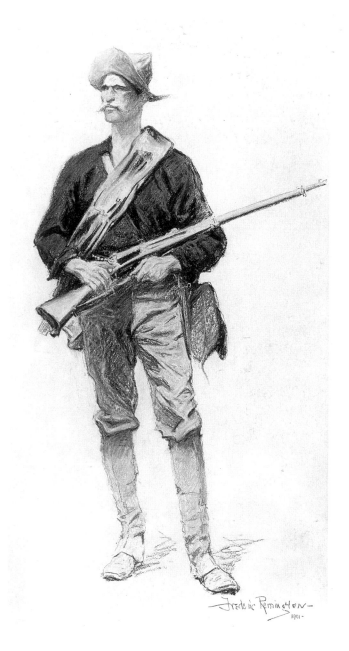

by God, then the birds ate the hoppers, by God, and we killed and ate the birds, by God, so that we were even in the long run, by God." Barracks accommodations were dirty, dark, vermin-infested, and overcrowded; each enlisted man shared his straw-stuffed pallet with a "bunkie." Sanitary conditions were poor enough that disease was responsible for far more casualties than Indian hostility. During the 1860s through 1880s, surgeons annually treated about 1,800 cases per 1,000 men, of which 1,550 were for disease and 250 for accidents, injuries, and combat wounds. (Thirteen out of 1,000 died—8 from disease, 5 from injuries—and 30 out of 1,000 were mustered out with disability discharges. Of the diseases, venereal infections were the most prevalent, with malaria, respiratory disorders, and gastrointestinal problems close behind. Cholera was an ever-present threat to western garrisons.)

The artist's admiration for the ill-equipped, wretchedly housed, poorly fed, and scarcely paid soldier of the West is evident in this straightforward sketch of a forthright character.

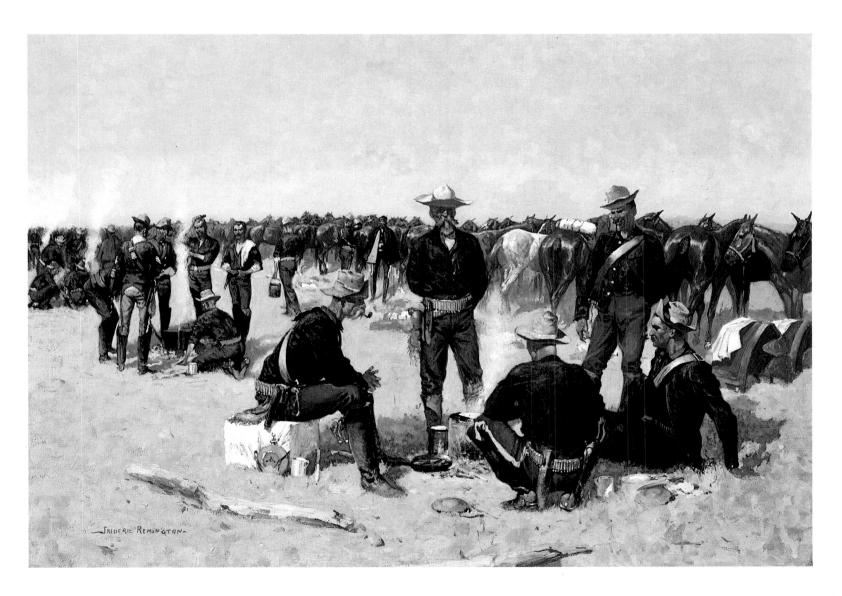

Frederic Remington (1861–1909)
Cavalryman's Breakfast on the Plains, c. 1892
Oil on canvas, (22 × 32 ⅛ in.)
Amon Carter Museum, Fort Worth, Texas

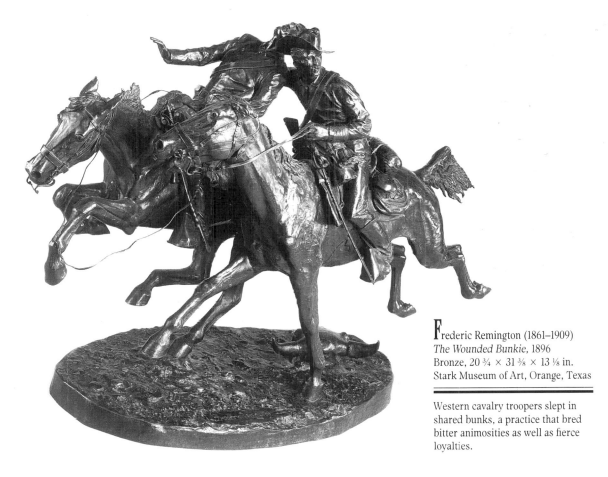

Frederic Remington (1861–1909)
The Wounded Bunkie, 1896
Bronze, 20 ¾ × 31 ⅜ × 13 ⅛ in.
Stark Museum of Art, Orange, Texas

Western cavalry troopers slept in shared bunks, a practice that bred bitter animosities as well as fierce loyalties.

In short, the army was not a good job. It is little wonder, then, that about half the enlisted men between 1865 and 1874 were poorly educated immigrants. Almost one-third of the enlisted men deserted in 1871, and reenlistment was generally low. Perhaps five or six thousand men at any given time could be described as veterans—soldiers with at least five years' experience. The rest were essentially raw recruits who received little or no combat training. Economy measures meted out precious few cartridges for rifle practice, and horsemanship was so poor that the men of the Second Cavalry manning Fort Phil Kearny along the Bozeman Trail in 1866 could not mount their horses without help.

Officers had their own problems, including low salaries (fourteen hundred dollars for a second lieutenant, thirty-five hundred for a colonel in 1870), subject to being cut at the annual whim of Congress, and dismal prospects for promotion. A stodgy seniority system meant that a second lieutenant could look forward to reaching the rank of major after a quarter-century of service; a colonelcy might take thirty-three to thirty-seven years. Not only was this discouraging to able men considering a military career, it made for a senescent officer corps. As General O. O. Howard reported in 1890, "almost all the captains of infantry and artillery are too old for duty involving marching on foot or even drill requiring continuous movement."

Understaffed and poorly staffed, the U.S. Army was up against Plains Indians, whose very culture exalted warfare and warriors. From childhood, braves learned extraordinary skill in horsemanship and weaponry, including the use of bow and arrow, lance, knife, and rifle. The best Indian warriors were experts in guerrilla tactics, a branch of warfare the regular army persistently refused to acknowledge, let alone develop proficiency in. And unlike the thinly spread soldiers, who were expected to pursue an aggressive course almost regardless of strength (or lack thereof), Indians generally attacked only when they possessed overwhelmingly superior numbers.

They enjoyed, too, the natural advantage of indigenous warriors pitted against "foreign" invaders. They had no choice but to believe in their fight. The army, however, was beset with ambivalence. Soldiers familiar with Indian acts of brutality—torture, mutilation, and the like—might be able to regard them as beasts to be exterminated plain and simple. But many soldiers came to respect Indians and to despise the injustice and abuse to which poorly conceived and indifferently or incompetently or maliciously executed federal policy had sub-

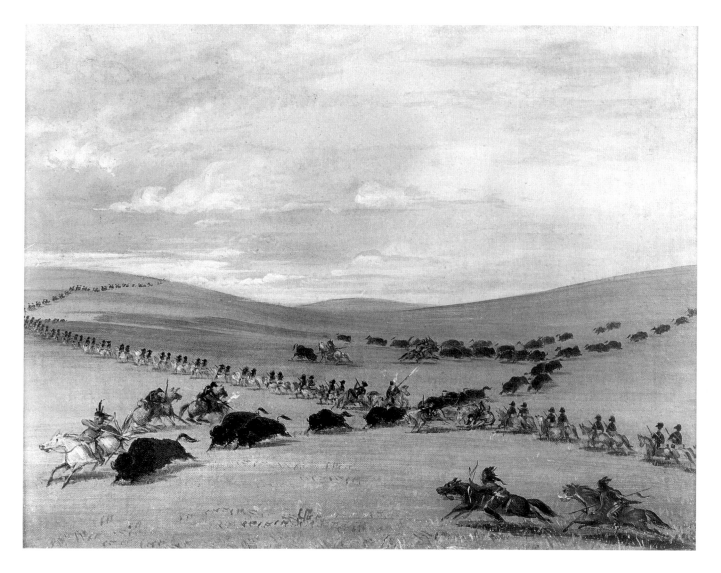

George Catlin (1796–1872)
The 1st Regiment of The United States Dragoons with Several Indian Hunters and Guides Meeting a Herd of Buffaloes in Texas, n.d.
Oil on canvas, 11 × 14 in.
Gilcrease Museum, Tulsa, Oklahoma

In the early days of the army's western operations, dragoons—mounted infantry who used their horses only for transportation, not in actual combat—were often preferred over cavalry.

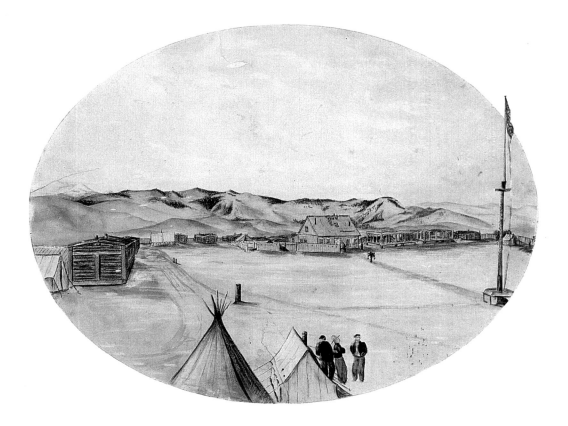

G̲ustavus Sohon (1825–1903)
Northwest Fort, 1855 (?)
Watercolor, 14 ¾ × 20 in.
Arthur J. Phelan, Jr., Collection

Born in East Prussia, Sohon came to
America in 1842 to escape
compulsory military service. After
working ten years as a bookbinder in
Brooklyn, he joined the U.S. Army
and served as a topographical artist
on Isaac Stevens's survey of a
northern transcontinental railroad
route. The name and location of the
fort pictured here are unknown.

jected them. Ambivalence also reigned at the highest
levels of government, as many legislators openly condemned military activity in the West as craven butchery.
Even among those who supported action against the Indians, contempt for the army was widespread.

Yet, for all his physical and, perhaps, spiritual advantages, the Indian was fatally handicapped in warfare
by the very features of his culture that elevated individual strength, cunning, skill, endurance, courage, and
honor. War chiefs were not the equivalents of generals;
they did not command their braves so much as they "led"
them through charisma and personal influence. Truly coordinated military action was usually impossible. On a
larger scale, the exaltation of individual virtue meant
that so-called tribes rarely acted with unity, and one
tribe rarely formed a strategically effective alliance with
another. Romantic hindsight notwithstanding, it is unlikely that Indians saw their wars with the whites as
struggles to preserve their race. War was a way of life,
fought for glory, plunder, and revenge, regardless of
whether the enemy was another tribe or the U.S. Army.
The culturally diverse Indians of the American West
never united against what they in all likelihood failed to
perceive as a common enemy.

NORTHWEST WARS

Much of California's gold country was inhabited by poor
bands of Indians whom whites collectively called "Diggers" because they eked out a meager subsistence digging roots and berries. Even the most romantic of white
observers could find little of the "noble savage" about
them, and California's governor blandly stated that "a

war of extermination will continue to be waged until the
Indian race becomes extinct." This, he said, "must be expected." Certainly, miners had no compunction about
sweeping the Diggers out of their path. In a remarkably
short time, 10 percent of the Digger population had been
killed by violent means—though, as usual, white diseases (as well as malnutrition and outright starvation)
felled even more. Before the gold rush, California was
home to perhaps a hundred thousand Indians. By the
end of the gold era, that population had been reduced by
two-thirds.

As was made tragically evident by the Whitman
massacre in 1847, the Indians farther north, in Oregon
country, did not suffer the white presence so meekly. Although timely intervention on the part of the Hudson's
Bay Company peaceably ransomed the hostages taken in
the Cayuse raid on the Whitman compound, Colonel
Cornelius Gilliam, leading 550 Oregon militiamen, was
intent on meting out punishment. What he did not pause
to consider was the guilt or innocence of those he intended to punish, for the Cayuses were by no means
unanimous in their support of Chief Tiloukaikt, who had
conducted the Whitman raid. Gilliam launched an attack
on the first Indian camp he could find, killing more than
a score of apparently peaceful Indians and suffering five
casualties himself.

While Gilliam was running amok among the Cayuses, Joel Palmer, appointed by the territorial governor
to head a three-man peace commission, was attempting
to calm neighboring tribes, especially the Nez Percé and
Palouse. Gilliam stubbornly sabotaged all peace efforts.
"Col Gilliam left the [peace] council in a huff," wrote one
of the men on Palmer's commission, "and declared he
has come to fight and fight he will."

The week after the abortive peace council, 250 Palouse warriors attacked Gilliam and his men, who were
appropriating cattle they assumed belonged to Cayuses.
Ten militiamen were wounded. Gilliam himself met his
end, not at the hands of Indians, but through his own
blundering clumsiness. He was trying to tether his horse,
caught the rope on the trigger of his rifle, and was killed.
Gilliam's removal did not stop the militia, however,
which continued to stalk Cayuses without success. Their
hostile meanderings did, however, rouse the ire of Wallawallas, Umatillas, Palouses, and Nez Percés, though the
militia finally retired before full-scale warfare erupted.
But, so far as the future of Indian-white relations in the
Northwest were concerned, the die had been cast.

By 1854, according to the local Indian agent, hostility between whites and Indians had become a kind of re-
flex "almost impossible to realize, except from personal
observation." Indians and whites fell into the habit of
shooting each other on sight. Settlers clamored for the intervention of the regular army, and then protested the
army's failure to pursue a straightforward course of
annihilation.

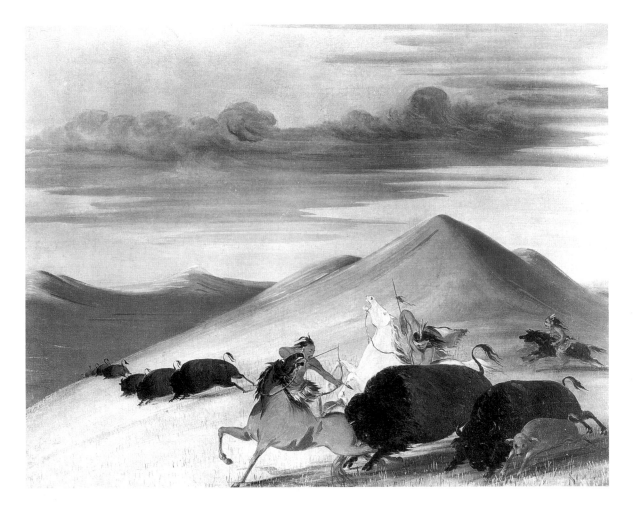

"During the season of the year whilst the calves are young, the male seems to stroll about by the side of the dam, as if for the purpose of protecting the young, at which time it is exceedingly hazardous to attack them, as they are sure to turn upon their pursuers, who have often to fly to each other's assistance."—George Catlin, *The Manners, Customs and Condition of the North American Indians*, 1841

Miller interpreted the Indians' buffalo-hunting prowess as something formal, almost a ballet.

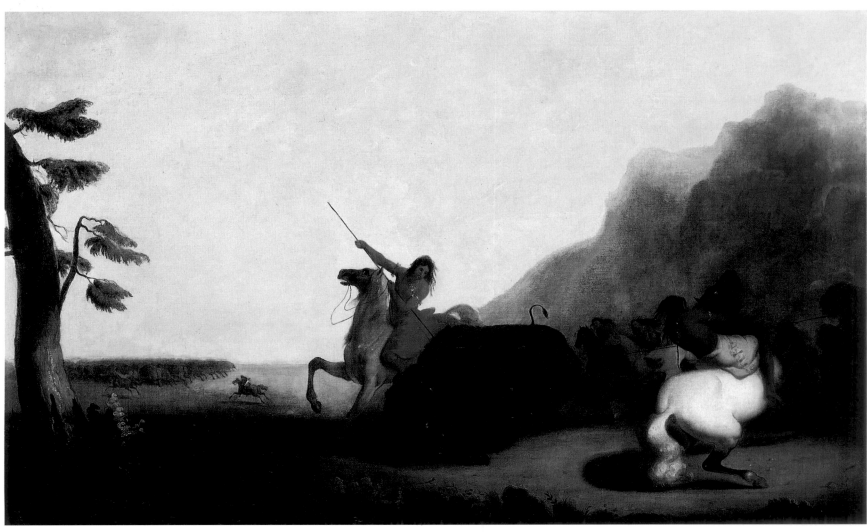

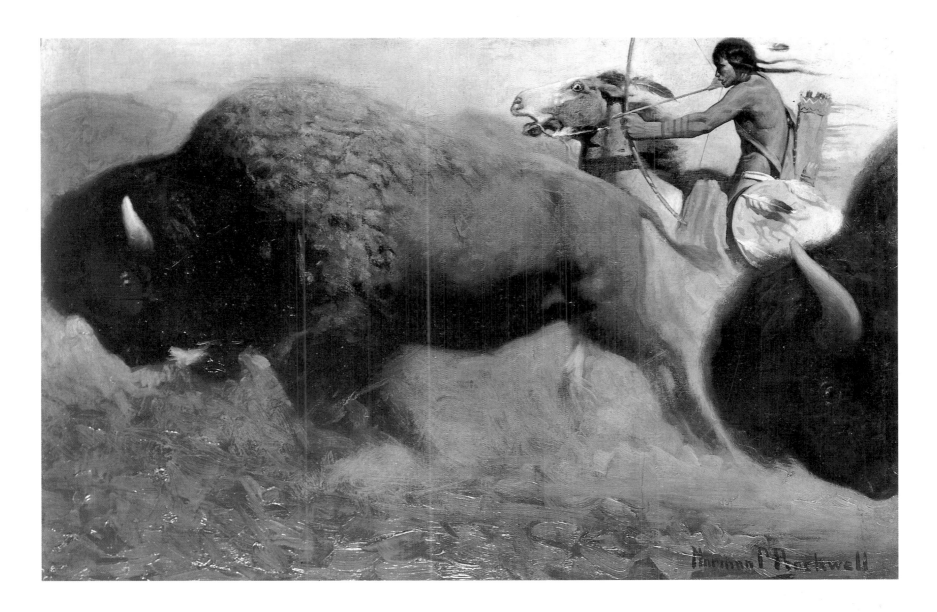

Norman Rockwell (1894–1978)
The Buffalo Hunt, 1915
Oil on canvas, 19 ½ × 31 ½ in.
The Rockwell Museum, Corning,
New York

Rockwell admirers would hardly
recognize this as the master's work:
no humor, no caricature, just speed,
grace, and danger at close quarters.

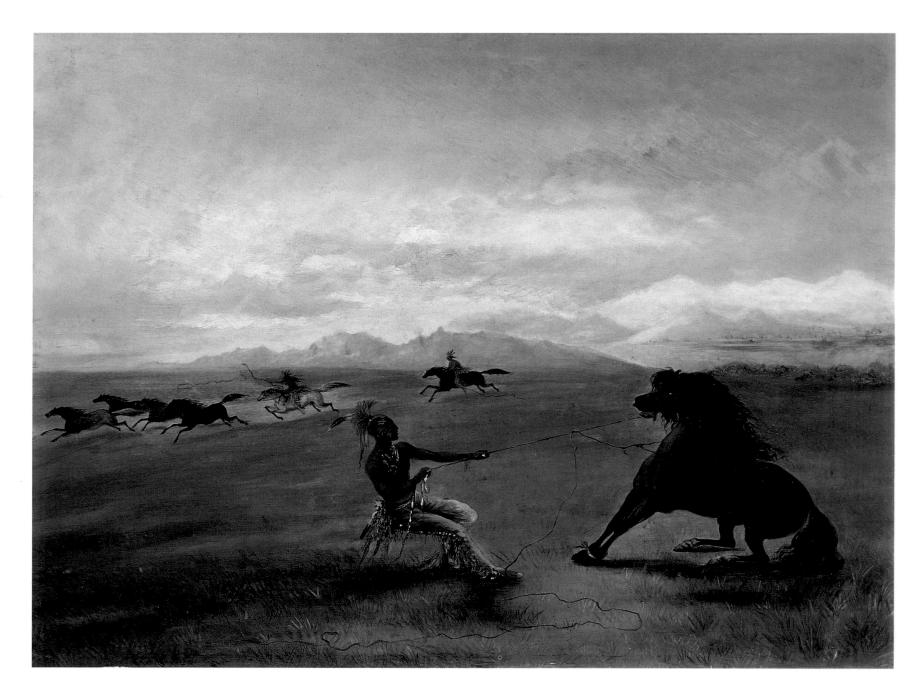

George Catlin (1796–1872)
Catching the Wild Horse, n.d.
Oil on canvas, 12 ¼ × 16 ½ in.
Gilcrease Museum, Tulsa, Oklahoma

Mustangs were greatly prized by Plains Indians, who wanted spirited animals.

General John E. Wool commanded the army's Department of the Pacific, charged with policing the Indian situation in the Northwest. Not only did the general refuse to annihilate the Indians, he repeatedly and publicly excoriated the citizenry of Oregon for their lust after Indian extermination. In the fall of 1855, the army found itself caught between Indians and settlers. As hostilities heated up in southern Oregon's Rogue River country, Captain Andrew Jackson Smith, commanding Fort Lane, found it necessary to offer Indian men, women, and children the protection of the fort. Nevertheless, a group of settlers raided an Indian camp in the shadow of the fort, killing twenty-three, including old men, women, and children. The next day, an Indian war party took revenge on the settlers, killing twenty-seven.

The bulk of General Wool's regulars were engaged in fighting the Wallawallas in what was called the Yakima War, so Captain Smith could do little with his small garrison until Wool was able to release reinforcements to him in the spring of 1856. At that time, too, the Rogue River chiefs known to the whites as Limpy, Old John, and George, weary of warfare, agreed to surrender to Smith at a place called Big Meadows. At the last minute, however, the chiefs thought better of it and instead mustered some two hundred warriors for an attack on Smith's fifty dragoons and thirty infantrymen. Two Indian women informed Smith of the planned attack, so that the captain had time to deploy his men on a readily defended hilltop. Nevertheless, when it came, the attack was fierce and protracted. The soldiers dug in the night after the first day of fighting, but morning revealed that some twenty-five troops had been killed or wounded. The Indians were massing for a final assault on the afternoon of May 28, 1856, when, with the good timing of a bad adventure novel, the promised reinforcements arrived, commanded by Captain Christopher C. Augur. Smith rallied his men to a downhill charge as Augur's infantry charged up from the rear, and the Indians were so utterly routed that, within the month, all had surrendered and meekly submitted to life on a reservation.

East of Cascades, Isaac Stevens, the youthful and aggressive governor of Washington Territory, was hastily concluding treaties binding the Indians to relinquish their lands in exchange for life on a reservation. The Yakima chief Kamiakin, revered among the tribes of the Columbia River basin, created an alliance that included, among others, the Wallawallas. As usual, hot-headed young warriors acted independently, killing six whites in September 1855. Kamiakin made the most of this premature action by sending a warning that the same fate would befall other whites who ventured east of the mountains. In October, a small force of regulars did reconnoiter the east face of the Cascades and were summarily pursued by five hundred Indians. In the meantime, militiamen managed to make matters worse by capturing the Wallawalla chief Peo-Peo-Mox-Mox during a peace parley and murdering him. The Oregonians retained the chief's ears and scalp as a trophy.

When the regulars finally marched, in the spring of 1856, five hundred strong, they found no one to fight. Chief Kamiakin and other hostiles had retreated eastward. The Yakima War was not wholly without effect, however, as Governor Stevens and others pressed for the removal of General Wool as commander of the Department of the Pacific, citing his lack of initiative in punishing the Indians. In May 1857, Wool was replaced by General Newman S. Clarke.

Kamiakin, now active east of the Columbia River, worked through 1857 and 1858 to foment a general uprising against settlers and gold seekers who were overrunning the country. In May 1858, 164 regulars out of Fort Walla Walla and under the command of Lieutenant Colonel Edward J. Steptoe were marching to the gold camp of Colville with the intention of impressing the Palouse, Spokane, and Coeur d'Alene Indians with the prowess of the U.S. Army.

When hundreds of mounted warriors descended on his column, it was Steptoe who was impressed. They did not attack, but they did demand that he and his men leave their country. The lieutenant colonel intended to do just that, ordering his men to turn back. But, on May 17, the Indians attacked the retreating column, killing two officers. When Steptoe reached a defensible hilltop position, he halted so that he could bring his howitzers to bear. That stratagem held the warriors at bay, but by nightfall it was clear to the regulars that they were in a bad way. Ammunition had dwindled to three rounds per man. Steptoe, in desperation, resolved to fight to the finish, go down in honor and a blaze of glory. His officers were less than enthusiastic about their colonel's plan and successfully argued for escape. Leaving their artillery behind, the regulars crept in darkness down the hill, circled behind the dozing Indian camp, and slinked back to the safety of Fort Walla Walla.

Outraged by this humiliation, General Clarke ordered Colonel George Wright to conduct a vigorous cam-

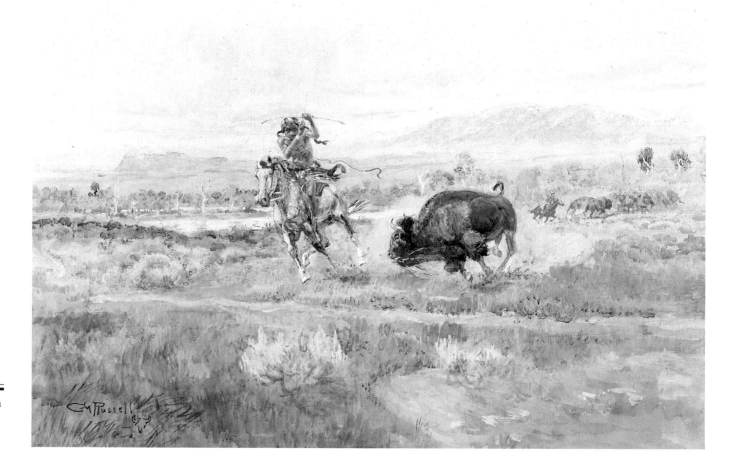

Charles M. Russell (1864–1926)
Fighting Meat, 1925
Watercolor, 20 × 29 ¾ in.
Montgomery Museum of Fine Arts;
The Blount Collection of American Art

The celebrated "cowboy artist" often exhibited a surprising delicacy in the depiction of inherently violent scenes.

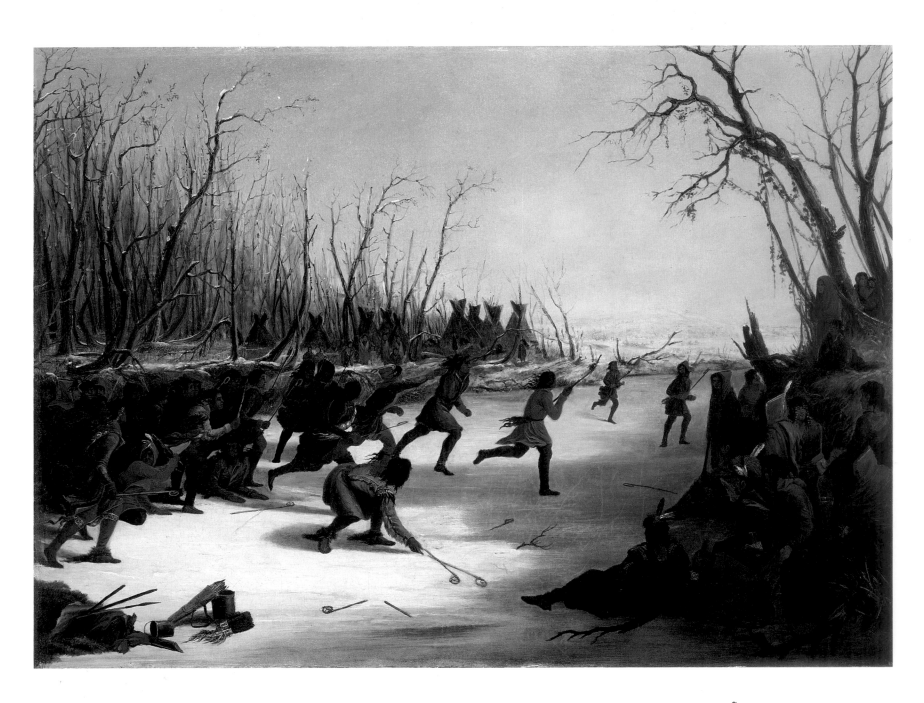

Seth Eastman (1808–1875)
*Ballplay of the Sioux on the St.
Peters River in Winter*, 1848
Oil on canvas, 25 ¾ × 35 ¼ in.
Amon Carter Museum, Fort Worth,
Texas

A heated game in a cold country.

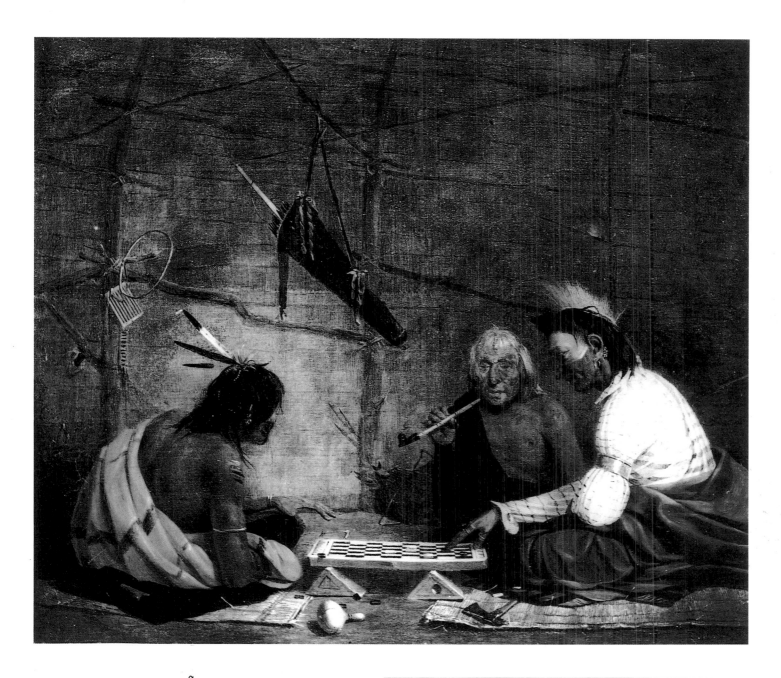

Charles Deas (1818–1867)
Winnebagos Playing Checkers, 1842
Oil on canvas, 12 ¼ × 14 ½ in.
Thyssen-Bornemisza Collection,
Lugano, Switzerland

Deas, best known for his
nightmarish visions of western life,
was also capable of quiet genre
scenes like this one.

John Mix Stanley (1814–1872)
Game of Chance, n.d.
Oil on canvas, 28 ¼ × 39 ⅜ in.
Gilcrease Museum, Tulsa, Oklahoma

Several western artists depicted
Indians playing white men's
games—a subject that greatly
intrigued contemporary Anglos.

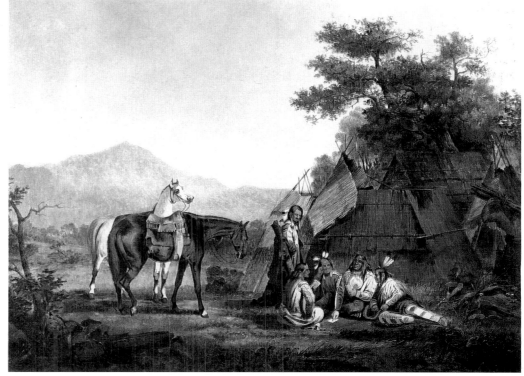

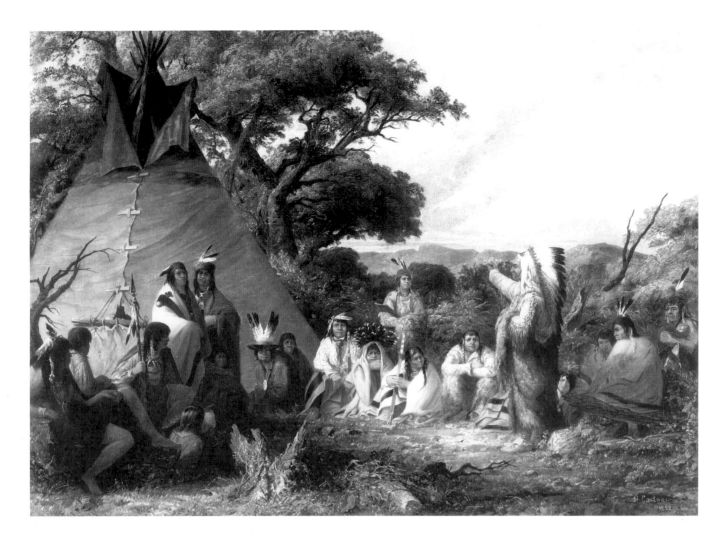

Seth Eastman (1808–1875)
The Indian Council, n.d.
Oil on canvas, 26 × 35 in.
Gilcrease Museum, Tulsa, Oklahoma

This painting, executed in
Washington, D.C., from sketches
made in the vicinity of Fort Snelling,
modern-day Minneapolis, reflects
the white man's fascination with
Indian government.

George Catlin (1796–1872)
Indian Council (Sioux), 1847
Oil on canvas, 25 ½ × 32 in.
Gilcrease Museum, Tulsa, Oklahoma

Typically, Indians made momentous
decisions only after protracted
councils. Chiefs were, of course,
important at such gatherings, but
their word was hardly final or
absolute.

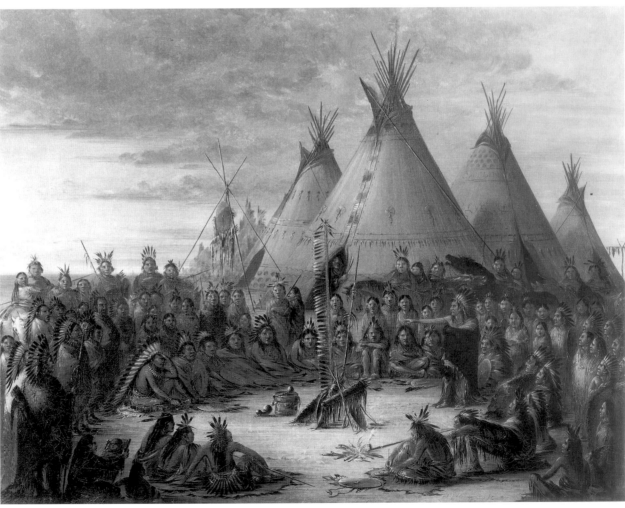

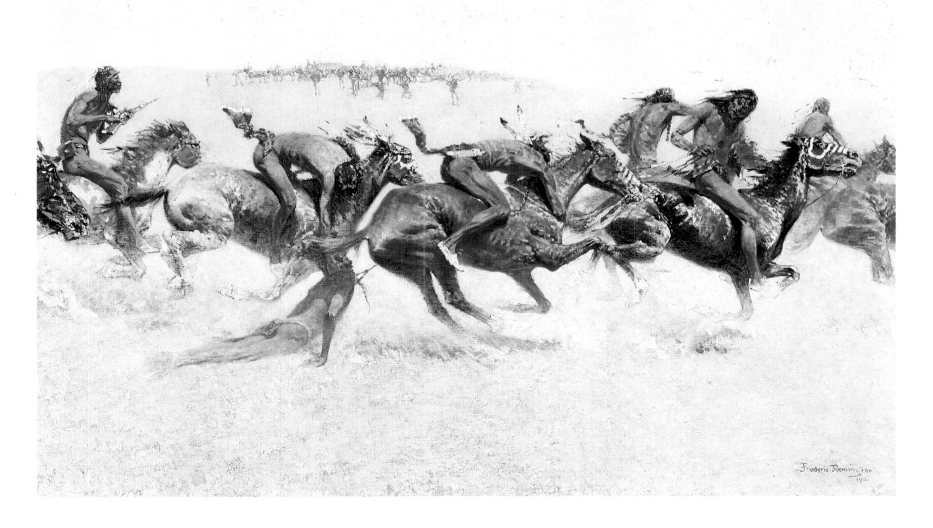

Frederic Remington (1861–1909)
Indian Warfare, 1908
Oil on canvas, 29 ½ × 50 in.
Gilcrease Museum, Tulsa, Oklahoma

Indians fought one another far more
often than they battled whites.

SETH EASTMAN

—

BORN 1808, BRUNSWICK, MAINE

DIED 1875, WASHINGTON, D.C.

—

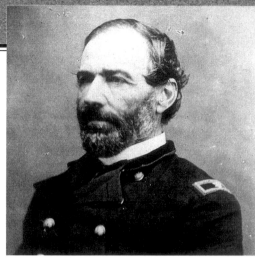

Anonymous, *Seth Eastman*, n.d. Photograph. National Portrait Gallery, Smithsonian Institution, Washington, D.C.

Graduating from West Point in 1829, Eastman successfully combined the careers of soldier and artist, serving as a topographical draftsman for a number of military land surveys and sketching and painting scenes of Indian life near the forts at which he was stationed.

In 1829, at Fort Crawford, on the Mississippi, in present-day Wisconsin, Eastman sketched the various Indians who regularly used the fort as a meeting place. He did the same at Fort Snelling (Minneapolis) on the Sioux frontier in 1830. When he was sent on a topographical reconnaisance in 1831, he made a series of drawings depicting the army's far-flung outposts and their environs.

Between 1833 and 1840, Eastman taught drawing at West Point while he himself studied with C. R. Leslie and Robert W. Weir. He also began exhibiting at the Apollo Gallery and at the National Academy of Design. After participating in the Seminole War during 1840–41, Eastman returned to Fort Snelling, where he continued his Indian studies, often working from daguerreotypes. After a tour of duty in Texas during 1848–49, Eastman was assigned the formidable task of illustrating Henry R. Schoolcraft's six-volume *History and Statistical Information Respecting . . . the Indian Tribes of the United States,* commissioned by the federal government and published between 1853 and 1856. Eastman also illustrated his wife's popular books about Indians, including *The Romance of Indian Life* and *American Aboriginal Portfolio* (both 1853) and *Chicora* (1854).

After more service in Texas and Utah followed by a stint in the office of quartermaster general during the Civil War, Eastman was retired with the brevet rank of brigadier general. In 1867, Congress commissioned him to paint Indian and fort scenes to decorate the Capitol.

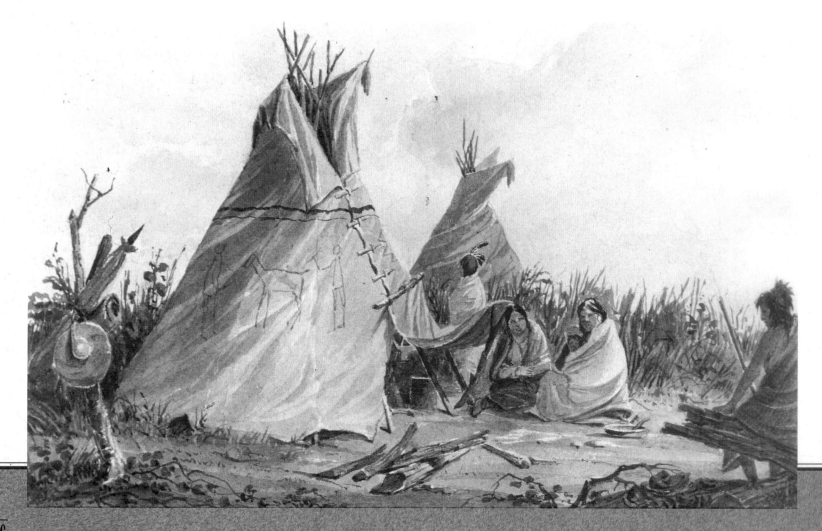

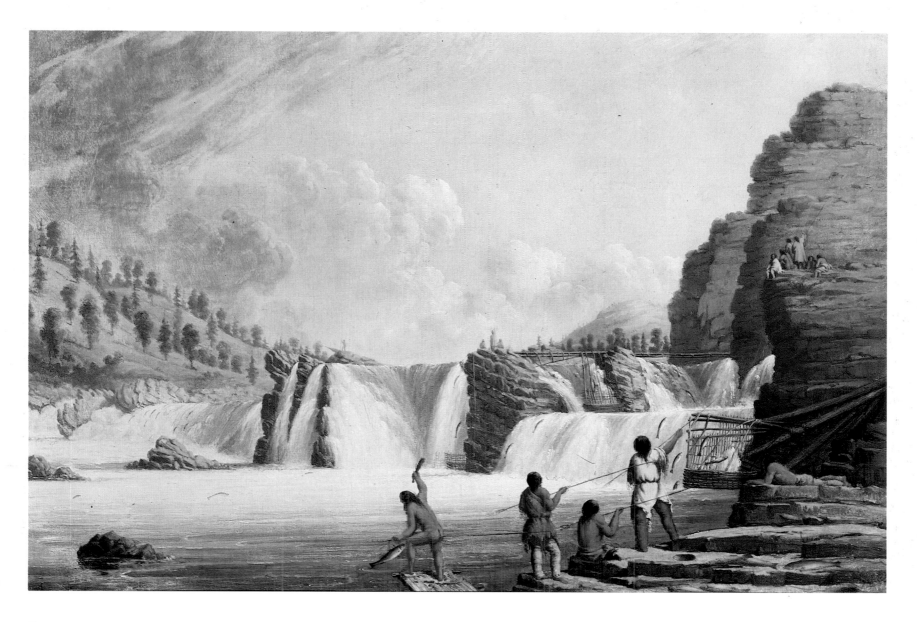

Paul Kane (1810–1871)
Falls at Colville, c. 1850
Oil on canvas, 19 × 29 in.
Royal Ontario Museum, Toronto

Spear fishing is an art for which the Indians of the Northwest coast are justly famous.

Seth Eastman (1808–1875)
Traveling Tents of the Sioux Indians Called a Tepe, 1847–49
Watercolor, 4 ¼ × 7 in.
The Saint Louis Museum of Art; Purchase: Fund Given by Western Electric Company

Accustomed to following the buffalo herds, many Plains tribes lived in these well-known portable dwellings. *(opposite)*

John J. Dalton (1856–1935)
Indian Buffalo Hunters in the Foothills of the Rocky Mountains, 1882
Watercolor, 27 × 40 in.
Royal Ontario Museum, Toronto, Canadian Collections

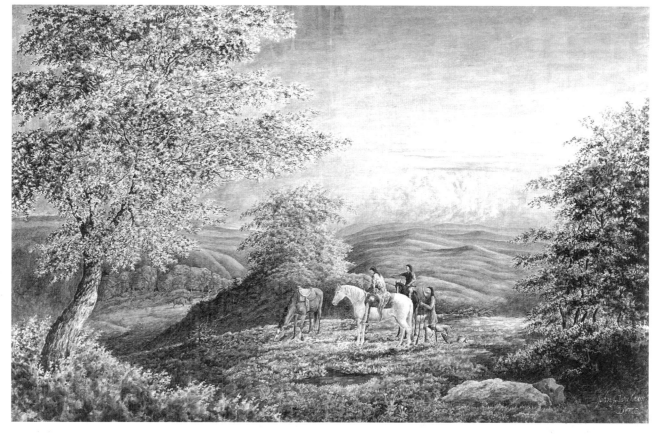

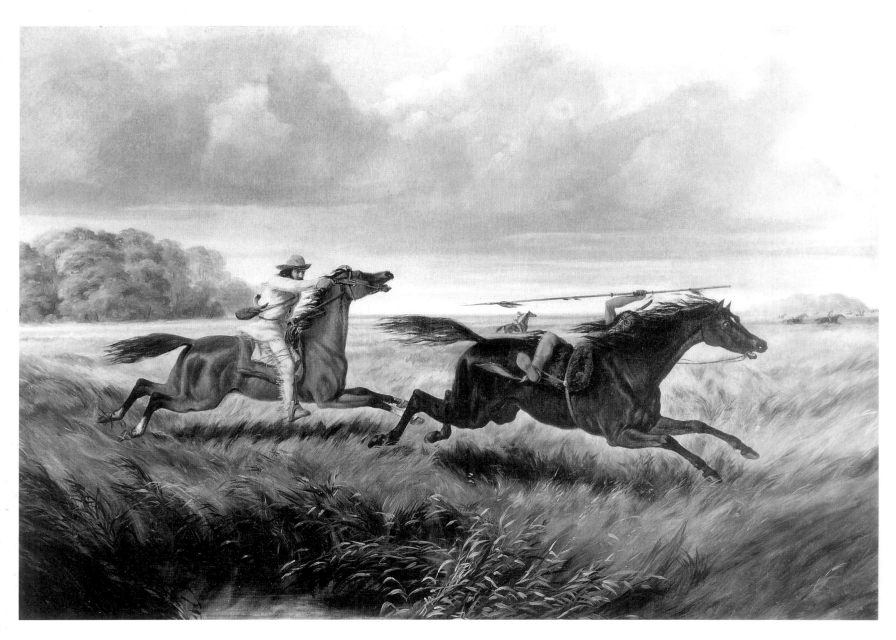

paign against the hostiles. "Make their punishment severe," the general admonished, "and persevere until the submission of all is complete." In a rare act of over-confident stupidity, the Indians gave Wright a perfect op-portunity to carry out his orders. About six hundred warriors met Wright's superior and better-armed force not guerrilla-style, but in the open on two battlefields—Spokane Plain (September 1) and Four Lakes (September 5)—suited to the kind of conventional warfare the army had been trained to fight.

Deeming his decisive victories insufficient "punish-ment," Wright marched from Indian camp to Indian camp, demanding delivery of those who had led the at-tack on Steptoe and his men. Fifteen braves were hanged, and others were made prisoner. Chief Ka-miakin, although he had been injured by artillery fire in the Battle of Spokane Plain, escaped to British Canada. The chief's brother-in-law, Owhi, approached Wright to make peace, was seized, and was forced to summon his son, the war leader Qualchin. Wright summarily hanged the young man in the presence of his father. In a subse-quent escape attempt, Owhi was shot and killed. Thor-

oughly dispirited, the tribes of the Columbia Basin made no more war, but resignedly marched to the reservations prescribed by Governor Stevens's treaties.

FIRST BLOOD IN THE SOUTHWEST

For as long as anyone could remember, the Apaches and Navajos had been raiding Mexican frontier settlements in New Mexico and Arizona. The United States, victorious in the war against Mexico, proposed to change all that. "From the Mexican government you have never received protection," General Stephen Watts Kearny declared on August 15, 1846, at the plaza of Las Vegas, New Mexico, as his Army of the West hoisted the Stars and Stripes. "My government . . . will keep off the Indians."

It was a bold promise that at first seemed possible to keep. The Mexican states of Chihuahua and Sonora had been so plagued by Apache raids that the Mexican government began offering generous bounties for Apache scalps. Not only Mexicans, but Americans, runaway slaves, and even Indians practiced this grisly form of what they called "backyard barbering." They did not

Arthur F. Tait (1819–1905)
The Pursuit, 1855
Oil on canvas, 30 × 44 ⅜ in.
Milwaukee Art Museum; Gift of
Edward S. Tallmadge

Adept at guerrilla-style tactics, few Indian warriors would allow themselves to be caught out in the open like this.

Arthur F. Tait (1819–1905)
On the Warpath, 1851
Oil on canvas, 33 × 44 in.
Courtesy of The Anschutz Collection

This extremely popular western artist, whose works were engraved for widely distributed Currier & Ives prints, never traveled west of the Mississippi, but he did collect authentic frontier gear for use as studio props. Working from a photograph of himself suitably attired, he created this image of a wary hunter drawing a bead on an unseen Indian enemy.

ARTHUR FITZWILLIAM TAIT

—

BORN 1819, NEAR LIVERPOOL, ENGLAND

DIED 1905, YONKERS, NEW YORK

—

Tait's western paintings, most of which depict exciting episodes in the lives of trappers, reached a wide audience and were highly influential since they were reproduced in many editions by Currier & Ives. Ironically, this artist, so instrumental in shaping the popular perception of the West, never crossed the Mississippi.

Son of a prosperous Liverpool shipping operator, Tait might have led the life of a well-to-do British urbanite had his father's business not faltered. When the family suffered serious financial reverses, young Tait was sent to live on a farm with relatives. There he learned to love animals, hunting, and fishing. His passion for the out-of-doors would eventually shape his artistic career.

That began with a clerkship in the Manchester gallery of Thomas Agnew, where Tait learned to appreciate paintings and prints, which he soon set about copying. He also persuaded the janitor of the Royal Institution in Manchester to open the doors early in the morning so that he might sketch plaster casts of classical sculpture before beginning his day's work at Agnew's. By nineteen, Tait was himself teaching drawing and studying the techniques of lithography. Seizing upon a contemporary fad for things "gothic," Tait found work as a draftsman and lithographer

for an ecclesiastical architecture firm and subsequently was commissioned by Saint Jude's Church in Liverpool to create a large print of the building.

After these successes, the artist turned his attention away from the past and squarely toward the present, preparing lithographs of the landscape of the early English industrial revolution, replete with tunnels, bridges, and railway stations. By the late 1840s, he had changed subjects again, producing oil paintings of animals and sporting scenes in the Scottish Highlands.

During the 1840s, Tait probably met George Catlin and assisted him in exhibiting his Indian Gallery in Liverpool; he may even have been part of Catlin's precocious Wild West show, which consisted of some twenty Englishmen dressed up as Indians and performing war dances and the like in order to promote attendance at the gallery. This experience may have encouraged Tait to immigrate to the United States in 1850.

Settling in New York, the artist met William Tylee Ranney, who loaned him frontier artifacts from his substantial collection so that the Englishman might capitalize on the excitement over things western generated by the gold rush. Tait was immediately successful and in 1852 was invited to submit work to the National Academy of Design exhibition. That year also, Tait began a series of trapper paintings for reproduction by Currier & Ives. Later in the decade, Currier & Ives sent Tait to the Astor Library, where he studied Catlin and Bodmer prints as the basis for two exciting prairie scenes, *The Pursuit* and *The Last War Whoop*, both painted in 1855. Two additional prairie canvases, *Buffalo Hunt* and *Life on the Prairie. The Trapper's Defense, "Fire Fight Fire,"* were painted in the early 1860s and soon after issued as Currier & Ives lithographs. These and a few other paintings constitute all of Tait's small but influential body of western work. From the mid 1860s until his death, the artist turned first to the lakes and woods of the Adirondack Mountains for his popular outdoor subjects, continuing to produce work for Currier & Ives, and then to scenes of Manhattan Island farm life just north of the city.

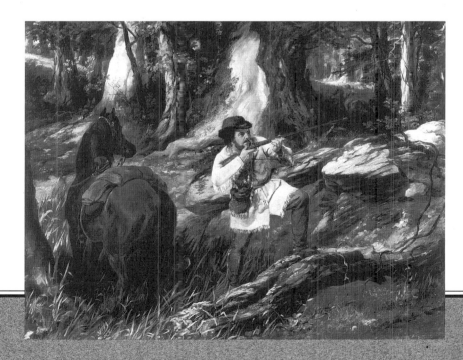

limit themselves to warriors, let alone warriors caught in the act of raiding, but would storm whole villages and kill every man, woman, and child they found. A special examination committee had been established to certify the authenticity of the scalps, but, as soon became evident to the bounty hunters, there was no way to distinguish between the scalps of friendly Indians and those of hostiles. So the harvest of death widened. Soon all Indians looked upon all whites as potential murderers, and a cycle of raids and counterraids ensued. (In fact, no one was safe from the scalper's knife. Many bounty hunters discovered that the examination committee was incapable not only of distinguishing friendly scalps from hostile, but couldn't tell the difference between Indian hair and Mexican. Remote Mexican villages, accustomed to enduring Apache raids, now fell victim to raids by the bounty hunters as well.) Although hatred of whites had become intense, the remarkable Apache chief Mangas Coloradas—Red Sleeves—was able and willing to distinguish between whites with whom he could ally himself and those he wanted to annihilate. He pledged friendship

to Kearny and proposed an alliance against their common enemy, the Mexicans. Although Kearny gladly accepted Mangas Coloradas's promise to stop raiding New Mexico, he declined his offer to invade Chihuahua, Sonora, and Durango with him; for Kearny was under orders to march to California.

Red Sleeves would have been a valuable ally. Born at the end of the eighteenth century, the chief grew into a giant of a man, standing six feet, six inches, and was consistently successful at outmaneuvering Mexican soldiers and volunteers. Tragically, though relations between the Apaches and the Americans were relatively peaceful during the 1840s and 1850s (this despite the fact that a number of Forty-Niners financed their westward trek by selling Apache scalps to the Mexicans), circumstances would change drastically in February 1861.

Cochise, chief of the Chiricahua Apaches, was a handsome man, except that his body was scarred with buckshot. Although his father, also a Chiricahua chief, had led the band in horse-stealing raids against the Mexicans, Cochise was inclined to like the Americans. He

Maynard Dixon (1875–1946)
Earth Knower, 1931, 1932, 1935
Oil on canvas, 40 × 50 in.
Collection of The Oakland Museum;
Bequest of Dr. Abilio Reis

The title of the painting and the visual similarities between the planes of the figure's face and clothing and those of the canyonland behind him signify the close identification of the Indian and the land—a symbiosis that transcended white ideas of mere ownership.

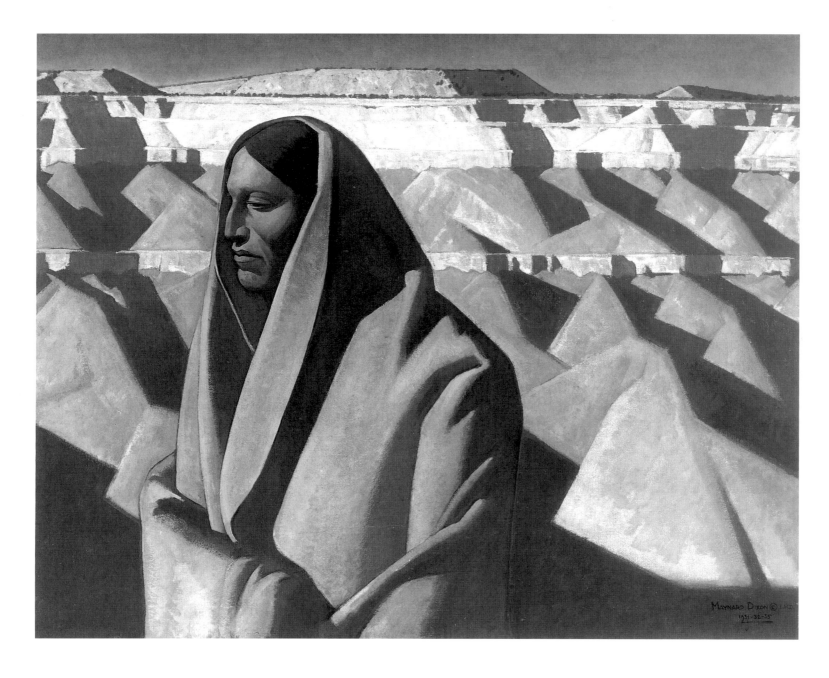

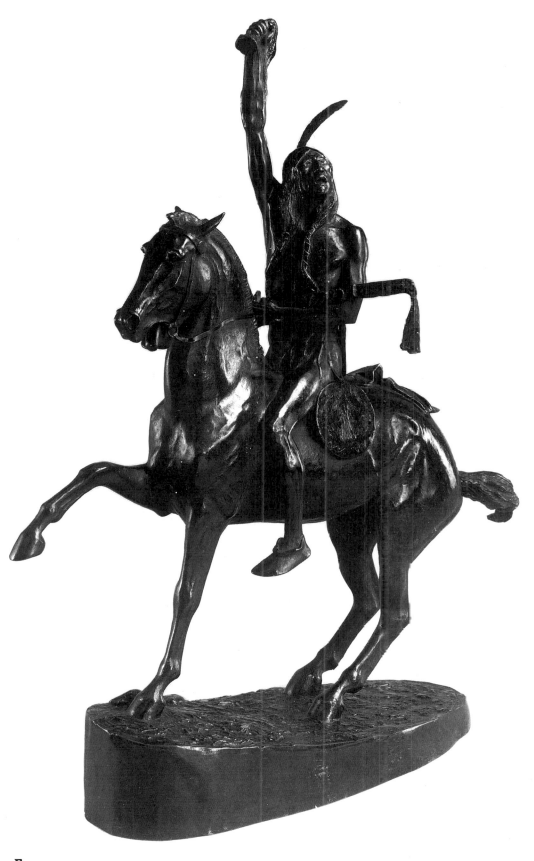

Frederic Remington (1861–1909)
The Scalp, 1898
Bronze, 25 ¾ × 21 ½ × 8 ¾ in.
Stark Museum of Art, Orange, Texas

The practice of scalping was not
exclusively the province of Indians.
The Mexican government, for
example, paid a bounty for slain
Apaches, and the scalp served as a
voucher when it came time to
collect.

and his people even had a contract with the Butterfield
Overland Mail to supply wood to the station at Apache
Pass.

About twelve miles from Fort Buchanan, Arizona,
lived a thoroughly disreputable rancher named John
Ward. His common-law wife, Jesúsa Martínez, had been
captured by Pinal Apaches and, during her captivity, had
borne a son named Felix. Late in 1860, a Pinal band
raided Ward's place and recaptured the child, rustling
some cattle as well. Ward, drunk at the time of the raid,
went to Fort Buchanan to tell its commander, Lieutenant
Colonel Pitcairn Morrison, that Chiricahua Apaches, led
by Cochise, had taken his boy and his cattle.

No one knows why three months passed before
Morrison dispatched Second Lieutenant George N. Bascom with sixty men to recover the boy and the cattle.
Bascom set up camp in Apache Pass, and Cochise, together with some relatives and friends, came there voluntarily to talk with him. Bascom demanded the return
of Ward's cattle and stepson, Cochise protested his innocence, and Bascom announced that he and his party
would be held captive until the boy and property were
returned. In a gesture fit for a matinee melodrama, Cochise drew his knife, slit the canvas of the conference
tent, and escaped. One of the warriors who followed his
chief out the hole was clubbed by a soldier and bayoneted in the gut by another. Six others were held
hostage.

Cochise gathered his warriors and raided the Butterfield station, killing one employee and taking another
prisoner. When a small wagon train passed by the station, Cochise captured it, along with the eight Mexicans
and two Americans who had been riding with it. The
Mexicans he ordered bound to the wagon wheels and
burned alive. The Americans—the two from the wagon
train and the station employee—he offered to exchange
for the six captives Bascom held.

Bascom refused. He also realized that the position
of his camp, in the middle of Apache Pass, was thoroughly vulnerable to attack by the Chiricahuas who surrounded him. He dispatched runners who sneaked
through the Indian lines and summoned reinforcements
from Fort Buchanan. Seventy dragoons under Lieutenant
Isaiah N. Moore arrived, only to find that Cochise and his
braves had vanished. The soldiers scouted the area and
found the bodies of the three American hostages, pierced
by lances and mutilated. Bascom took his own prisoners,
as he explained in his official report, "to the grave of
[the] murdered men, explained through the interpreter
what had taken place, and my intentions, and bound
them securely hand and foot, and hung them to the nearest trees."

Cochise responded with a vow to exterminate all
Americans in Arizona. In this way a drunken rancher's
false accusation gave rise to a quarter-century of
bloody war.

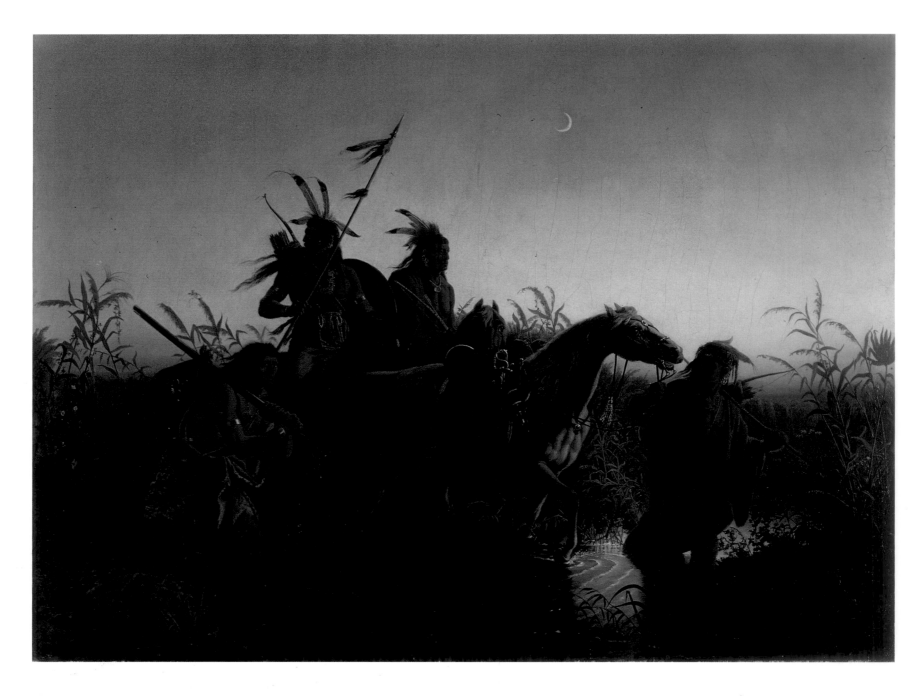

Charles Wimar (1828–1862)
The Captive Charger, 1854
Oil on canvas, 30 × 41 in.
The Saint Louis Art Museum; Gift of
Lillie B. Randell

Horses were coveted battle trophies,
especially fine cavalry mounts like
this one.

Charles M. Russell (1864–1926)
Stolen Horses, 1898
Oil on academy board, 18 × 24 in.
The Rockwell Museum, Corning,
New York

Horse stealing was a way of life for
many Plains tribes, whose culture
did not share in the white man's
worship of private property.

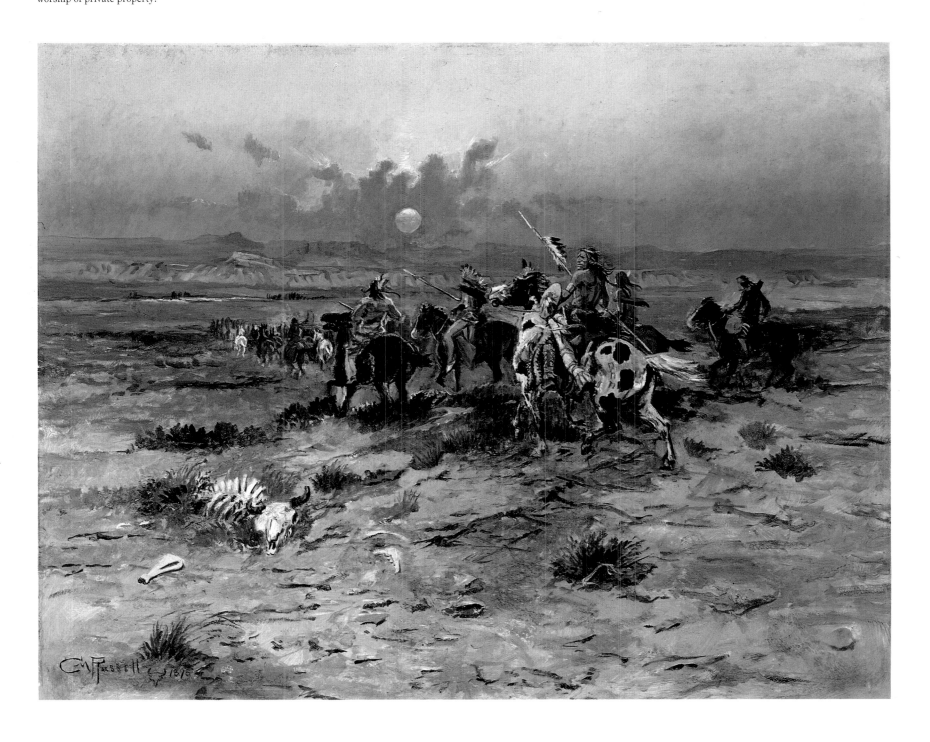

The Navajos, linguistically and culturally related to the Apaches, had eluded the attempts of late eighteenth-century missionaries to Christianize them and were feared throughout New Mexico and Arizona by whites and other Indians alike. They raided farms and settlements, including the Hopi village of Oraibi in 1837, nearly wiping it out. Mexican troops were powerless against them. When, in 1846, during the Mexican War, Lieutenant Colonel Alexander Doniphan encountered a party of five hundred Navajos near Bear Springs, New Mexico, they negotiated a peace treaty. Between the signing of that treaty and 1849, when Lieutenant Colonel John Washington negotiated another, the United States launched five expeditions against marauding Navajo bands.

On July 19, 1851, Lieutenant Colonel Edwin V. Sumner assumed command of the Ninth Military Department, which was responsible for much of the Southwest. Sumner had earned the sobriquet "Bull-head" when, reportedly, a musket ball struck him in the head and bounced off. *Bull-head* also described his obstinate determination to prevail. He pulled his troops out of the towns in which they had been garrisoned and set them to building a chain of forts, including Fort Defiance, which, gradually, at least hampered Navajo raids and brought the Indians in for peace talks.

New Mexico's governor, James S. Calhoun, was as

level headed as Sumner was bull headed and began negotiating a workable peace. But, before the peace was consolidated, he became desperately ill, appointed an acting superintendent of Indian affairs to stand in for him, and left Santa Fe to return home. He died en route. The unsympathetic Sumner assumed—illegally—the role of acting governor, overruling the efforts of John Greiner, the acting superintendent Calhoun had named. Nevertheless, peace generally prevailed until the summer of 1852, when William Carr Lane arrived to serve as the new territorial governor. Unlike Sumner, he believed that "it is better to feed the Indians, than to fight them" and negotiated generous treaties with the Navajos and the Jicarilla Apaches. Lane's efforts were foiled this time not by Sumner but by Congress, which failed to vote the twenty-thousand-dollar appropriation needed to administer the treaties. The Jicarillas, disappointed by the failure of their treaty, vigorously raided the countryside. The Navajos, except for an occasional raid, remained generally quiet for several years, even after a band of Utes asked them to unite in an alliance against the whites.

But the spring of 1856 brought renewed Navajo raids followed by punitive expeditions against them, escalating tensions on the frontier over the next two years. One spring day in 1858, some Navajos argued with soldiers from Fort Defiance who had been grazing their

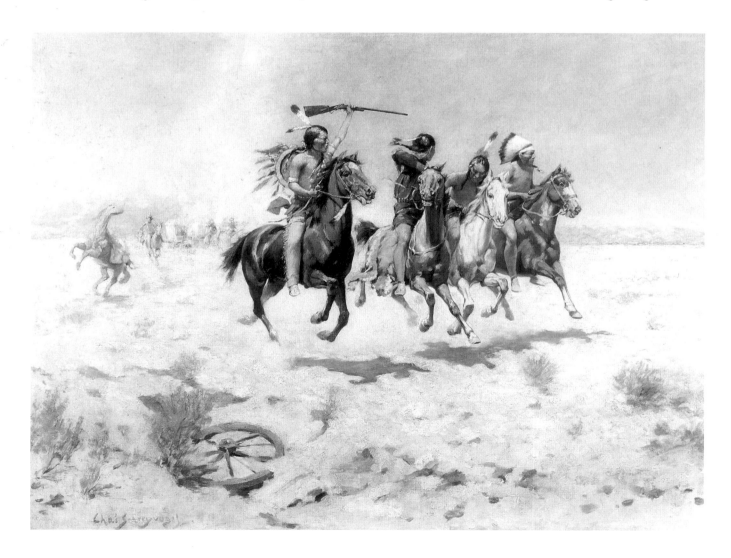

Charles Schreyvogel (1861–1912)
In Hot Pursuit (Attackers), c. 1900
Oil on canvas, 25 × 34 in.
Courtesy of The Anschutz Collection

Two interpretations of Indian harassment.

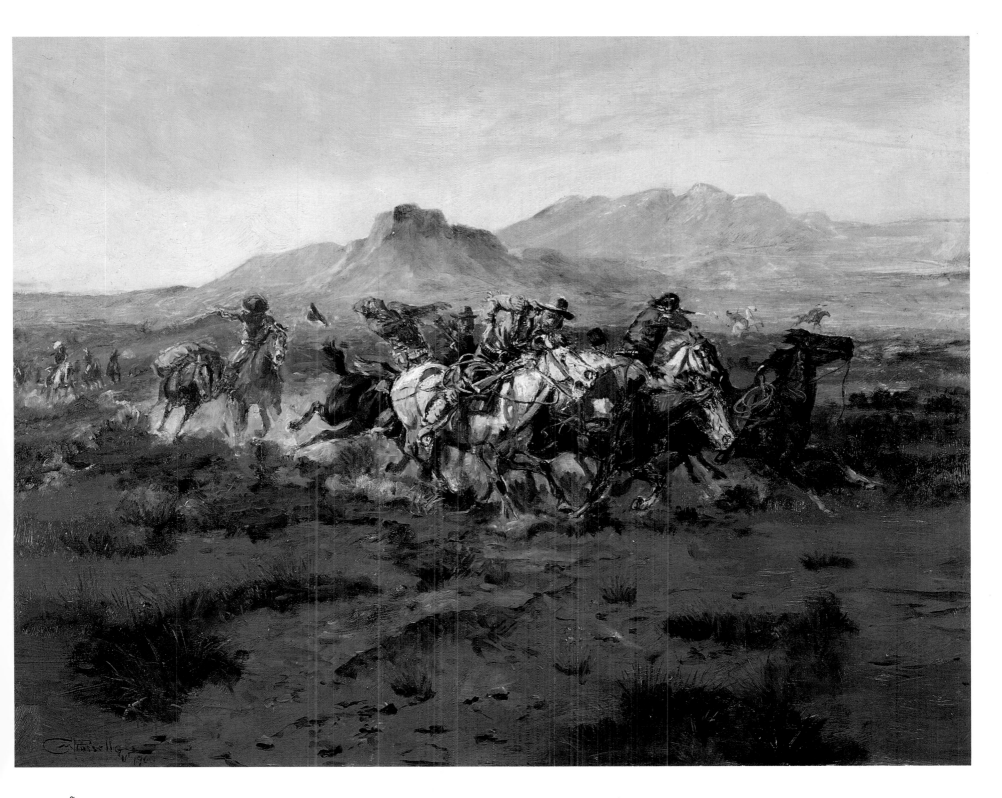

Charles M. Russell (1864–1926)
The Attack, 1900
Oil on panel, 18 ½ × 24 ⅜ in.
Amon Carter Museum, Fort Worth,
Texas

Frederic Remington (1861–1909)
A Dash for the Timber, 1889
Oil on canvas, 48 ¼ × 84 ⅛ in.
Amon Carter Museum, Fort Worth,
Texas

Remington was a master at this kind
of frieze-like action—riders
advancing abreast—a visual motif
that would become very familiar,
later in the century, to fans of
western movies. *(overleaf)*

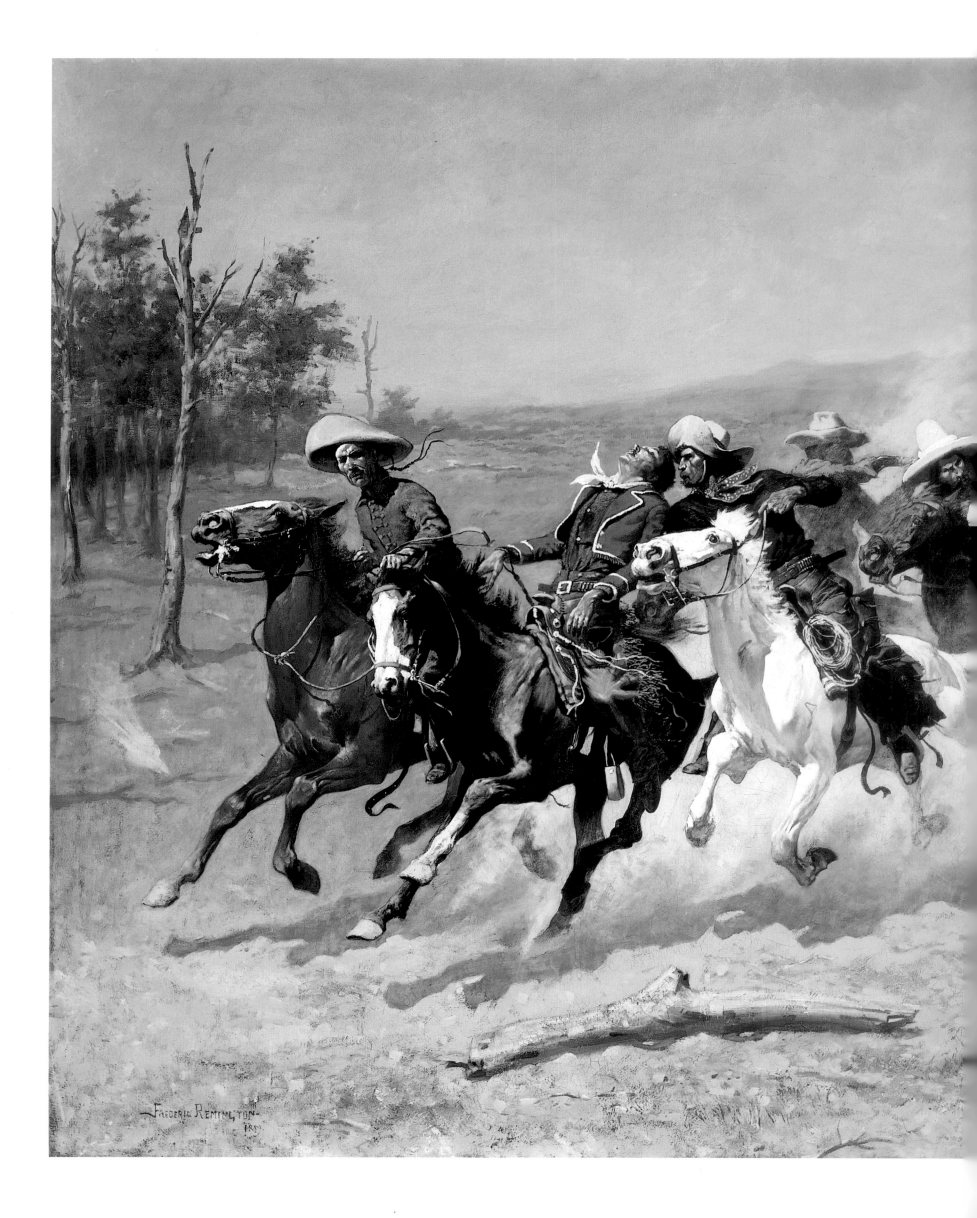

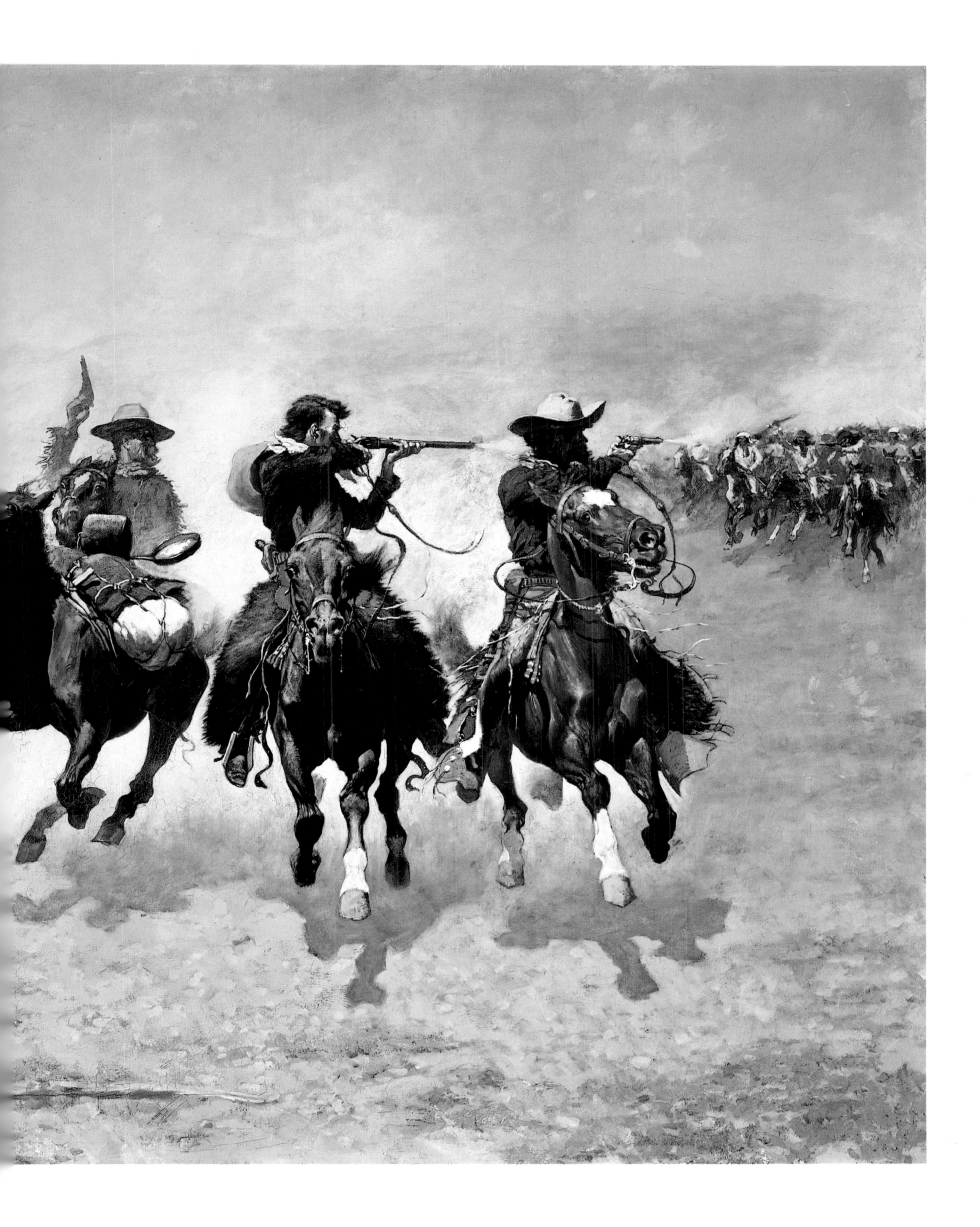

horses on land claimed by the Apache chief Manuelito. A few months later, Manuelito defiantly set his stock to graze on the land. Major Thomas H. Brooks, commander of Fort Defiance at the time, ordered his men to slaughter sixty of Manuelito's animals as a warning to clear off the disputed land. On July 7, Navajos shot volleys of arrows into a soldiers' camp, and on the twelfth, a Navajo warrior murdered Brooks's black servant, Jim. The major demanded that the Navajos produce the murderer, meanwhile preparing a substantial punitive expedition involving volunteers and Ute Indians in addition to regulars. General John Garland, who had replaced Bull-head Sumner as commander of the Ninth Military Department, not only approved Brooks's plans, but dispatched Lieutenant Colonel Dixon S. Miles to Fort Defiance to put them into operation.

Miles summoned to Fort Defiance a Navajo leader named Sandoval, telling him that unless he produced Jim's murderer by eight o'clock on the morning of September 9, the war would begin. On September 6, Sandoval informed Miles that the murderer had been captured and would be brought in. The next day, however, Sandoval told Miles that the prisoner had died of wounds he had sustained during capture. One day before the deadline, the Navajos brought the body into Fort Defiance. It was that of an eighteen year old; the murderer was known to be at least forty. It was a freshly killed corpse; Sandoval said the man had been dead four days. War commenced with a punitive expedition to Canyon de Chelly, Arizona, where soldiers burned fields of corn and a peach orchard; they killed six Indians and appropriated six thousand sheep. The army conducted a raid on the village of another Navajo leader, Zarcillos Largos, wounding him at least three times and capturing forty warriors. The Navajos conducted retaliatory raids and even attacked Fort Defiance.

By the next month, the Ninth Military Department had yet another new commander, Colonel Benjamin Bonneville, the celebrated western explorer, now superannuated and, unlike General Garland, desiring no war. However, he was a good soldier, and dispatched Lieutenant Colonel Miles and Major Electus Baccus to lead assaults against the Navajos. Little was actually accomplished—except for the burning of what Miles believed to be Manuelito's village—but the show of force was enough to prompt the Indians to sue for peace.

As usual, the terms of peace were dictated in a punitive spirit. There was no talk, no negotiating. The Americans read a treaty that compelled the Navajos to accept all blame for everything that had occurred, that set back farther west the boundary of their land and forbade their crossing the boundary for any reason, that required payment of fourteen thousand dollars in damages for livestock losses, that required all white captives to be released, that asserted the United States' right to send soldiers through Navajo country at any time and build

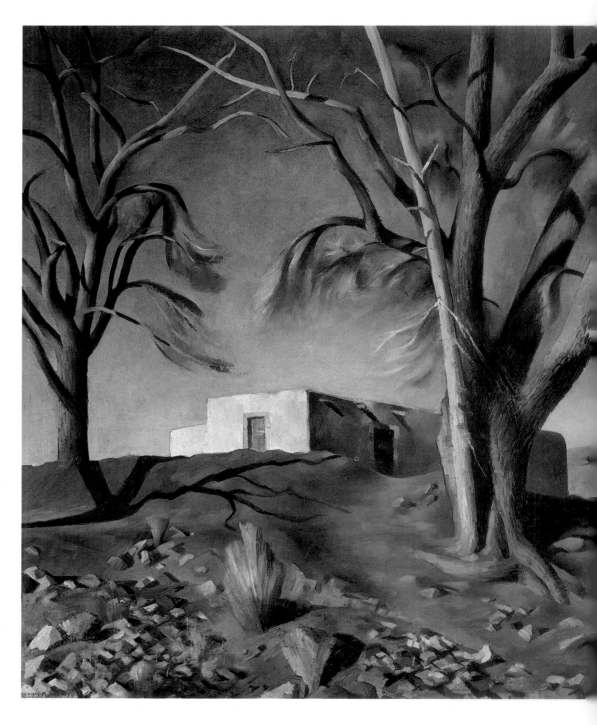

forts there, that proclaimed that the entire Navajo nation would be held culpable for the actions of any individual Navajo—and that made the Indians promise they would not harbor the murderer of poor Jim.

The remarkable thing is that the Navajos actually did try to comply with the unreasonable "Bonneville Treaty," as it was called. Some of the fourteen-thousand-dollar indemnity was paid—in the form of livestock—and some captives were returned. But by the middle of 1859, Ute Indians had begun raiding the Navajos, who retaliated against them and stole some New Mexican sheep while they were at it. New Mexico Indian superintendent James L. Collins ordered that the Navajos' "chastisement must be more severe, they must be well punished and thoroughly humbled." A new offensive was prepared, which again brought the Indians to a peace conference. This time, however, the Navajo chief Huero refused to

Kenneth Miller Adams (1843–1921)
New Mexico Landscape, n.d.
Oil on canvas, 40 ⅛ × 36 ⅛ in.
Stark Museum of Art, Orange, Texas

Considered as mass and plane, ancient adobe can seem very modern.

sign a treaty, claiming that such pieces of paper bound the Indians, not the whites.

By the beginning of 1860, raids were almost a daily occurrence. Far from being able to administer a severe chastisement, the army was powerless to stop the unremitting Indian violence. On April 30, a thousand warriors attacked Fort Defiance, which was ordered abandoned on May 4. By the end of 1860, the Santa Fe *Gazette* estimated that the Navajos had killed three hundred persons during the first six months of the year and had destroyed or stolen property worth $1.5 million. Colonel Thomas T. Fauntleroy was sent to replace Bonneville, but was ordered to concentrate his undermanned forces against the Comanches and Kiowas, who were raiding mail routes in Texas. The outraged governor of New Mexico Territory called for a volunteer force, though before it could be assembled, Fauntleroy received reinforcements and announced that he would launch a full-scale expedition against the Navajos.

More than 500 regulars were joined by 470 civilian volunteers in the expedition. While the regulars did little damage to the Navajos, the volunteers burned enough crops and captured enough cattle to prompt the Indians,

yet again, to seek peace. The so-called Canby Treaty was signed by fifty-four Navajo leaders—more than had signed any previous document—which gave the army reason to hope that this peace, at long last, would be an enduring one. The fact was that the Navajos were prepared to sign anything in order to gain some respite from destruction of their crops and appropriation of their cattle.

But there was to be peace for no one, not in the West and not in the East, either; for the North and the South, by this time, had gone to war with one another.

EARLY WARS ON THE PLAINS

Whereas the Apaches and Navajos in the far Southwest discriminated—for a time, at least—between Mexicans and Americans, directing most of their raids against the former, the Kiowas and Comanches of the southern plains plundered Mexicans and Americans alike. As with the Apaches and Navajos, raiding was a way of life for the Kiowas and Comanches. In 1851, the United States attempted to negotiate a grand treaty with several Plains tribes—Sioux, Cheyennes, Arapahos, Crows, Gros

F rederic Remington (1861–1909)
Cavalry in an Arizona Sandstorm,
c. 1889
Oil on canvas, 22 ³⁄₁₆ × 38 ³⁄₈ in.
Amon Carter Museum, Fort Worth,
Texas

One of many miseries troopers faced was the sometimes hostile climate of the desert Southwest.

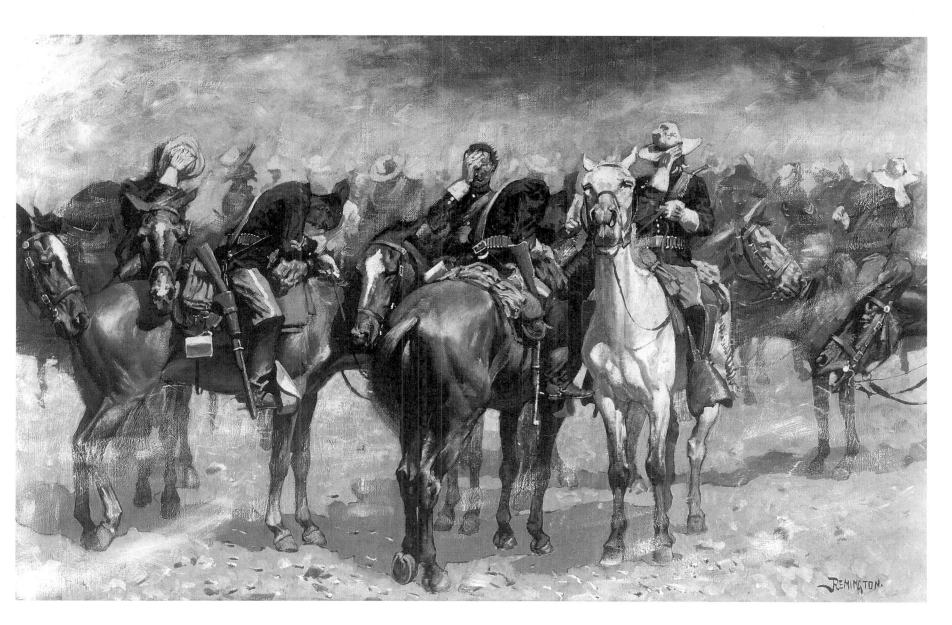

EARNEST MARTIN HENNINGS

—

BORN 1886, PENNSGROVE, NEW JERSEY

DIED 1956, TAOS, NEW MEXICO

—

After high school in Pennsgrove, Hennings studied briefly at the Pennsylvania Academy of the Fine Arts and then for five years at the Art Institute of Chicago, followed by two at the Royal Academy in Munich, where fellow students included Walter Ufer and Victor Higgins. Hennings returned to Chicago at the outbreak of World War I, in 1914, working as a muralist and a commercial artist.

Hennings attracted the attention of former Chicago mayor Carter Harrison, a patron of the arts, who suggested that the painter investigate Taos. He visited the village in 1917, becoming a resident in 1921—though he also traveled widely in Europe and North Africa.

The artist's favorite subject was the Indian, whom he typically posed against a bright background of intense fall foliage or with a few well-chosen props. For all their detail and realism, the paintings have a strongly stylized decorative dimension and are "prettier" than what one might expect from an artist of the rugged West.

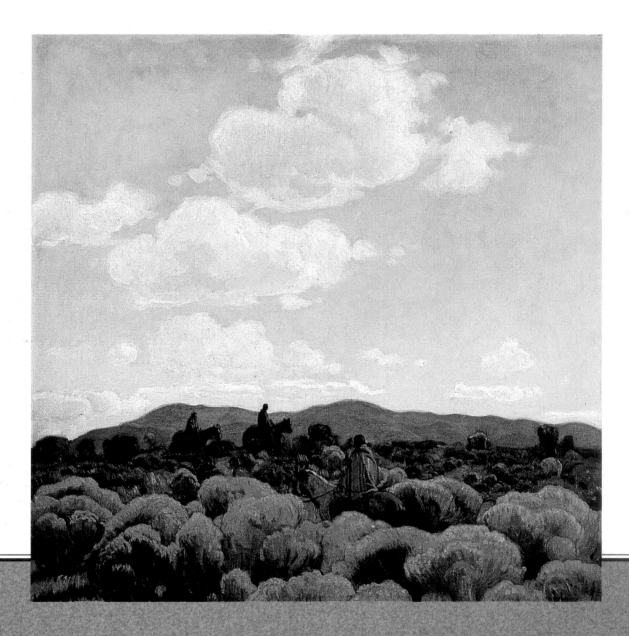

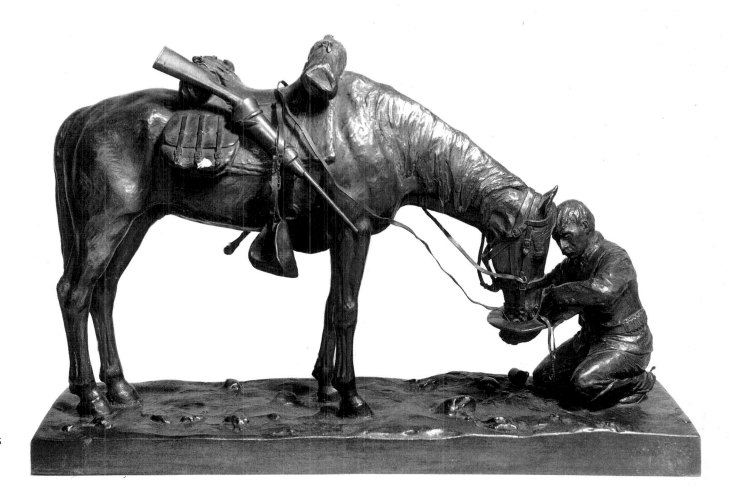

Charles Schreyvogel (1861–1912)
The Last Drop, 1904
Bronze, H. 12 in.
Collection of The Newark Museum;
Gift of Joseph S. Isidor, 1925

A cavalry trooper looks to the needs
of his horse before his own.

E. Martin Hennings (1886–1956)
Edge of the Sage, 1936
Oil on canvas, 30 × 30 in.
Santa Fe Collection of Southwestern
Art

Ventres, Assiniboins, Arikaras, Shoshones, Pawnees, and Kiowas and Comanches—calling chiefs to a big council at Fort Laramie. The Kiowas and Comanches stubbornly refused to come to the 1851 council, but did attend treaty talks later at Fort Atkinson, on the Arkansas River. The object of both the Fort Laramie treaty and the Fort Atkinson treaty was to confine Indians to what the documents called "territories," but that were, in fact, reservations. The Kiowa and Comanche chiefs signed, to the great satisfaction of the government. But the signatures meant virtually nothing, since the chiefs were not sovereigns; as far as the chiefs themselves were concerned, all signing signified is that they would receive gifts from the large stockpile of trade goods that accompanied the treaty council. The Kiowas and Comanches continued to raid Texas, as they had for generations.

After the Mexican War, the U.S. Army built a chain of seven forts from the Red River to the Rio Grande, but the frontier of settlement quickly overran them. In 1852, another half-dozen forts were established farther west, but they were garrisoned by a force of regulars numbering fewer than three thousand (in 1854), charged with patrolling four hundred miles of frontier as well as the Mexican-American border. It was during this period that various volunteer groups, most notably the Texas Rangers, were formed in an effort to accomplish what the undermanned regulars could not.

When the so-called Mormon War erupted in 1857, much of the Second Cavalry left Texas for Utah, whereupon the Nokoni Comanches launched a massive raid,

killing a number of whites and stealing some five hundred horses. Texas Governor Elisha M. Pease called for volunteers and immediately dispatched a company of Rangers to pursue the raiders. Early the next year, Pease's successor, Governor Hardin R. Runnels, sent Texas Ranger Captain Rip Ford with 215 men across the Red River, to punish the Comanches on their home territory. Ford encountered and fought warriors of the Kotsoteka Comanche tribe, killing seventy-six of them, including Chief Iron Jacket. Though Ford lost only one Ranger and one Indian scout, he was forced to withdraw after his victory because he was short on supplies.

In the fall of 1858, regular troops under Major Earl Van Dorn joined the Texas Comanche campaign. On October 1, 1858, he moved against a Comanche village of 120 lodges presided over by Chief Buffalo Hump, killing fifty-six warriors and two women and burning the lodges. Van Dorn, however, was shot with arrows through the wrist and navel. Though his wounds were pronounced mortal, he lived to fight more Comanches between the Arkansas and Red rivers, most notably defeating a band of them in the Battle of Cripple Creek during the spring of 1860. Forty-nine warriors died and five were wounded.

Despite such decisive victories, the raiding continued unabated. A group of Texans, disgusted with the regular army's inability to halt the raids, took out their hatred on the first group of Indians they encountered. It was a small party that had a special pass from the white agent in charge of their reservation giving them permis-

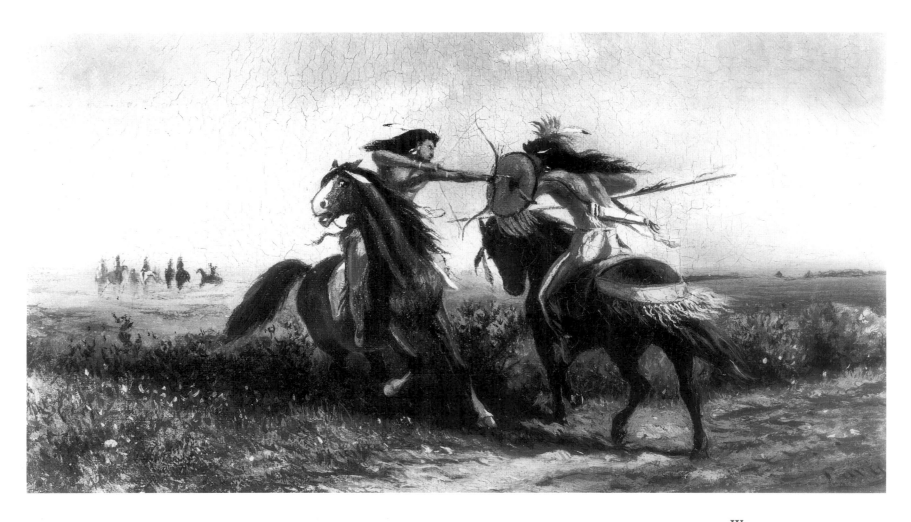

William de la Montagne Cary (1840–1922)
Indians Jousting, c. 1875
Oil on canvas, 5 11/16 × 10 3/8 in.
The Rockwell Museum, Corning,
New York

The title of the painting underscores
the unwillingness of most
nineteenth-century whites to see
Indians for themselves. Here they
are "elevated" to knighthood.

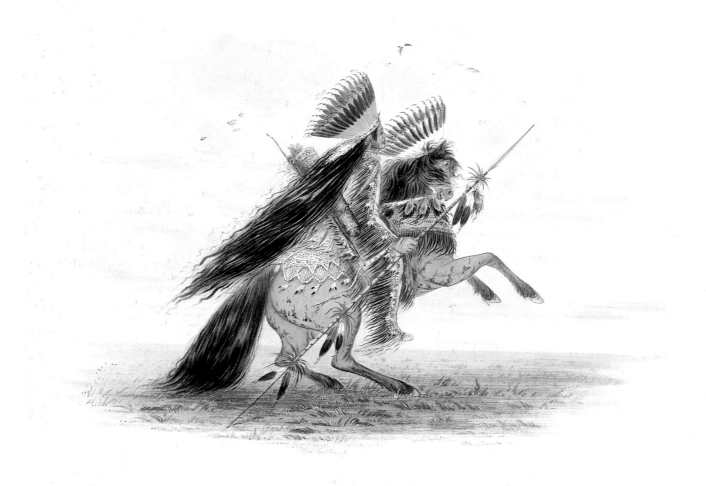

George Catlin (1796–1872)
*Pa-ris-ka-roo-pa from the Album
Unique,* 1852
Pencil and watercolor on paper,
17 1/4 × 22 5/8 in.
Stark Museum of Art, Orange, Texas

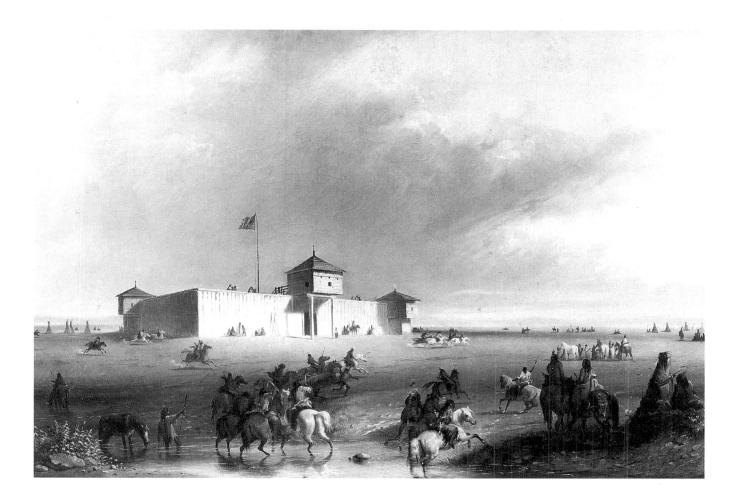

Alfred Jacob Miller (1810–1874)
Fort Laramie, 1851
Oil on canvas, 18 × 27 in.
Gilcrease Museum, Tulsa, Oklahoma

Alfred Jacob Miller (1810–1874)
Interior View of Fort Laramie, 1837
Watercolor on paper, 10 ¼ × 14 in.
Gilcrease Museum, Tulsa, Oklahoma

The earliest western forts were not
built by the army, but by fur
companies. Originally called Fort
William, Fort Laramie was built on
the banks of the Laramie River near
the upper Missouri in the 1830s by
William Sublette and Robert
Campbell of the Rocky Mountain Fur
Company.

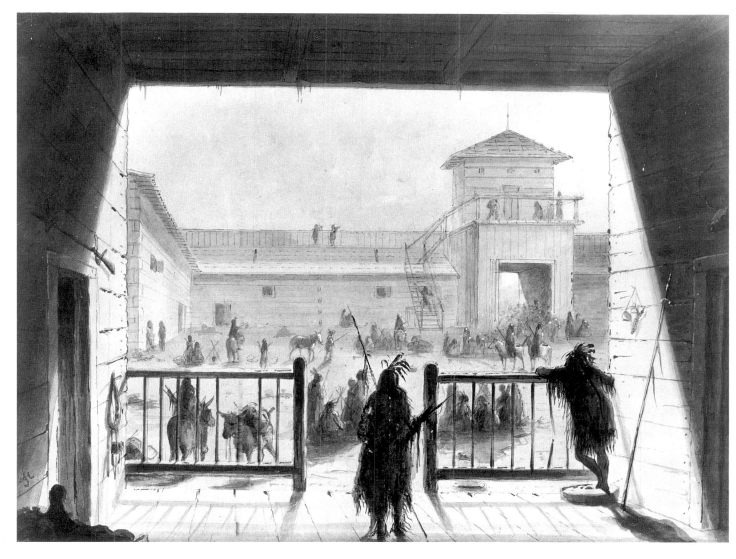

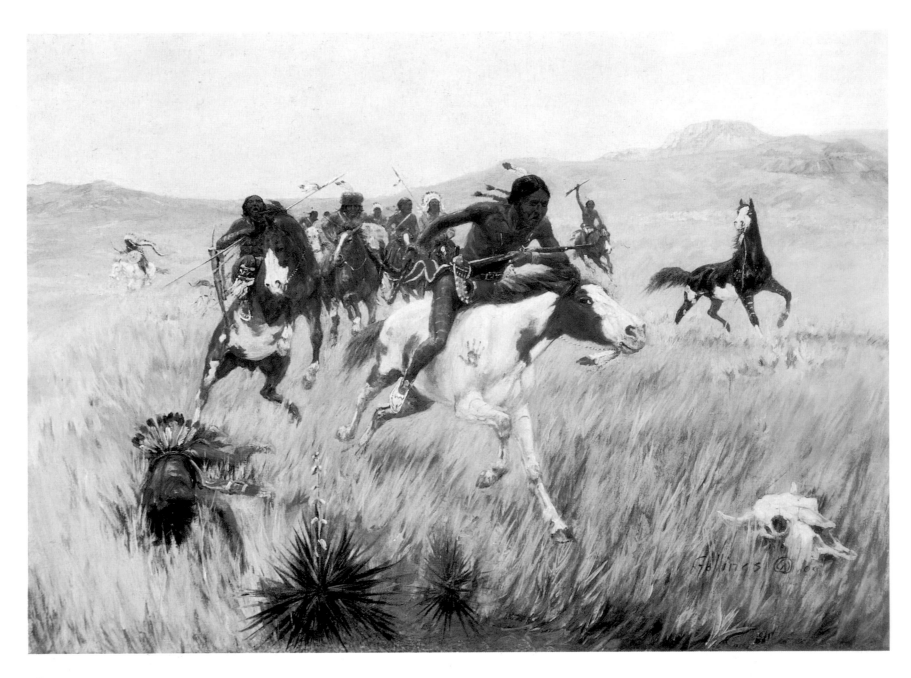

sion to scout out grazing land for their horses. The pass notwithstanding, the Texans killed four men and three women and wounded most of the rest of the party. Governor Runnels ordered the arrest of the Texans, but the Texas Rangers refused to execute the order, and a grand jury refused to hand up indictments—instead recommending that the citizens be praised for performing a public service.

The incident prompted federal officials to move the southern Comanches to Indian Territory—present-day Oklahoma—but the Texans were not satisfied even with this removal. On May 23, 1859, 250 volunteers led by John Robert Baylor entered the soon-to-be-vacated Texas reservation, demanding that all Indians guilty of crimes be turned over to them. A fight developed between Baylor's group and the Indians as U.S. Army regulars stood by and watched. Governor Runnels called out the militia against the Baylor band, but had to withdraw them when they threatened to join Baylor in the slaughter of the reservation Comanches. Indian Superintendent

Robert Neighbors hurriedly evacuated his Comanche charges from their two Texas reservations and delivered them to a reservation in Oklahoma. Returning to Texas, Neighbors was slain by a Texan who thought the Indian superintendent was harboring renegades.

Nothing seems simpler—or more horrifying—than Indian-white relations in Texas. In reality, they were more complex. Although southern Comanche tribes preyed upon Texans, those in the north and west enjoyed a peaceful trading relationship with Americans, especially those living in New Mexico. They traded stolen goods—even captive women and children—taken from Texas, in return for arms, ammunition, liquor, and the like. As early as the 1820s, this commerce had become a regular feature of southwestern life. Annual caravans of traders known as Comancheros trafficked in the goods Indians desired. Poor New Mexicans and Pueblo Indians, the Comancheros occupied the lowest rung of New Mexico society. "Dirty filthy looking creatures," one traveler described them; and another was horrified by their nasty

William E. Gollings (1878–1932)
Warfare on the Plains, n.d.
Oil on canvas, 28 × 39 in.
Courtesy of The Anschutz Collection

Born in Idaho, Gollings was raised in rural Michigan and New York and in Chicago. At age eighteen he left his family and took up the hobo's life in the West, eventually becoming a cowboy. When he was twenty-five, Gollings ordered some oil paints through the Montgomery Ward catalog and began to record what he already knew was the vanishing world of the cowboy.

William de la Montagne Cary
(1840–1922)
The Captive White Child, 1875
Oil on canvas, 11 ⅝ × 23 ½ in.
The Rockwell Museum, Corning,
New York

It was not uncommon for Indians to
adopt captured white children and
raise them in the ways of the tribe.

Henry F. Farny (1847–1916)
Among the Foothills, 1892
Gouache on paper, 8 × 14 in.
Berry-Hill Galleries, New York

Two artifacts associated with the
peripatetic life of the Plains Indian
are in evidence here: the tepee,
light, easily erected, easily
dismantled, and readily portable,
and the travois, the simplest vehicle
of the plains.

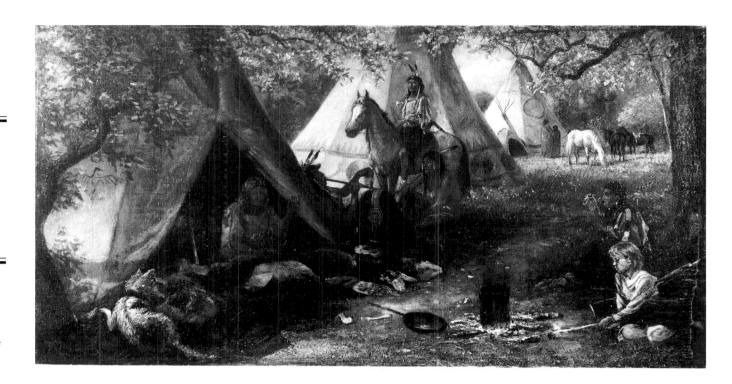

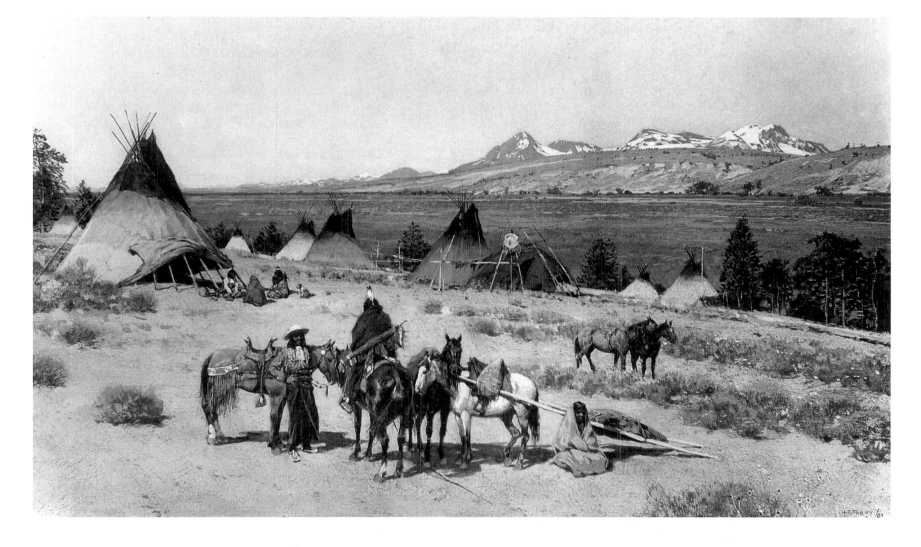

habit of catching their lice and eating them.

The American administration in New Mexico did not know whether to ignore, condone, or condemn the Comanchero trade. For while the Comancheros did reward Indians for their depredations in Texas, they also helped keep the peace in New Mexico, and they regularly ransomed white captives, purchasing them in Texas and selling them in New Mexico. While Indian Superintendent James S. Calhoun was appalled by this practice, he frequently resorted to the Comancheros as the only viable means of recovering captives. Of course, it was true that the captives were taken in the first place for the purpose of wholesaling them to the Comancheros, who, in turn, sold them at retail, for a profit.

The delicate, if thoroughly distasteful, economy of Texas–New Mexico–Comanche–Comanchero relations was upset during the mid to late 1850s as Comanches were caught in a pincers between Texas Ranger campaigns that drove them west and increasing white settlement of New Mexico, which pushed them east. In March 1858 a band of Comanches raided Samuel Watrous's ranch on the Canadian River in New Mexico, killing the ranch foreman, burning the buildings, and driving off the cattle. The next year, they attacked a group of surveyors who had come into the Canadian River valley. Indeed, they stepped up raiding generally, concentrating on ranches but always avoiding sheepherders, for no other reason than that Comanches had traditionally been friendly with herders.

In 1860, approximately 850 regulars were broadcast

Joseph Henry Sharp (1859–1953)
War Talk, before 1942
Oil on canvas, 18 × 22 ½ in.
Courtesy of The Anschutz Collection

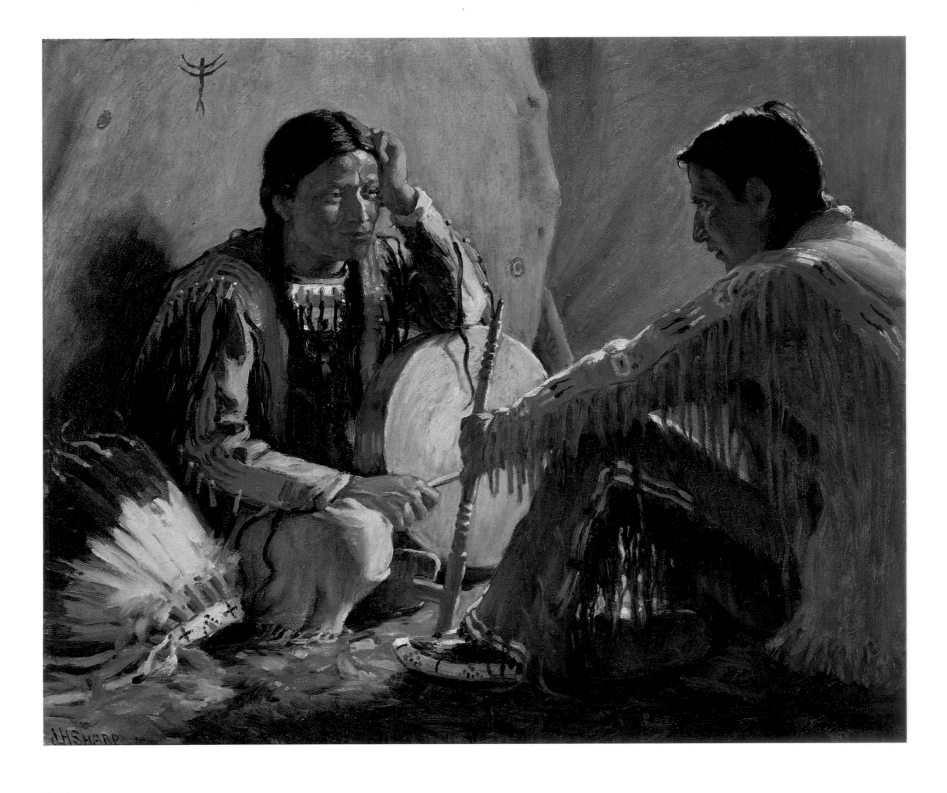

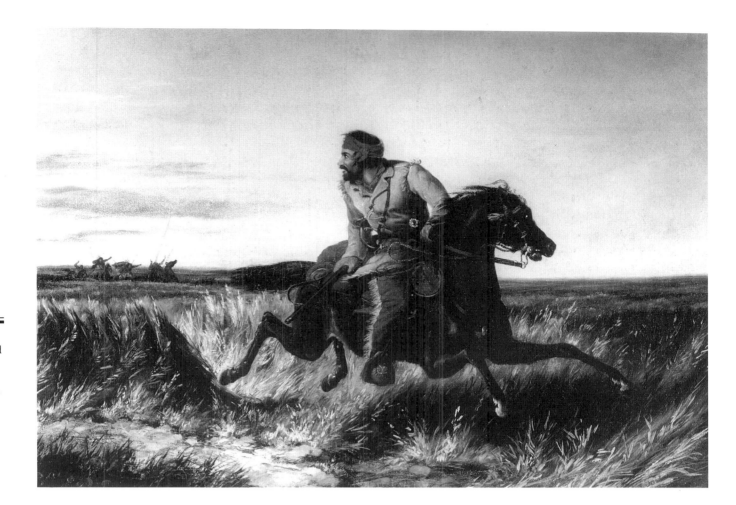

across the Texas plains, charged with finding and killing Comanches. Comancheros supplied the soldiers with a great deal of misinformation, and the expedition accomplished little. When Lieutenant Colonel George B. Crittenden at Fort Union realized that the Comancheros were probably warning Indians of impending attacks, he organized a secret expedition consisting of sixty men who attacked a Comanche village of 150 lodges, destroying it, killing ten Indians, and appropriating forty horses. This action seems to have brought about a Comanche negotiation attempt during May 10–11, 1861, at Alamo Gordo Creek, which resulted in a short-lived truce. As raiding resumed in eastern New Mexico, ranchers, who had complained that the army was doing little to fight the Comanches, now blamed the soldiers for "unprovoked attacks" that incited the Indians to further raids. While this bickering was going on, the outbreak of the Civil War suddenly necessitated the withdrawal of soldiers from New Mexico. Whereas withdrawal of troops from Apacheria (as the region controlled by the Apaches was called) had triggered raiding with a vengeance, in eastern New Mexico the withdrawal brought peace, as Comanches resumed their practice of looting Texas to trade in New Mexico.

As bad as conditions were in the Far Southwest and the southern plains, it was the central and northern plains that were destined to see the fiercest and most protracted Indian warfare. It started on August 18, 1854, when High Forehead, a Brulé Sioux, shot an arrow into the flank of an ox belonging to a wagon train passing through the North Platte valley of Wyoming, near Fort Laramie. The Mormon owner of the ox put in a complaint at the fort, and Lieutenant John L. Grattan was dispatched to the Indian camp of Chief Brave Bear with thirty infantrymen and two small cannon. When High Forehead declined to give himself up, Grattan opened fire on the village, fatally wounding Brave Bear. The full fury of the Brulé warriors was turned against Grattan's small band. One trooper survived long enough to return to Fort Laramie, where he later died of his wounds.

Seizing upon the "Grattan Massacre" as sufficient cause, Secretary of War Jefferson Davis ordered General William S. Harney to punish the Brulé Sioux. Leading six hundred men out of Fort Kearny, Nebraska, he was heard to declare, "By God, I'm for battle—no peace."

But what happened couldn't be called a battle. Chief Little Thunder, successor to Brave Bear, gathered his band of 250 about him and simply waited for Harney's approach. On September 3, 1855, Harney's infantry attacked from the south, and his dragoons moved in from the north. It was a rout, as 85 Indians perished and 70 women and children were taken captive. The Sioux would learn to call Harney "The Butcher."

Harney continued his march into the very heart of Sioux country, the Black Hills, but no Indians offered a fight. At Fort Pierre, a former fur-trading post, Harney held a peace conference with chiefs of the Teton Sioux. The chiefs signed a treaty that endured for years.

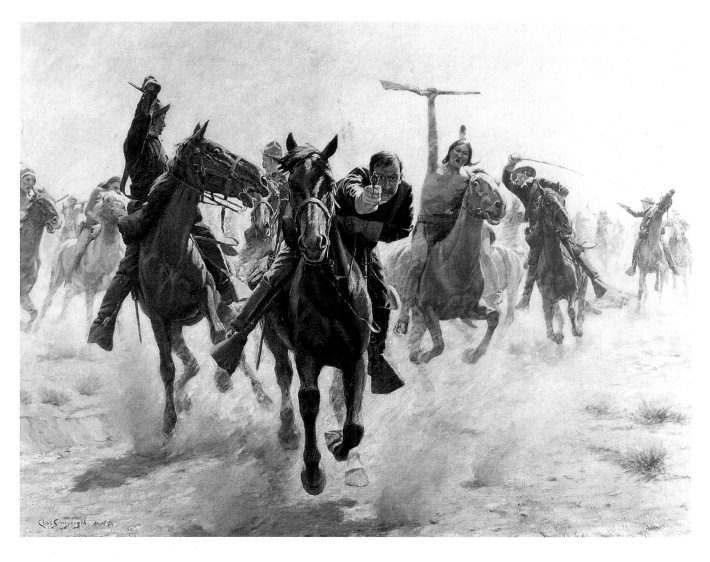

Charles Schreyvogel (1861–1912)
Breaking through the Line, n.d.
Oil on canvas, 39 × 52 in.
Gilcrease Museum, Tulsa, Oklahoma

This artist was fond of taking direct
aim at the viewer. It was a dramatic
visual device he used frequently.

In Nebraska, the Cheyennes were raiding commerce along the Platte Road. Bull-head Sumner campaigned in Nebraska and western Kansas, meeting a band of three hundred Cheyennes along the Solomon River. The cavalrymen faced the Indians pretty equally matched, but the warriors thought they had an edge, having washed their hands in a lake whose waters, according to a medicine man, would protect them from bullets. About to attack, Bull-head gave the order: "Sling—carbine. Draw—saber. Gallop—march! Charge!"

The Indians panicked and were cut to pieces. For the water's magic was against bullets, not sabers. Sumner's troops pursued the fleeing band for seven miles. Like the Sioux, the Cheyennes now sued for peace. They would remain relatively peaceful until Colonel John M. Chivington provoked war with them in 1864.

BLUE, GRAY, AND RED

The Civil War in the West was not the same epic struggle that raged in the East. No great cities were lost or won. No decisive strategic ends were achieved. Men fought, and men died—a great many of them Indians. In some places, most notably the Far Southwest, withdrawal of federal troops to other battlegrounds gave Indians license to raid; but in many other places, the massed presence of troops was a good excuse to pursue and kill Indians. After all, many settlers and army officers were convinced that the Indians had sided with Confederate interests.

Kansas experienced a prelude to the war during the 1850s when, with Nebraska, it was created by Congress as a "popular sovereignty" territory—that is, a territory empowered to vote for or against slavery within its boundaries, without interference from the federal government. A series of four constitutional conventions were convened between 1855 and 1859 alternately espousing antislavery and proslavery policies. During this period, free state and proslavery factions fought so bitterly—perhaps two hundred persons died—that the territory became known nationally as "Bleeding Kansas." An organized antislavery guerrilla movement got under way on the eve of Civil War, in 1858, with the formation of the Jayhawkers. Almost immediately, "Doc" Charles R. Jennison, a New Yorker transplanted to Kansas, used the abolitionist banner of the Jayhawkers as a screen behind which he and his men raided western Missouri, robbing, looting, and murdering. Soon known as the "Independent Mounted Kansas Jayhawkers"—officially the Seventh Kansas Regiment—they pillaged the pro-South town of Harrisonville, Missouri, in July 1861. In December of that year they raided and occupied Independence, terrorizing, robbing, and killing virtually at random. Following this outrage, Doc Jennison was relieved of command, but in 1863 he and the Jayhawkers reemerged as the Red Legs, named for the red leggings they wore, and resumed depredations against western Missouri.

Early in the war, southern Missouri saw two substantial battles, at Wilson's Creek (August 10, 1861) and at Pea Ridge (March 6–8, 1862). Missouri's pro-South governor, Claiborne F. Jackson, had hurriedly convened, at the town of Neosho, a session of the legislature. In the absence of a quorum, pro-South representatives passed a secession ordinance. Nevertheless, the Battle of Pea Ridge brought most of Missouri under federal control, although guerrilla fighting continued, aggravated first by Union General John C. Frémont's blustering ineptitude. Famed as a western explorer and prime mover of the California Bear Flag Rebellion, Frémont was commissioned a major general at the outbreak of the Civil War and put in command of western forces. One of his

Charles Schreyvogel (1861–1912)
Dead Sure, 1902
Oil on canvas, 19 ¾ × 15 ¾ in.
The Rockwell Museum, Corning,
New York

The tomahawk at the lower left tells us that the trooper's bullet found its mark.

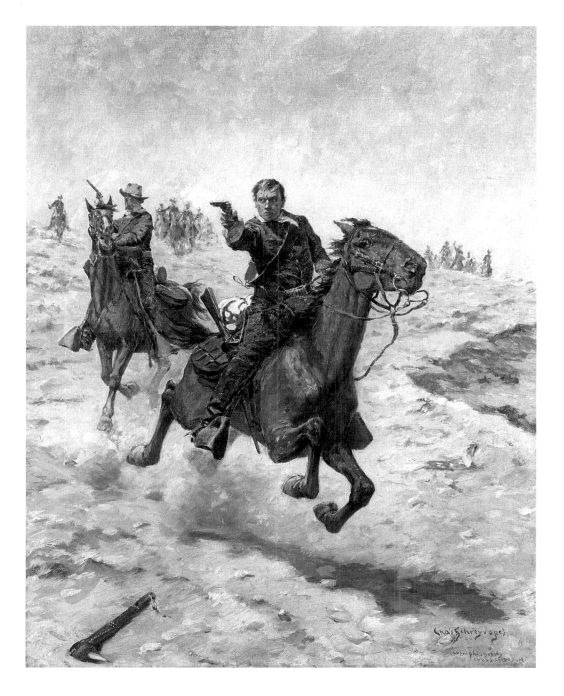

first acts, in 1861, was to proclaim the emancipation of Missouri slaves and the confiscation of property belonging to Southern sympathizers. The effect of this was an increase in guerrilla warfare between Missourians, and the transfer of Frémont from a short-lived command in the West to a short-lived command in West Virginia.

Guerrilla conflicts between Missouri and Kansas reached a crescendo in 1863 when, on August 21, William Clarke Quantrill led 450 raiders to the abolitionist stronghold of Lawrence, Kansas, and blithely—there is no other word for it—massacred 150 townspeople and burned much of the town. Quantrill, born in Ohio in 1837, taught school for a time in Ohio and in Illinois before he moved west and embarked on a career as a gambler and horse thief. Blond and coldly handsome—those who saw him remembered his steely, heavy-lidded eyes—Quantrill proved a charismatic leader. He and his small band of raiders were taken into the regular Confederate army after they participated in the capture of Independence during August 1862. It was under Quantrill's tutelage that Frank and Jesse James and the Younger brothers, Cole and Jim, learned the art of ambush and of handling the Colt revolvers that were the raiders' weapons of choice. Perhaps they also learned a code of killing that knew no moral boundaries, as Quantrill stopped at nothing to accomplish his objective, including wearing captured federal uniforms to surprise the enemy. At Baxter Springs, Kansas, 65 of a troop of 100 federals were slain when Quantrill and his men approached them in Union blue. Quantrill himself was killed on May 10, 1865, by Union guerrillas as he traveled through Kentucky, reportedly on his way to Washington, D.C., where he planned to assassinate President Lincoln.

Farther west, Texas was a major problem for the North. Pro-Union governor Sam Houston was forced out of office when the state seceded in February 1861, and General David E. Twiggs, federal commander of the army's Department of Texas, soon surrendered all property and supplies to the Confederates. Union forces enjoyed a temporary victory in October 1862 when a seaborne squadron captured Galveston. The town, a crucial Confederate supply point, was occupied by federal troops in December, but quickly retaken by Confederates aboard riverboats that had been converted to gunboats. By 1863, the Union threw a blockade around Galveston, which reduced but did not stop the flow of Confederate supplies. Combined with Admiral David G. Farragut's capture of New Orleans in April 1862, however, the blockade helped sever Texas and the rest of the Confederate West from the Confederate states east of the Mississippi.

In the meantime, Texas Confederates under Colonel John Robert Baylor took Fort Bliss in El Paso during July of 1861 and marched into the Mesilla valley of New Mexico, taking Fort Fillmore and Fort Stanton, whereupon Baylor proclaimed the Confederate Territory of

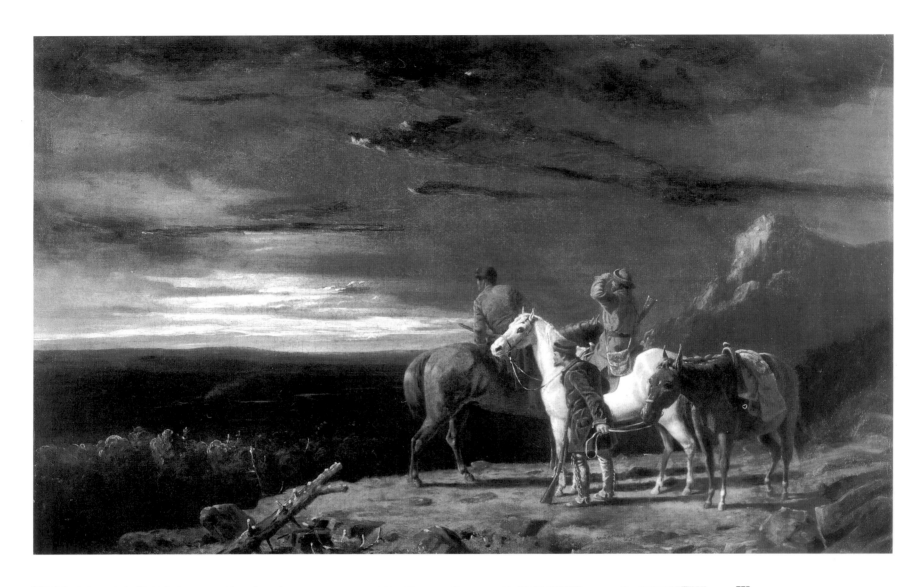

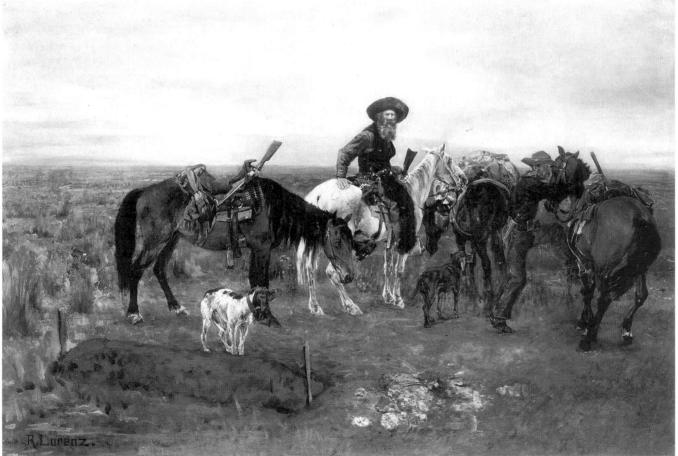

William Tylee Ranney (1813–1857)
The Scouting Party, 1851
Oil on canvas, 22 × 36 in.
Thyssen-Bornemisza Collection,
Lugano, Switzerland

This painting enjoyed considerable
contemporary popularity in the form
of a lithograph engraved for the Art-
Union.

Richard Lorenz (1858–1915)
Burial on the Plains, n.d.
Oil on canvas, 42 × 60 in.
Courtesy of The Anschutz Collection

Ralph Albert Blakelock (1847–1919)
Western Landscape, n.d.
Oil on canvas, 34 ¼ × 60 in.
The Newark Museum; Gift of the
Board of Directors of the National
Newark and Essex Bank

Maverick son of a New York City doctor, Blakelock left college in 1866 to paint landscapes. Eschewing the course of European study virtually mandatory for "serious" nineteenth-century American artists, Blakelock sketched in the West from 1869 until about 1872, even taking up residence among various Indian tribes. His later style, developed some years after his western period, was a romantic Impressionism so different from the work of his contemporaries that the artist was unable to sell his paintings. He and his large family—nine children—descended into abject poverty, and Blakelock himself became violently insane. He was confined to an asylum for the last twenty years of his life.

Arizona (which included all of present-day Arizona and New Mexico south of the thirty-fourth parallel) and named himself governor. Baylor's efforts were followed during the winter of 1861–62 by a larger Confederate invasion led by General Henry H. Sibley and aimed at the capture of all of New Mexico, seizure of the Colorado silver mines, and possibly the occupation of Southern California. Sibley moved up the Rio Grande, intent on taking Fort Union, at the time the best-provisioned Union post in the Southwest.

It was the headquarters of Colonel Edward R. S. Canby, commander of the Department of New Mexico under whom Sibley—his brother-in-law—had served as a major just a few months before. As the Texas invaders threatened, Canby had his hands full with Navajo raids in New Mexico and unauthorized, highly provocative New Mexican counterraids. Learning that the majority of New Mexicans were loyal to the Union, Canby hastily sought to organize them as the First and Second Regiments of New Mexican Volunteers. This gesture, however, failed to bring the volunteers under Canby's control. Lieutenant Colonel Manuel Chaves, second in command of the Second Regiment, was placed in charge of Fort Fauntleroy at Ojo del Oso on August 9 with a detachment of 210 officers and men. As the Canby Treaty of February 1861 had promised, Chaves's men began distributing rations, including liquor, to the Navajos in Au-

gust and September. A careless, festival atmosphere prevailed, and, along with the liquor, came gambling. A series of horse races were run, the featured event being a contest between Chief Manuelito on a Navajo pony and an army lieutenant on a quarter horse. Many bets were laid.

Early in the race it was apparent that Manuelito had lost control of his mount, which soon ran off the track. The horse's rein and bridle, the Indians claimed, had been slashed with a knife. Despite Indian protests, the "judges"—all soldiers of the Second New Mexican Regiment—declared the quarter horse the winner. The soldiers formed a victory parade into the fort, as the angered Navajos stormed after them, only to have the gates shut in their faces. One Navajo tried to force his way in. A sentinel shot and killed him. Then Colonel Chaves turned his troops on the five hundred or so Navajos gathered outside the fort. One New Mexican, Captain Nicholas Hodt, disgusted by what was happening, depicted the carnage in a memorandum read into the Congressional Record:

The Navahos, squaws, and children ran in all directions and were shot and bayoneted. I succeeded in forming about twenty men. . . . I then marched out to the east side of the post; there I saw a soldier murdering two little children and a woman. I halloed immediately to the soldier

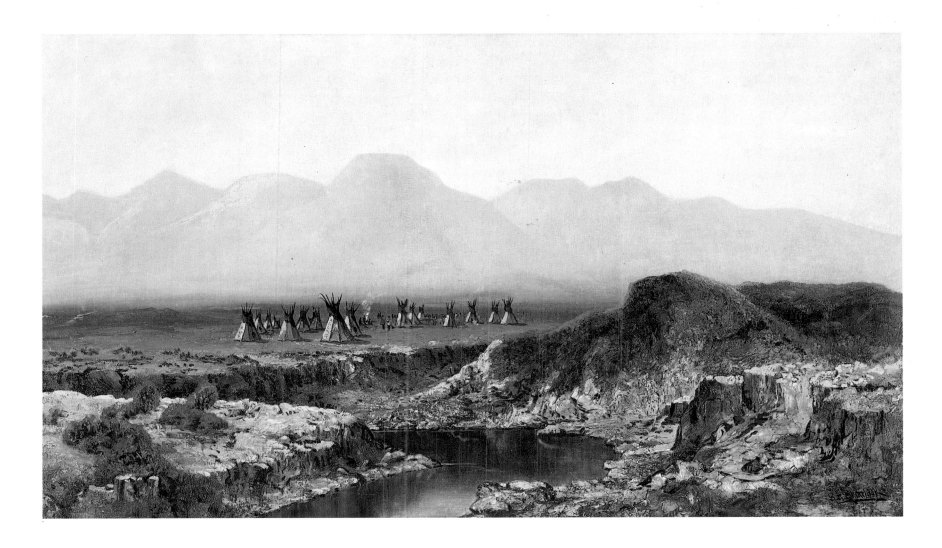

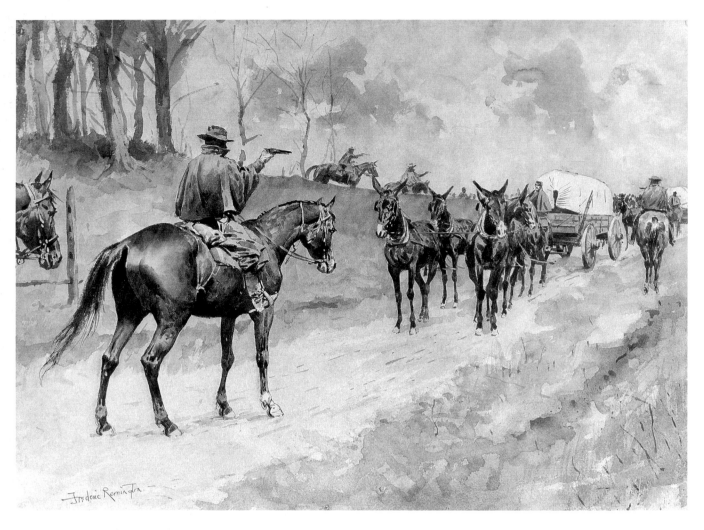

to stop. He looked up, but did not obey my order. . . .
Meanwhile the colonel had given orders to the officer of
the day to have the artillery brought out to open upon
the Indians. The sergeant in charge of the mountain
howitzers pretended not to understand the order given,
for he considered it an unlawful order; but being cursed
by the officer of the day, and threatened, he had to exe-
cute the order or else get himself in trouble.

Thirty or forty Navajos were killed. The rest fled
and began a campaign of raiding. After relieving Chaves
and arresting him, Canby ordered John Ward, the Indian agent, to attempt to persuade the Indians to gather
at Cubero, where they could be given the "protection" of
the government during the impending Confederate invasion. Canby's primary aim, of course, was to concentrate
the Indians where they could be watched and kept from
alliances with rebel forces. Canby dispatched the celebrated Kit Carson, commander of the First Regiment of
New Mexican Volunteers, to move vigorously against any
Navajos who persisted in raiding. He was ordered to take
no prisoners.

It was on February 21, 1862, that the anticipated
contest between Sibley and Canby took place at Val-
verde, New Mexico. The result was a Confederate victory. Sibley next took Santa Fe and pressed on toward
Fort Union. En route, at La Glorietta Pass, the Confederates encountered a Union force under the command of

Colonel John Slough. In a battle sometimes called "the
Gettysburg of the West," March 26–28, Slough's regulars, reinforced by Colorado volunteers rushed to the
scene by Governor William Gilpin, defeated the Texans.
Major John M. Chivington, soon to become infamous for
his unbridled policy of Indian extermination, led a flanking party that destroyed the Confederates' supply train.
Sibley's invaders were forced to retreat from New
Mexico.

Simultaneously with the victories of Slough and
Chivington, Brigadier General James Henry Carleton
was sweeping through the Southwest with his "California
Column" of Union regulars. They pushed the Confederates out of Arizona—fighting the westernmost battle of
the Civil War, at Picacho Peak on April 15, 1862—and
southern New Mexico. By the end of 1862 the short-lived
Confederate Territory of Arizona was no more, and both
Arizona and New Mexico were securely in Union hands.

Carleton's work was by no means finished. With the
rebels out of the way, he now turned his attention to the
raiding Mescalero Apaches and Navajos. A New Englander, born in Lubec, Maine, in 1814, James Henry
Carleton first saw action as a militiaman in 1838, during
the so-called Lumberjack War between his home state
and New Brunswick, Canada. Discharged from the militia in 1839, he collected letters of recommendation from
his commanding officers, passed a test in Washington,
D.C., and was commissioned a second lieutenant of dra-

JULES TAVERNIER

—

BORN 1844, PARIS

DIED 1889, HONOLULU

—

A pupil of Felix Barriès, Tavernier gained some recognition as a landscape and genre painter, exhibiting his work in the Paris Salon from 1865 to 1870. After service in the Franco-Prussian War, he immigrated to the United States, apparently hounded out of France as a Communist.

In New York, the artist found work as an illustrator for the *Graphic* and *Harper's,* which sent him in 1873 with Paul Frenzeny on a cross-country sketching tour to San Francisco. Their work was published from 1873 to 1876. The series depicted scenes of western emigration as well as a cattle drive across Indian Territory, and rail and stagecoach journeys.

When Tavernier reached San Francisco in 1874, he was elected to the Bohemian Club and soon set up a studio where he produced western and Indian scenes based on his illustration. Although his paintings sold well, the artist's work habits were so erratic and his life-style so extravagant that he was continually dunned for bad debts. In 1884, Tavernier's friends raised enough money to send the artist to Hawaii to escape his creditors and the sheriff.

Tavernier continued to work in Hawaii, painting island landscapes, but was a virtual prisoner because of his debts. He died of acute alcoholism.

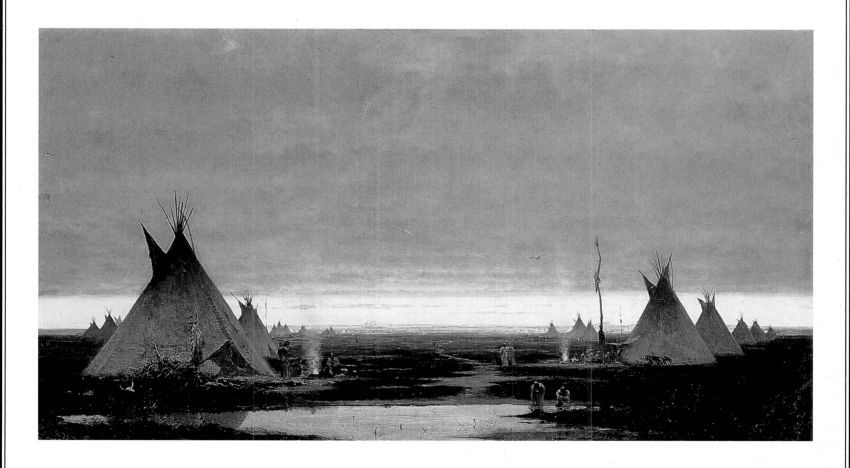

goons. He served in several western posts and fought in the Battle of Buena Vista during the Mexican War. He next turned his attention to the Mescalero and Jicarilla Apaches as well as Navajos, becoming a disciple of total warfare against the Indian and advocating a scorched earth policy. To hone his skills, he came back east briefly in 1856, to Philadelphia, where he studied European cavalry methods, including those of the Cossacks. In 1858, Carleton took seven hundred recruits to California (via the Isthmus route), where he served under his longtime friend, General Edwin V. Sumner. With the outbreak of the Civil War, Major Carleton was promoted to colonel and given command of a volunteer outfit, the First California Regiment of Infantry—better known as the California Column.

Since the "Bascom Affair"—the capture and execution of Cochise's relatives on unfounded charges of theft and kidnapping—settlements and trade routes between El Paso and Tucson had felt the wrath not only of Cochise's band of Apaches, but those led by his ally, Mangas Coloradas. The federal abandonment of Forts Buchanan, Breckinridge, and Fillmore in the face of the Confederate invasion of New Mexico was interpreted by the Apaches as a sign that the "bluecoats" feared *them,* so that when, in July 1862, more bluecoats were seen approaching from the west, the Apaches were ready to fight.

It was the van of Carleton's California Column, 119 infantry men and 7 cavalrymen equipped with two howitzers, led by Captain Thomas L. Roberts. On July 15 they marched into Apache Pass and were ambushed by 700 warriors under Cochise. As had happened on previous occasions, the soldiers were saved by their howitzers, and Roberts sent 6 of the cavalrymen back to warn the wagon train that was following him. Apaches pursued the messengers, hitting the horse of one. Private John Teal used the carcass of his mount as a breastwork and fired rapidly with his modern breech-loading carbine. These Apaches were apparently familiar only with the old muzzle loaders and, instead of attacking Teal, merely circled his position, taking an occasional potshot. The private returned fire, hitting what he called "a prominent Indian," after which the others retreated.

That "prominent Indian" was none other than the six-foot, six-inch-tall Mimbres Apache chief Mangas Coloradas, whose height made him a good target. His men took him to Mexico, where they forced a physician in Sonora to extract the bullet, and the chief recovered, resuming his raids against settlers and miners and skirmishing with Carleton's troops. For some reason, on January 17, 1863, Mangas Coloradas agreed to meet with Captain E. D. Shirland, who was serving under Brigadier General Joseph R. West, commander of the southern sector of Carleton's Department of New Mexico. Despite his flag of truce, the chief was seized and delivered to West's camp.

The official story is that West informed Mangas Coloradas that, because he had come voluntarily, he would not be executed, but that "the remainder of his days would be spent as a prisoner" and that his life was "forfeit" if he attempted escape. According to the official report, he made three escape attempts and was shot and killed on the third. An American prospector present at West's camp had a different story, reporting that West told his troopers, "Men, that old murderer has got away from every soldier command and has left a trail of blood for five hundred miles on the old [Butterfield] stage line. I want him dead or alive tomorrow morning, do you understand. *I want him dead."* According to the prospector, guards heated bayonets in the campfire and applied them to the chief's feet. When he rose up to protest, the guards emptied their muskets into him point-blank, then shot him four times in the head with their pistols.

Like E. R. S. Canby, whom he had replaced as commander of the Department of New Mexico, Carleton called upon the services of the redoubtable Indian fighter Kit Carson. Born in the North Carolina backcountry in 1809, Carson learned the ways of the wilderness early. His parents destined him for a legal career, and he had three years of schooling in Missouri, to which the family moved in 1812, but the death of his father in 1818 compelled the boy to stay at home to tend to the planting and harvesting. His mother apprenticed him to a saddlemaker in 1825, from whom the young man bolted the following year to join a Santa Fe trading caravan as a herder. He remained in New Mexico, becoming a trapper, Indian fighter, and trailblazer. He served with distinction in the Mexican War, after which he settled with his Mexican wife near Taos, to farm. In 1853, he was appointed Indian agent for the Utes, a post he held for the next seven years, by all accounts serving with honesty, intelligence, and compassion—qualities hard to come by in the generally corrupt, callous, and inept Indian agency system. Having resigned as agent at the outbreak of Civil War, Carson was not wholly prepared to follow Carleton's order to him of September 1862, to pursue Mescalero Apaches and hold no "council . . . with the Indians, nor any talks. The men are to be slain whenever and wherever they can be found."

Carson did pursue the Mescaleros, but he also arranged for five chiefs to visit Santa Fe for talks with Carleton. En route, two of the chiefs met a detachment of soldiers commanded by Captain James (Paddy) Graydon, in civilian life a saloonkeeper. Graydon offered them beef and flour for the journey, and the two parties went on their way, only to meet again a short time later. For some reason—no one knows why—Graydon went into the chiefs' camp, liquored them up, and shot them dead, the chiefs and their men. Three other chiefs did reach Santa Fe and informed General Carleton that they no longer had the heart to fight. "Do with us as may seem good to you," the chiefs told Carleton, "but do not forget we are men and braves."

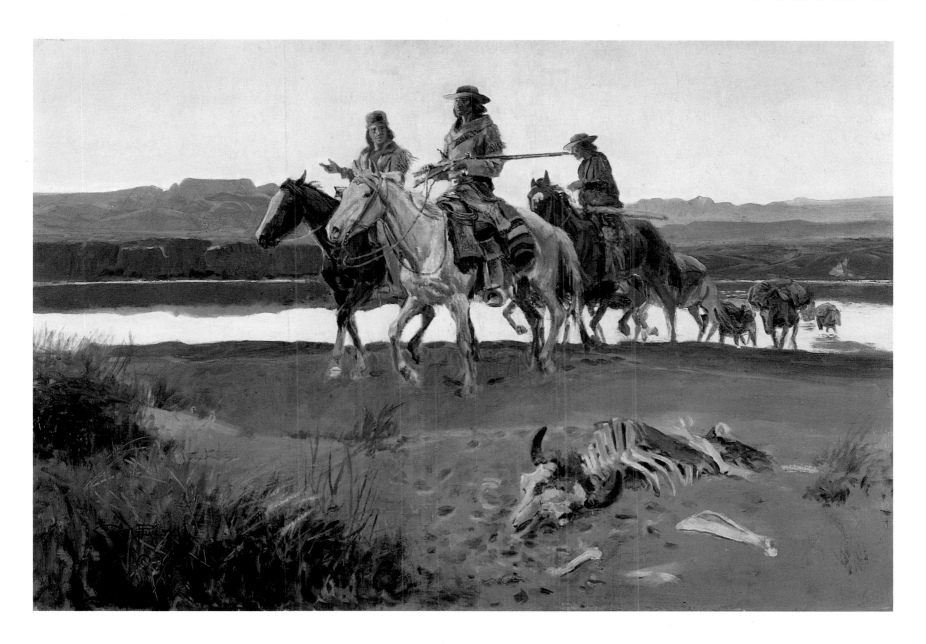

Charles M. Russell (1864–1926)
Carson's Men, 1913
Oil on canvas, 24 × 35 ½ in.
Gilcrease Museum, Tulsa, Oklahoma

The serene strength of this painting conveys much about Kit Carson's personality. Famed as a deadly effective Indian fighter, Carson nevertheless persistently counseled peace.

What Carleton proposed to do with them—and, shortly, with the Navajos as well—was to round them up and send them to a forty-mile-square reservation at the Bosque Redondo on the Pecos River in New Mexico. Carleton's own board of officers, dispatched to inspect the site, reported negatively on it, but Carleton thought it ideal: fifty miles remote from any white settlement (except for Fort Sumner, which would guard it), but close to sources of water and game, including buffalo plains. Carleton replied to the Mescalero chiefs that there would be no peace unless they and their people marched to the Bosque. Many Mescaleros fled to Mexico; others marched to the Bosque Redondo.

Meanwhile, many of the Navajos were also wearying of the unceasing warfare Carleton was waging against them. When eighteen important Navajo chiefs, including the renowned Delgadito and Barboncito (but not the ever-recalcitrant Manuelito), came to Santa Fe seeking terms of peace, Carleton replied harshly. Later, Carleton sent word to Delgadito and Barboncito that "we have no desire to make war upon them and other good Navajoes; but the troops cannot tell the good from the bad, and we cannot nor will tolerate their staying as a peace party among those upon whom we intend to make war." Their only alternative to war, Carleton told them, was to take their people to the Bosque Redondo reservation. He set a deadline of July 20, 1863, after which "every Navajo that is seen will be considered as hostile and treated accordingly . . . after that day the door now open will be closed." Barboncito replied: "I will not go to the Bosque. I will never leave my country, not even if it means that I will be killed."

When July 20 came and went, Kit Carson set out with 736 men and officers to make war on the Navajos. Thirteen warriors were dead before the end of the month and 11 women and children in captivity. Far more significant was the widespread destruction of Navajo fields and orchards. Carleton offered a twenty-dollar bounty for each horse or mule captured and a dollar for each sheep. Although Navajo raiding continued—ten thousand sheep stolen in August alone—the Indians did begin to surrender to confinement at the Bosque Redondo: 51 at the end of September, 188 in November, more than 500 in January. By March, a total of 2,138 Navajos were sent from

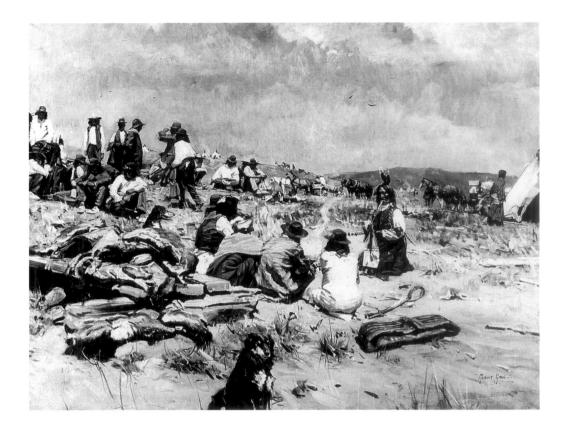

W. Gilbert Gaul (1855–1919)
Issuing Government Beef, n.d.
Oil on canvas, 30 × 42 in.
Gilcrease Museum, Tulsa, Oklahoma

By concentrating them on
reservations, the government
deprived the Indians of most means
of self-subsistence and made them
dependent on a federal dole. Rations
often consisted of condemned beef
rejected for U.S. Army consumption.

William Tylee Ranney (1813–1857)
Hunting Wild Horses (The Lasso),
1846
Oil on canvas, 36 × 54 in.
Gene Autry Western Heritage
Museum, Los Angeles

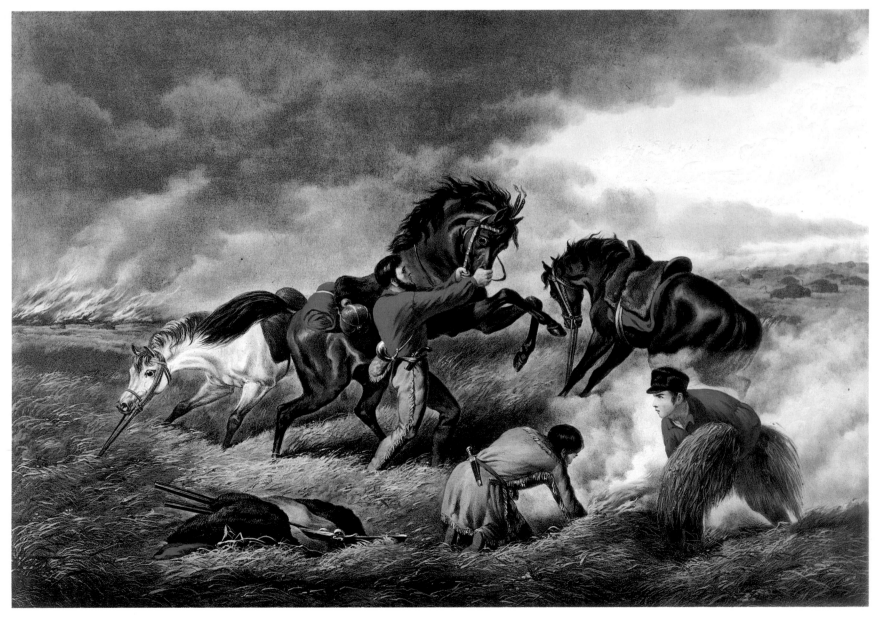

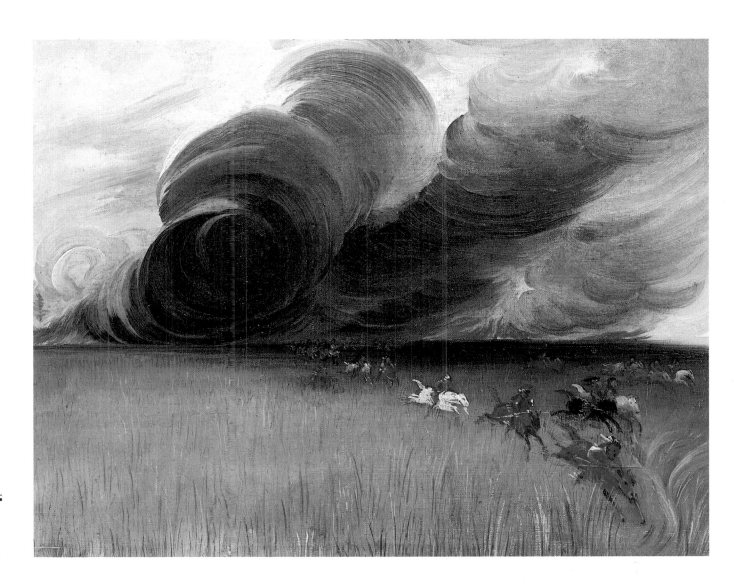

George Catlin (1796–1872)
Prairie Meadows Burning, 1832
Oil on canvas, 11 × 14 ⅛ in.
National Museum of American Art,
Smithsonian Institution;
Gift of Mrs. Joseph Harrison, Jr.

Lightning frequently touched off
prairie blazes. Indians also
deliberately set grass fires in order
to flush out game, especially buffalo.

Fort Canby, New Mexico, to the Bosque.

That is when the nightmare began. Although government wagons were furnished to transport the very young, the old, and the infirm, the remainder marched. Conditions at Fort Canby were deplorable, and 126 Navajos died there of dysentery. More died en route to the Bosque itself; reportedly, some, no longer able to march, were shot by their soldier escorts. Eventually, 8,000 Navajos crowded the reservation. There were never sufficient rations to feed them. General Carleton pleaded for 2 million pounds of food, 13,000 yards of cloth for clothing, 7,000 blankets, 20 spinning wheels, 50 mills for grinding corn, farm implements, seeds, and—lastly—600 cotton handkerchiefs. While Congress did appropriate funds, the amount fell short of what was needed. Attempts to teach the traditionally peripatetic Navajos and Apaches sedentary farming techniques failed. By 1864, conditions at "Fair Carletonia'—as the soldiers referred to the Bosque—were desperate. Finally, four years later, Manuelito, Barboncito, and other chiefs were permitted to journey to Washington, D.C., to inform President Andrew Johnson of conditions at the reservation. A month later, peace commissioners visited the Bosque Redondo and concluded that the Navajos "had sunk into a condition of absolute poverty and despair." A treaty was concluded on June 1, returning the Indians to their homeland and declaring it their new reservation.

Indian conflict was not confined to the Southwest and southern plains. The Santee Sioux of Minnesota initially accepted the policy of "concentration" that the Apache and Navajo had so vigorously resisted. Clearly, however, resentment smoldered among them, as they were confined to a narrow strip of land along the upper Minnesota River, hemmed in by growing numbers of Scandinavian and German immigrants and, as usual, prey to a corrupt Indian agency system that diverted funds and supplies guaranteed them by treaty. On August 17, 1862, four Santee men were journeying home after a disappointing hunting trip. One of the hunters dared another to kill a white man. By the end of the day, the Indians had killed five settlers.

The act of violence fanned the flames of resentment into a raging blaze. For some years, the Santees had been split into a militant faction and a party of peace, led by Chief Little Crow. Now the militants took command, pressuring Little Crow to lead his people into war. The very day after the first five killings, some 400 settlers were massacred. Forty-six Minnesota militiamen blundered into the rampage; half their number returned to Fort Ridgely, joining some 300 refugees and a small volunteer garrison of 155. On August 20 and 22, Little Crow led 800 warriors against the fort. As usual, it was howit-

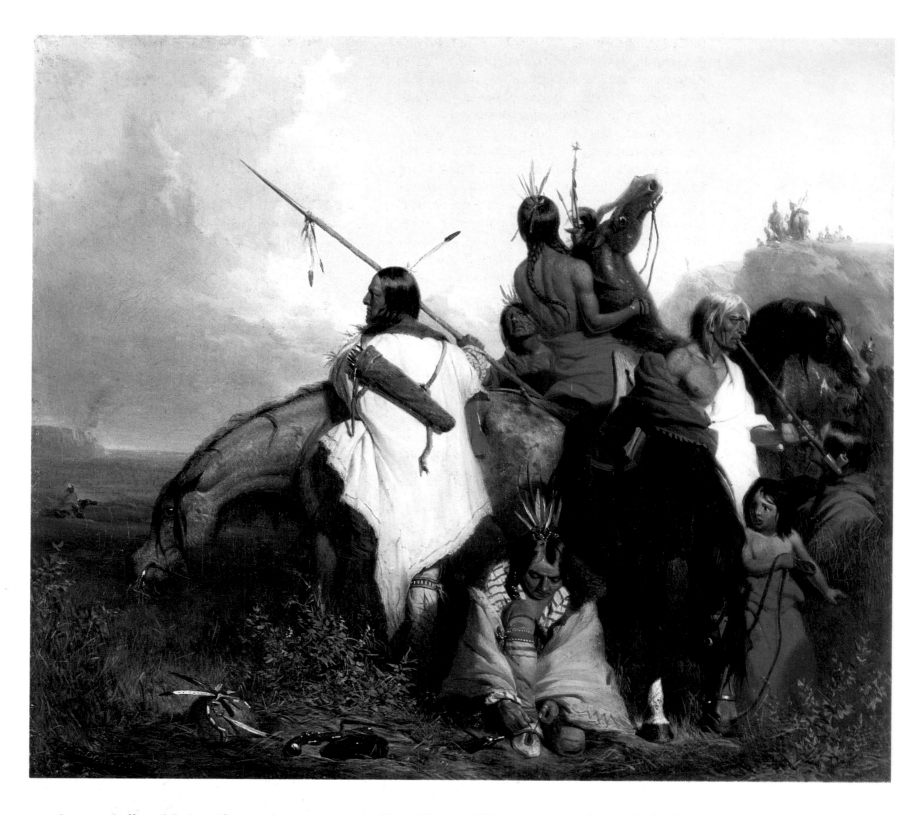

zers that staved off annihilation. After cannister grape-shot had felled 100 warriors, Little Crow withdrew. "With a few guns like that," remarked one Santee, "the Dakotas could rule the earth."

On August 23, a war party of 350 Sioux raided the town of New Ulm. This time, however, the Indians had lost the element of surprise. Townsmen, reinforced by settlers from the surrounding area, forced the Indians to withdraw after a day-long fight. The cost to New Ulm: 100 dead and wounded, 190 buildings burned to the ground. In a single, deadly week of August 1862, 800 Minnesota settlers died.

In September, a relief column, 1,600 strong, led by

Henry Hastings Sibley (not to be confused with the Confederate Sibley) marched into the Minnesota River valley. Seven hundred Sioux challenged this force at Wood Lake on September 23. The Indians were soundly defeated. Within three days, 400 white captives were released, and during the next two weeks some 2,000 Sioux surrendered to Sibley, who hastily convened a military tribunal to try individual Santees accused of specific crimes. Three hundred three Indians were sentenced to be hanged. The remaining 1,700 were transferred to Fort Snelling (present-day Minneapolis)—a hellish march, as angry whites stoned and clubbed many; a baby was snatched from the arms of its mother and beaten to

Charles Deas (1818–1867)
A Group of Sioux, 1845
Oil on canvas, 14 ⅛ × 16 ½ in.
Amon Carter Museum, Fort Worth, Texas

This artist's works are characteristically intense, rich, and charged with nervous energy. The Indian group is massed with a nod toward classical composition, but the traditional triangle is irregular here; each figure is rapt in his own activity, the horses exude explosive energy, and the child's face betrays a wary anxiety.

death. In the meantime, President Abraham Lincoln, doubting the absolute justice of Sibley's tribunal, personally reviewed the 303 death sentences. On December 6 the president notified Sibley that he should "cause to be executed" 39 of the 303 convicted, the balance to be held "subject to further orders." Nevertheless, the 38 hangings (one Indian was given a last-minute reprieve) at Mankato constituted the largest mass execution in American history. (In their carelessness, two Indians not on Lincoln's list were hanged. Only after the lapse of nine years was this fact admitted. "It was a matter of regret that any mistakes were made," declared an official. "I feel sure they were not made intentionally." It is said that one of those hanged had saved a white woman's life during the raiding.)

Far from bringing hostilities on the plains to an end, the defeat of Little Crow marked the beginning of eight years of warfare with the Sioux. The theater of battle shifted from Minnesota to Dakota territory, where Sibley—now commissioned a brigadier—and another general, Alfred Sully, succeeded in stirring to war Santee Sioux refugees and the Teton Sioux as well as the Cheyennes. In Colorado, when Governor John Evans failed to secure mineral-rich Cheyenne and Arapaho hunting grounds in exchange for reservations, he called upon Colonel John M. Chivington, military commander of the territory, to force the Indians out.

He had chosen the right man for the job. A former Methodist minister, Chivington was known as the fighting parson, with a hatred of Indians that was exuberant in its rabidity. He declared in an 1864 speech made in Denver that all Indians should be killed and scalped, including infants. "Nits make lice!" was the way he put it. A militant faction of the Cheyennes, a group of young warriors known as the *Hotamitanio,* or Dog Soldier Society, provided Chivington with sufficient incidents for him to declare the Cheyenne to be at war. He launched a number of attacks, which provoked Indian counterraids. To combat the crisis they had themselves created, Governor Evans and Colonel Chivington formed the Third Colorado Cavalry, comprised of short-term, hundred-day enlistees drawn mainly from Colorado's tough mining camps.

The trouble was that, come winter, a number of Indians, led by Black Kettle, an older chief opposed to the youthful and tempestuous Dog Soldiers, were asking for peace. Through the sympathetic commander of Fort Lyon, Major Edward Wynkoop, they sought an audience with Governor Evans. To Wynkoop, Evans replied: "But what shall I do with the Third Colorado Regiment if I make peace? They have been raised to kill Indians, and they must kill Indians." Nevertheless, Evans and Chivington met with the Cheyennes and Arapahos and told them that those Indians who wanted peace should "submit to military authority" by laying down their arms at a local fort. They left the meeting and marched to Sand Creek, about forty miles northeast of Fort Lyon, where they planned to talk with Major Wynkoop, who issued rations to them. The army, however, would not long tolerate Wynkoop's humane attitude, and on November 5,

Charles M. Russell (1864–1926)
Council of War, c. 1892
Watercolor on paper, 22 ½ × 35 in.
Amon Carter Museum, Fort Worth, Texas

Indian politics were usually democratic to the point of anarchy. Major decisions were debated and decided in often protracted councils, as so-called chiefs, though important, enjoyed no sovereign powers.

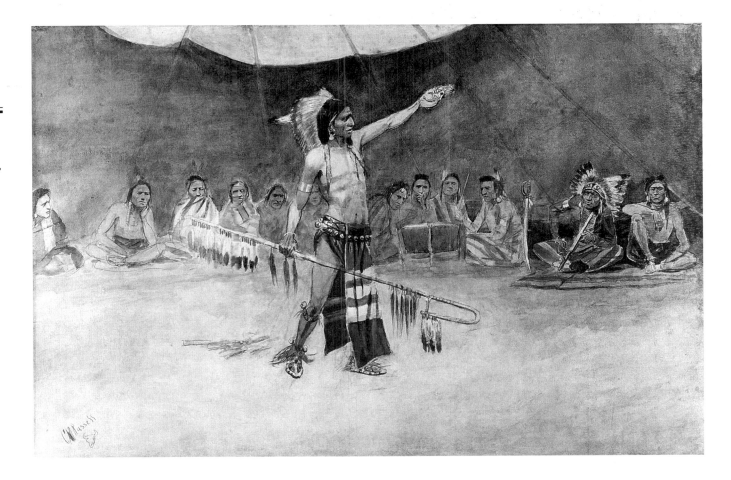

ALFRED JACOB MILLER

—

BORN 1810, BALTIMORE

DIED 1874, BALTIMORE

—

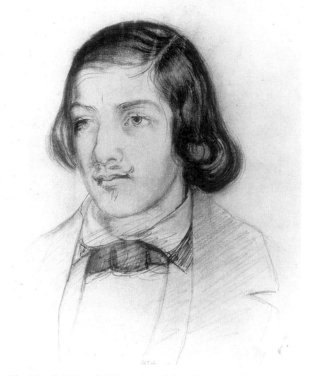

Alfred Jacob Miller, *Self Portrait,* n.d. Pencil on paper, 9 × 7 ⅝ in.
Joslyn Art Museum, Omaha, Nebraska

Son of a well-to-do grocer, Miller began to study drawing at Dr. Craig's school before becoming a student of Thomas Sully in 1831–32. In 1833, he embarked upon the European grand tour fashionable for young men of means and, through the good offices of the United States consul in Paris, gained entrance to the Ecole des Beaux-Arts as its only American student. After further study at the English Life School in Rome, Miller returned home—though he had first to convince French customs officials that the paintings he was carrying out of the country were his copies of Old Masters, not the originals.

In spite of the auspicious opening of his career, Miller's first Baltimore studio failed, and the artist relocated in New Orleans. There he was discovered by Captain William Drummond Stewart, a wealthy Scottish nobleman who had toured the West a number of times. He proposed now to take Miller with him in order to create a pictorial record of his latest excursion. With a party of American Fur Company men, the artist and his patron embarked from the vicinity of present-day Kansas City, Missouri, in 1837, traveling the embryonic Oregon Trail to the Rockies. Miller depicted the rich variety of the trapper's life, including the annual rendezvous, as well as Shoshones, Nez Percés, Flatheads, and Crows. The rendezvous alone attracted about three thousand Indians. Although young Miller did not enjoy life on the frontier, he did record it faithfully and in profusion.

After his return to New Orleans and Baltimore in 1838, the artist worked up his sketches into eighteen finished oils. In 1840,

he accepted Stewart's invitation to be his guest at Murthly Castle in Scotland to paint additional western scenes to decorate his hunting lodge. He also delivered to his patron a portfolio of eighty-three drawings and watercolors.

Miller returned to Baltimore in 1842 and spent the rest of his life there, painting (among other works) a large number of western oils and watercolors for public consumption. Though he presumably continued to work from his field sketches, his later painting became increasingly stylized, conventional, decorative, and further removed from the vivid immediacy of firsthand impression.

one of Chivington's command, Major Scott J. Anthony, relieved Wynkoop as commander of the post. His first action was to cut the Indians' rations and to demand the surrender of their weapons. Out of sheer meanness, Anthony even ordered his men to fire on a group of unarmed Arapahos, who had approached the fort to trade buffalo hides for rations.

By the end of November, most of the Third Colorado had gathered at Fort Lyon. Black Kettle and his Cheyennes were still camped peacefully at Sand Creek, believing they had abided by Evans's and Chivington's order to submit to military authority, believing they were at peace. Chivington deployed his seven-hundred-man force, which included four howitzers, around the camp. When three of Chivington's officers, Captain Silas Soule and Lieutenants Joseph Cramer and James Connor, protested that an attack on a peaceful village was murder and nothing but murder, Chivington barely restrained himself from striking Cramer. "Damn any man who sympathizes with Indians!" he roared. "I have come to kill Indians, and believe it is right and honorable to use any means under God's heaven to kill Indians."

Black Kettle sought to calm his people, who were alarmed at the presence of a surrounding army. He hoisted an American flag and white flag of truce over his tepee. That is when the troops opened fire and charged. The unarmed Indians, warriors, old men, women, and children, ran in panic. Unspeakable atrocities were committed: children's brains were beaten out with clubs, women were gutted like fish ("I saw one squaw cut open with an unborn child . . . lying by her side," reported Captain Soule), warrior corpses were castrated ("I saw the body of White Antelope with the privates cut off," reported Soule, "and I heard a soldier say he was going to make a tobacco pouch out of them"). Two hundred Cheyennes, two-thirds of them women and children, and nine chiefs were killed. Black Kettle escaped.

The massacre galvanized the Indians' resolve to fight, as Sioux, Arapahos, and Cheyennes united in a spasm of savage raids during January and February of 1865. Except for Black Kettle, who still desperately hoped for peace, the Indians moved north, to the Powder, Tongue, and Yellowstone rivers, gathering more allies for a quick strike against the military presence in Colorado. On July 26, 1865, one to three thousand warriors attacked a cavalry detachment at Upper Platte Bridge and destroyed an army supply train before withdrawing for the fall buffalo hunt. In response, General Patrick E. Connor, commander of the northern plains, dispatched a force of three thousand into the Powder

Alfred Jacob Miller (1810–1874)
Indian Village, 1850
Oil on canvas, 30 ¼ × 48 ¼ in.
Amon Carter Museum, Fort Worth, Texas

While his depiction is picturesque and tinged with romanticism, Miller effectively suggests the transient nature of an Indian "village."

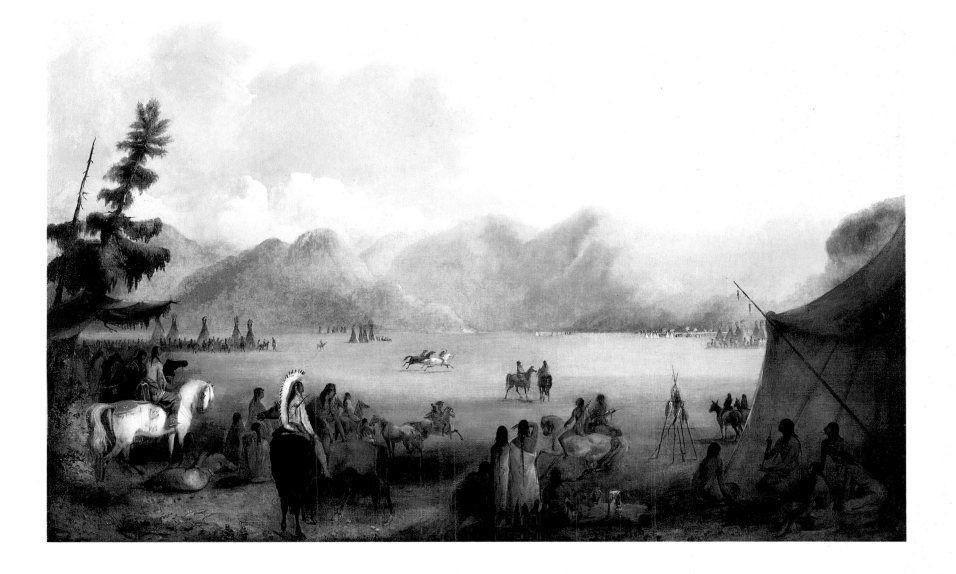

River country and destroyed one Arapaho village and engaged the Sioux. The early onset of winter storms forced the abandonment of the campaign, as Connor's men nearly starved to death. The campaign had cost some twenty million dollars and had produced little result—except to help convince Congress to *reduce* troop numbers and military appropriations. The end of the Civil War had not released soldiers to fight the Indians, but had triggered a frenzy for rapid demobilization. With its manpower limited, the army was told to confine itself to patrolling and protecting trade and travel routes.

VICTORY AND DEFEAT

While the end of the Civil War did not bring a rush of reinforcements to the western frontier, it did free up for western service two able and aggressive commanders, General William Tecumseh Sherman and Sherman's second in command, General Philip H. Sheridan. Neither man suffered ambivalent feelings about combat. During the recent conflict between the states, both had amply demonstrated a commitment to "total war," that is, warfare not limited to one army fighting another, but against

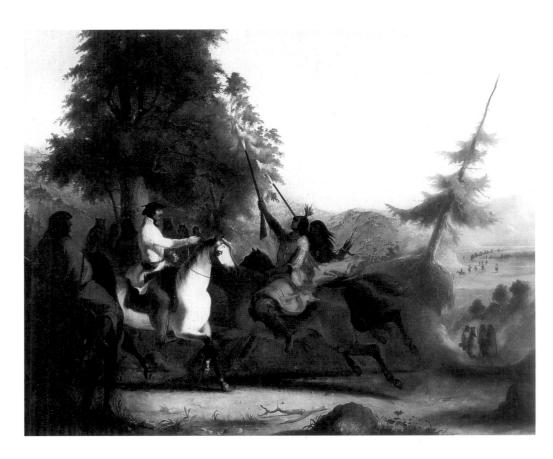

Alfred Jacob Miller (1810–1874)
Sir William Drummond Stewart Meeting Indian Chief, n.d.
Oil on canvas, 33 × 42 in.
Gilcrease Museum, Tulsa, Oklahoma

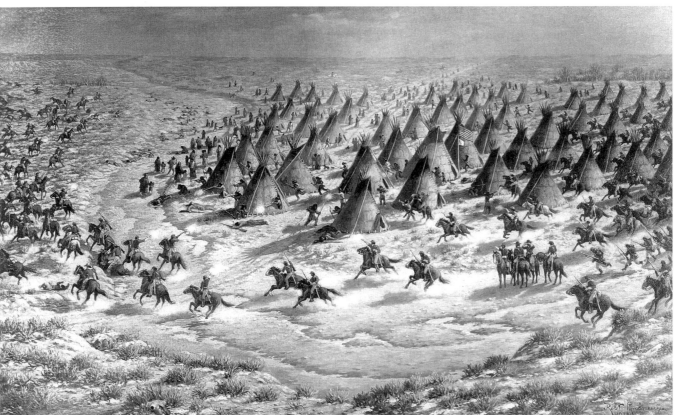

Robert Lindneux (1871–1970)
The Sand Creek Massacre, 1936
Oil on canvas, 32 ¼ × 52 in.
Colorado Historical Society

This self-proclaimed historian of the West was born in New York in 1871 and died ninety-nine years later in Denver. Note that the artist faithfully depicts the American flag Black Kettle raised above a flag of truce in a vain attempt to signify his allegiance and peaceful intentions.

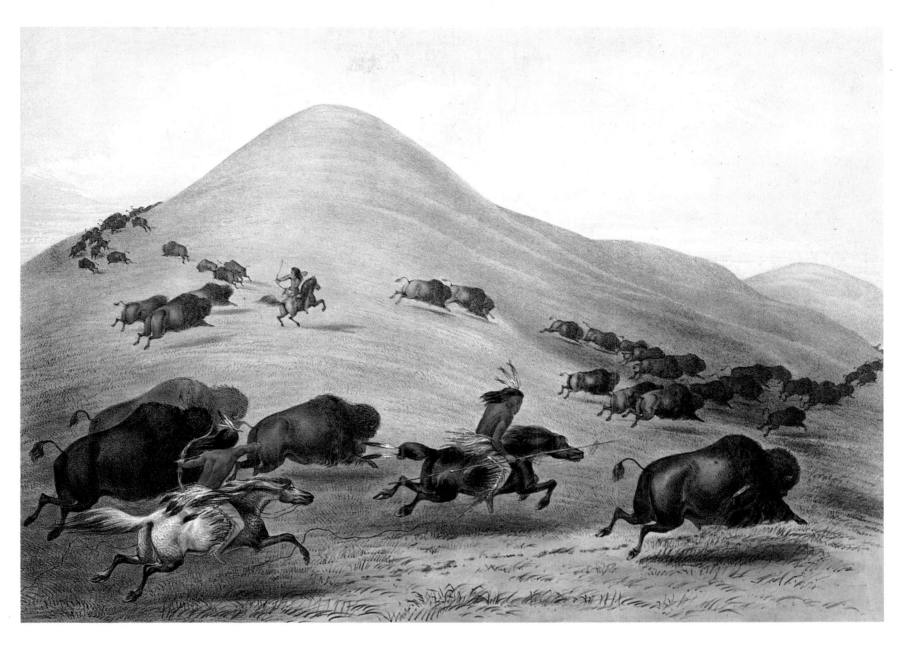

George Catlin (1796–1872)
Buffalo Hunt, Chase
Lithograph from *Catlin's North American Indian Portfolio*, 1845
Courtesy Library of Congress

the entire enemy population, soldiers and civilians alike. The swath of charred ruins Sherman left as a token of his "march to the sea" was the South's lesson in the new combat. Yet Sherman realized that the postwar army he commanded was hardly adequate to a comparable task. He craved a year or two of peace on the plains in order to effect a transition between the disbanding volunteer forces and the installation of the regular army. He also desperately needed time to whip his raw and poorly trained regiments into shape. Accordingly, a series of treaties was signed with the plains tribes: the Kiowas, Comanches, Kiowa-Apaches, Cheyennes, and Arapahos in the southern plains; the seven tribes of the Teton Sioux, and the Yankton Sioux in the northern plains.

The peace was broken first in the north. While the Tetons had agreed to withdraw from the vital Bozeman Trail and allow whites free passage on it, Chief Red Cloud was concerned that doing so would merely open his land to invasion. He went to Fort Laramie to negotiate terms with the peace commissioners there. During the discussions, an infantry column commanded by Colonel Henry B. Carrington marched into the fort. Their

mission, Red Cloud heard, was to build forts to protect the Bozeman Trail. "The Great Father sends us presents and wants us to sell him the road," Red Cloud observed, "but White Chief goes with soldiers to steal the road before Indians say Yes or No." Red Cloud now refused to agree to allow whites to use the trail.

Meanwhile, Carrington established three forts, Fort Reno and Fort Phil Kearny (his headquarters) in Wyoming, and Fort C. F. Smith in Montana. Red Cloud struck the forts before they were completed, forcing Carrington's soldiers into a desperate defensive posture. Rather than spend time preparing his troops for combat—two-thirds were raw recruits—Carrington kept them hard at the task of building forts that were far more complicated and elaborate than frontier conditions and harassment from hostile Indians warranted. His officers bridled under their timid and obsessive commander. One of them, Captain William J. Fetterman, sick of cowering in a stockade fort, boasted that with eighty men he could ride through the entire Sioux nation. On December 6, 1866, Indians attacked a wagon train hauling wood on a road near the Bozeman Trail. Carrington sent Fetter-

BERT GREER PHILLIPS

—

BORN 1868, HUDSON, NEW YORK

DIED 1956, SAN DIEGO, CALIFORNIA

—

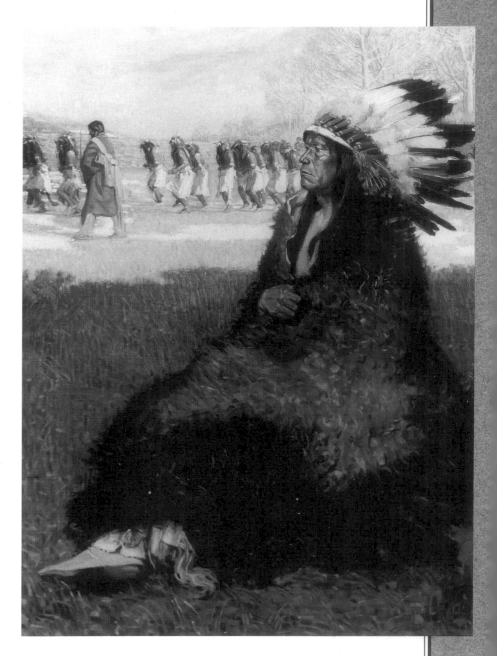

Raised near a Mohican battlefield, Phillips grew up steeped in the Indian world of James Fenimore Cooper. When he and Ernest Blumenschein suffered a broken wagon wheel near Taos during a sketching tour of the Southwest, Phillips fell in love with the Indian village and settled in it immediately, thereby becoming the first of the full-time Taos artists.

After early study at the Art Students League and the National Academy of Design in New York, Phillips painted watercolor landscapes in England during 1894 and, the next year, enrolled at the Académie Julian in Paris. It was there that fellow student Joseph Henry Sharp told him (and Blumenschein) about Taos. In 1912, Phillips became one of the six founding members of the important Taos Society of Artists.

For sixty years, Phillips painted vivid, high-keyed oils of Pueblo Indian life. While many of his Taos colleagues turned increasingly to a modernist aesthetic, Phillips remained a romantic visionary, his paintings nevertheless firmly anchored in the here and now by such realistic touches as the scrupulous delineation of Indian artifacts, of which Phillips amassed a fine and extensive collection.

Will Connell, *Bert Phillips,* 1932. Photograph. The Harwood Foundation Museum, Taos, New Mexico.

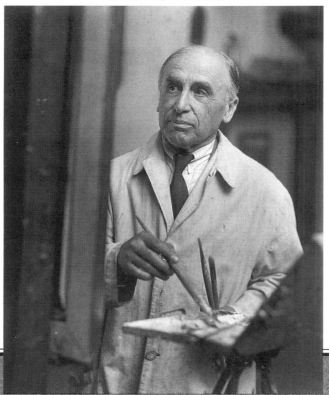

Bert Greer Phillips (1868–1956)
Captain of the Buffalo Dance, 1916
Oil on canvas, 40 × 30 in.
Courtesy of The Anschutz Collection

American artists delighted in the Indian's celebrated stoicism even as the federal government sought resigned compliance from the red man.

man and another officer, Lieutenant Horatio S. Bingham, with thirty cavalrymen to drive the Sioux west while he himself, with twenty-five mounted infantrymen, would cut them off from behind.

The maneuver was a disaster, as the inexperienced soldiers panicked and stampeded out of control. Lieutenant Bingham was shot through with arrows as he tried to rally the forces, and Carrington, distracted by engagement with another band of Indians, never arrived to join forces with Fetterman's troops. The soldiers were forced to withdraw to Fort Phil Kearny.

On December 21, the Indians again attacked the wood train. This time, they massed between fifteen hundred and two thousand warriors, who hid in ravines and along a ridge near the trail. Again, Carrington dispatched Fetterman to relieve the besieged train, warning him not to pursue the Indians beyond Lodge Trail Ridge, but to remain on the wood road, merely drive them off, and then retire. This time, Fetterman hand picked a force of forty-nine experienced infantrymen. Lieutenant George W. Grummond followed him out of the stockade with twenty-seven cavalrymen. Captain Frederick H. Brown and two civilians came along to see the fight.

Fetterman had no intention of following Carrington's order to keep to the wood road and do nothing more than relieve the wood train. He marched his men away from the road and toward the Bozeman Trail itself, disappearing behind the Sullivant Hills. The sound of heavy gunfire alarmed Carrington, who sent forty infantry and dismounted cavalrymen under the bibulous Cap-

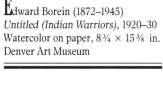

Edward Borein (1872–1945)
Untitled (Indian Warriors), 1920–30
Watercolor on paper, 8¾ × 15⅜ in.
Denver Art Museum

tain Tenodor Ten Eyck to assist Fetterman. Reaching the summit of the ridge, they saw hundreds of warriors. Along the road to Peno Valley, they discovered the naked and mutilated bodies of Fetterman and his command: counting Grummond's cavalry, eighty men.

Though no one was left alive to tell the tale, it was clear that the brash Fetterman had blundered into a trap set by a daring young Oglala Sioux warrior named Crazy Horse. He led a small decoy party that lured Fetterman beyond Lodge Trail Ridge and into a valley of death. It was the kind of fight the Indians favored: ambush from concealment at close quarters and with overwhelming superiority of numbers. For the army, it was a stunning defeat and a bitter humiliation.

The Sioux did not repeat their triumph on August 1 and 2, when they attacked a group of hay cutters near Fort C. F. Smith in the so-called Hayfield Fight, and woodcutters near Fort Phil Kearny in the Wagon Box Fight (so named because the soldiers took refuge behind a makeshift corral of wagon boxes). By the time of these skirmishes, the army had replaced the cumbersome muzzle-loaded weapons that Fetterman had had with much more efficient breech loaders. The Indians were stunned by the rapidity of the soldiers' fire, suffered substantial casualties, and withdrew—but they did not make peace.

To the south, on the central plains, Major General Winfield Scott Hancock, a Civil War hero, launched an offensive intended to intimidate the Cheyennes and Kiowas below the Arkansas River. In the summer of 1867, he

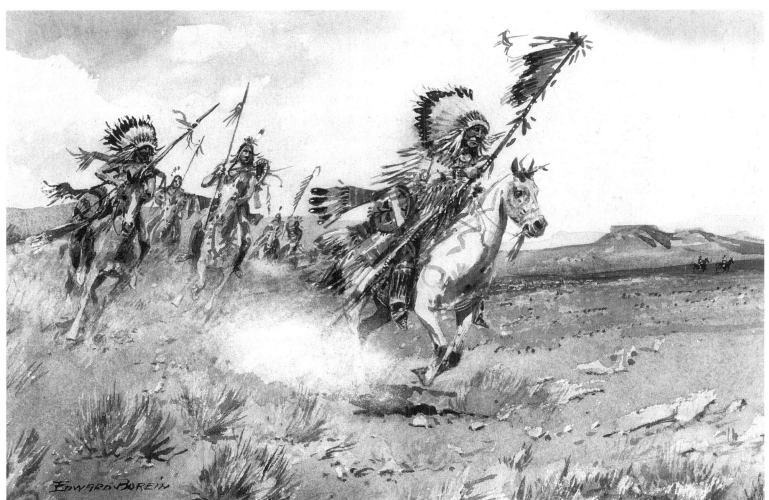

(JOHN) EDWARD BOREIN

—

BORN 1872, SAN LEANDRO, CALIFORNIA
DIED 1945, SANTA BARBARA, CALIFORNIA

—

After leaving school at age seventeen, Borein worked for a saddler, learning in detail about western equipage, and then went on to do odd jobs for a local rancher. He spent a month in 1891 at the San Francisco Art Association Art School, where he met Maynard Dixon, who would gain notice as an important painter of the desert country. Leaving art school, Borein hired on as a cowboy at the Jesús Maria Rancho in Santa Barbara and then at a ranch in Malibu. The owner, who admired the young man's sketches, staked him to an extended sketching tour of Mexico. When he returned, Borein joined the San Francisco *Call* as a staff artist, earning eight dollars a week—even less than cowboy pay.

With Dixon, Borein toured the Sierras, Carson City, and parts of Oregon and Idaho in 1901, returning to Mexico two years later. It was during this trip that he began making watercolors.

Borein set up as an advertising illustrator, working in a rented Oakland studio from 1904 to 1907. By that time, the world of fine art beckoned, and Borein took off for New York, where his studio became a gathering place for such visiting westerners as Charlie Russell, Dixon, Olaf Carl Seltzer, and Will Rogers. After a brief return to Oakland in 1909 and a sketching tour in Oregon, Borein established himself in New York as a sought-after illustrator for such popular periodicals as *Harper's*, *Collier's*, *Sunset*, *Western World*, and *Century*. He became intrigued by etching in 1911, seeking advice on techniques from the great American Impressionist Childe Hassam. He also studied at the Art Students League.

After his marriage in 1921, the artist settled in Santa Barbara, where he enjoyed lifelong prosperity as "the cowpuncher artist."

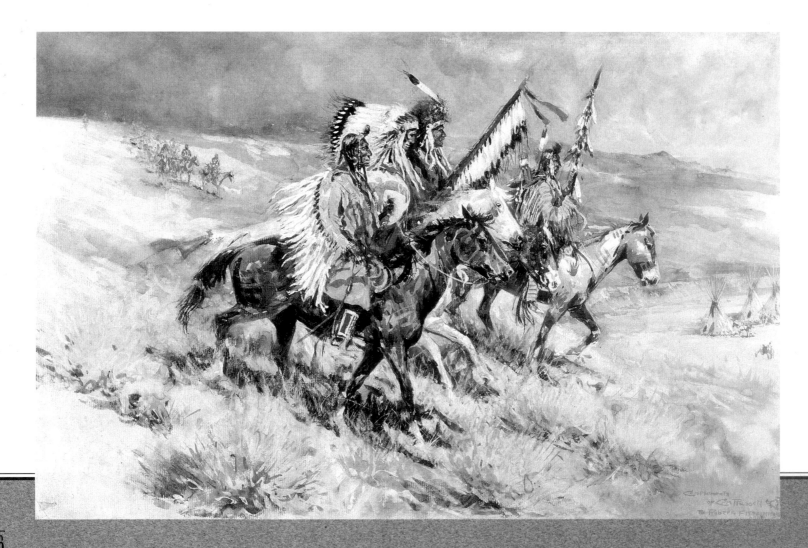

Gerald Cassidy (1879–1934)
The Buffalo Dance, c. 1924
Oil on canvas, 57 × 46 in.
Courtesy of The Anschutz Collection

The buffalo was central to Plains
Indian subsistence, religion, and
culture. It was not the army that
defeated the Plains Indians, but the
inexorable disappearance of the
buffalo.

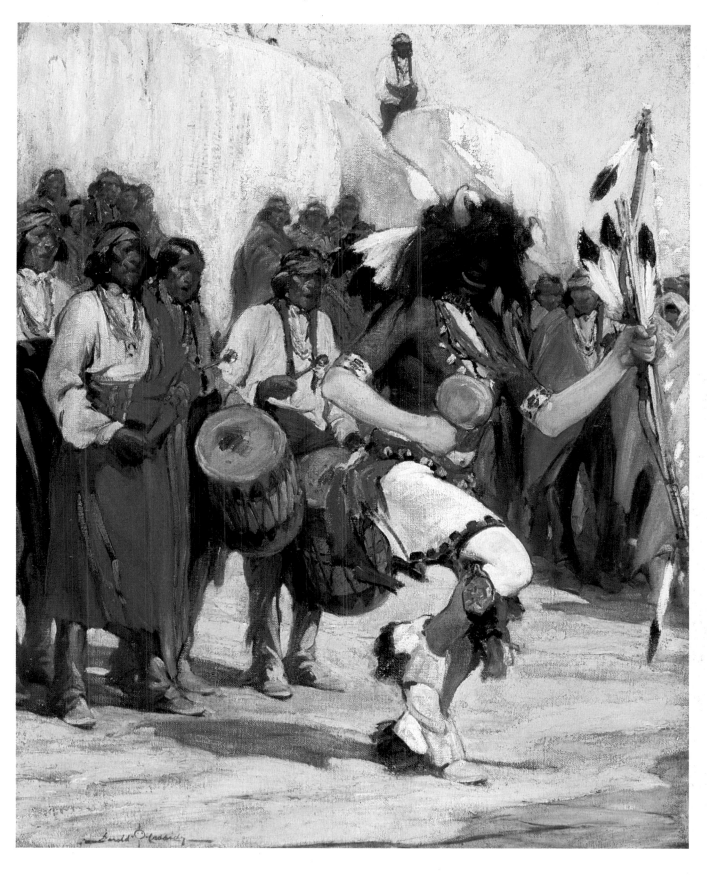

Edward Borein (1872–1945)
Victorious Warrior, c. 1902
Gouache and watercolor on paper,
12 ½ × 18 ⅝ in.
Amon Carter Museum, Fort Worth,
Texas

summoned Cheyenne chiefs to Fort Larned, Kansas, where he lectured them on the might of the army. The next day, Hancock and a column of soldiers marched to a combined Cheyenne and Sioux village to deliver the same message to more chiefs. Doubtless recalling the horror of Sand Creek, the women and children of the village scattered for the hills as they saw the soldiers approaching. Although Hancock instructed his principal field officer, Lieutenant Colonel George Armstrong Cus-

ter, to surround the village to prevent the men from escaping as well, by morning the lodges were all deserted. "This looks like the commencement of war," Hancock summarily declared.

At twenty-five, Custer had attained the brevet rank of major general in the Civil War, earning a reputation as a brilliant, if erratic and egotistical, cavalry commander. The flamboyant, yellow-haired "boy general" was, like many other officers, reduced in rank at the conclusion of

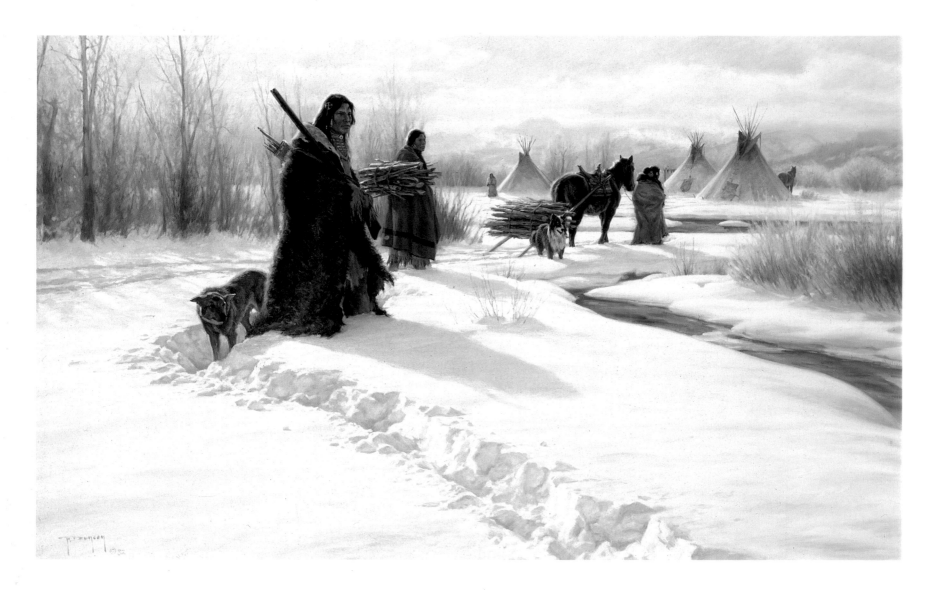

the war. He was determined to fight Indians and fight them unrelentingly. Acting on Hancock's orders, he led his Seventh Cavalry in hot pursuit of the fleeing Cheyenne and Sioux. Through the long summer he and his men followed the chase, always in vain, as the Indians terrorized Kansas. Finally, Custer and the Seventh, exhausted, had to withdraw.

Costly and futile, "Hancock's War" prompted a peace movement, and commissioners negotiated two sets of treaties, at Medicine Lodge Creek, Kansas, in 1867, and at Fort Laramie the next year. The Medicine Lodge treaties established Cheyenne, Arapaho, Kiowa, Comanche, and Kiowa-Apache reservations in Indian Territory, and the Fort Laramie treaties gave to Red Cloud most of what he had fought for, including the designation of the Powder River country as "unceded Indian territory," the establishment of a Great Sioux Reservation in all of present-day South Dakota west of the Missouri, hunting privileges outside the reservation "so long as the buffalo may range thereon in such numbers as to justify the chase" (which was to prove a significant proviso), and the abandonment of the Bozeman Trail forts. The latter was less of a concession than it may at first seem, since the transcontinental railroad was rapidly pushing west and rendering the trail obsolete anyway.

Yet, as usual, the treaties did not bring peace. The Cheyennes were still divided into peace factions versus Dog Soldiers, who would not brook confinement to any reservation. Together with Brulé and Oglala Sioux, Northern Cheyennes, and Arapahos, the Dog Soldiers continued to raid throughout 1868 in western Kansas and eastern Colorado, killing seventy-nine settlers, wounding nine, and stealing a great deal of stock. As to the Kiowas and Comanches, in February 1868, Indian agent Jesse Leavenworth arrived at their new reservation in Indian Territory, and found himself without rations to give to the winter-hungry Indians. Several thousand Indians engaged in raids on Texas, in between which they terrorized Leavenworth and his agency as well as the agency of the peaceful Wichita Indians. When Kiowa and Comanche parties burned that agency, Leavenworth decamped and handed in his resignation, whereupon the Indians launched new raids on Texas.

The Cheyennes were agitating for the guns and ammunition that the Medicine Lodge treaty had promised. But Tall Bull, a Dog Soldier chief, had led a raid on a neighboring Indian village, and the Indian Bureau refused to issue the weapons until, pressured by repeated threats, it finally yielded and distributed arms. However, two hundred Cheyennes who had not heard about the

Robert Duncan (b. 1952)
Winter Fuel, 1982
Oil on canvas, 30 × 48 in.
Private collection

O. E. Berninghaus (1874–1952)
Winter Hunt, 1917
Oil on canvas, 22 × 28 in.
Courtesy of The Anschutz Collection

Winter was as hard on Indians as it was on the soldiers who pursued them.

OSCAR EDMUND BERNINGHAUS

—

BORN 1874, ST. LOUIS, MISSOURI

DIED 1952, TAOS, NEW MEXICO

—

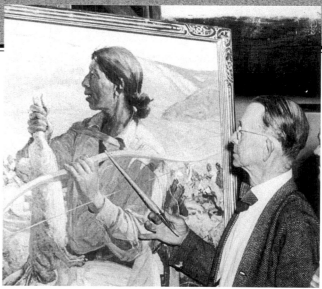

Anonymous, *Oscar Edmund Berninghaus*, c. 1945. Photograph.
The Harwood Foundation Museum, Taos, New Mexico.

Berninghaus's only formal art training was three terms in the night program of the St. Louis School of Fine Arts, but, as the son of a lithograph salesman, he had been steeped in traditions of popular illustration since early childhood. Even as a boy, he was selling his own illustrations to St. Louis newspapers, and he made a living as an illustrator before attempting a career as a "fine" artist.

In 1899, the Denver and Rio Grande Railroad invited him to tour and sketch in the West. A brakeman suggested that he stop in Taos, twenty-five miles distant from the Rio Grande's right of way and, at the time, a remote Pueblo Indian settlement. After his first visit, Berninghaus returned every summer until 1925, when he took up full-time residence, becoming a specialist in the sensitive but unsentimental depiction of Pueblo Indian life. Berninghaus was one of the founders of the Taos Society of Artists in 1915.

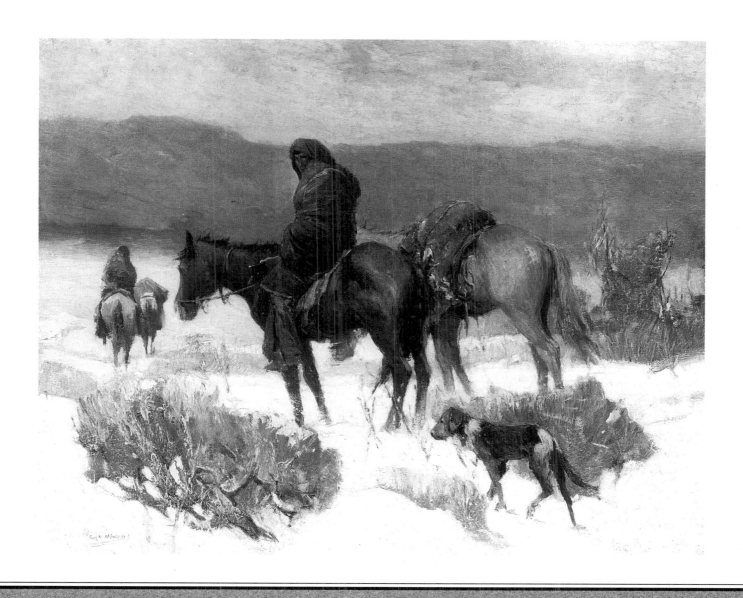

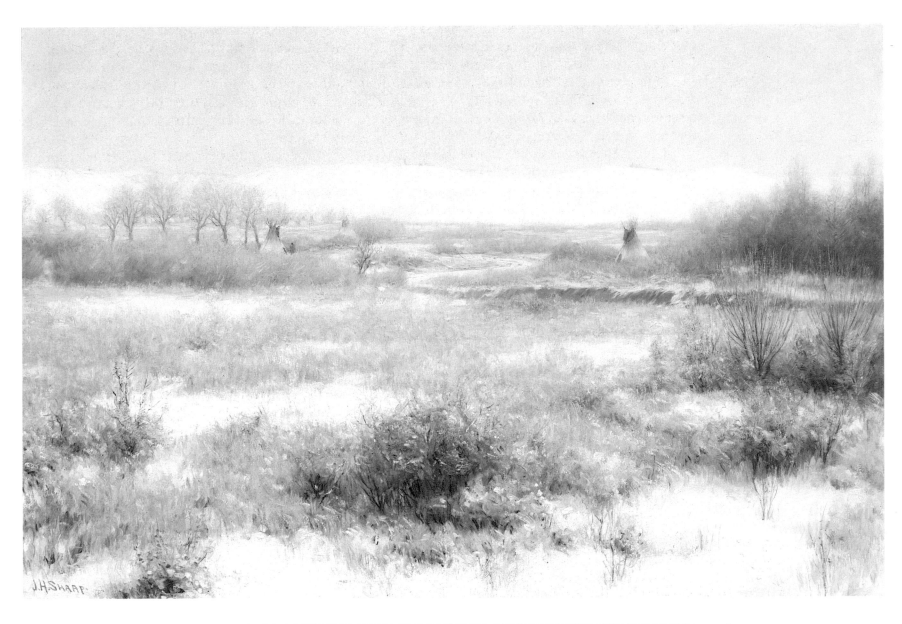

Joseph Henry Sharp (1859–1953)
Winter Encampment on the Plains,
1919
Oil on canvas, 24 × 36 in.
Courtesy of The Anschutz Collection

The soft contours and colors of
winter stubble give little hint of the
formidable adversary the season
could become.

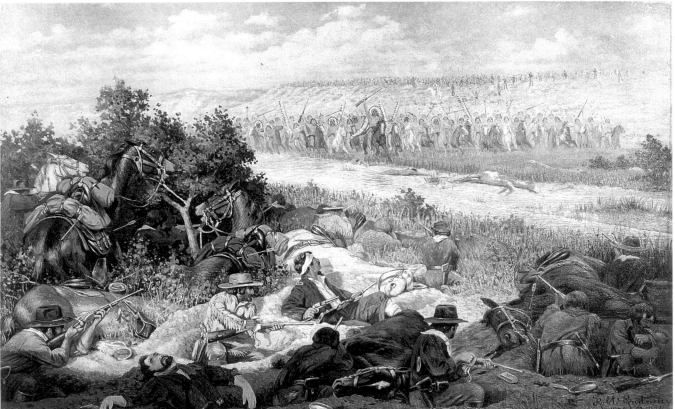

Robert Lindneux (1871–1970)
The Battle of Beecher's Island, n.d.
Oil on canvas, 30 ¼ × 46 in.
Courtesy of the Colorado Historical
Society

An effective evocation of a desperate
stand: note the slain horses used as
breastworks.

distribution raided settlements on the Saline and Solomon rivers, killing fifteen men, raping five women, burning ranches, and running off stock. The peace factions of the Cheyennes as well as the Arapahos headed for the reservation in Indian Territory. The Dog Soldiers and other warlike factions renewed their raids throughout western Kansas and eastern Colorado.

General Sheridan, who had replaced General Hancock as commander of the region, decided that an aggressive winter campaign would be the most effective means of dealing with the hostiles. With food in short supply, the Indians were particularly vulnerable during the harsh winter months on the plains. In the meantime, he dispatched Major George A. Forsyth with fifty handpicked plainsmen to patrol settlements and travel routes. On September 17, 1868, the small company encountered six or seven hundred Dog Soldiers and Oglala Sioux in western Kansas. Forsyth's party took refuge on an island in the all but dried-up Arikara Fork of the Republican River. Fortunately for the group, they were armed with repeating carbines, which twice turned back the Indians' headlong charges. One of the Cheyennes' most capable war chiefs, Roman Nose, restrained himself from joining the first two charges because he had broken his protective medicine by inadvertently eating bread that had been touched by a metal fork—the eating utensil of whites. Yet by the third charge, he could no longer resist and joined the fray, even though he knew it meant certain death. A bullet tore through his chest and killed him.

Disheartened by the death of Roman Nose, the attackers broke off the charge and, instead, laid siege to the island. As half the company lay dead or wounded, two messengers managed to slip through the Indian lines and travel ninety miles to Fort Wallace. A relief column arrived on the eighth day of the siege and drove off the Indians. The defenders had been subsisting on their dead horses.

The winter campaign Sheridan devised was three pronged. One column would approach from Fort Bascom, New Mexico, another from Fort Lyon, Colorado, and the third from Fort Dodge, Kansas, under Custer. They would converge upon the Indians' winter camps on the Canadian and Washita rivers, in Indian Territory. The yellow-haired commander led his Seventh Cavalry to a Cheyenne camp on the Washita, surrounded it, and, to strains of the famed regimental tune "Garry Owen," charged into the sleeping village, shooting down many warriors as they emerged from their tepees.

Then the Seventh found itself under counterattack by warriors from nearby camps. Custer held his position, slaughtering nine hundred Indian ponies and setting tepees ablaze. At dusk, he marched his men toward the Indian camps downstream, as if he intended to attack them. Seeing this, the Indians broke off their assault and prepared to defend the other camps. At nightfall, Custer and the Seventh Cavalry quietly slipped out of the Washita Valley. The list of casualties was an ugly one: five soldiers killed and fourteen wounded, plus fifteen missing, whose bodies were discovered later. Among the Indians killed was the peace chief, Black Kettle, and his

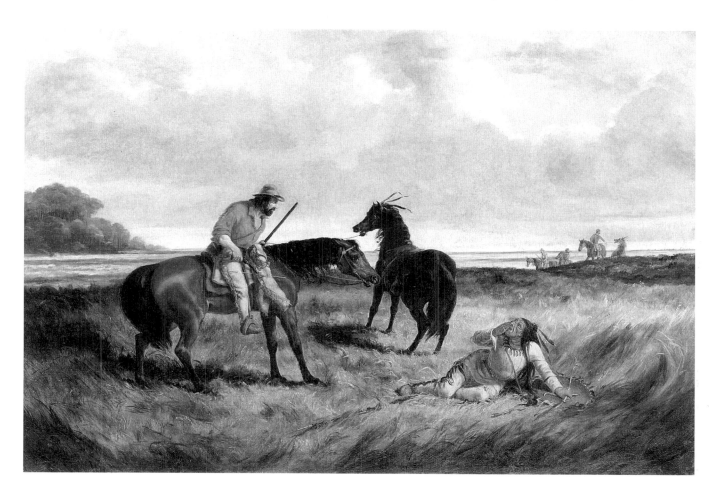

Arthur F. Tait (1819–1905)
The Last War Whoop, 1855
Oil on canvas, 30 × 44 in.
Milwaukee Art Museum; Gift of
Edward S. Tallmadge

Although Indians were often defiant in defeat, the usual practice among most combative tribes was for the vanquished warrior to sing his "death song" when he saw that the end was imminent. The song was personal, unique, and of great religious significance; it was not a barbaric "whoop."

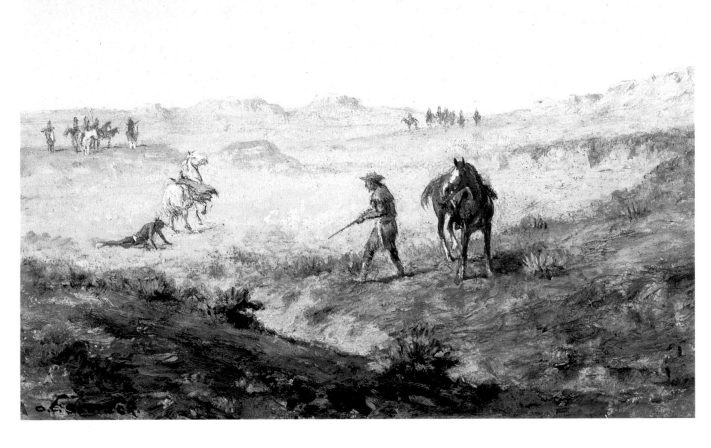

Olaf Carl Seltzer (1877–1957)
Buffalo Bill's Duel with Yellow Hand,
1933
Oil on board, 4 ¼ × 5 ½ in.
Gilcrease Museum, Tulsa, Oklahoma

Shortly after the Custer massacre at the Little Bighorn, Buffalo Bill was scouting for Colonel Wesley Merritt in Nebraska. On July 17, 1876, Bill fought the Cheyenne subchief Yellow Hand (more properly called Yellow Hair) at War Bonnet Creek, a "duel" celebrated in subsequent dime novels devoted to Buffalo Bill.

wife, cut down as they were riding double on a pony in a desperate attempt to escape the attack.

The battle on the Washita and the Christmas Day Battle of Soldier Spring, fought against Comanches on the north fork of the Red River, suggested that the winter strategy was effective. However, it was almost as hard on the troops as it was on the Indians. Travel and supply during winter storms presented a logistical nightmare. It was not until March 1869 that Custer again launched his Seventh against the Cheyennes, who had moved west, into the Texas Panhandle. At Sweetwater Creek, Custer discovered the villages of Medicine Arrows and Little Robe, but he dared not attack, because he knew that the Indians held two white women hostage. He called for a parley, and during the talks seized four chiefs. He sent one back with surrender terms, demanding that the hostages be released or he would hang the other three. The Cheyennes complied and, even more, lost their heart for fighting. They surrendered, with a promise to return to their reservation.

The Dog Soldiers, however, led by Tall Bull, did not give up. They decided to join forces with the Northern Cheyennes in the Powder River country. On July 11, 1869, the Fifth Cavalry, commanded by Major Eugene Carr, and numbering in its rank a scout named William F. Cody—Buffalo Bill—surprised the Dog Soldiers' camp at Summit Springs, Colorado. Tall Bull was killed, and the cavalry's victory was total, with far-reaching ef-

fects. The Dog Soldiers were finished in western Kansas, and the rest of the Cheyennes joined their brethren from Sweetwater Creek in retiring to the reservation.

Yet it was during this time that another of the many shifts in United States Indian policy occurred. General Ulysses S. Grant succeeded Andrew Johnson as president and, even before his inauguration, announced a new policy of peace toward the Indian—"conquest by kindness," he called it. Accordingly, Grant turned to the most pacific group of people he could think of, the Quakers, in order to find Indian agents.

One such was Lawrie Tatum, who left his Iowa farm to administer the Kiowa-Comanche reservation in Indian Territory. Big and hairless, he was called by his charges Bald Head Agent. Texans soon found other names for him, as the reservation Indians, instigated by the Kiowa chief Satanta, indulged in frequent raids, only to retreat back into the reservation, from which the army was debarred. In May 1871, Satanta, Satank, Big Tree, Eagle Heart, Big Bow, and about a hundred braves lay in ambush on Salt Creek Prairie, Texas. They let pass unmolested a small wagon train; for the medicine man had predicted a larger one would follow. Sure enough, a tenwagon train came later in the day. Only four of the train's twelve teamsters escaped massacre; the wagons were burned, and forty-one mules were stolen. Ironically, the smaller train had carried a much bigger prize—General William Tecumseh Sherman, on a tour of inspection.

The general was appalled by Agent Tatum's inability to regulate his charges, and, after Satanta boasted to Tatum about having led the Salt Creek massacre, demanding more arms and ammunition for even more raids, the Quaker agent himself was willing to cooperate with the army. The most important Kiowa chiefs, including Satanta, were summoned to Fort Richardson, where they were told they would meet General Sherman. In a moment of high drama, Satanta boasted to Sherman that he had been responsible for Salt Creek. Sherman replied by announcing that he, Satanta, as well as Satank and Chief Big Tree, were under arrest for murder. Satanta reached for a pistol concealed beneath his blanket, whereupon Sherman signaled, and the shutters of the fort commander's residence flew open. A squadron of black cavalrymen trained their carbines on the Indians.

Talks proceeded until Stumbling Bear shot an arrow at Sherman. His aim was deflected by a soldier. Lone Wolf pointed his carbine at the general, but the fort commander seized the weapon, and the two tangled on the ground. The three chiefs were shackled, loaded into wagons, and, under heavy escort, sent off to Texas. Satank, singing his death song, tore the flesh from his wrists and removed his handcuffs. Taking a penknife he had concealed, the Indian stabbed one of his guards in the leg. From the wagon behind the one carrying Satank, a soldier fired two shots, fatally wounding the chief in the chest. Satanta and Big Tree stood trial in a Texas state court, were convicted, and were sentenced to hang. In re-

sponse to pressure from the Department of the Interior and from humanitarian groups, the sentences were commuted to prison terms. In 1873, responding to more pressure, the governor of Texas released Satanta and Big Tree.

If the release of the two chiefs was intended to placate the Indians into leaving the Texas frontier alone, it did not succeed. And despite the government's demonstration of its peaceful intentions, little was done to improve poor conditions at the reservations. Worse, the plains were crawling with white buffalo hunters who were driving the animals to extinction, killing them for their hides alone. The buffalo was of paramount importance in Plains Indian culture. The herds were the Indians' chief source of food and clothing, and, as long as vast numbers of the animals ranged freely, the encroachment of ranchers and farmers was limited. The Indians of the plains rightly saw that the herds were being exterminated, and they knew that, when the buffalo vanished, so would their traditional way of life.

By the summer of 1874, with Indians raiding the Texas Panhandle at will and with the reservation system a shambles, the army was given permission to carry its offensives into the reservations themselves. General Sheridan and his lieutenants, General John Pope and General Christopher C. Augur, planned a campaign of convergence upon the Staked Plain region of the Panhandle, with columns closing in from Fort Sill, Indian Territory, from Texas, from New Mexico, and from Kan-

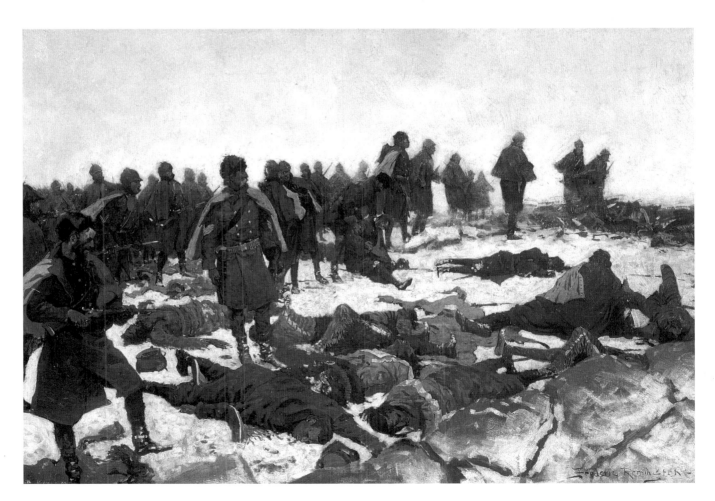

Frederic Remington (1861–1909)
Battle of War Bonnet Creek, n.d.
Oil on canvas, 26 ½ × 39 in.
Gilcrease Museum, Tulsa, Oklahoma

sas. The crack Fourth Cavalry, under Colonel Ranald Mackenzie, swept through a combined Kiowa-Comanche-Cheyenne village, killing only three Indians, but destroying the village as well as fifteen hundred ponies, and so disheartening the inhabitants that most surrendered to the local agencies. Through the winter and spring, an infantry command under Colonel Nelson A. Miles pursued and defeated the Kwahadi Comanches, who, for the first time in their history, consented to retire to a reservation. With the southern plains essentially secured, Sheridan took the vital precaution of exiling seventy-four militant chiefs to Castillo de San Marcos, a former Spanish fortress in St. Augustine, Florida. Satanta was sent again to the Texas state penitentiary, where, despairing in captivity, he committed suicide by leaping from a window in 1878.

The northern plains presented a very different picture. Some Sioux, Cheyennes, and Arapahos retired to the reservations, resigned to live on the government dole. Red Cloud and Spotted Tail—a Brulé Sioux—became leaders of these "reservation Sioux," locked into a seemingly perpetual contest with the Indian agency on the one hand and the restless young warriors on the other. The reservations were often places of violence. Those groups that shunned the reservation—mainly the Oglala, Hunkpapa, and Miniconjou Sioux and factions of the Northern Cheyennes, as well as some Yankton, Teton, and Santee Sioux—remained militant. Among them, Crazy Horse,

an Oglala, and Sitting Bull, of the Hunkpapas, were gaining legendary status as warrior chiefs. Indeed, the very name of Sitting Bull had become among the Indians a word (as one white scout observed) for "all that was generous and great." In his forties during the 1870s, swarthy and broad-shouldered, with a penetrating gaze, Sitting Bull had nothing but contempt for his reservation brethren, who, he said, made themselves "slaves to a piece of fat bacon, some hard-tack, and a little sugar and coffee."

Provoked by the inexorable white incursion into their lands, the Sioux of the northern plains raided settlements in Montana, Wyoming, and Nebraska. Sitting Bull, in particular, menaced survey parties laying out the Northern Pacific in 1873. A year later, George Armstrong Custer, leading a military expedition in the Black Hills, discovered gold. Within another year—and in flagrant violation of treaty—thousands of whites swarmed the Black Hills in search of ore. The army made some gestures of interference, but the only hope for a peaceful resolution of the crisis was government purchase of the Black Hills. As the ground most sacred to the Sioux people, however, the Black Hills were not for sale. At the end of 1875, therefore, the tribes were issued an ultimatum: report to an agency and reservation by January 31, 1876, or be hunted and killed as hostiles.

The deadline came and went, and General Sheridan prepared to launch two campaigns. The first never got started. Colonel Custer was supposed to lead his Seventh

Charles M. Russell (1864–1926)
Wild Meat for Wild Men, 1890
Oil on canvas, (20 ¼ × 36 ⅛ in.)
Amon Carter Museum, Fort Worth, Texas

Thousands of pounds of angry buffalo were rounded up for the kill by Indian horsemen so skilled that they could relinquish the reins to wield the bow.

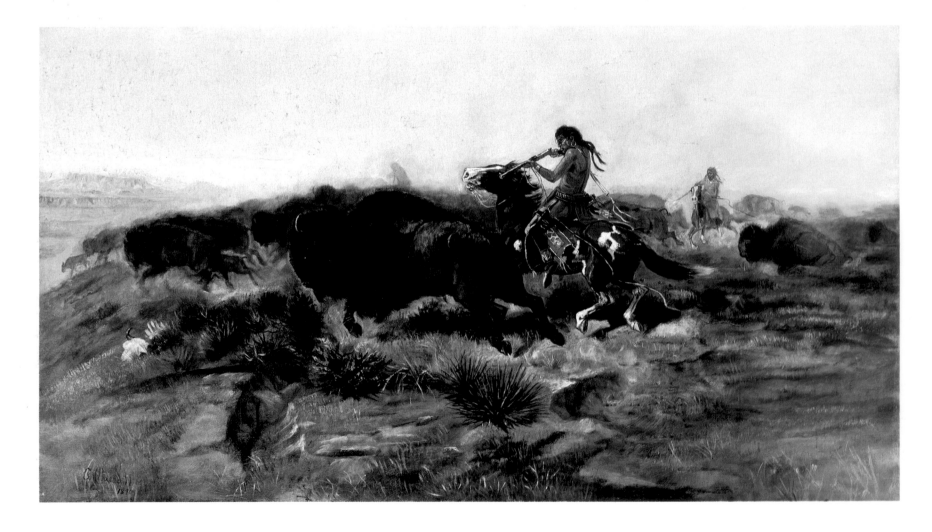

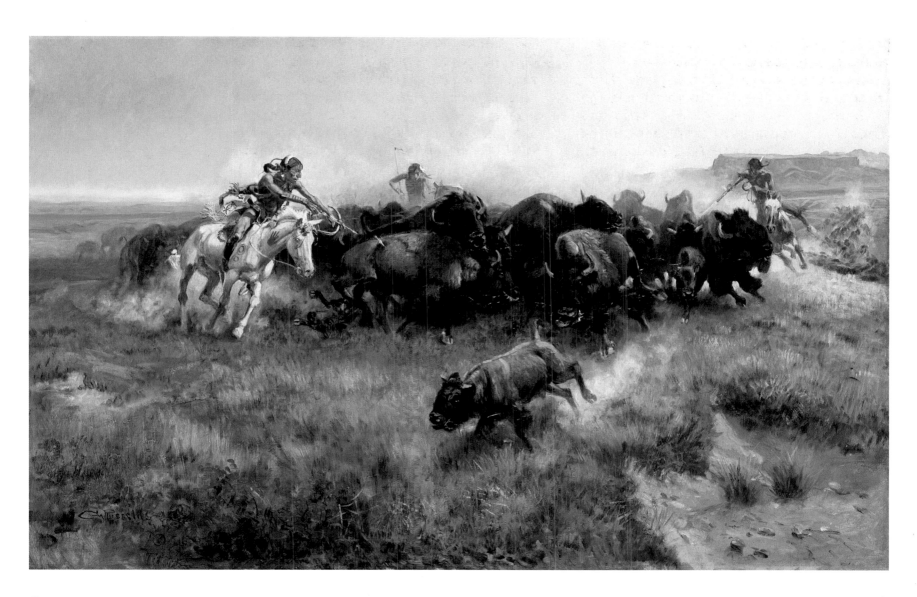

Charles M. Russell (1864–1926)
The Buffalo Hunt No. 39, 1919
Oil on canvas, 30 ¼ × 48 ¼ in.
Amon Carter Museum, Fort Worth,
Texas

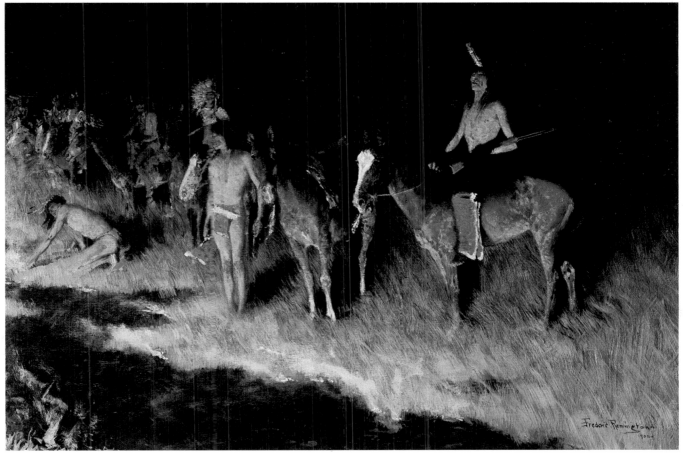

Frederic Remington (1861–1909)
The Grass Fire, 1908
Oil on canvas, 27 ⅛ × 40 ⅛ in.
Amon Carter Museum, Fort Worth,
Texas

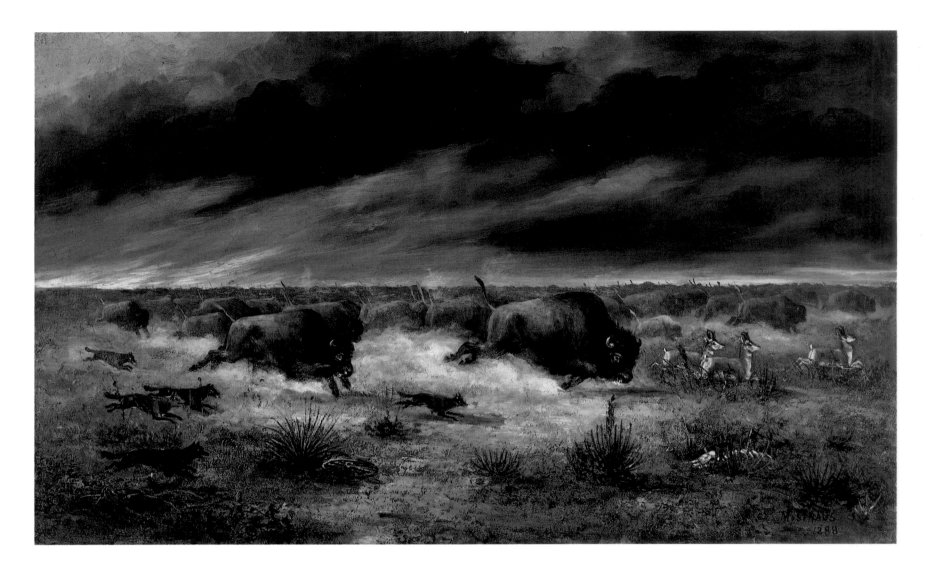

Meyer Straus (birth and death dates unknown)
Herd of Buffalo Fleeing from a Prairie Fire, 1888
Oil on canvas, 17 ⅞ × 29 ⅞ in.
Amon Carter Museum, Fort Worth, Texas

Indians used fire to flush out buffalo herds for hunting.

Cavalry westward from Fort Lincoln, but was repeatedly foiled by heavy snow. General George Crook did lead nine hundred men out of Fort Fetterman, Wyoming, on March 1, 1876, and, battling storms and cold, scoured the Powder River country for Indians. After three discouraging weeks, a trail was found, and Crook dispatched Colonel Joseph J. Reynolds with a large complement of cavalry to attack a village of 105 lodges. Although taken by surprise, the Oglalas and Cheyennes counterattacked so effectively that Reynolds was forced to withdraw back to Crook and the main column. Crook retreated to Fort Fetterman—and brought charges against Reynolds for mismanaging both the attack and the retreat. General Sheridan dismissed the charges, realizing that the severity of the weather was to blame for the colonel's poor showing. If winter combat made the Indians more vulnerable, as Sheridan believed, it also took a terrible toll on the attackers. "General," Reynolds complained to William Tecumseh Sherman, "these winter campaigns in these latitudes should be prohibited. . . . The Month of March has told on me more than any five years of my life."

Crook's abortive winter campaign did little damage to the Indians; worse, it galvanized them into a large fighting force under the able leadership of Crazy Horse and Sitting Bull. Late in the spring of 1876, Sheridan ini-

tiated another campaign of convergence: General Alfred Terry led a force from the east (including Custer and his Seventh), Colonel John Gibbon approached from the West, and Crook marched out of Fort Fetterman. They converged on the Yellowstone, even as the Indians were traveling that way. Early in June, on the Rosebud Creek, the Indians held a religious ceremony known as a Sun Dance, at which Sitting Bull announced that he had had a vision. It was of many, many soldiers "falling right into our camp."

On the morning of June 17, General Crook, with more than a thousand men, halted for a rest at the head of the Rosebud. Crow and Shoshone scouts attached to Crook's column sighted Sitting Bull's Sioux and Cheyennes as they descended upon Crook's position and gave sufficient warning to avert disaster. Even so, the Indians withdrew only after a six-hour fight; Crook's column had taken severe punishment and was also forced to retreat. Following the Rosebud battle, the Indians established a camp that was soon augmented by the arrival of agency Indians who left the reservation for the spring and summer. The camp grew to a village of about seven thousand people.

In the meantime, General Terry's column united with Colonel Gibbon's at the mouth of the Rosebud. Both men were unaware of Crook's retreat. The officers of both commands, including George A. Custer, convened in the cabin of the Yellowstone steamer *Far West* to lay out a campaign strategy. They figured they would find the Sioux encampment on the stream that the Indians called the Greasy Grass and that white men called the Little Bighorn.

Custer was to lead his Seventh up the Rosebud, cross to the Little Bighorn, and proceed down its valley from the south as Terry and Gibbon marched up the Yellowstone and Bighorn to block the Indians from the north. In that way, Sitting Bull's forces would be caught between the two columns.

On the morning of June 22, to the tune of "Garry Owen," the six hundred men of the Seventh passed in review before Terry, Gibbon, and Custer. Shaking hands with his fellow officers, Custer set off to join his men. General Gibbon called after him: "Now, Custer, don't be greedy, but wait for us."

"No," Custer replied, "I will not."

Seizing on this exchange and on Custer's reputation as a brash and heedless fire eater, some historians have laid the blame for the Little Bighorn disaster entirely at the feet of the young colonel. The fact is that Gibbon's

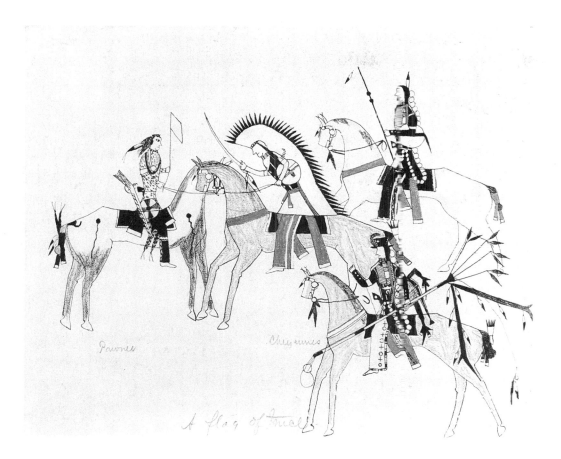

Buffalo Meat (1847–1917)
A Flag of Truce, 1876
Pen and ink, graphite and colored pencil on paper, 8 ¾ × 11 ¼ in.
Amon Carter Museum, Fort Worth, Texas

Cheyenne and Pawnee cease hostilities for a parley.

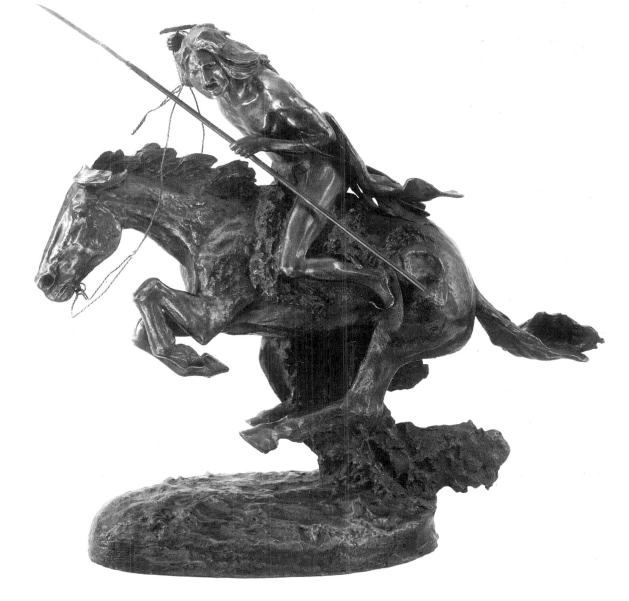

Frederic S. Remington (1861–1909)
The Cheyenne, 1901
Bronze, H. 24 in.
The Rockwell Museum, Corning, New York

Remington entertained no sentimental visions of the Cheyenne warrior as a "noble savage." Here he is a terrible engine of doom.

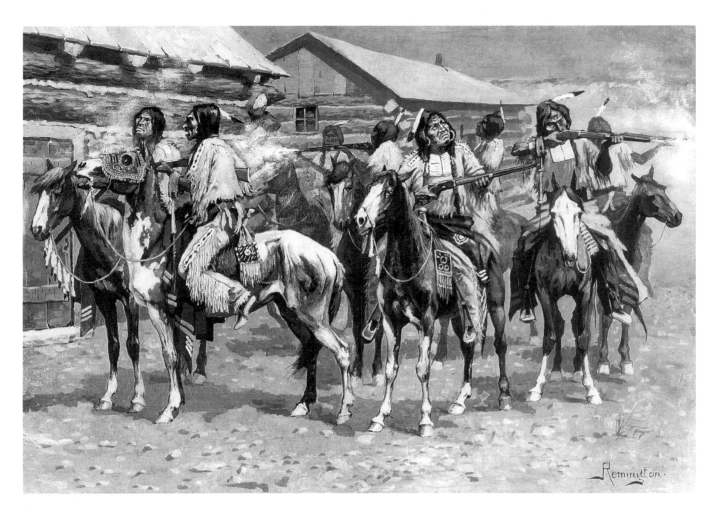

Frederic Remington (1861–1909)
Crow Indians Firing into the Agency,
1887
Oil on paper, 17 ⅞ × 25 ⅛ in.
Amon Carter Museum, Fort Worth,
Texas

Poorly run and rife with heartless
corruption, the Indian agency and
reservation system kindled
numerous revolts and other acts of
violence.

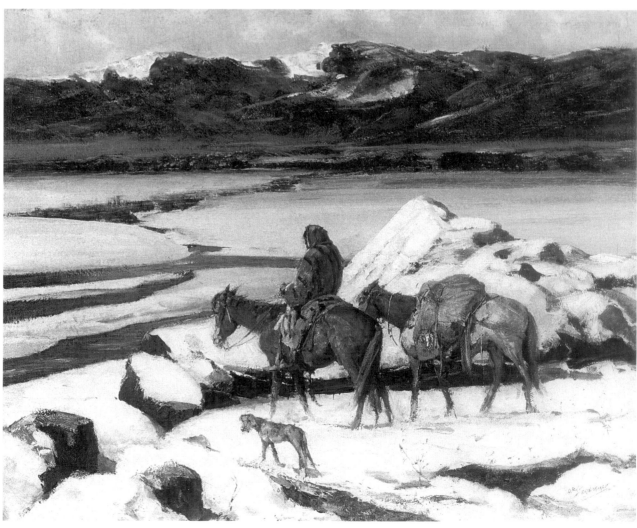

O. E. Berninghaus (1874–1952)
On the Trail, 1908
Oil on canvas, 16 × 20 in.
The Warner Collection of Gulf States
Paper Corporation, Tuscaloosa,
Alabama

HENRY F. FARNY

—

BORN 1847, RIBEAUVILLE, ALSACE, FRANCE
DIED 1916, CINCINNATI

—

Farny's family settled in Warren, Pennsylvania, after leaving France in 1853. Here the boy became fascinated with the local Seneca Indians. After the family moved to Cincinnati in 1859, Farny was apprenticed to a lithographer and, six years later, published a two-page spread of Cincinnati views in *Harper's Weekly*. After three years of European study, Farny returned to Cincinnati and illustration work. He shared a studio with the painter Frank Duveneck; with him, Henry Twachtman, and Frank Dengler, he next studied in Munich. Returning to the United States, Farny made a thousand-mile canoe trip down the Missouri River in 1878.

In 1881, the artist began a series of Indian sketches, including portraits of Sitting Bull and depictions of the politically charged Ghost Dance. He received many assignments from the popular illustrated magazines, including one from *Harper's*, to cover the completion of the Northern Pacific Railroad in 1883.

Throughout the remainder of his career, Farny continued to travel in the West, sketching as well as collecting a vast store of Indian artifacts with which he stocked his Cincinnati studio. By the 1890s, Farny turned increasingly to easel painting in that studio, creating genre scenes emphasizing the contrasts between white and Indian civilizations, of which the 1904 *Song of the Talking Wire* (p. 212) is a particularly moving example.

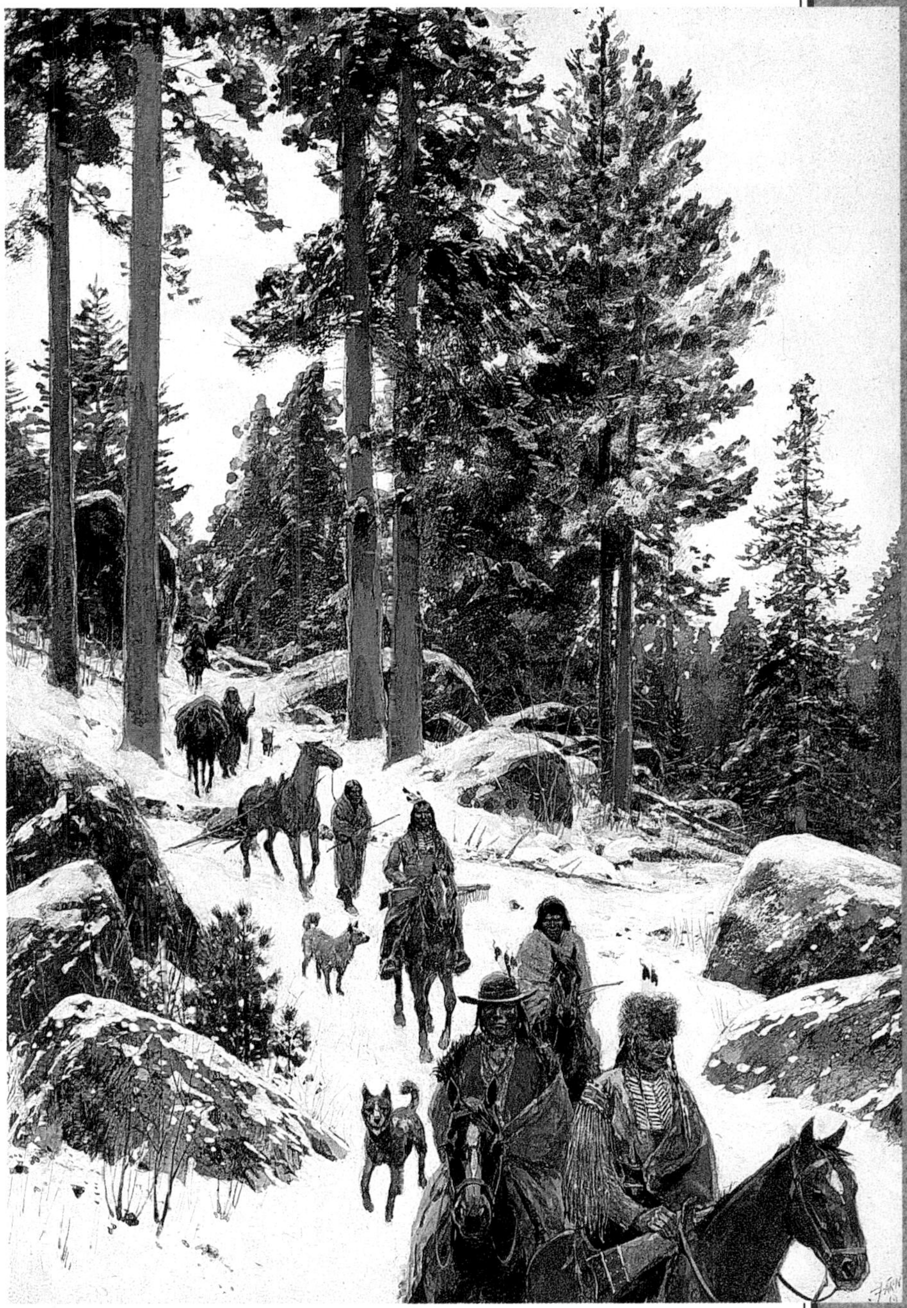

Henry F. Farny (1847–1916)
On the Trail in Winter, 1894
Gouache on paper, 15 ¾ × 10 ⅞ in.
The Rockwell Museum, Corning,
New York

EDGAR SAMUEL PAXSON

BORN 1852, EAST HAMBURG, NEW YORK

DIED 1919, MISSOULA, MONTANA

—

His long hair, goatee, and generous moustache marked Paxson as a man of the frontier. He came west, to Montana, in 1877, working as ranch hand, hunting guide, dispatch rider, freighter, driver for the Overland Stage Company, and scout in the Nez Percé war of 1877–78. It was not until 1879 that he brought his wife and child, whom he had left in Buffalo, New York, to Deer Lodge, Montana, where he painted action-filled canvases, sharply delineating classic frontier character types, while supporting his family as a commercial artist, sign painter, theatrical set painter, and saloon decorator.

His early education had been in a one-room log school-house and at a Quaker academy in upstate New York. His first training as a painter came from his father, who worked as a sign painter and decorator.

In 1881, Paxson moved from Deer Lodge to Butte, where there was greater demand for what he had to offer. A Montana National Guardsman, the artist served in the Philippines during the Spanish–American War and settled in Missoula in 1905. He is best known for *Custer's Last Stand,* completed in 1899 after years of labor. The artist's mural work appears in the Montana State Capitol at Helena and in the Missoula County Court House.

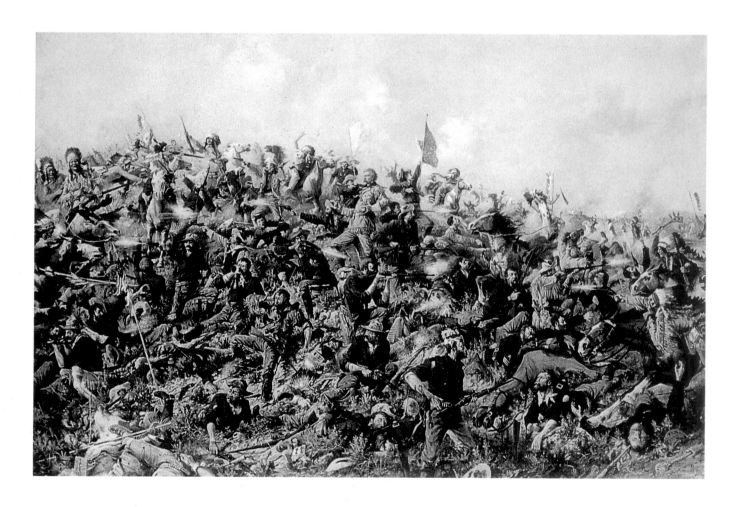

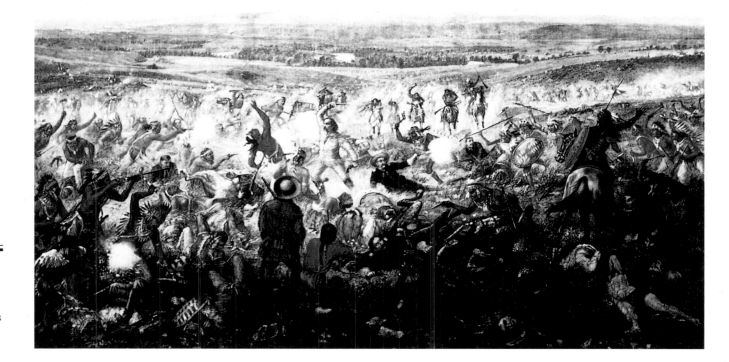

Otto Becker (1854–1945)
Custer's Last Fight, 1896
Lithograph, 39 ½ × 49 ½ in.
Aneheuser-Busch, St. Louis

This German-born artist was
commissioned by the Anheuser-
Busch brewing company in 1895 to
copy Cassily Adams's *Custer's Last
Fight* for a color lithograph. Adams's
work, owned by the brewery, was
subsequently destroyed in a fire.

Edgar Samuel Paxson (1852–1919)
Custer's Last Stand, 1899
Oil on canvas, 70 ½ × 106 in.
Buffalo Bill Historical Center, Cody,
Wyoming

Probably the most familiar depiction
of the Custer debacle, *Custer's Last
Stand* is also the artist's best-known
work.

admonition was jocular. It was never part of the *Far West*
plan to join forces before engaging the Indians. The idea
was for whoever made contact first to fight, driving the
Indians into the other half of the pincers; and it was assumed that Custer's highly mobile Seventh would be the
first to make contact. It is true that Custer was supposed
to follow the Rosebud beyond the point where the Indians' trail was expected to turn west, so that he would
cross to the Little Bighorn Valley south of the Indians'
position, thereby insuring the enemy would be caught
between the Seventh Cavalry and the forces of Gibbon
and Terry. And it is true that Custer departed from the
plan. He found the Indian trail, but it was much fresher
than anticipated, which meant that the Indians were not
in the upper valley of the Little Bighorn, but very close
by. To continue up the Rosebud would carry the Seventh
far from the Indians' position. Instead, Custer sent out
scouts to follow the trail and locate the Indian village.

He planned to attack on June 26, the day Gibbon
and Terry were scheduled to reach their position at the
mouth of the Little Bighorn, but on June 25, the scouts
not only discovered a Sioux camp, but also warriors lurking nearby. Custer decided that he could not wait a day
to attack; the Sioux would spot him and flee. The yellow-
haired colonel led his men across the divide between the
Rosebud and the Little Bighorn. He dispatched Captain
Frederick W. Benteen with three troops, 125 men, to the
south, in order to make sure that the Sioux had not, in
fact, moved into the upper valley of the Little Bighorn. As
Custer approached the Little Bighorn River, he spotted

about forty warriors and sent Major Marcus A. Reno,
with another three troops, after them. The plan was for
Reno to pursue the warriors back to their village while
Custer, with his remaining five troops, charged the village from the north.

And here were the true sources of catastrophe. Custer had not seen the village, and he was maneuvering in
entirely unfamiliar terrain. Neither Custer nor his commanding generals had any idea of how many warriors
they were going up against. Later estimates put the number at anywhere from fifteen hundred to six thousand.
Custer's combined strength was six hundred—and that
had been split up.

Reno's squadron of 112 men was overwhelmed by
masses of Sioux. He ordered his command to dismount
and set up a skirmish line. When his left flank came
under attack, he ordered a retreat to a cottonwood grove.
Again, his position was infiltrated. He ordered his men to
mount up for a run to the bluffs across the river. By the
time his troopers had reached this position—some forty-
five minutes after they had first engaged the enemy—
their number had been reduced by about half.

Where—Reno must have agonized—was Custer?
The colonel had ascended a bluff, had seen the vast
Sioux encampment and had seen Reno advancing for the
attack. Custer called for his trumpeter, Giovanni Martini, and handed him a note to deliver to Captain Benteen, ordering him to bring the ammunition packs and
join the fight. Martini was the last surviving cavalryman
to see George Armstrong Custer alive.

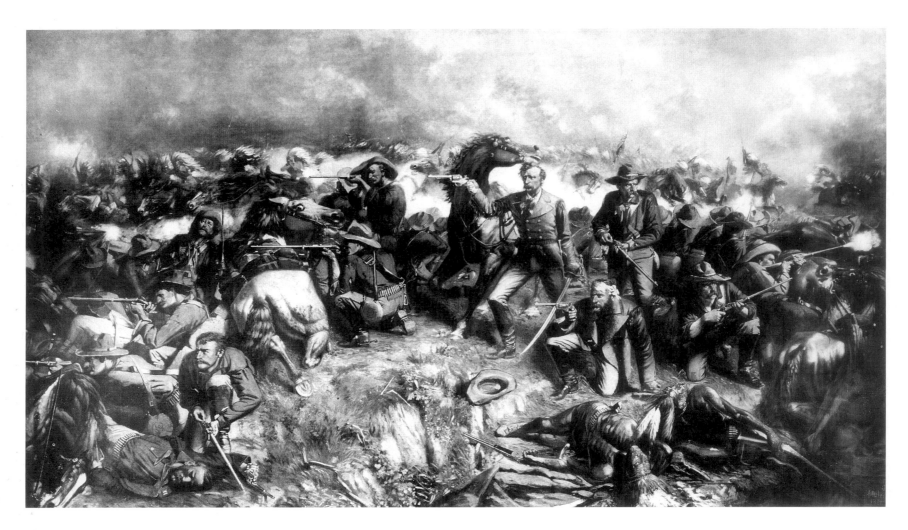

Warriors led by a Hunkpapa chief named Gall surged across the Little Bighorn, pushing the troopers back. As Gall pressed from the south, Crazy Horse pushed in from the north. Within an hour, Custer and his men were dead.

In the meanwhile, Benteen, having received Custer's note, united with the remnant of Reno's command as it withdrew from the Little Bighorn Valley. When the sound of firing was heard, signifying that Custer was engaged, a number of officers wanted to ride off in his support. Reno refused—but some did go, only to return when warriors riding back from the Custer fight blocked their way.

The combined forces of Reno and Benteen—368 officers and men—dug in on the bluffs and fought off a day-long siege. On the next day, June 26, the siege was renewed, continuing until early afternoon. Finally, the entire village moved off to the south as Generals Terry and Gibbon approached from the north. Casualties among the combined commands of Reno and Benteen were heavy.

Far grimmer, of course, was the Custer battlefield, littered with the naked and mutilated corpses of some two hundred men. The body of Custer, found near his personal pennant—beside which he had taken his last stand—had been stripped naked. But the attackers in this one instance had refrained from scalping and mutilation.

While the disaster at the Little Bighorn moved Congress to increase army strength in the West by twenty-five hundred cavalry privates and won for the military control of the Sioux agencies, its principal effect was to demoralize Generals Crook and Terry. They spent the rest of the summer of 1876 in futile and desultory pursuit of Sioux, who had already scattered and headed east after the Custer fight. Crook did destroy a small Sioux camp on September 9 in the Battle of Slim Buttes, but it wasn't until November that his able commander of the Fourth Cavalry, Ranald Mackenzie, won a significant victory in the Bighorn Mountains against a Cheyenne band led by Dull Knife. In January, Brigadier General Nelson A. Miles, with a small command of five hundred infantrymen, engaged Sioux and Cheyenne warriors under Crazy Horse. The Battle of Wolf Mountain was fought in a severe snowstorm, but when it was over, Miles was able to boast that he had "taught the destroyers of Custer that there was one small command that could whip them as long as they dared face it." Bear's Coat, as the Cheyennes called Miles, dogged them as well as Crazy Horse's Oglala Sioux through the winter until, in the spring of 1877, the Cheyennes surrendered on the Yellowstone. Sitting Bull and his Hunkpapas fled to Canada, but Crazy Horse brought the Oglala to the Red Cloud Agency and surrendered there.

Crazy Horse proved restive on the reservation, an "incorrigible wild man, silent, sullen, lordly and dictato-

John Mulvany (1844–1906)
Custer's Last Rally, c. 1881
Oil on canvas, 132 × 240 in.
Courtesy Library of Congress

This Irish-born artist claims the distinction of having painted the first depiction of the Custer disaster. When the poet Walt Whitman saw the painting in New York in 1881, he pronounced it "altogether a Western phase of America . . . deadly, heroic to the uttermost; nothing in the books like it."

Thomas Hart Benton (1889–1975)
Custer's Last Stand, 1943
Oil on canvas, 42 × 48 in.
Albrecht Art Museum; Purchased with funds donated by the Enid and Crosby Kemper Foundation

Judging from the satanic nose and witchlike set of Custer's chin, it is doubtful that Benton's sympathies lay with the Seventh Cavalry's fallen commander.

THOMAS HART BENTON

BORN 1889, NEOSHO, MISSOURI

DIED 1975, KANSAS CITY, MISSOURI

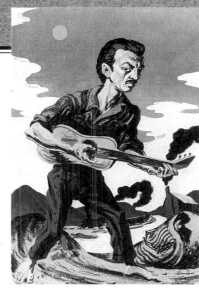

Harry Sternberg, *Thomas Hart Benton*, 1944. Serigraph, 18 ⅝ × 12 ⅜ in.
National Portrait Gallery, Smithsonian Institution.

Son of a congressman and grand nephew and namesake of the fiery nineteenth-century Missouri senator and promoter of western expansion, Thomas Hart Benton left his family's home near the Ozarks when he was seventeen to study at the Art Institute of Chicago. He moved on to Paris in 1908, where he studied at the Académie Julian until 1911.

Benton returned to New York and tried to apply the lessons of European modernism to his work—but with little success. After America's entry into World War I, the artist worked as an architectural draftsman for the U.S. Navy. Partly due to this experience, he turned away from his European training in abstraction and toward the stylized, anecdotal historical realism for which he would become famous.

Between 1926 and 1935, Benton taught at New York's Art Students League (where one of his students was Jackson Pol-lock) and traveled widely throughout the United States, including the Far West, Texas, and New Mexico. His wanderings not only inspired popular regional artworks, they also convinced him that the New York art scene was insular, stultifying, and—as Benton put it—"diseased." He returned to his native Missouri in 1935 and became director of painting at the Kansas City Art Institute.

Benton is best known for his murals in numerous public buildings—the largest being the 45,000-square-foot work in the Missouri State Capitol, executed in 1935–36. Of heroic proportions, Benton's mural work nevertheless avoids the well-worn heroic subjects. The Missouri Capitol mural, for example, depicts such figures as Jesse James and the forsaken Frankie and faithless Johnny of the popular ballad.

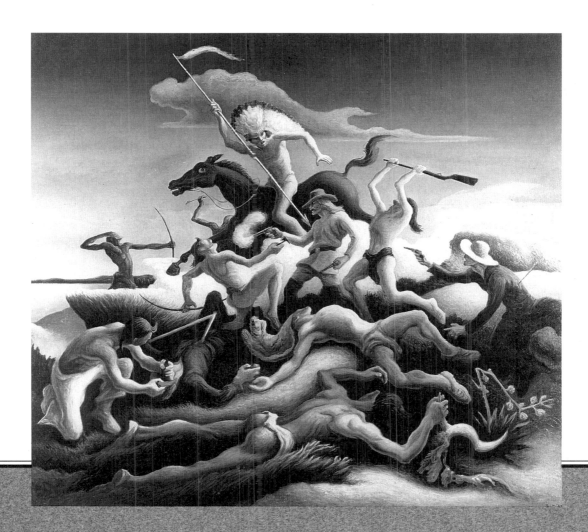

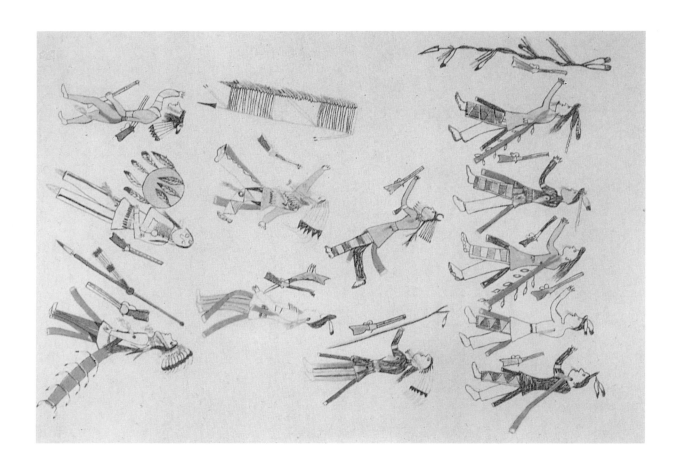

Red Horse (birth and death
dates unknown)
Battle of The Little Big Horn, c. 1876
Crayon and pencil on manila paper,
24 × 36 in.
Historical Pictures Service, Chicago

A chilling Sioux report of the results
of battle: dead Sioux, dead
cavalrymen, and Sioux returning
from combat.
(this page and opposite top)

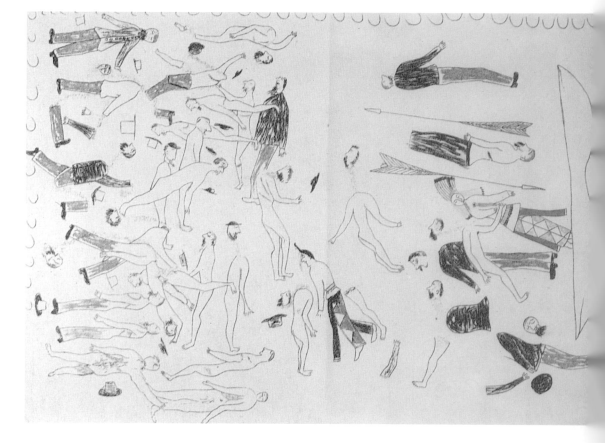

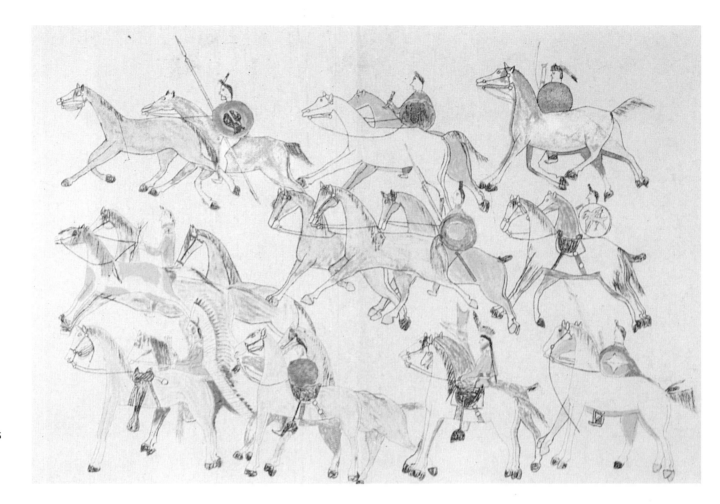

White Bird (birth and death dates unknown)
Battle of The Little Big Horn,
1894–95
Painted on muslin, 67 ½ × 98 in.
Courtesy of The West Point Museum collection, United States Military Academy, West Point, New York

A starkly schematic narrative depiction of the Custer fight by an Indian combatant. *(below)*

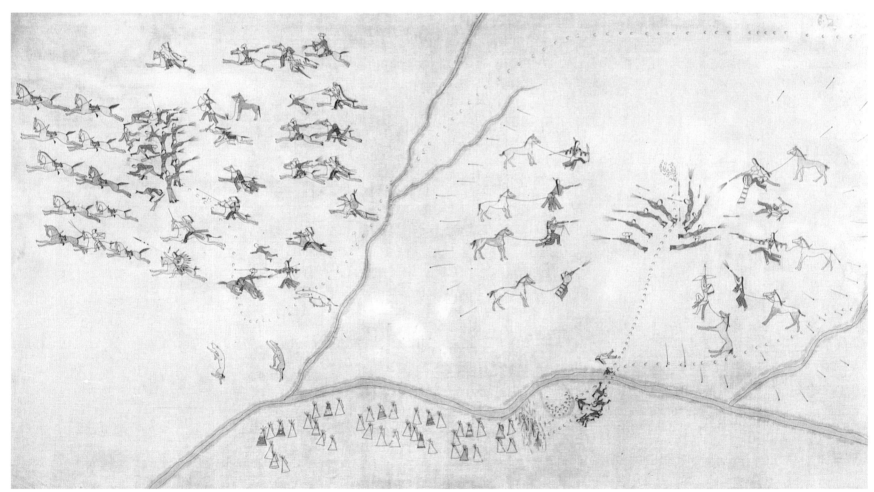

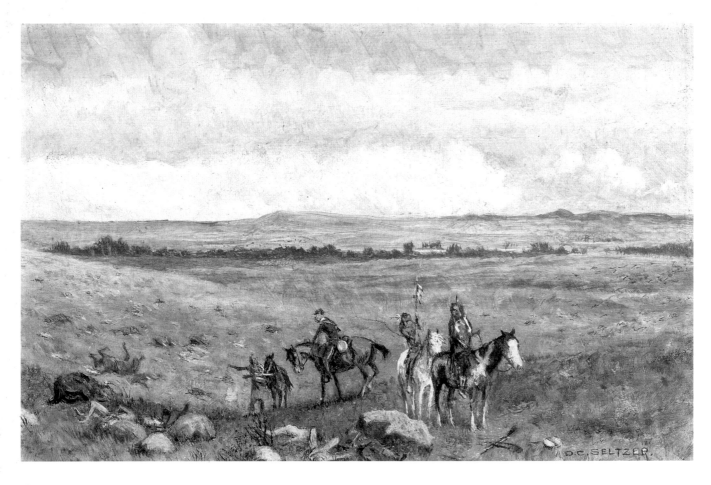

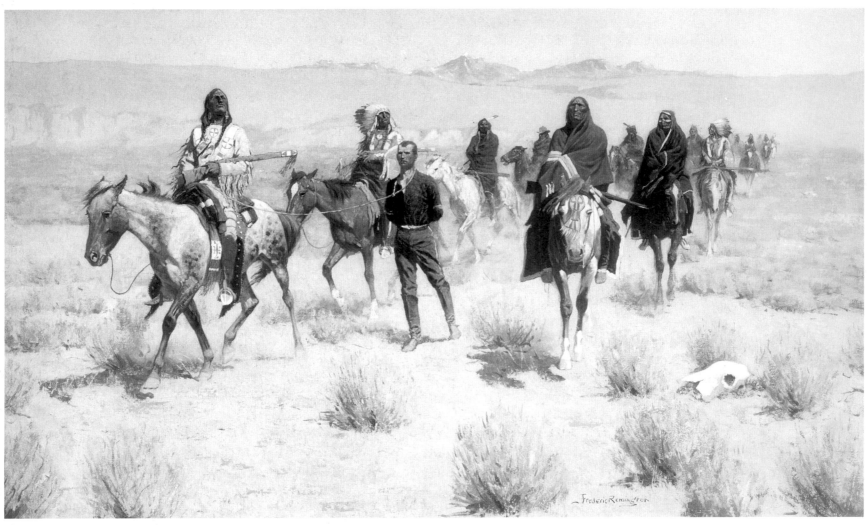

C H A R L E S

S C H R E Y V O G E L

—

BORN 1861, NEW YORK

DIED 1912, HOBOKEN, NEW JERSEY

—

The career of Charles Schreyvogel, one of the most exciting painters of western life, especially cavalry subjects, was marked by poverty, struggle, and frustration. His birth and upbringing were geographically and culturally distant from the West. Born in New York's Lower East Side slums, he sold newspapers and worked as an office boy until his parents moved to Hoboken. There the boy began to carve meerschaum pipes, was apprenticed to a gold engraver, became a die sinker, and, in 1877, a lithographer. Within a few years, he had established himself as a lithographic artist and supplemented his income by teaching drawing.

In 1887, through the assistance of patrons, he was able to study in Munich with Carl Marr and Frank Kirchbach. After three years, he returned to New York, supporting himself again as a lithographic artist while painting portraits, landscapes, and even ivory miniatures—all without financial success.

In 1893 he sketched personalities from Buffalo Bill's Wild West Show, earning enough money to spend the balance of the year touring the West, where he made studies of Utes, western army life, and cowboys. He brought back to his Hoboken studio a collection of western gear, which he used in creating his finished paintings. None of these works sold, however, and he finally offered one, *My Bunkie*, to a restaurant on consignment. When the restaurant owner refused to display it properly, hanging it in a dark corner, the artist angrily took it back and entered it in the 1900 National Academy Exhibition—with so little hope of success that he did not even bother to leave his address with exhibition officials.

The painting won first prize—$300—but, as no one at the academy had ever heard of Schreyvogel, the painter was located with some difficulty. After the exhibition prize, the artist enjoyed "overnight" success. When the contentious Frederic Remington condemned Schreyvogel's military paintings as "half-baked stuff," his soldier subjects rose to his defense, voicing their approval of how he had depicted them.

In contrast to such artists as Remington and Russell, Schreyvogel worked slowly and painstakingly, scrupulously researching his subjects and executing large canvases. While his output was relatively limited, his work was widely reproduced. The artist enjoyed his hard-won success for little more than a decade, succumbing to blood poisoning in 1912, contracted from a chicken bone that had lodged in his gum.

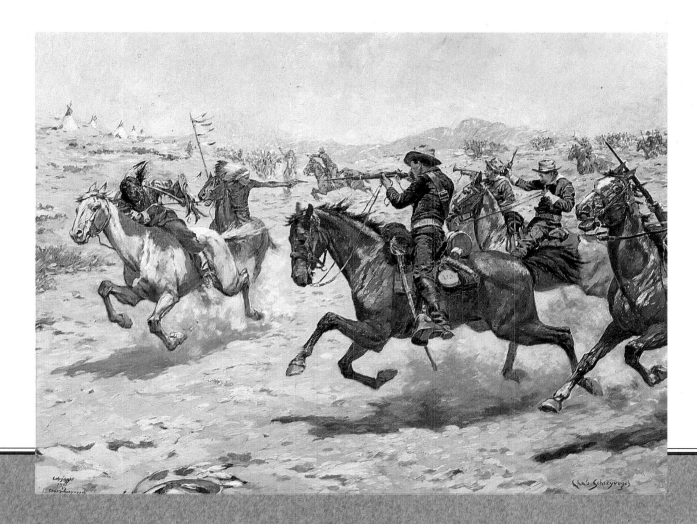

rial," as the Indian agent described him. Fearing that he would stir the reservation to revolt, General Crook ordered his arrest and confinement. Taken into custody on September 5, 1877, he was stabbed to death in a scuffle involving soldiers and Indians. It is unclear whether he was mortally wounded by his own hand, the knife of another Indian, or a soldier's bayonet.

In October 1877, General Terry, with the cooperation of the North-West Mounted Police, located Sitting Bull in Canada and attempted to persuade him to come back to a reservation in the United States. Faced with winter famine and unwelcome by Canadian tribes who did not want to share with them the little game that was available, his Hunkpapas were defecting in small bands. Sitting Bull spat at Terry in 1877—"You come here to tell us lies. Go home where you came from"—but on July 19, 1881, with the last two hundred of his people remaining to him, the chief surrendered at Fort Buford, Dakota Territory.

In the Northwest, the Nez Percés were sharply divided into "treaty" and "nontreaty" factions. An 1863 gold rush prompted a revision of an earlier treaty that had defined the boundaries of the Nez Percé reservation. The new treaty excluded the mineral-rich lands from the reservation. Those Indians whose homes remained within the revised boundaries signed the treaty; those who were dispossessed by the revision refused to sign. Prominent among the latter was the revered Chief Joseph, who re-

pudiated the treaty and lived with his people in land now technically beyond the reservation. However, few whites were interested in that particular area, and Joseph was left in peace. In 1873, two years after Joseph's death, President U. S. Grant even set aside part of the Wallowa Valley as a reservation, but then Oregon settlers began to covet the land for grazing, whereupon Grant reopened the tract to white settlement.

General Oliver O. Howard, a one-armed warrior known as the "praying general" on account of his strong Christian and humanitarian leanings, was named head of a negotiating committee charged with convincing the nontreaty Nez Percés to vacate the disputed lands in return for compensation in goods and money. Young Joseph, who had become chief upon the death of his father, and another Nez Percé leader, Old Toohoolhoolzote, met with Howard at Lapwai, the reservation headquarters. While the general was sympathetic to their position—indeed, he agreed that Old Joseph had not sold the Wallowa Valley—the conference broke down after the two refused to sell out. Frustrated, Howard declared that the Indians had one month to move to the reservation or be driven off by force.

Young Joseph and the other chiefs knew that war would be fruitless. With their people, they marched off to the reservation. As usual, however, it was one thing for the chiefs to agree to the whites' terms and another for the tribe's young men to obey. While traveling to the

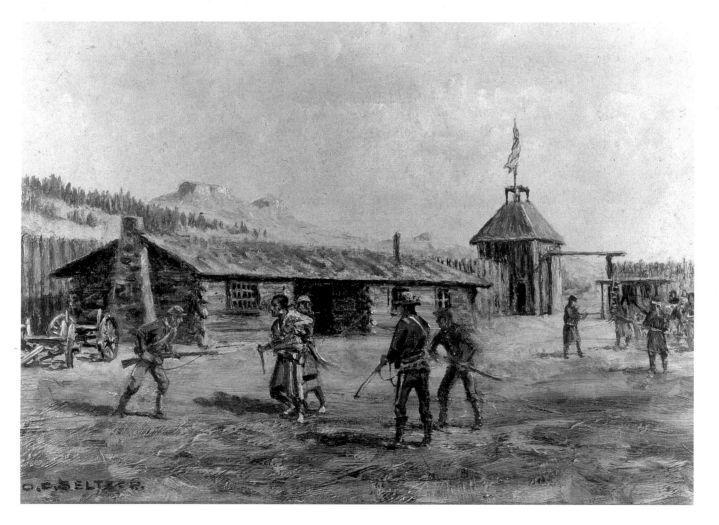

Olaf Carl Seltzer (1877–1957)
*The Stabbing of Crazy Horse—
Sept. 5, 1877,* 1935
Oil on board, 4 ¼ × 6 ½ in.
Gilcrease Museum, Tulsa, Oklahoma

Victorious against Custer, Crazy Horse was apprehended by soldiers of General Crook's command on September 5, 1877. Two days later, a group of soldiers and Indians attempted to disarm the defiant chief. In the struggle, Crazy Horse was fatally stabbed—whether by a soldier, an Indian, or even by his own hand is not known.

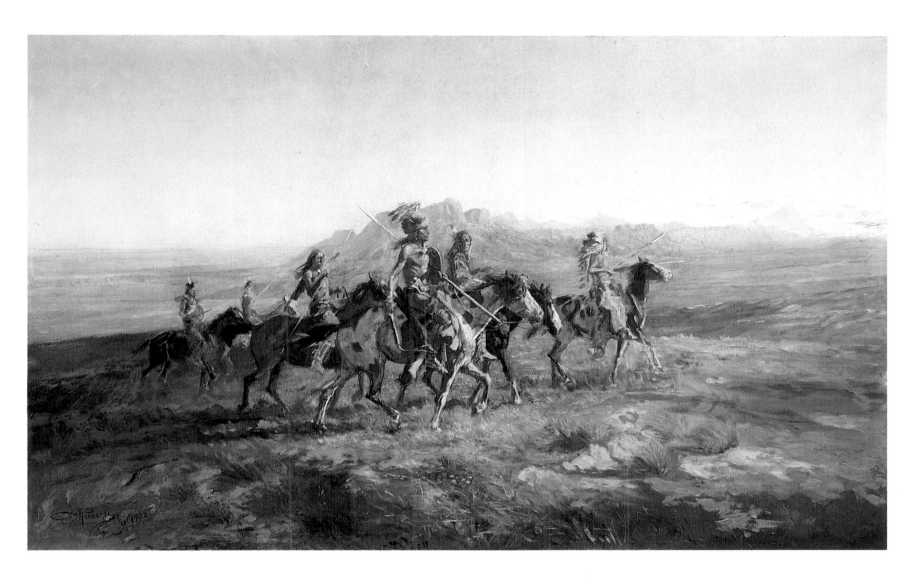

Charles M. Russell (1864–1926)
Sun River War Party, 1903
Oil on canvas, 18 × 30 in.
The Rockwell Museum, Corning,
New York

Russell often depicted Indians with greater formality of technique than he employed with his cowboy subjects, which usually convey the spontaneous feeling of a deft sketch.

reservation, some young warriors, fired up on liquor, killed a number of whites. A hundred cavalrymen from Fort Lapwai were dispatched, but were soundly defeated in the Battle of White Bird Canyon on June 17, 1877. Howard responded by leading a force of four hundred infantry and cavalry in a three-week-long pursuit of the Nez Percés. On July 11, the Battle of Clearwater began. After two bloody days of combat, the Indians were routed. Exhausted by the battle, Howard failed to pursue the scattering bands.

It was not until August 9 that the army made contact with the Nez Percés again when Colonel John Gibbon, leading 15 officers, 146 enlisted regulars, and 45 volunteers, surprised a camp on the Big Hole River, Montana. Under the leadership of Chief Looking Glass, the Indians quickly rallied and counterattacked, killing 2 of Gibbon's officers, 22 regulars, and 6 civilians, and wounding 5 more officers, 30 enlisted men, and 4 civilians. Indian losses were also heavy—at least 89 dead—but Gibbon was sent dragging back to his station as the Nez Percés fled across the newly established Yellowstone National Park.

Howard gave chase. The Seventh Cavalry, under Colonel Samuel D. Sturgis, attempted to block the Indians' escape route. But the Nez Percés evaded both Howard and Sturgis until September 13, when the Seventh

Cavalry engaged them at the site of present-day Billings, Montana. Sturgis lost three men killed and eleven wounded—and, once again, the Nez Percés got away.

The Nez Percés sought haven among the Crows, but soon discovered that Crow scouts had been fighting on the side of the bluecoat officer they had just evaded. They determined to press northward, to Canada, where, they trusted, Sitting Bull would welcome them as brothers. But first, Looking Glass counseled, the people needed a rest. Thinking they had left the soldiers far behind, the Nez Percés slowed their march. On September 30, they were camped just forty miles south of the Canadian border, on the northern edge of the Bear Paw Mountains. There, with 350 to 400 men, Nelson A. Miles attacked. But the Indians had had time to take up positions in a cutbank south and east of their camp, from which they were able to mow down 60 of Miles's cavalrymen. The dashing commander pulled back and settled into a siege, which lasted through six snowy, miserable days, from September 30 to October 5. On October 4, General Howard arrived with a small escort, but left command to Miles.

During this time, the Indians held council. Chief Joseph argued for surrender. Looking Glass and White Bird wanted to fight. On October 1, under a flag of truce, Joseph went to meet Miles to negotiate surrender terms.

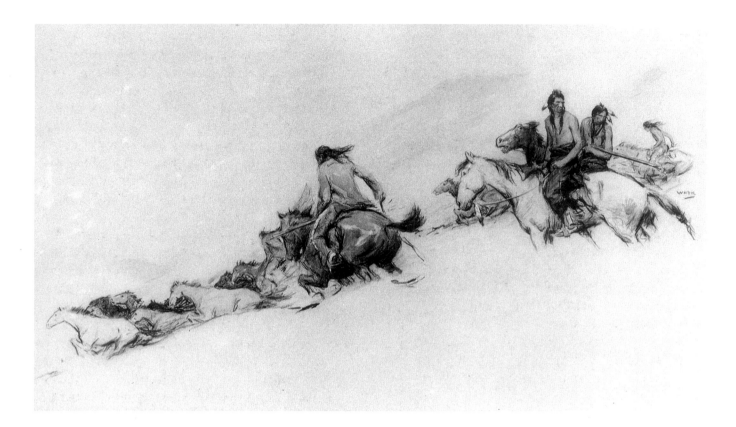

W. H. D. Koerner (1878–1938)
Crow Raiders, 1931
Charcoal and watercolor, 15 × 28 in.
Charles B. Goddard Center for the Visual and Performing Arts, Ardmore, Oklahoma

The object of most Plains Indian raids was the acquisition of horses.

Talks broke down, and Miles decided to hold the chief. But one Lieutenant Lovell H. Jerome, apparently believing that the Indians were about to surrender, carelessly wandered into their lines and was seized. Miles exchanged Joseph for the errant lieutenant. On October 5, after another fruitless debate among Joseph and Looking Glass and White Bird, Joseph again prepared to meet Miles. Leaving the council, Looking Glass was struck in the forehead by a stray bullet and killed.

Chief Joseph went to Miles and spoke:

I am tired of fighting. Our chiefs are killed. Looking Glass is dead. Toohoolhoolzote is dead. The old men are all dead. It is the young men who say yes or no. He who led on the young men [Joseph's brother, Ollokot] is dead. It is cold and we have no blankets. The little children are freezing to death. My people, some of them, have run away to the hills, and have no blankets, no food; no one knows where they are—perhaps freezing to death. I want to have time to look for my children and see how many of them I can find. Maybe I shall find them among the dead. Hear me, my chiefs! I am tired; my heart is sick and sad. From where the sun now stands I will fight no more forever.

Thus ended the epic of the Nez Percés. For three months, 800 strong, they had traveled over seventeen hundred miles of extraordinarily rugged terrain, eluding the army at each turn. About 120 died on the trek. After his retirement to the reservation, Chief Joseph spent many years petitioning the United States government for permission to return to the Wallowa Valley. Although he was aided in his efforts by Generals Miles and Howard,

the land was never regained, and Joseph died in the Colville Reservation in 1904.

Farther west, in Idaho and Oregon, the Northern Paiutes and Bannocks were being stirred to war by a Bannock chief named Buffalo Horn. Incursions of white settlement depleted game and even camas roots, a staple that the Indians dug for on Camas Prairie, ninety miles southeast of Boise, Idaho. The right to dig for camas was guaranteed by explicit treaty, but by 1878 settlers' hogs were destroying the roots, and on May 30 Buffalo Horn launched a raid into southern Idaho. When a party of civilian volunteers killed Buffalo Horn on June 8, his 200 warriors rode to Oregon, where they found Paiute allies under the leadership of a militant medicine man named Oytes and a chief known as Egan. The new alliance fielded about 450 warriors against a slightly larger number of soldiers led by General Howard, who pursued his quarry with determination, engaging them in repeated combat through most of the summer and finally driving the Paiutes to the Yakima Reservation in Washington and the Bannocks to their reservation on the Snake River.

In western Colorado and eastern Utah, miners were working the silver strikes of the 1870s, lusting after new territory to prospect. They pressed for permission to invade the Ute reservation in Colorado. In the meantime, the Ute agent, Nathan C. Meeker, was attempting to force the free-ranging Indians to take up lives as sedentary farmers. He demanded that they begin plowing their ponies' grazing land. When, on September 10, 1879, a Ute medicine man known as Johnson complained to Meeker that plowing the grazing lands would starve the horses, the agent replied: "You have too many ponies. You had better kill some of them." This so infuriated Johnson that he threw Meeker out his own front door. The agent telegraphed back east that he and the agency were in danger. Major Thomas T. Thornburgh, commanding 175 infantry and cavalrymen, was ordered to Meeker's relief.

The sight of a column of troops served only to stir the Utes to greater hostility. Meeker himself asked that Thornburgh personally approach the agency for a parley. The major agreed, and the talks were arranged, but at the last minute Thornburgh decided to move 120 cavalrymen closer to the agency, just in case. The Utes, believing they were about to be attacked, confronted the soldiers on the trail. It was a tense face-off, and when the major's adjutant waved his hat—apparently in greeting—either an Indian or a soldier took it for a signal. A shot was fired, and the Battle of Milk Creek began.

Thornburgh was among the first slain, felled by a rifle bullet above the ear. The troops retreated across the creek and took refuge behind their wagon train, which had been defensively circled up. A week-long siege ended when two of the defenders were able to sneak

Cyrennius Hall (1840–1904)
Chief Joseph (Hinmaton-Yalaktit),
1878
Oil on canvas, 22 ¼ × 18 in.
National Portrait Gallery, Smithsonian Institution

After months of pursuit by the U.S. Cavalry, Chief Joseph led his Nez Percé to surrender and, with it, life on a reservation. His speech of capitulation has haunted the white American conscience since the day it was spoken, October 5, 1877.

through the Indian lines and summon reinforcements.

All of this was too late for Agent Meeker. He and nine other agency employees had been killed and the agency buildings burned. Mrs. Meeker, her daughter, and another woman and her two children were taken captive. Generals Sherman and Sheridan were all for a vigorous campaign of punishment, even though it would mean the death of the captive women. However, Secretary of the Interior Carl Schurz, an Indian agent named Charles Adams, and a peace-counseling old Ute chief called Ouray managed to negotiate the release of the captives without further bloodshed. By 1880, this proud tribe was living on reservations in eastern Utah and southwestern Colorado.

In the rugged Lost River valley of northern California and southern Oregon, a small tribe of about three hundred people was trying to live in something like harmony with the miners who had come into the region. The Modocs, a hunting and gathering people, were by nature aggressive, having terrorized white immigrants along the Applegate Trail during the 1850s. But by the 1860s, the Modocs, led by Kintpuash—whom the whites called Captain Jack—wanted peace. The trouble was that they were not willing to accept subsistence on a reservation, especially one they shared with the Klamath Indians who, resenting intrusion into their land, made life unpleasant for the Modocs. Instead, they settled on the Lost River, near Tule Lake, getting their living for some seven years by trade with the neighboring white settlers. By the 1870s, as more and more whites poured into the region, pressure mounted for the Modocs' removal. Finally, on November 29, 1872, a force of forty cavalrymen entered Captain Jack's camp and proceeded to disarm the Indians. A scuffle between a trooper and an Indian resulted in an exchange of fire. The Modocs scattered unharmed; several soldiers were hit.

With fifty warriors, Captain Jack hid in the twisted, otherworldly landscape of the Lava Beds south of Tule Lake, a place the Indians called the Land of Burnt-Out Fires. On January 17, 1873, Lieutenant Colonel Frank Wheaton attempted to flush out the Indians with a force of 309 men. Nine of Wheaton's men were killed, and 28 were wounded. Not only had the army failed to kill or capture any Modocs, no soldier had even *seen* the enemy.

Unable to dislodge the Modocs by force of arms, General Edward R. S. Canby, commander of the Department of the Columbia, decided to try diplomacy and formed a peace commission including himself, a Methodist preacher named Eleaser Thomas, a former superintendent of Indian affairs, Alfred B. Meacham, and another official, L. S. Dyar.

Under a flag of truce, Canby began talks with Captain Jack by demanding unconditional surrender. Jack asked that he be given "this Lava Bed for a home. I can live here; take away your soldiers, and we can settle everything. Nobody will ever want these rocks; give me a home here."

When neither side backed down, Jack withdrew to his camp. Confident that the general could be made to change his mind, Captain Jack urged persistence and patience. Other Modocs wanted to murder Canby and the other peace commissioners as a warning to all whites. Jack pointed out that such a killing would only result in redoubled efforts at pursuit and, most likely, the annihilation of the Modocs. Berating Jack as a weak woman and coward, the militant Modocs goaded him into committing murder. "All who want me to kill Canby," Jack said to his warriors, "raise to your feet." When a majority did just that, Jack declared with resignation, "I see you do not love life nor anything else. . . . I will ask [Canby] many times. If he comes to my terms I shall not kill him."

On Good Friday, April 11, 1873, despite warnings from the Modoc wife of his interpreter, Edward Canby and the other three commissioners held council with Captain Jack. The general passed out cigars to all present and began the council by promising to take the Modocs to a good country. As he had told his fellow warriors, Jack answered each of the commission's demands with his own single demand to be allowed to live in the Lava Beds.

Tempers flared. Another Modoc, Hooker Jim, donned Meacham's overcoat, which had been draped over the commissioner's saddle, strutted about in it, and asked, "You think I look like Meacham?"

The commissioner attempted to go along with the Indian's joke, offering Hooker Jim his hat. "Take it and put it on; then you will be Meacham."

"You keep a while. Hat will be mine by and by."

The threat was all too evident. Canby tried to make Jack understand that "only the Great Father in Washington" could withdraw the troops.

"I want to tell you, Canby," repeated Jack, "we cannot make peace as long as these soldiers are crowding me. If you ever promise me a home, somewhere in this country, promise me today. Now, Canby, promise me. . . . Now is your chance."

"General," Meacham implored, "for heaven's sake, promise him."

Another Modoc, Schonchin John, leaped to his feet: "You take away soldiers, you give us back our land! We tired talking. We talk no more!"

"Ot-we-kau-tux-e," Jack called out: *All ready!* He drew a pistol, pointed it at Canby's face, pulled the trigger—and the hammer clicked; the weapon failed to fire. The general stared in astonishment as Captain Jack pulled the trigger again. This time there was a loud report, and Edward Canby fell back dead (some accounts say that he was stabbed as well as shot), the only U.S. Army general killed in the Indian wars.

Reverend Thomas was also slain, and Meacham was wounded; L. S. Dyar escaped without harm. Jack

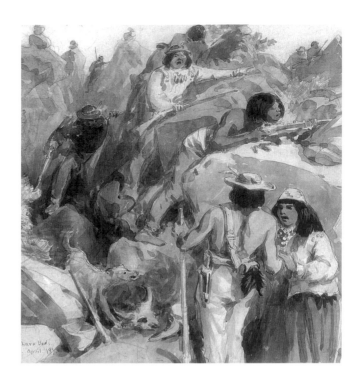

William Simpson (1823–1903)
The Modoc Indians in the Lava Beds, 1873
Watercolor, 16 ½ × 11 in.
Peabody Museum, Harvard University

and his warriors fled to the Lava Beds, where they were pounded by mortar fire and invaded by infantry. But the Modocs always eluded their enemy. On April 26, they sighted a reconnoitering party of sixty-six soldiers and a dozen Indian scouts eating lunch in an entirely vulnerable spot. With twenty-two braves, Scarfaced Charley attacked, killing five officers, twenty men, and wounding another sixteen. "All you fellows that ain't dead," Charley called out, "had better go home. We don't want to kill you all in one day."

Even in the face of these victories, the Modoc warriors began to realize that continued resistance was ultimately futile. By the middle of May, the Modocs had scattered. It remained for troops under Jefferson C. Davis (no relation to the Confederate president) to hunt them down and bring the ringleaders to justice for the murder of Edward Canby. On June 1, a cavalry detachment found Captain Jack and his family hiding in a cave, coaxed them out, and took them prisoner. Captain Jack, Boston Charley, Black Jim, and Schonchin John were hanged.

APACHE FINALE

By the early 1870s, after more than a decade of continual warfare, all of the Apaches retired to reservations in Arizona and New Mexico—except for the Chiricahua Apaches, led by Cochise. The "praying general," Oliver O. Howard, employed Thomas J. Jeffords, the only white man who enjoyed the respect of Cochise, to search out the chief and his people and arrange a parley. In the fall of 1872, Howard and Cochise finally met and began two weeks of discussion to determine the fate of the Chiricahuas. Although Howard hammered away at a reservation along the Rio Grande, Cochise insisted that he wanted Apache Pass, where full-scale hostilities had begun in 1861, promising now to keep the peace. At length, Howard agreed.

Content with his reservation, Cochise kept his promise not to fight. Other Apache bands, who had marched off to the reservations well before Cochise, became so disgusted with reservation life that they began raiding. Lieutenant Colonel George Crook, employing small, highly mobile forces, moved against them, enaging Apache war parties at least twenty times, killing perhaps two hundred braves. By the end of March 1873 Apaches began surrendering, and by fall some six thousand had been concentrated on reservations again.

In 1875 it was decided to take the concentration of the Apaches a step further by abolishing the four separate reservations in Arizona and New Mexico and removing all of the Apaches to one large reservation, San Carlos, in Arizona. Cochise had died in 1874, and the Chiricahuas lacked the leadership that might have kept them together in resistance. When they were ordered to San Carlos in 1876, about half went, and the remainder

scattered into Mexico. The Warm Springs Apaches were ordered to the reservation the following year. Again, some scattered, some marched to San Carlos.

It was an awful place, barren, hot, disease ridden. The agency, as usual, provided insufficient rations and distributed poorly what little it had. In this place of discontent and misery, two militant leaders rose up, Victorio and Geronimo. Victorio made the first break from San Carlos on September 2, 1877, when he led more than 300 Warm Springs Apaches and a few Chiricahuas out of the reservation. For a month Victorio and his people resisted the ever-pursuing soldiers, but were finally compelled to surrender at Fort Wingate, New Mexico. After the surrender, however, they were permitted to return to their homeland at Ojo Caliente while the government debated their fate. Within a year the order came to return to San Carlos. Most did return, but Victorio, together with 80 warriors, headed for the hills and tried in vain to return to Ojo Caliente. In 1879 he even attempted to settle with the Mescalero Apaches on their reservation, but it was not to be. On September 4, 1879, Victorio and

Frederic Remington (1861–1909)
Aiding a Comrade, c. 1890
Oil on canvas, 34 5/16 × 48 1/8 in.
The Museum of Fine Arts, Houston;
The Hogg Brothers Collection, Gift
of Miss Ima Hogg

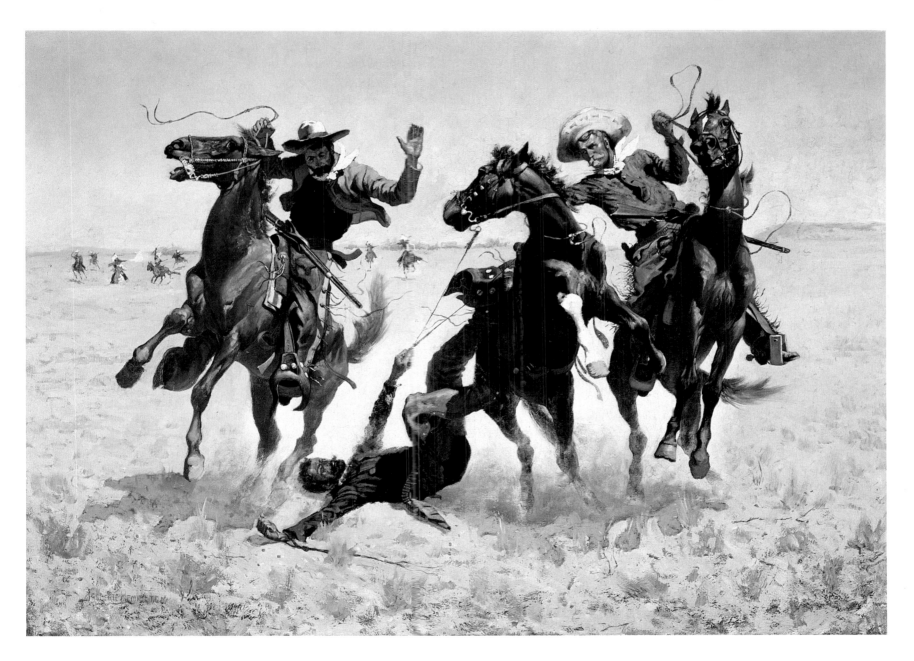

60 warriors raided the camp of Troop E, Ninth Cavalry, killing eight soldiers, and stealing forty-six horses. An influx of Mescaleros brought Victorio's strength to some 150 men, who terrorized the Mexican state of Chihuahua, much of western Texas, southern New Mexico, and Arizona.

Mexican and American forces cooperated in pursuit of Victorio, who managed to elude them for over a year. By the fall of 1880, however, Victorio's warriors began to wear out. Colonel George P. Buell joined his forces with Mexican irregulars commanded by Colonel Joaquín Terrazas to bring Victorio to ground in Chihuahua. As it became clear that they were about to make contact with the Indians, Terrazas ordered Buell and his troops out of the country. The honor of destroying Victorio would belong to a Mexican officer.

During October 15–16, 1880, Terrazas engaged Victorio at the Battle of Tres Castillos. The fighting was hand to hand, "man against man," as Terrazas reported, "the combatants wrestling with each other and getting hold of each other's heads." In addition to Victorio, seventy-seven Indians died, including sixteen women and children. Those who escaped made their way back to New Mexico and eventually united with Geronimo in a last-ditch effort to escape confinement at the San Carlos reservation.

Even among the Apaches, Geronimo—Goyahkla

was his Indian name—was considered (as one said) "a true wild man." He rode with the Nednhi band of Chiricahua Apaches, who lived in the Sierra Madre of Mexico. When he turned up at the Ojo Caliente reservation in New Mexico in 1877, agent John P. Clum had him apprehended and taken to San Carlos. After a year there, he escaped to Mexico again but returned to San Carlos in 1880, after being pursued by Mexican troops.

During this period at San Carlos there arose a prophet among the Apaches, Nakaidoklini, who preached the resurrection of the dead and a return to the good old days when the Apaches ruled the Southwest. He trained celebrants of his religion to invoke the spirits by means of a dance, anticipating the so-called Ghost Dance religion that would soon be introduced among the Sioux. Whites saw the religion of Nakaidoklini as dangerous and liable to foment rebellion. On August 30, 1881, Colonel Eugene A. Carr, commanding Fort Apache, led seventy-nine regulars, twenty-three White Mountain Apache scouts, and nine civilians to seek out Nakaidoklini at his village and, as San Carlos agent J. C. Tiffany put it, have him "arrested or killed or both."

With the medicine man in custody, Carr's troops set up camp outside the village. About one hundred followers of Nakaidoklini attacked the encampment. The White Mountain scouts mutinied, killing their captain. A sergeant shot and killed Nakaidoklini, and Carr's command

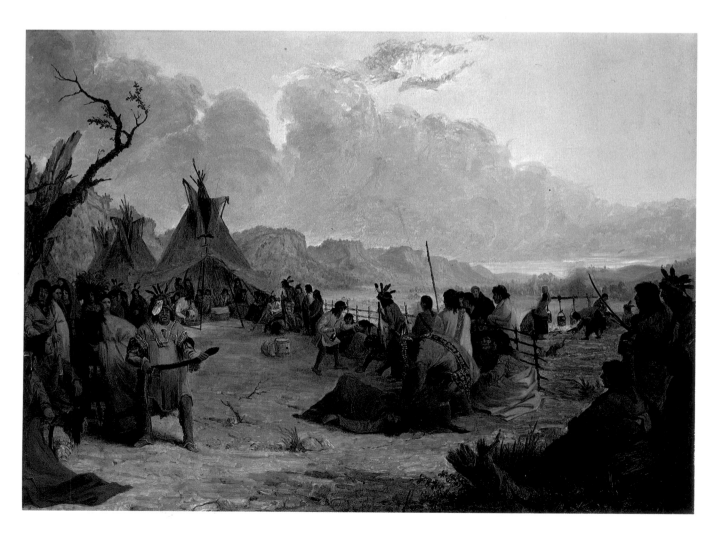

Seth Eastman (1808–1875)
Medicine Dance, 1848
Oil on canvas, 25 ½ × 35 ½ in.
Courtesy of the Buffalo Bill Historical Center, Cody, Wyoming

Eastman successfully combined a career as an army officer with that of a painter, serving on several army surveys as a topographical draftsman; his precision of line and acuteness of eye are apparent here.

314

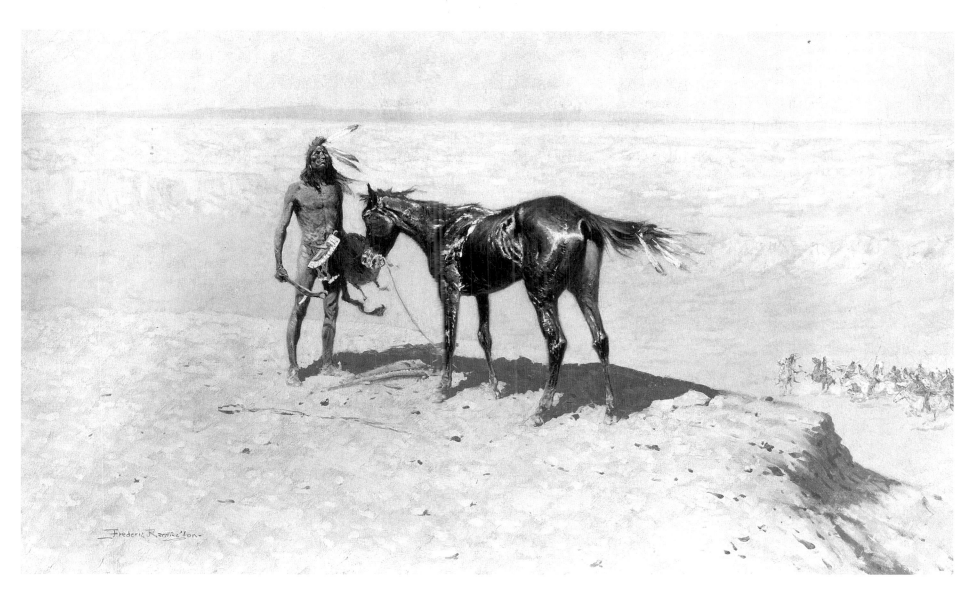

Frederic Remington (1861–1909)
Ridden Down, 1905
Oil on canvas, 30 × 51 ¼ in.
Amon Carter Museum, Fort Worth,
Texas

His horse spent, a lone warrior
prepares to meet his doom.

barely escaped the swarm of attackers. No sooner had the soldiers retired to Fort Apache than the Indians attacked them there. Newspapers carried headlines announcing that Carr's entire command had been butchered, and army regulars rushed into the San Carlos area from all over the Southwest. By the end of September, Nachez—son of Cochise—Juh, Chato, and Geronimo, with seventy-four braves, were again heading for Mexico, where they united with the survivors of the Battle of Tres Castillos. In April 1882 a war party stormed back to San Carlos, killed the reservation police chief, and forced the leader of the Warm Springs Apaches, Loco, along with several hundred Indians, to return to Mexico with them. Later, in July, White Mountain Apaches, followers of the slain Nakaidoklini, came back to San Carlos and killed the new police chief, along with three of his officers.

These raids moved the army to replace Major General Orlando B. Willcox with General George Crook as commander of the Department of Arizona. Crook set about recruiting scouts from among the White Mountain Apaches themselves and, with 193 of them as well as a troop of cavalry and a substantial supply train, pursued Apache raiders into the most remote reaches of the Sierra Madre in Mexico. On May 15, Crook's troops attacked the encampment of Chato. It was a significant action; for the Indians had assumed that their wilderness

position was undiscoverable and, in any event, impregnable. Leaders, including Geronimo, came to parley with Crook.

The general took a very hard line, telling them that Mexicans as well as Americans were tired of their "depredations" and that his intention was not to take them prisoner, but "to wipe them out." Crook told them that Mexican troops were approaching as well and that the "best thing for them to do was to fight their way out if they thought they could do it. I kept them waiting for several days," Crook later reported. "Jeronimo and all the chiefs at last fairly begged me to be taken back to San Carlos." Actually, only the Warm Springs Apaches immediately returned to San Carlos; Geronimo and the Chiricahuas took their time, arriving not until March 1884.

The reservation did not remain quiet for long. General Crook had many rules for the San Carlos Reservation, among them a prohibition against a form of booze called tiswin. The Indians defied the ban in May 1885, and Geronimo, Nachez, Chihuahua, and the venerable chief Nana, with 134 others, ran from the reservation and headed for Mexico. Crook had to give chase, making, as usual, liberal use of Indian scouts. But the Apaches always eluded their pursuers, all the while terrorizing the citizenry of Arizona and New Mexico. Nevertheless, the army pressed the chase, even crossing into Sonora, Mexico. By January 1886, the renegades were tiring of life on the run. They sent a squaw to the camp of Captain Emmet Crawford, commander of Apache scouts, with a message that Geronimo wanted to talk about surrender.

The conference was set for January 11. On the morning of that day, Captain Crawford was awakened by his sentries and told that troops were approaching. At first, Crawford believed it was another column of Apache scouts, and he yelled out to them in Apache. The advancing soldiers opened fire.

For they were not Apache scouts, but Mexican militiamen. Crawford climbed up a rock and waved a white handkerchief. "Soldados Americanos," he called out to the Mexicans. Another volley was fired, and Emmet Crawford lay mortally wounded. His scouts, enraged, traded fire with the Mexicans. Although the Sonoran governor and the Mexican government later apologized for the "accidental" shooting of Crawford, it has never been clear just how accidental the attack was. The Sonorans resented the incursion of American soldiers and, even more, Apache scouts into their territory, especially since the scouts often fell to looting and rustling. Moreover, the Mexican government paid the militiamen not a salary, but a bounty on scalps—and there was no way to tell whether a scalp had belonged to a hostile Apache or an Apache scout.

Although the peace conference had been thus tragically postponed, it took place two days later at Canyon de los Embudos, on March 25, 1886. General Crook adopted the demeanor that had served him well at the peace conference two years earlier. "I'll keep after you and kill the last one," he told Geronimo, Nachez, Chihuahua, and Nana, "if it takes fifty years." This time, however, he offered only one alternative to death: two years of exile in the East. After long conference among themselves, the Apaches accepted. On the way to Fort Bowie, Arizona, the place agreed upon for the formal surrender, Geronimo encountered a whiskey peddler and, always a hard-drinking man, tied one on. Thus fortified, he bolted, taking twenty men and thirteen women with him. Compounding Crook's chagrin was a telegram from Philip Sheridan ordering him to retract the surrender conditions to which the Indians had agreed and demand unconditional surrender. Exhausted, discouraged, morally unable to comply with Sheridan's order, General George Crook asked to be relieved of command. Sheridan dispatched Nelson A. Miles to take his place.

Miles disdained the use of Apache scouts, preferring to rely exclusively on army regulars. He sent a strike force under Captain Henry W. Lawton to run Geronimo to ground. Lawton's men chased the Indians through the whole of the summer of 1886, penetrating Mexico as far as two hundred miles south of the border without once actually engaging the enemy. The chase had taken its toll, however, and by the end of August, Geronimo was ready to talk. Lieutenant Charles Gatewood accepted the hazardous assignment of venturing into Geronimo's

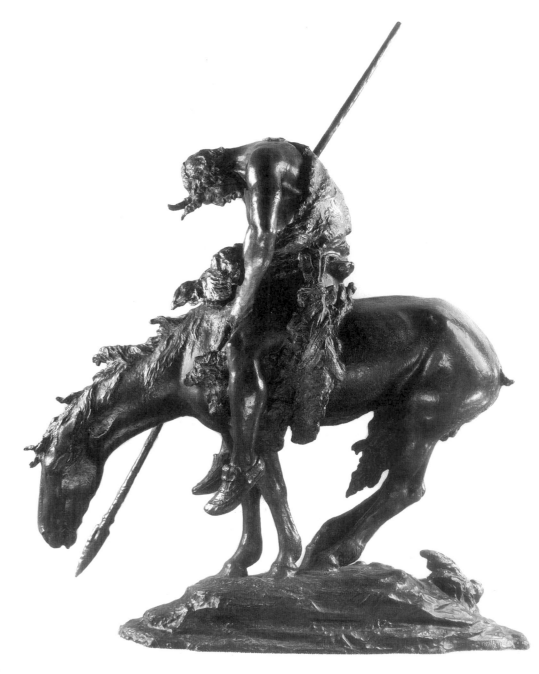

camp, accompanied only by two Indian guides, to persuade the Apaches to accept what, in fact, Crook had demanded, exile to a Florida prison until President Grover Cleveland determined his fate. At first Geronimo announced that he would accept confinement only at San Carlos, but when Gatewood told him that all the Warm Springs and Chiricahua Apaches had already been moved to Florida, the dispirited warrior agreed to surrender to General Miles, who sent him out of Fort Bowie and on his way to Florida to the strains of "Auld Lang Syne" played by the regimental band. Eventually, the Chiricahuas and Warm Spring Apaches would be permitted to return to the West, but only as far as a reservation in Oklahoma. Geronimo died, age eighty, at Fort Sill, Oklahoma, in 1909.

GHOST DANCE

By the middle 1880s, the United States contained 187 reservations—181,000 square miles of land—harboring 243,000 Indians. With the final surrender of Geronimo,

James Earle Fraser (1876–1953)
End of the Trail, modeled c. 1894; cast c. 1908
Bronze, H. 44 ½ in.
The Rockwell Museum, Corning, New York

A small-scale study for a sculpture executed for the Panama-Pacific Exposition in 1915. In 1913 the artist designed the Indian-head nickel.

Joseph Henry Sharp (1859–1953)
Early Moonlight, Little Horn, Montana, n.d.
Watercolor on paper, 19 ½ × 14 ¼ in.
Stark Museum of Art, Orange, Texas

Luminous and tranquil, Sharp's canvas suggests the Indians' tenuous hold on the twentieth century.

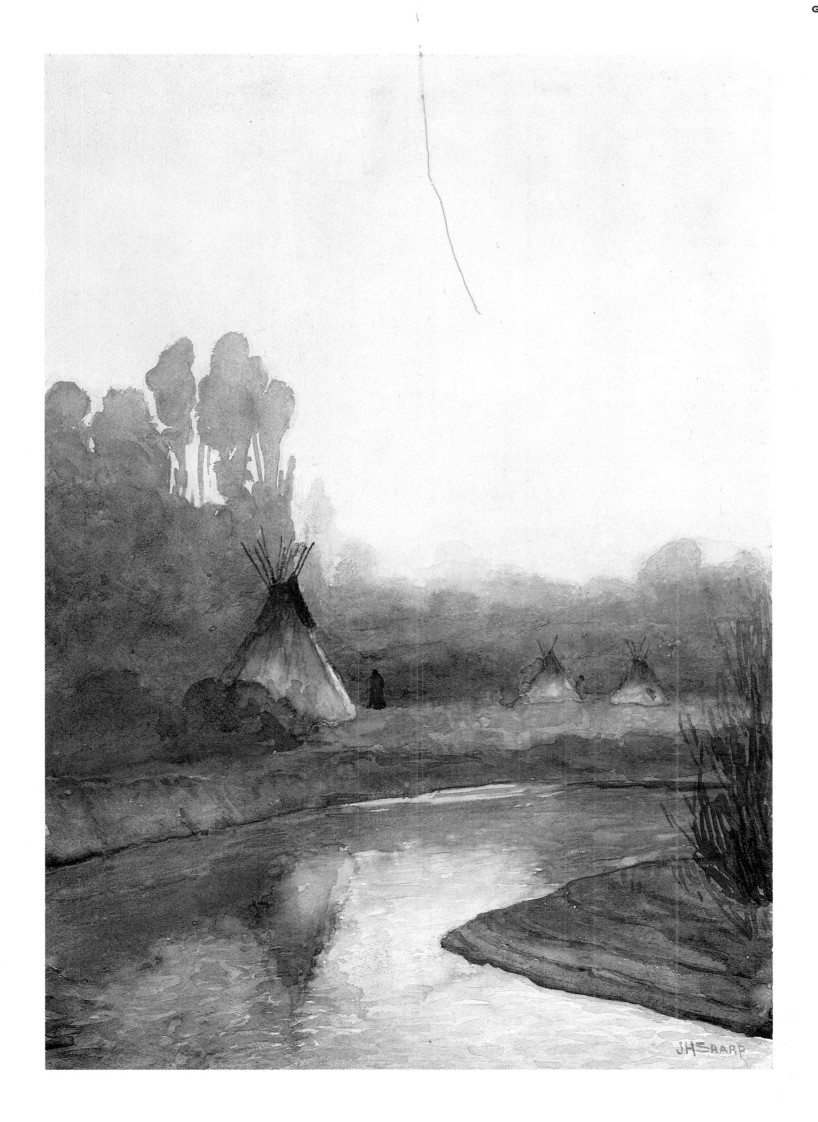

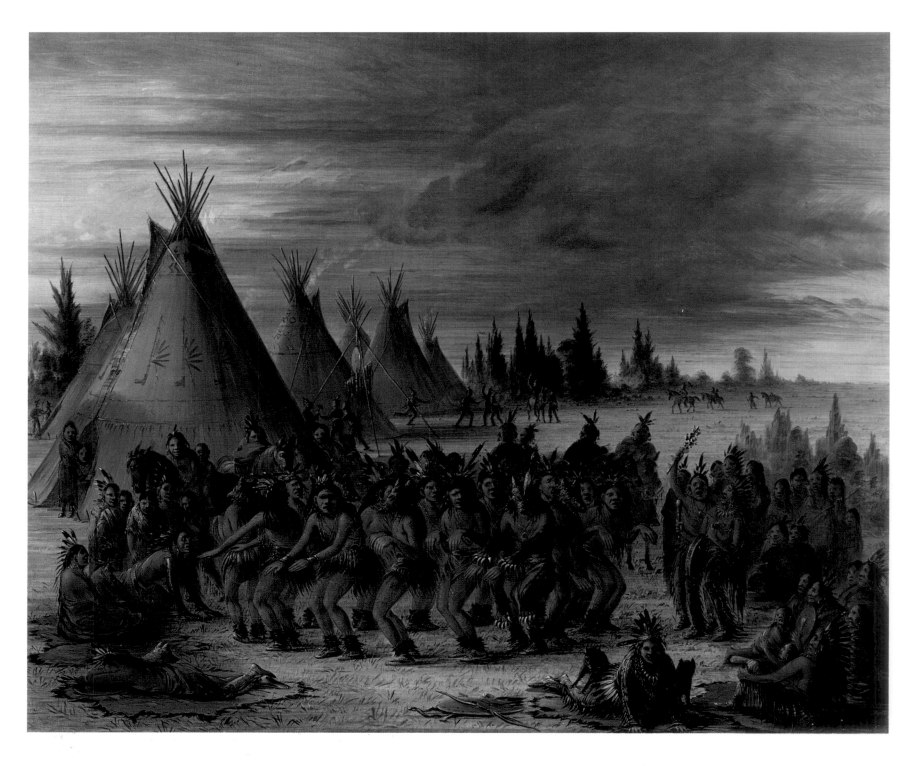

the last significant Indian resistance was neutralized. But there were still two final melancholy acts left to play out.

While almost a quarter of a million Indians were confined to reservations, not all of them had relinquished their identity and way of life. Sitting Bull, presiding over the Hunkpapas at the Standing Rock Reservation, stubbornly refused to cooperate with the agent in charge and did all he could to avoid contact with the white world. At its best, the reservation system was an undermanned and inefficiently run bureaucracy. At its worst—and that meant more often than not—it was a corrupt and cruel machine that failed even to maintain the Indians at a decent level of subsistence or to provide elementary sanitation. Out of the hunger, disease, and despair that afflicted the reservations in the 1880s arose a prophet,

Wovoka, a Paiute shaman's son who had spent part of his life with a white rancher's family and had imbibed Indian as well as Christian religious traditions. Wovoka was moved to preach, and he preached of a new world coming, one in which only Indians dwelled and in which buffalo were again plentiful. The generations of dead Indians would come back to life in the new world, and all would live in bliss. To propitiate this millennium, Wovoka counseled, all Indians must dance the Ghost Dance and must observe peaceful ways: "Do no harm to anyone."

Soon, many of the western reservations were alive with Ghost Dancing. Among the Sioux, however, Wovoka's injunction to peace was suppressed. Short Bull and Kicking Bear urged hastening the day of deliverance by a

George Catlin (1796–1872)
The Bear Dance (Sioux), 1847
Oil on canvas, 25 × 32 in.
Gilcrease Museum, Tulsa, Oklahoma

"All the world have heard of the '*bear dance*,' though I doubt whether more than a very small proportion have ever seen it. The Sioux . . . are fond of bear's meat, and must have good stores of 'bear's-grease' laid in, to oil their long and glossy locks, as well as the surface of their bodies. And they all like the fine pleasure of a bear hunt, and also a participation in the bear dance. . . ."—George Catlin, *The Manners, Customs and Condition of the North American Indians*, 1841.

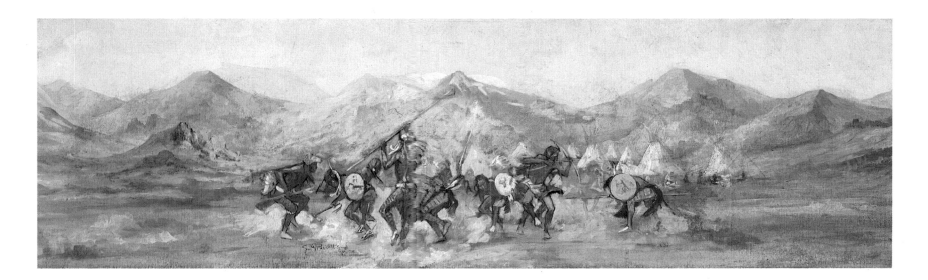

Charles M. Russell (1864–1926)
The Indian War Dance, 1906
Oil on canvas, 14 ¾ × 50 ⅛ in.
Amon Carter Museum, Fort Worth,
Texas

Dance served a central and complex
role in many Indian cultures. Most
white observers were incapable of
distinguishing between a war dance
and the Ghost Dance, which was in
essence pacific, and saw all Indian
dancing as frenzied and menacing.

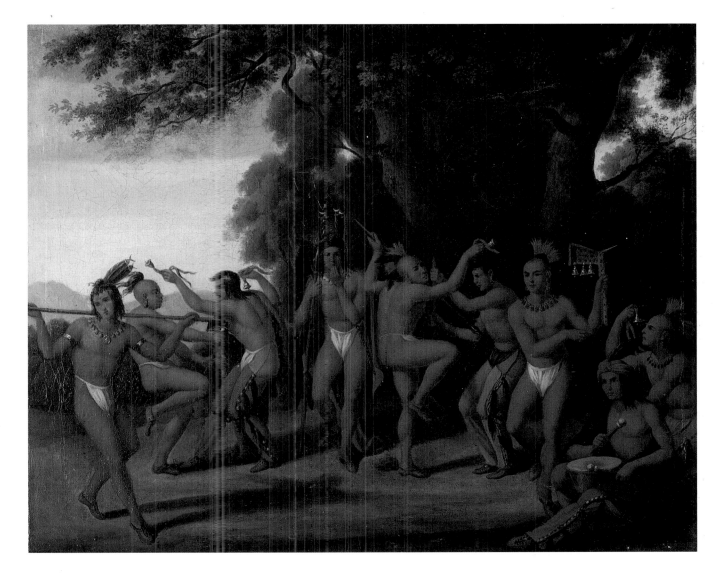

Ferdinand Flor (1793–1881)
Indian Dance, 1838
Oil on canvas, 20 × 24 ½ in.
W. Graham Arader III Gallery

JOSEPH HENRY SHARP

BORN 1859, BRIDGEPORT, OHIO

DIED 1953, PASADENA, CALIFORNIA

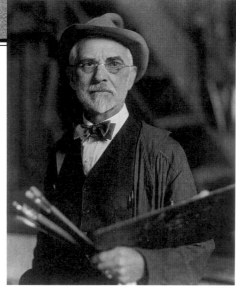

Will Connell, *Joseph Henry Sharp*, 1932. Photograph. The Harwood Foundation Museum, Taos, New Mexico.

Called a "latter-day George Catlin" because of the ethnographic accuracy and scope of his Indian portraits, Sharp had perhaps the broadest western painting experience of all the Taos painters. Deaf from age fourteen, he left public school for study at the McMicken School of Design and, later, at the Cincinnati Art Academy. He studied with Charles Verlat in Antwerp, after which he returned to the United States and made a sketching trip to New Mexico, California, and the Columbia River, devoting his attention primarily to Indians. He went to Europe again in 1886, where he studied with Karl Marr in Munich and then traveled with fellow Cincinnatian Frank Duveneck to Italy and Spain. When he returned to Cincinnati he taught life classes at the art academy from 1892 to 1902.

In 1893, the artist made his first trip to Taos, producing a sketch of and commentary on the Pueblo Indian harvest dance, which was published in *Harper's Weekly*. He made his last voyage to Europe in 1895, when he went to Paris for study at the Académie Julian, where he met Ernest Blumenschein and Bert Phillips, both of whom he convinced to visit Taos.

By the turn of the century, Sharp was spending his summers in the West, sketching Indian portraits, which he would work into finished paintings back in Cincinnati during the winter. In 1901, the federal government commissioned Sharp to paint portraits of Indians who had fought George Armstrong Custer at the Little Bighorn, and for that purpose the artist built a studio and cabin next to the battlefield. He painted approximately two hundred portraits.

In 1912, Sharp settled permanently in Taos, becoming that same year a founding member of the Taos Society of Artists.

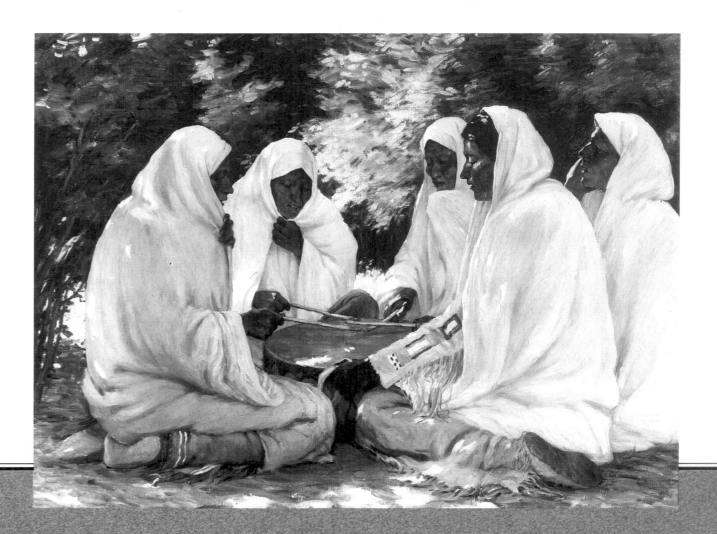

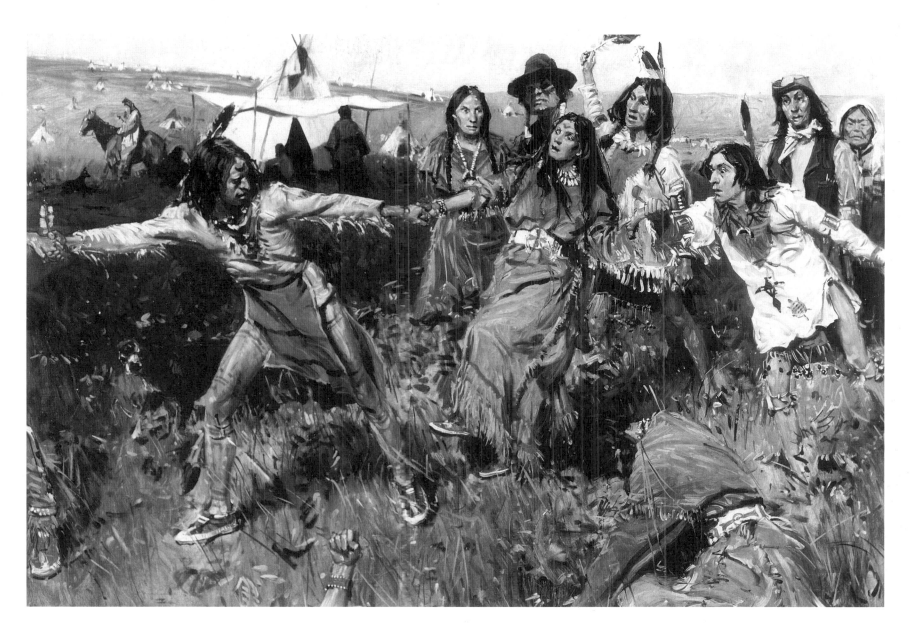

W. Gilbert Gaul (1855–1919)
Ghost Dance, after 1890
Oil on canvas, 22 × 33 in.
Courtesy of The Anschutz Collection

Joseph Henry Sharp (1859–1953)
The Gift Dance Drummers, c. 1910–1920
Oil on canvas, 30 × 40 in.
The Rockwell Museum, Corning, New York

Sharp had a keen appreciation of the spiritual nature of the Pueblo Indians among whom he lived in Taos.

campaign to obliterate the white man. They even fashioned a "ghost shirt," which, they said, was infallible armor against white men's bullets.

"Indians are dancing in the snow and are wild and crazy," Pine Ridge Reservation agent Daniel F. Royer frantically telegraphed Washington in November 1890. "We need protection and we need it now."

On November 20, cavalry and infantry reinforcements arrived at Pine Ridge and at the Rosebud Reservation. Far from discouraging the Sioux under Short Bull and Kicking Bear, the army presence galvanized their resolve. Some three thousand Indians gathered on a plateau at the northwest corner of Pine Ridge called the Stronghold. Brigadier General John R. Brooke, commander of the Pine Ridge area, attempted to defuse the situation by sending emissaries to talk with the "hostiles." To Brooke's commanding officer, Nelson A. Miles, such parleys were insufficiently decisive. He decided to move his headquarters to Rapid City, Dakota Territory, and prosecute the campaign himself.

While Miles was preparing to move, Sitting Bull, at Standing Rock Reservation, began actively espousing the Ghost Dance doctrine. That reservation's agent, James

McLaughlin, as level-headed as John Brooke was hysterical, decided that the old chief would have to be arrested and removed from the reservation—but not by a show of soldiers. The operation should be carried out as quietly as possible, using the reservation's own Indian policemen. General Miles had another idea. He called upon Buffalo Bill Cody, by this time universally famous on account of his Wild West Show, to remove the chief. After all, Sitting Bull had for a time appeared in Buffalo Bill's show, and it was known that Cody was the only white man Sitting Bull trusted.

McLaughlin was appalled by the notion of importing a popular showman to carry out what should be a quiet, expeditious, and dignified operation calculated not to inflame an already incendiary situation. When Buffalo Bill arrived at Standing Rock on November 27, McLaughlin saw to it that he was waylaid by the commandant of nearby Fort Yates, Lieutenant Colonel William F. Drum, who drank with Cody all night at the officers' club while McLaughlin moved to have the showman's authority rescinded.

But the man had not been born who could drink Buffalo Bill Cody under the table. In the morning, steady

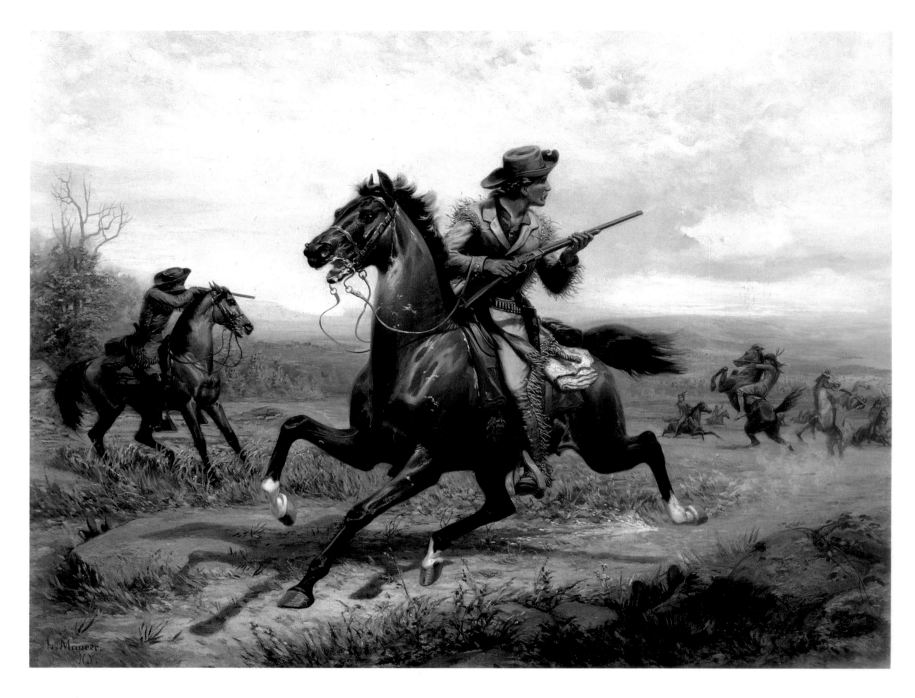

as ever, he set out for Sitting Bull's camp—only to be delayed further by McLaughlin's henchmen, just long
enough for the arrival of orders canceling Cody's mission. The old showman, in a bad mood, set off for Chicago without having even met with Sitting Bull.

No sooner had agent McLaughlin dealt with Buffalo
Bill than matters came to a crisis as Short Bull and Kicking Bear invited Sitting Bull to join them and their people
at the Stronghold in the Pine Ridge Reservation. The
agent dispatched forty-three reservation policemen on
December 15 to arrest Sitting Bull before he could slip
out of Standing Rock Reservation. The officers surrounded the old chief's cabin as Lieutenant Bull Head,
Sergeant Red Tomahawk, and Sergeant Shave Head entered the cabin.

The chief had been sleeping. "What do you want
here?" he asked.

"You are my prisoner," explained Bull Head. "You
must go to the agency."

Sitting Bull asked leave to put his clothes on.

When they came out with their prisoner, a crowd
had gathered. Catch-the-Bear called out to all assembled:
"Let us protect our chief." With that, he leveled his rifle
at Bull Head, fired, and hit him in the side. The policeman spun about with the force of the bullet, discharging
his own weapon as he did so, at close range, into Sitting
Bull's chest. Sergeant Red Tomahawk shot him in the
back of the head. As the band of police officers tangled
with Sitting Bull's people, the dead chief's horse, which
Buffalo Bill had given Sitting Bull when he was part of
the Wild West Show, was apparently stimulated by the
noise of the crowd. He began to perform his old circus
tricks.

So ended the tragedy's penultimate act. But General
Miles had one more Ghost Dancer to arrest. His name
was Big Foot, and he led the Miniconjou Sioux, who were
living on the Cheyenne River. Ironically, Big Foot had
personally given up the Ghost Dance religion; for he saw

Louis Maurer (1832–1932)
Buffalo Bill Fighting Indians, c. 1885
Oil on canvas, 27 × 36 in.
Courtesy of The Anschutz Collection

Best known as a staff artist for
Currier & Ives and later as a
lithographer in his own right,
Maurer made his first extended trip
west in 1885 as the guest of Buffalo
Bill himself.

Willard Midgette (1937–1978)
"Sitting Bull Returns" to the Drive-In, 1976
Oil on canvas, 108 ¼ × 134 ⅛ in.
National Museum of American Art, Smithsonian Institution;
Gift of Donald B. Anderson

A sardonic comment on the American Indian in Anglo culture and society.

John Hauser (1858–1913)
Sioux Camp at Wounded Knee, 1904
Watercolor, 12 × 20 in.
Gilcrease Museum, Tulsa, Oklahoma

Born in Cleveland, Ohio, Hauser studied in the United States and abroad and taught art in the Cincinnati public schools. In 1891 he traveled to New Mexico and Arizona; determining to specialize in the depiction of Indian subjects, he made annual visits to the Indian reservations from 1891 on. The Sioux nation adopted him as Straight White Shield.

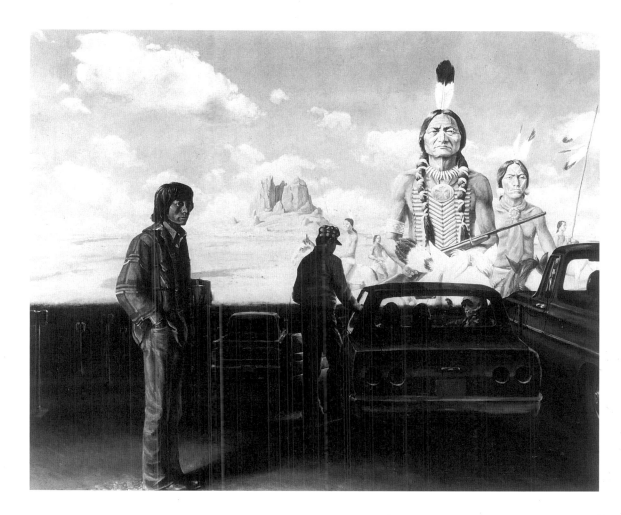

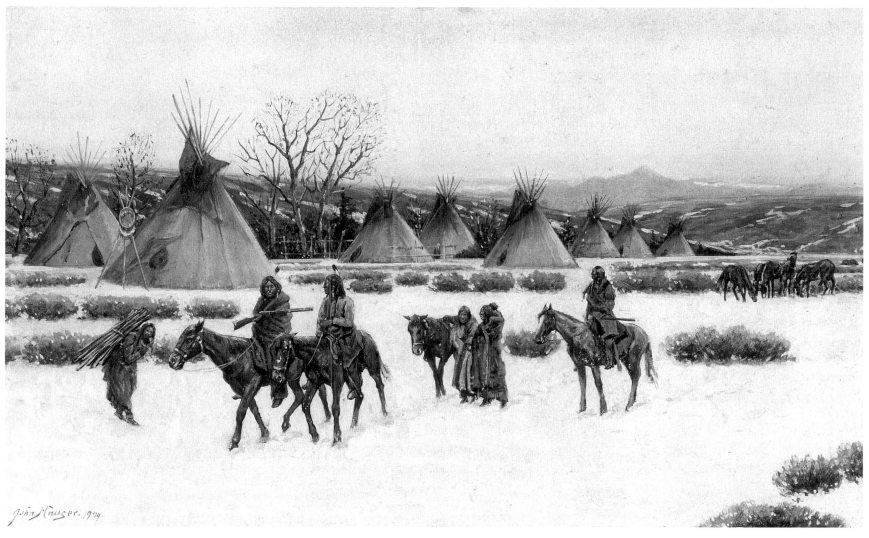

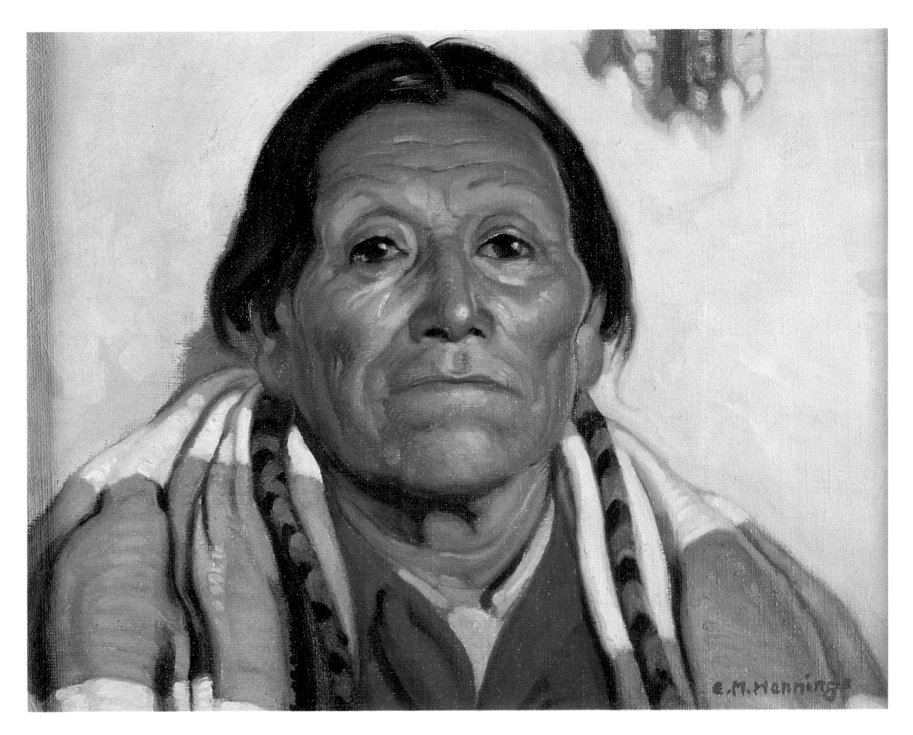

E. Martin Hennings (1886–1956)
Taos Indian, 1953
Oil on canvas, 8 × 10 in.
Santa Fe Collection of Southwestern
Art

that it preached desperation and futility. Miles didn't know this. He also didn't know that Chief Red Cloud, a Pine Ridge leader friendly to the whites, had asked Big Foot to come to the reservation in order to use his influence to reconcile the Stronghold party to surrender. When the general learned that Big Foot was headed for the Stronghold, he assumed that it was to *join* Short Bull, Kicking Bear, and the other hostiles. Miles threw a dragnet across the prairies and badlands to intercept all Miniconjous and Big Foot in particular.

When a squadron of the Seventh Cavalry located Big Foot and about 350 Miniconjous on December 28, 1890, they were camped near a stream called Wounded Knee Creek. Big Foot was huddled miserably in his wagon, suffering from pneumonia. During the night, more troops moved into the area, so that by the morning of December 29, 500 soldiers, under Colonel James W.

Forsyth, surrounded the camp. Four Hotchkiss guns—small, deadly howitzer-like cannon—were trained on the camp from the surrounding hills. Forsyth's mission was to disarm the Indians and take them to the railroad, so that they could be removed from the "zone of military operations." No one expected a fight.

But as the soldiers searched the camp for guns, Yellow Bird, a medicine man, began dancing, urging his people to fight, telling them that the ghost shirts they wore would protect them.

Black Coyote, whom another Indian described as "a crazy man, a young man of very bad influence and in fact a nobody," raised a Winchester above his head as the soldiers were collecting weapons. He shouted that he had paid much money for the rifle, that it was his, that nobody was going to take it.

The troops spun him around. A rifle fired—perhaps

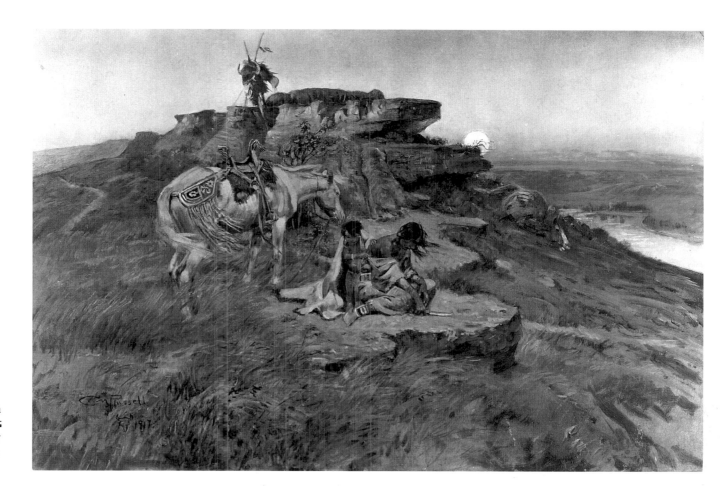

Charles M. Russell (1864–1926)
Her Heart Is on the Ground, 1917
Oil on canvas, 23 × 35 in.
Gilcrease Museum, Tulsa, Oklahoma

Raucously realisic in his depiction of
the cowboy, Russell indulged a more
romantic vision of the Indian.

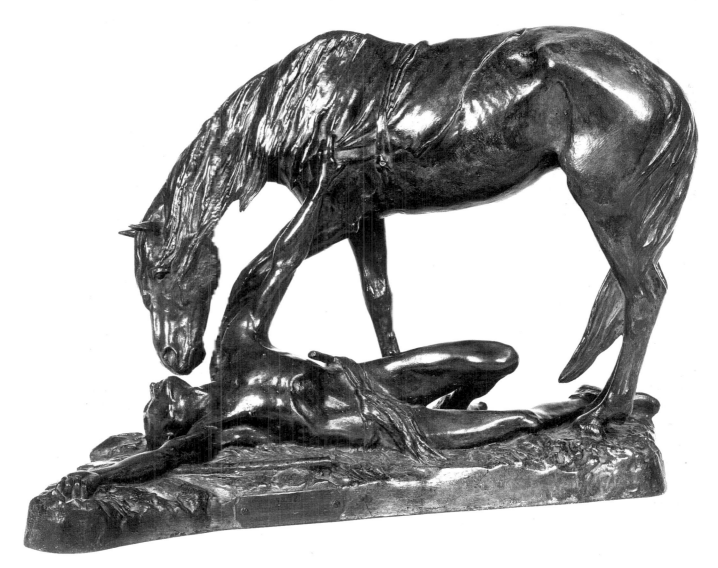

Gutzon Borglum (1867–1941)
The Fallen Warrior, c. 1891
Bronze, 10 ⅞ × 15 ⁵⁄₁₆ × 7 ⁵⁄₁₆ in.
Gilcrease Museum, Tulsa, Oklahoma

A sentimental sculpture by the artist
who would go on to carve Mount
Rushmore.

(JOHN) GUTZON DE LA MOTHE BORGLUM

—

BORN 1867, NEAR BEAR LAKE, IDAHO
DIED 1941, CHICAGO

—

SOLON HANNIBAL BORGLUM

—

BORN 1868, OGDEN, UTAH
DIED 1922, STAMFORD, CONNECTICUT

—

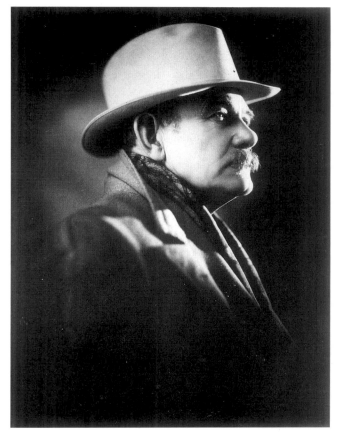

Anonymous, *Gutzon Borglum*, 1934. Photograph. The National Park
Service, Mount Rushmore National Memorial

Sons of an immigrant Danish woodcarver-turned-physician, the Borglum brothers both became noted western artists.

Gutzon began, like his father, as a carver before he was apprenticed to a Los Angeles lithographer and then to a fresco painter in the early 1880s. He left Los Angeles for San Francisco in 1885 to study at the Art Association and then returned to paint western subjects for a group of benefactors who sent him to the Académie Julian and Ecole des Beaux-Arts in Paris about 1888.

It was in Paris that he turned to sculpture, and between 1895 and 1901, when he exhibited in Paris and London, he was identified as a disciple of Auguste Rodin. In 1902, he came to New York, where he opened a studio and taught at the Art Students League. Driven by an irrepressible need to express himself on an epic scale, Gutzon Borglum conceived the idea of "sculpture with dynamite," designing and, from 1927 until his death in 1941, executing the titanic group of presidents' heads carved into Mount Rushmore.

Although Solon Borglum was, understandably enough, overshadowed by his brother, who was also his first teacher, the younger artist earned a reputation as a fine sculptor, particularly of horses. Until 1894, he was a working cowboy, an experience that gave him an intimate knowledge of his animal subjects. His training at the Cincinnati Art School, 1895–97, included close study of equine as well as human anatomy. He returned to the West for a time at the turn of the century, mainly to study Indians at the Crow Creek Reservation in South Dakota. He opened a studio in New York in 1900, working there until 1907, when he and his wife moved to Silvermine, Connecticut, and a studio-home the artist christened "Rocky Ranch." Solon Borglum exhibited at the epoch-making Armory Show of 1913.

Serving with the French army in World War I, the middle-aged Borglum, severely wounded, was decorated with the Croix de Guerre. After the war, he founded the School of American Sculpture, but he never fully recovered from his battle injuries, and died at the age of fifty-four.

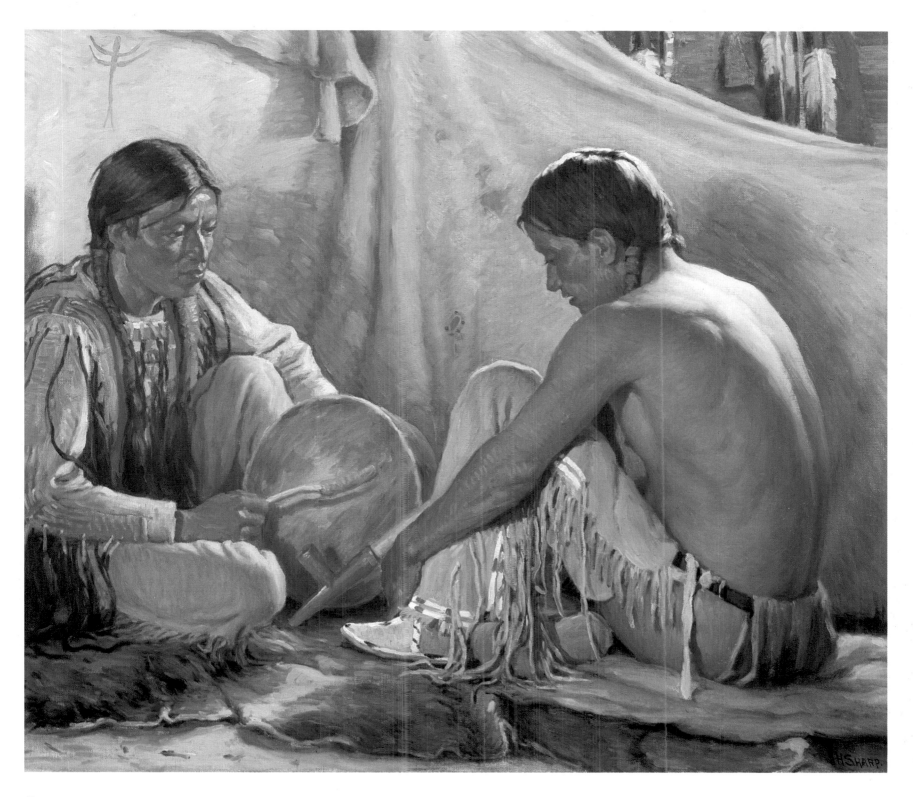

Joseph Henry Sharp (1859–1953)
The Pipe Song, 1923
Oil on canvas, 25 × 30 in.
Museum of Western Art, Denver

it was Black Coyote's, perhaps not; perhaps it was accidental, perhaps not.

Both sides opened fire—though only a few of the Indians had arms. Hand-to-hand combat commenced. Then the Indians began to flee. At that point, the Hotchkiss guns opened up on the camp, firing almost a shell a second at men, women, children.

"We tried to run," Louise Weasel Bear said, "but they shot us like we were buffalo."

It was over in less than an hour. Big Foot and 153 other Miniconjous were known to have been killed. So many others limped or crawled away that it is impossible to know just how many finally died—perhaps 300 of the 350 who had been camped at Wounded Knee Creek. Army losses were 25 killed and 39 wounded, mostly the victims of wild Hotchkiss rounds.

Briefly, hostile as well as friendly Sioux factions united and, on December 30, ambushed the Seventh Cavalry. But elements of the Ninth Cavalry came to the rescue. General Miles marshalled thirty-five hundred troops around the Sioux holdouts, all the while urging their surrender and pledging good treatment. Formal capitulation came on January 15, 1891. The Indian wars were over.

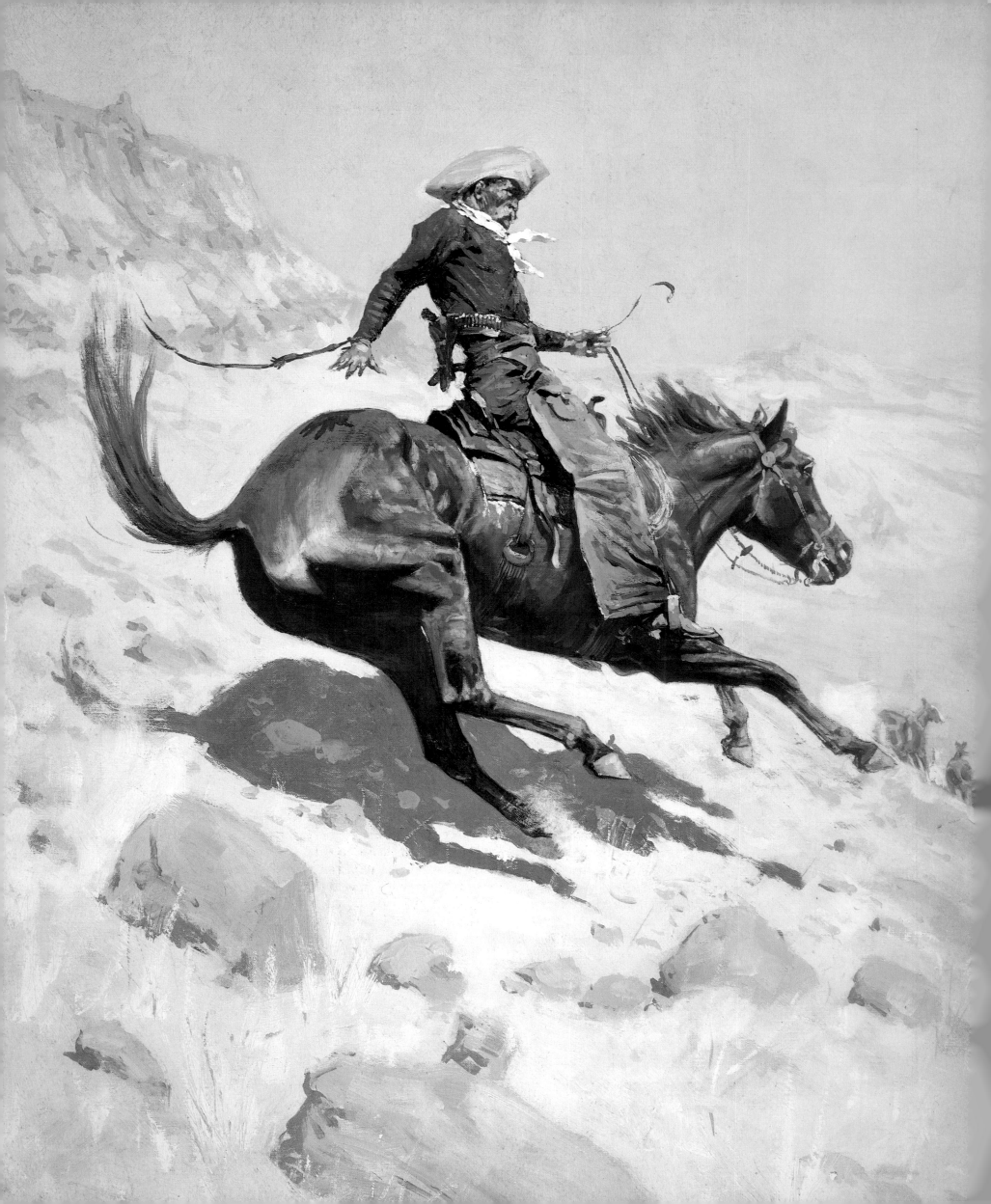

R ANCH
AND HOMESTEAD

T o successive generations, the West offered up fur, then gold, then grass—grass and space—elements that could be transmuted into beef, and the beef into fortunes of money and a way of life that has yet to loose its mythic hold on America. Until the end of the eighteenth century, livestock were being grazed in the Appalachian Piedmont, mostly on public lands, and then driven to northeastern urban centers such as Baltimore and New York for slaughter. As the population of the Piedmont increased, the cattlemen were pushed westward, where the grass grew more sparsely but where more open land was available, which meant that more cattle could be kept under surveillance and, therefore, that productivity and profits increased. By 1800, cattle were being grazed on the lower Mississippi in Louisiana. Twenty years later, the industry had penetrated as far as the Red River in Arkansas.

By early mid century, the westward-moving herds began to interbreed with the wild herds that were the descendants of cattle brought by the Spanish of the Southwest. Juan de Oñate had brought stock into New Mexico as early as 1598, and conquistadors had introduced cattle to California and Arizona as well. Much of this early stock was slaughtered in the Pueblo Revolt of 1680, but some ran wild, and, after Popé and the other renegade Pueblo Indians were put down, cattle were reintroduced. The largest herds were those raised in the Spanish missions. For example, by 1770, Misión La Bahía del Espíritu Santo, near Goliad, Texas, controlled forty thousand head. Until the secularization laws enacted by republican Mexico in 1833–34, cattle raising made many of the missions wealthy indeed. In California, during its Spanish as well as its Mexican period, cattle were the very basis of the region's economy.

For Texas cattlemen, the Mexican War provided a bonanza in the form of army beef contracts. Texans even began to drive cattle to New Orleans, whence they were shipped east. Between this period and the Civil War, Texans started to drive some cattle north, to fatten on the grass of public lands before being shipped east, and thus the range cattle industry came into being. The Civil War, however, brought a Union blockade, which prevented shipment. As a result, Longhorns ran wild on the Texas prairies, growing to a vast herd of some five million head by the end of the war. When the Confederate sons of Texas returned home after Appomatox, many found these free-ranging animals the only visible assets left to them and set about hiring on as cowboys, rounding up the cattle, branding them, and trailing them to market. The war had depleted the North's supply of beef animals, so that a Longhorn

Frederic Remington, *The Cowboy,* 1902. Detail; see page 342 worth four dollars in Texas fetched forty or fifty dollars in northeastern markets. Moreover, as the army moved into the West to prosecute the Indian wars, and as the government needed to feed the Indians who were themselves being herded onto the western reservations as a result of those wars, federal beef contracts became plentiful again.

For a time the cattle empire of Texas was bounded by San Antonio, Corpus Christi, and Laredo, a region of good and well-watered grasslands. But as the demand for meat grew, the herds began to outgrow even this vast area. Whereas immediately following the Civil War, Texas cattle were raised to maturity on vast ranches within that state and then shipped to market for slaughter, from the 1870s on Texans began driving larger and larger herds of young animals, yearlings and two-year-olds, to northern ranges, where pasturelands were particularly rich and capable of nurturing fat cattle. After two or three years on these ranges, the animals were ready for slaughter. Texas still served as the cradle of the cattle industry, but between 1870 and 1880 the number of cattle in Kansas increased from 374,000 to 1,534,000; in Nebraska from 80,000 to 1,174,000; in Colorado from 70,000 to 790,000; Montana, 37,000 to 428,000; Wyo-

ming, 11,000 to 521,000; and Dakota Territory, 12,000 to 141,000.

By 1880, individuals and corporations from all over the United States were investing in cattle. Foreign investors poured in as well, especially from Great Britain—and Scotland in particular—which had an insatiable appetite for beef. Methods of refrigerated transport were developed to make transatlantic shipment possible, and the Scots cattlemen brought their expertise in breeding to the United States, raising fatter and choicer beeves to satisfy the discriminating European market.

AN EMPIRE OF COWS

Edward Everett Dale was an Oklahoma cowboy, rancher, and, finally, a Harvard Ph.D. historian. His varied background gave him a unique perspective on the imperial qualities of the western American experience. As we have seen, the American West was the stage for many empires: Spanish, English, French, American, as well as the abortive imperial ventures of men, like Aaron Burr, who would be king. The cattle industry, Dale wrote in his 1942 classic *Cow Country,* established its empires as well:

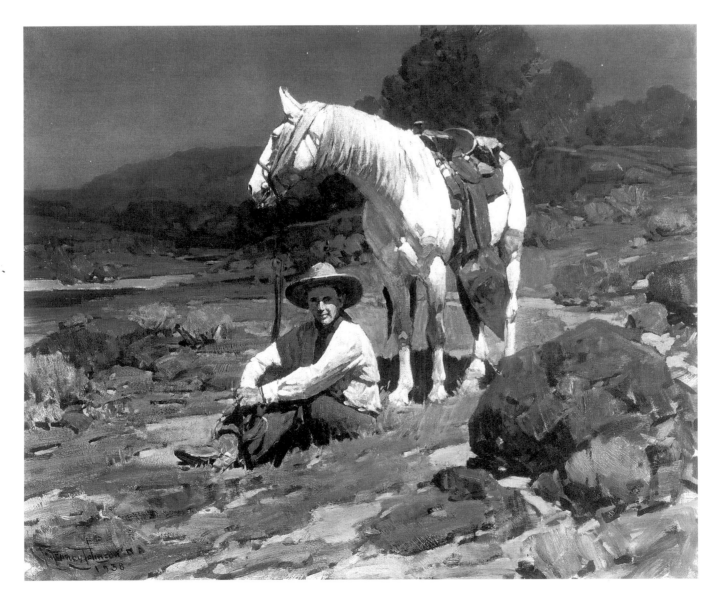

Frank Tenney Johnson (1874–1939)
Ranchero, 1938
Oil on canvas, 25 ⅛ × 30 ⅛ in.
Amon Carter Museum, Fort Worth, Texas

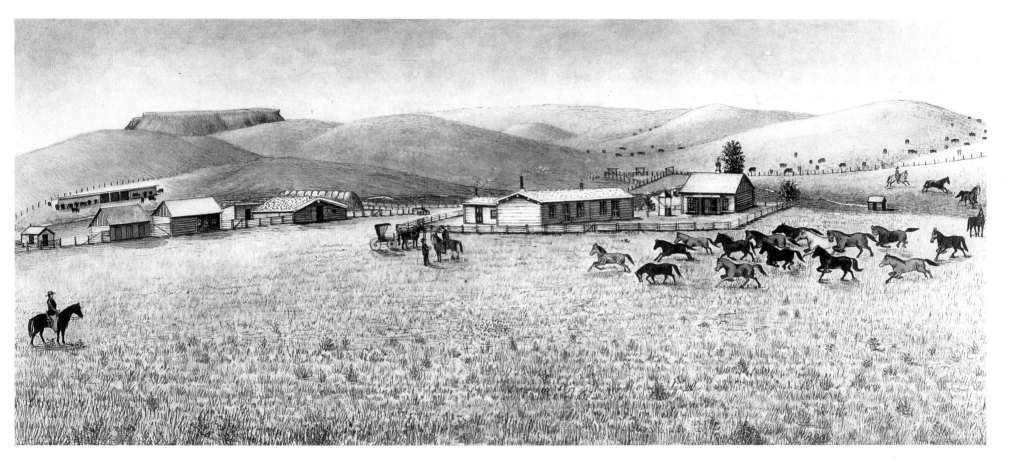

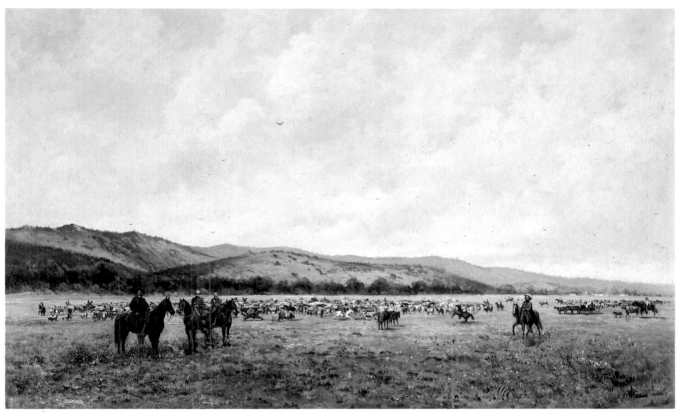

Merritt Dana Hougton (1846–1918)
Ranch Scene, c. 1875
Pen and ink wash on paper mounted
on paperboard, 13 ⅜ × 25 ⅜ in.
Amon Carter Museum, Fort Worth,
Texas

A Wyoming ranch by an artist born
in Michigan and based, during most
of his career, in Laramie.

Jules Tavernier (1844–1889)
*El Rodeo, Santa Margarita, Califor-
nia*, 1884
Oil on canvas, 36 × 60 in.
Arthur J. Phelan, Jr., Collection

The painting shows a spring
roundup ("rodeo," in the original
sense of the word) on a ranch some
twenty miles north of San Luis
Obispo. It was commissioned by the
owner of the ranch, General P. W.
Murphy, who is depicted astride his
horse, overseeing the roundup.

*In time there developed on the western plains a curious
American feudalism strongly reminiscent of the feudal
order of medieval Europe. The headquarters ranch
house of the great ranchman might be neither large nor
pretentious and yet as the central point for the administration of a wide region it was not entirely unlike the
castle of some medieval landgrave. His cattle ranged
over an extent of territory larger than that held by many
a German princeling. [The celebrated XIT Ranch, for example, covered three million acres of Texas.] His riders
were quite as numerous as the knights and men at arms
of the feudal baron. His brand or distinguishing mark—
the spur, pitchfork, rocking chair, flying H, three circles,
or the jingle bob—might be even more widely known
than was the bleeding heart of the Douglases, the white
lion of the Howards, the clenched hand and dagger of
the Kilpatricks, or the blue falcon of Marmion. Conflicts
between rival groups of ranchmen as in Johnson County
and Lincoln County wars were not entirely unlike the
border wars of Scotland. . . . Chivalry, in the original and*

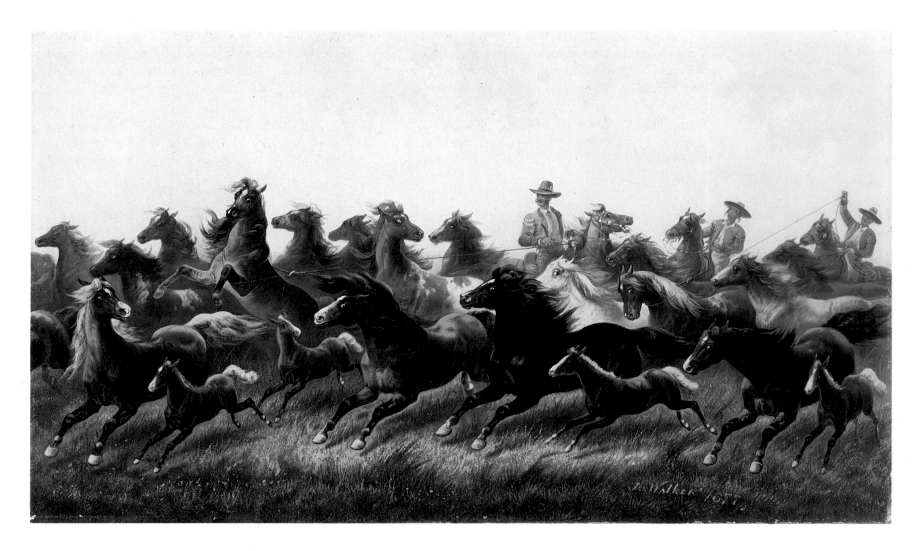

James Walker (1819–1889)
Roping Wild Horses, 1877
Oil on canvas, 14 × 24 in.
Gilcrease Museum, Tulsa, Oklahoma

Tamed, but not broken of spirit, the wild horse was greatly prized by California vaqueros and, later, the cowboys of the great cattle drives.

truest sense of the term, prevailed; for though the range rider was not sworn to protect pure womanhood, he would probably go farther in that direction than did the cavaliers of that older age "when knighthood was in flower." Tests of skill and prowess were also in order, for though the pastoral empire had no tilts or tournaments, the rodeo or roping contest furnished a very satisfactory substitute. Certain bad men appeared in the Cow Country and in time the half legendary figures of Billy the Kid, Clay Allison, John Wesley Hardin, Tom Starr, Sam Bass, Bill Doolin, and the Daltons became clothed with the same glamour of romance which clusters about the names of Robin Hood, Rob Roy, and Rinaldo Rinaldini. Some parallel may even be found between such organizations as the great livestock associations and the Templars, Hospitaliers, and Knights of Jerusalem. Both types of organization had great power and influence, extended over a wide region, and at times seemed almost to overshadow the regularly constituted authority of government.

On the thrones of these American empires sat the so-called cattle barons. By the mid 1880s some thirty or forty men controlled twenty million acres of the United States and owned about one-third of the cattle in the West. They were men of varied backgrounds. John Wesley Iliff was one of the first cattlemen to ranch the Colorado plains. Born in Ohio, the son of a livestock breeder, Iliff turned down his father's offer of $7,500 to buy an Ohio farm. "No!" he said. "Give me $500 and let me go West." Dominating some 150 miles of range along the South Platte River, Iliff amassed a fortune that allowed this pious teetotaler to found the Iliff School of Theology in Denver.

John Benjamin Kendrick drove a Longhorn herd for a wealthy Texas rancher in the late 1870s, married his employer's daughter, and acquired ranches near the east slope of the Bighorn Mountains in Wyoming and Montana. Whereas Iliff was a graduate of Wesleyan University, Kendrick never got beyond the seventh grade, but he not only became a millionaire, he went on to a brilliant political career as Wyoming governor and senator.

Then there was Abel Head—"Shanghai"—Smith, as "uncouth as the cattle he drove." He left an apprenticeship at his uncle's general store in Virginia, stowed away on a schooner bound for Indianola, Texas, and began working on a ranch. At one point early in his career, he owned a mere eleven acres, yet ran fifty thousand head of cattle. Eventually he acquired a million acres. Smith introduced the Brahma cattle breed into the United States on account of its resistance to the dreaded Texas fever. The breed became the basis for numerous herds found throughout the country.

Alexander Hamilton Swan, backed by $3,750,000 in Scottish capital, came to control or own six hundred thousand acres from Nebraska to Wyoming and amassed holdings worth $50 million. Swan's ranching company staged Wyoming's first rodeo. Like many another cattle baron, however, Swan was wiped out by the blizzard of 1886–87. Unlike others who were more resilient, Swan suffered a complete emotional collapse and ended his days in an asylum.

Antoine Amedée Marie Vincent Manca de Vellombrosa, Marquis de Morès came to the United States from France after marrying a rich banker's daughter. He went to the Dakota Badlands in 1883 and organized the Northern Pacific Refrigerator Car Company, established a ranch, and built a slaughterhouse, intending to ship dressed meat back east. By 1887 the enterprise folded, and de Morès had lost at least $1.5 million, most of which had been put up by his father-in-law. Leaving the Badlands and the United States, the marquis attempted to build a railroad through French Indochina but was foiled when the government refused to award him a concession. He then turned his attention to organized anti-Semitism but was killed in 1896 by North African anticolonialists.

Granville Stuart, whom we have seen in an earlier chapter as the Montana founder of the nation's most notorious vigilante movement, also pioneered Montana ranching. His approach to ranching was similar to his execution of justice. He dispatched his men to poison sheepmen's dogs and to run troublesome homesteaders off the range. An important territorial official, Stuart was driven out of the cattle business by the disastrous winter of 1886–87 and later served as United States minister to Uruguay and Paraguay under President Grover Cleveland.

Without doubt, the most famous cattle baron was Charlie Goodnight, who was born on a farm in southern Illinois in 1836 and came to the Brazos River country of Texas with his family in 1845. It was a land of longhorns running wild—some 300,000 head in 1845—and Charlie naturally grew into the life of a cowboy, gathering the animals and driving them to market for local ranchmen. In 1856, the young cowhand partnered with his stepbrother in tending 430 cows of the C V Ranch. For pay, the boys were given every fourth calf that was born. By 1860 they owned 180 head.

Goodnight joined the Confederate cause during the Civil War, serving as a Texas Ranger. He was mustered out a year before the war ended and set out to gather his herd, which had grown to five thousand head. Goodnight and his stepbrother borrowed against this herd to buy out the entire C V herd, which they supplemented by cattle "appropriated" from the open range, thereby swelling their holdings to eight thousand animals.

At this time, most ranchmen were driving their cattle to Kansas railheads for shipment east. Goodnight determined to pioneer a route to Colorado, where he knew that mining operations and Indian-fighting military outposts were creating a ready market for beef. Charlie

Henry Miller (birth and death dates unknown)
View of Bakers Ranch, Cal.,
c. 1856–57
Watercolor, sepia wash, and gouache on paper, 18 × 25 3/8 in.
Amon Carter Museum, Fort Worth, Texas

A prosperous California ranch at mid century: note the Chinese hired hands.

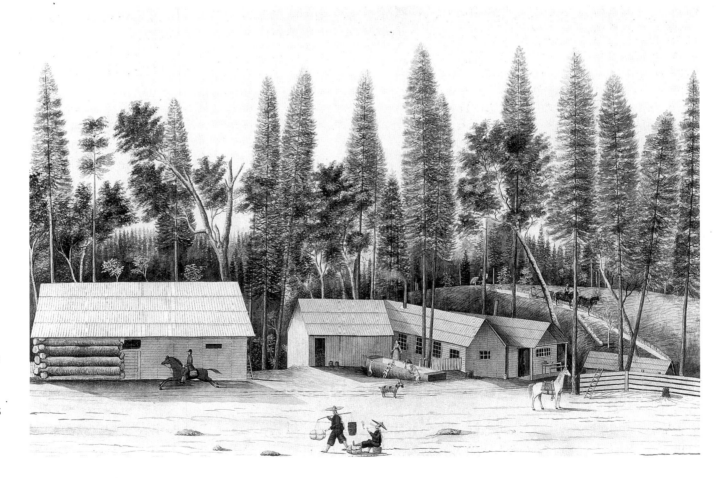

met Oliver Loving, an oldtime cattleman who had driven cattle as far as Illinois in 1855 and was the first man ever to trail animals to Colorado. In 1866 the pair gathered two thousand head and, with eighteen riders, followed the Southern Overland Mail route to the head of the Concho River. Goodnight and Loving liberally watered their stock for the dry trip ahead. Nevertheless, the herd moved eighty miles before more water was encountered, and some three hundred cattle were lost; another hundred were trampled to death in the stampede that was triggered when they finally reached a watering place. Despite such hazards, the drive was a financial success, netting Goodnight some twelve thousand dollars in gold.

Oliver Loving succumbed to another hazard of the trail a year later when he was ambushed by five hundred Comanche warriors and shot in the arm and side. Although he escaped capture, traveling seven days without food, he died at Fort Sumner of an infection. The post physician, unfortunately typical of the medical men serving in the army, felt himself too inexperienced to perform a life-saving amputation.

Goodnight, however, continued to drive cattle along the Goodnight-Loving Trail between Texas and Colorado until 1870, when he decided that he had had enough of such hazardous and demanding work. He decided to establish a ranch near Pueblo, Colorado, along the Arkansas River, married, settled down, and trailed up a ranch herd from Texas. By 1873, Goodnight had become one of

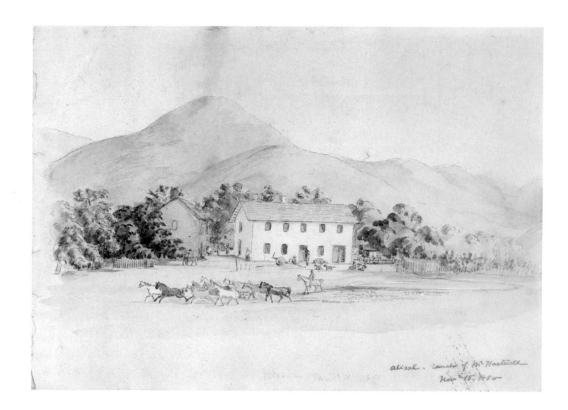

the wealthiest ranchers on the northern range, but, like all big cattlemen, he depended heavily on bank credit to provide the cash flow necessary to maintain his enterprise. With other Colorado ranchers he formed the Stock Growers Bank of Pueblo, aiming to beat high interest rates. A financial panic rocked the nation in 1873 and, as

Alfred Sully (1820–1879)
El Alisal Rancho, ca. 1850
Arthur J. Phelan, Jr., Collection

This ranch, part of a land grant obtained by William E. P. Hartnell, an English merchant who settled in the Salinas area about 1822, became the site of California's first college, which Hartnell opened in January 1834.

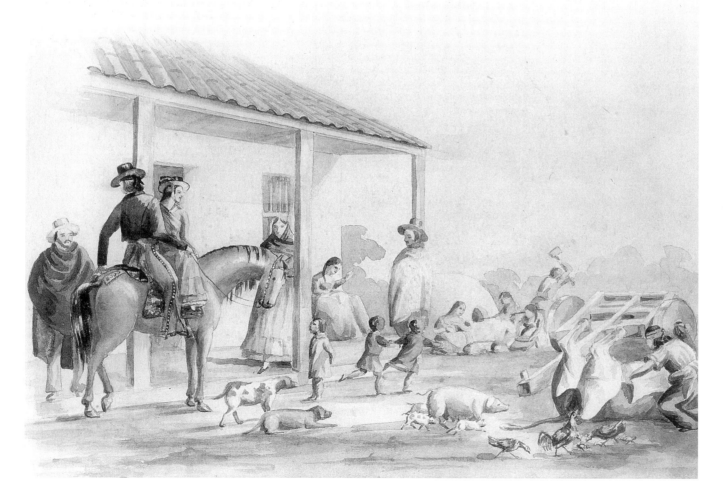

Alfred Sully (1820–1879)
Monterey, California, Rancho Scene, n.d.
Watercolor on paper, 8 × 10 ¾ in.
Collection of The Oakland Museum; Kahn Collection

Son of Thomas Sully, one of America's most respected and successful portrait painters, Alfred Sully graduated from West Point in 1841 and saw action against the Seminoles in Florida and served during the Mexican War. In 1848 he was stationed at Monterey, where he boarded with the family of Don Manuel Jimeno, whose daughter he married. This sketch is of Jimeno's ranch.

Willard Schouler (1852–1930s)
Ranch Hand, Wyoming, 1888
Oil on panel, 8 ¼ × 10 ¼ in.
Arthur J. Phelan, Jr., Collection

This obscure artist may have painted *Ranch Hand* on commission from the Bay State Livestock Company, owners of the J. H. D. Ranch. The cowboy is not your typical Tom Mix Anglo-American, but appears to be of Hispanic origin.

W. H. D. Koerner (1878–1938)
The Trusty Knaves, 1931
Oil on canvas, 24 × 58 in.
Courtesy of The Anschutz Collection

Viewed from the standpoint of economics, cowboys were at the bottom of the vocational ladder. But such a view leaves out all the gallantry and romance that has grown up about this most demanding profession.

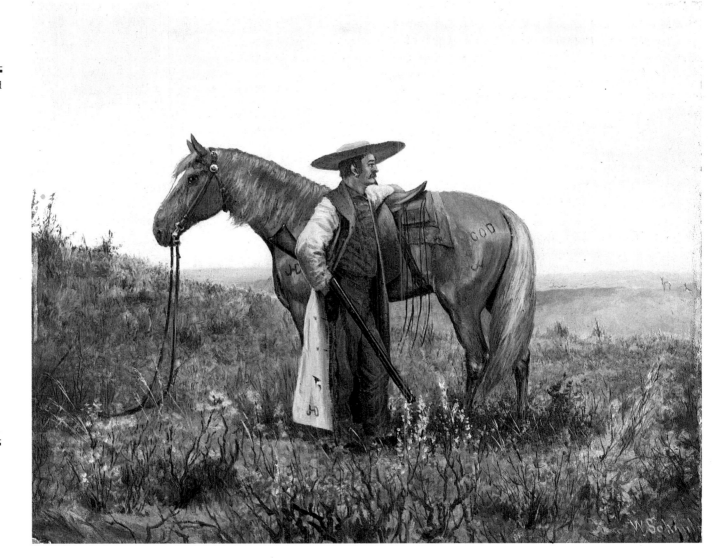

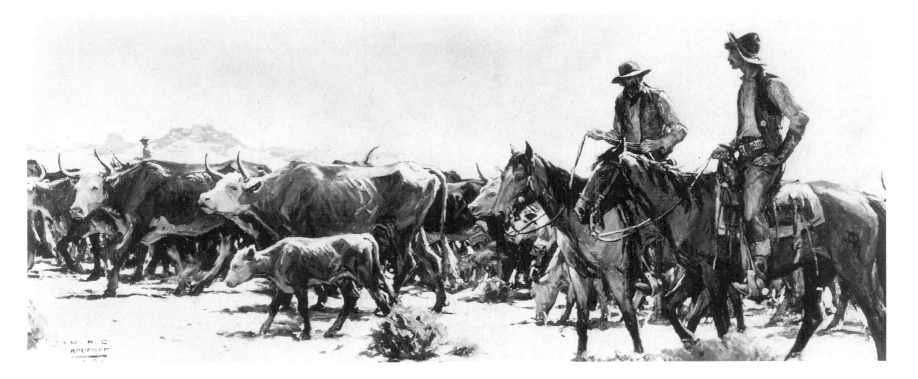

Goodnight later put it, "wiped me off the face of the earth."

In 1876, the ruined rancher, now trailing a herd of sixteen hundred through the Texas Panhandle, came across the Palo Duro Canyon, which widened into a vast pastureland, well watered, sheltered, and naturally fenced in by high bluffs. He built corrals and a modest house and stocked the new ranch with what remained of his Colorado herd. Next, Goodnight invited John and Cornelia Adair, a wealthy couple he had met in Denver, who had a yen for the ranching life, to settle on and invest in the Palo Duro ranch.

Goodnight took the young Irishman's initials—J A—for his brand and, with half a million dollars borrowed from him, bought up twenty-four thousand acres of public land, making his purchases in a highly strategic pattern that actually enabled him to control much more land than he actually purchased; it was a land grab typical of the big ranchers. He erected some fifty houses and a small village as a headquarters. Beginning with two thousand blooded bulls—valued at $150,000—Goodnight grew the herd to a hundred thousand.

RIDERS OF THE RANGE

If cattle barons were at the top rung of the West's feudal ladder, cowboys were, depending on how you look at them, not much lower—or at the very bottom. Edward Everett Dale called them latter-day knights, and, indeed, their vocation required courage, honor, and self-reliance in uncommon quantity. Noble, too, is the image of the lone rider, beholden to no one, free in a country untrammeled by the petty vagaries of civilization. On the other hand, no less a personage than the daughter of Karl Marx, Eleanor Aveling, traveling with her husband on a tour of the American West, saw the cowboy as a wage slave: "no class is harder worked, none so poorly paid for their services." Even she, however, was taken with the cowboys she saw in Buffalo Bill's Wild West Show, admiring the "ease and grace and simple refinement of these most manly men."

Knight errant or wage slave, no other occupation has captured the American imagination as that of the cowboy. Even when one strips away the thick veneer of romanticism that tenaciously clings to his image, the sheer grit that remains is material enough for continued admiration and mythologizing. But there is very little romance about the motives that led most men to become cowboys. A large number were discharged Confederate soldiers, who returned to a South so broken by war that all opportunity had been obliterated. Many cowboys were not Anglos, but Mexicans, Indians, and blacks, what a later age would euphemistically call "disadvantaged groups." One in seven western cowboys was a black man, usually a former slave, and, like blacks in the East, subject to racial hatreds and abuse. The lonely,

dirty, dangerous work of cowpunching was, for men like these, often the only available means of getting a living.

The pedigree of all cowboys—black, white, red—is founded not in the freedom of the plains, but in the slavery of Spanish America. When the herds of the great Spanish missions in the Far Southwest had grown too large for the priests to handle themselves, they trained mission Indians—under Spanish colonial law, free, but in fact slaves to the mission and its surrounding ranchos—as horsemen. These *vaqueros*—from the Spanish *vaca*, "cow"—had to learn to rope steers with a loop of braided rawhide rope known as *la reata*—a lariat. They had to learn what to do once they had caught the animal in the loop. *Dar la vuelta*—making a turn—described the act of wrapping the end of the lariat around the saddle horn in order to jerk a roped steer to a halt. Americans later transformed the Spanish term to "dally" roping. Even the *chaparreras,* leather trousers the vaquero wore to keep his legs from getting cut up on brush and chaparral, found a counterpart in the cowboy's chaps. The word *vaquero* itself suffered an American translation as buckaroo.

Frederic S. Remington (1861–1909)
An Arizona Cowboy, 1901
Pastel and graphite on paper,
30 × 24 in.
The Rockwell Museum, Corning,
New York

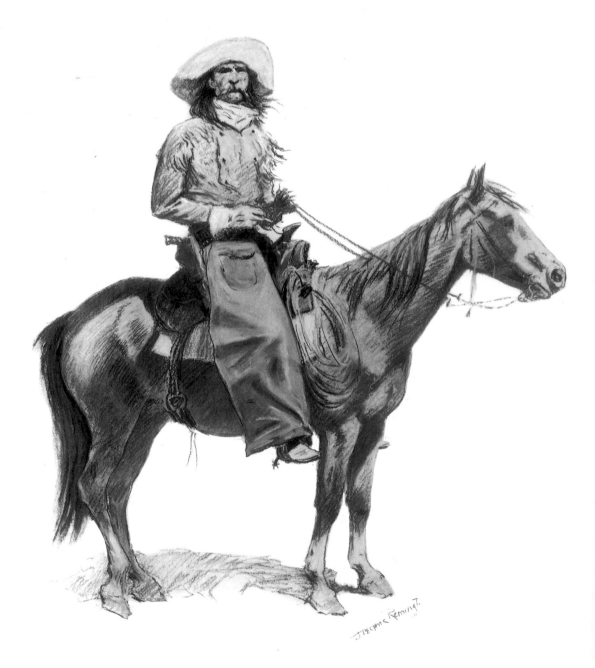

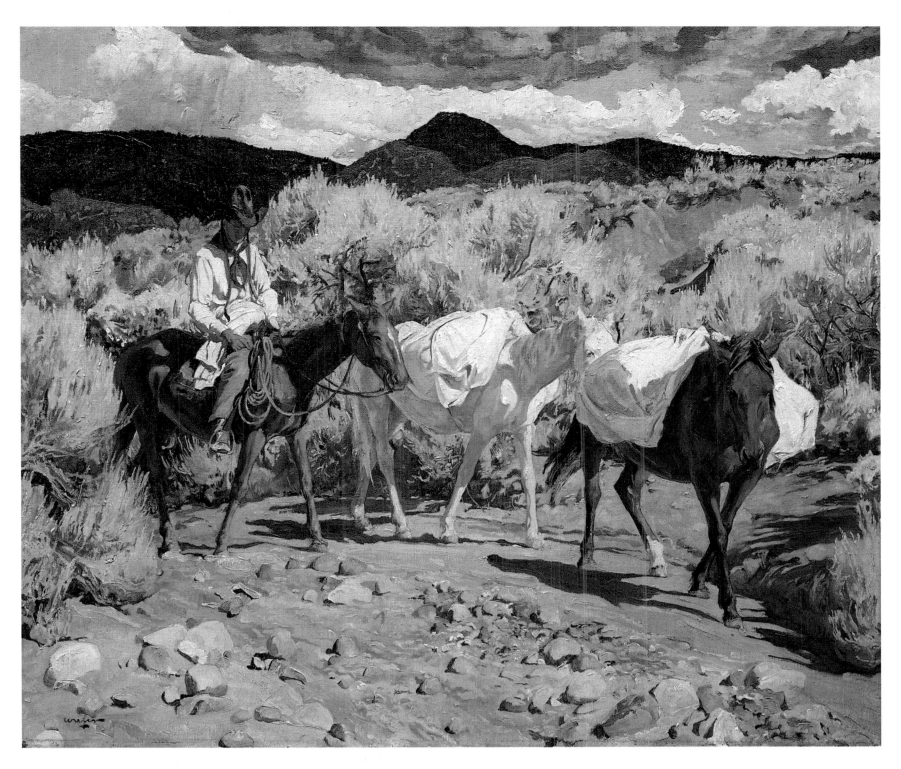

Walter Ufer (1876–1936)
Taos Indian and Pack Horse or *His Kit*, n.d.
Oil on board, 25 ⅛ × 30 ¼ in.
Stark Art Museum, Orange, Texas

Though little boys at play have traditionally divided their forces into cowboys and Indians, in the working West, the two groups were often indistinguishable from one another.

On the ranch, the cowboy's principal job was to ride over an assigned stretch of range and tend the cattle. This included rough veterinary work, such as treating wounded animals with strong disinfectants like concoctions of pitch and carbolic acid to kill the blowflies that hatched in open sores. It included rescuing animals from quicksand-like bog holes, pulling them out by the horns. When a herd of Longhorn steers became rambunctious, it was sometimes necessary for the cowboys to corral large numbers of animals and dehorn them—saw or chop off their horns—to prevent them from injuring one another. Castrating calves was another chore, which was often done at the same time as branding. While the calf was roped and down for the one operation, the other could be performed as well. Castration not only made the

animals more tractable, it tended to fatten them up, though the cowboy had to be careful to observe castrated animals for signs of blowflies on the wound, lest his employer lose an animal to infection. In particularly dry months, the cowboy often had to double as a fire warden, quenching dangerous brush fires before they developed into full-scale conflagrations that could stampede a herd and consume precious grazing land.

The cowboy also was responsible for rounding up the cattle scattered across the range. Roundups, which took place twice a year, in the spring and fall, were to the rancher what harvest was to the farmer. Mature steers were gathered for shipment to market, yearlings and two-year-olds might be herded for a long drive to another range, and calves had to be roped and branded in

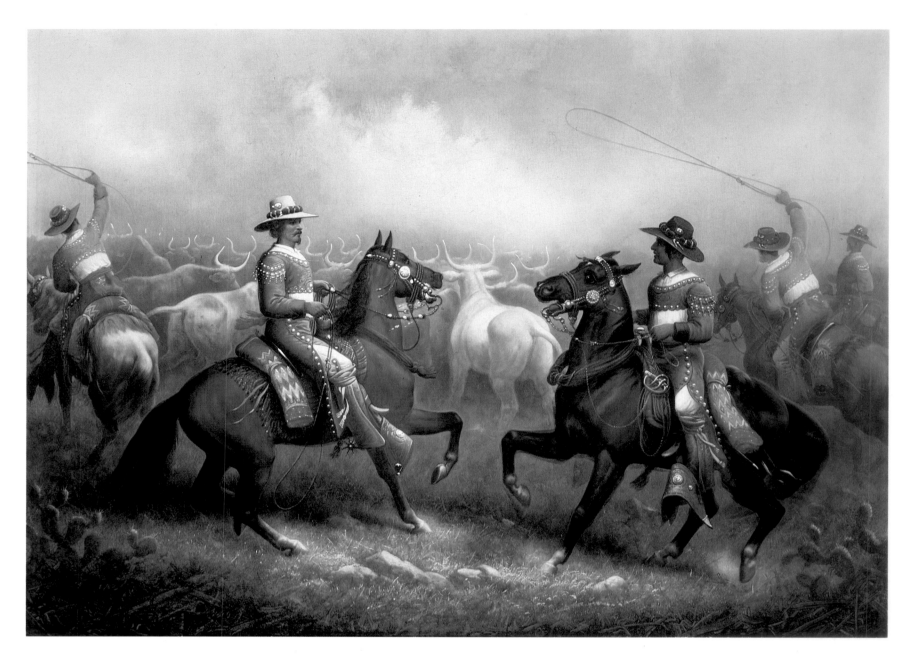

order to identify them as the property of a particular ranch.

All of the work required expert horsemanship, and a great deal of it involved skillful and hazardous roping. To "bust a herd quitter," for example, the cowboy galloped after the steer, threw his rope around its horns, rode up parallel with him, catching the rope under his hind leg, then turned his horse at a forty-five-degree angle to the steer's path so that the rope became tight, turning the steer's head and flipping him over by the hind legs. The animal, now turned around, on his back, and facing the herd, would usually get up and meekly join his fellows—if he hadn't been badly injured or killed. Of course, the cowboy also risked injury and death. An ornery steer could pull both horse and rider down. Fingers could get caught in, and cut off by, a rope suddenly jerked taut by eight hundred pounds of beef on the hoof.

In fast-paced and hazardous work involving cattle, the horse was the cowboy's most critical tool. Through a combination of training and instinct, the good cow horse

knew how to move among and dominate cattle. The most valuable mounts were cutting horses, used to cut out—or separate—cattle from the herd, as, for example, a calf to be branded. These horses had a special "feel" for working with stock. The rider would gesture toward the calf to be cut, and the horse would chase it and prod it just enough to separate it from the herd without spooking the animal. Nevertheless, few cowboys grew sentimental about their horses. Indeed, few cowboys possessed their own horses. The animals were the property of the ranch, and in the fourteen-hour day he worked, the cowboy would exhaust at least two mounts.

When they weren't riding the range, ranch cowboys lived in a pastoral slum known as the bunkhouse. It was always a crude structure, built of logs or planks, often with a dirt floor. If there was any paint on the walls, it was whitewash. Often, the walls were papered with newsprint to preserve warmth—for heating devices were rare, and few bunkhouses boasted even a crude fireplace. The newspapers pasted on the walls also provided reading material. Above all, bunkhouse inmates and vis-

James Walker (1819–1889)
California Vaqueros, 1876–77
Oil on canvas, 31 × 46 in.
Courtesy of The Anschutz Collection

The direct ancestor of the American cowboy was the California vaquero. Cowboys who call themselves buckaroos—a word derived from vaquero—still pride themselves on their fancy duds *(above)*

Charles M. Russell (1864–1926)
Cowboy Camp During the Roundup, 1887
Oil on canvas, 23 ½ × 47 ¼ in.
Amon Carter Museum, Fort Worth, Texas

More primitive than the artist's usual work, this painting nevertheless suggests some of the intense activity associated with a roundup *(opposite top)*

Charles M. Russell (1864–1926)
Jerked Down, 1907
Oil on canvas, 23 × 36 ¾ in.
Gilcrease Museum, Tulsa, Oklahoma

What happens when you rope one
steer and another gets in the way?
Nothing very pleasant—especially if
you are roping by the "hard-and-
fast" method, in which the near end
of the rope is securely tied to the
saddle horn of the cutting horse.
Horse, cowboy, and the steer that
fouled the line are all in great
danger. *(below)*

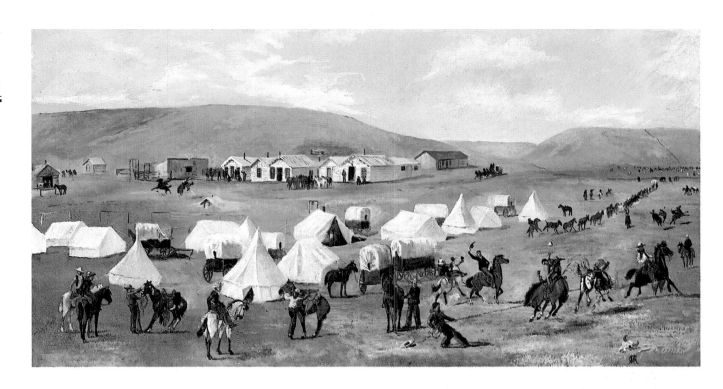

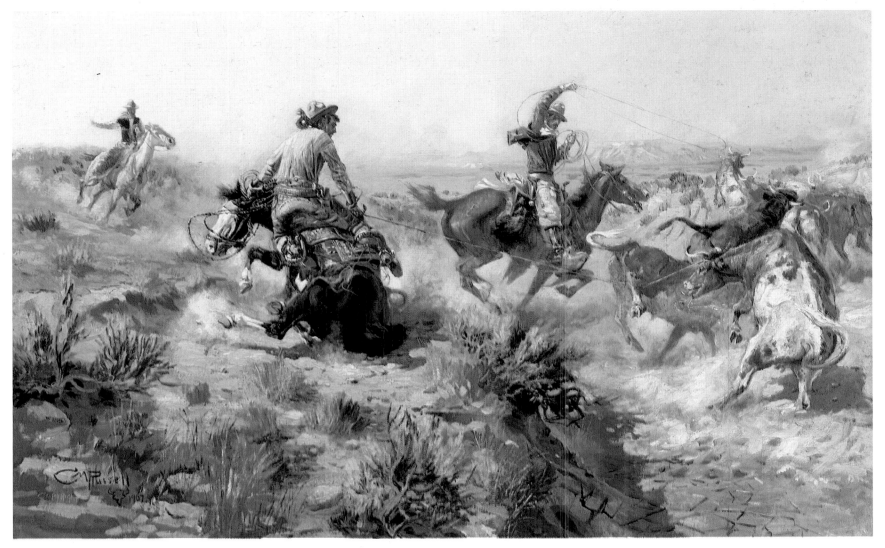

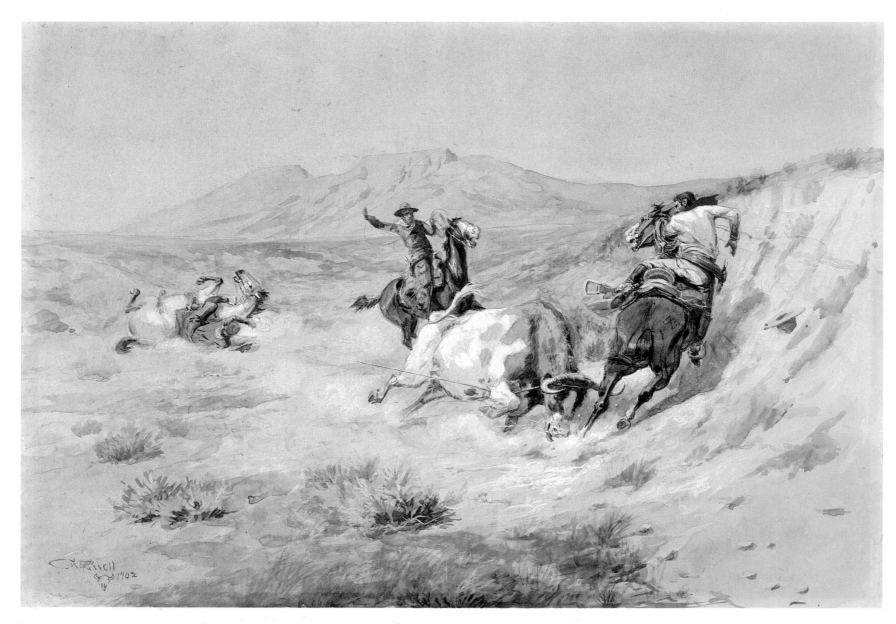

Charles M. Russell (1864–1926)
One Down, Two To Go, 1902
Watercolor, 20 × 30 in.
The Rockwell Museum, Corning,
New York

The hazards of rounding up "herd
quitters."

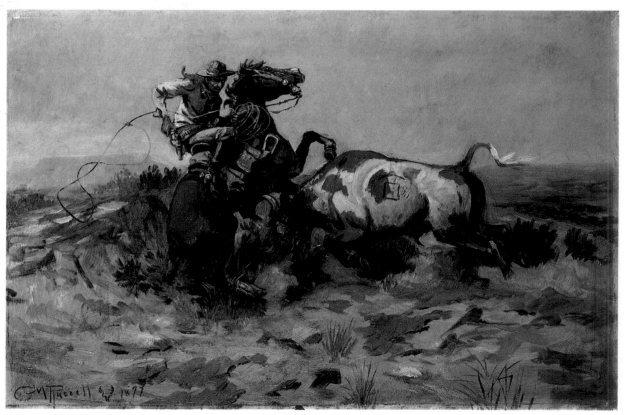

Charles M. Russell (1864–1926)
A Dangerous Situation, 1897
Oil on canvas, 12 ¼ × 18 ¼ in.
Stark Museum of Art, Orange, Texas

A man could get killed being a
cowboy.

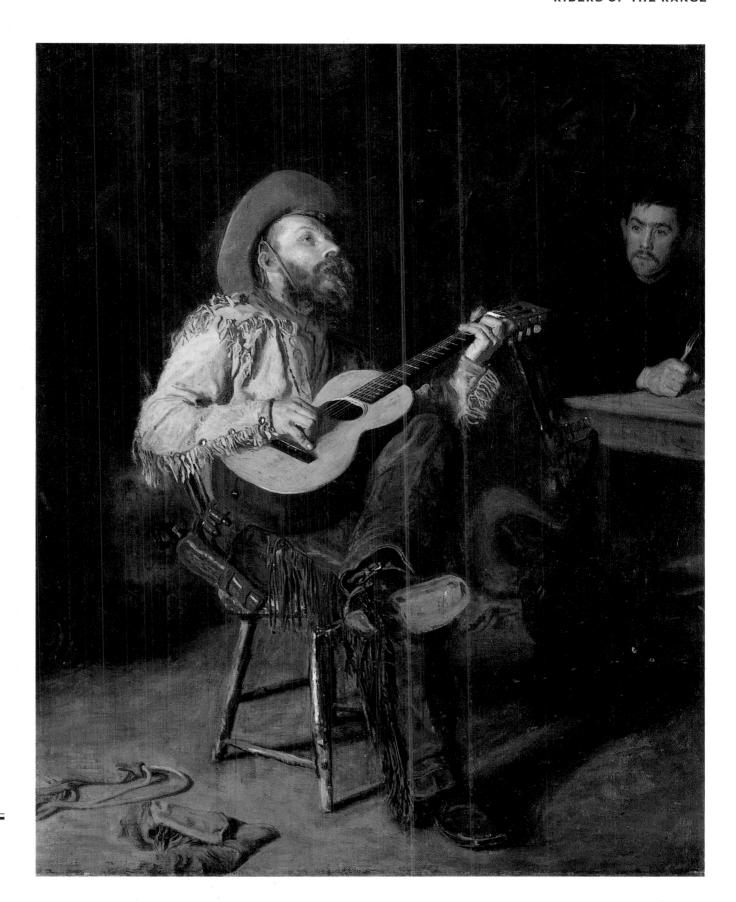

Thomas Eakins (1844–1916)
Home Ranch, 1888
Oil on canvas, 24 × 20 in.
Philadelphia Museum of Art; Given
by Mrs. Thomas Eakins and Miss
Mary Adeline Williams

The great Philadelphia master
captures the cowboy's melancholy
side. Note the listener's—
anguished?—grasp of the fork.

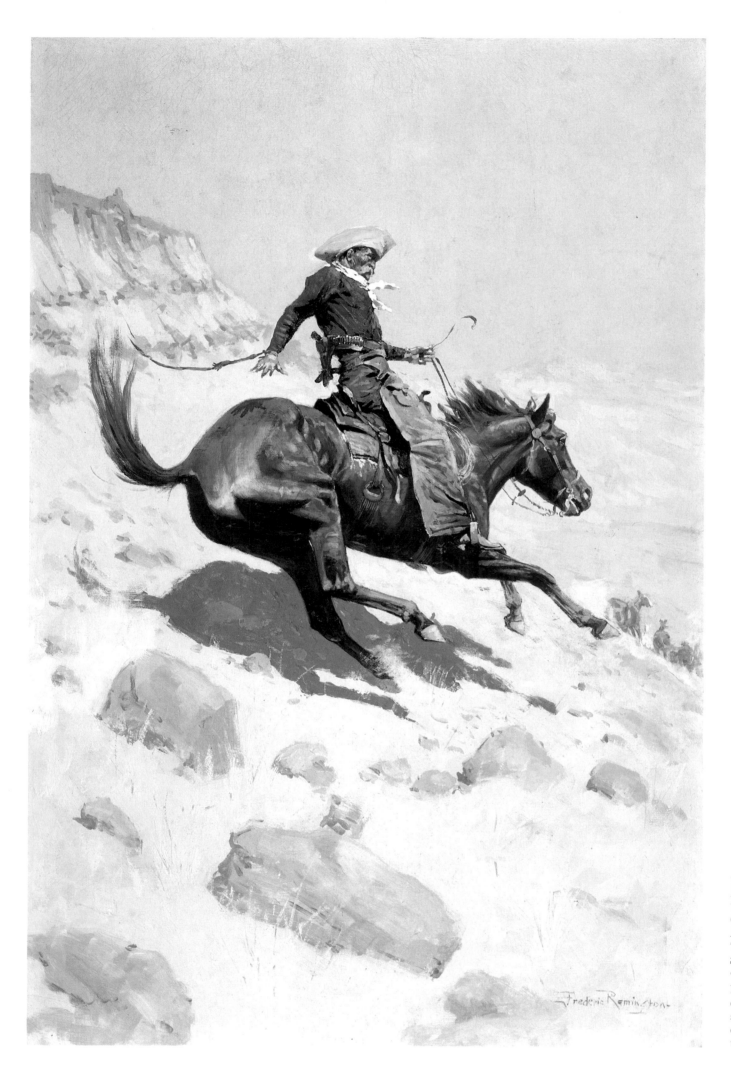

Frederic Remington (1861–1909)
The Cowboy, 1902
Oil on canvas, 40 ¼ × 27 ⅜ in.
Amon Carter Museum, Fort Worth,
Texas

The cowboy, struggling to keep
himself on his mount and his horse
on its feet as he negotiates a steep
slope at high speed, provides an
opportunity for the artist to render
the animal's beautiful musculature.

Charles M. Russell (1864–1926)
Just a Little Pain, c. 1898
Watercolor and graphite on paper,
13 ⅜ × 10 ⅜ in.
Amon Carter Museum, Fort Worth,
Texas

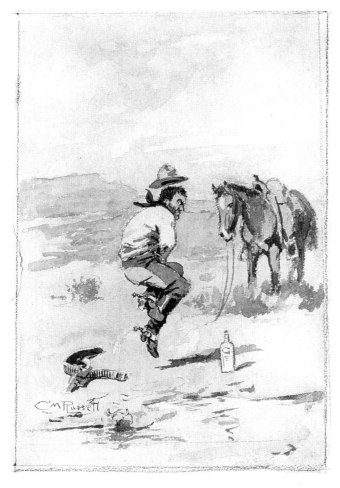

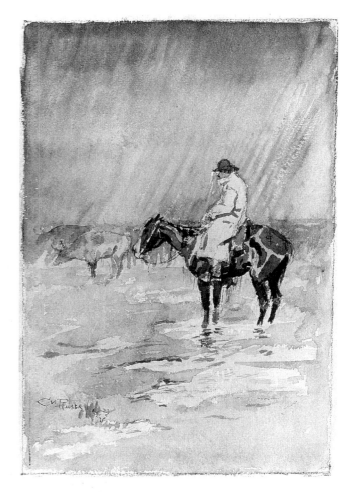

Charles M. Russell (1864–1926)
Just a Little Rain, c. 1898
Watercolor, opaque white, and
graphite on paper, 13 ⅛ × 10 ¾ in.
Amon Carter Museum, Fort Worth,
Texas

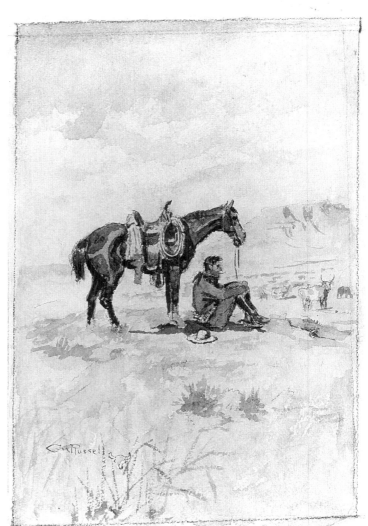

Charles M. Russell (1864–1926)
Just a Little Sunshine, c. 1898
Watercolor and graphite on paper,
13 ⅛ × 9 ⅞ in.
Amon Carter Museum, Fort Worth

Episodes in a cowboy's life—titled
with the appropriate western
understatement.

itors alike remember the aroma of the place: sweat, manure, boots, lamp oil. As to housekeeping, one eyewitness summed it up succinctly: "clothes were hung on the floor, so they wouldn't fall down and get lost." Or there was cowboy-historian Charlie Siringo's vignette of bunkhouse life on Shanghai Pierce's Rancho Grande: we "made an iron-clad rule that whoever was caught picking grey backs [body lice] off and throwing them on the floor without first killing them, should pay a fine of ten cents for each and every offense."

Not that a cowboy's bunkhouse entertainment was limited to picking lice. A good deal of time was passed in playing cards, reading—though, usually, few books were available—and playing guitar, banjo, fiddle, jew's harp or singing sentimental ballads. Tall tales were swapped, some crude, some downright obscene, a good many of them very funny in the dry, drawling vein that cowboy humorists like Will Rogers later popularized. Edward Everett Dale, in *Cow Country*, recalls a typical specimen:

. . . the usual Saturday afternoon crowd of loafers was gathered about a crossroads store in western Arkansas. Looking up the road toward the west, they saw a little cloud of dust approaching and as it came nearer they saw a most astonishing spectacle—a man in a two-wheeled cart to which was hitched a pair of mountain lions. The man himself was an unkempt, bearded individual with two six-shooters buckled about his waist and a bowie knife in his belt. A huge wild cat with a spiked collar about its neck sat on the seat beside him and the man was driving his fearsome team with a live rattlesnake for a whip. He pulled up in front of the store with a loud Whoa! laid down his rattlesnake, and asked: "Has anybody here got anything to drink?" There was a moment's silence and then one man diffidently stated that he had a little corn whisky. "Corn whisky is no sort of drink for a man," roared the newcomer, "ain't you got no sulphuric acid?" After another pause someone remarked that there was some in the store. "Bring me a quart of it," cried the newcomer. It was brought and, draining the liquid in a few gulps, the visitor picked up his rattlesnake, gathered up the lines and said: "Well, cats, we've got to be goin'. Much obleeged, men." Then one of the goggle-eyed crowd summoned up courage to ask: "Stranger, whare be ye frum? We ain't seen anybody like you in these parts afore. Whare do you live at anyhow?" "I'm frum Oklahomy," said the stranger. "To tell you th' truth, men, th' damned Ku Klux is gettin' so bad out there it's runnin' all of us sissies out."

Charles M. Russell (1864–1926)
A Mix Up, 1910
Oil on canvas, 30 × 48 in.
The Rockwell Museum, Corning,
New York

Getting tangled in rough rope with eight hundred pounds of live beef tied to one end was no joke for horse or rider.

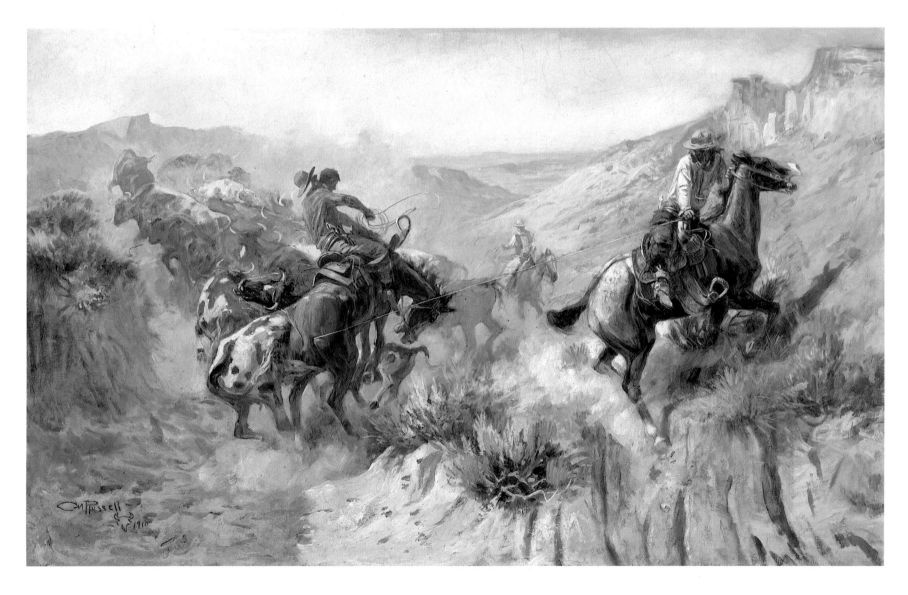

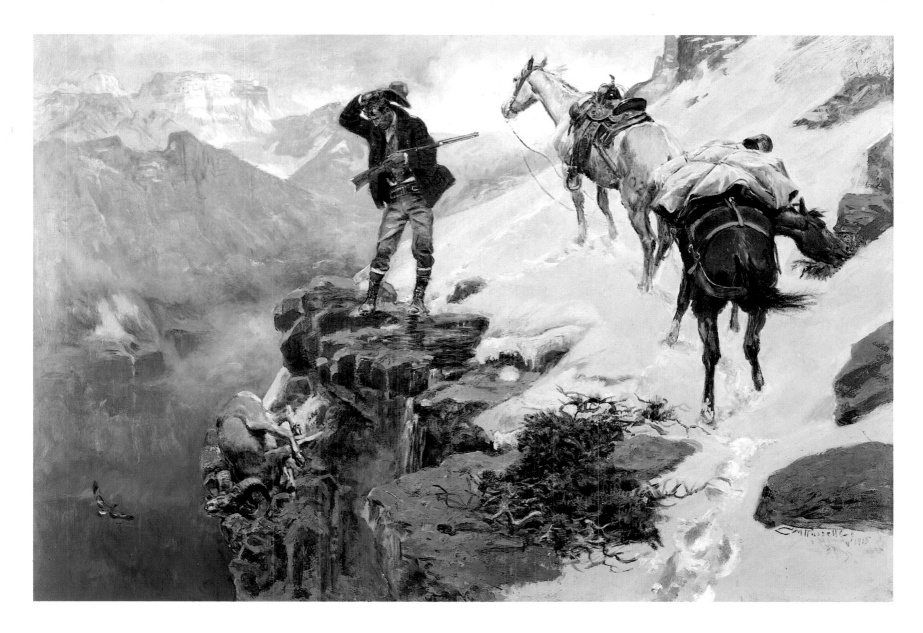

Charles M. Russell (1864–1926)
Meat's Not Meat 'Till It's in the Pan,
1915
Oil on canvas, 23 × 35 in.
Gilcrease Museum, Tulsa, Oklahoma

The West offered great bounty.
Usually, the real problem was
getting at it.

One of the oldest bunkhouse stories, according to Dale, is

that of Hank Blevins who, reaching Kansas City with a trainload of cattle, repaired to a swell restaurant for dinner. At the next table a girl and two men were giving their orders:

"Waiter," said the girl, "I want a thick steak, a rare steak please."

"Bring me a steak, too," said one of the men, "and I want mine very rare."

"I'll have a steak myself," said the next man, "but I want it extremely rare. Just sear the outside a little."

"Waiter," said Hank, when it came his turn, "just cripple him and drive him in. I'll eat him."

Despite its discomforts, most cowboys appreciated the bunkhouse for the fellowship it offered. Outside of it, much of the cowboy's work was solitary and tedious. For days at a time, a lone cowboy might be assigned to "ride the line," to patrol the perimeter of a particular range or pasture and keep his employer's stock from straying beyond it. Even with the development and widespread use

of barbed wire, riding the line was still an important duty; for ranch fences required continual repair and maintenance. Riding the line meant spending days or even weeks far from other human beings, holing up at night in a line camp, which was usually a one-room dugout or half dugout equipped with a door, a fireplace, and a straw-tick cot. It was work like this, lonely, distant from companions, from a woman's touch, from the warmth of a family, that has indelibly tinged the cowboy's story with melancholy, despite his vaunted freedom, his acts of prowess in the face of danger, and his boisterous good humor.

The most demanding test of a cowboy's mettle was the trail drive, a task of epic proportions. A herd of cattle—perhaps as small as 500 head or as large (in one record-breaking instance) as 15,000—had to be moved either to northern ranges for maturing (as was sometimes done with Texas cattle) or to market at railhead cattle towns like Abilene, Ellsworth, and Dodge City, Kansas, Pueblo and Denver, Colorado, and Cheyenne, Wyoming. Distances involved were often greater than a thousand miles over four principal trails: the Shawnee, from Brownsville, Texas, to Kansas City, Sedalia, and St.

CHARLES MARION RUSSELL

—

BORN 1864, ST. LOUIS, MISSOURI
DIED 1926, GREAT FALLS, MONTANA

—

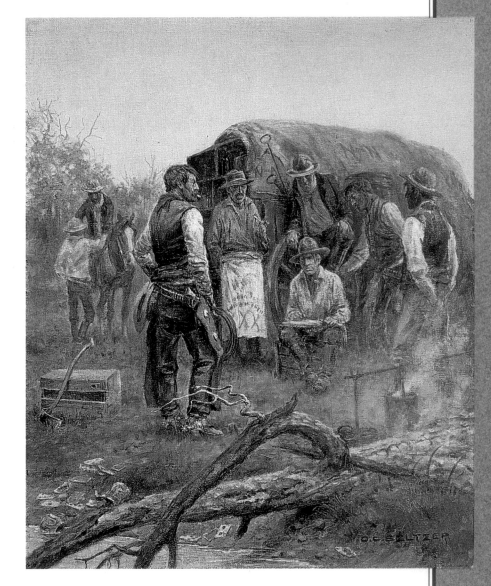

A poor student, young Charlie Russell was sent by his father to a New Jersey military academy in 1879. He lasted one term before his father, in desperation, allowed him to go out west as a Montana sheepherder. Russell soon drifted off from this job, worked as a hunter and trapper for about two years, and then took a place as night wrangler on a trail drive. Russell continued as a wrangler and cowboy for about eleven years. Toward the end of this period, in the terrible winter of 1887, he was driving five thousand head of cattle for Kaufman and Stadler, who were headquartered in Helena, Montana. Aware of the devastation the weather was visiting upon all range cattle, Kaufman wrote Russell's trail partner, Jesse Phelps, inquiring about the condition of the herd. Phelps hardly knew where to begin his reply, so Russell found a two-by-four-inch scrap of paper, took out the watercolors with which he liked to sketch, and painted a starved steer standing in a snow drift, about to collapse, eyed by hungry coyotes. Russell titled it *Waiting for a Chinook*—a wind that would bring a break in the weather. "Send 'em that," he told Phelps. Later, the watercolor, often reproduced, became known as *Last of the 5,000*. The painting, a small and eloquent monument to the end of the range cattle industry, was the start of Russell's career as a cowboy artist.

His reputation spread through reproduction of work in popular magazines and through exhibition by his first "collectors," saloon keepers throughout cattle country. After he married in 1896, it was Russell's wife, Nancy Cooper, who took on the job of managing her husband's career, seeing to it that his work commanded the prices it deserved. By the turn of the century, the artist was sculpting in bronze. It was his habit to carry a lump of clay in his pocket so that he could "sketch" a subject for later development into a finished sculpture. Though he was ignored by critics, by 1911, his works were selling in eastern mar-

kets for what the artist called "dead man's prices," and by the 1920s his fortune was secure.

Russell painted thousands of pictures, including the marvelous watercolors that often illustrate his letters to friends. Subject matter was generally drawn from his days as a cowboy, and, according to the artist himself, he always worked from memory, never using a model. With Frederic Remington, Charles Russell is undoubtedly the best known of western artists.

Louis, Missouri; the Chisholm, from various points in Texas to Abilene, Ellsworth, and Dodge City; the Western, from San Antonio, Texas, to Dodge City, and on to Fort Buford, at the fork of the Missouri and Yellowstone rivers in Dakota Territory; and the Goodnight-Loving, from the middle of Texas to Cheyenne. Hazards of the trails were almost beyond counting: storms, floods, drought, stampede, rustlers, hostile Indians (for three of the trails stretched right through Indian Territory), and limitless variations on all of these. Usually, cowboys were hired at the ratio of one for each 250 head of cattle—though some drovers got by with a ratio of one to 400. If the average herd size was 2,500 head of cattle, that meant that the average cowboy crew consisted of ten men. Their pay was about a hundred dollars for three or four months' work.

The drive began with a roundup of animals on the home range, followed by a process of cutting out animals from the main herd to make up the trail herd. If the cattle were being driven to northern ranges, they might be yearlings and two-year-olds. If they were destined for a drive directly to market, they were five to seven years old. Assembling the trail herd might take several weeks, depending on its size and the extent of the range. While this work was going on, the rancher made ready the equipment necessary for the drive, including a covered chuck wagon drawn by four mules. This vehicle carried food, bedding, and other supplies. Fitted into the back of the wagon was the chuck box, which contained flour, sugar, dried fruit, coffee, pinto beans, plates, cups, cut-

lery, salt, lard, baking soda, vinegar, chewing tobacco, rolling tobacco, a sourdough jar, matches, molasses, coffeepot, whiskey, skillets, and dutch ovens. The back door of the chuck box swung down when it was opened, forming a neat table for the preparation of food.

Before setting off, and after the herd was assembled, one crucial chore remained. The trail herd was often gathered from cattle that had been owned several years as well as cattle purchased from others. Usually, the cattle bore several different brands. It was necessary, then, to "road brand" the animals in order to identify them further.

The personnel who conducted the trail drive included a trail boss—sometimes the owner of the ranch, sometimes a hired foreman—a cook, a wrangler, and the cowboys. The trail boss was responsible for many thousands of dollars' worth of cattle and for the safety and welfare of his men. While his authority was absolute, he did not hold himself aloof and above his cowboys. Although he was paid far more than they—about $125 per month—he did the same hard and hazardous work. The cook was also paid somewhat better than the average cowboy, for he was crucial to an outfit's morale. The wrangler held the humblest position on the trail drive and, indeed, was something of an apprentice, often a lad of fourteen years or so. His job was to round up the horses each morning, driving them into a makeshift "corral" consisting of ropes stretched from each end of the chuck wagon. Five to ten horses had to be provided for each rider, which meant that the wrangler had forty-five

Olaf Carl Seltzer (1877–1957)
Charley Russell about 1891 Sketching in the Judith Basin, Montana, 1927
Oil on board, 12 × 10 in.
Gilcrease Museum, Tulsa, Oklahoma

Charles M. Russell (1864–1926)
Bronco Busting. Driving in. Cow Puncher, 1889–90
Oil on canvas, 20 ⅛ × 30 ⅛ in.
Amon Carter Museum, Fort Worth, Texas

Russell at his best—depicting the cowboy at work.

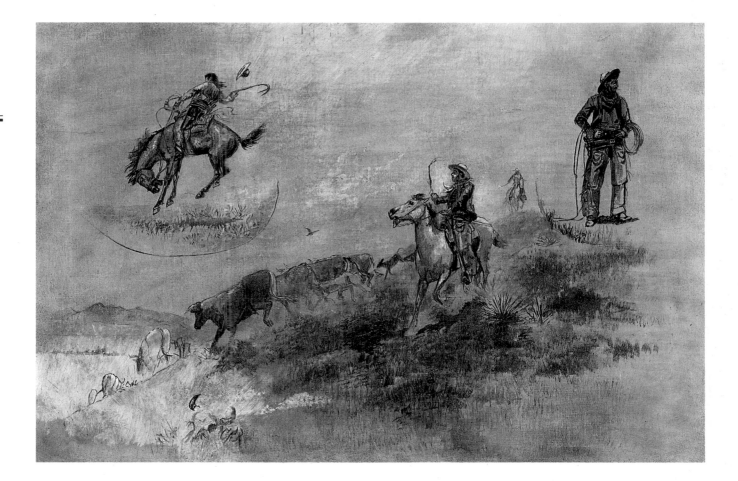

W. H. D. KOERNER

BORN 1878, LUN, GERMANY

DIED 1938, INTERLAKEN, NEW JERSEY

A popular western illustrator, William Henry David Koerner instilled in his work an aura of myth and legend partly through sophisticated handling of broken color and so-called "commercial impressionism," a technique he learned through study with the illustrator Frank Breckenridge.

Koerner, aged two, was brought to Clinton, Iowa, in 1880. At sixteen he was working for the *Chicago Tribune* as a staff artist for the starvation wage of five dollars a week. During this period he attended classes at the Art Institute and at the J. Francis Smith Art Academy. After a brief stint in 1904 as art editor for a magazine out of Battle Creek, Michigan, illustrating short stories and poetry, Koerner came to New York for study at the Art Students League from 1905 to 1907. He next moved to Wilmington, Delaware, at the time a mecca for fine illustrators, and worked as an illustrator while he studied with Howard Pyle (N. C. Wyeth was a fellow pupil) until 1911.

By the 1920s, Koerner had reached the top ranks of magazine illustrators, specializing in western subjects. He traveled widely in the West and maintained for a time a summer studio in a log cabin near the Crow reservation in Montana. For most of his mature career, however, his base of operations was a studio at Interlaken in rural New Jersey, which the artist amply stocked with Indian and other western artifacts.

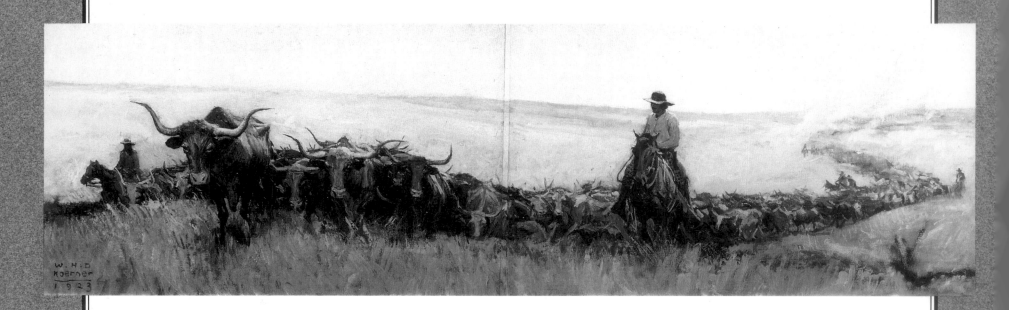

W. H. D. Koerner (1878–1938)
Trail Herd to Wyoming, 1923
Oil on canvas, 22 ¼ × 72 ¼ in.
Courtesy Buffalo Bill Historical
Center, Cody, Wyoming

These Texas cattle are being trailed
to northern pastureland for
maturing and fattening.

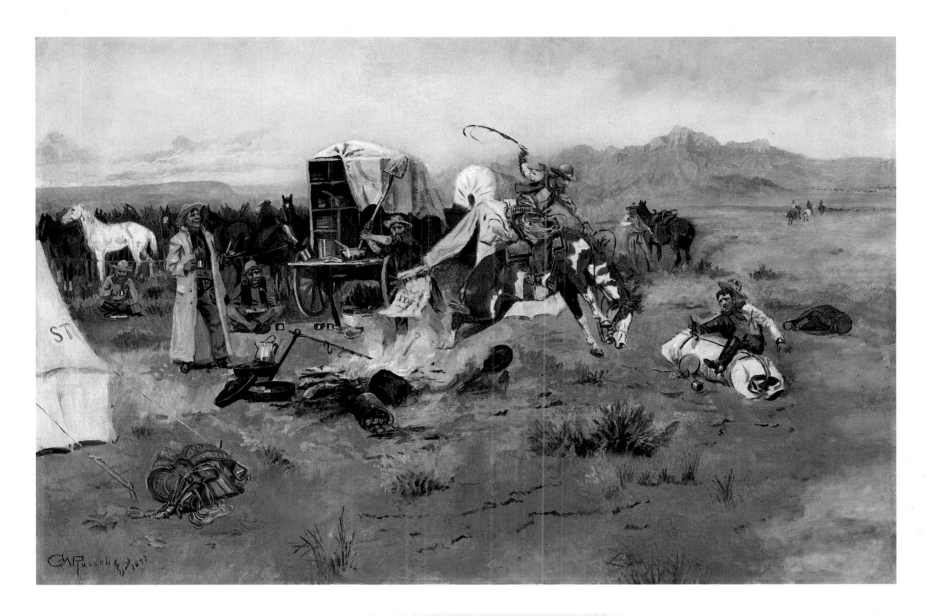

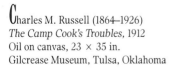harles M. Russell (1864–1926)
Bronc in Cow Camp, 1897
Oil on canvas, 20 ⅛ × 31 ¼ in.
Amon Carter Museum, Fort Worth,
Texas

Control of an unbroken horse is hard
won, not granted. This painting
provides a good view of the trail-
drive chuck wagon with its fold-
down table. It also shows an article
of cowboy attire almost as familiar
as the Stetson and boots: a yellow
rain slicker.

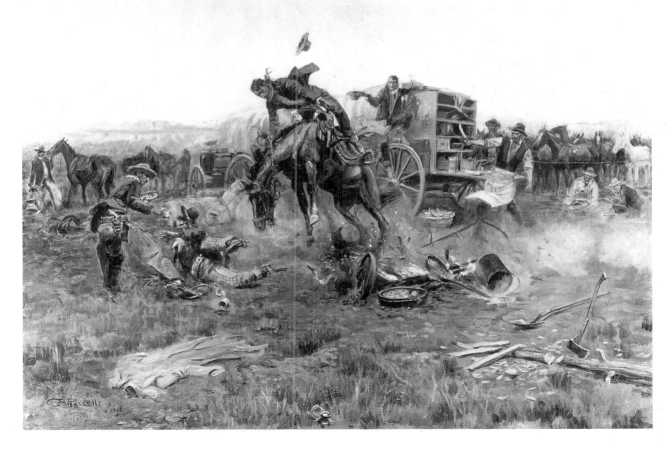

Charles M. Russell (1864–1926)
The Camp Cook's Troubles, 1912
Oil on canvas, 23 × 35 in.
Gilcrease Museum, Tulsa, Oklahoma

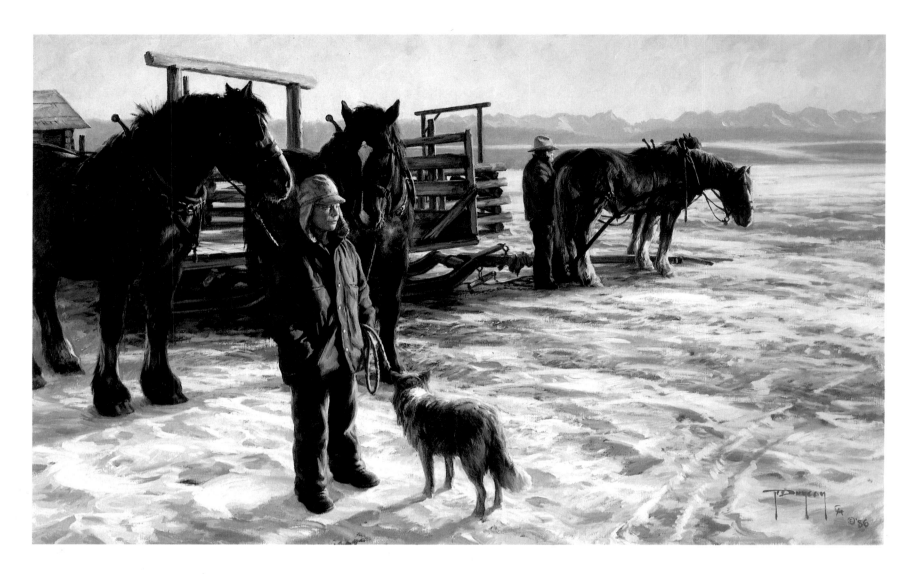

to ninety ponies to look after: the "saddle band" or *remuda* or *caballada,* sometimes anglicized to "cavvy yard," "cavalry yard," or just plain "cavvy." As to the cowboys, they were assigned specific positions relative to the herd. Out ahead of the herd, the procession was led by the trail boss. At the front of the herd, flanking it, were the point men; behind them, the swing riders; behind them, the flank riders; and behind the herd, the cowboys riding drag. Customarily, the cowboys rotated among these positions.

The drive usually commenced in early April, when the grass had risen sufficiently to insure good pasturage. The first several days on the trail were the most difficult, requiring all the skill the trail boss and his men could muster. The cattle had to be "road broke," accustomed to moving along the trail. The boss had to judge whether it was best to drive the cattle hard during these first few days in order to get them used to the trail as quickly as possible and to tire them out sufficiently so that they would not be restive at night, or to go easy on them, so as not to make them skittish.

A nervous herd was a drover's greatest misery. Skittish animals tended to stampede, especially at night, when the slightest noise—a peal of distant thunder, the cry of a coyote, the rustle of a cowboy's rain slicker— might spook a herd. An unchecked stampede was like a

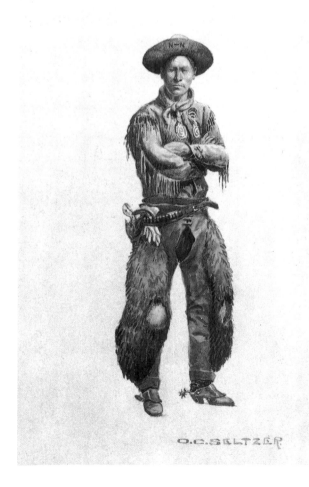

sudden squall at sea and potentially as deadly. At the very least, a stampede meant hours of riding to round up the strayed animals.

After these first critical days, the drive settled into a hard routine of early rising, a breakfast of strong cowboy coffee (with eggshells in it, to settle the grounds), sourdough biscuits, beef steak or bacon, and syrup and dried fruit. After eating, the men went to the wrangler's improvised corral and caught and saddled their horses of choice. They then rode out to the herd, relieving the night watch, who came in for their breakfast and to change horses.

Under the cowboys' watchful gaze, the cattle were allowed to graze until nine o'clock or so and were gradually drifted up toward the north, strung out into a mile-long column.

While all of this was taking place, the cook had washed up and packed up his portable kitchen. He hitched his four-mule team to the chuck wagon and, while the herd was still grazing, rode out ahead five to seven miles to a spot that had been scouted out by the trail boss where there was a stream or other source of

water for the cattle. Here he set up the wagon for the afternoon meal. When the herd reached the spot—by around noon, if all went well—the cattle were spread out so that they could graze and drink. After the men ate and the washing up was done, the cook drove the wagon out beyond the herd to the spot designated as the night campsite, again near a stream, where the cattle could be well watered. After the evening meal, those who were not on night guard duty could swap stories before they stretched out for sleep. The first-shift night guards circled slowly around the herd, singing, perhaps, to calm the animals and prevent their being spooked into a stampede. At eleven, the second-shift guards rode out to relieve the first. Guards on this shift had to be wary, since cattle usually got up around midnight to stretch and walk about. The riders had to take care to keep the animals from walking too far, lest they stray from the herd or start the entire herd moving. At two in the morning, the last shift took over until dawn.

Life on the trail was hard at best, and it often got much harder. Heavy rain made the cowboy's work particularly miserable as well as dangerous when the herd

Frederic Remington (1861–1909)
The Stampede, 1908
Oil on canvas, 27 × 40 in.
Gilcrease Museum, Tulsa, Oklahoma

The mere rustle of cowboy's rain slicker could trigger a stampede during a cattle drive; thunder and lightning were almost guaranteed to set off a nervous herd.

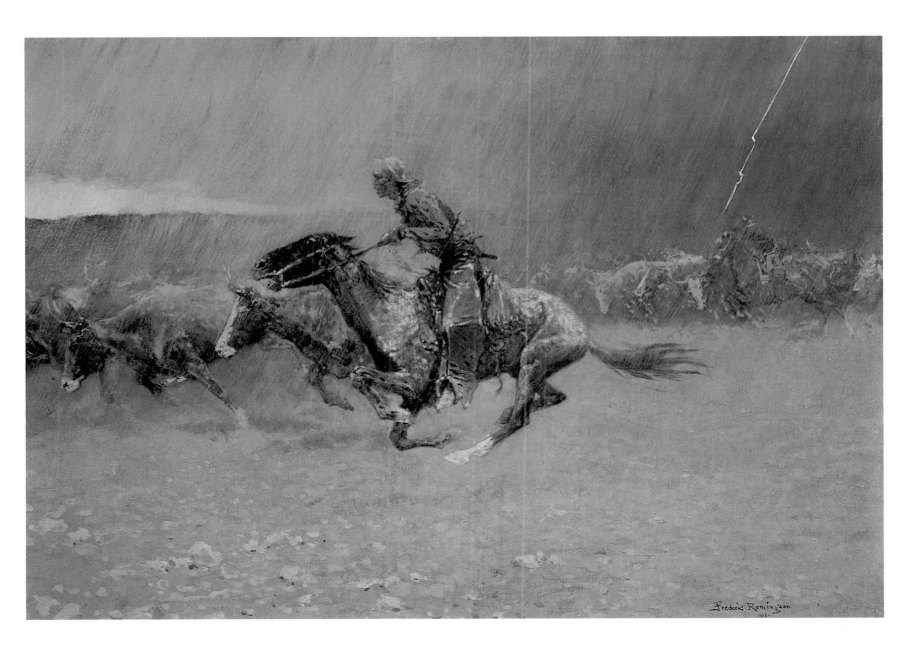

had to ford swollen streams. Getting the chuck wagon across sometimes involved cutting two large cottonwood logs, lashing them to the sides of the wagon, and floating the impromptu barge across. As to the cattle, they would have to be made to swim to the other side. It was often an all-day affair inducing the lead animals into the water and then prodding unwilling stragglers. If the river were wide and deep, the animals might attempt to turn back in the middle of the crossing. Those behind the leaders would follow, but then the leaders would end up following *them,* creating what cowboys called a "mill." The cattle would swim around and around and, if not promptly broken up, drown.

Nighttime might or might not bring relief. If the herd got spooked into a stampede, all riders had to be roused, mount their night horses, and gallop out in search of the herd leaders. The object was to turn these animals so that the others would follow, creating a mill. Once the mill was established, the riders had to circle it in order to keep the herd from breaking out across the prairie again. There was nothing to do but let the mill run its course and hope the animals would tire sooner rather than later. Sometimes the cowboys were kept riding, round and round, all night.

Indian hostility was less of a problem to drovers than popular fiction and film have suggested, although it is true that the first several years of the big trail drives across Indian Territory saw some violence. For the most part, however, bands of Indians would approach the trail boss and demand some tribute of beeves. Rarely was a cattleman in danger of outright attack if he refused to bargain, but he did run the risk of having the Indians return at night to stampede the herd. On the other hand, with some two hundred miles of Indian Territory to tra-

W. Herbert Dunton (1878–1936)
The Shower, c. 1914
Oil on canvas, 32 × 25 in.
Courtesy of The Anschutz Collection

Frank Tenney Johnson (1874–1939)
A Fresh Mount, 1932
Oil on canvas, 36 ¼ × 46 in.
Amon Carter Museum, Fort Worth, Texas

Members of the "night guard" change horses. A cowboy commonly exhausted two mounts during his trail shift.

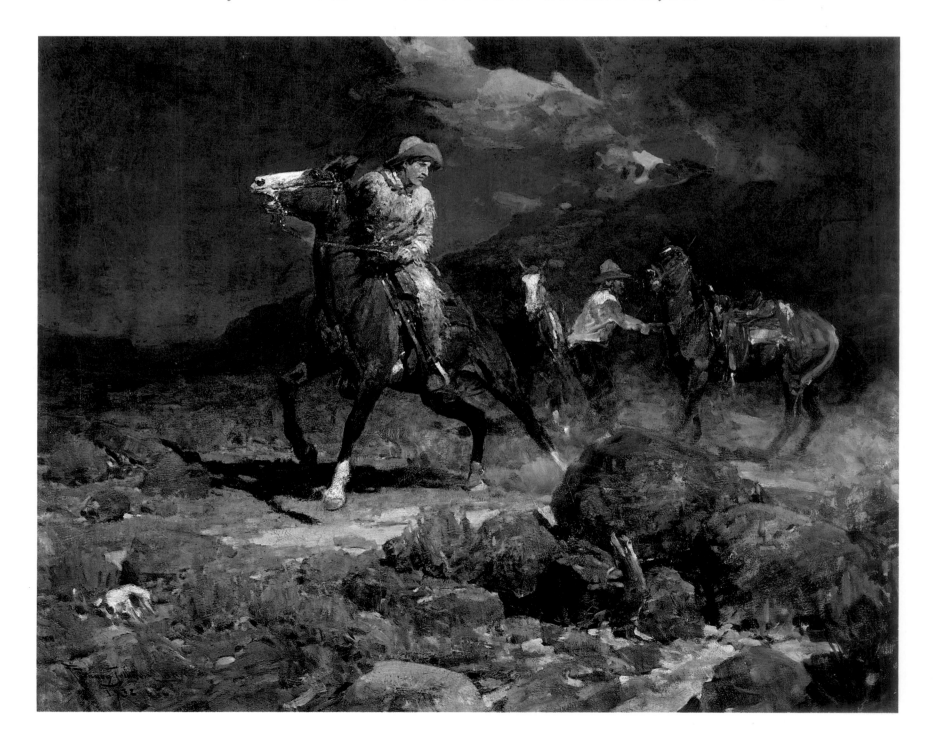

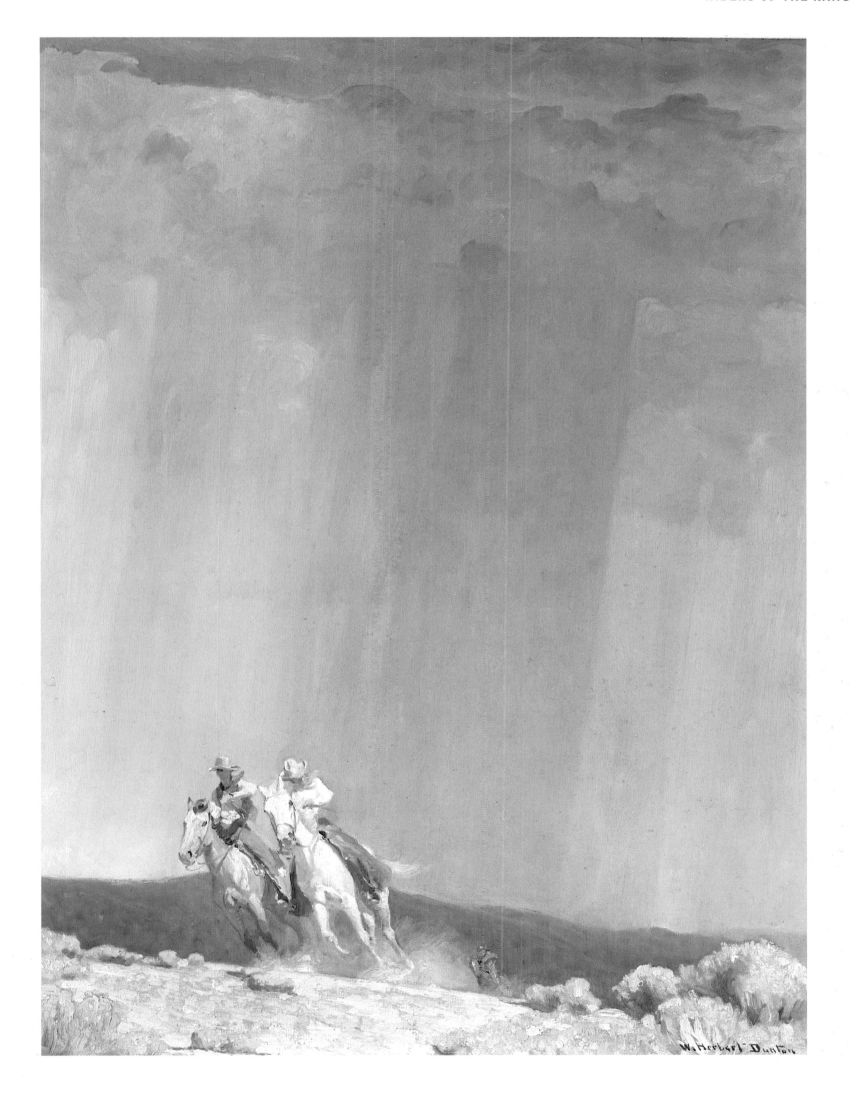

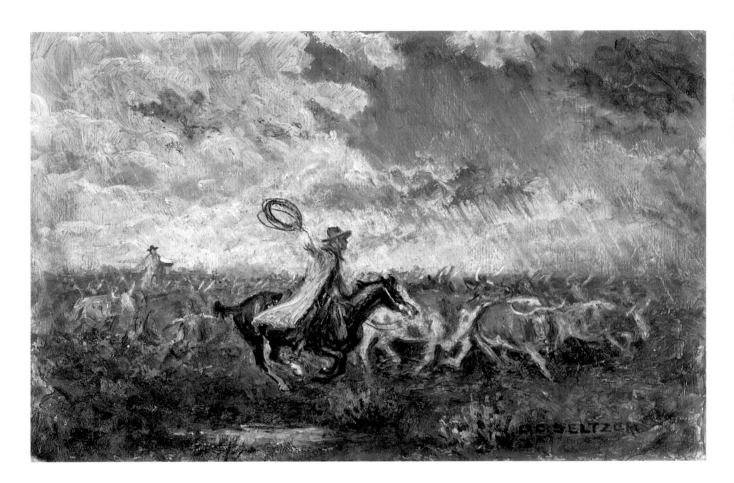

Olaf Carl Seltzer (1877–1957)
The Cattle Stampede, 1934
Oil on board, 4 × 6 in.
Gilcrease Museum, Tulsa, Oklahoma

It was jobs like this in weather like
this that made the cowboy's daily
life so damned hard.

verse, a trail boss could not afford to be overly generous, or he would find his (or his employer's) stock greatly diminished. Negotiations between Indians and trail bosses, as Edward Everett Dale recorded, were sometimes as sharp as they were dry: "I'll give you two but not six," a trail boss told a Kiowa.

"Two not enough," said the old Kiowa haughtily. "You give me six or I'll come with my young men tonight and stampede your cattle." "Well," replied the boss, "when you come tonight be sure to bring a spade with you." "Why spade?" asked the chief. "Well," said the foreman, "the cook broke the handle out of our spade yesterday, and when you come to stampede my cattle I aim to kill you and unless you bring a spade along we can't bury you."

The old Kiowa got two beeves.

More dangerous were cattle raiders, who would fall upon a herd, shoot at the cowboys, stampede the herd, and appropriate the strays. Equally violent, on some occasions, were the Kansas farmers whose croplands were trampled by herds and whose own livestock was in danger of infection by Texas fever (a disease carried by the Texas Longhorns, which did not become sick, but that was fatal to northern-bred cattle). Many drovers encountered self-appointed, shotgun-toting border guards. "Bend 'em west, boys," one trail boss called to his men during a showdown at the Kansas line. "Nothing in Kansas anyhow, except the three suns—sunflowers, sunshine, and those sons of bitches."

Sometimes, violence between trail drivers, sheepherders, and homesteader-farmers (about whom we shall hear more shortly) erupted into ugly episodes of vigilante "justice" and even full-scale range wars.

Sheepherding, a major western agricultural industry, never worked upon the American imagination the kind of magic conjured up by the world of the ranchman and cowboy. Cattlemen always looked upon the sheepman with contempt, at times mounting to hatred. The harsh fact was that sheep and cattle could not coexist on the same range. Sheep grazed grass down to the very roots and then tended to cut up the roots with their sharp hooves, leaving nothing behind for cattle and often destroying pasturage. (Cattlemen carried their grievance a step beyond this very real problem, believing that sheep could ruin pasturage merely by walking across it. Glands between a sheep's toes secrete a sticky fluid, which cattlemen incorrectly believed made the grass unpalatable to cattle.) In Wyoming, a vigilante gang of masked cattlemen killed four thousand sheep, using clubs, guns, and even dynamite. Other gangs practiced "rimrocking," driving sheep off sheer cliffs. A flock of one thousand was destroyed this way in Colorado. Oftentimes, it was not only the animals who suffered, as cattlemen and sheepmen opened fire on one another.

Sheepmen were not the only "enemy" the cattlemen encountered as they expanded their holdings by laying claim to, preempting, or simply occupying government lands as grazing range. In the Lincoln County War in New Mexico (1878–81) one set of cattlemen faced off against another, and in the Johnson County War in Wyoming (1892) big ranchers took up arms against homesteaders.

The stage was set for the Lincoln County conflict when cattleman John Chisum began pushing his herds into the Pecos Valley during the early 1870s, preempting government lands in this region, which was already notorious for its lawlessness. He eyed lucrative U.S. government contracts to supply soldiers and Indian reservations with beef. But squared off against him was Lawrence G. Murphy, a powerful Santa Fe merchant, entrepreneur, and financier. Murphy had crucial political connections and financial control of the area's small ranchers that gave him a virtual monopoly on the government beef contracts. The two sides were unevenly matched until 1875, when a lawyer named Alexander McSween and an Englishman-turned-rancher named John Tunstall joined forces with Chisum against the monopoly.

At this time, however, Murphy sold his interests to James J. Dolan and James H. Riley, who soon found themselves losing business to the firm of Chisum, McSween, and Tunstall. As his business grew, Chisum appropriated more and more government land, which turned many smaller ranchers against him. Other ranchers were beholden to Dolan and Riley for credit, as they had been to Murphy. Yet still others saw an alliance with Tunstall and McSween—if not directly with Chisum—as a means of breaking the political and economic stranglehold exerted by Dolan and Riley and the so-called "Santa Fe Ring," a political cabal.

When, on February 18, 1878, John Tunstall was murdered by Dolan supporters, Lincoln County erupted into war. County law enforcement was entirely dominated by the Santa Fe Ring, and Sheriff William Brady refused to arrest the murderers of Tunstall, even though he had warrants. Instead, he took into custody two of Tunstall's employees, Fred Waite and a teenager whose name was Henry McCarty but who called himself William Bonney or Billy the Kid.

Some say Henry—or Billy—was born in New York City; others believe it was in Marion County, Indiana. During the Civil War, Billy moved with his parents and his older brother Joe to Kansas. After his father died, the family moved to New Mexico, where Billy's mother married William H. Antrim in 1873. She succumbed to tuberculosis the following year, and Billy, a year after her death, was arrested (as the *Grant County Herald* put it) "upon the charge of stealing clothes from Charley Sun

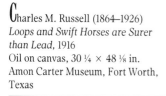

Charles M. Russell (1864–1926)
Loops and Swift Horses are Surer than Lead, 1916
Oil on canvas, 30 ¼ × 48 ⅛ in.
Amon Carter Museum, Fort Worth, Texas

Yet another hazard of the trail—handled expertly by California vaqueros.

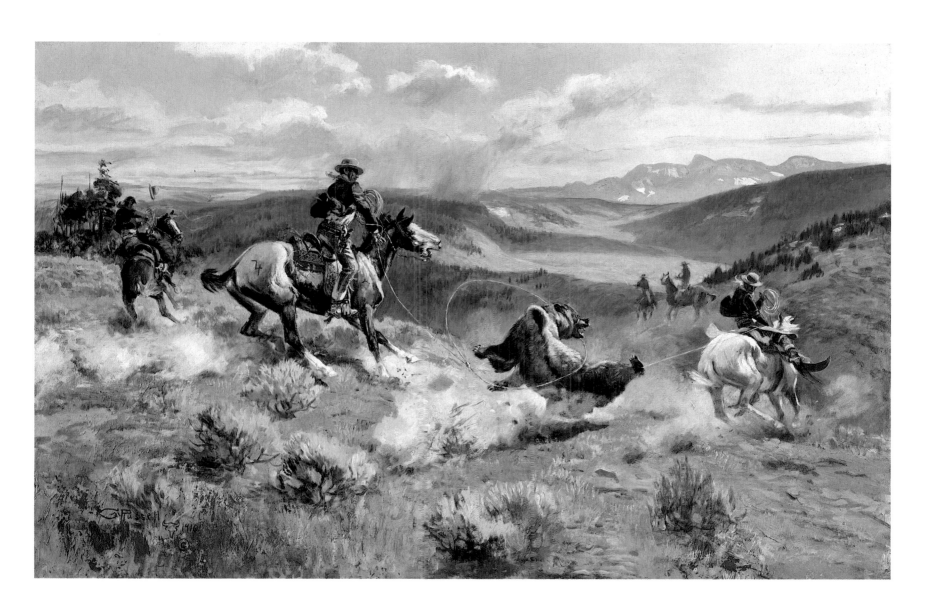

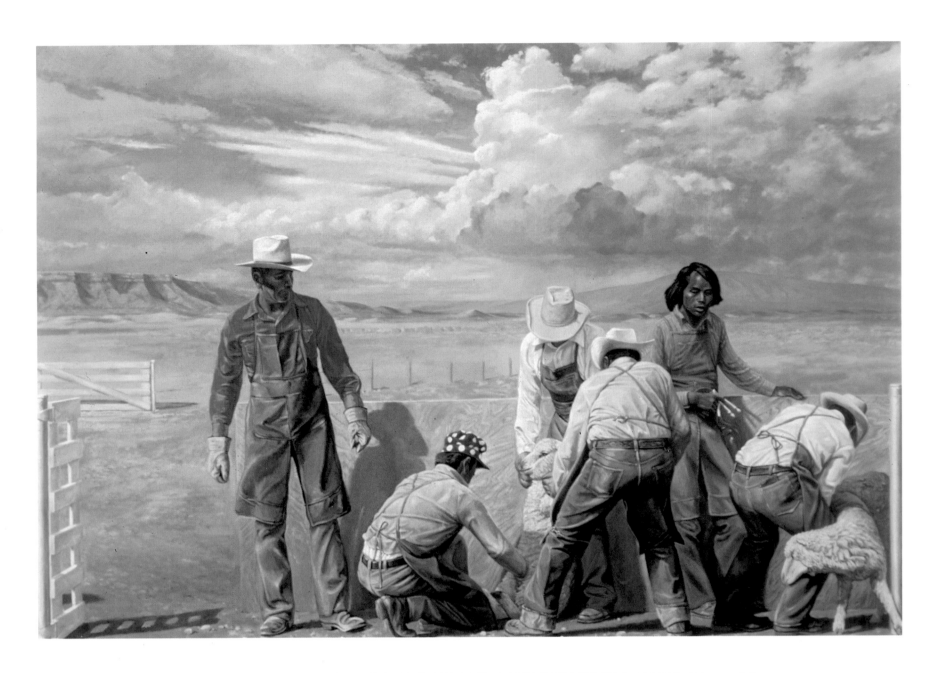

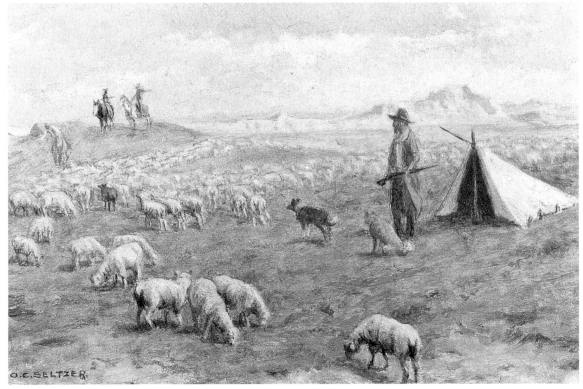

Willard Midgette (1937–1978)
Processing Sheep, 1976
Oil on linen, 108 ¼ × 156 ½ in.
Phoenix Art Museum; Museum purchase with funds provided by Mr. and Mrs. Kemper Marley

This modern depiction of sheep handling suggests why the profession never enjoyed the romance associated with the cattle trade.

Olaf Carl Seltzer (1877–1957)
Sheepmen vs. Cattlemen, 1934
Oil on board, 11 × 16 in.
Gilcrease Museum, Tulsa, Oklahoma

The oil and water of the range: cattle versus sheep interests. Cattlemen claimed—with some justification—that sheep ruined pastureland, leaving nothing for cattle.

and Sam Chung, celestials sans cue." It is doubtful whether Billy actually committed this petty theft, but it did give him an opportunity to practice—successfully—escaping from jail.

For the next two years Billy worked as a laborer, teamster, and cowboy until August 17, 1877, when the seventeen-year-old had an argument with one F. P. Cahill in George Adkins's saloon in Fort Grant, Arizona. Cahill, a big Irish blacksmith, threw the slightly built Billy onto the saloon floor and slapped his face. That's when the boy drew his revolver and shot him. Cahill died the next day. Indicted for "criminal and unjustifiable murder," Billy was jailed to await trial. He made the second prison break of his career and returned to New Mexico. There he started working on the Lincoln County ranch of John Tunstall, only to end up in the clutches of Sheriff Brady.

After Brady was forced to release him for lack of evidence, Billy swore to avenge the murder of his employer, and joined a posse of "Regulators" led by Dick Brewer, Tunstall's foreman, in pursuit of the Englishman's killers. They captured two of the chief suspects, Frank Baker and William Morton, who subsequently made a break for it, seizing a gun from one of the posse, William McCloskey, and wounding him fatally before galloping down the trail. After a furious volley of gunfire, both Baker and Morton were felled. Billy claimed credit.

The Kid next determined to kill Sheriff William Brady and, with four accomplices, set an ambush for him behind a low adobe wall on the main street of Lincoln. About midmorning, Brady walked by, accompanied by his deputy, George Hindman, and Billy Matthews, Jack Long, and George Peppin. The Kid and his men opened fire, mortally wounding both Brady and Hindman, slightly wounding Matthews, and missing Long and Peppin; all three of the latter dashed for cover. When Billy and Fred Waite ventured out to steal the Winchesters belonging to the sheriff and his deputy, Matthews opened fire, wounding both outlaws slightly and sending them off to their horses and galloping away.

Between April and July of 1878, Billy the Kid was deeply embroiled in the fruitless violence of the Lincoln County War, which reached its crescendo in the so-called Five Day Battle of July 15–19. With ten others, the Kid holed up in Alexander McSween's adobe house doing battle with the Dolan faction, who were laying siege against them. After a four-day exchange of gunfire, troops from Fort Stanton arrived, and the McSween place was set ablaze.

With only three of his adobe's twelve rooms intact, McSween, unarmed, walked outside, a Bible clutched to his chest. A volley of gunfire cut him down.

Others attempted escape and met with similar fates—except for the Kid, who somehow negotiated the storm of lead uninjured. He subsequently turned himself over to the authorities in exchange for amnesty granted

by the territorial governor, the popular novelist Lew Wallace (Ben-Hur). As his trial approached, however, Billy the Kid became jittery and bolted, forming a band of cattle thieves that ranged as far as the Texas Panhandle and becoming involved in one shooting scrape after another.

In Bob Hargrove's saloon in Fort Sumner, New Mexico, the Kid was tipped off that a gambler named Joe Grant was out to kill him. On the night of January 10, 1880, Billy approached Grant and asked if he could admire the man's ivory-handled revolver. Grant handed it over, and Billy saw that there were only three bullets in the cylinder. Before returning the piece to Grant, Billy turned the cylinder so that it would next fire on an empty chamber. Sure enough, Grant challenged Billy later in the evening, stuck his gun in the outlaw's face, pulled the trigger—and *click*. Billy the Kid drew his own weapon and discharged a slug squarely into Grant's head.

There followed a number of deadly exchanges between Billy and lawmen until December 19, 1880, when the Kid and five henchmen arrived in Fort Sumner, New Mexico, and were met by Sheriff Pat Garrett and a posse, who ordered the outlaws to surrender. Instead, they wheeled their horses about and ran. All but one escaped. Garrett trailed them to a rock house in Stinking Springs on December 23 and ordered his men to kill Billy the Kid on sight. One of the Kid's gang, Charlie Bowdre, ignorant of the lurking posse, ventured out the door. Garrett thought he was the Kid and gave the signal to fire. Bowdre staggered back into the house, badly hit. Billy put a gun in the doomed man's hand and told him, "They've murdered you, Charlie, but you can get revenge. Kill some of the sons-of-bitches before you die." Billy shoved him back out the door, but Bowdre did not manage a shot. He stumbled forward and died at Pat Garrett's feet. Later that day, Billy and his three surviving followers surrendered to Sheriff Garrett.

Tried, convicted, and sentenced to death, Billy the Kid was held in the Lincoln County Courthouse to await hanging. About six o'clock on the evening of April 28, 1881, Billy asked one of his guards, J. W. Bell, to let him use the outhouse. On the way back upstairs to his cell, Billy slipped his small hands out of the handcuffs that bound them, raced past Bell (despite being manacled with leg irons), and broke open a weapons locker. (Some accounts report that a weapon had been planted in the outhouse.) Billy told the hapless guard to put up his hands. Instead, he turned and fled. Billy shot him, and Bell was mortally wounded by a slug ricocheting off the staircase wall.

Bell died in the arms of Godfrey Gauss, who ran to give warning to another of Billy's guards, Bob Olinger, who had been out at the time of the escape. Olinger had not treated the Kid well during his incarceration and had just that morning tormented him with a shotgun. It was that very shotgun with which Billy now armed himself.

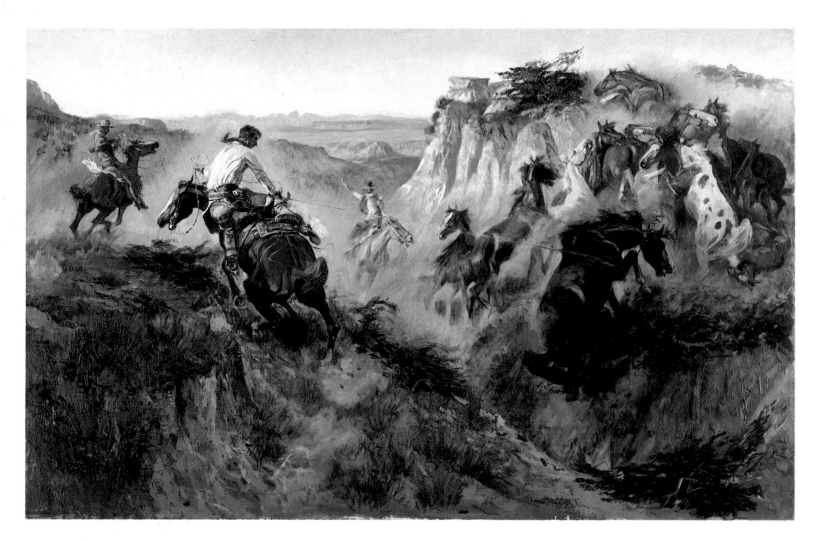

Then, still shackled, he hobbled to a window. As Olinger rushed across the street toward him, the Kid called out "Hello, Bob" and discharged both barrels of the shotgun: one barrel after "Hello," the other after "Bob."

"You won't follow me anymore with that gun," Billy said, tossing the shotgun down beside the corpse. Exchanging a few calm words with bystanders, he rode out of town—coolly, if awkwardly, on account of the leg irons.

Billy the Kid holed up at a sheep camp near Fort Sumner. On Wednesday evening, July 14, 1881, he came to the fort, some have said, to see Celsa Gutiérrez, Pat Garrett's sister-in-law, who, by some accounts, was Billy's sweetheart. Others say he came to the fort to see another woman, Paulita Maxwell. In any case, it is probable that Paulita's brother, Pete Maxwell, informed Garrett that Billy was in the vicinity of the fort; perhaps, if Billy was seeing his sister, he wanted to bring the doomed relationship to an end. Whether Billy, in fact, visited Paulita—or Celsa—that night before he was killed is impossible to say. Sheriff Pat Garrett's self-serving account of the death of Billy the Kid is entirely unreliable, as are, in varying degrees, all of the others. Most plausible is that of Francisco Lobato, the sheep-herder with whom Billy was hiding out near Fort Sumner: "On the night he was killed, [Billy] and I went to Fort Sumner together. We were hungry and stopped at

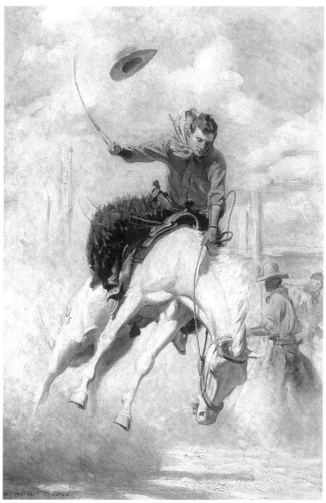

Charles M. Russell (1864–1926)
Wild Horse Hunters, 1913
Oil on canvas, 30 ⅛ × 47 in.
Amon Carter Museum, Fort Worth, Texas

Indians were not the only equestrians who prized the spirit of free-ranging horses.

W. Herbert Dunton (1878–1936)
Bronco Buster, c. 1905
Oil on canvas, 39 × 25 in.
The Rockwell Museum, Corning, New York

Most horses don't take naturally to being ridden; they have to be broke—and that often means a very rough ride.

OLAF WIEGHORST

—

BORN 1899, JUTLAND, DENMARK

DIED 1988, EL CAJON, CALIFORNIA

—

Like many of the best traditional "cowboy artists," Wieghorst was first a working cowboy—but his knowledge of horses extended even further. Educated in the public schools of Copenhagen Wieghorst was a child acrobat, an apprentice shopkeeper, a farm hand, and a sailor—all before he had reached age twenty. From his father, a display artist, photo retoucher, and engraver, he inherited a talent for art and began painting in 1916. While he was still in Denmark, Wieghorst became interested in the American "Wild West."

Employed as an able seaman, he jumped ship in New York City in 1918 and enlisted in the U.S. Cavalry for duty on the Mexican border. He served three years as a horseshoer, also learning rodeo riding and trick riding. He left the service in Arizona, where he found work on the Quarter Circle 2C Ranch, adopting its brand as his painting signature.

In 1923, Wieghorst returned to New York and enrolled in the city's police academy, becoming a member of the Police Show Team of the Mounted Division in 1925. During this period, Wieghorst also began painting seriously, but it was not until 1940 that he secured an agent to market his work for direct sale as well as reproduction. By 1942, the artist was also executing bronzes.

Wieghorst retired from the police department in 1944 and moved to El Cajon, California, painting full time and specializing in horses, which, the artist once remarked, "have been my life."

Olaf Wieghorst (1899–1988)
Bucking Bronco, n.d.
Oil on artist's board, 20 × 16 in.
Amon Carter Museum, Fort Worth,
Texas

Few western painters knew horses better than Wieghorst, who worked not only as a cowboy out West, but as a member of the New York City Mounted Police show team.

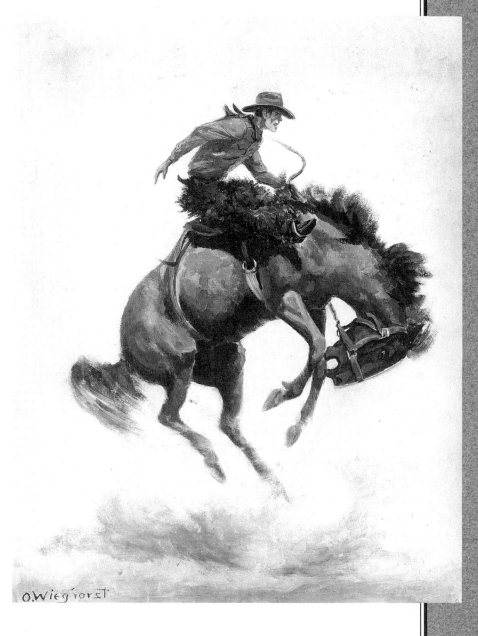

Jesús Silva's to eat. Billy wanted some beefsteak and asked Silva if he had any fresh meat. Silva replied that he had none but had helped Pete Maxwell kill a yearling that morning. He told the Kid he could get all he wanted if he went over to Maxwell's for it."

Coincidentally, Garrett, John Poe, and Tip McKinney rode into Fort Sumner at this time, around midnight. Garrett went into Maxwell's bedroom while Poe and McKinney waited outside. "It was probably not more than thirty seconds after Garrett had entered Maxwell's room," recalled Poe, "when my attention was attracted . . . to a man approaching. . . . I observed that he was only partially dressed and was both bareheaded and barefooted, or rather, had only socks on his feet, and it seemed to me that he was fastening his trousers as he came toward me. . . ."

Although Garrett's account claims that the Kid was armed with a double-action .41, it seems certain that all he carried was a butcher knife.

"Quién es?" Billy asked the two men, Poe and McKinney, who were loitering before Pete Maxwell's door. "Quién es?"

The Kid stepped past the silent men and into Maxwell's room.

"Pedro, quién es son estos hombres afuera?"

"That's him," Pete Maxwell said to Garrett, and the sheriff fired at the dimly visible silhouette. The second shot went wild, but the first had found its mark. Billy the Kid was dead.

The later Johnson County War in Wyoming did not gestate a legendary badman like Billy the Kid, but it did show just how far rangeland violence—this time between homesteaders and ranchers—could go. In 1892, the big cattlemen of Wyoming decided to take steps to end the rustling that had been plaguing them for some years. Most of the rustling seemed to be concentrated about 250 miles from Cheyenne, in Johnson County, where cowboys, having left the employ of the big ranchers, would take up government homesteads and rustle up their own herds at the expense of their former employers.

Rustling was always hard to prove in court, and even when the ranchers could come up with convincing evidence, juries tended to side with the homesteading cowhands rather than the mighty ranchers. Failing to ob-

Charles M. Russell (1864–1926)
Smoke of a .45, 1908
Oil on canvas, 24 ⅜ × 36 ¼ in. Amon Carter Museum, Fort Worth, Texas

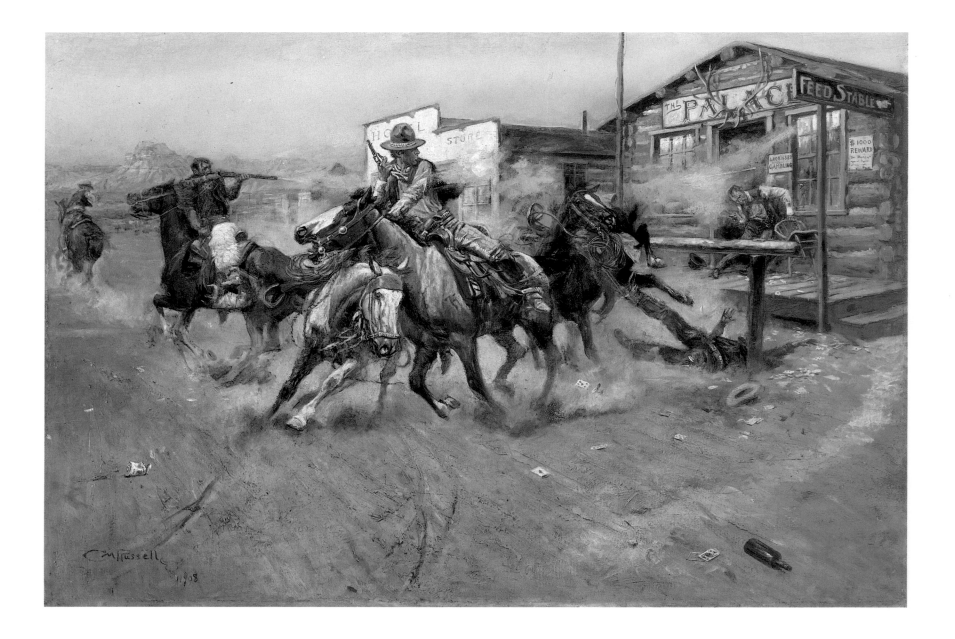

Edward Borein (1872–1945)
Cowbow Chasing Longhorn Steer,
n.d.
Watercolor on paper, 18 ¼ × 19 ⅞ in.
Collection of The Oakland Museum;
Museum Donor's Acquisition Fund

A stringy animal, its meat far from
choice, the hearty Longhorn was
nevertheless the basis of the Texas
cattle industry and the range cattle
industry that developed from it.

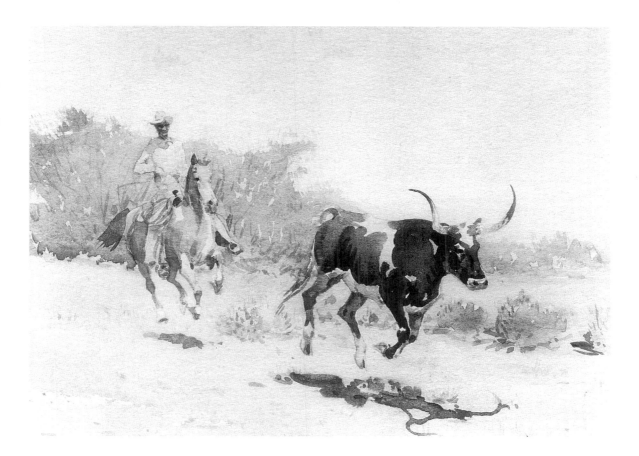

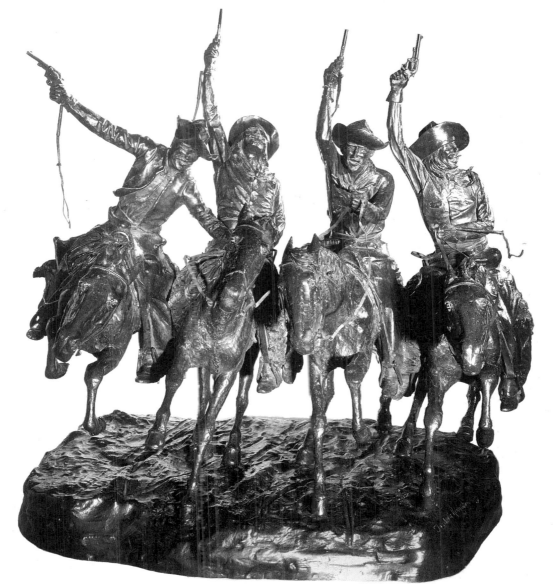

Frederic Remington (1861–1909)
*Comin' Through the Rye (Off the
Range),* 1902
Bronze casting, H. 27 ¼ in.
Gilcrease Museum, Tulsa, Oklahoma

The artist's most celebrated
sculpture embodies all the abandon
and high spirits easterners have
perpetually celebrated and envied in
the cowboy. Confronted with this
end-of-the-cattle-drive behavior,
however, respectable residents of
the West's cattle towns entertained
very different emotions.

tain satisfaction from the courts, the ranchers hired "detectives"—thugs, really—who freely ambushed-suspected rustlers and murdered them.

The most notorious incident was the assassination of Cattle Kate and her partner, Jim Averill. Kate, whose real name was Ella Watson, served Sweetwater, Wyoming, as a prostitute and madam, and also took in cowboys' washing and ironing. The 170-pound woman and her partner extended their enterprise to cattle rustling and established a corral where the appropriated animals could be branded and held for transportation elsewhere. The summary execution of Kate and Averill did nothing to discourage rustling, but only put the small ranchers up to more rustling.

In retaliation, the cattlemen used their Wyoming Stock Growers' Association to compile what today would be called a "hit list." Forty-six vigilantes—Invaders or Regulators, as they alternately called themselves—led by Frank Wolcott and Frank H. Canton, took a special Union Pacific train from Cheyenne, where the Stock Growers' Association had just concluded its meeting, to Casper. From that town they set out on horseback after the condemned men. The Regulators surprised two of them, Nate Champion and Nick Ray, at the KC Ranch. Ray was killed first, and Champion held off the forty-six Invaders for twelve hours before he was smoked out and then shot. But the vigilantes' brutal triumph was short-

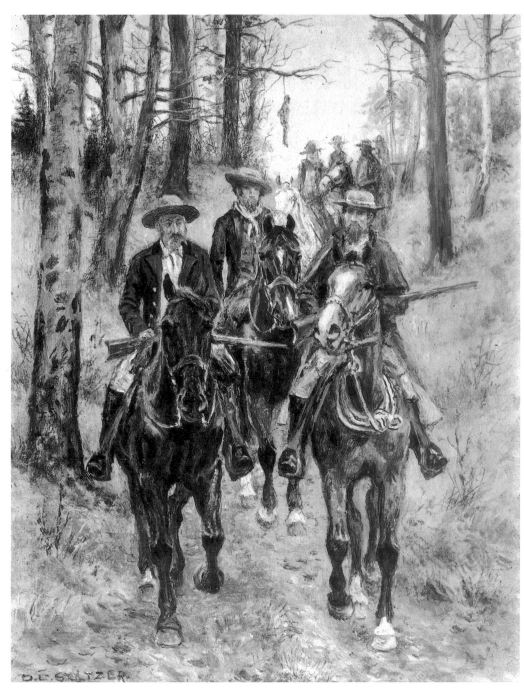

Olaf Carl Seltzer (1877–1957)
Vigilante Ways, n.d.
Oil on board,
6 × 4 ½ in.
Gilcrease Museum, Tulsa, Oklahoma

Commissioned to paint a series of miniatures depicting Montana history, Seltzer could hardly have left out vigilantism—for which the state was justly infamous.

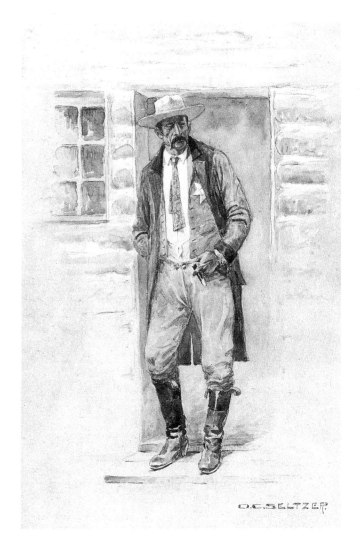

Olaf Carl Seltzer (1877–1957)
Sheriff, 1928
Watercolor, 12 × 7 in.
Gilcrease Museum, Tulsa, Oklahoma

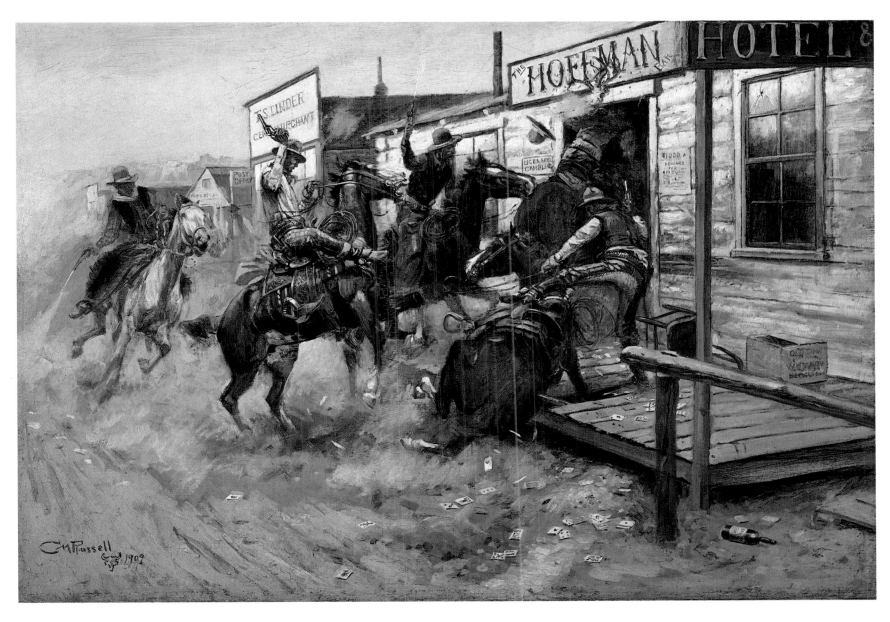

Charles M. Russell (1864–1926)
In Without Knocking, 1909
Oil on canvas, 20 ⅛ × 29 ⅞ in.
Amon Carter Museum, Fort Worth,
Texas

In this, one of his most popular
paintings, Russell captures the
boisterous, unfettered, and
irresponsible side of cowboy life that
has always appealed to suburban
folk with tedious jobs in the city.

lived, as the sheriff of Johnson County rounded up a posse of some two hundred outraged citizens who hunted down the Regulators and surrounded them at a ranch thirteen miles south of the county seat. Acting Governor Amos Barber called on two U.S. senators to help him obtain the intervention of federal troops, who arrived in time to prevent casualties beyond the deaths of two Regulators.

Over the vehement protests of Johnson County authorities, who demanded that the vigilante invaders stand trial at the county seat, the cavalry escorted the men to Cheyenne. Extraordinary legal maneuvering resulted in dismissal of all charges. However, back in Johnson County, small ranchers and other citizens were looting property belonging to the Regulators. It took twelve troops of cavalry and a federal marshal with a posse to restore order.

SIXGUNS AND CITIZENS

We shall see that it was a combination of homesteaders, homesteading legislation, barbed wire, and ecological catastrophe that brought to a close the days of the long

cattle drive over the open range. But before those days vanished forever, the end of the trail, as far as the individual cowboy was concerned, was a dusty, devilish place called a cattle town.

The towns—most of them were in Kansas—served as points of transfer from the trail to the rails. Beef brokers concluded major purchases on the basis of a handshake, and the cattle were off to the great cities of the East. For the cowboy, a cattle town was a place to get a bath, a shave, a woman (three hundred prostitutes in the small town of Wichita), and a drink (in many towns, saloons outnumbered other buildings two to one). It was also easy for a cowboy to gamble away his entire wages in a night and have nothing to show for three or four months on the trail except his saddle sores.

Like the mining towns of the late 1840s and 1850s, cattle towns sprung up fast, bred more than their share of rowdiness and lawlessness, and, in some cases, went bust almost as fast as they had come into being. But there were also important differences between the two kinds of town. Whereas the mining settlement generally grew from a camp that was established wherever a collection of mining claims happened to be, the typical

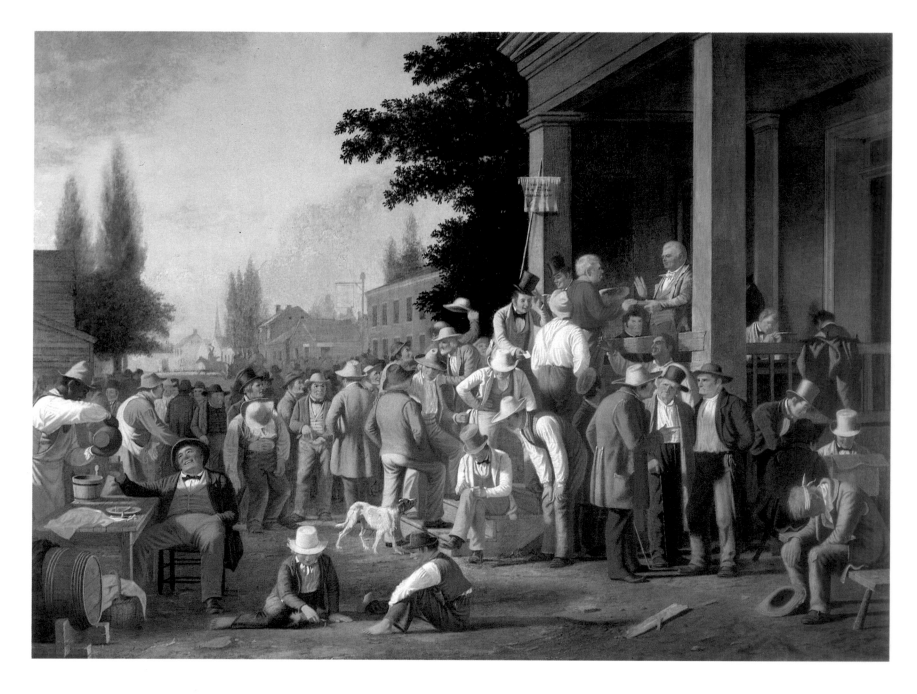

George Caleb Bingham (1811–1879)
The Country Election, 1851–52
Oil on canvas, 35 ⁷/₁₆ × 48 ¾ in.
The Saint Louis Art Museum;
Museum Purchase

Cattle towns were just an extreme form of the West's easy-going brand of democracy. In this Missouri hamlet, the wheels of government are lubricated with a popular western beverage.

cattle town was founded with considerably more deliberation, usually by a land speculator or other entrepreneur, either adjacent to the railroad or near enough to a line that the railroad company could be induced to extend its tracks to the town. While the population of a mining town often consisted exclusively of miners and the merchants who supplied their needs, cattle towns had a seasonal population of rowdy cowboys (with the attendant complement of gamblers, outlaws, and "soiled doves") and a year-round population of more stable citizens who served the farming economy that generally grew up around the towns. In cattle towns where this stable element managed to take a solid hold, citizens began to demand a degree of law and order as well as civilized amenities not found in the mining towns. Thus established, many of the cattle towns survived the end of the trail drive era in the late 1880s and continued to prosper. Often, the local farmers, through measures legal as well as extralegal, hastened the transition from a cattle-

based economy to one based on agriculture.

Abilene, Kansas, the first of the cattle towns, was the prototype of all those that followed. It began as an idea in the mind of Joseph Geiting McCoy, son of a wealthy Springfield, Illinois, beef dealer. Two of McCoy's friends returned from Civil War service in the Southwest, full of stories about the millions of Longhorns grazing freely over the Texas plains. There was money to be made in that much beef, McCoy realized, but that depended on the animals reaching a market beyond Texas. It came to him that the "southern drover and northern buyer" needed a place where they "could meet upon an equal footing, and both be undisturbed by mobs or swindling thieves." McCoy took a train bound for Salina, Kansas, in 1867 the western end of the Union Pacific. His intention was to convince the Salinans to support his scheme. On the way west, his train was forced to stop for an hour so that workmen could repair a bridge. McCoy got off the train to stretch his legs and found himself in

Abilene, "a small, dead place,' he later wrote, "consisting of about one dozen log huts."

McCoy reboarded the train and reached Salina, only to find the population quite uninterested in what he had to offer. On the way back east, he tried Junction City—but land there was too dear. That left Abilene. On the plus side was its location on the Union Pacific Eastern Division (later called the Kansas Pacific) and the fact that Kansas farmers had not yet moved that far west. Negatives were many, however: the town lacked a railroad station, cattle pens, and loading ramps; it lacked population; it lacked amenities; and it was within the Kansas quarantine zone meant to bar Texas fever–infected cattle.

In the best western tradition, McCoy took these drawbacks merely as so many obstacles to be overcome. He obtained the assurance of the governor of Kansas that the quarantine would not be enforced. He obtained from the Union Pacific a commitment to build the necessary switches and sidings and to carry cattle at five dollars a carload. (These rates, a bargain indeed, were nevertheless very much in the railroad's best interest. The problem with western service—from the railroads' point of view—was that a great deal of freight went west, but little returned, which meant that cars often rolled east empty. Transportation of livestock would go far to reduce the imbalance of trade.) McCoy also purchased 250 acres of town land and collected additional backers from among his brothers and friends, including T. C. Henry and W. W. Sugg. The latter rode some two hundred

miles into Indian Territory, promoting Abilene among the drovers in transit with their herds.

Within two months, McCoy was constructing stock pens, a scale capable of weighing a score of cattle at a time, a livery stable and other buildings, and an eighty-room hotel to accommodate drovers and beef brokers. Joe McCoy had first laid eyes on Abilene in the spring of 1867; by August, the cattle began to arrive; on September 5, twenty carfuls set off for Chicago; by November, the end of the season, some one thousand cars had pulled out of the new town. Next season, when a Texas fever panic threatened to cut short McCoy's enterprise, the entrepreneur staged a grand buffalo hunt and put together a Wild West show that anticipated Buffalo Bill's by fifteen years. The hoopla successfully stifled thoughts of the fever.

By the early 1870s, the dusty streets of Abilene were lined with false-front buildings that harbored stores, blacksmith's shops, doctor's offices, and banks—the latter showing a marked bias toward the cattlemen, lending money to them at the rate of 3 or 4 percent, while demanding from farmers as much as 36 to 60 percent interest. There were churches and schools. There were emporia that catered to the cowboy's taste for such finery as fancy hats and boots. There were saloons, like the Bull's Head and the Alamo. The Drover's Cottage hotel occupied a prominent corner. And there were the fragrant stockyards

Concentrated a half-mile from downtown Abilene was the "Devil's Addition," haunt of the cattle town's regiment of soiled doves, calico queens, or nymphs du prairie. But prostitution was the most innocuous affront to law and order to be found in Abilene. "Murder, lust, highway robbery and whores run the city day and night," declared one newspaper. Yet, through its first three cattle seasons, Abilene lacked law enforcement officials of any kind. Concerned citizens petitioned for the right to incorporate and to elect city officials, who set about establishing a long list of municipal ordinances, which were published in the local newspaper and posted on billboards along roads leading to town. These signs provided cowboys with ample target practice.

T. C. Henry, Abilene's first administrative executive and provisional mayor, put out the call for a city marshal. Two candidates came out, one after the other, and, one after the other, turned the job down. Then Henry found handsome, handlebar-mustachioed Thomas J.—Bear River Tom—Smith, a former New York City police officer, railroadman, and railroad town marshal. Appointed marshal of Abilene in June 1870, Smith quickly made a name for himself by effectively controlling violent situations without the use of firearms. Indeed, he adamantly refused to carry a weapon within city limits. When a fellow known as Big Hank came into town with a sixgun in his belt in deliberate and flagrant violation of the town's ordinance prohibiting firearms,

Richard Lorenz (1858–1915)
Following a Trail, c. 1900
Oil on canvas, 12 × 14 in.
Arthur J. Phelan, Jr., Collection

German born, Lorenz studied in Weimar before immigrating to Milwaukee in 1886. The following year he headed west, apparently getting work as a Texas Ranger. After a dozen years, he returned to Milwaukee, where he taught art and painted western subjects. His most celebrated pupil was Frank Tenney Johnson.

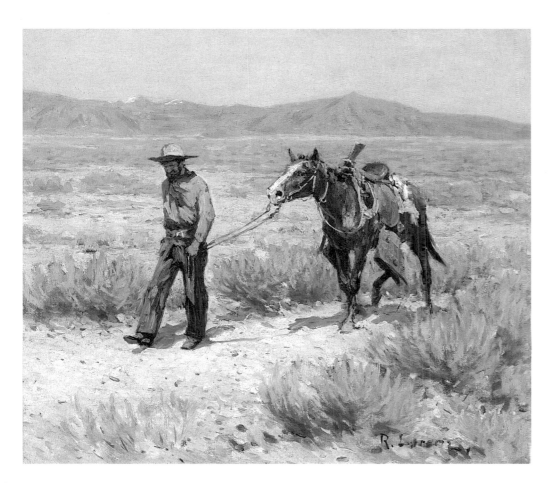

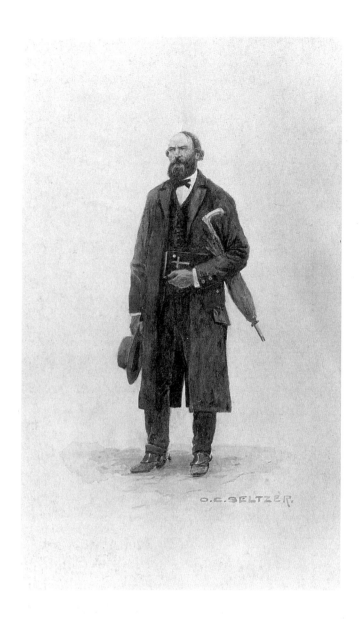

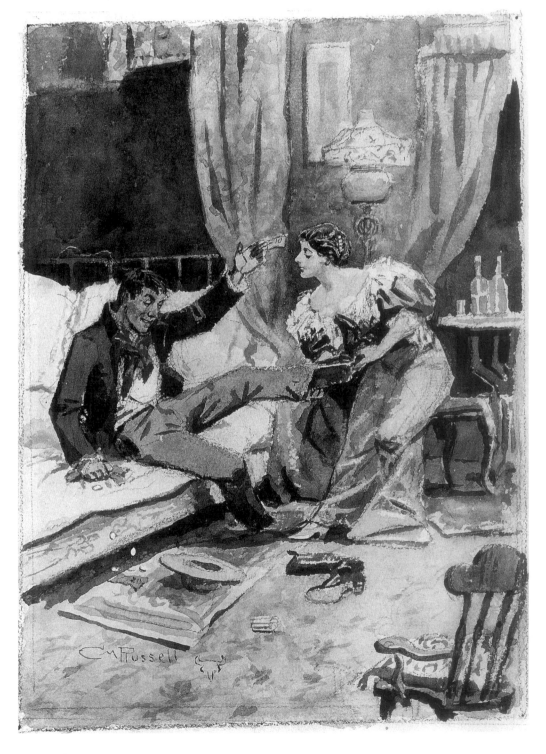

Olaf Carl Seltzer (1877–1957)
Circuit Rider, 1929
Watercolor, 12 × 7 in.
Gilcrease Museum, Tulsa, Oklahoma

The far-flung towns of the West were often unable or unwilling to support a full-time preacher. The spiritual needs of such places were served by itinerant circuit riders, who made the rounds of several towns.

Charles M. Russell (1864–1926)
Just a Little Pleasure, c. 1898
Watercolor, gouache, and graphite on paper, 13 ⅜ × 10 ⅜ in.
Amon Carter Museum, Fort Worth, Texas

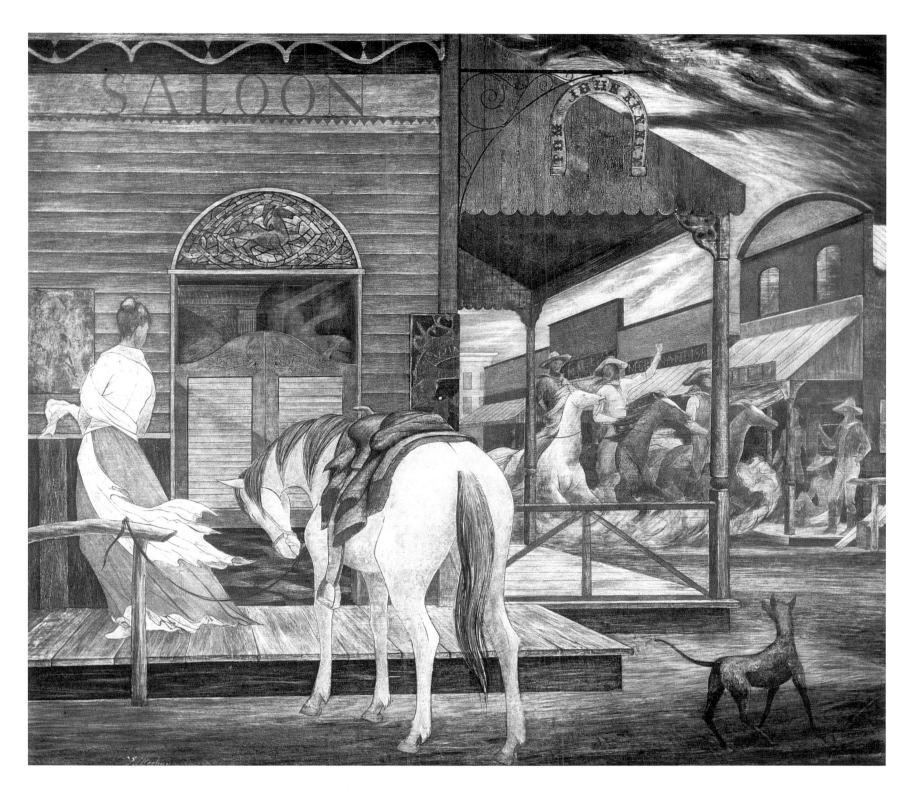

Frank Mechau (1903–1946)
Saturday P.M., 1942
Tempera on board, 30 ¼ × 36 ⅛ in.
Denver Art Museum

Raised in Colorado, Mechau
financed his art education by prize
fighting and working as a railroad
cattle hand. After a year at the
University of Denver (1923–24) and
another at the Art Institute of
Chicago (1924–25), Mechau moved
to New York and then on to Europe,
where he was influenced by the
Cubists. His painting career lasted
only some sixteen years; by the time
of his death, he had produced about
sixty canvases.

Smith demanded the piece. Big Hank refused. Smith
hauled off and hit him across the jaw, took the gun, and
sent him out of town. News of this exploit rapidly made
the round of the cowboy camps outside of town, and one
cowhand, Wyoming Frank, bet his friends that he could
show down the marshal. Frank strode into town on Sunday morning, found Bear River Tom, and spoke a few
choice words to him. The marshal quietly asked for his
gun. Some say that Smith backed Wyoming Frank into a
saloon, floored him with a well-aimed punch, took his
gun, and ordered him out of town. Others hold that
Frank actually drew his weapon, and the marshal, un-
flinching, slugged the cowboy, took the gun, and pistol-
whipped the offender with it.

Unfortunately, Bear River Tom Smith did not hold
his job for long. On October 23, 1870, a homesteader
named Andrew McConnell, who lived a few miles outside of Abilene, returned to his dugout sod house after a
day of deer hunting. He saw his neighbor John Shea
driving some cattle across his land. The two men had
words, and Shea sought to resolve the conflict with his
pistol. He pulled the trigger twice, but the weapon failed
to discharge. As Shea was cocking the hammer for a
third attempt, McConnell, who had been leaning on his
rifle, raised the weapon and fired point-blank into Shea's
heart. McConnell went to fetch a doctor and turned himself in. The testimony of another homesteader, Moses
Miles, secured McConnell's immediate release, but other

neighbors of Shea—who had left a widow and three children—cast doubt on the testimony. A warrant was issued for McConnell's arrest, but the county officer who tried to serve it was driven off the homesteader's property. Bear River Tom volunteered to do the job and, accompanied by a deputy, rode out to McConnell's dugout.

Smith found McConnell and Miles together and began to read the warrant. Without warning, McConnell shot the marshal in the right lung, but Smith, who on this occasion outside the Abilene city limits wore a gun, managed to return fire, slightly wounding his assailant. The two injured men began wrestling. In the meantime, Miles exchanged fire with Smith's deputy, J. H. McDonald, who wounded Miles but then, unaccountably, fled. Miles immediately turned on Smith and beat him to the ground with his gun. Miles and McConnell dragged the unconscious marshal about ten yards from the dugout, where Miles took up an axe and used it to decapitate Bear River Tom. (Both Miles and McConnell were captured within three days, tried, convicted, and given long prison terms.)

Who would be fool enough to replace Bear River Tom Smith as marshal of what the newspapers were calling "the meanest hole in the state"? Joe McCoy turned up a likely candidate, James Butler Hickok, who had earned a memorable nickname after he had backed down a lynch mob during the Civil War. A woman who witnessed that event shouted, "Good for you, Wild Bill!" and the name stuck.

Hickok was born on May 27, 1837, in the sleepy village of Troy Grove, Illinois, the son of a farmer and merchant who was also active in the abolitionist movement, helping fugitive slaves escape through the Underground Railroad. Hickok soon gained a reputation not only as the best shot in northern Illinois, but as a man handy with his fists. A teamster by trade, he brawled with one Charlie Hudson, beating him so badly that the eighteen-year-old Hickok thought he was dead. He fled to St. Louis and then to "Bloody Kansas," at the time in turmoil over the slave issue. True to his father's convictions, Hickok joined the Free-State Militia under General Jim Lane.

In 1858, Hickok was elected constable of Monticello Township, worked also as a farmhand, and then worked his own homestead claim before joining Russell, Majors & Waddell as a wagon master. While leading a train through Raton Pass, along the Santa Fe Trail, Hickok was attacked by a bear, which he managed to kill with his pistols—but not before it had severely mauled him. The firm sent him to Santa Fe and to Kansas City for medical treatment and then gave him a light-duty post at Rock Creek Station in Nebraska.

Rock Creek revealed another side of Hickok. Dave McCanles lived with his family on a ranch across the creek from the Russell, Majors & Waddell station and kept a mistress, Sarah Shull, in a house nearby. Mc-

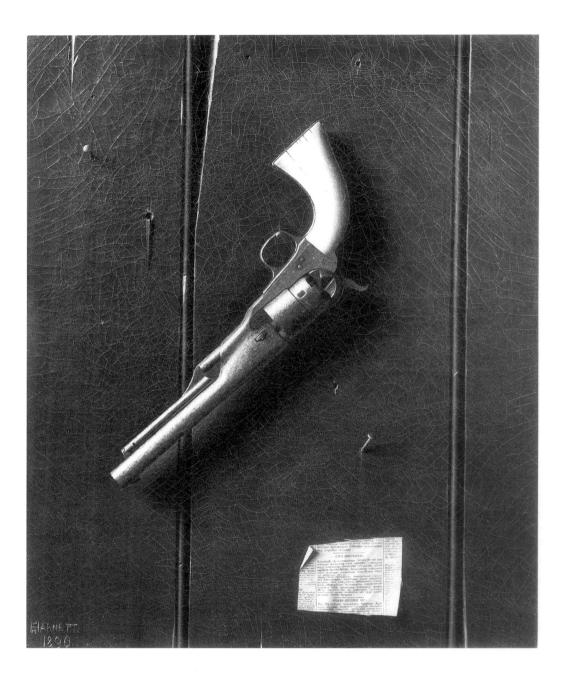

William Michael Harnett (1848–1892)
The Faithful Colt, 1890
Oil on canvas, 22 ½ × 18 ½ in.
Wadsworth Atheneum, Hartford;
Ella Gallup Sumner and Mary Catlin
Sumner Collection

A trompe l'oeil tour de force depicting the ultimate arbiter of western disputes.

Canles had a financial dispute with the freighting company and, even more, had a personal animosity toward Hickok, who had been seeing Sarah. McCanles delighted in egging Hickok on by calling him "Duck Bill"—a reference, perhaps, to his protruding lips—and "hermaphrodite." On July 12, McCanles showed up at the station and was met by stationmaster Horace Wellman's common-law wife. Hickok refused to come outside. McCanles went around to a side door and saw Hickok hiding behind a curtain. "Come out and fight fair," McCanles challenged, threatening to come in and drag him out.

"There will be one less son-of-a-bitch when you try that," Hickok returned.

McCanles stepped inside, and Hickok shot him dead.

Hearing the shot, McCanles's twelve-year-old son, Monroe; McCanles's cousin, James Woods; and James Gordon, one of McCanles's ranch hands, came running toward the station. Monroe found his father and cradled his lifeless body in his arms as Woods approached the kitchen door. Hickok shot him twice, then spun around on Gordon, who was coming through the front door. Wounded, both Woods and Gordon fled, but station-master Wellman and the station's stable hand, Doc Brink, gave chase. Wellman, brandishing a hoe, caught up with Woods and hacked him to death. Brink polished off Gordon with a shotgun blast.

After seeing some Civil War service, probably at the Battle of Pea Ridge, Wild Bill moved on to Springfield, Missouri, where he set up as a professional gambler. In Springfield, he had another gunfight involving rivalry over a woman. While playing cards at the Lyon House on the night of July 21, 1865, Wild Bill had words with a former Union soldier named Dave Tutt over the affections of a certain Susanna Moore. They arranged a showdown for six o'clock the next evening in the town square.

A crowd gathered for the event. Hickok and Tutt faced off, Wild Bill calling out, "Don't come any closer, Dave," as Tutt approached from about seventy-five yards. Tutt drew his revolver and shot, missing his mark

at that range. Hickok coolly steadied his weapon with both hands and squeezed off a clean shot. The round slammed into Dave Tutt's chest, killing him instantly. Hickok duly surrendered himself to the local authorities and was acquitted after a brief trial.

The Springfield duel is about as close as real western gunfighters ever got to the classic showdown depicted in popular fiction, western films, and television. There was no such thing as the fabled "quick draw," in which one man attempted to pull his weapon faster than the other. Indeed, many gunfighters didn't even carry their weapons in a holster, but merely stuffed a revolver in a belt, waistband, or pocket. In truth, even the famed Colt .44 was inaccurate at any distance, and a gunfighter's primary object was not to shoot first, but simply to hit what he was shooting at.

Most western gunfights consisted of an exchange of more or less wild fire without fatality. Fights in which the parties involved really meant business, however, were seldom as "clean" as the Hickok–Tutt duel. The blood feud between Hugh Anderson and the brothers McCluskie, Mike and Arthur, was western mayhem at its worst.

It started in another Kansas cattle town, the short-lived and violent village of Newton, where Mike Mc-Cluskie, a railroad strongman, killed a Texas gambler named William Bailey and left town. Bailey's friend, Hugh Anderson, a sometime cowboy and sometime bartender, swore to avenge the killing. On August 19, 1871, McCluskie returned to Newton and spent the night at the faro table in Perry Tuttle's dance hall. At one in the morning, Hugh Anderson entered the establishment, approached McCluskie, and shouted, "You are a cowardly son-of-a-bitch! I will blow the top of your head off." Anderson fired point-blank and hit his man in the neck.

McCluskie rose as best he could, drew his gun, and pulled the trigger. The hammer clicked on a bad cartridge. Anderson shot McCluskie in the leg; he fell, and his gun discharged on impact. Anderson pumped another slug into the prone man's back.

In the meantime, other cowboys in the dance hall had opened fire. When the shooting stopped, four cowboys, in addition to McCluskie, lay mortally wounded. Two others recovered from gunshot wounds. Anderson had been hit twice in the leg, and, although a warrant was issued for his arrest, friends rushed him out of town.

Anderson returned to Kansas in 1873 and tended bar at Harding's Trading Post in the miserable little settlement of Medicine Lodge. Some time in June, Mike McCluskie's brother, Arthur, rode into Medicine Lodge with a guide named Richards, who entered the trading post and delivered Arthur McCluskie's challenge to a knife or gun fight. Since McCluskie was a large man, Anderson elected to fight with pistols. He closed the bar, announcing that he "had a chore to do."

A crowd gathered to watch as the two men took up

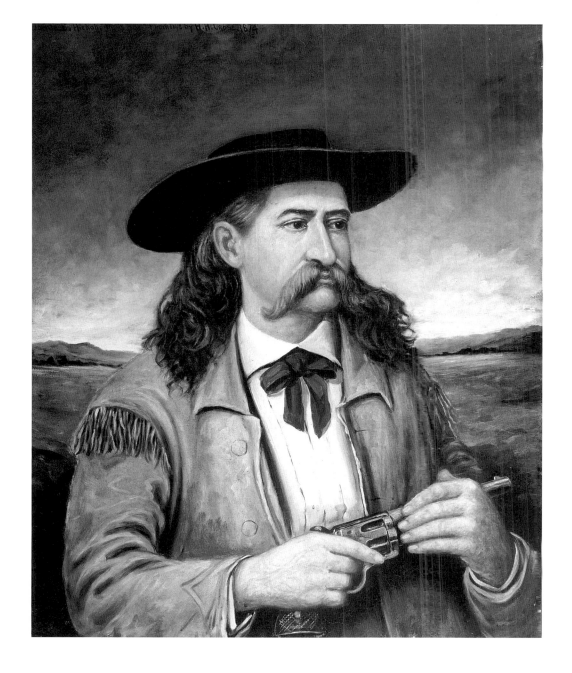

Henry H. Cross (1837–1918)
Wild Bill Hickok, 1874
Oil on canvas, 30 × 25 in.
Gilcrease Museum, Tulsa, Oklahoma

Son of an abolitionist father and capable himself of heroism in that cause, the legendary Hickok was, among many other things, part lawman and part cold-blooded killer. His last vocation was that of a professional gambler. He was shot while playing poker in Deadwood's Saloon No. 10 and died clutching his winning hand.

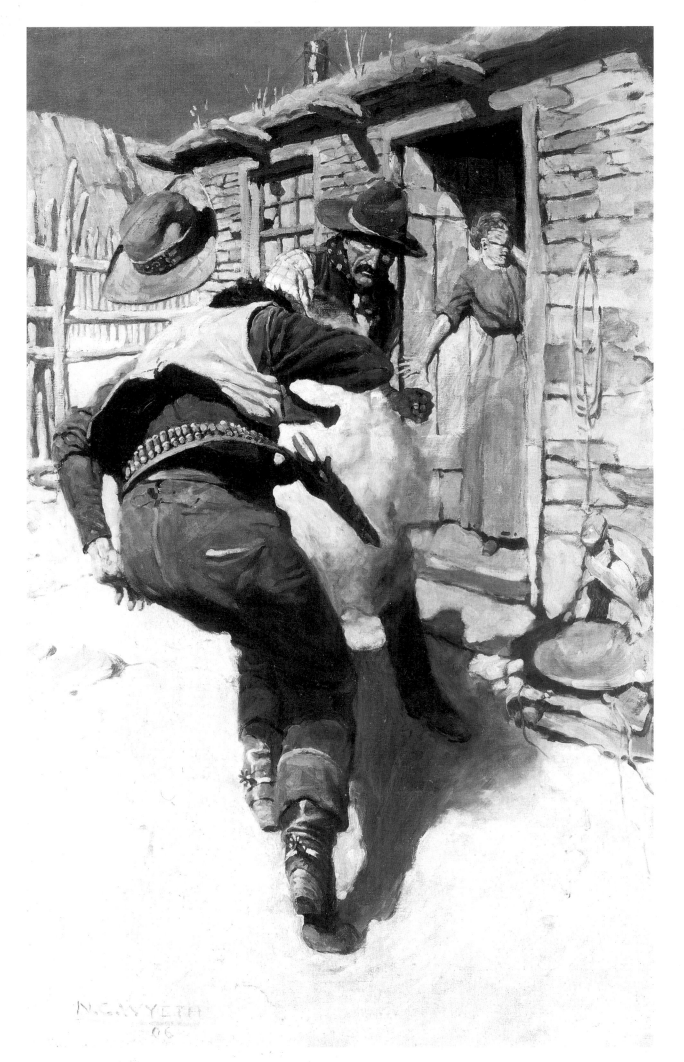

N. C. Wyeth (1882–1945)
*Hahn Pulled His Gun and Shot Him
Through the Middle,* 1906
Oil on canvas, 37 ⅞ × 23 ⅞ in.
Stark Museum of Art, Orange, Texas

An illustration for popular western
fiction, the scene Wyeth depicts here
is nevertheless close to reality. Most
western gunfighting was done at
pointblank range. The vaunted
"showdown" at a hundred paces was
a rarity, and the outcome of such
duels was seldom fatal. The "faithful
Colt," like all early handguns in the
West, was notoriously inaccurate
and unreliable.

N. C. WYETH

—

BORN 1882, NEEDHAM, MASSACHUSETTS

DIED 1945, CHADDS FORD, PENNSYLVANIA

—

Father of the important and very popular realist artist Andrew Wyeth and grandfather of the almost equally well-known Jamie Wyeth, Newell Convers Wyeth made his mark as one of the nation's greatest romantic illustrators in the manner of his teacher, Howard Pyle.

After study at Mechanics Art High School, the Massachusetts Normal Art School, and Eric Pape's Art School—all in Boston—Wyeth became the student of C. W. Reed and then of Pyle, in company with W. H. D. Koerner, Frank Schoonover, and other important illustrators. The best-loved of Wyeth's three thousand plus illustrations are those he executed for Scribner's "Juvenile Classics" series, twenty-five books, most of which con-

tinue to be popular as illustrated by Wyeth.

The artist's western work was done early in his career. Indeed, his first published illustration was a bucking bronco commissioned by *The Saturday Evening Post* in 1903. *Scribner's* sent him on a western illustrating assignment in 1904, and *Outing* commissioned work in 1906.

Later in his career, Wyeth began to turn to fine art, especially tempera and mural work, executing murals for the Missouri State Capitol and the National Episcopal Cathedral in Washington, D.C. His career was cut short by an automobile accident, which killed him as well as a young grandson.

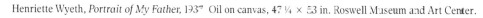

Henriette Wyeth, *Portrait of My Father,* 1937 Oil on canvas, 47 ¼ × 53 in. Roswell Museum and Art Center.

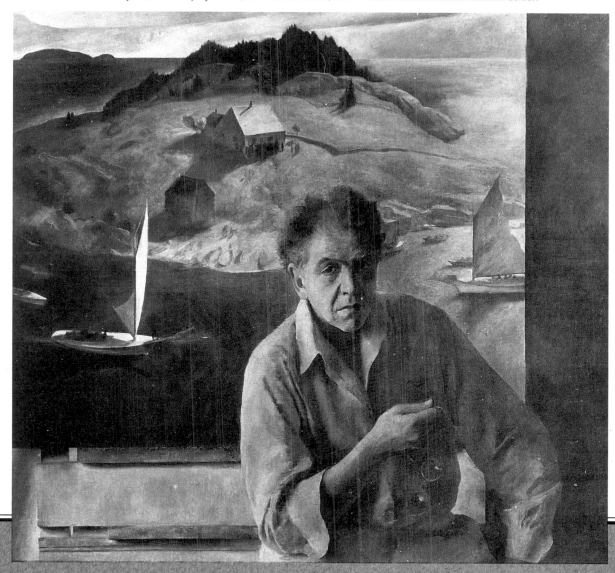

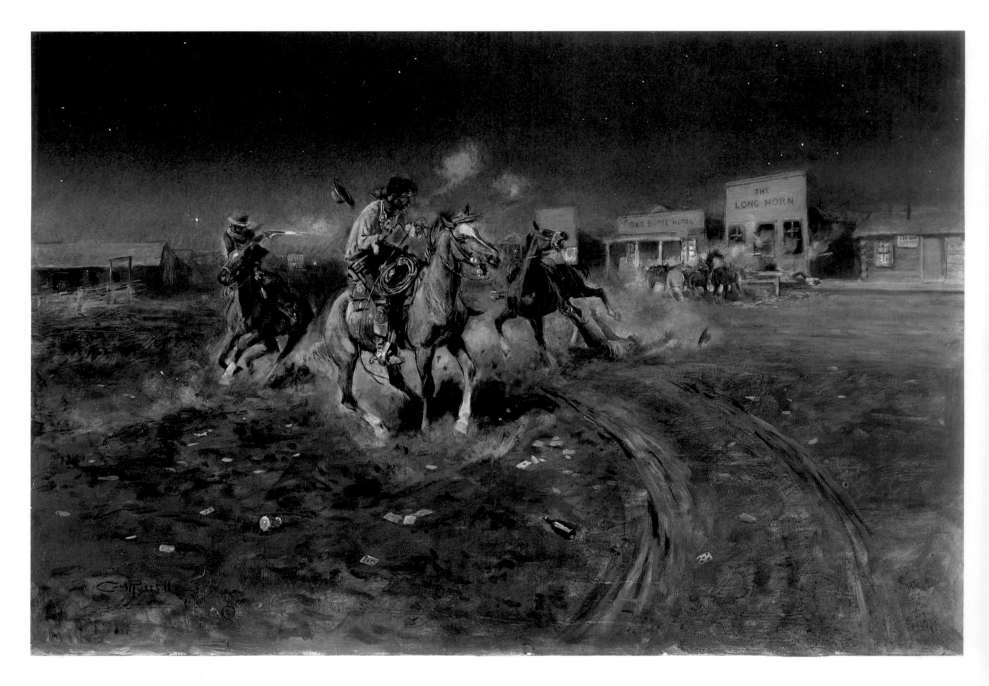

Charles M. Russell (1864–1926)
When Guns Speak, Death Settles Disputes, n.d.
Oil on canvas, 24 ⅛ × 36 ⅛ in.
Gilcrease Museum, Tulsa, Oklahoma

Late night, liquor, cards, cowboys, and firearms: a volatile combination.

positions back to back, twenty paces apart, and, at a signal, spun around firing. The first shots went wild. McCluskie's second shot shattered Anderson's arm, and the man collapsed to his knees in agony, but managed to send a bullet into Arthur McCluskie's mouth. Spitting teeth and blood, McCluskie charged his fallen opponent, who continued to fire, hitting the raging bull of a man in the leg and abdomen.

McCluskie went down. Then he looked up, aimed his weapon, and sent a slug into Anderson's stomach. The bartender rolled onto his back, but he was still alive. McCluskie, knife in hand, crawled over to him. Members of the crowd tried to stop the proceedings at this point, but Anderson's "second," the owner of the trading post, insisted that the fight be continued to the finish. By the time McCluskie reached Anderson, the latter had managed to sit up and draw his own knife. Anderson slashed McCluskie's neck; McCluskie, in return, stabbed Anderson in the side; and both men died.

After his more formal but nevertheless fatal Springfield contest, Wild Bill Hickok moved to Fort Riley, Kansas, where he served as a scout for George Armstrong Custer's Seventh Cavalry, ran unsuccessfully for the office of sheriff of Ellsworth County, Kansas, and then became a deputy U.S. marshal. On one occasion Wild Bill was assisted by Buffalo Bill in transporting prisoners to Topeka. Hickok also saved the day in Colorado, during September of 1868, when he and a group of cattlemen were attacked by Cheyennes. Hickok was chosen to make a dash for help and did so, accomplishing his mission with only a minor leg wound.

In August 1869, Wild Bill succeeded in getting elected to the office of sheriff of Ellis County, Kansas, the seat of which was Hays City, yet another hazardous cattle town made even more raucous by the presence of the Seventh Cavalry nearby. The very month he was elected, Wild Bill gunned down a drunken cavalry trooper for resisting arrest. The next month, Hickok and his deputy, Peter Lanihan, were called to put down a disturbance in a saloon. Hickok ordered Samuel Strawhim to stop busting up the saloon. The man turned on the sheriff, a full-fledged riot commenced, and Hickok calmly put a bullet through Strawhim's head, thereby bringing the trouble to an abrupt halt.

The next summer, Hickok himself became the center of a drunken brawl with Seventh Cavalry troopers in Drum's Saloon. Five soldiers threw the lawman down and began kicking him, whereupon Wild Bill started shooting, wounding two cavalrymen, one fatally. The incident cut short his service to the county, as Bill left town and turned up briefly in Niagara Falls, New York, fronting a Wild West show called "The Daring Buffalo Chase on the Plains." When that venture flopped, Bill returned to Kansas, where McCoy hired him as Abilene's second marshal at $150 per month plus a percentage of fines collected.

His single shoot-out at Abilene began as a response to a breach of decorum. Phil Coe and Ben Thompson, Texas gamblers who opened the Bull's Head Saloon, decorated their establishment with a realistic depiction of that which makes a bull a bull. It is a measure of the

town's growing maturity at this point that a group of irate citizens prevailed upon the city council to order the removal of the offensive symbol. Wild Bill was dispatched to see that the job was done, and, as a result, bad feelings grew up between him and Coe. On October 5, 1871, Coe led about fifty Texans in a wild session through Abilene, forcing several citizens to buy drinks for them—including Marshal Hickok. Wild Bill warned them to behave and alerted his deputy, Mike Williams, to the trouble. Williams, however, received a telegram summoning him to the bedside of his ailing wife in Kansas City. He decided to take the 9:45 P.M. train.

At nine in the evening a shot was heard. Hickok told Williams to stay where he was and went out to investigate. He found Phil Coe surrounded by a knot of rowdies. Coe protested that he was just shooting at a dog, but the hot-headed marshal had had enough. He

Frank Tenney Johnson (1874–1939)
Night at the Trading Post, 1928
Oil on canvas, 36 × 46 in.
Courtesy of The Anschutz Collection

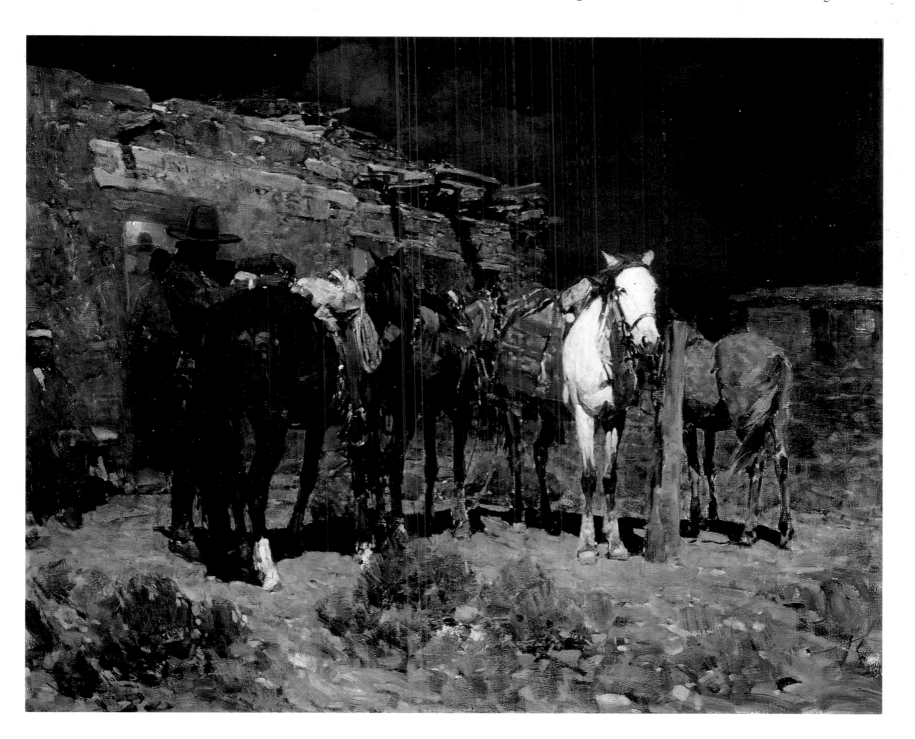

went for his gun, whereupon Coe took a pot shot, hitting Wild Bill's coattails. Hickok leveled his piece and fired at Coe, who was just eight feet away. The slug tore through the man's stomach and went out his back. "I've shot too low," the marshal was heard to say. Coe fell to the ground, discharging his revolver as he did so, sending a bullet harmlessly between the lawman's legs.

It was then that Mike Williams ran through the crowd to assist Wild Bill. Instinctively, the marshal spun around and fired at the approaching figure, striking the deputy twice in the head, killing him instantly. Coe was taken away to die—it took three agonizing days—and some bystanders were treated for minor wounds. Hickok paid for Williams's funeral expenses and hung up his gun for good, although it is impossible to say if he did so out of a sense of guilt: "As to killing," Wild Bill once said, "I never think much about it. I don't believe in ghosts, and I don't keep the lights burning all night to keep them away. That's because I'm not a murderer. It is the other man or me in a fight, and I don't stop to think—is it a sin to do this thing? And after it is over, what's the use of disturbing the mind?"

At any rate, the incident did have a dramatically sobering effect on Abilene, Kansas. Hickok was fired: "He acted only too ready to shoot down, to kill outright," one citizen opined. More important, the "Farmers' Protective Association and Officers and Citizens of Dickinson County" abruptly ended Abilene's days as a cow town, publishing a manifesto in various Kansas and Texas newspapers "respectfully" requesting "all who have contemplated driving Texas Cattle to Abilene . . . to seek some other point of shipment, as the inhabitants of Dickinson will no longer submit to the evils of the trade."

As to the legendary Wild Bill Hickok, he returned to the East to make a living as a performer in Buffalo Bill's Wild West Show. Suffering from gonorrhea, Hickok was gradually losing his eyesight. He seems to have hit a low point in Cheyenne, Wyoming, where he was arrested several times in 1876 for vagrancy. He made a stab at a settled life that year by marrying a circus owner named Agnes Lake but, within two weeks of the wedding, was off to the gold fields near Deadwood, Dakota Territory. He wrote to his bride that he was hard at work prospecting. Actually, he was hard at work in Deadwood Saloon No. 10, gambling. On August 2, Wild Bill was being cleaned out in an afternoon game. At 4:10 P.M. a drifter named Jack McCall drank off a shot of whiskey, drew a superannuated Colt, and walked up behind Hickok. Wild Bill had just been dealt his first winning hand of the afternoon—a queen and two pairs, aces and eights—when McCall discharged a round into the back of his head.

"Take that!" said the drifter.

Wild Bill slumped to the floor, still gripping his cards.

The Saloon No. 10 bartender, a man with the re-markable name of Anson Tipple, leapt over his bar to tackle McCall. The assassin pulled the trigger, but this time the hammer only clicked. (Indeed, the slug that killed Wild Bill was the only nondefective round in the chamber.)

Frank Massie, who had been sitting across from Wild Bill, took in the arm the round that had passed through Hickok's skull. He ran out of the saloon. "Wild Bill shot me!" he screamed, assuming the slug had come from Hickok's gun. As to McCall, he was subsequently hanged.

Dodge City, Kansas, was the longest-lived of the cattle towns, surviving ten tumultuous seasons from the mid 1870s to the mid 1880s and racking up an unparalleled reputation for violence.

DECEMBER 23, 1872: Even before it became a full-fledged cattle town, Dodge City was a rough place. William L. ("Buffalo Bill") Brooks, a long-haired lawman who would end his days at the end of a lynch mob's rope for stealing cattle, quarreled with a Santa Fe Railroad yardmaster, squared off with him, and exchanged shots—three each. Brooks was slightly wounded, but his third shot winged a bystander and went on to kill the railroad man.

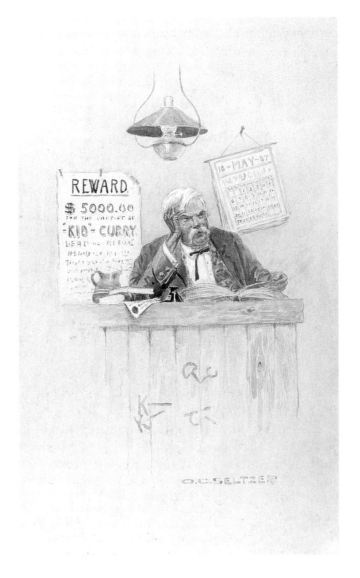

Olaf Carl Seltzer (1877–1957)
Circuit Judge, 1928
Watercolor, 12 × 7 in.
Gilcrease Museum, Tulsa, Oklahoma

Towns of insufficient size to warrant a full-time magistrate were served by circuit judges.

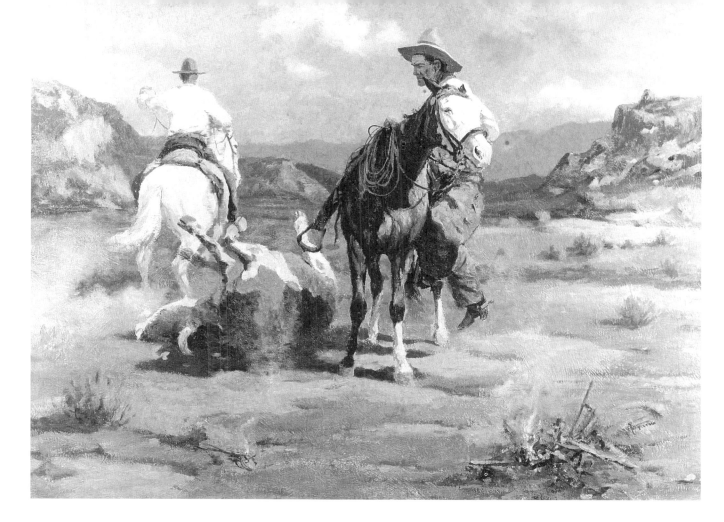

Frank Tenney Johnson (1874–1939)
Branding, c. 1925
Oil on canvas, 36 ⅜ × 46 ³⁄₁₆ in.
The Rockwell Museum, Corning,
New York

The practice of branding, universal
among the great ranchers and
drovers of the West, did not
originate with them, but with the
Spanish conquerors of the New
World, who branded slaves as well
as cattle.

DECEMBER 28, 1872: Uninfluenced by the Christmas
spirit, Buffalo Bill Brooks decided to settle an old score
with a saloonkeeper named Matthew Sullivan. Without
ceremony, he strolled to Sullivan's saloon, stuck his gun
through an open window, shot his man—and walked off
scot free.

MARCH 4, 1873: Brooks picked a fight with a buffalo
hunter, Kirk Jordan. That was a mistake. The man leveled his buffalo gun and fired as Brooks jumped behind
two water barrels. The slug blew through both barrels,
but was stopped by the second barrel's iron hoop. Buffalo Bill offered his apologies and lived without further
gunplay until July 28, 1874, when he was lynched near
Caldwell, Kansas.

SEPTEMBER 25, 1877: A. C. Jackson, a cowboy, rode
into town firing his revolver in the air. He was confronted by the sheriff and deputy marshal, the brothers
Masterson, Bat and Ed. Bat ordered Jackson to halt. "I
am going to skip out for camp," announced the cowboy
firing twice more. The brothers fired on the cowboy, hitting his horse, which conveyed Jackson safely out of
town before it collapsed and died.

NOVEMBER 5, 1877: Deputy Marshal Ed Masterson
was called to break up a fight between Texas Dick Moore
and Bob Shaw at the Lone Star Dance Hall. Masterson
ordered Shaw to surrender his weapon. In lieu of compliance, Shaw took a shot at Moore, whereupon Masterson
hit Shaw over the head with the butt of his gun. Shaw
spun around and opened fire on Masterson, who took a
bullet in the right breast; it passed through and out
under the right shoulder blade, temporarily paralyzing
the deputy marshal's right arm, so that he dropped his
revolver. Masterson bent down, picked up the weapon

with his left hand, and shot Shaw in the left arm and left
leg. A shot from either Shaw or Masterson hit Moore in
the groin. Everyone ultimately recovered—and, after all,
the deputy marshal *had* succeeded in breaking up the
fight.

APRIL 9, 1878: Half a dozen drunk cowboys were acting up at the Lady Gay. With Deputy Nat Haywood, Ed
Masterson—now full marshal—walked over to the saloon to quiet the rowdies down. He ordered one of the
revelers, Jack Wagner, to surrender his pistol, as firearms were illegal in Dodge City. The marshal disarmed
the cowboy without incident and gave the gun to A. M.
Walker, Wagner's boss. Unfortunately, Walker was just
as drunk as Wagner and returned the pistol to the cowboy. The pair then decided to go after Masterson and
Haywood. Masterson tangled with Wagner, trying to
wrest the weapon from him. When Haywood came forward to assist, Walker and another cowhand forced him
back at gunpoint. Walker poked his gun in Haywood's
face, pulled the trigger, and the piece failed to discharge.
In the meantime, whether accidentally or deliberately,
Wagner's gun went off, sending a slug through Masterson's gut and out his back. The powder flash set the marshal's clothes aflame. Nevertheless, he drew his gun and
squeezed off four shots. One bullet hit Wagner in the
stomach; three hit Walker. The faces of two gawking citizens were grazed by flying lead.

Wagner retreated into Peacock's saloon, collapsed,
was carried away, and died the next day. Walker, his
lung perforated, his right arm shattered, ran through
Peacock's and out the back door, where he collapsed
(eventually, he recovered). Masterson, whose clothing
was still on fire, walked two hundred yards and into an-

other saloon, where he announced to George Hinkle, "George, I'm shot." He collapsed and was carried to his brother Bat's room, where he died within a half hour.

JULY 26, 1878: Wyatt Earp, deputy marshal of Dodge, and another Masterson brother, Jim, a deputy sheriff, rushed to break up a group of three or four cowboys who were firing their guns into the air about three in the morning. The cowboys and the lawmen traded fire, and then the cowboys rode off. One, George Hoy, a convicted cattle rustler, was hit in the arm and fell off his horse. He died of infection four weeks later.

APRIL 5, 1879: "Cockeyed Frank" Loving had words with Levi Richardson over a woman. Later, the two men confronted one another across a gambling table in the Long Branch Saloon.

"You damn son-of-a-bitch," said Loving, "if you have anything to say about me why don't you come and say it like a gentleman."

"You wouldn't fight."

"You try me and see!"

Richardson drew his gun; Loving went for his. Richardson shot and missed, but when Loving tried to return fire, the hammer clicked without effect. Loving dashed behind a pot-bellied stove. Richardson fired twice more. The saloon crowd dived for cover. Loving pumped several shots into Richardson, who continued to fire as he fell back against a table. Richardson was hit in the chest, side, and right arm; Loving was slightly scratched.

APRIL 16, 1881: Jim Masterson, co-owner, with A. J. Peacock, of the Lady Gay Dance Hall and Saloon, was quarreling with his partner over the tenure of Al Updegraff, a bartender Peacock had hired and Jim wanted to fire. At one point, the three men exchanged shots. Jim telegraphed his brother Bat, who had left Dodge City in 1879 and was living in Tombstone, Arizona, to return to Dodge City to help resolve the situation. At 11:50 A.M., Bat Masterson stepped off the train and immediately saw Peacock and Updegraff walking together. Bat ran through the crowded street, stopped about twenty feet from the pair, and called out: "I have come over a thousand miles to settle this. I know you are heeled—now fight!"

The three began shooting and were joined by two men from a saloon (perhaps Jim Masterson and Charlie Ronan). In the intense fusillade, one bystander was struck in the back and Updegraff was hit in the right lung. While all five men paused to reload, Sheriff Fred Singer and Mayor A. B. Webster appeared on the scene, brandishing shotguns. Updegraff recovered. Bat paid a modest fine and took the next train out of town.

APRIL 30, 1883: A reform administration was elected to office and sought to clean up Dodge City. Luke Short, variously a farmer, cowboy, whiskey peddler, army scout, dispatch rider, gambler, and co-owner of the Long Branch Saloon, fired his gun at Special Policeman and City Clerk L. C. Hartman, who had arrested three female

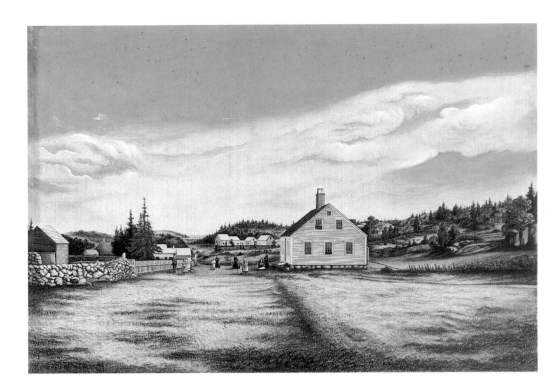

Look closely. The figures in the middle distance are playing croquet—an unlikely enough sport in rough-and-ready California. The architecture of the house suggests that these settlers came from New England.

"singers," employees of the Long Branch. Hartman hit the dirt, and Short, thinking he had killed him, walked away. Hartman fired on him, but Short disappeared into the night. Lawyers for the city filed charges against Short, whose own lawyers brought countercharges against the city. Run out of town, Short soon returned, accompanied by a "peace commission" consisting of Wyatt Earp and Bat Masterson, among others, calculated to intimidate the new city fathers. No violence resulted, but neither did the administration back down, and Short resumed his career as gambler and saloon owner in Fort Worth, Texas.

JULY 18, 1884: "Mysterious Dave" Mather had been a horse thief, a stagecoach robber, a train robber, a gambler, deputy marshal of Dodge City, and deputy sheriff of Ford County until he was defeated in his bid for Dodge City constable in February 1884. Tom Nixon, a former buffalo hunter, replaced Dave as deputy marshal, and on July 18, at nine in the evening, an old feud between the two men erupted into a gunfight. The two argued outside the Dodge City Opera House. Mysterious Dave stood at the top of the Opera House steps; Nixon was on the ground. Nixon suddenly pulled his gun and fired at Mather. Sheriff Pat Sughrue disarmed Nixon, who posted eight hundred dollars bail and walked free until . . .

JULY 21, 1884: Nixon was standing on the corner, by the Opera House. At 10:00 P.M. Mather approached the building, drew his Colt .45, and in the darkness whispered, "Tom. Oh, Tom." Nixon turned, and Mysterious Dave Mather fired. "Oh," groaned Tom Nixon, "I'm killed" and collapsed in the dirt. Dave continued to fire into the lifeless body, one of his rounds passing through its target and critically wounding a cowboy onlooker. Mather surrendered himself to Sheriff Sughrue, stood trial, and was acquitted of murder. He farmed for a short time, became involved in another fatal gunfight, in Ashland, Kansas, in 1885, was arrested, posted bail, jumped bail, and became city marshal of New Kiowa, Kansas. In 1887 he took a hotel job in Long Pine, Nebraska, and a year later disappeared forever. It is rumored that he was a descendant of Cotton Mather, the great Puritan exponent of the doctrine of Original Sin.

Of course, crime and violence were not the exclusive province of the classic Kansas cattle towns, and no discussion of western outlawry, no matter how cursory, could ignore the fabled Shoot-out at the O.K. Corral or the equally legendary career of the James brothers, Frank and Jesse.

Wyatt Berry Stapp Earp, born on March 19, 1848, in Monmouth, Illinois, was a farmer, railroad section hand, buffalo hunter, horse thief, bunco artist, prospector, saloonkeeper, gambler—and law officer. In 1875 he was a policeman in Wichita, in which capacity he nearly shot himself while making an arrest, often "forgot" to turn over fines he had collected from the town's complement of soiled doves, and was himself arrested for fighting. Fired from the force, he became a policeman in Dodge City, later moving up to deputy marshal, serving also as a church deacon, and getting soundly beaten in a fist fight with a cowboy named Red Sweeney in a dispute over a dance hall girl.

In September 1879, he left Dodge for Las Vegas, New Mexico, stopping in Mobeetie, Texas, where he briefly engaged in a bunco scheme with Mysterious Dave Mather. Later in the year, Earp and his brothers Morgan, James, Virgil, and Warren moved to Tombstone, Arizona, where they were joined by the most famous dentist the West has ever known, John Henry "Doc" Holliday, who practiced a great deal more gambling and drinking

Peter Moran (1841–1914)
New Mexico, 1864–81
Oil on canvas, 28 × 36 in.
Courtesy of The Anschutz Collection

A charming reminder that life in a western town was not all gunplay.

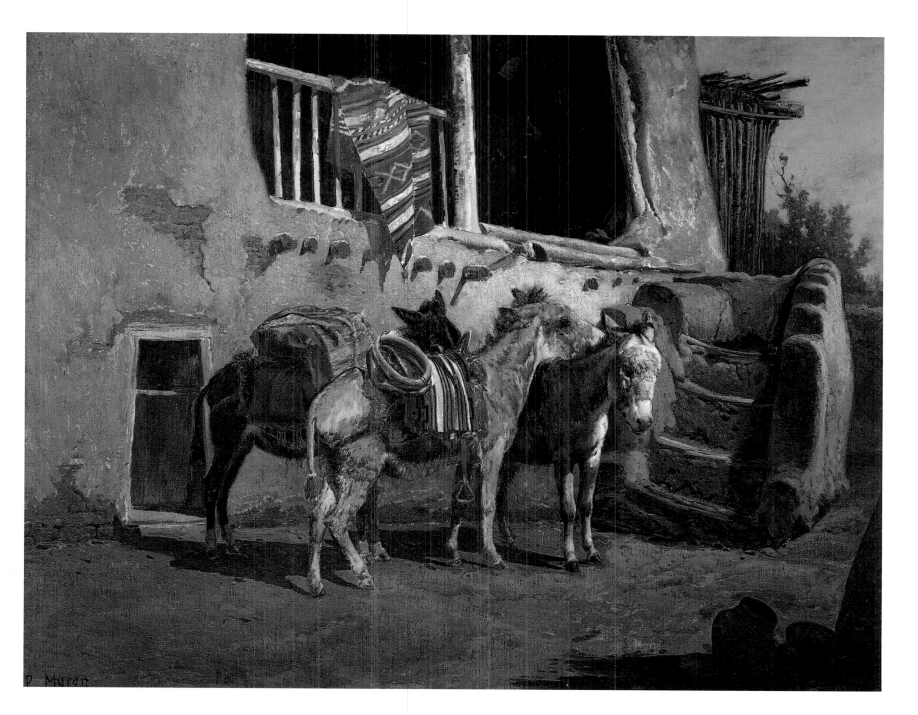

than dentistry, before he succumbed to tuberculosis at age thirty-five.

The Earps attempted to establish themselves as solid citizens of Tombstone, investing in real estate, associating with prominent businessmen, and joining the Republican party. In October 1880, Virgil became the town marshal. Wyatt tried, unsuccessfully, to win election to the office of Cochise County sheriff. James became a bartender.

The brothers' rise to respectability was threatened by a growing feud with N. H. "Old Man" Clanton and his sons, Ike, Phin, and Billy, who lived, for the most part, by cattle rustling. Southern Democrats, they were the frequent targets of editorials in the *Tombstone Epitaph*. In March 1881, the Kinnear and Company stage was attacked, and two men were killed. Wyatt saw his chance to gain the sheriff's post that had so far eluded him. He would arrest the robbers. After weeks of fruitless searching, however, Wyatt approached Ike Clanton, who, Earp

knew, was well acquainted with the robbers. Earp promised Clanton the reward money for the capture of the robbers if he would reveal the whereabouts of their hideout; all Earp wanted was the credit. Ike was only too happy to sell out his friends, but the deal disintegrated when the gang was shot and killed by others. Now the abortive deal between Earp and Clanton became a threat to both of them, if word of it got out.

Throughout the summer of 1881, charges and countercharges, threats and counterthreats were exchanged between the Clantons and the Earps. The Earps' friend Doc Holliday was arrested in June on suspicion of having been involved in the stagecoach robbery. Charges were dropped, but the reputation of the Earp brothers was tarnished. The Clantons encouraged what may have been well-founded rumors circulating about town that the Earps were involved in rustling and other shady enterprises. Next, a friend of Wyatt publicly accused Ike Clanton of having betrayed his friends, the dead stage-

Edmund F. Ward (1892–1978)
Enter the Law, 1924
Oil on canvas, 21 × 28 in.
Gilcrease Museum, Tulsa, Oklahoma

The loneliest job in the West.

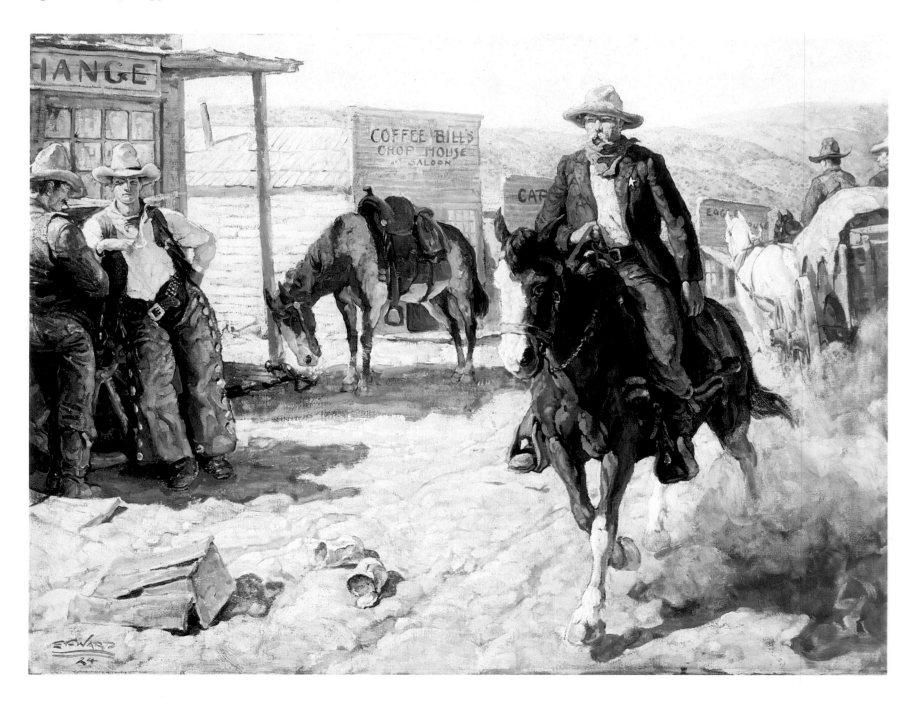

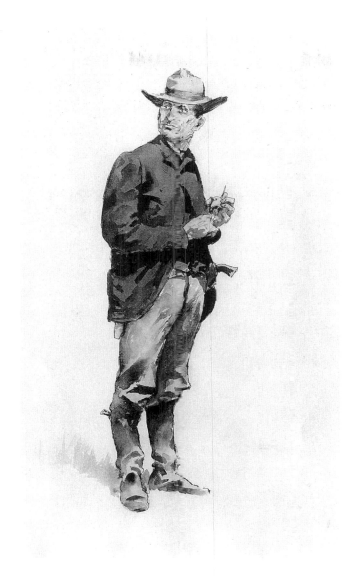

Frederic Remington (1861–1909)
I Settle My Own Scores, 1891
Watercolor, 15 × 8 ½ in.
Arthur J. Phelan, Jr., Collection

This illustration for a *Harper's Weekly* serial, "The Jonah of Lucky Valley" by Howard Seely, depicts "Sheriff Townsend" cleaning the "chamber of his revolver, still gazing at his prostrate foe," the "outlaw Jim White."

coach robbers. Ike, in turn, accused Wyatt of having betrayed their secret transactions, and on the night of October 25, 1881, Ike boasted that the Earps would pay for violating his confidence. The next day, Virgil Earp arrested Ike and hauled him into court, but he was quickly released. Not, however, before Wyatt Earp encountered Ike's friend, a rancher and rustler named Tom McLaury, had words with him, and finally cracked him over the pate with his pistol. Later the same day, Wyatt antagonized Tom's brother, Frank, when he ordered the man to remove his horse from the boardwalk.

"Take your hands off my horse!" Frank growled.

"Keep him off the sidewalk," Earp warned. "It's against the city ordinance."

One hour after this exchange, town marshal Virgil Earp recruited his brothers Wyatt and Morgan as well as Doc Holliday to help him arrest the Clantons and the McLaurys. Sheriff John Behan knew this meant trouble and tried to intervene. He was simply ignored as the Earp brothers and Doc Holliday approached Ike and Billy Clanton, the McLaury brothers, and William Claiborne (a rustler so short they called him Billy the Kid) outside the O.K. Corral.

"You sons of bitches," Wyatt said, "you've been looking for a fight and now you can have it!"

"Throw up your hands!" ordered Marshal Virgil Earp.

Morgan shot Billy Clanton. Wyatt drew his pistol from his right trousers pocket and opened up on Frank McLaury. Ike Clanton, unarmed, ran to Wyatt, grabbed his left arm, and begged him to stop shooting.

"The fighting has now commenced. Go to fighting or get away," Wyatt said.

Ike and Claiborne ducked into a nearby photo studio, and the gunplay continued. When it was all over, Billy Clanton and both McLaurys lay dead or dying. Virgil, Morgan, and Doc Holliday were all wounded. Wyatt was just fine.

The Earps and Holliday were exonerated at a hearing, which determined that they had been acting in their capacity as "peace officers." The citizens of Tombstone, however, were not so forgiving. Virgil Earp lost his job as marshal, and Wyatt's aspirations to the office of sheriff were finally and forever dashed. In the wake of the shoot-out at the O.K. Corral came a series of vengeance shootings. On December 28, 1881, at 11:30 P.M., Virgil Earp was ambushed as he left the Oriental Saloon. Buckshot badly injured Virgil's arm, and, because the doctor was forced to remove some four inches of bone, he never regained full use of it. On March 18, 1882, Morgan Earp was playing billiards at Hatch's Billiard Parlor. At 10:50 P.M., as Morgan was chalking up, several men crept to the rear door of the building and fired two shots. One of the slugs ripped through the right side of Morgan's stomach, shattered his spine, and exited, slightly wounding a bystander. Morgan was carried to an adjacent room and laid out on a sofa, surrounded by his brothers Wyatt, Virgil, James, and Warren. When an attempt was made to stand the injured man on his feet, he gasped out, "Don't, I can't stand it. This is the last game of pool I'll ever play." Most attributed Morgan's assassination to Clanton sympathizers Frank Stilwell, Pete Spence, a gambler named Freis, Florentino Cruz, and Indian Charley.

Wyatt determined to exact revenge, teaming up with Doc Holliday to kill Frank Stilwell. Wyatt, Holliday, and Warren Earp next killed Florentino Cruz. Wyatt also dispatched Curly Bill Brocius, known to have rustled cattle in company with the McLaury brothers. Wyatt Earp successfully avoided arrest and prosecution for all of this work, dying in Los Angeles from natural causes in 1929, aged eighty-one, a few months after meeting Stuart N. Lake, who began work on his biography. (A tireless self-promoter in his old age, Earp had unsuccessfully tried to get William S. Hart to play him in a movie.)

As should be apparent from the story of the cattle towns, not all cowboys were gunslingers and not all gunslingers were cowboys—though a good many were. The most common vocation for a gunfighter was the lawman's trade, and close behind came that of the cowboy. In different ways, both partake of the spirit of frontier lawlessness most of us, at some level of consciousness, envy—no matter how difficult and even unrewarding a cowboy's life really was or how brutal, bloody, and mean the deeds of the gunman.

This said, it is still difficult to account for the legendary status of two outlaws who were not cowboys—or gamblers, or lawmen gone bad, or anything other than professional thieves and murderers. Yet the "Ballad of Jesse James" sums up the popular view: "Jesse James was a lad who killed many a man," the ballad begins (actually, in nine gunfights he killed at most four men and may have killed as few as one):

He robbed the Glendale train.
He took from the rich and he gave to the poor.
He'd a hand and a heart and a brain.

Frank James was born in 1843 and Jesse in 1847, the sons of a Baptist preacher in Clay County, Missouri. The father went off to the California gold fields, where he died when Jesse was three and Frank seven. The boys' mother, Zerelda, hastily remarried and just as hastily took steps to dissolve the marriage because the new stepfather was mean to Frank and Jesse. In 1855, she married Dr. Reuben Samuels, a quiet, passive, and compliant man.

Growing up in Missouri on the eve of the Civil War, the boys were continually acquainted with violence. When the war finally broke out, Frank James joined the notorious Confederate guerrilla William Quantrill. Jesse joined up later, in 1864, serving under Quantrill's lieutenant, Bloody Bill Anderson, and taking part in the murderous raid on Centralia, when two dozen unarmed Union soldiers were shot down in cold blood. In 1865, while trying to surrender to Union forces, Jesse himself was shot and gravely wounded. He recovered and, with his brother Frank and the Younger boys, Cole (who had also served with Quantrill), James, Bob, and John, embarked in earnest on a life of crime.

The gang's first robbery took place on February 13, 1866—though there is some doubt as to whether this maiden voyage included Frank and Jesse; indeed, Jesse may have been bedridden at the time, still recovering from a lung wound received in the service of Quantrill. For that matter, it is not always possible to identify just who participated in any of the robberies, since the gang members always wore full masks. In any case, a dozen men rode into Liberty, Missouri, two of whom walked into the Clay County Savings Bank, drew revolvers, locked the cashier and his young son in the bank's vault, and stuffed some sixty thousand dollars, currency, into a single wheat sack. The accomplices outside the bank, meanwhile, got spooked and opened up on passersby, killing a college student named George Wymore.

Two years later, a gang of eight, including Frank and Jesse James and Cole and Jim Younger, went back east to rob the Southern Bank of Kentucky in Russellville. The Kentucky cashier was less compliant than the man in Liberty, Missouri, and Jesse had to fire a number

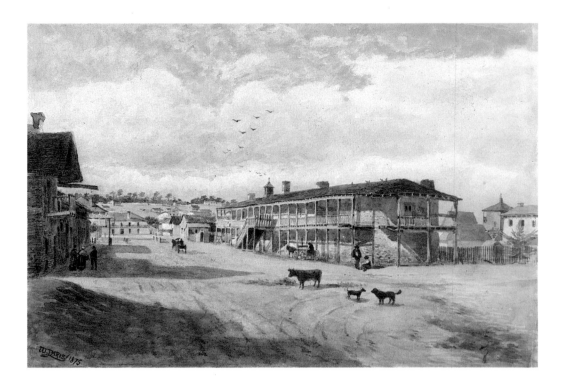

T. Walter Paris (1842–1906)
Town Scene, 1875
Watercolor, 9 ¾ × 13 ⅞ in.
Arthur J. Phelan, Jr., Collection

An architect and painter, Paris traveled to Utah and California during 1875–76. The town pictured here is unidentified, but the present owner of the watercolor speculates that it is in Wyoming, somewhere along the Central Pacific Railroad.

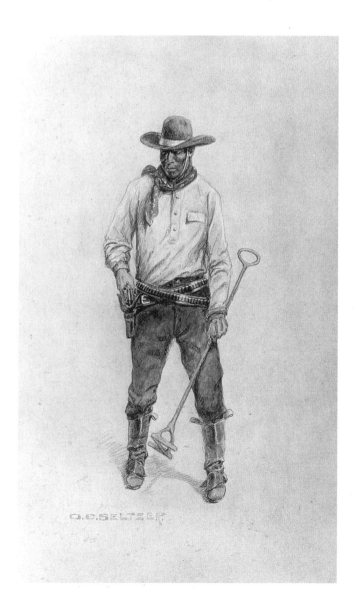

Olaf Carl Seltzer (1877–1957)
Cattle Rustler, 1928
Watercolor, 12 × 7 in.
Gilcrease Museum, Tulsa, Oklahoma

The rustler is shown with the principal tools of his trade, the branding iron and the sixgun.

of "warning" shots his way before Morton Barkley finally handed over the money. The gunfire brought bank president Nimrod Long running from home, where he had been eating lunch. The president shouted, burst through the back door, and tangled with Jesse until the outlaw wrenched his gun hand free and fired two shots, one of which grazed Long's head and sent him crashing to the floor.

Jesse, in a panic, shouted to his cohorts that he had killed the bank president, and the gang, grabbing about twelve thousand dollars, ran for their horses. Long, meanwhile, shook off his muzziness, sounded the alarm, and was fired on by the retreating bandits.

Next year, Jesse and Frank were back in Missouri, where, on December 7, they walked into the town of Gallatin's only bank and asked to speak with the owner, John W. Sheets. The boys, it seems, harbored a grudge against Sheets, who had served the Union in the Civil War. While talking "business" with Sheets, one of the brothers drew a revolver and shot the man twice at point-blank range, killing him instantly. A clerk was also fired upon and hit, but he was able to run into the street and summon aid. Meanwhile, the James boys had managed to collect a sackful of cash, and crashed out the

front door. One of the brothers was unable to steady his horse sufficiently to mount it, so they galloped away on a single pony until they were able to appropriate another from an unwilling farmer.

The boys holed up at their stepfather's Clay County farm, which fell under siege on December 15, surrounded by four men eager for the three-thousand-dollar reward now on the Jameses' heads. Just as Deputy Sheriff John Thomason approached the Samuels farmhouse, Frank and Jesse galloped headlong out of the barn. Shots were fired, and the posse gave chase until Deputy Thomason leaped off his horse, intending to use his mount to steady his aim across the saddle. Before he could squeeze off a shot, the riderless horse bolted, pulled alongside the fleeing brothers, one of whom shot the steed dead.

April 29, 1872, found Frank, Jesse, Cole Younger, and two others at the Deposit Bank in Columbia, Kentucky. Guns were pulled and the cashier confronted. "Bank robbers!" cashier R. A. C. Martin shouted. It was his last utterance on earth; one of the gang shot him dead. Following a brief scuffle with bystanders, the bandits collected a paltry six hundred dollars and ran.

The next reported appearance of at least Jesse

N. C. Wyeth (1882–1945)
The James Brothers in Missouri,
n.d.
Oil on canvas, 25 × 42 in.
Gilcrease Museum, Tulsa, Oklahoma

A great illustration by a great illustrator: the boys never looked so good.

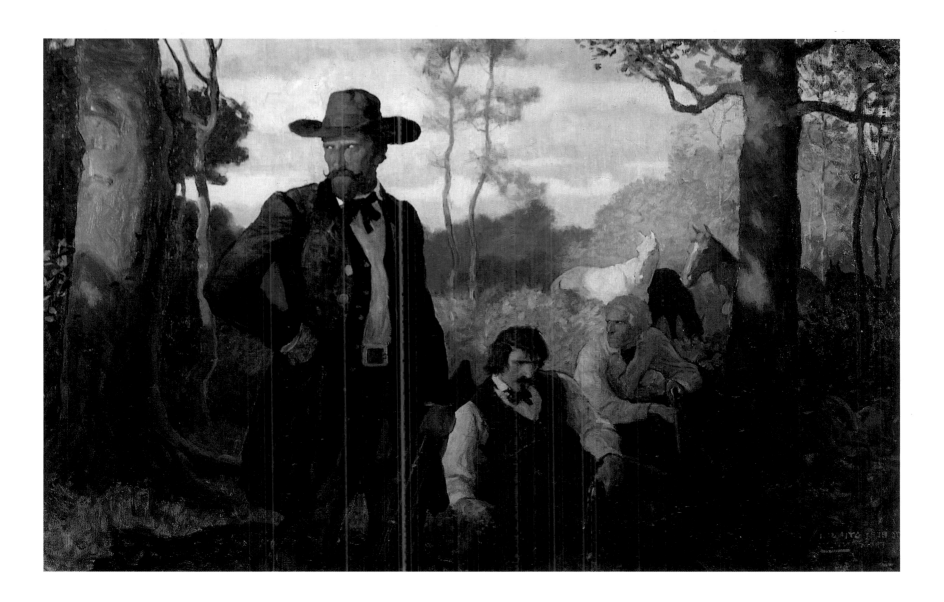

James was on September 26, 1872, when he and two other mounted men robbed Ben Wallace, ticket seller at the Kansas City Fair, of the contents of his tin cash box. Wallace did not allow himself to be relieved of his take easily and grappled with Jesse, who decided to resolve the matter with his revolver. His shot went wild, however, hitting a little girl in the leg. The three galloped off into the woods.

The next year, the James–Younger gang began robbing trains, and the frustrated railroads hired Pinkerton detectives to hunt the boys down. When one of the Pinkerton men, John W. Wicher, turned up dead—shot in the head and heart—near the Samuels farmstead on March 10, 1874, it was generally assumed that the James boys were the murderers. Whoever was guilty, this incident did not, however, interfere with Jesse's personal life as, on April 23, 1874, he married his lifelong sweetheart, Zee Mimms. She would bear him a son and a daughter.

The next year, on the night of January 5, tragedy visited the James boys' family when unidentified persons—strongly rumored to have been Pinkerton detectives—tossed a railroad flare into the Samuels farmhouse, killing the nine-year-old half-brother of Frank and Jesse and blowing away (or necessitating the amputation of) their mother's arm. If this act really was railroad harassment and the work of Pinkerton men, it backfired badly, enflaming public opinion against the heartless railroads and almost moving the Missouri state legislature to grant the James boys and their accomplices amnesty.

But then the James–Younger gang decided to try a job distant from Missouri. Eight members of the gang rode to Northfield, Minnesota, on September 7, 1876, to rob the First National Bank there. Three of the gang

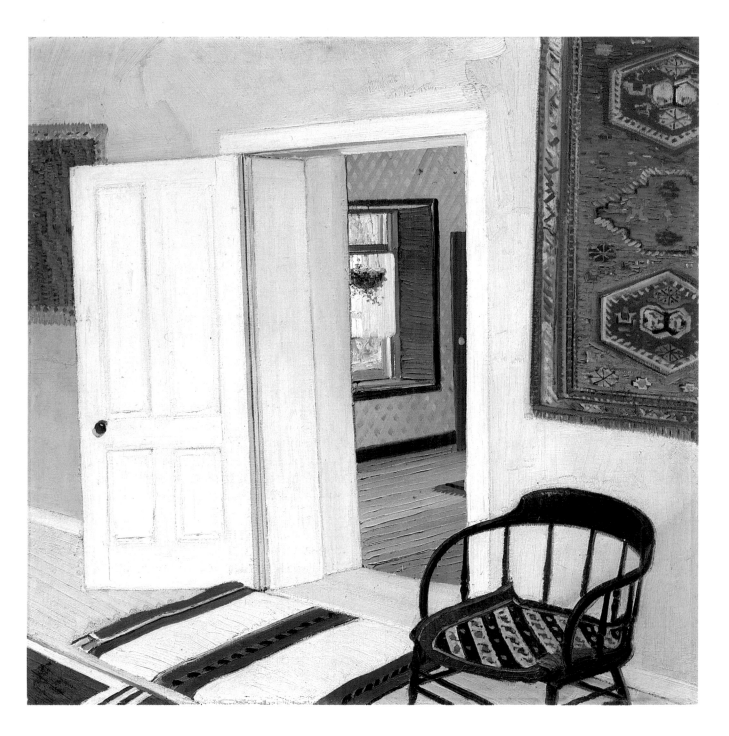

William Victor Higgins (1884–1949)
Adobe Doorway, n.d.
Oil on board, 30 × 30 in.
Stark Museum of Art, Orange, Texas

Amid the gun smoke and blood of many western settlements it is all too easy to overlook places of quiet beauty.

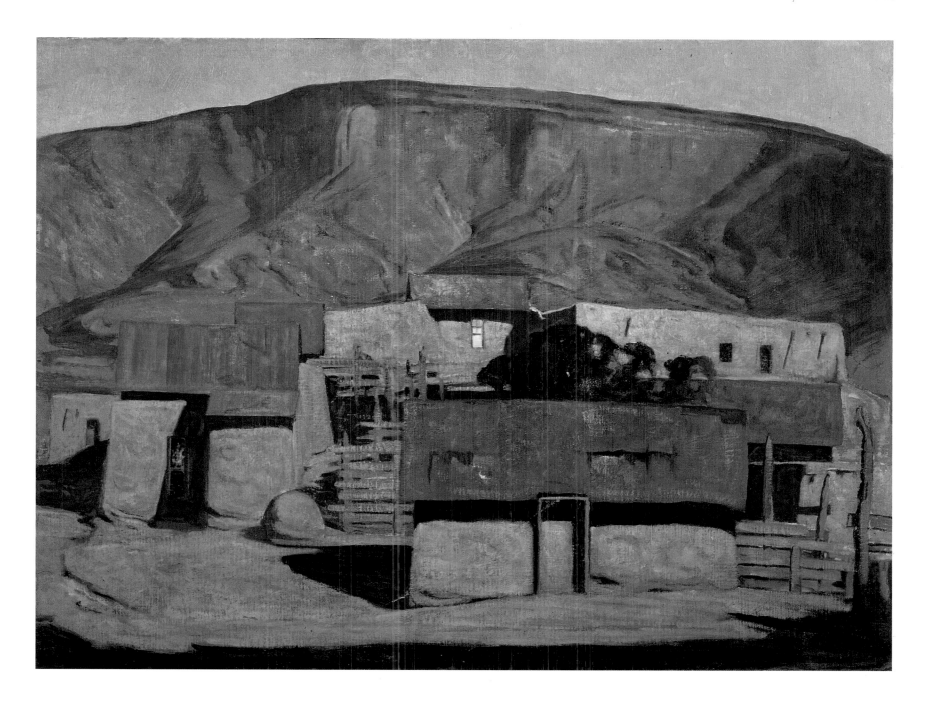

Carl Redin (1892–1944)
Village in Moonlight, n.d.
Oil on canvas, 30 × 38 in.
Courtesy of the Albuquerque Museum, Albuquerque High School Collection

Even today, the West is dotted with the ghostly remains of settlements like this one.

waited on the outskirts of town while five rode in. Two of those stayed outside the bank, minding the horses, while the three others entered, demanding loot. Cashier Joseph L. Heywood refused, whereupon one of the bandits slashed his throat and then, for good measure, shot him. Teller A. E. Bunker ran outside to summon help, but was cut down by a bullet in the shoulder.

The ruckus did alert a number of townsmen, however, who began firing on the outlaws, killing Clell Miller and William Stiles and gravely wounding Bob Younger. The remainder of the gang fought its way out of town, killing a local named Nicholas Gustavson.

Cole Younger later reported that Jesse wanted to abandon or "finish off" the badly injured Bob Younger so that the gang could move faster. When Cole refused to leave his brother, Frank and Jesse set off on their own. Within days, another gang member, Charlie Pitts, was killed by a posse, and Bob, Cole, and Jim Younger were captured.

For the next three years the Jameses lay low in Nashville, Tennessee, living under various aliases. They resurfaced in October 1879, robbing a train at Glendale Station, Missouri. On July 15, 1881, six men posing as passengers, including the James brothers, boarded a Chicago, Rock Island and Pacific train at Winston, Missouri. When conductor William Westfall entered the smoking car to collect fares, Jesse (most likely), dressed in a linen duster, blocked the aisle. He pulled a gun from under his garment and told Westfall to put up his hands. Instead, the conductor abruptly spun about—and was shot in the back. He staggered out the door, and Jesse (again, presumably) pumped another shot into Westfall, sending him over the railing of the rear observation platform. Several of the bandits then opened fire, killing one passenger.

Other gang members forced their way into the locomotive cab and ordered the engineer to stop the train on a siding. The robbers then broke into the express car, pistol-whipped the messenger inside, took his key, and opened the safe, after which the gang disappeared into the night.

While the Jameses made good their escape, the Winston robbery was at last to prove their undoing. As a result of its attendant mayhem, the state of Missouri offered five thousand dollars each for Frank and Jesse James, dead or alive, a reward impossible for some to resist.

Jesse was living in St. Joseph, Missouri, under the name of Thomas Howard. On April 3, 1882, the outlaw was engaged in one of those myriad domestic tasks that might occupy any husband and father of two. He was standing on a chair, straightening a picture. Robert Ford, a new member of the James gang, who had joined up with the intention of killing Jesse and collecting the reward, entered the room and shot him in the back. "The dirty little coward," ended the "Ballad of Jesse James," "That shot Mr. Howard/And laid poor Jesse in his grave."

A few months after the death of his brother, Frank James turned himself in, was tried twice for robbery and twice acquitted. Partly owing to public opinion, which discouraged testimony against him, and partly due to the effectiveness of the gang's masked disguise, the state was unable to assemble a convincing case. The outlaw died quietly in 1915.

SODBUSTERS

On May 27, 1862, Abraham Lincoln signed into law the Homestead Act, authorizing any citizen or immigrant who intended to become a citizen to select any surveyed but unclaimed parcel of public land up to 160 acres, settle it, improve it, and, by living on it five years, gain title to it. Alternatively, after six months' residence, one could "preempt" the land by purchasing it for $1.25 an acre. Or a homesteader could exercise preemption to augment his original 160-acre claim, though few settlers could ante up the $50 for the minimum purchase of 40 acres the government required. It was also possible to add to the original grant by means of a "timber claim." Planting 10 acres of timber-producing trees on the poorly forested prairie would entitle the claimant to an additional 160 acres of land—not that it was easy for trees to take root in the hard-packed prairie sod.

Although the Homestead Act was formulated expressly to avert the greedy speculative abuses to which western land grants had traditionally been subject, the unscrupulous nevertheless found loopholes in the law. To begin with, federal land agents were few and far between, making it virtually impossible to inspect claims and enforce the provisions of the act. The law carefully specified that homesteaders must secure their claim by constructing a house at least twelve by twelve, with windows. Some speculators perfected their multiple claims by building such a house on wheels, so that it could be trundled from claim to claim. Others, noting that the language of the twelve-by-twelve provision failed to specify feet or inches, set dollhouses, twelve inches by twelve inches in plan—complete with miniature windows—on each of their claims. Abuses like these were practiced not only by solitary speculators, but by railroads and mining companies, which claimed and preempted land by means of "dummy entrymen" hired to file as if they were legitimate homesteaders. Although homestead claims would eventually encroach on and close off the open range, even major ranchers managed to acquire vast tracts of homestead land.

Despite its imperfections, the Homestead Act opened the West to millions. The railroads, which had been granted alternating sections of public lands along their rights of way, also had acreage to offer settlers. It was more expensive than the government lands, but it was plentiful and often richer and better watered. The railroads propagandized prairie lands not only throughout the United States, but in Europe as well, advertising the availability of millions of Edenic acres to accommodate millions of immigrants. The government program and the railroad campaigns brought to the West a new kind of settler: not the solitary, self-indulgent trapper, not the prospector with restless dreams of instant wealth, not the bachelor soldier, not the cowboy—knight errant or social outcast—but the farmer and his family. The new settlers brought with them no lust for sudden riches, no aspirations to empire, no hankering after a lawless life. For a family requires responsibility, stability, and liberty within law. A family needs civilization, and the presence of families builds civilization. With the homesteaders—sodbusters, as they were called—the West came of age. Around these people grew no legends or wistful mythologies, for they were too much like you and me. Only stronger.

Typically, the family would send the father or the older sons in advance to stake out a claim and build a house before the mother and other children followed. The prairie was a forbidding place, vast as a sea, flat, lonely, and forlorn, subject to extremes of weather—a hundred degrees of summer heat, forty degrees below zero in winter—periodically plagued by ravenous insects, its soil hard packed and reinforced by a massive tangle of roots, resistant to the plow, mostly unforested, often unwatered—at least on the surface—and scoured by a wind as mournful as it was unrelenting. Yet it was from these very elements that the sodbuster would build his family's life.

First, there was the sod itself. In the absence of timber, the hard, stubborn earth would provide shelter. Usually, the first sod structure a homesteader built was a somewhat elaborated hole in the ground called a dugout. A rectangle was laid out on a rising slope of land or a knoll, and sod was excavated to a depth of about six feet.

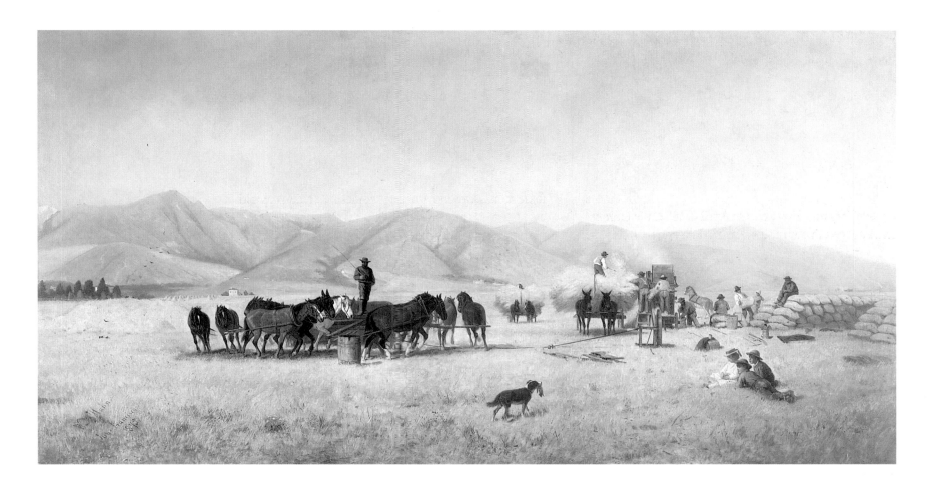

Carl William Hahn (1829–1887)
Harvest Time, 1875
Oil on canvas, 36 × 70 in.
The Fine Arts Museums of San Francisco; Gift of Mrs. Harold R. McKinnon and Mrs. Harry L. Brown

Born in Saxony, Hahn studied in Dresden, Düsseldorf, Paris, and Naples before immigrating to New York some time before 1871. In the early 1870s, after a brief interlude in Boston, Hahn moved to San Francisco and made sketching trips throughout the Napa Valley, Yosemite, and the Sierras. *Harvest Time* is the quintessential image of California's agricultural bounty.

George Caleb Bingham (1811–1879)
The Squatters, 1850
Oil on canvas, 25 × 30 in.
Museum of Fine Arts, Boston; Bequest of Henry L. Shattuck in memory of the late Ralph W. Gray

Bingham, an unsuccessful Whig candidate for the Missouri state legislature, had little affection for squatters, whose political allegiances were almost always Democratic. Nevertheless, here he portrayed them with sensitivity. The wistful look on the young man's face and the hard, resigned expression of the old man suggest the uncertainty of the squatters' perpetually transient status.

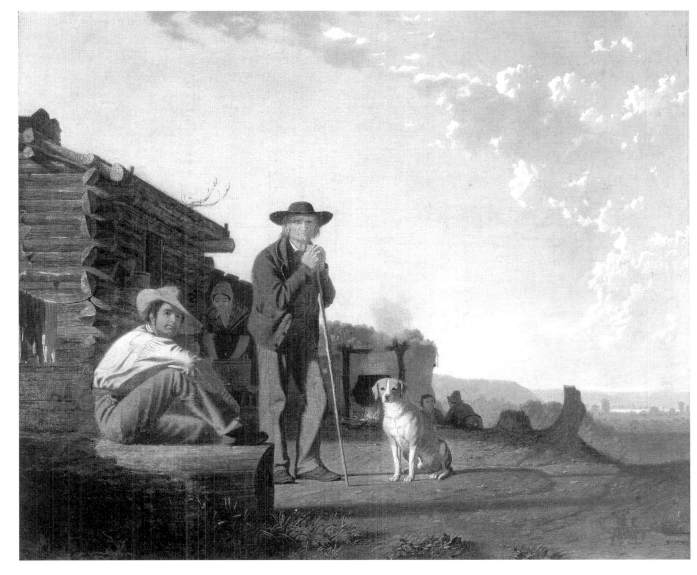

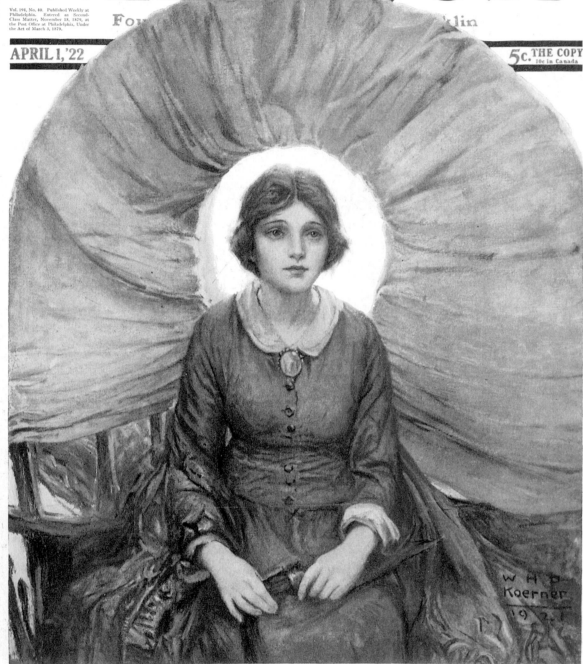

THE SATURDAY EVENING POST

Vol. 194, No. 40. Published Weekly at
Philadelphia. Entered as Second-
Class Matter, November 18, 1879, at
the Post Office at Philadelphia, Under
the Act of March 3, 1879.

Founded A.D. 1728 by Benj. Franklin

APRIL 1, '22

5c. **THE COPY**
10c in Canada

Beginning **THE COVERED WAGON—By Emerson Hough**

W. H. D. Koerner (1878–1938)
The Madonna of the Prairies, 1922
Oil on canvas, 36 × 30 in.
© 1928 Curtis Publishing Co.

A sentimental illustration for a
sentimental story—but it suggests
the maturing West's hunger for the
civilizing stability of families and
family life.

Next, using "bricks" cut from the tough sod, walls were raised to a height of two or three feet. The structure was roofed over with boards, straw—and more sod. The family would live here, raise its first subsistence crops, and then build a more substantial above-ground house, with real windows and doors, but, most likely, still constructed of sod bricks. Special plowshares were developed specifically for cutting strips of sod that could be chopped into the needed bricks, and sod houses—soddies, they were called—became ubiquitous across the prairies. Thick-walled—three feet was not unusual—and well-insulated, the soddies were nevertheless difficult to maintain. Roofs leaked constantly. Dirt and debris fell from the ceiling and walls. Mice, snakes, and insects, including plagues of lice and bedbugs, thrived in the earthen walls and dirt floors. Yet, raised from the land, a

William Tylee Ranney (1813–1857)
Prairie Burial, 1848
Oil on canvas, 14 × 20 in.
Courtesy of the Anschutz Collection

The usual cause of death on the
overland emigrant trek was not
Indian attack, but disease—
especially dysentery and cholera.

Currier & Ives (after Frances Flora
Palmer)
*The Pioneer's Home/On the Western
Frontier*, 1867
Museum of the City of New York

The classic log cabin was suited to
forested areas. On the prairie, where
trees were scarce, pioneers built
their houses of sod—which popular
artists deemed insufficiently
picturesque to portray on canvas,
much less engrave for a mass-
produced lithograph.

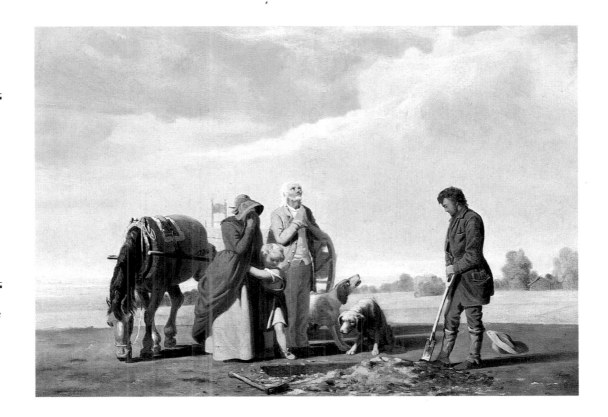

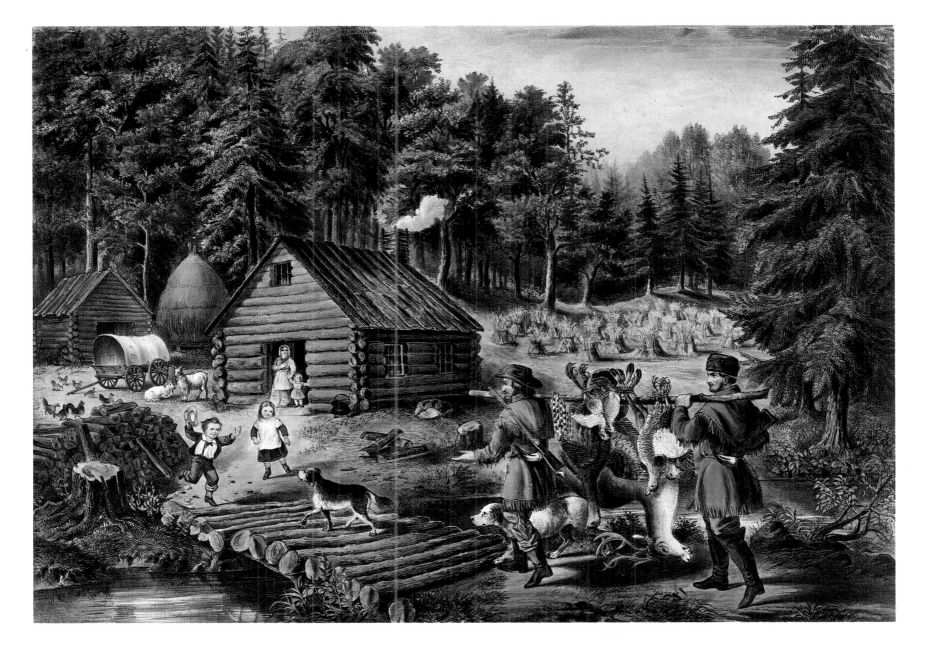

soddy was cheap, sturdy, and essentially fireproof. And for most settlers, it was the first home they had ever owned.

Busting the sod into crop rows was back-breaking work and, until plows of tempered iron or steel were developed in the 1860s, sometimes impossible work. For those many homesteaders whose claims were distant from creeks and streams, there was the added task of digging a well. Since most settlers could not afford to hire a drilling rig, the work had to be done by hand, with pick and spade, sometimes to depths approaching three hundred feet. The dangers of working in such a hole included cave-ins, obviously, but also asphyxiation from such subterranean gases as methane and carbon monoxide. After all the work, of course, there was no guarantee that the well would find water. Once a sodbuster hit bedrock or shale without having tapped into the water table, he had to start all over, sinking a shaft elsewhere.

After water was struck, it needed to be pumped to quench the thirst of livestock and to irrigate fields. The motive power for the pump was provided by the prairie wind. In 1854 a Connecticut tool-shop tinkerer named David Halladay invented a windmill with a vane that allowed it to pivot into the wind and that used centrifugal force to adjust the pitch of the mill blades so that the gusty, frequently violent winds would not tear them apart. A crankshaft transformed the rotary motion of the mill into the up-and-down action needed to operate a pump. Wind power could move hundreds of gallons of water a day.

As to the emotional desolation of prairie life, that may have been the most valuable natural resource of all. If the endless space and driving winds did not make a man insane, they reinforced the solidarity of the family as a bulwark against loneliness, despair, and danger. These conditions of the prairie also served to unite neighbor with distant neighbor, whereas, in the past, western vocations had tended to make "neighbors" at best unwelcome and at worst enemies. A trapper wanted no competition; a prospector wanted his claim all to himself; an open-range cattleman needed space and more space, untrammeled by anyone, least of all "neighbors." But sodbusters treasured companionship and community, and if their claims were in the vicinity of a rough-and-ready cattle town, their influence usually transformed the prairie Gomorrah into a decent village or substantial city.

It is no wonder that the homesteader's world was little compatible with that of the cowboy and cattleman. Farming required settlement; range cattle culture demanded movement. Cattle drives trampled the sodbuster's crops; the sodbuster's barbed wire fences denied the cattleman free pasturage.

The invention of barbed wire transformed the face of the West. Before its advent, homesteaders either avoided open land, farming only in forested areas well

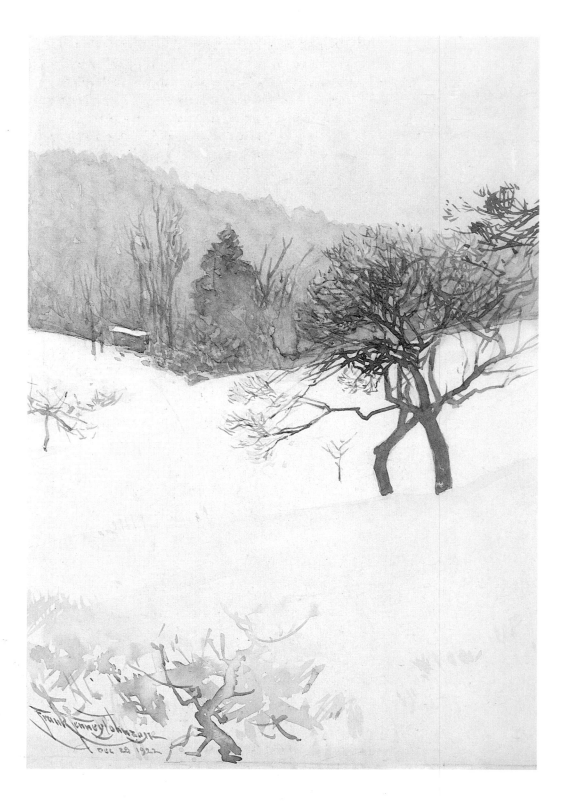

provided with cheap timber for fencing, or tried to create "fences" by planting osage orange hedges, or simply endured the damage periodically wrought by cattle. There were no other choices, since the cost of fencing homestead land in unforested areas more than equaled the cost of purchasing better private land in more humid regions; that is, the cost of fencing threatened to make a mockery of the Homestead Act. "For every dollar invested in livestock," an 1871 government report declared, "another dollar is required for the construction of defenses to resist their attacks on farm production."

In 1873, Joseph Farwell Glidden, a farmer in De Kalb, Illinois, saw at the De Kalb County Fair an exhibit

Frank Tenney Johnson (1874–1939)
Winter in Wyoming, 1922
Watercolor on board, 14 ⅛ × 10 in.
Stark Museum of Art, Orange, Texas

The stark monochrome of a deep western winter could yield a scene of Oriental delicacy.

of barbed wire fencing invented by Henry M. Rose. Glidden improved Rose's prototype and applied for a patent on October 27, 1873. The spur wires on Glidden's version were held in place by a two-braid length of wire that not only made the fencing strong but also was readily adaptable to mass production. Glidden began manufacturing the wire in De Kalb in 1874, taking a partner the next year, then selling out his interest for sixty thousand dollars plus royalties the next. The purchaser of Glidden's patent, Washburn & Moen Manufacturing Company, produced 2.84 million pounds of barbed wire in 1876. In 1880 it was making 80.5 million pounds and had become one of the nation's largest and wealthiest industrial concerns.

Cattlemen were among the first users of barbed wire. It made possible better breeding on Texas ranches because blooded animals could be fenced off from "mongrels" and bred exclusively with other blooded animals. The fencing also reduced the number of cowboys needed to patrol the range, since fencing a line effectively confined animals to their home range. Moreover, barbed wire promoted the drilling of wells in otherwise unwatered ranges, thereby expanding available pastureland. A rancher who was reluctant to invest in a well on unprotected land, spending money for water that anybody's stock might use, would eagerly finance a water project when he was sure it was for his use alone. Finally, despite legislation against the practice, some cattlemen even began fencing the public lands for use as exclusive grazing ranges.

But barbed wire also damaged stock, and a horse whose tendon was severed by a barb could be badly lamed. Between the ranchers' own use of barbed wire on the public range and the homesteaders' employment of it to protect crops, the days of the long trail drive were clearly coming to an end. There were wire-cutting incidents and fence "wars," but the rapid ramification of railroad networks, which meant that most cattle ranges were coming within easy reach of railheads, and the widespread legislative acceptance of barbed wire made strong-arm tactics to preserve the open range futile.

Although no cattleman realized it at the time, the range cattle industry had peaked in 1885. Profits were high, and high profits brought a lust for expansion,

Currier & Ives
The Western Farmer's Home, 1871
Museum of the City of New York

One key to the success of these popular print publishers was their unerring sense of the American public's dreams and ideals—embodied here in a neat, bright vision of an agrarian West.

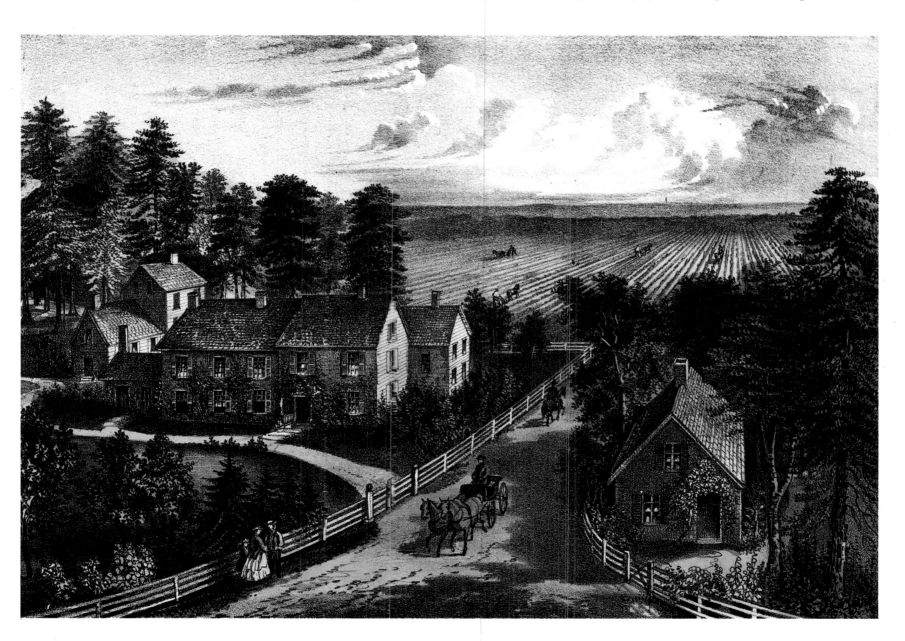

which in turn brought a need for borrowed money—and lots of it—which, in 1885, was readily available, as banks were eager to make loans against cattle. Flush, the ranchers overstocked the range; for money to purchase cattle proved more abundant than good grass.

The winter of 1885 was a relatively mild one, but the autumn had seen heavy rains, which, as cattlemen said, "soaked the strength out of the grass." Despite the tolerable winter weather, then, the herds fared poorly on the overstocked and inadequate pasturage, suffering considerable losses and the thinning and weakening of those animals that survived into spring. When the terrible winter of 1886–87 hit the already beleaguered herds with bottomless temperatures and blizzard after blizzard, staggering losses—80 to 90 percent—wiped out almost every major cattleman on the northern plains.

Artist Charlie Russell, a working cowboy in charge of five thousand head owned by a Helena, Montana, company, was queried by his employers as to the condition of their investment. Russell painted his reply on a two-inch by four-inch scrap of paper and sent it off. *Waiting for a Chinook*, depicting a lonely and emaciated steer standing in a deep snowdrift as if waiting for the end as it is eyed by a hungry coyote, not only launched Russell's career as an artist, but may also serve as a visual epitaph for the range cattle industry. From now on, those cattlemen who survived to pick up the pieces of their shattered empires would have to husband the animals with more discipline and care, breeding heartier stock, and fencing what was left of the open range.

THE CENSUS OF 1890

Explored, surveyed, marked off, claimed, sold, bought, given away, fenced, closed. In 1890 the United States Bureau of the Census declared that it could no longer desig-

Joseph Henry Sharp (1859–1953)
Prayer to the Spirit of the Buffalo, c. 1910
Oil on canvas, 29 × 39 in.
The Rockwell Museum, Corning, New York

By the time Sharp painted this highly formal composition, the spirit was about all that was left of the buffalo—once so numerous that they blackened the vast plains. White hunters decimated their ranks, trail drivers usurped their grazing lands, and sodbusters fenced off their ranges.

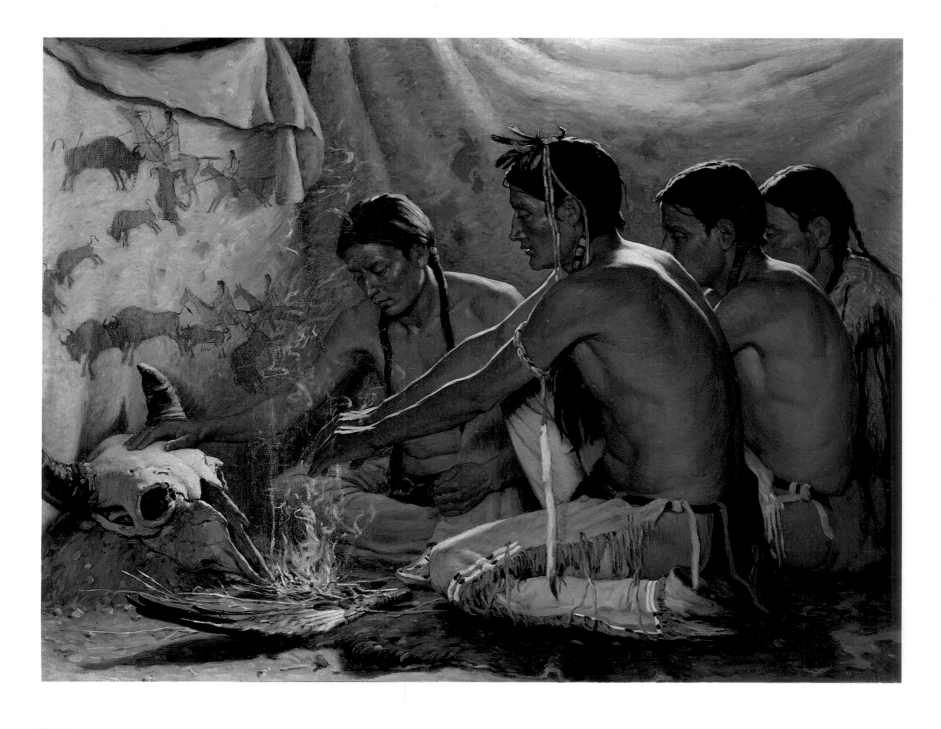

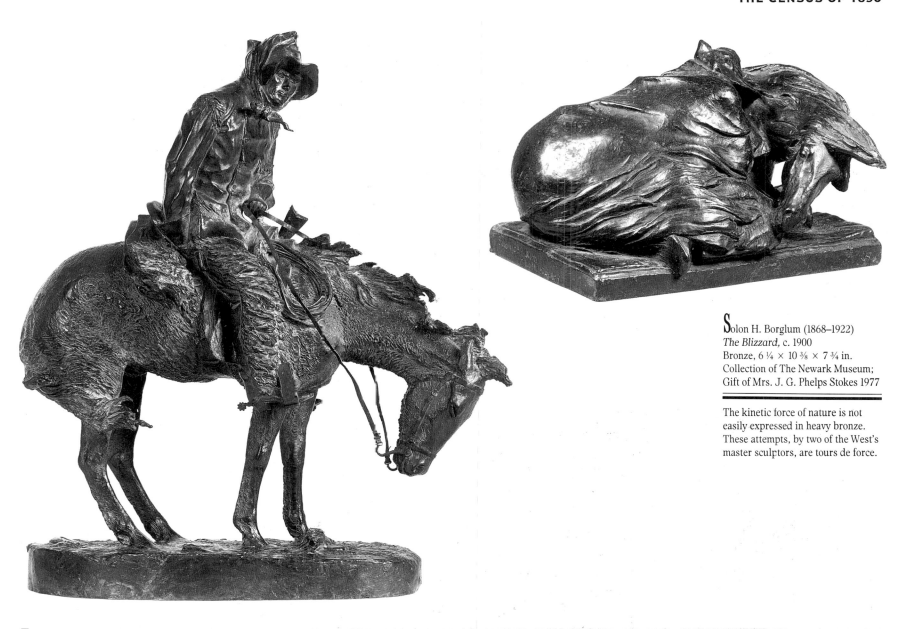

Solon H. Borglum (1868–1922)
The Blizzard, c. 1900
Bronze, 6 ¼ × 10 ⅜ × 7 ¾ in.
Collection of The Newark Museum;
Gift of Mrs. J. G. Phelps Stokes 1977

The kinetic force of nature is not
easily expressed in heavy bronze.
These attempts, by two of the West's
master sculptors, are tours de force.

Frederic Remington (1861–1909)
The Norther, 1900
Bronze casting, H. 22 in.
Gilcrease Museum, Tulsa, Oklahoma

Charles M. Russell (1864–1926)
Waiting for a Chinook, 1886
Watercolor on paper, 3 × 4 ½ in.
Montana Stockgrowers Association

"This is the real thing painted the
winter of 1886 at the OH ranch,"
Russell noted on this watercolor
executed on a postcard. It was the
picture that launched his career as
an artist.

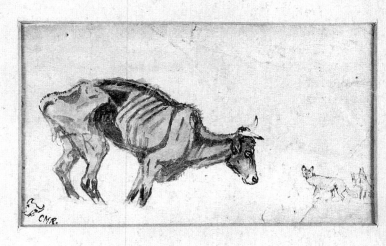

This is the real thing
painted the winter of 1886
at the OH ranch
C M Russell

This picture is Chas.
Russell's reply to my
inquiry as to the
condition of my cattle
in 1886. L E Kaufman

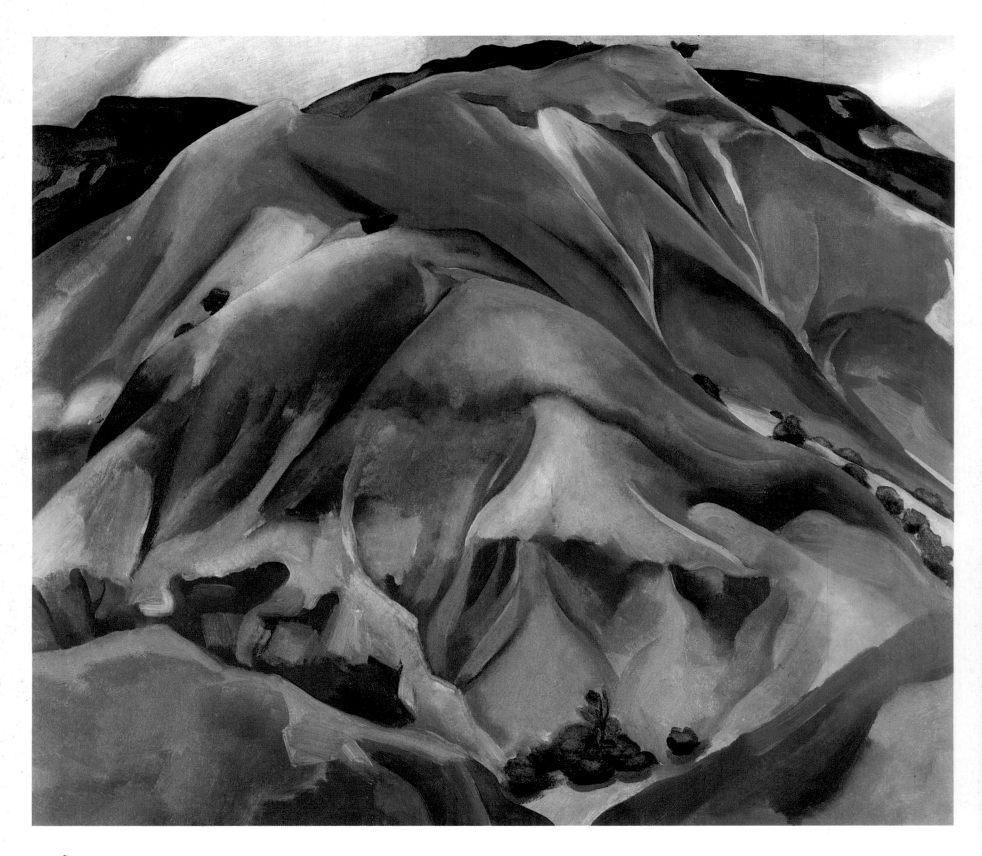

Georgia O'Keeffe (1887–1986)
The Mountain, New Mexico, 1931
Oil on canvas, 30 × 36 in.
Collection of Whitney Museum of
American Art, New York; Purchase

O'Keeffe was one of the few
genuinely modern artists whose
works capture the spirit, look, and
feel of the southwestern landscape.

Georgia O'Keeffe (1887–1986)
From the Plains I, 1953
Oil on canvas, 47 $\frac{11}{16}$ × 83 $\frac{5}{8}$ in.
Marion Koogler McNay Art Museum,
San Antonio, Texas; Gift of the Es-
tate of Tom Slick

GEORGIA O'KEEFFE

—

BORN 1887, SUN PRAIRIE, WISCONSIN
DIED 1986, ABIQUIUI, NEW MEXICO

—

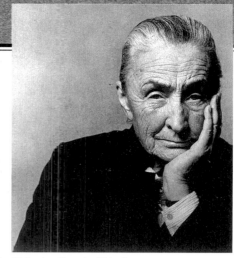

Phillipe Halsman, *Georgia O'Keeffe*, 1967. Photograph. © Yvonne Halsman 1990

One of the giants of twentieth-century art, Georgia O'Keeffe was transformed by the landscape of New Mexico even as she transmuted it into austere monuments of modern art energized by a powerful, impersonal sensuality. Rarely has an artist developed so fully symbiotic a relationship with her environment.

She studied first at the Art Institute of Chicago, then moved to New York as the student of William Merritt Chase at the Art Students League in 1907. At Columbia University, she studied with Arthur Dow from 1914 to 1915, also teaching art herself in South Carolina and Texas during 1912–18.

In 1916, the great photographer and cultivator of contemporary artists Alfred Stieglitz discovered and exhibited O'Keeffe's work. He married the artist in 1924.

O'Keeffe first visited New Mexico in 1917. Gradually, her art became less abstract and more representational as she explored the landscape near Taos. In 1929, on an extended Taos visit, O'Keeffe began to distill the monumental essence of the New Mexican landscape, refining it and studying it in terms of light and shadow. She returned to the Southwest summer after summer, settling permanently in New Mexico in 1949, concentrating her art upon the topography and other physical features of the Southwest: hills, flowers, the bleached bones of cattle. She depicted, too, the hand of man upon this beautiful but unforgiving country, painting crosses, adobe churches, and other buildings. She was one of the few painters of the western land to integrate her subject successfully into the mainstream of modern art, and she was one of even fewer modern artists to gain virtually universal admiration from critics and public alike.

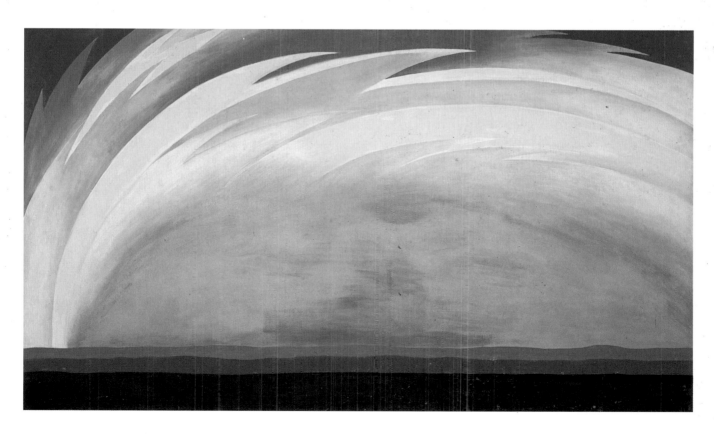

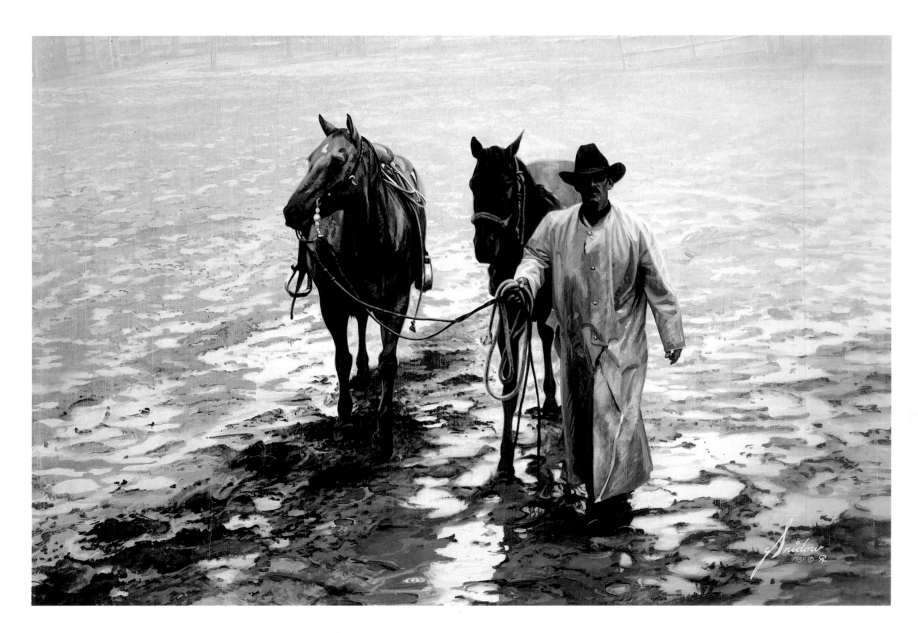

nate the boundaries of a western frontier by means of population statistics. Prior to 1890, the bureau had designated the frontier as a line demarcating areas of settlement with a population density of more than two persons per square mile. That clear demarcation no longer existed. The last of the cheap, arable lands had been taken. The Bureau of the Census concluded that the American frontier was "closed."

At least one historian, Frederick Jackson Turner, greeted the news from the census bureau as something of a national amputation. The inexorable push westward, Turner argued in a famous paper of 1893, had molded the character of the United States: "That coarseness and strength combined with acuteness and inquisitiveness; that practical, inventive turn of mind, quick to find expedients; that masterful grasp of material things, lacking in the artistic, but powerful to effect great ends; that restless, nervous energy; that dominant individualism, working for good and for evil, and withal that buoyancy and exuberance which comes from freedom—these are the traits of the frontier, or traits called out elsewhere because of the frontier." Now, Turner predicted, with the western direction closed off, the nation would be pro-

pelled to imperialist ventures overseas; the laboring masses, which previously found freedom from oppression in the limitless West, would now organize into powerful unions to fight oppression from which there was no longer geographical escape; and the national body politic would turn away from individualism and privatism to something approaching socialism.

In the years since 1893, many have found fault with Turner's sweeping and, perhaps, simplistic "frontier theory." Yet, in broad outline, his predictions have proven remarkably accurate. Nevertheless, the great historian did fail to appreciate two truths. First, Americans, most emphatically including those Americans at and beyond the frontier, were anything but "lacking in the artistic." Quite the contrary, the great West inspired a great body of artistic achievement, as this volume amply demonstrates.

That the western experience produced so much art—on canvas and in bronze, as well as in prose, on film, and in folklore—points up Turner's second mistaken conclusion. The demographical "closing" of the western frontier, momentous as it may have seemed, could never close the West to the American imagination.

Gordon Snidow (b. 1936)
Headin' For the Barn, n.d.
Gouache on illustration board,
24 × 36 in.
The First National Bank of Belen,
New Mexico

A contemporary photorealistic depiction charged with changeless western feeling.

James Bama (b. 1926)
Bill Smith—Number One, 1974
Oil on board, 22 ½ × 24 in.
National Cowboy Hall of Fame and
Western Heritage Center

Rodeo, a sporting display of courage
and skill, grew out of necessity; in
their line of work, cowboys need an
abundance of courage and skill.

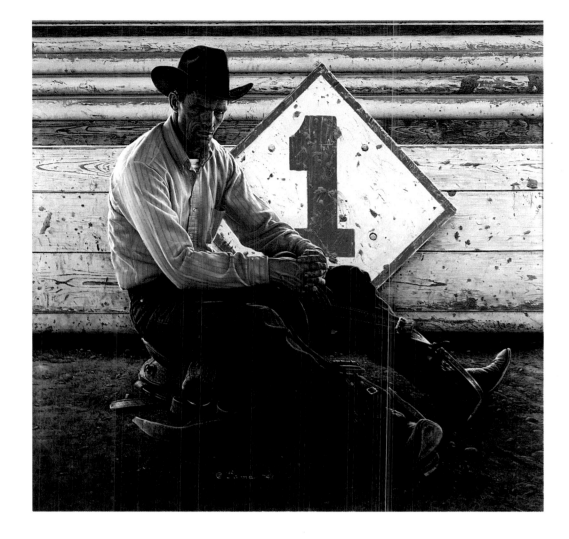

Robert Duncan (b. 1952)
A Late Feeding, 1984
Oil on canvas, 34 × 60 in.
Private collection

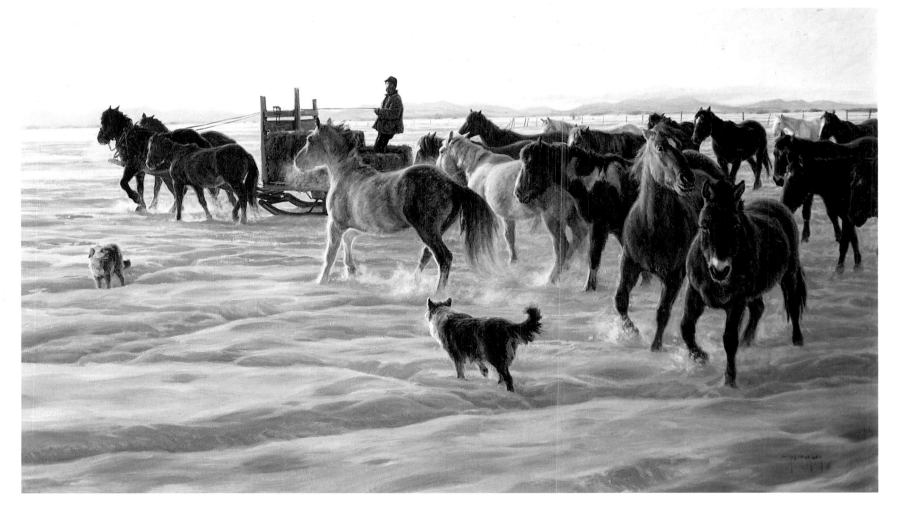

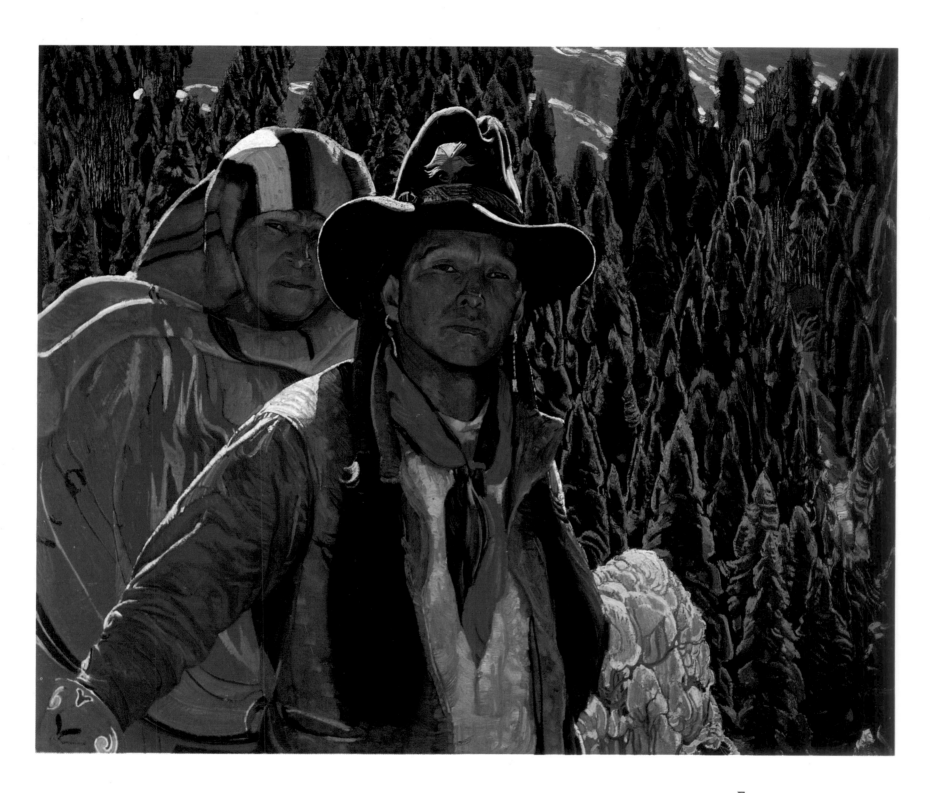

Ernest L. Blumenschein (1874–1960)
Star Road and White Sun, 1920
Oil on canvas, 45 ½ × 54 ½ in.
Courtesy of the Albuquerque Museum, Albuquerque High School Collection

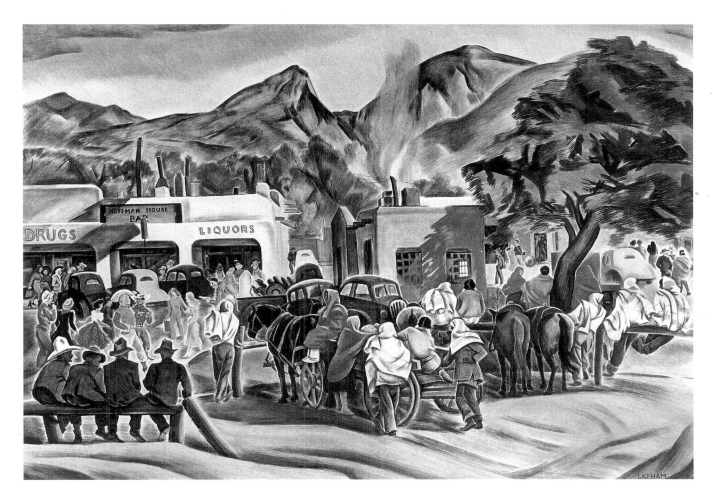

Barbara Latham (1896–1989)
Tourist Town—Taos, n.d.
Tempera on panel, 24 × 35 ¾ in.
Roswell Museum and Art Center;
Gift of the Artist

When Ernest Blumenschein and Bert
Phillips stumbled on it in 1898, Taos
was a little-visited Indian town.
Before mid century, it had become a
western tourist mecca.

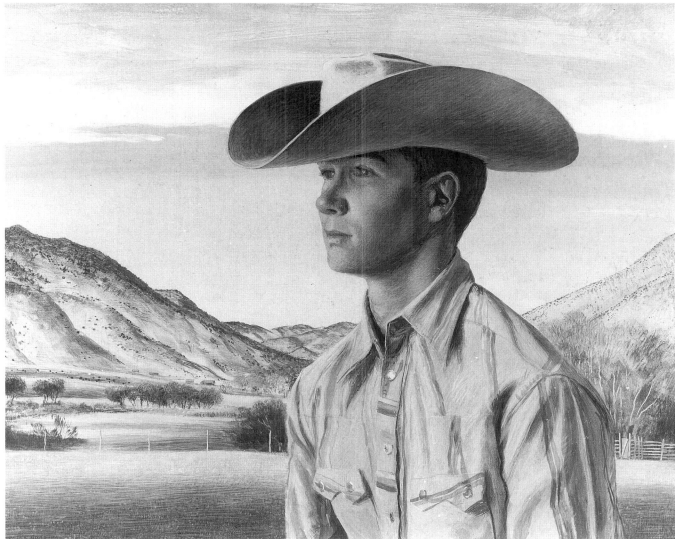

Peter Hurd (1904–1984)
Portrait of Gerald Marr, 1952
Tempera on masonite, 22 ¼ × 30 ⅜
in.
Colorado Springs Fine Arts Center;
Gift of the Percy Hagerman Memo-
rial Fund

The frank, open spirit of the West
survives into the middle of the
twentieth century—and beyond.

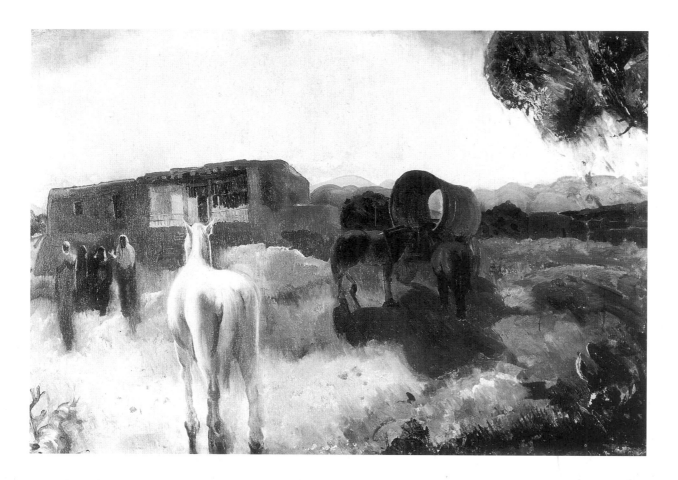

George Bellows (1882–1925)
Chimayo, 1917
Oil on canvas, 30 × 40 in.
Museum of Fine Arts, Museum of
New Mexico; Anonymous Gift

New Mexican adobe: a fragile
building material that nevertheless
endures.

Albert Bierstadt (1830–1902)
The Emerald Pool, 1870
Oil on canvas, 76 ½ × 119 in.
The Chrysler Museum, Norfolk,
Virginia

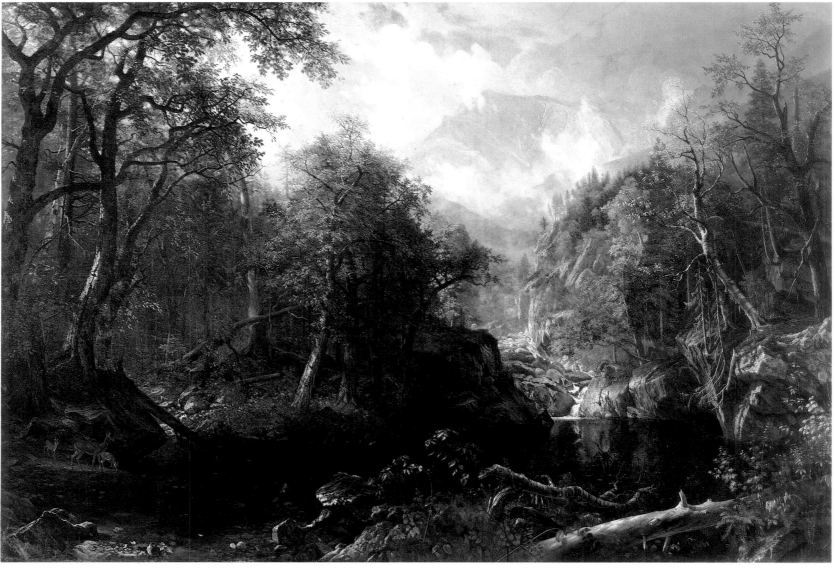

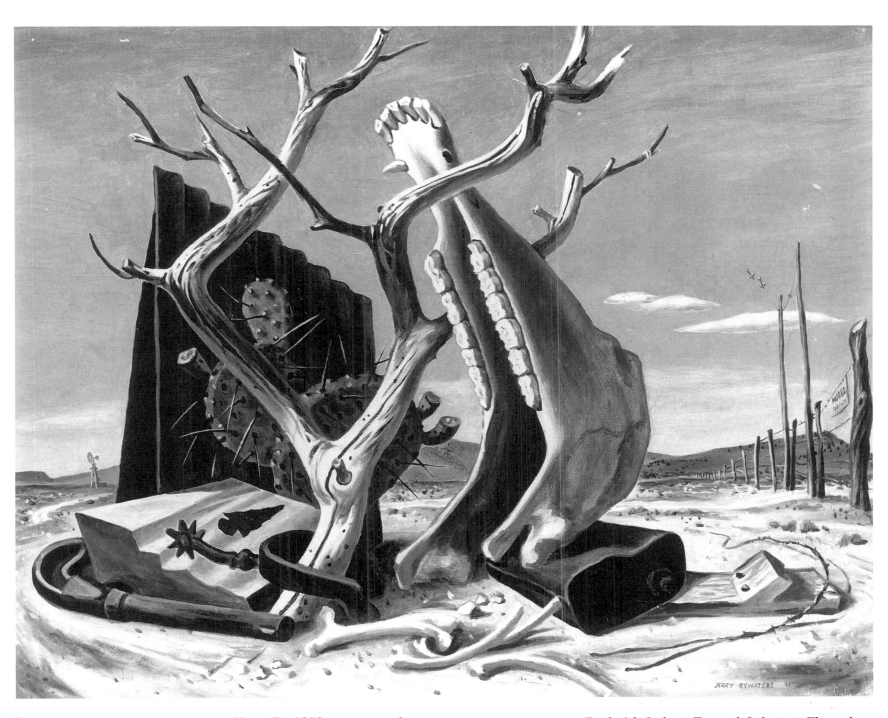

Jerry Bywaters (1906–1989)
On the Ranch, 1941
Oil and tempera on masonite,
19 ⅞ × 25 ⅞ in.
Dallas Museum of Art; Dealey Prize,
Thirteenth Annual Dallas Allied Arts
Exhibition

A distinguished teacher, writer, and
museum director, Bywaters studied
at the Tate, Louvre, and Prado. He
was also influenced by the frescoes
of Orozco and Rivera in Mexico.
With very little exaggeration, the
artist transforms the detritus of the
West—old and new—into an eerie,
surreal composition.

Henry David Thoreau seemed to express our nation's restless urge to push back the western frontier when he wrote in a mid-nineteenth-century essay titled "Walking," "Eastward I go only by force; but westward I go free. . . . I must walk toward Oregon, and not toward Europe. And that is the way the nation is moving, and I may say that mankind progress from east to west." Yet Thoreau never did go west himself, let alone try to live there; for he knew that the actual movement west was almost beside the point. The point was the *urge* and the *spirit* that the westward movement expressed. In *A Week on the Concord and Merrimack Rivers,* published in 1849, Thoreau wrote, "The frontiers are not east or west, north or south, but wherever a man *fronts* a fact."

Frederick Jackson Turner left that out. The real frontiers lie within, and places as spectacular, beautiful, vast, hellish, dangerous, and demanding as the American West serve finally to make men—and women—*front* the varied facts of their own existence: physical, spiritual, private, social, and universal. That is an enduring truth of life and of that expression of life we call art. The American West flashed and sparked, developed and changed with a speed that startles even our hypersonic and electronic age. But the artworks here and the story they illustrate excite us in the way that no "closed" history, over and done with, ever could. No, the frontier did not close, not in 1890, nor will it in 2090.

It cannot.

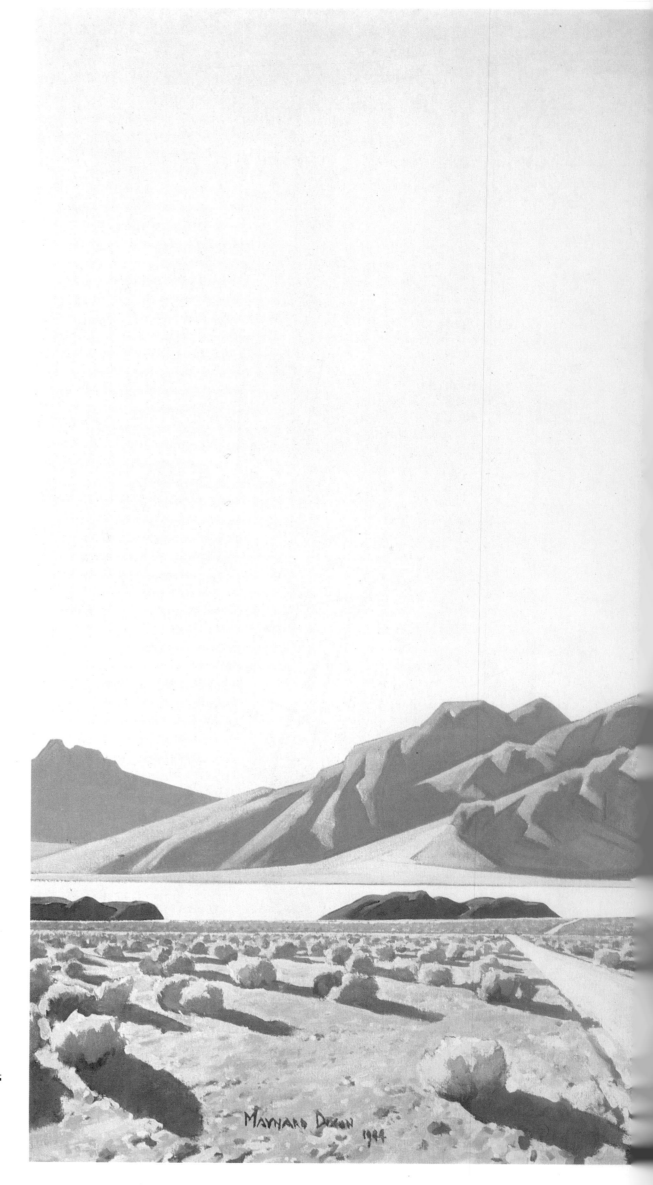

Maynard Dixon (1875–1946)
Desert Southwest, 1944
Oil on canvas, 40 × 36 in.
Courtesy of the Anschutz Collection

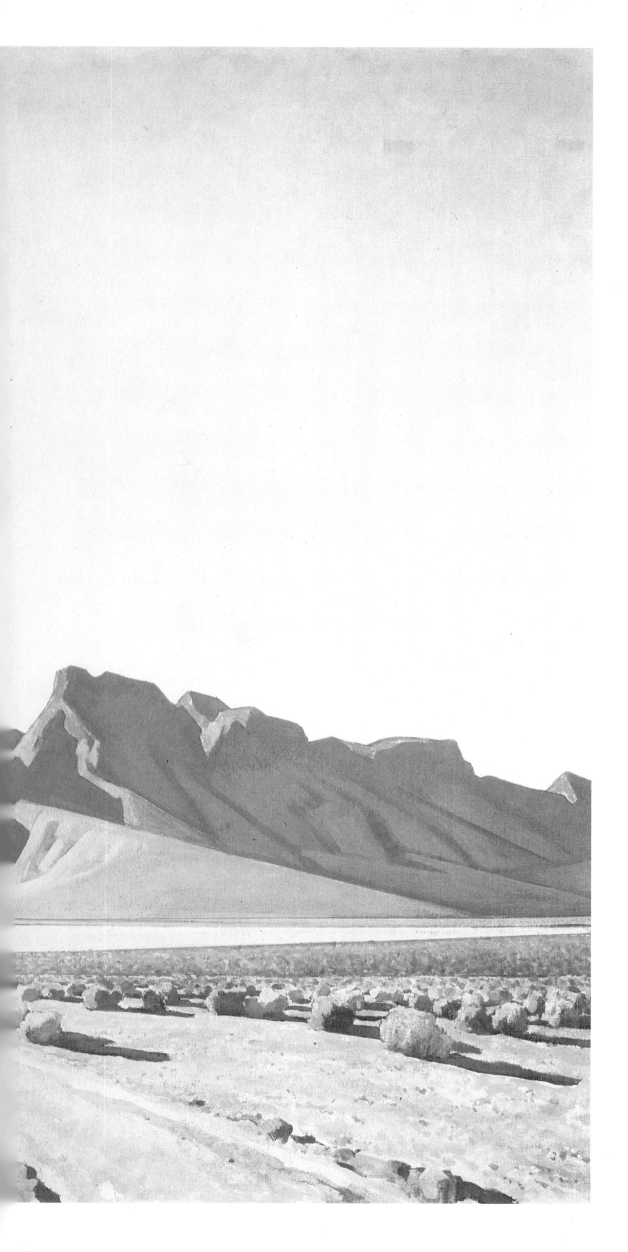

ACKNOWLEDGMENTS

Most numerous and generous among those it is a pleasure to thank are the collectors, museums, historical societies, and other private, local, state, and federal institutions from whose holdings we have reproduced paintings, prints, photographs, and sculptures. Their names are found in the captions that accompany the illustrations throughout this book.

It is equally a pleasure to acknowledge the creativity, expertise, good will, good humor, and support of the staff of Abbeville Press. In particular, I wish to thank picture editor Massoumeh Farman-Farmaian for her tireless work in obtaining illustrations and permission to reproduce them, and production supervisor Hope Koturo, who ensured that the color reproduction, printing, and manufacture of this book met Abbeville's rigorous standards. Senior editor Walton Rawls got me started on this project and has faithfully shepherded it through each of its stages. Elaine Luthy, manuscript editor, saved me from innumerable stupidities; she also created this book's magnificent index. Robin James, copy chief, saw to it that all corrections (plenty of those) were properly implemented. Abbeville's managing editor, Susan Costello, provided much sage advice on final revisions.

Perhaps the real "star" of any large illustrated book is the designer. It was my good fortune to work with Julie Rauer on this one—and that was an even greater good fortune for the many artists, living and dead, who are represented in this volume. Practitioners of a great artistic tradition deserve the great showcase Julie has given them.

It is difficult for me to imagine this book without the contribution of everyone I just mentioned—though I suppose it might have come into existence, in some diminished form or other, even in the absence of one or two of them. However, without the imagination, confidence, and support of Abbeville's president, Robert E. Abrams, there would be no *Art of the Golden West*. He commissioned the book in the first place and has kept the faith—his *and* mine—throughout the process of its creation.

Anita and Ian, my wife and son, gave their time to this project no less than I did. I thank them, and I hope they will long enjoy the book.

—Alan Axelrod

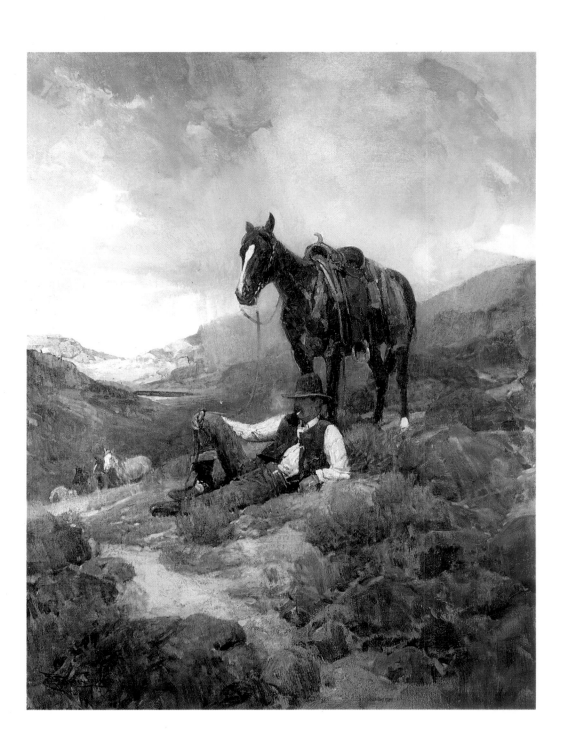

Frank Tenney Johnson (1874–1939)
A Morning Shower, 1927
Oil on canvas, 36 × 28 in.
The Rockwell Museum, Corning,
New York

SOURCES

Abbey, Edward. *Desert Solitaire.* New York: McGraw-Hill, 1968.

Adams, Celeste Marie, et al. *America: Art and the West.* New York: Harry N. Abrams, 1986.

Adams, Ramon F. *Burs Under the Saddle: A Second Look at Books and Histories of the West.* Norman: University of Oklahoma Press, 1964.

———. *More Burs Under the Saddle: Books and Histories of the West.* Norman: University of Oklahoma Press, 1979.

Albuquerque Museum. *The Alberquerque High School Collection.* Albuquerque, New Mexico: The Albuquerque Museum and Albuquerque High School, 1986.

Alexander, Michael, ed. *Discovering the New World: Based on the Works of Theodore de Bry.* New York: Harper and Row, 1976.

American-Australian Foundation for the Arts and International Cultural Corporation Limited. *America: Art and the West.* New York: Harry N. Abrams, 1986.

American Heritage. *Indians of the Plains* New York: Harper and Row, 1960.

Amon Carter Museum of Western Art. *Amon Carter Museum of Western Art: Catalogue of the Collection 1972.* Fort Worth, Texas: By the museum, 1973.

Anderson, Dennis R. *Three Hundred Years of American Art in the Chrysler Museum.* Norfolk, Virginia: By the museum, 1976.

Anonymous. *Our Great Indian War. The Miraculous Lives of Bill (Mr. Wm. Rhodes Decker) and Miss Marion Fannin,* 1876; reprinted in Washburn, vol. 86.

———. *Mrs. Huggins, the Minnesota Captive,* 1864; reprinted in Washburn, vol. 86.

Anschutz Collection. *Masterpieces of the American West: Selections from the Anschutz Collection.* Denver: The Anschutz Collection, 1983.

Ashbaugh, Don. *Nevada's Turbulent Yesterday.* Los Angeles: Westernlore Press, 1963.

Askins, Charles. *Texans: Guns and History.* New York: Winchester Press, 1970.

Athearn, Robert G. *Union Pacific Country.* Chicago: Rand, McNally, 1971.

Atherton, Lewis. *The Cattle Kings.* Bloomington: Indiana University Press, 1961.

Axford, Joseph Mack. *Around Western Campfires.* New York: Pageant Press, 1964.

Bard, Floyd C. *Horse Wrangler: Sixty Years in the Saddle in Wyoming and Montana.* Norman: University of Oklahoma Press, 1960.

Barnard, Edward S., ed. *Reader's Digest Story of the Great American West.* Pleasantville, New York: Reader's Digest, 1977.

Beal, Merrill D. *"I Will Fight No More Forever": Chief Joseph and the Nez Percé War.* Seattle: University of Washington Press, 1963.

Berry, Don. *A Majority of Scoundrels: An Informal History of the Rocky Mountain Fur Company.* New York: Harper's, 1961.

Berry-Hill Galleries, Inc. *American Paintings.* New York: Berry-Hill, 1981.

———. *American Paintings III.* New York: Berry-Hill, 1985.

———. *American Paintings IV.* New York: Berry-Hill, 1986.

Billington, Ray Allen. *The Far Western Frontier 1830–1860.* New York: Harper & Brothers, 1956.

Bowman, John S., ed. *The World Almanac of the American West.* New York: World Almanac, 1986.

Brandon, William. *Indians.* New York: American Heritage, 1985.

Breihan, Carl W. *Great Gunfighters of the West.* San Antonio: The Naylor Company, 1962.

———. *Great Lawmen of the West.* New York: Bonanza Books, 1963.

Broder, Patricia Janis. *American Indian Painting and Sculpture.* New York: Abbeville Press, 1981.

———. *The American West: The Modern Vision.* Boston: A New York Graphic Society Book Published by Little, Brown, 1984.

———. *Bronzes of the American West.* New York: Harry N. Abrams, n.d.

———. *Fifty Great Paintings of the Old American West.* New York: Crown, 1979.

———. *Great Paintings of the Old American West.* New York: Abbeville Press, 1979.

Brodie, Fawn. *No Man Knows My History: The Life of Joseph Smith.* New York: Knopf, 1945; revised ed., 1971.

Brooks, Juanita. *The Mountain Meadows Massacre.* Palo Alto, California: Stanford University Press, 1950.

Brown, Dee. *Bury My Heart at Wounded Knee.* New York: Holt, Rinehart and Winston, 1970.

———. *The Gentle Tamers.* New York: Putnam's, 1958.

———. *Hear That Lonesome Whistle Blow—Railroads in the West.* New York: Holt, Rinehart, 1977.

Brown, John A. *Indians of the Pacific Northwest.* Norman: University of Oklahoma Press, 1981.

Browne, Linda Fergusson. *J. Ross Browne: His Letters, Journals, and Writings.* Albuquerque: University of New Mexico Press, 1969.

Burns, Walter Noble. *The Saga of Billy the Kid.* Garden City, New York: Garden City Publishing Co., 1925.

Butler Institute of American Art. *Sixty Years of Collecting American Art: An Index to the Permanent Collection.* Youngstown, Ohio: Butler Institute, 1979.

Capps, Benjamin. *The Great Chiefs.* Alexandria, Virginia: Time-Life Books, 1975.

Chapin, Louis. *Charles M. Russell: Paintings of the Old American West.* New York: Crown, 1978.

———. *Fifty Charles M. Russell Paintings of the Old American West.* New York: Crown, 1978.

———. *Frederic Remington.* New York: Crown, 1979.

Chittenden, Hiram M. *The American Fur Trade of the Far West.* 1902; reprint ed., Lincoln: University of Nebraska Press, 1986.

Cleland, Robert Glass. *This Reckless Breed of Men: The Trappers and Fur Traders of the Southwest.* New York: Knopf, 1950.

Conger, Robert N. *Texas Rangers: Sesquicentennial Anniversary, 1823–1973.* Fort Worth: Heritage Publications, 1973.

Coolidge, Dane. *Fighting Men of the West.* New York: Dutton, 1932.

Covey, Cyclone, tr. and ed. *Cabeza de Vaca's Adventures in the Unknown Interior of America.* New York: Collier, 1961.

Crawford, Thomas Edgar. *The West of the Texas Kid, 1881–1910.* Norman: University of Oklahoma Press, 1970.

Cunningham, Eugene. *Triggernometry: A Gallery of Gunfighters.* New York: Press of the Pioneers, Inc., 1934.

Custer, Elizabeth. *Boots and Saddles.* 1885; reprint ed., Norman: University of Oklahoma Press, 1977.

Czestochowski, Joseph S. *The American Landscape Tradition: A Study and Gallery of Paintings.* New York: Dutton, 1982.

Dale, Edward Everett. *Cow Country.* Norman: University of Oklahoma Press, 1942.

———. *Frontier Ways: Sketches of Life in the Old West.* Austin: University of Texas Press, 1959.

Dalton, Emmett, and Jack Jungmeyer. *When the Daltons Rode.* Garden City, New York: Doubleday, Doran and Co., 1931.

De Voto, Bernard. *Across the Wide Missouri.* Boston: Houghton Mifflin, 1947.

Dick, Everett. *The Sod-House Frontier: 1854–1890.* New York: D. Appleton-Century, 1937.

———. *Vanguards of the Frontier.* New York: D. Appleton-Century, 1937.

Dimsdale, Thomas J. *The Vigilantes of Montana: Being a Correct and Impartial Narrative of the Chase, Trial, Capture, and Execution of Henry Plummer's Notorious Road Agent Band.* 1866; reprint ed., Norman: University of Oklahoma Press, 1953.

Dobie, Frank J. *The Longhorns.* Boston: Little, Brown, 1941.

Dodge, Richard Irving. *The Plains of the Great West and Their Inhabitants.* 1875; reprint ed., New York: Archer House, 1959.

Douglas, Branch E. *The Cowboy and His Interpreters.* New York: Appleton, 1926.

Drago, Harry Sinclair. *Notorious Ladies of the Frontier.* New York: Dodd, Mead, 1969.

Driver, Harold E. *Indians of North America.* 2d ed., rev. Chicago: University of Chicago Press, 1969.

Duffus, R. L. *The Santa Fe Trail.* New York: Longmans, Green, 1930.

Dunlop, Richard. *Great Trails of the West.* New York: Abingdon Press, 1971.

Dykstra, Robert R. *The Cattle Towns.* New York: Knopf, 1968.

Earp, Josephine Sarah Marcus. *I Married Wyatt Earp: The Recollections of Josephine Sarah Marcus Earp.* Tucson: University of Arizona Press, 1976.

Eccles, W. J. *France in America.* New York: Harper and Row, 1972.

Ehle, John. *Trail of Tears: The Rise and Fall of the Cherokee Nation.* New York: Anchor Books/Doubleday, 1988.

Eldredge, Charles C., et al. *Art in New Mexico: Paths to Taos and Santa Fe.* New York: Abbeville Press, 1986.

Elliott, J. H. *The Old World and the New 1492–1650.* Cambridge: Cambridge University Press, 1972.

Elman, Robert. *Badmen of the West.* Secaucus, New Jersey: Ridge Press, Inc., 1974.

Fairbanks, Jonathan, et al. *Frontier America: The Far West*. Boston: Museum of Fine Arts, Boston, 1975.

Faulk, Odie B. *Crimson Desert: Indian Wars of the American Southwest*. New York: Oxford University Press, 1974.

———. *The Geronimo Campaign*. New York: Oxford University Press, 1969.

Fehrenbach, T. R. *Lone Star: A History of Texas and the Texans*. 1968; reprint ed., New York: American Legacy Press, 1983.

Fiedler, Mildred. *Wild Bill and Deadwood*. New York: Bonanza Books, 1965.

Flint, Timothy. *Biographical Memoir of Daniel Boone: The First Settler of Kentucky; Interspersed with Incidents in the Early Annals of the Country*. 1833; reprint ed., New Haven, Connecticut: College and University Press, 1967.

Forbis, William H. *The Cowboys*. Alexandria, Virginia: Time-Life Books, 1973.

Frantz, Joe B., and Julian Ernest Choate, Jr. *The American Cowboy: The Myth and the Reality*. Norman: University of Oklahoma Press, 1955.

Frémont, John Charles. *The Expeditions of John Charles Frémont*. 3 vols. Champaign: University of Illinois Press, 1970.

Fulton, Maurice Garland. *History of the Lincoln County War*. Tucson: University of Arizona Press, 1968.

Garrett, Pat F. *The Authentic Life of Billy the Kid*. Norman: University of Oklahoma Press, 1954.

Gibson, Arnell Morgan. *The American Indian: Prehistory to the Present*. New York: Heath, 1980.

Gibson, Charles. *Spain in America*. New York: Harper & Row, 1966.

Gilbert, Bil. *The Trailblazers*. Alexandria, Virginia: Time-Life Books, 1973.

Glanz, Dawn. *How the West Was Drawn: American Art and the Settling of the Frontier*. Ann Arbor, Michigan: UMI Research Press, 1978, 1982.

Greever, William S. *The Bonanza West: The Story of the Western Mining Rushes, 1848–1900*. Norman: University of Oklahoma Press, 1963.

Gregg, Josiah. *Commerce of the Prairies*. 1844; reprint ed., Indianapolis: Bobbs-Merrill, 1970.

Griffiths, D., Jr., *Two Years' Residence in the New Settlements of Ohio, North America: With Directions to Emigrants*. London: Westley and Davis; Jackson and Walford; Toller, Kettering; Abel and Wheeler, Northampton; Tomalin and Potts, Daventry, 1835.

Grinnell, George Bird. *The Fighting Cheyennes*. 1915; reprint ed., Norman: University of Oklahoma Press, 1956.

Hafen, Leroy R., ed. *The Mountain Men and the Fur Trade of the Far West*. 10 vols. Spokane, Washington: Arthur H. Clark, 1965–72.

Hagwood, John A. *America's Western Frontier: The Exploration and Settlement of the Trans-Mississippi West*. New York: Knopf, 1967.

Haley, J. Evetts. *The XIT Ranch and the Early Days of the Llano Estacado*. 1929; reprint ed., Norman: University of Oklahoma Press, 1967.

Hassrick, Royal B. *Cowboys and Indians: An Illustrated History*. New York: Promontory Books, 1976.

———. *The Sioux*. Norman: University of Oklahoma Press, 1964.

Hawke, David. *The Colonial Experience*. Indianapolis: Bobbs-Merrill, 1966.

Hertzog, Peter. *A Dictionary of New Mexico Desperadoes*. Santa Fe: Press of the Territorian, 1965.

Hine, Robert V. *The American West: An Interpretive History*. Second ed. Boston: Little, Brown, 1984.

Hoffman, Charles Fenno. *A Winter in the West*. 2 vols. New York: Harper & Brothers, 1835.

Hollon, W. Eugene. *Frontier Violence: Another Look*. New York: Oxford University Press, 1974.

Horn, Huston. *The Pioneers*. Alexandria, Virginia: Time-Life Books, 1974.

Hungerford, Edward. *Wells Fargo: Advancing the American Frontier*. New York: Random House, 1949.

Hunter, John Dunn. *Memoirs of a Captivity Among the Indians of North America*. 1824; reprint ed., New York: Schocken Books, 1974.

Hutchinson, W. H. *The World, the Work, and the West of W.H.D. Koerner*. Norman: University of Oklahoma Press, 1978.

Irving, Washington. *The Adventures of Captain Bonneville, U.S.A., in the Rocky Mountains and the Far West*. 1837; reprint ed., Norman: University of Oklahoma Press, 1961.

———. *Astoria; or Anecdotes of an Enterprise Beyond the Rocky Mountains*. 1836; reprint ed., Norman: University of Oklahoma Press, 1964.

———. *A Tour on the Prairies*. 1835; reprint ed., Norman: University of Oklahoma Press, 1956.

Jackson, Joseph Henry. *Anybody's Gold: The Story of California's Mining Towns*. New York: Appleton-Century Company, Inc., 1941.

Jahns, Pat. *The Frontier World of Doc Holliday*. New York: Hastings House, 1957.

James, Jesse, Jr. *Jesse James, My Father*. Independence, Missouri: Sentinel Publishing Co., 1899.

Jennings, Francis. *Empire of Fortune: Crowns, Colonies, and Tribes in the Seven Years War in America*. New York: W. W. Norton, 1988.

———. *The Invasion of America: Indians, Colonialism, and the Cant of Conquest*. New York: W. W. Norton, 1976.

Johnson, Dorothy M. *Famous Lawmen of the Old West*. New York: Dodd, Mead, 1963.

Johnson, William Weber. *The Forty-Niners*. Alexandria, Virginia: Time-Life Books, 1974.

Josephy, Alvin M., Jr. *The Nez Percé and the Opening of the West*. New Haven: Yale University Press, 1965.

Keleher, William A. *Violence in Lincoln County, 1869–81*. Albuquerque: University of New Mexico Printing Plant, 1957.

Kovinick, Phil. *The Woman Artist in the American West 1860–1960*. Fullerton, California: Muckenthaler Cultural Center, 1976.

Kroeber, A. L. *Handbook of the Indians of California*. New York: Dover, 1976.

Ladner, Mildred D. *O. C. Seltzer: Painter of the Old West*. Norman: University of Oklahoma Press, 1979.

Lake, Stuart N. *Wyatt Earp: Frontier Marshal*. Boston: Houghton Mifflin, 1931.

Lamar, Howard R., ed. *The Reader's Encyclopedia of the Great American West*. New York: Crowell, 1977.

Langford, Nathaniel Pitt. *Vigilante Days and Ways*. Missoula: University of Montana Press, 1957.

Lavender, David. *Bent's Fort*. Garden City, New York: Doubleday, 1954.

———. *The Great West*. Boston: Houghton, Mifflin, 1987.

———. *Land of Giants: The Drive to the Pacific Northwest, 1750–1950*. Lincoln: University of Nebraska Press, 1956.

Leonard, Zenas. *Narrative of the Adventures of Zenas Leonard, a Native of Clearfield County, Pa. Who Spent Five Years in Trapping for Furs, Trading with the Indians &c., &c., of the Rocky Mountains*. Clearfield, Pennsylvania: D. W. Moore, 1839.

Lewis, Marvin, ed. *The Mining Frontier: Contemporary Accounts from the American West in the Nineteenth Century*. Norman: University of Oklahoma Press, 1967.

Lewis, Meriwether, and William Clark. *The History of the Lewis and Clark Expedition*. 1893; reprint ed., New York: Dover Books, n.d.

Lummis, Charles F. *The Land of Poco Tiempo*. New York: Scribner's, 1893.

Manchester, Robert C. *Boundless Realism: Contemporary Landscape Painting of the West*. Corning, New York: The Rockwell Museum, 1987.

Martin, Charles L. *A Sketch of Sam Bass, the Bandit: A Graphic Narrative*. 1880; reprint ed., Norman: University of Oklahoma Press, 1956.

Martin, Douglas D. *Tombstone's Epitaph*. Albuquerque: University of New Mexico Press, 1951.

Matthiessen, Peter, ed. *North American Indians*. Modern abridgement of George Catlin, *Letters and Notes on the Manners, Customs and Condition of the North American Indians Written During Eight Years' Travel (1832–1839) Amongst the Wildest Tribes of North America (1844)*. New York: Penguin, 1989.

McCracken, Harold. *The Charles M. Russell Book: The Life and Work of the Cowboy Artist*. Garden City, New York: Doubleday, 1957.

McShine, Kynaston, ed. *The Natural Paradise: Painting in America 1800–1950*. New York: The Museum of Modern Art, 1976.

Miles, Nelson A. *Serving the Republic: Personal Recollections and Observations of General Nelson A. Miles*. 1896; reprint ed., New York: Da Capo, n.d.

Miller, Alfred Jacob. *The West of Alfred Jacob Miller*. Norman: University of Oklahoma Press, 1951.

Monaghan, Jay. *The Great Rascal: The Life and Adventures of Ned Buntline*. Boston: Little, Brown, 1952.

———. *Custer: The Life of General George Armstrong Custer*. Norman: University of Nebraska Press, 1959.

Moody, Ralph. *The Old Trails West*. New York: Crowell, 1963.

Morgan, Dale. *Jedediah Smith and the Opening of the West*. Lincoln: University of Nebraska Press, 1953.

Morrison, Samuel Eliot. *The Oxford History of the American People*. 3 vols. 1965; reprint ed., New York: New American Library, 1972.

Mulder, William, and Russell Mortensen. *Among the Mormons: Historic Accounts by Contemporary Observers*. New York: Knopf, 1958.

Murray, Keith A. *The Modocs and Their War*. Norman: University of Oklahoma Press, 1959.

Museum of Fine Arts, Houston. *A Guide to the Collection*. Houston: By the museum, 1981.

Nash, Roderick. *Wilderness and the American Mind*. Revised ed. New Haven: Yale University Press, 1967.

National Geographic Society. *Historical Atlas of the United States*. Washington, D.C.: National Geographic Society, 1988.

Neihardt, John G. *Black Elk Speaks: Being the Life Story of a Holy Man of the Oglala Sioux*. 1932; reprint ed., Lincoln: University of Nebraska Press, 1961.

Nevin, David. *The Soldiers*. Alexandria, Virginia: Time-Life Books, 1974.

———. *The Texans*. Alexandria, Virginia: Time-Life Books, 1975.

The Newark Museum. *American Art in the Newark Museum*. Newark, New Jersey: By the museum, 1981.

Novak, Barbara. *Nature and Culture: American Landscape and Painting, 1825–1875*. New York: Oxford University Press, 1980.

Nuttal, Thomas. *A Journal of Travels into the Arkansa Territory, during the Year 1819*. Philadelphia: Thomas M. Palmer, 1821.

O'Dea, Thomas F. *The Mormons*. Chicago: University of Chicago Press, 1957.

O'Gorman, Edmundo. *The Invention of America: An Inquiry into the Historical Nature of the New World and the Meaning of Its History*. Bloomington: University of Indiana Press, 1961.

O'Neal, Bill. *Encyclopedia of Western Gunfighters*. Norman: University of Oklahoma Press, 1979.

O'Neill. Paul. *The Rivermen*. Alexandria, Virginia: Time-Life Books, 1975.

Opler, Morris. *Western Apache Raiding and Warfare*. Tucson: University of Arizona Press, 1971.

Orr-Cahill, Christina, ed. *The Art of California: Selected Works from the Collection of the Oakland Museum*. Oakland: The Oakland Museum Art Department and Chronicle Books, 1984.

Osgood, Ernest Staple. *The Day of the Cattleman*. Minneapolis: University of Minnesota Press, 1929.

Tyler, Ron, et al. *American Frontier Life: Early Western Painting and Prints.* New York: Abbeville Press, 1987.

Parkman, Francis. *The Discovery of the Great West.* Boston: Little, Brown, 1869.

———. *The Oregon Trail; Sketches of Prairie and Rocky-Mountain Life.* Boston: Little, Brown, 1872.

Parsons, John E. *The Peacemaker and Its Rivals: An Account of the Single Action Colt.* New York: Morrow, 1950.

Paul, Rodman Wilson. *California Gold: The Beginning of Mining in the Far West.* Cambridge: Harvard University Press, 1947.

Phillips, Paul C. *The Fur Trade.* Norman: University of Oklahoma Press, 1961.

Pike, Zebulon. *The Journals of Zebulon Montgomery Pike with Letters and Related Documents.* 2 vols. Norman: University of Oklahoma Press, 1966.

Quinn, David B., ed. *North American Discovery Circa 1000–1612.* New York: Harper & Row, 1971.

Raine, William MacLeod. *Famous Sheriffs and Western Outlaws.* New York: Doubleday, 1929.

Randolph, Edmund. *Beef, Leather and Grass.* Norman: University of Oklahoma Press, 1981.

Rawls, Walton. *The Great Book of Currier & Ives' America.* New York: Abbeville Press, 1979.

Reader's Digest. *Story of the Great American West.* Pleasantville, New York: The Reader's Digest Association, Inc., 1977.

Renner, Frederic G. *Charles M. Russell: Paintings, Drawings, and Sculpture in the Amon Carter Museum.* New York: Harry N. Abrams, 1974.

Richardson, Edgar P., et al. *Charles Willson Peale and His World.* New York: Abrams, 1983.

Rickey, Don, Jr. *Forty Miles a Day on Beans and Hay: The Enlisted Soldier Fighting the Indian Wars.* Norman: University of Oklahoma Press.

Riegel, Robert Edgar. *The Story of the Western Railroads—From 1852 Through the Reign of the Giants.* New York: Macmillan, 1926.

Rockwell-Corning Museum. *The Painters' West: A Selection from the Rockwell Collection of Western Art.* Corning, New York: By the museum, 1976.

Rosa, Joseph G. *The Gunfighter: Man or Myth?* Norman: University of Oklahoma Press, 1969.

———. *They Called Him Wild Bill: The Life and Adventures of James Butler Hickok.* 2d ed. Norman: University of Oklahoma Press, 1964.

Rossi, Paul A., and David C. Hunt. *The Art of the Old West: From the Gilcrease Institute.* New York: Knopf, 1971.

Roswell Museum. *Roswell Museum and Art Center: Guide to the Collections.* Roswell, New Mexico: By the museum, 1983.

Ryan, Kathleen Jo, et al. *Ranching Traditions: Legacy of the American West.* New York: Abbeville Press, 1989.

St. Louis Art Museum. *The St. Louis Art Museum: Handbook of the Collections.* St. Louis: By the museum, 1975.

Samuels, Peggy and Harold. *Samuels' Encyclopedia of Artists of the American West.* New York: Castle, 1985.

Santee, Ross. *Lost Pony Tracks.* New York: Scribner's, 1953.

Schimmel, Julie. *Stark Museum of Art: The Western Collection.* Orange, Texas: The Stark Museum of Art, 1978.

Scott, Gail R. *Marsden Hartley.* New York: Abbeville Press, 1988.

Scott, Rev. James L. *A Journal of a Missionary Tour Through Pennsylvania, Ohio, Indiana, Illinois, Iowa, Wiskonsin, and Michigan.* Providence, Rhode Island: By the author, 1843.

Smith, Duane A. *Rocky Mountain Mining Camps: The Urban Frontier.* Bloomington: Indiana University Press, 1967.

Smith, Helena Huntington. *The War on Powder River: The History of an Insurrection.* New York: McGraw-Hill, 1966.

Smith, Henry Nash. *Virgin Land: The American West as Symbol and Myth.* Cambridge: Harvard University Press, 1950.

Smith, Rex Alan. *The Carving of Mount Rushmore.* New York: Abbeville Press, 1985.

Spicer, Edward H. *Cycles of Conquest: The Impact of Spain, Mexico, and the United States on the Indians of the Southwest.* Tucson: University of Arizona Press, 1962.

Splete, Alan P. and Marilyn D., eds. *Frederic Remington—Selected Letters.* New York: Abbeville Press, 1988.

Stebbins, Theodore E., Jr., Carol Troyen, and Trevor J. Fairbrother. *A New World: Masterpieces of American Painting 1760–1910.* Boston: Museum of Fine Arts, Boston, 1983.

Sutton, Ann and Myron. *The American West: A Natural History.* New York: Random House, n.d.

Thompson, Gerald. *The Army and the Navajo: The Bosque Redondo Reservation Experiment.* Tucson: University of Arizona Press, 1976.

Turner, Frederick. *Beyond Geography: The Western Spirit Against the Wilderness.* New York: Viking, 1980.

Turner, Frederick Jackson. *Frontier and Section: Selected Essays.* Englewood Cliffs, New Jersey: Prentice-Hall, 1961.

Tuska, Jon. *Billy the Kid: A Bio-Bibliography.* Westport, Connecticut: Greenwood Press, 1983.

Tuska, Jon, and Vicki Piekarski. *The Frontier Experience: A Reader's Guide to the Life and Literature of the American West.* Jefferson, North Carolina: McFarland, 1984.

Twain, Mark. *Life on the Mississippi.* 1883; reprint ed., New York: Bantam, 1981.

———. *Roughing It.* 1872, reprint ed., Berkeley: University of California Press, 1972.

Tyler, Ron. *Visions of America: Pioneer Artists in a New Land.* New York: Thames and Hudson, 1983.

Underhill, Ruth. *The Navajos.* Norman: University of Oklahoma Press, 1956.

Utley, Robert M., and Wilcomb E. Washburn. *Indian Wars.* 1977; rev. ed., Boston: Houghton Mifflin, 1987.

Utley, Robert M. *Frontier Regulars: The United States Army and the Indian, 1866–1891.* New York: Macmillan, 1973.

Van Every, Dale. *The Final Challenge: The American Frontier 1804–1845.* 1964; reprint ed., New York: William Morrow, 1988.

Vestal, Stanley. *Dodge City: Queen of Cowtowns.* New York: Bantam, 1957.

Viola, Herman J. *The Indian Legacy of Charles Bird King.* Washington, D.C.: Smithsonian Institution Press and Doubleday and Co., 1976.

Walker, Henry Pickering. *The Wagonmasters.* Norman: University of Oklahoma Press, 1966.

Washburn, Wilcomb, comp. *The Garland Library of Narratives of North American Indian Captivities.* Vol. 86. New York: Garland, 1978.

———. *The Garland Library of Narratives of North American Indian Captivities.* Vol. 87. New York: Garland, 1977.

Waters, Frank. *The Earp Brothers of Tombstone.* London: Neville Spearman Ltd., 1962.

Webb, Walter Prescott. *The Great Plains.* New York: Ginn, 1931.

———. *The Texas Rangers.* Austin: University of Texas Press, 1935.

Wellman, Paul I. *Death on the Prairie: The 30 Years' Struggle for the Western Plains.* 1934; reprint ed., Lincoln: University of Nebraska Press, 1987.

Wheeler, Keith. *The Railroaders.* Alexandria, Virginia: Time-Life Books, 1973.

———. *The Townsmen.* Alexandria, Virginia: Time-Life Books, 1975.

Whitman, S. E. *The Troopers: An Informal History of the Plains Cavalry, 1865–1880.* New York: Hastings House, 1962.

Winther, Oscar Osburn. *Express and Stagecoach Days in California.* Palo Alto, California: Stanford University Press, 1963.

Wright, John S. *Letters from the West; or a Caution to Emigrants.* Salem, New York: Dodd & Stevenson, 1819.

Wyeth, John B. *Oregon; or a Short History of a Long Journey from the Atlantic Ocean to the Region of the Pacific, By Land.* Cambridge, Massachusetts: Printed for the author, 1833.

INDEX

Italic page numbers refer to captions and illustrations; **boldface** numbers refer to artist biographies.

Hubert O. Shuptrine (b. 1936)
The Tribesman, 1982
Egg tempera and watercolor on paper, 15 ¾ × 19 ½ in.
Collection of the Montgomery Museum of Fine Arts, Montgomery, Alabama; The Blount Collection

Even in the face of prejudice and hatred, generation after generation has recognized the stoic dignity fostered by most Indian cultures.

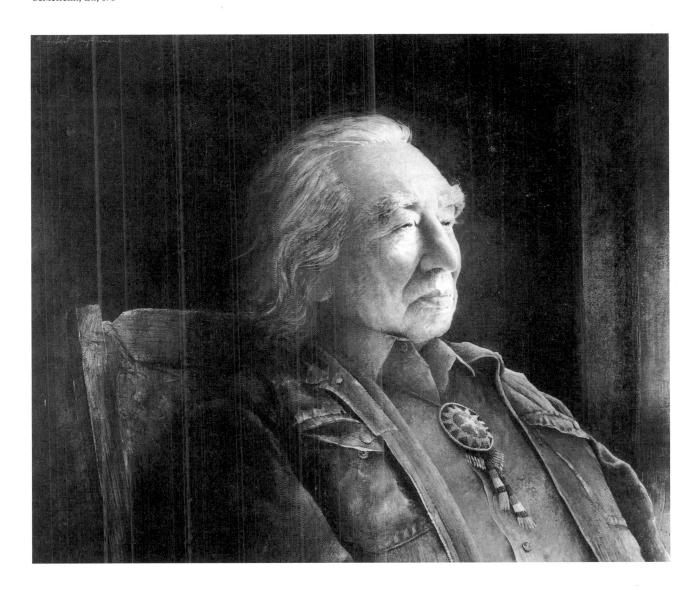